EUROPE: PAST, PRESENT AND FUTURE

CROATIA

PAST, PRESENT AND FUTURE PERSPECTIVES

EUROPE: PAST, PRESENT AND FUTURE

Additional books and e-books in this series can be found on Nova's website under the Series tab.

EUROPE: PAST, PRESENT AND FUTURE

CROATIA

PAST, PRESENT AND FUTURE PERSPECTIVES

MATKO MARUŠIĆ
EDITOR

nova
science publishers
New York

Library of Congress Cataloging-in-Publication Data

Names: Marušić, Matko, 1946- editor.
Title: Croatia: past, present and future perspectives / Matko Marušić (editor), University of Split, Croatia.
Identifiers: LCCN 2020031390 (print) | LCCN 2020031391 (ebook) | ISBN 9781536183009 (paperback) | ISBN 9781536183849 (adobe pdf)
Subjects: LCSH: Croatia--History. | Croatia--Politics and government--20th century. | Croatia--Relations--20th century.
Classification: LCC DR1535 .C763 2020 (print) | LCC DR1535 (ebook) | DDC 949.72--dc23
LC record available at https://lccn.loc.gov/2020031390
LC ebook record available at https://lccn.loc.gov/2020031391

Published by Nova Science Publishers, Inc. † New York

CONTENTS

Preface	The Past Affecting the Present and the Future	**vii**
How To Pronounce Croatian Words		**xvii**
Part I: Croatian History Timeline		**1**
Chapter 1	Overview of the Croatian History from the 7th Century to the Accession of the Republic of Croatia to the European Union in 2013 *Karmen Perković*	**3**
Chapter 2	The Croatian Language *Sanda Ham*	**79**
Chapter 3	The Croatian Question in Austria-Hungary at the Beginning of the Twentieth Century: Between Federalism and Trialism *Željko Holjevac*	**135**
Chapter 4	Field Marshal Svetozar Boroević and the Way to Croatian National Unification *Darko Richter*	**147**
Chapter 5	Alojzije Stepinac: Profile in Courage *Esther Gitman*	**175**
Chapter 6	Can Communism Have a Human Face? The Testimony of a Prominent Croatian Catholic Intellectual Smiljana Rendić from the Mid-Sixties in Yugoslavia *Marino Erceg*	**219**
Chapter 7	Croatian Spring: The Croatian National Reform Movement in Socialist Yugoslavia (1967 – 1972) *Josip Mihaljević*	**245**
Chapter 8	The Croatian War of Independence (1991 – 1995) *Andrijana Perković Paloš*	**267**

Part II: Past in Present and Future 295

Chapter 9 Croatian-Serbian Relations in the 19th and 20th Century 297
Mihovil Biočić

Chapter 10 Understanding History in Croatia Today: A Missed Opportunity in the Film "Diary of Diana Budisavljević" 369
Igor Vukić

Chapter 11 Croatia: Future Perspectives: The SWOT Analysis 385
Matko Marušić

About the Editor 415

Index of Names 417

Index of Terms 423

PREFACE

THE PAST AFFECTING THE PRESENT AND THE FUTURE

Matko Marušić*
Editor

On December 13, 1886, the great Croatian statesman and Viceroy Ivan Mažuranić, also a poet and linguist, delivered a speech in the Croatian Parliament, during which he stated: "I trust in the State of Croatia, in her past, present, and, with God's help, her future." (Hrvatski Sabor 2020). Mažuranić made the statement eight centuries after Croatia had lost its freedom (1102), and one century before it regained it (1991). Delivered during hard times for Croatia, the statement defines both the centuries-old desire of the Croats to have a free and independent state and their lasting desire for freedom. Foreign forces attempted to prevent the establishment of a free Croatian state and subsequently tried to stamp out the Croatian nation in all aspects of life. They did so through unfair taxation, deleterious monetary policies and territorial seizures. Most importantly, however, they focused their efforts on eliminating that which is the essence of a national identity: its language, faith, and history. The Croatian language was saved by a narrow margin on a number of occasions (see Chapter 2). Meanwhile, the people's faith remained strong despite innumerable executions of Croatian priests, destruction of churches, and prosecutions of believers and clergy (Kožul 1998). The historic narrative about Croatia is so severely distorted that the positive parts of Croatian history are still neglected, while the negative parts are exaggerated (Sadkovich 2005), and a number of issues remain controversial.

Today, in peace, democracy and prosperity, when Croatia is a member of the European Union (EU) and NATO, its present and future do not differ significantly from those of other EU countries. However, its history grows increasingly more controversial, because the new freedom has allowed scientific research of previously forbidden ("unpopular", unpleasant) topics, and newly acquired data indicate gross distortions in many previously accepted

* Corresponding Author's Email: matko.marusic@gmail.com.

accounts. Historians from communist times still hold positions of authority and remain resistant to new findings, so that the controversy has moved from the academic to the political and public arenas, deepening the divisions between left and right in society. There is therefore no doubt that the Croatian past significantly affects its present and its future!

The Warped History of Croatia

Since 1102, Croatia was ruled by various foreign regimes as part of different kingdoms and federations. Nonetheless, the yearning for freedom never wavered. This is why these various regimes feared Croatian determination to fight for freedom, so they took all possible steps to suppress it. One such method of suppression was the manipulation of Croatian history. Most of the information published on Croatia, from cheap propaganda (Danas 2019) to respectable history books (Koulouri and Repe 2016) is incomplete or biased.

Croatian historical narratives of the 20th century are especially distorted (Štefan 1999). Under the Serbian royal regime from 1918 to 1941, the oppression was so harsh that two prominent Croatian historians, Ivo Pilar (New York Times 1931a; Lipovčan 2006) and Milan Šufflay (Einstein and Mann 1931; New York Times 1931a, b) were simply murdered by the state police. The Franciscan monk and prolific historian Dominik Mandić (Jolić 2014) was forced to emigrate and never returned, and all his books were banned until 1990. Stjepan Radić, the president of the Croatian Peasant Party and the political father of the nation in the early 20th century, was assassinated along with two of his party members in the Yugoslav Parliament in 1928, during a session (New York Times 1931b). This murder triggered the formation of the Ustasha movement, which brought about demographic catastrophe for the Croatian nation in World War II (WWII) and its reputation after the war. The fact that Vlatko Maček, the leader of the Croatian Peasant Party, the most influential Croatian political figure at that time (successor of the murdered Stjepan Radić), who declined the Nazi offer to create an independent state of Croatia, is often neglected in historical research (Tomasevich 2001). Even today, the shameful alliance of the Croatian Ustasha government with Nazi Germany is misused to denigrate Croats and intimidate them to give up their national restoration and pride. The tactics of those trying to falsify and distort the narrative of Croatian history were, and still are, to inflate and emphasize the negative and hide or deny any positive elements (e.g. the case of Cardinal Stepinac, see Chapter 5) of that part of Croatian history. This behavior continues to the present time, as the resistance to the collection, analysis and publication of scientific data about that period in history. This book addresses some of the most heated historical controversies.

The mortal blow to Croatian historiography occurred in 1945 with the communist extermination of Croatian intellectuals and elites, including entrepreneurs, soldiers, reporters, clergy and politicians, and the establishment of a communist regime. This regime aimed to erase all parts of existing culture and replaced them with those that conformed to the goal of achieving a communist society, as was done in Stalin's Soviet Union. In particular, this included interventions in Croatian history and language. From 1945 to 1990, in Tito's Yugoslavia, Croatia had no freedom of speech, it had limited or non-existent access to information other than communist propaganda; and school curricula were packed with lies and half-truths so that students learned to love communism, Yugoslavia and Tito, as well as to hate free- market capitalism. In consequence, students dismissed entrepreneurship, national history and Western culture. Almost all Croatian efforts towards national liberation were depicted as backward, wrong or chauvinist, sometimes even fascist, in nature. Both the country and the world have been flooded with innumerous lies about Croats and Croatia (see Lozo, 2017). After Croatian independence in 1990/1991, Croatia faces a rediscovery of its past and conflicts that arise from these emerging truths. Nonetheless, the conflicts elicited by the clash of old and new narratives may turn out to be of the utmost importance for Croatia's future.

Freedom and Independence Allow an Evidence-Based Study of History

The arrival of independence in 1990 brought Croatia many different things, including a war. Among them was the disclosure of incredible past events, much more appalling than the old tales and legends told by parents and grandparents. A different version of Croatian history started to emerge in public life. New things still keep emerging, almost daily, and elicit a raging public dispute that significantly affects history (Geiger and Grahek Ravančić 2018), politics (see Danas 2019), public communication (see Kosanović 2019) and even education (see Paar and Šetić 2017). New research is vehemently rejected and criticized by established public figures that have retained positions of power, carried over from the former communist regime. These include most prominent historians, reporters, writers and politicians. Their criticism purports to be more authoritative, because the "new" history, with rare exceptions (Matković 2017; Vukić 2019 b), is mostly published in local media or history journals and in the Croatian language (Horvat et al. 2015; Razum 2015; Pilić and Matković 2014; Lozo 2017; Geiger and Grahek Ravančić 2018; Vukić 2019 a, b). Such sources may be inherently less credible so it is easy to attack them with insults, ignore them, or to proclaim the topics to be taboo. However, much of this new research has been confirmed by forensic findings in the field; the most stunning and unquestionable examples are discoveries of mass graves of Croats massacred by Tito's partisans in 1945 (Tolstoy 1991; Jurčević 2012; Leljak 2015; Vukić 2016).

The notorious WWII Jasenovac camp, led by the Ustasha regime (Pečarić 2001; Kevo 2008; Jakir 2012), illustrates the best challenge of addressing these emerging stories and research. In communist Yugoslavia, all school children were taught that 700,000 civilians, mostly Serbs, were killed in Jasenovac. This was written in Yugoslavian textbooks, encyclopedias, and, very often, in newspapers as well. This figure was not to be questioned for fear of severe consequences. For instance, the late Dr. Franjo Tuđman, the first President of the free and democratic Republic of Croatia, was sentenced to two years imprisonment in the former regime for claiming in one of his books that the number of victims in Jasenovac ranged from 30,000 to 40,000. The key evidence of his crime presented at the court was the Yugoslav Military Encyclopedia which gave the number as 600,000 victims (Knežević and Mihaljević 2018).

In 1985, Bernstein, Hitchcock and Blake made the film *A Painful Reminder: Evidence for All Mankind* in which they wrote that Jasenovac had 20,000 victims (Bernstein et al 1985), but the film was never shown in Yugoslavia until it was aired in 1990 on Croatian television. The multitude of estimates and claims on the number of Jasenovac victims was thoroughly presented in the works of Croatian historian Vladimir Geiger; the range of that number extends from 2,238 to 1,110,929 (Geiger 2013). Today, *The Public Establishment Memorial*

Park Jasenovac in Jasenovac, Croatia (the official Croatian name is *Javna ustanova Spomen park Jasenovac*, JUSP (http://www.jusp-jasenovac.hr/Default.aspx?sid=6467) lists each individual victim by name, and this figure amounts to approximately 84,000 (Benčić 2018). At the same time, the Jasenovac Research Institute in New York (https://jasenovac.org/), which also lists the names of victims, maintains a list comprising some 600,000 names, ignoring the JUSP list (and vice versa). A number of contemporary historians still insist on (at least) 700,000 victims, among them M. Bulajić (see Krušelj 2001), R. Israeli (see Gitman 2019), G. Zuroff (see HINA 2015), and Greif (see Kosanović 2019). Historians like them openly oppose any further research and different opinions and interpretations. They even proclaim that they have a "cosmopolitan approach" (Subotic 2018), which means that their statements should be unquestionable and immune to scrutiny. Subotić writings (2018) are just one of thousands examples of Serbian strategy defined as early as in 1941, in Valerian's Memorandum (see Chapter 9). Fifty years later, Philip S. Cohen described this strategy as "desecrating the Holocaust" (Cohen 1993). The best answer to that "approach" was given by one of the greatest Croatian historians, Mirjana Gross. Writing about questions of objectivity and bias in history research, she said: "Numerous historians assure the readers that their fragmentary and promising research results are the "full truth" and refuse the possibility of alternative interpretations. Instead of that, it should be natural and acceptable that other historians examine the evidence and set forward different opinions, if they do not do so without arguments and solely by ideological-political allegations. Eventually every statement becomes obsolete and requires revision, which I affirmed with this book." (Gross 1996, 381).

During the last decade, controversies regarding the Jasenovac camp grew stronger because new data indicated a rather different picture. The publication of three forensic excavations of mass graves from Tito's regime at the suspected graves on the location of Gradina, where hundreds of thousands of victims were presumed (Danas 2019; see HINA 2015, and Kosanović 2019) brought about additional complications. More than 100 boreholes were made at the site. Many did not contain any human remnants but some did: in total, the remains of 440 persons of equivocal origin and times of deaths were identified (Pilić and Matković 2014). Pilić and Matković (2014) also argue that Jasenovac camp was not closed in 1945 but was used by communist regime for next several years. Data challenging the very character of the Jasenovac camp were presented in Vukić's (2019 a, b) books on Jasenovac. Informatics experts Nikola Banić and Mladen Koić studied systematically the list of victims on the JUSP-Jasenovac website and published some 60 articles revealing so many inaccuracies on the list, which then casts doubt about the entire list. A rather intriguing finding came from an analysis of the birth years of the listed victims which showed significant anomalies. For example, the number of victims listed as born in 1900 is more than twice the number listed as born in 1899 and in 1901. This would be statistically highly unlikely. In contrast, a similar analysis of birth years of the victims from Buchenwald revealed no such discrepancies (Koić and Banić 2001).

What is the Truth?

Science is a human endeavor and thus cannot reach an absolute truth which would be exempt from additional scrutiny. Human truth is an "unfinished jigsaw puzzle" in which some parts may still be missing without our knowledge, and even without any notion of what the shape and meaning of those parts might be. However, we can detect falsehoods – mistakes, biases, inaccuracies, even malevolent intent. Conclusions and inferences that do not agree with research data must be treated as untrue. When research data is questionable, inaccuracies can be detected, and the findings rechecked and corrected. This means that, in cases of disagreement, everybody interested in the subject is obliged to consider and reassess the contradictory data. Reexamination of what were once considered truths is not shameful but a part of the natural process of acquisition and maturation of human knowledge (Popper 1968, Mohr 1977).

The logic of modern science brings us back to the case of Croatian history: the data that are controversial must be analyzed objectively (by all sides) and conclusions must be made in accordance with the most reliable evidence, including the identification of knowledge gaps that require more research. This was the unanimous conclusion of the Council for Facing the Consequences of Nondemocratic Regimes (Vijeće za suočavanje 2018) which was established by the Croatian government on March 2, 2017, when public disputes on several historic themes had become too heated (Government of the Republic of Croatia 2017). Among other things, the Council proclaimed that good practice for dealing with the past would be to engage in historiographic research via scientific exploration of sources, critical inquiry, non-selective choice of facts, and the publication of newly discovered materials. This includes the availability of archival materials and new research to reveal the death toll of past undemocratic regimes, including the Independent State of Croatia (NDH) during WWII and communist Yugoslavia afterwards, as well as a dignified commemoration at the places of death and sacrifice. Manipulation and discrepancies in the research about victims from previous undemocratic regimes continue to be an impediment for seeing the historical truth, for culture of dialogue, and ultimately for peaceful civilian life (Vijeće za suočavanje 2018).

The Book

This book offers information on key elements of Croatian history and its importance for the present. It also urges further rigorous academic research on certain issues that need to be assessed and reconciled with extant knowledge. The contributors are renowned historians, as well as experts from different research fields, for example medicine and linguistics. They provide their view of what we know (and what we still do not know) about the past, present and future Croatia and what they consider important, interesting, controversial and challenging. All chapters were reviewed by at least three reviewers from an expert team of reviewers. Dr. Žarko Domljan graduated in art history and English, in parallel with a secondary music school education (French horn). He was the first President of the Croatian Parliament (Sabor) in 1990-1992, and Vice-President in the next two mandates. Dr. Goran Kardum is a professor of psychology at the University of Split (Split, Croatia), and is a learned, critical, and objective researcher; in 2019 he received the University of Split Award for Excellence in Research. Dr. Neven Karlovac is an engineer and entrepreneur (retired Chief Executive Officer), Croatian-American, and a proficient English speaker; he also edited all texts in this book with his son Harvey Karlovac, attorney and international trade professional. Finally, I was honored by the assistance of the professor of history of the University of Split, Dr. Edi Miloš, whose research expertise is Croatian history in the 20th century. We also thank a number of experts and colleagues who provided informal review of early versions of the texts and whose critical comments were most valuable in shaping the individual chapters. The reviewers and the authors were known to each other. In a number of cases the authors and reviewers communicated directly until both sides were satisfied with every sentence in respective chapters. The review documentation is kept by me as the editor of the book.

REFERENCES

Bernstein, Sidney, Alfred Hitchcock and Brian Blake. 1985. *Movie A Painful Reminder: Evidence for All Mankind.* New York: First Run Features/Icarus.

Benčić, Andriana. 2018. "Koncentracijski logor Jasenovac: konfliktno ratno nasljeđe i osporavani muzejski postav." *Polemos: časopis za interdisciplinarna istraživanja rata i mira* XXI(41): 37-63. ["Concentration Camp Jasenovac: Conflicted Heritage of War and Contested Museum Exhibition". *Polemos: Journal for Interdisciplinary Research of War and Peace*].

Cohen, Philip J. 1993. *Desecrating the Holocaust: Serbia's Exploitation of the Holocaust as Propaganda*. Philip J. Cohen.

Danas. 2019. "Politika. Brnabić: Da se ne zaborave zločini u Jasenovcu i da se ne relativizuje karakter NDH. ["Politics: The Crimes in Jasenovac should not be Forgotten, and the Character of NDH should not be Relativized"]. Accessed April 5, 2020. https://www.danas.rs/politika/brnabic-da-se-ne-zaborave-zlocini-u-jasenovcu-i-da-se-ne-relativizuje-karakter-ndh/.

Einstein, Albert, and Heinrich Mann. 1931. *Appeal to the International League of Human Rights. Berlin.* Accessed February 14, 2020. http://www.croatianhistory.net/etf/einste.html.

Geiger, Vladimir. 2011. "Ljudski gubici Hrvatske u Drugom svjetskom ratu koje su prouzročili 'okupatori i njihovi pomagači' Brojidbeni pokazatelji (procjene, izračuni, popisi)." *Časopis za suvremenu povijest* 43(3):699-749. ["Human Losses of Croatia in World War II Caused by 'Occupators and their Collaborators' (Estimations, Figures, Lists"). *Journal for Contemporary History* 43(3):699-749].

Geiger, Vladimir. 2013. Numerical Indicators of the Victims of the Jasenovac Camp, 1941-1945 (Estimates, Calculations, Lists). *Review of Croatian History* 9/2013(1):151-187.

Geiger, Vladimir, and Martina Grahek Ravančić. 2018. "Jasenovac i Bleiburg između činjenica i manipulacija". In *Jasenovac – manipulacije, kontroverze i povijesni revizionizam, Zbornik radova*, edited by Andriana Benčić, Stipe Odak, Danijela Lucić, 19-64. Jasenovac: Javna ustanova Spomen područje Jasenovac. [Jasenovac and Bleiburs between facts and manipulations. In *Jasenovac –manipulations, controversies and historic revisionism, Collection of Papers*, edited by Andriana Benčić, Stipe Odak, and Danijela Lucić, 19-64. Jasenovac: Public Establishment Memorial Park Jasenovac].

Gitman, Esther. 2019. "Book Review: Raphael Israeli, The Death Camps of Croatia: Visions and Revisions, 1941–1945. New Brunswick, NJ: Transaction Publishers, 2013." *Journal of Cold War Studies* 22(1):266-268.

Government of the Republic of Croatia. 2017. *Odluka o osnivanju Vijeća za suočavanje s posljedicama vladavine nedemokratskih režima, 2. ožujka 2017.* [*Decision on Constitution of Council for Facing the Consequences of Nondemocratic Regimes from*

March 2nd. 2017]. Accessed February 20, 2020. https://vlada.gov.hr/UserDocsImages/Vijesti/2018/02%20velja%C4%8Da/28%20velja%C4%8De/Odluka%20o%20osnivanju%20i%20%C4%8Dlanovi.pdf.

Gross, Mirjana. 1996. *Suvremena historiografija: korijeni, postignuća, traganja.* [*Contemporary historiography: Roots, Achievements, Quests*]. Zagreb: Novi liber.

Hina. 2015. "Zuroff o genocidu u NDH: Stepinac je bio Pavelićev duhovni savjetnik." [Zuroff on Genocide in the NDH: Stepinac was Pavelić's Spiritual Advisor]. *Index reporting what Zuroff said for the Belgrade daily 'Politika'*, Belgrade, July 14, 2015. Accessed January 6, 2020. https://www.index.hr/vijesti/clanak/Zuroff-o-genocidu-u-NDH-Stepinac-je-bio-Pavelicev-duhovni-savjetnik/830695.aspx.

Horvat, Vladimir, Igor Vukić, Stipo Pilić, and Blanka Matković. 2015. *Jasenovački logori – istraživanja.* Zagreb: Društvo za istraživanje trostrukog logora Jasenovac. [*Jasenovac Camps – Research.* Zagreb: Association for Research of the Triple Camp Jasenovac].

Hrvatski Sabor. 2020. *Govor Ivana Mažuranića u Saboru 13. prosinca 1886.* [*The Speech of Ivan Mažuranić in Sabor (Croatian Parliament) on December 13, 1886*]. Accessed February 14, 2020. https://www.sabor.hr/hr/o-saboru/povijest-saborovanja/znameniti-govori/govor-ivana-mazuranica-u-saboru-13-prosinca-1886.

Jakir, Aleksandar. 2012. "Memories in Conflict. Remembering the Partisans, the Second World War and Bleiburg in Croatia." In *Balkan Memories: Media Constructions of National and Transnational History*, edited by Tanja Zimmermann,187-205. Bielefeld: Transcript.

Jolić, Robert, editor. 2014. "Dr. fra Dominik Mandić (1889.-1973.)." *Zbornik radova sa znanstvenog simpozija održanog u prigodi 40. obljetnice njegove smrti (Mostar – Široki Brijeg, 24. i 25. listopada 2013.).* Hercegovačka franjevačka provincija Uznesenja BDM – Franjevačka knjižnica Mostar – Hrvatski institut za povijest, Mostar – Zagreb. [*Franciscan Dr. Dominik Mandić. Collection of Papers from Scientific Symposium on the Occasion of 40 years of His Death (Mostar – Široki Brijeg, October 24 and 25, 2013).* Herzegovian Franciscan Province of Ascension of Blessed Virgin Mary – Franciscan Library Mostar – Croatian Institute for History, Mostar – Zagreb].

Jurčević, Josip. 2012. *Prikrivena stratišta i grobišta jugoslavenskih komunističkih zločina.* Zagreb: Dokumentacijsko informacijsko središte – DIS. [*Hidden Scaffolds and Graveyards from Communist Crimes.* Zagreb: Documentary Information Center – DIS].

Kevo, Mario. 2008. "ICRC Delegate's Visit to Concentration Camps of Jasenovac and Stara Gradiška in the Summer of 1944." (In Croatian and German). *Časopis za suvremenu povijest* [*Journal of Contemporary History*]. 40(2):547-584.

Knežević, Domagoj, and Josip Mihaljević. 2018. "Political trials against Franjo Tuđman in Socialist Federal Republic of Yugoslavia." *Review of Croatian History*, 14(1):353-381.

Koić M, and Nikola Banić. 2018, "Koić i Banić: Gdje su ostale lažne jasenovačke žrtve?" [Koić and Banić: Where are the Remaining False Victims from Jasenovac?]. *Narod*, April 22. Accessed January 28, 2020. https://narod.hr/hrvatska/koic-banic-ostale-lazne-jasenovacke-zrtve.

Kosanović, Saša. 2019. "Štampači Jasenovca." *Novosti* (Zagreb). [Editors of Jasenovac. *News* (Zagreb)], October 6. Accessed January 22, 209. https://www.portalnovosti.com/stampaci-jasenovca.

Koulouri, Christina, and Božo Repe, editors. 2016. *Wars, Divisions, Integration (1990-2008).* Volume 2. Teaching Contemporary Southeast European History. Source Books for

History Teachers. Thessaloniki, Greece: Center for Democracy and Reconciliation in Southeast Europe (CDRSEE).

Kožul, Stjepan. 1998. "Svećenici žrtve progona u Hrvatskoj nakon II. Svjetskog rata" ["Priests Victims of Prosecution after World War II"]. *Croatica Christiana Periodica* 22(41):177-202.

Krušelj, Željko. 2001. "Dr. Milan Bulajić – Guardian of Greater-Serbian 'Genocidomania'." In Pečarić, Josip. *Serbian Myth about Jasenovac*. p. 9-29. Zagreb: Naklada Stih.

Leljak, Roman. 2015. *Huda jama – strogo čuvana tajna*. Zagreb: Društvo Huda jama. [*Huda jama – Strictly Guarded Secret*. Zagreb: Association Huda Jama].

Lipovčan, Srećko. 2006. "A Portrait of Ivo Pilar." *PILAR – Croatian Journal of Social Sciences and Humanities* Year I, Issue 2(2):11-16.

Lozo, Stjepan. 2017. *Ideologija i propaganda velikosrpskoga genocida nad Hrvatima*. Split: Naklada Bošković. [*Ideology and propaganda of Greater-Serbian genocide over Croats*. Split: Edition Bošković].

Matkovic, Blanka. 2017. *Croatia and Slovenia at the End and After the Second World War (1944-1945): Mass Crimes and Human Rights Violations Committed by the Communist Regime*. Boca Raton, FL: BrownWalker Press.

Mohr Hans. 1977. *Lectures on structure and significance of science*. New York-Heidelberg: Springer Verlag.

New York Times. 1931a. "Einstein Accuses Yugoslavian Rulers in Savant's Murder." Published on May 6. Accessed January 31, 2020. http://www.croatianhistory.net/etf/nyt.html.

New York Times. 1931b. *Raditch Left Tale of Yugoslav Plot*. Published on August 23. Accessed January 31, 2020. http://www.croatianhistory.net/etf/raditch.pdf.

Paar, Vladimir, and Nevio Šetić, editors. 2017. *Prilozi za raspravu o obrazovnoj i kurikulnoj reformi. Kritike i vizije. Recenzije članova Znanstvenoga vijeća za obrazovanje i školstvo Hrvatske akademije znanosti i umjetnosti*. Zagreb: Hrvatski pedagoško-književni zbor. [*Contributions for Discussion on Curricular Reform. Critiques and Visions. Reviews of the Members of the Scientific Committee for Education and School of Croatian Academy of Sciences and Arts*. Zagreb: Croatian Pedagogic-Literary College]. Accessed April 7, 2020. http://hpkz-napredak.hr/wp-content/uploads/sites/387/2017/07/Prilozi-za-raspravu-o-obrazovnoj-i-kurikularnoj-reformi-Crvena-knjiga_kb.pdf.

Pečarić, Josip. 2001. *Serbian Myth about Jasenovac*. Zagreb: Naklada Stih.

Pilić, Stipo, and Blanka Matković. 2014. "Poslijeratni zarobljenički logor Jasenovac prema svjedočanstvima i novim arhivskim izvorima." *Radovi Zavoda za povijesne znanosti HAZU u Zadru* 56:323-408 ["Post-War Concentration Camp Jasenovac: Witness Testimonies And Newer Archival Sources". *Publications of Department for History Sciences of the Croatian Academy of Science and Art in Zadar* 56:323-408].

Popper, Karl. 1968. *The logic of scientific discovery*. London: Hutchinson.

Razum, Stjepan. 2015. "Dr. Stjepan Razum: Obavješćujem hrvatsku javnost da sam otkrio veliku prijevaru u Jasenovcu." ["Dr. Stjepan Razum: Hereby I Inform Croatian Public that I Discovered Gross Fake in Jasenovac"]. *Hrvatski tjednik* June 11, 559:18-29.

Sadkovich James J. 2005. "(E) Is Image Everything? American Stereotypes of Croatia." *Text for a Talk Delivered in Chicago on April 26, 2005*. Accessed January 8, 2020. http://www.croatia.org/crown/articles/6254/1/E-Is-Image-Everything-American-Stereotypes-of-Croatia.html.

Subotic, Jelena. 2018. "Political Memory, Ontological Security, and Holocaust Remembrance in Post-Communist Europe". *European Security*, 27:3, 296-313.

Štefan, Ljubica. 1999. *Mitovi i zatajena povijest.* [*Myths and Supressed History*]. Zagreb: "K. Krešimir": Slovo M, 1999.

Tolstoy, Nikolai. 1986. *The Minister and the Massacres*. London: Century Hutchinson.

Tomasevich, Jozo. 2001. *War and Revolution in Yugoslavia 1941-1945*. Stanford, California: Stanford University Press.

Vijeće za suočavanje – Vijeće za suočavanje s posljedicama vladavine nedemokratskih režima. 2018. *Dokument dijaloga: temeljna polazišta i preporuke o posebnom normativnom uređenju simbola, znakovlja i drugih obilježja totalitarnih režima i pokreta*. Zagreb veljače 28. 2018. [Council for Facing the Consequences of Nondemocratic Regimes. 2018, February 28. *Document of Dialogue: Basic Starting Points and Recommendations on Special Normative Regulation of Symbols, Emblems and Other Signs of Nondemocratic Regimes*]. Accessed February 19, 2020. https://vlada.gov.hr/UserDocsImages/Vijesti/2018/02%20velja%C4%8Da/28%20velja%C4%8De/Dokument%20dijaloga.pdf.

Vukić, Igor. 2019a. *Jasenovac iz dana u dan* Zagreb: Naklada Pavičić. [*Jasenovac from Day to Day*. Zagreb: Edition Pavičić].

Vukić, Igor. 2019b. *Labour camp Jasenovac*. Zagreb: Igor Vukić.

Vukić, Ina 2016. "The Haunting Reminders of Depravity of Communist Crimes." In *Ina Vukic – Croatia: People, Politics, History, Economy, Transition from Communism to Democracy*. October 5. Accessed February 25, 2020. https://inavukic.com/2016/10/05/the-haunting-reminders-of-depravity-of-communist-crimes/.

How To Pronounce Croatian Words

The Croatian Language is written in the Latin alphabet like English but with some different signs. Pronunciation of different letters is often different than in English, but it almost never changes, and that makes it considerably easier to learn. Here is a quick guide to Croatian pronunciation together with some examples:

Letters with diacritical signs
ć and č are both pronounced like "ch," as in **ch**op *(by many Croatians, others properly say ć more softly)*
š is pronounced like "sh," as in hu**sh**
ž is pronounced like the "s" in trea**su**re.
đ is pronounced like the "j" in **j**ewel

Same letters with different pronunciation
c is pronounced like "ts," as in ca**ts**
j is pronounced like the "y" in **y**oung
u is pronounced like the "oo" in b**oo**t

Same letters with same pronunciation (sometimes)
a is pronounced like the "a" in f**a**ther
e is pronounced like "e" as in m**e**n
g is pronounced like "g," as in **g**ood
h is pronounced like the "h" in **h**ouse
i is pronounced like "i" as in split
o is pronounced like the "o" in f**o**rd
s is pronounced like the "s" in **s**plit
t is pronounced like the "t" in spli**t**
z is pronounced like the "z" in **z**oom

Same letters with same pronunciation (always)
b, f, k, l, m, n, p

Letters not used in the Croatian language
q, w, x, y

Examples of Croatian names (with approximate English equivalents)

Petar Krešimir (Petar Kreshimir)
Stjepan Radić (Styepan Radich)
Franjo Tuđman (Franyo Toojman)
Matko Marušić (Matko Marooshich)

PART I: CROATIAN HISTORY TIMELINE

In: Croatia: Past, Present and Future Perspectives
Editor: Matko Marušić
ISBN: 978-1-53618-300-9

Chapter 1

OVERVIEW OF THE CROATIAN HISTORY FROM THE 7TH CENTURY TO THE ACCESSION OF THE REPUBLIC OF CROATIA TO THE EUROPEAN UNION IN 2013

Karmen Perković*
Primary School Ivana Gorana Kovačića, Zagreb, Croatia

ABSTRACT

Croatian state was created after Croats had arrived at the Adriatic in the 7th century. On June 7, 879, Duke Branimir received recognition from Pope John VIII, which made Croatia an internationally recognized state. Shortly after, Croatian state advanced from a duchy to kingdom, reaching its peak in the 10th century during the reigns of Tomislav and Stjepan I Držislav, and later in the 11th century when Petar Krešimir IV and Dmitar Zvonimir ruled.

In 1102, the Kingdom of Croatia entered a personal union with the Kingdom of Hungary, having maintained its legal and political autonomy. Starting in the 15th century, and peaking in the 16th century, many parts of Croatia fell under the Ottomans, whereas the Adriatic coast went to the Republic of Venice. To resist Otomans, in 1527 Croatian nobility elected Ferdinand of the House of Habsburg as King of Croatia.

After the fall of the Republic of Venice 1797, Croatian provinces Istria and Dalmatia fell under the Habsburgs (later Austro-Hungarian Monarchy). Croatian lands did not unite not even after provinces Bosnia and Herzegovina passed from Ottomans to Habsburgs in 1878, but the Kingdom of Croatia, whose capital was Zagreb, kept its political and legal autonomy held by the Ban (Viceroy) and the Sabor (Croatian Parliament).

After World War I in 1918, Croats and their lands, pressured by the victorious countries, entered into a new union – the Kingdom of Serbs, Croats, and Slovenes. There the Croats lost centuries-long statehood (with the discontinuation of Sabor) and were subjected to persecution. Repression reached its peak in 1929, when three Croatian representatives in the Yugoslav Parliament, among them Stjepan Radić, very popular leader of Croatian Peasant Party, were murdered during the session in the Parliament in Belgrade. This led to the dictatorship of the king Alexander and even greater repression.

* History teacher; Correspondence to: karmen.p62@gmail.com.

The multinational country, dominated by Serbs, fell apart in April 1941 under the attack of Axis powers.

After the assassination of Stjepan Radic and in response to violence against Croats, a Zagreb lawyer Ante Pavelić emigrated, and in 1930 founded in Italy an organization "Ustasha – Croatian Revolutionary Organization." Its goal was to win an independent state of Croatia by arms, because after all what happened Pavelić saw no hope in negotiations with Serbs. The Independent State of Croatia was established in 1941 by the Ustasha as a Germany's ally, and ended in May 1945.

Under communist rule, the second Yugoslavia was founded, and Croats once again were oppressed and lived in a dictatorship. With the fall of communism, in May 1990, after the first democratic elections in the history of Croats, Croatian multiparty parliament (Sabor) was formed. In August 1991 the unrest of Serbian minority started and grew into a full-scale aggression with the aim of forming Greater Serbia. Serbs in Croatia, backed by Yugoslav Federal Army, occupied 25% of the Croatian territory and proclaimed a Serbian republic. In 1991, Sabor proclaimed independence from Yugoslavia, and Republic of Croatia became internationally recognized in 1992. Up to 1995, it liberated its occupied territories, in 2009 joined NATO, and in 2013 became the 28th member of the European Union.

Keywords: Croatia, history; Croatian Kingdom; Hungarian-Croatian Kingdom; Ottoman conquests, Croatia; Croatia, in the Habsburg Monarchy; Croatia, countries in the Austro-Hungarian Monarchy; Croats, in the First World War; Kingdom of Yugoslavia; Second Yugoslavia; Communist government, Croatia; Communism, fall of; Greater Serbia; Croatia, Homeland War; Croatia, international recognition

The Rise of the Croatian State in the Early Middle Ages to the 12th Century

Historians still cannot determine with certainty the origin of the Croats, the ancestral homeland they lived in before their migration, and what directions they came from to the present-day Croatia. The exact time frame of the settlement is also questionable. There are a number of different theories about origin that have not been fully elucidated. The best known are Indo-European-Slavic, Germanic-Carpathian, Germanic-Gothic, Carpathian-Illyrian, Carpathian-Thracian, Iranian, Iranian-Caucasian and others (Mužić 1989, 10-18; Matasović 2019, 81-94).

Name, Origin, and Settlement

There are two Greek inscriptions from the turn of the 2nd to the 3rd century as material evidence of the origin of Croats. On the inscriptions found at the mouth of the river Don, the name Horoathos or Horuathus can be read. They are assumed to be of Iranian origin. Greek inscriptions fit into a broader historical context. They were associated with the great Iranian colonization under the leadership of Persian King Darius the Great in the 6th century BC. The Persian kingdom extended from India in the east to central Europe in the west and Poland in the north of Europe. Historian Ćurić writes that there were numerous Harauvatis from the Old Kingdom of Harauvatya in the ranks of Darius's army. He also cites creation of the White,

Western Croatian Kingdom in the Carpathian Mountains. Based on these data, he refers to ethnic assimilation of immigrant Iranians with Slavic indigenous people they had found in the area (Ćurić 1991, 10-11).

Although many historians disagree over the origin of the name Croat, available information about the migration of Croats in the 7th century indictes that the Croats were already slavicized during the migration to the south. They lived according to Slavic customs. Furthermore, the Croatian name was also used until the 11th century by people in Greater or White Croatia around the city of Krakow in Poland and northeastern Czech Republic. We learn about the ancestral land of the Croats from the Byzantine source of Emperor Constantine VII. Porphyrogenitus, who cites the same information in his work "On the Management of the Empire" in the 10th century. He sets the arrival of the Croats from their ancestral homeland in the 7th century during the reign of the Byzantine emperor Heraclius (610 – 641). In the same work, Emperor Constantine states that in the 7th century the Byzantine emperor Heraclius summoned Croats from White Croatia as allies against the Avar-Slavic and Persian invasions of Constantinople, then the capital of the Byzantine Empire. According to Constantine VII Porphyrogenitus, Croats came to Dalmatia to expel the Avars. One group of Croats descended from the Carpathians and the Baltic Sea into the former Roman province of Illyria. After a successful victory over the Avar tribes, Croats settled in Dalmatia. Some of them conquered Illyria and Pannonia. In the same work, Constantine mentions a group of Croats who separated under the leadership of five brothers and two sisters. According to the legend, their names were: Kluk, Lobel, Muhlo, Kosenc, and Croat, and sisters Tuga and Buga (Mužić 2007, 249-259).

Fleeing the Avar-Slavic invasion, the indigenous population took refuge in inaccessible places, mountains, islands or within the ramparts of Dalmatian cities. Inhabitants of the demolished Roman city of Salona took refuge in the nearby Diocletian's Palace (today the city of Split), and refugees from Epidaurus (today Cavtat) fled to the gorgeous islet of Ragus. This is where the city of Dubrovnik (Ragusa) developed in the early middle Ages. Several cities, such as Zadar and Trogir, as well as islands Krk, Osor, and Rab, survived the Avar-Slavic invasion. The same cities and islands fell under Byzantine rule (Mužić 2010, 266-271; Gračanin, H. 2008, 67-69).

Before the arrival of Croats, ancient culture flourished in the same area for centuries. Christian faith was already deeply rooted. Salona was a flourishing city and one of the largest in the Roman Empire. The Arena of Pula, remains of the Temple of Augustus, ruins of Salona and the Diocletian's Palace, where life in medieval Split took place, and Narona (Vid at Metković) are testimonies of that time. In older historiography, the prevailing view was that Croats, as a barbarian people, had a negative attitude towards the established ancient culture. This view has been changing lately, especially after Radoslav Katicic published a capital work called "Litterarum studia" in which, on the basis of philological research and documents, he showed that Croatian early medieval literacy and culture did not develop in conflict with ancient culture, but on the contrary, in symbiosis with it (Katičić 2007, 760).

Due to its geographical location, Istria was not exposed to the consequences of Slavic - Croatian migrations. In the history of the Salonitan Church, historian Thomas the Archdeacon in the 13th century states that Croats upon their arrival did not live in the cities but roam the hills and forests. Later they mixed with the natives, gradually acquiring the ancient cultural heritage and the Christian faith. Immigrating to the hinterland of the eastern Adriatic coast, accepting Frankish and Byzantine influence, Croats became part of European history and culture in the early Middle Ages (Macan and Holjevac 2013, 13).

Territorial Division and Acceptance of Christianity

After the assimilation of newly arrived Croats with indigenous peoples, new territorial divisions began to form in the area as embryonic states. Croats established several smaller communities called Sklavinija, which were divided into counties, smaller territorial units headed by prefects (Figure 1). Elders of lineages joined into tribal alliances so they could more easily defend themselves against the enemy. At the head of a tribal alliance was a duke or a prince. These were the beginnings of the first Croatian state – the Principality of Croatia. (Macan and Holjevac 2013, 16).

The principalities of Croatia were situated in an area of conflict of interest of the then greatest medieval empires, The Frankish Empire and Byzantium. The conflict ended with the Peace in Aachen, the aftermath of which also affected Croatia: the Frankish Empire and the Byzantium in 812 divided the Croatian lands. Byzantium kept the Dalmatian cities and islands (Zadar, Trogir, Krk, Osor and Rab). Croatia and Lower Pannonia fell under the Frankish rule (Mužić 2010, 281-285).

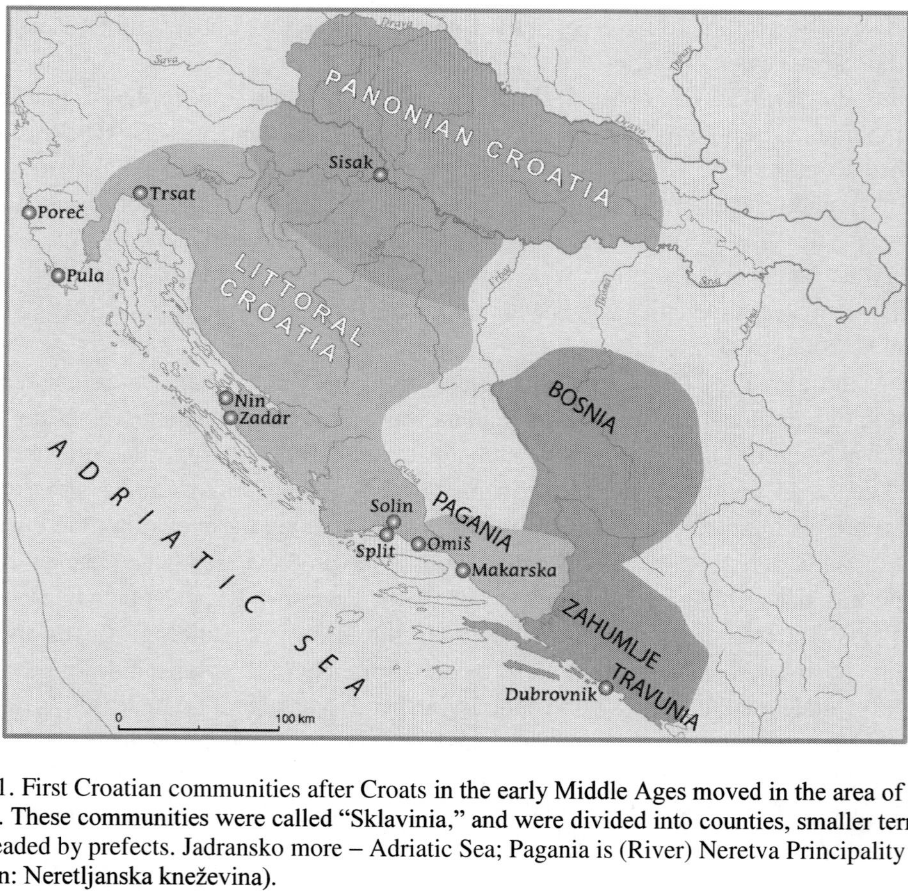

Figure 1. First Croatian communities after Croats in the early Middle Ages moved in the area of today's Croatia. These communities were called "Sklavinia," and were divided into counties, smaller territorial units headed by prefects. Jadransko more – Adriatic Sea; Pagania is (River) Neretva Principality (in Croatian: Neretljanska kneževina).

According to the Byzantine Emperor Constantine VII Porphyrogenitus, Croats were pagans upon their arrival. They believed in a multitude of gods, fairies, and natural powers. The dead were buried with food, drinks and other items, thus prepared for the afterlife. Material remains from ancient Croatian graves are evidence of pagan religious practices. The Christian faith was more widely accepted through Frankish missionaries and Benedictines from the west. Croats in southern Sklavinias accepted Christianity a little bit later through involvement of Byzantine and Roman missionaries. The best known material evidence for acceptance of Christianity by immigrant Croats is the baptismal font of Duke Višeslav and the lintel in the St. Cross Church in the city of Nin, the first ecclesiastical center in Croatia (Mužić, I. 2010, 285-286; Macan and Holjevac 2013, 17).

Croatian Principalities in the 9th Century

We have no written historical records about the early history of Croatian rulers in the 7th century, but only material ones. From the graves of Croatian dignitaries in which were found jewelry, horse spurs, and the remains of weapons we can conclude that there was a tribal hierarchy in the first Croatian principalities (Milošević 2016, 240-262).

After the peace of Aachen, Croats west of the Raša River in Istria fell in 788 under the Frankish rule; Slavic worship and the Glagolitic script connected them with other Croatian tribes. The rest of the Croatian principalities also gradually fell under the rule of the Frankish Empire (Mužić, I. 2007, 127).

The first known princes from the 8th century mentioned in two Croatian states, northern and southern, are Višeslav (about 800- 810) and Vojnomir. Višeslav ruled in the southern Croatian state from the Adriatic Sea to Gvozd, called Littoral or White Croatia (see Figure 1). Vojnomir ruled Pannonian Croatia from Gvozd to Drava; he recognized Frankish rule and was succeeded by Prince Ljudevit Posavski (about 810 – 823) who, however, rose agains the Franks. Ljudevit Posavski resisted 10 Frankish campaigns and his courage and resistance shook the Frankish rule in the Croatian principalities. At the same time Višeslav's successor in White Croatia Duke Borna (about 810–821) sided with the Franks and entered the war against Ljudevit; he wanted to unite the Croatian principalities from the Adriatic Sea to the Drava river and needed Frankish support against the Byzantine rule in Dalmatia (Mužić 2007, 157).

The Frankish Empire in the west and the Byzantine's in the east were getting weaker at this time and the situation was exploited by new rising powers, the Ugri (Hungarians) and the Arabs, who had consolidated in southern Italy. Furthermore, Venetians grew stronger in the west as a merchant power engaged in maritime trade with Byzantium. The Venetians needed the eastern Adriatic coast to protect their way to Byzantium, which caused Venice's centuries-old wars with the Croatian rulers. Major conflicts arose during the reign of Croat Prince Mislav and Prince Družak of Neretva and their pirates who beat Venetian merchants on several occasions. The conflicts lasted until 887, when the Venetian doge Kandian died in the naval battle of Makarska and for some time the Venetian efforts to rule over the eastern Adriatic coast were stopped.

The Trpimirović Dynasty

On the Croatian throne, in White Croatia, Prince Mislav was succeeded by Prince Trpimir (845–864) by whom the Croatian ruling dynasty was called Trpimirović. Prince Trpimir reigned as an independent ruler.

Trpimir's Grant from 852 mentions for the first time the Croatian name in a document written Latin: "Trpimir, by the grace of God, prince of the Croats (dux Croatorum)." Another material evidence, carved in stone, is the inscription "For Prince Trpimir (Pro duce Trepimiro)" from the town of Rižinica near Klis.

In Trpimir's time, Rižinice near today's city of Split was the center of education. On Trpimir's demand, Benedictines from the Frankish Empire came to Rižinice to a restored monastery. They spread literacy, culture, and faith. Trpimir was a rather knowledgeable ruler. From the report of Benedictine Gottschalk, to whom Trpimir gave refuge, we learned about progress in the economy and the expansion of education (Mužić 2010, 286-287).

Trpimir had three sons who were to succeed him (Petar, Zdeslav and Muncimir); however he was not succeeded by any of them but by Prince Domagoj (about 864-878), from another ruler's family. This led to a series of conflicts between supporters of Domagoj, an ally of the Franks, and Trpimir's sons who allied with the Byzantium. Byzantine fleet devastated the Dalmatian coast while Neretva pirates attacked Venetian ships on their way to Byzantium. Prince Domagoj crushed the opposition. Pope John VIII writes to the "famous prince" Domagoj to be gentle with the conspirators and strict with the pirates. Domagoj led the wars with the Venetians until his death. In Venetian records, Domagoj is referred to as the "worst Croatian prince" (Mužić 2010, 285-289). Prince Domagoj, however, with his firm rule secured Croatia's independence (Macan and Holjevac 2013, 45).

After some strife, Domagoj was succeeded by his son Branimir. During Branimir's reign (879–892), Croatia freed itself from the Byzantine rule and became an independent state with reliance on Pope John VIII In a document called the June Charter, issued on June 8, 879, Pope John VIII blessed Branimir, his people, and Bishop Theodosius whom Branimir appointed the Archbishop of Dalmatia in Split (Mužić 2007, 195-204).

This historical document is a testimony to the first international recognition of the independence of the Croatian state. Monument dedicated to prince Branimir is in the town of Nin (Macan and Holjevac 2013, 22, 45-46). As material evidence, five stone fragments in Latin, bearing Branimir's name, prove that he was a powerful ruler. The most famous one is the inscription from Šopot near the town of Benkovac, which reads "BRANIMIRO COM (ES) DVX CRVATORV(M)." Prince Branimir was a powerful prince who ruled a strong and independent state. His reign was peaceful, and both Venetians and Byzantines paid the "tribute of peace." The monument to Prince Branimir is located in the town of Nin (Mužić 2007, 198-204; Josipović 2018, 145-151).

With Pope's blessing, Archbishop Theodosius was granted permission to conduct mass in Croatian language. This led to arrivals of students who were taught by the Byzantine philosopher Methodius in Moravia. Methodius' students found refuge in Croatia, especially in Kvarner and Istria and middle Dalmatia. Upon arrival, they introduced a new script, the Glagolitic, which was thereafter used in the Croatian Church. Slavic worship was also performed in Glagolitic script. Branimir will not be succeeded by his son, but briefly by Muncimir (892–910), son of Prince Trpimir, and father of King Tomislav (Klaić 1975, 275-277).

Croatian Kingdom in 10th and 11th Century

Descendants of Trpimir regained the throne with Prince, later King Tomislav (914–928). Tomislav united for the first time all principalities of Croatia into a single state: Pannonian Croatia, White and Red Croatia, and partly Pagania with the islands of Vis, Brač, and Hvar. The kingdom of Tomislav stretched from the river Raša in Istria to Srijem and the river Drina, where it bordered Bulgaria, and to Zahumlje. He also successfully defeated the invasions of the Hungarians from the north and the Bulgarians from the east. As an ally to Byzantium in the war with the Bulgarians, he conquered all Dalmatian cities and islands that belonged to the Byzantine Empire. The record of the Byzantine emperor Constantine VII Porphyrogenitus testifies to the strength of Tomislav's military and naval forces. Emperor Constantine VII states that the Croatian principality at that time had an army of 100,000 infantrymen and 60,000 cavalrymen, and a navy of 80 sagens (larger ships) and 100 condors (smaller ships). In 925, Tomislav took the title of king in the presence of the people at the Duvno field near today's Tomislavgrad. Pope John X in his letter acknowledged Tomislav's royal title (Klaić 1975, 276-293).

During the reign of King Tomislav, two church councils were held, in 925 and 928. At the first church council in 925 Archbishop Ivan of Split was elected as the Archbishop of Croatia. At the second, in 928, Glagolitic priests were allowed to hold Glagolitic masses which were a turning point for Croatian worship thanks to the leadership of Bishop Gregory of Nin. The famous monument to Gregory of Nin in the city of Split is the work of the sculptor Ivan Meštrović. Glagolitic script became a strong part of Croatian cultural heritage, and still is to this day (Klaić 1975, 293-312). King Tomislav's rule was reflected not only in territorial and economic gains but also in the unity of the Croatian people. Tomislav also improved domestic matters and consolidated the ancient Croatian culture, and he is regarded as one of the greats of Croatian history. King Tomislav's monument is located on the eponymous square in Zagreb.

The strength of Tomislav's kingdom was briefly maintained by his successors, Trpimir II and Krešimir I (Margaritoni 2003, 11) and started declining during Tomislav's grandson Miroslav's time (945-949). Conflicts for the throne ensued during successive reigns of, Mihajlo Krešimir II, Stjepan I Držislav, Svetoslav Suronja, Krešimir III and Gojslav, and Stjepan I.

There were many clashes and repeated territorial losses and gains during these difficult times. Venetians took advantage of the weakness in the country by attacking the principality of Neretva. In 950, Hungarians crossed into eastern Slavonia and Srijem. Dalmatian cities and islands again fell under Byzantine rule but they were soon returned to Croatia. Stjepan I arrived on the Croatian throne (about 1030–1058). During his reign, the restoration of the Croatian kingdom began, with short-term conflicts with the Venetians (Margaritoni 2003, 12-13).

The "golden age" of the Croatian kingdom will follow during the reign of King Peter Krešimir IV (1058–1074). Petar Krešimir restored the unity of the Croatian kingdom and brought it to its pinnacle of development and rise. The territory of the Croatian Kingdom included principalities from the Drava River to the Adriatic Sea and Slavonia, Bosnia, and Neretva Principality. Through his strong rule, he took advantage of international opportunities of that time as Byzantium fought Turkish Seljuks and Normans in southern Italy. Petar Krešimir IV governed the Dalmatian cities and islands. He bore the title: "King of Croatia and

Dalmatia." King Peter Krešimir's royal capital initially was Biograd and later Nin (both near today's city of Zadar) where he held a separate court. Other cities such as Skradin and Šibenik, first mentioned in 1066, grew stronger. He gave some cities self-government. Feudalisation of society began. In the feudal hierarchy, county prefects and nobles acquired estates and shared inheritance rights over estates. New families were receiving noble titles. Towards the end of his reign, King Krešimir IV sided with the Bulgarians and the Duklians against the weakened Byzantine Empire. The Normans used this political opportunity and in 1074 invaded the Croatian coast. In these conflicts, Petar Krešimir IV was taken into captivity and his fate is unknown (Klaić 1975, 360-361). Monument to King P. Krešimir IV is located in his hometown Šibenik (Macan and Holjevac 2013, 48-49).

King Krešimir IV distributed grants to churches and monasteries, which were, in return, strong supporters of his reign. Then, in 1054, the religious schism led to the division of the Church into Western-Catholic and Eastern-Orthodox. The Croatian state came under the protection of Western, Catholic Christianity (Klaić 1975, 357-361). With Popes'support and in the presence of his envoy Maynhard, a third major church council was held in Split in 1060. According to the conclusions of the council, priests were forbidden to marry and wear long hair and beards. Among other things, it was forbidden to marry among relatives. The Benedictine ranks grew stronger in the territory from Istria to Split. One of the most famous is the monastery of St. Mary in Zadar.

King Peter Krešimir IV died without a successor. Dmitar Zvonimir (1075–1089), today called Zvonimir, a grandson of Trpimir, was the only candidate for the throne as Ban and a new ruler because Krešimir's nephew Stjepan withdrew to priory. Dmitar Zvonimir was crowned in 1075 in Solin in the church of St. Peter and was confirmed as the "King of Croatia and Dalmatia." He received royal signs of honor from the Pope's envoy Gebizon: flag, scepter, crown and sword, and swore his allegiance to the pope and the Catholic Church. He ruled from the town of Knin and strengthened his rule in Slavonia. He married Jelena "The Beautiful" of the Hungarian Arpadović dynasty, sister of the Hungarian king Ladislav. With Arpadović's assistance, Zvonimir incorporated north Adriatic islands to White Croatia (Macan and Holjevac 2013, 50).

Zvonimir briefly fought with Byzantium. His reign was marked by universal progress and prosperity in economic, cultural and political sense. It was the culmination of the "golden age" of the Croatian kingdom before it lost its independence. Zvonimir, like his predecessor, continued to donate possessions to the Catholic Church and monasteries. The process of feudalisation continued. One of the most important deeds of endowment was the one King Zvonimir donated to the Glagolitic Monastery of St Lucy in Baška on the island of Krk. As a way of thanking King Zvonimir, the Glagolitic priests carved a text written in Glagolitic script and Croatian in stone, the Baška (Baščanska) Tablet, the most precious monument of the Croatian language preserved in its entirety (Figure 2). In addition, it is the refrence to the sovereign title in the Croatian language: "... Zvanimir, King of Croatia. ..." Today, the Baška tablet is kept in the Croatian Academy of Sciences and Arts in Zagreb (Klaić 1975, 378; Galović, T. 2018, 265-286).

Since Zvonimir's son Radovan died very young, Zvonimir died without a successor. Little is known about Zvonimir's death in Croatian history. According to the legend, the good king Zvonimir was killed by the members of the Croatian nobility in the Knin field who refused to join the Crusade war for Zvonimir. Another assumption is that King Zvonimir died from natural causes. The monument of the king Zvonimir in Knin is the work of the sculptor Guberina (Nemet 2006, 73-89).

Figure 2. Baščanska tablet, a monument written in the Croatian script Glagoljica. It was created about 1100. This most valuable stone monument was preserved in its entirety. The name of the Croatian ruler King Zvonimir was mentioned in the Croatian language for the first time. Today it is kept in the Croatian Academy of Sciences and Arts in Zagreb.

Conflicts over succession ensued after Zvonimir's death. Zvonimir's widow Jelena "The Beautiful" demanded by her hereditary right that her brother Ladislav Arpadović, son of Bela I, of the Hungarian Arpadović dynasty, ascend to the throne. Part of Croatian nobility supported Jelena, while the rest elected Petar Svačić ("Snačić") (1091?–1097). Petar, with country's capital in Knin, was to maintain Croatian independence with the help of Byzantium. Ladislav I Arpadović entered Croatia in 1091, and without a fight took over the territory that stretched from Hungary accross river Drava to Mount Gvozd (today Petrova Gora). In 1094 Ladislav founded the Diocese of Zagreb. As Byzantium was opposed to the Hungarian expansion in Croatian regions, it summoned the Kumans to fight the Hungarians. The Kumans were Turkish tribes that invaded Moldova and Wallachia to get to Hungary. Consequently, King Ladislav had to withdraw from Croatia. He left his nephew Almosh as a co-ruler. In 1097 Hungarian King Koloman, the heir to Ladislav I Arpadović, defeated Petar Snačić, the last Croatian king, in the Battle of Gvozd. Mount Gvozd has since been named Petrova Gora. With the death of Peter Snačić, the Croatian kingdom reigned by national rulers was gone forever (Margaritoni 2003, 15).

With the Gvozd victory, Koloman (1102–1116) became the master of Pannonian Croatia from Gvozd to White Croatia on the South. He occupied Biograd and signed a contract with the Venetians in 1098 to obtain estates on the Croatian coast. In order to avoid a larger scale conflict with the powerful Croatian nobility, Koloman concluded in 1102 a settlement called Pacta Conventa with the most prominent Croatian nobles of the lineages Kačići, Šubići, Snačići, Kukari, Čudomirići, Mogorovčići, Gusići, Karinjani and Lapčani, Polečići, Lačinići, Jamometići and Tugomirići. According to the settlement, the high Croatian nobility retained all its privileges and possessions, and tax exemption. The Croatian nobles became Koloman's co-rulers and they recognized Koloman as their king. They committed themselves to war at their own expense south of the river Drava, and at the king's expense from the river Drava North.

In 1102, Koloman was crowned as Hungarian-Croatian King in Biograd, a town on the Adriatic Sea. It was the first personal union in Croatian history, which will later be repeated several times. With this event, Croatia and Hungary became the states that shared the same ruler. Croatia retained the right to choose a Ban (Viceroy), as the King's governor. It also kept a separate parliament (Sabor), tax system, money, and the military (Margaritoni 2003, 15-16; Tanner 2001, 16; Macan and Holjevac 2013, 51).

Croatian Culture and Literacy in the Early Middle Ages

Art which was created during the period of the reign of the national Trpimirovic dynasty we call ancient Croatian art. It belongs to the period of pre-Romanesque style in the 9th and 10th centuries in Western Europe. The influence of Frankish and Byzantine art is evident in architecture, arts, and literature. In Byzantine-influenced architecture, churches of circular, rectangular or cross shape with a dome, larger or smaller in size, were built. One of the most beautiful is the church of St. Donatus in Zadar. Out of smaller churches, the church of the St. Cross in Nin and the church of The Holy Trinity in Split stand out (Jarak 1998, 119-128).

Rectangular churches with a bell tower were built under Frankish influence. As an example of Frankish influence on ancient Croatian architecture, it is worth mentioning the church of St. Spas at the source of the Cetina river (Jurković 1995, 55-80).

Church of St. Peter in Priko near Omiš is a unique example of a mixed Byzantine – Frankish style, rectangular in shape with a dome. The early Croatian pre-Romanesque churches were decorated with furniture. These were mostly altar partitions, pulpits and baptisteries. Furniture was carved of stone with intertwining ornaments. The architecture was influenced by Italian and Frankish craftsmen who came to Croatia in the 9th century. Until the 11th century, ornaments called "pleter" were decorated with plant motifs such as vine leaves, lilies, grapes or crosses. In the 11th century a human figure appeared in the art. The depiction of the Virgin, found in the Diocese of Knin, is one of the oldest such ornaments with a human figure as well as a relief from the 11th century baptistery of Split which shows a king, his emissary, and his subject. Two slabs of the altar partition from St. Nediljica church in Zadar with scenes from the life of Christ are also preserved. On the altar partitions we find records of the names of saints or Croatian rulers who, by donating grants, encouraged the construction of churches. Names of these Croatian national rulers are mentioned: Trpimir, Branimir, Stjepan Držislav, Zvonimir. In addition to construction and the arts, literacy spread with the spread of Christianity. Latin alphabet was the oldest. Many inscriptions and documents were written in the Latin alphabet. Also, monks of different orders wrote and copied various books, documents or charters in Latin script in the 9th century (Ivančević 1986, 58-59).

With the arrival of Glagolitic priests and monks in Croatia at that time, the Glagolitic script developed and spread. Methodius' students, who found refuge in the Croatian principality, spread the Glagolitic script from Kvarner, Istria, Lika to northern Dalmatia. Because Byzantium was in conflict with Rome, it sought to spread Glagolitic and Slavic worship through its influence in the territory of Byzantine Dalmatia. Numerous Glagolitic monuments have been created in the area of Istria and Kvarner, including the islands of Cres, Lošinj, Ilovik, Unije and Susak and others. The unique Istrian territory stands out with a lot of medieval towns situated on hills: Motovun, Grožnjan, Završje, Buzet, Buje, Roč, Hum. Of the oldest records written in stone we can point out: Hum inscription, Grdoselski fragment, Plomin inscription, Krk inscription, Supatarski ulomak and Valun plate (Nazor 2008, 28-32), and the most beautiful monument the Baška Tablet (Galović 2018, 265-285).

February 22 was proclaimed the Day of Croatian Glagolitic Studies. The day commemorates the printing of the first Croatian book Missal by the Law of the Roman Court in 1483 (Paro 1984, 91-110).

The Arpadović and the Anjou on the Croatian Throne Until the 15th Century

After the fall of the Croatian rulers, the Hungarian dynasty Arpad (in Croatian Arpadović) took over the Croatian lands. King Koloman bore the title "King of Hungary, Croatia and Dalmatia".

Croatia during the Arpadović Reign

Koloman ruled the area from the Drava river to the Adriatic Sea. Most of the Dalmatian cities recognized Koloman's authority. This was recorded by having Koloman's name engraved on the bell tower of the church of St. Mary in Zadar. Koloman confirmed old privileges of the Dalmatian cities and exempted them from paying taxes. Due to the great distance from the Hungarian court, Arpadović's power in Dalmatia was weaker than in Slavonia, which was territorially closer (Klaić 1976, 278-291).

In Dalmatia, the Croatian noble families grew stronger as co-rulers: Bribir Šubić, Nelipčić, Kačić, and Frankopan families. The Dalmatian cities were in frequent conflict with Venice. They changed their rulers, passing from the hands of Arpadović into the hands of the Venetians and vice versa. The Venetians used the 4th Crusade to briefly overtake Zadar in 1202, abandoning it in 1203 after they ravaged it and destroyed it. They also tried to conquer Dubrovnik but failed. Dubrovnik enjoyed the protection of the Normans and quickly became independent through the maritime and overland trade with the hinterland. Dubrovnik also defended independence against the Serbian prince Miroslav from the Nemanjić dynasty. It signed numerous trade agreements with cities in the Mediterranean but also in the hinterland; the Kulin Ban Charter of 1189 is a written record of Dubrovnik trade between Dubrovnik and Bosnia. In 1184, the two parties concluded a peace treaty on free navigation (Vrana 1955, 5-57).

Arpadović dynasty formed counties in Slavonia, which then became royal counties. The counties were managed by the county prefect. He, as the king's commissioner, had judicial, administrative, and military authority. From the 12th to the 15th centuries, the following counties were established in Slavonia: Zagreb, Varaždin, Križevci, and Virovitica, Požega, Vukovar, and Srijem County. In Slavonia, Koloman replaced the tax paid in marten fur, called kuna or a marturine, with a monetary tax.

After his victory over the Byzantine army in 1186, King Koloman acquired a treaty which formally ended Byzantine rule over the Dalmatian cities and islands. With Koloman's death, a period of feudal power struggles ensued. During the reign of Bela III (1172–1196) the areas of Srijem, Croatia, and Dalmatia from the rivers Krka to Neretva were returned to the Hungarian-Croatian crown. His authority was recognized by the Bosnian Ban Kulin.

At the same time, the feudalization of society continued in Croatian lands. Royal power weakened in favor of powerful feudal families. In the west these were the Frankopan, princes of Krk; the Šubić, princes of Bribir; the Nelipčić, dukes of Cetina; the Kačić, princes of Omiš, famous for pirating; and the Kurjaković, dukes of Krbava. In Slavonia, the power of Princes Babonići strengthened. However, Bela III successfully maintained his dominance and improved economic and political circumstances in the kingdom. Especially Coastal cities flourished, with urban aristocracy and rich merchants thriving. The second son of Bela III, Andrija (Andrew) II Arpadović (1205–1235), failed to consolidate his rule, both because of international circumstances and because Croatian noble families grew stronger (Klaić 1976, 307-315; Tanner 2001, 18-19).

Due to frequent encroachment by the high nobility, lower nobility requested from Andrew II assistance and protection of their rights. In order to calm the situation in the kingdom, in 1222 King Andrew II issued a document called the Golden Bull, confirming the privileges and protection of the lower nobility. The successor of Andrew II, Bela IV (1235-1270), also tried to weaken the power of high nobles. They, however, took advantage of the Tatar invasion of Hungary in 1241and resisted obedience to the king. The Tatars defeated King Bela IV's army and forced the king to flee via Zagreb to Dalmatia. King Bela IV was hiding briefly in Zagreb's Gradec (Old Town), which was ravaged by the Tatars. In Dalmatia, he first took refuge in the well-fortified Trogir and later he moved to the islands. When the Tatars withdrew, King Bela IV began to encourage the construction of forts and cities by granting them privileges. In 1242 he granted Gradec, by charter, the Golden Bull, the status of a free royal city (Klaić 1976, 316-324). All such cities enjoyed royal protection and authority. Citizens elected a city judge, independently governed the city, and exercised the right to hold trade fairs.

The reign of Bela IV was weaker in areas south of the Kupa River. Powerful Croatian noble families took advantage of this, especially the Subic princes and the Frankopan princes. The center of the Šubić administration was the town of Bribir near Šibenik. Today, there is a large archeological site called Bribirska glavica.

The peak of high nobility feudal power lasted from the late 13th to the early 14th century during the reign of Prince Paul I Šubić. Paul I held the title "Ban of Croatia and Lord of Bosnia." His authority stretched from Dalmatian cities to White Croatia and Bosnia (Tanner, M. 2001, 21-23; Karbić, D. 2008, 44-60).

Bela IV was succeeded by his son Stjepan V (Stephen V). He established family ties with the Anjou royal dynasty of Naples. The only male offspring from the Arpadović dynasty was his son Andrew III, the Venetian (1290–1301) who recognized the Šubić family as co-rulers.

The Anjou court, the Pope, and Rudolf Habsburg did not recognize Andrew III as the King of Hungary-Croatia. They proposed an Anjuvin, Karl Martel, and later his son Karl I Robert, to assume the throne. After the death of Andrew III, who had no successor, Juraj Šubić went to the kingdom of Naples and brought Karl I Robert to the Croatian throne. Karl I Robert (1301–1342) was crowned in the Hungarian city of Ostrogon as Hungarian-Croatian king. Thus, a new dynasty, the Anjuvins, started ruling over Croatian lands and continued until the 15th century (Tanner 2001, 24; Karbić 2004, 1-26).

Croatia during the Reign of the Anjou Dynasty

Since the strong rule of Croatian aristocratic families in the time of Arpadović led to the collapse of royal authority, Karl I sought to weaken the power of Croatian nobility. He consolidated his reign in Hungary and Slavonia. In Croatia, powerful Princes Šubić of Bribir interfered with his efforts; however, other Croatian nobles sought to diminish the power of the Šubić clan and gave Karlo (Karl Robert) I an opportunity. In a military campaign in 1322, he defeated Mladen II, the son of Pavao Šubić. However, Karl I, who was striving for absolute power, failed to defeat other aristocratic families south of Gvozd, including the powerful Nelipčić family based in Knin. He was also unable to prevent Venice from conquering most of the Dalmatian cities.

What Karl I Anjou failed to accomplish in Croatian lands was achieved by his son and successor Ludovik I (1342–1382). Ludovik I restored royal authority in Croatia and diminished the power of all noble Croatian families. He managed to pacify almost all lands south of Gvozd in military campaigns. The Nelipčić nobles handed over Knin to Ludovik in exchange for the Cetina estate. To the princes of the Šubić family and Pavao III Šubić, King Ludovik I Anžuvinac (Anjou) offered a new estate called Zrin in Slavonia in exchange for the fortified cities Klis, Skradin, and Omiš in Dalmatia. The Šubić family was called Zrinski ever since but never regained its former power.

With Croatia secured, Ludovik I was able to to go to war with Venice. Fighting was heavy, particularly in Istria and around Zadar, but Ludovik inflicted several defeats on the Venetians and they signed a peace treaty in Zadar on February 18, 1358, by which the Venetians renounced all their possessions on the Croatian coast, and the entire Adriatic coast down to Durres, Albania. The event was recorded on a silver chest made by Ludovik's wife, Elizabeta Kotromanić, and located today in the altar of the church of St. Šimun (Simon) in Zadar (Klaić 1976, 610-625; Jakšić 2019, 1-27).

Dubrovnik recognized the Croatian-Hungarian king, freeing itself from Venetian rule. By marrying Elizabeta Kotromanić, Ludovik I also received the lands of Hum and Završje as dowry. Thus, for the first time since the reign of King Zvonimir, all Croatian lands were united under the rule of King Ludovik I Anjou – but not for long. After his death in 1382, Croatian nobility rebelled and so did Bosnian nobility, and many conflicts ensued over the succession to the throne. Ultimately, Sigismund of Luxembourg (Croatian: Žigmund Luksemburški), who married Ludovik's daughter Marija (Maria), seemed to prevail, but his opponents took advantage of his absence and temporary disappearance in the war with the Ottomans and brought in a new candidate for the Croatian throne, Ladislav of Naples (in Croatian: Ladislav Napuljski).

With the return of the "missing" Sigismund from the battlefield in Nikopol to Croatia, a "Bloody Assembly" took place in Križevci. The new ruler Ladislav and all his supporters led by Stjepan Lacković were killed by Sigismund and his followers, and the rebellion was crushed. Tragically, in the short time he was in power, Ladislav of Naples managed to sell in 1409 all rights to Dalmatia to the Venetian Doge for 100,000 ducats. From that point, Croatian state remained for 400 years without the Dalmatian coast (Klaić 1976, 661).

Dubrovnik and Istria

The earliest history of the city of Dubrovnik is poorly known. In the middle Ages, Dubrovnik, as Ragusa, recognized Byzantine rule. In the 12th century Dubrovnik was proclaimed a commune governed by the local nobility. At that time Dubrovnik was running a successful hinterland trade, especially with Bosnia; the trade was recorded in the charter of Kulin Ban from 1189 (Vrana 1955, 5-57). The Dubrovnik commune also made trade agreements with Italian cities. With the growth of Venice in the 13th century, Dubrovnik became stagnant in development. More favorable circumstances came after the Peace of Zadar in the 14th century, when Dubrovnik recognized the supreme authority of King Ludovik I in exchange for military protection. In the 15th century Dubrovnik became a Republic with a high level of independence. The city was ruled by patrician nobility. Soon Dubrovnik with its fleet gained a reputation in maritime trade in the Mediterranean. Famous diplomats of Dubrovnik made an agreement with the Pope, which allowed navigation and trade with Islamic countries. At the time of Ottoman rule in neighboring Croatian territories, the people of Dubrovnik paid their tribute to the Ottomans. Dubrovnik's policy with the Ottomans enabled them to freely trade and navigate in the Ottoman Empire, as well as in the Atlantic (Tanner, M. 2001, 24-25; Macan and Holjevac 2013, 75- 80).

Although the majority of its population was Croatian, Istria was never a part of the Croatian kingdom. With the arrival of the Croats in Istria in 7th century they occupied the interior of the peninsula. The Roman population withdrew to the cities on the coast. Thus, Istria remained divided between Roman cities and Croatian villages. In the early Middle Ages, it was ruled by Byzantine, Frankish, and German emperors. From the mid-13th century, Venice took over the coast. The central part of Istria consisted of a self-governing Pazin County, which in the 15th century fell under the rule of the Austrian Habsburg family. From then until the collapse of Venice in 1805, Istria was divided between the Habsburgs and Venice (Yriarte 1999, 15-40).

Croatian Culture from the 12th to the 15th Century

Romanesque art appeared in Croatian lands for the first time in the 12th century. In the coastal cities, the Romanesque flourished, as is evident in the monuments of sacral architecture of the period. Particularly in the construction of cathedrals – the Cathedral of St. Stošija in Zadar, St. John in Trogir, Cathedral St. Tripun in Kotor, and St. Krševan in Zadar. Romanesque sculpture decorated churches with depictions of biblical motifs, such as the doorways of Andrew Buvina in the Split Cathedral and the portal of craftsman Radovan at Trogir Cathedral. Dubrovnik has remarkable cloisters of Franciscan and Dominican orders. Paintings were present in murals, icons or miniatures that decorated the books.

However, in the interior of Croatia and in Istria Gothic art was prevalent. Among the sacral buildings in Gothic style some of the most beautiful are the Cathedral of Mary's Assumption and Saint Stephen and Ladislav in Zagreb (1093), and St. John Kapistran church in Ilok (1349). The portal of the church of St. Mark in Zagreb (1261) is a fine exemple of gothic sculpture, and the chest of St. Šimun in Zadar (1380) is a jewelry masterpiece.

Croatian literature also developed. It was written in four scripts: Latin, Glagolitic, and Croatian and Bosnian Cyrilic, and three languages: Latin, Croatian, and Old Slavic. Most preserved books of this period consist of missals, evangelicals, and other church books used in liturgy. In addition to biographies of saints, chronicles were written, such as the 13th-century Salonitan History of Toma Arhiđakon (Thomas the Archdeacon). The most famous works written in the Glagolitic script from that time are the Missal of Hrvoje Vukčić Hrvatinić, the Novak Missal, and the Povalj Charter from the Island of Brač written in Croatian Cyrillic. In the 13th century, the first town bylaws and statutes were written in Dalmatia. The oldest such codification is the Korčula Statute from 1265. The Vinodol Code from 1288 was written in Glagolitic script. The Vinodol Code is also a legal document governing the feudal relations of the noble Frankopan family and their subjects (Kolanović 1993, 85-98; Galović 2019, 869-894).

HUMANISM AND THE RENAISSANCE IN CROATIA

The period of humanism and the Renaissance in Western Europe marks a time of prosperity from the 14th to the 16th century. Croatian territories however were going through a difficult time during this period, which was marked by Ottoman conquests. At that time, only the Republic of Dubrovnik enjoyed independence. Yet even in this time of isolation, notable individuals left a deep and lasting mark on science, literature and the arts. It is these Croatian intellectuals who, through their works, described the most violent conflicts and sufferings of Croats under the Ottoman rule.

To the Split literary circle belongs the "father of Croatian literature" Marko Marulić (1450--1524). One of Marulić's most famous works is "Judita," an epic that sought to encourage citizens of Split and other Dalmatian cities to fight the Ottomans. Judita was written in 1501 and it was written in Croatian (Lokós 2008, 189-198). "The Prayer Against Turks" is also a well-known work by Marulić. Most of the works he wrote in Latin but also in Italian and Croatian. He was known at home and in Europe as a skillfull writer whose texts were easy to read. His works have been translated to many European languages. Some of them he illustrated himself. Monuments to him have been erected in the cities of Split, Mostar, Vukovar, and Knin as well as in Chille, also in Zagreb in front of the state archives building (Cattaneo 2013, 145-149). Marulić's figure is shown on the 500 kuna Croatian banknote.

At the beginning of the 16th century, one of the most famous playwrites was Marin Držić from Dubrovnik. In his works, Držić mocked the weaknesses and flaws of his fellow citizens. The best-known Držić's comedy is "Dundo Maroje" from 1551, still performed in Croatia. Other works are "Pomet" (1548), "Tirena" (1549), "Novela od stanca" (1550) "Džuho Kerpeta" (1554), "Skup" (1555), "Plakir" (1556), and a tragedy "Hekuba" (1559) (Kunčević 2008, 7-44; Delić-Gozze 2004, 125-133).

Another citizen of Dubrovnik, humanist Benedict Kotruljević (1416-1469), was renowned in Europe. Most of his life he spent at the court of King Alfons V of Naples (Croatian: Alfons V Napuljski). He wrote the first guide on trade and bookkeeping (1458), today in the National Library of Malta, and books "On the Skill of Trading" (Ital. "Della mercatura et del mercante perfetto"), "About Sailing" (1464) (Ital. "De navigatione"), "On the Nature of Flowers" (Ital. "Della natura dei fiori"), and in Latin "On the Choice of Wife" ("De uxore ducenda").

At the same time, Petar Hektorović and Hanibal Lucić were active members of the literary circle on the island of Hvar. Petar Hektorović (1487-1527) was an erudite poet. He wrote "bugarščice" (an old Slavic epic poetry form), and patriotic and lyric songs. He designed his summer villa Tvrdalj in Starigrad on the island Hvar, where today stands a monument to him. His main work is "Fishing and Fishermens' Grumbling" (in Croatian "Ribanje i ribarsko prigovaranje") (published 1568).

Hanibal Lucić (1485-1553) was a poet. His drama "The Slave Girl" (in Croatian "Robinja") is the first secular drama written in Croatian. Original manuscripts of Petar Hektorović and Hanibal Lucić are stored in the Croatian Academy of Sciences and Arts in Zagreb.

Humanist scientist Marko Antony de Dominis (1560-1624) born in the town of Rab on the namesake island, was a university professor of physics and philosophy at the University of Padua, and the Archbishop of Split. He studied light dispersion to explain the phenomenon of rainbow. In his work "Euripus seu de fluxu et reflex maris Sentential" (1624) he explained the origin of high and low tide. He accepted the heliocentric system in opposition to the official position of the Catholic Church and in 1624 was arrested, killed, and burned with his books (Martinović 2002, 67-145).

Among the greatest Croatian scientists of the era is certainly Faust Vrančić (1551-1517), historian, lexicographer, and inventor born in Šibenik. Faust's parachute (Homo Volans) presaged the modern parachute. In addition to numerous inventions in the field of mechanics (Machinae novae), he compiled the first multilingual dictionary. Although he died in Venice, his remains are located today on the island of Prvić, in the church of St. Mary. Today in Prvić there is a beautiful interactive museum dedicated to this Croatian great (Lisac 2012, 37-47).

Croatian humanist intellectuals were diplomats at many European courts and were also often tutors of noble children. Ivan Vitez of Sredna was a teacher of the future King Matthias Corvinus (Croatian: Matijaš Korvin) and his nephew Ivan Česmićki (lat. Jannus Panonius) wrote books on astronomy and also poetry. Corvinus' court also included theologian Matija Vlačić Ilirik and sculptor Ivan Duknović (Tomorad 2011, 165- 191).

Juraj Julije Klović, a representative of miniature painting in Croatia and Europe, had the most impact in Renaissance painting. He was known as the "Michelangelo of Miniatures." Klović painted numerous church books in miniatures (Hrvatska enciklopedija 2020, Klović, Julije). Another painter who stood out was Nikola Božidarević from Dubrovnik, who decorated the interiors of many churches.

Until the 16th century, Renaissance art outside Italy was almost non-existent. However, on Croatian soil, at that time, architectural masterpieces were built. Builder Juraj Dalmatinac in 1431 built the cathedral in Šibenik without the use of mortar. He decorated the cathedral with 72 carved heads of his fellow citizens. Construction of Šibenik's cathedral lasted for about 100 years. It was completed by Juraj Dalmatinac's son-in-law Nikola Firentinac in 1536. Today, the Cathedral of Šibenik is on the UNESCO World Heritage List.

On the Croatian coast, construction of palaces, castles, and mansions was popular at that time. The mansion of Petar Sorkočević, the Rector's palace in Divona, and the city walls of Dubrovnik are also on the UNESCO World Heritage List (Čorić 2013, 37-47).

In the area of Bosnia and Herzegovina and in the Dalmatian hinterland many tombstones (Croatian: stećci), mainly from the 14th and 15th century, were built until the 16th century (Hrvatska enciklopedija 2020, Stećci). They are under the protection of UNESCO.

At the same time, fortifications were built in the interior of Croatia for defense against the Ottoman threat in Karlovac, Slavonski Brod, Sisak (Kljaić 2013, 121-156).

THE RISE OF THE OTTOMAN EMPIRE AND ITS EXPANSION IN CROATIA AND EUROPE

The Ottoman Empire is the name for an Empire that began in the late 13th century on the border with Byzantium in northwest Asia Minor. At the head of the state was the tribal leader Osman. By uniting the tribes, Osman began campaigns of conquest, which his descendants continued for three centuries on Croatian soil. The Ottoman Empire ended only after World War I. Europe first faced the Ottoman conquest in 1354 when the Byzantine fortress of Cimpe in the Gallipoli peninsula fell. The Ottomans successfully penetrated the Balkan Peninsula with continuing military campaigns. In a short time, Bulgaria fell under Ottoman rule. In 1389, in the battle of Kosovo, Serbia became an Ottoman vassal land. King Sigismund of Luxembourg tried to stop the penetration of the Ottomans into the Kingdom of Croatia and Hungary but was badly defeated in the battle of Nikopol in 1396. The Ottoman invasion of the West was briefly stopped by the Mongols. After the Mongols' withdrawal in 1453, Sultan Mehmed II conquered Constantinople and the millennial Byzantine Empire disappeared forever.

The organization of the Ottoman Empire was based on a timar-spahi system. At the head of the state was the Sultan. The Grand Vizier collected taxes and he was in charge of military conquest. The conquered areas were divided into large provinces, pashaluks, and smaller areas, sandžaks. The core force of the Ottoman army was the elite infantry units of janissaries and horsemen. Spahis were feudal nobles who received land from the sultan for their military contribution. Timar (land) was not hereditary but returned to the Sultan after Spahi's death. Janissaries (in Croatian: janjičari) were professional soldiers and a product of the military system which took children of conquered Christians, converted them to Islam, and gave them aigorous military training. In Croatian literature and history, this method of recruiting Ottoman infantry is called the "Danak u krvi" (A tribute in blood) (Dragić 2001, 123-139).

The Turkish Conquests in Croatia

The Hungarian-Croatian King Matijaš Korvin (Matthias Corvinus) established a military system in Bosnia, in Jajce and Srebrenica Banovina, which for 60 years provided a shield against Turkish conquests on Croatian lands. After the fall of Bosnia in 1463 and the death of the last Bosnian king, Stjepan Tomašević, the Ottomans frequently penetrated into Croatian territories (Botica 2014, 322-326) pushing westward towards Austria.

Croatian provinces Lika and Gorski Kotar were devastated. The Croatian population was leaving the devastated and looted areas en masse. Many of the Croatian civilian population were taken by the Ottomans into slavery as spoils of war. After the death of King Matthias Corvinus (Tomorad 2011, 165-191), the Croatian nobility and bans from the most respected Croatian families, Zrinski and Frankopan, led the struggle against the Ottomans. In 1493, Croatian Ban Emerik Derenčin decided to oppose the Turkish army of Jakub Pasha. Ban was joined by Croatian nobles, led by the experienced Frankopan princess. The Frankopans suggested that the Ottoman army be ambushed in nearby gorges and straits. Ban Derenčin however decided to face the Ottomans in Krbavsko Field. It was a crushing defeat for the Croatian army where a large majority of Croatian nobility were killed or captured. This event was recorded in the Glagolitic script by a monk Martinac in the 2nd Novljan Breviary (Lokmer 2004, 19-28).

The remaining Croatian nobles sought help from European rulers by pointing out that the Ottomans were threatening the rest of Europe as well, mostly without success. Croatia was left alone to defend itself against the Ottoman invasions. Notably, Ban Petar Berislavić successfully resisted Ottoman attacks. He became famous in 1513 at the Battle of Dubica, which became known throughout Europe (Peričić 1971, 258-266). During his rule, the Turks failed to conquer even a fraction of Croatian territory.

In 1520, Sultan Suleiman the Magnificent came to the Ottoman throne. During Suleiman's reign, the Ottoman Empire reached the peak of its power. Suleiman planned a conquest of Western Europe. With the conquest of Belgrade in 1521, Suleiman the Magnificent tried to open the passage to Europe through Hungary. His intention was to conquer Vienna. In 1526, Hungarian-Croatian King Louis II of Hungary (Croatian: Ludovik II Jagelović) decided to oppose Sultan Suleiman's superior army in the Battle of Mohács Field. The Croatian-Hungarian army at the time was divided into three parts: Transylvanian under the command of Ivan Zapolja, Hungarian under the command of King Louis II of Hungary, and the third and smallest one led by Croatian Prince Krsto Frankopan from Ozalj. However, Louis II did not wait for the military assistance of Zapolja and Frankopan but faced the enemy only with his own Hungarian army. It was a crushing defeat and the Hungarian army and most of the Hungarian nobility was destroyed. King Louis II fled the battlefield and drowned crossing a stream. The Hungarian-Croatian throne was left without a successor.

The Habsburg Dynasty on the Croatian Throne

After the death of Ludovik II Jagelović, the Croatian and Hungarian nobility had to choose a new king. Most of the Croatian nobility were inclined to the Habsburg dynasty. However, the Croatian Parliament met in the fortress of Cetin on January 1, 1527, and Croatian nobility elected Austrian Archduke Ferdinand I Habsburg as their king. On that occasion, the Cetin Charter was signed. By that charter, Ferdinand swore to protect the Croatian lands and to maintain fortifications at the border. He also confirmed all privileges that Croatian nobility received from previous rulers. Hungarian nobility, however, elected Ivan Zapolja as king with the support of some Slavonian nobles led by Krsto Frankopan. After a long war for the throne, Zapolja's party lost and the Hungarian-Croatian kingdom, created in 1102, ceased to exist.

Continued Defensive War against the Ottomans

The war of succession among Croatian nobles further weakened Croatia's defense against the Ottomans. While Ferdinand I was preoccupied with fighting Ivan Zapolja, he was not able to deliver on his promises to the Croatian nobility, and Croatia suffered the greatest territorial losses of all time. With the fall of Obrovac (1527), the connection between the north and the south of Croatia was broken. By occupying Udbina, the Ottomans gained Lika and Krbava. The victory of the Ottomans in Bosnia in 1528 at Jajce pushed back the line of Croatian defense to Bihać. On his first march to Vienna, the army of the Sultan Suleiman I the Magnificent stopped on August 5, 1532, and besieged Kiseg (Hungarian: Kőszeg, the last stronghold in Hungary on the border with Ottomans. It was defended by a small garrison with Croatian military commander Nikola Jurišić, who was King Ferdinand of Habsburg's diplomat. The battle lasted until August 30, 1532 (Hrvatska enciklopedija 2020, Kőszeg). After 25 days of siege Vizier Ibrahim Pasha proposed a settlement. Hostages were exchanged and the Turks withdrew.

In 1537, the Ottomans reached the Adriatic coast through Klis, the last royal fort in the south. With the fall of Klis under Ottoman rule, its brave defender Petar Kružić was killed and his surviving soldiers sailed to the northern Adriatic coast. The whole Dalmatia, except for the towns on the coast, fell under Ottoman rule. At the same time in the interior, the Ottomans conquered the territory from Slavonia to Čazma. After the conquest of Slavonia, Sultan Suleiman I the Magnificent decided to attack Vienna again. This time the army of the powerful Sultan was stopped in 1566 by a heroic Croatian Ban Nikola Šubić Zrinski at the Siget Fort (Hungarian: Szeged) in southern Hungary. After a month-long siege of Siget and in vain waiting for military reinforcement from the Habsburgs, the Ban with about a hundred of his fellow soldiers rushed out from the burning fort in a doomed counterattack. Before the assault Zrinski told his soldiers: "I, Nikola, Count Zrinski, promise first to His Mighty Lord, then to His Majesty our glorious monarch, to our piteous Homeland and to you, my knights, that I would never leave you but with you I will live and die, good and evil endure, so help me God!" Both Ban Zrinski and Sultan Suleiman died at Siget. The Sultan's death was kept secret so as not to affect the outcome of the battle. The Ottoman army gave up the march to Vienna once again. The death of Suleiman the Magnificent was the beginning of the end of the Ottoman expansion in Europe. The courage of Ban Nikola Šubić Zrinski is known in history as the victory of the "new Leonidas." Siget was initially defended by 2,500 Croatian soldiers to 100,000 Suleiman's. The earthly remains of Nikola Zrinski today lay in the tomb of the Zrinski family near the Croatian city of Čakovec. The memorial park in Siget (Szeged, Hungary) displays the figures of Nikola Šubić Zrinski and Suleiman the Magnificent. Nikola Zrinski is celebrated in Croatia as a great national hero. Croatian composer Ivan pl. Zajc composed the opera "Nikola Šubić Zrinski" in the 19th century and it is still performed in Croatia (Banov 2018, 111-133).

The Zrinski family's Fort Gvozdansko also fell. It was defended by 300 soldiers under the commands of captains D. Doktorović, J. Gvozdanović, N. Ožegović and A. Stepšić. The Ottoman army had 10,000 soldiers. Fort Gvozdansko fell on January 13, 1578, after Ferhat Pasha's fifth assault. Due to a particularly severe winter, the army and civilians of Gvozdansko froze to death in their positions. The Pasha ordered that the dead be buried according to Catholic custom, with military honors. The remaining surviving population was exempt from taxes. The Fort Gvozdansko's bloody fate was repeated in World War II: on Christmas Day 1941 Chetniks and partisans killed and expelled civilians and burned down devastated houses and a church (Borovčak 2019).

The culmination of the Ottoman conquests occurred in 1592 with the fall of Bihać. The Croatian Parliament called the remaining small part of its territory that was still free from the Ottoman rule "The remains of the remains of the once glorious Kingdom of Croatia" or

"Reliquiae reliquiarum." After Bihać, the Ottomans made their way to the fort of Sisak. With the conquest of the fort, they planned to pave the way for the conquest of Zagreb. The Bosnian Pasha, Hasan Pasha Predojević, set off in the summer of 1593 with a large army to Sisak. The fort of Sisak was defended by the troops of the Croatian Ban Toma Erdödy and the victory of the Ban's army, reinforced by the king's troops, at the Battle of Sisak, marked a turning point in the war with the Ottomans (Sikirić 1992, 371-374). The Ottoman conquests were halted, and the 100 years of ravages of Croatian lands were over (Latinčić and Vuković 2018, 384-387).

Military Frontier – A System of Defence against the Ottomans

After the Battle of Sisak, the Habsburgs decided to establish a more effective defense of their borders in order to prevent the Ottoman invasion of Vienna. For this purpose, they built a defense system with military formations – the Military Frontier (in Croatian: Vojna Krajina) divided into three regions. In the area south of the Kupa River, Croatian Krajina was established, with its center in the town of Karlovac. Between the Drava and Sava rivers, with headquarters in Varaždin, was the Slavonian region. Between the Sava and Kupa there was the Banska region (Figure 3).

In addition to Austrian commanders, the Habsburgs were recruiting into the army refugees from the conquered Ottoman border areas, mostly Vlachs. The Vlachs were an ancient nomadic Orthodox population who after fleeing the Ottomans settled in depopulated Croatian estates. They refused to pay taxes and came into conflict with Croatian nobles who owned the land. Despite all past courageous efforts of Croatian bans and knights in the defense of Vienna and Europe, the Habsburgs sided with the Vlachs and King Ferdinand II issued in 1630 the Vlach Statutes. The Article 1 of the Statutes said "…Let Vlachs from all captain areas (Croatian "kapetanija") as many as there are of them, even the young men older than 18, stay ready to swiftly, with joint forces, expel Turks and enemies at the price of life and blood…" These laws gave the Vlachs the right to self-government, free trade, and personal freedom in exchange for military service. The Vlachs were Orthodox and, with the appearance of the Serbian Kingdom in 19th century they self-identified as Orthodox Serbs – and today are a part of the Serbian minority in Croatia (Heka 2019, 26-45).

One of the consequences of the Ottoman conquests was the massive emigration population from the Military Frontier to the west and south. Croatian population fled before the Ottomans to Burgenland (Austria), Hungary (and Slovakia), and the Italian province of Molise. Vlachs, a population of the Orthodox faith, remained in the abandoned Croatian lands. Religious and ethnic structure of the population changed in these areas, which would significantly influence future events in Croatian history. The remaining population in Croatia and, for the most part, the Christian population in the Bosnian Pashaluk embraced Islam as the new religion (Beus 2018, 503-534).

Croatian fugitives who after the fall of Klis fled to Senj, called Uskoks, had many conflicts with the Ottomans and with the Venetians. They were supported by the Habsburgs who went to war with Venice for dominance in the Adriatic. The Uskok war lasted from 1615 to 1617. According to the peace agreement, the Habsburgs relocated these fugitives from Senj inland to the area around Otočac and Žumberak (Gruenfelder 2003, 211-252).

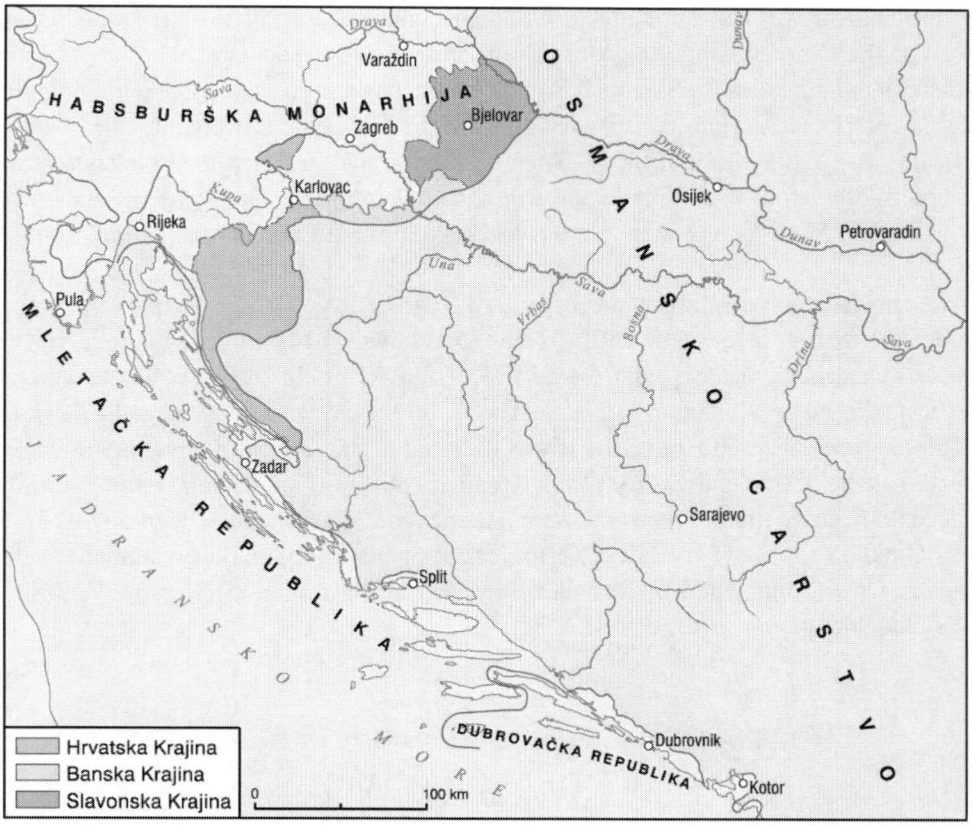

Figure 3. The formation of the Military Frontier (Croatian: Vojna Krajina), the defense system against the Ottomans in the 16th Century: Slavonian Krajina (from the River Drava to Kupa with the center in Varaždin), Banska Krajina between rivers Sava and Kupa), and Croatian Krajina (from the River Kupa to the Adriatic Sea with the center in Karlovac).

Reformation and Catholic Renewal in Croatia

The appearance of Protestantism in Europe led to bloody wars in its aftermath. The culmination of religious conflicts was the Thirty Years' War (1618-1648) that affected most of European countries. The Catholic side was led by the Habsburgs, while Denmark and Sweden led the Protestant military forces. Because Croatian countries were within the Habsburg Empire, Croatian soldiers were recruited into the Habsburg army and participated in the Thirty Years' War. Croatian soldiers and noblemen distinguished themselves with extraordinary courage under the command of Nikola Zrinski who was appointed General of all Croats on December 27, 1647, by the Emperor Ferdinand III. Croatian Light Cavalry and Infantry were recognizable by their headscarves, which they tied to their uniforms in a special way. This stylish accessory garment is today recognized worldwide as a men's accessory, the tie or cravat (Huzjan, V. 2008, 103-120). In addition, the Stockholm Military Museum holds a large number of flags of Croatian regiments from the Thirty Years' War. A legend has it that the Swedish King Gustav II Adolf himself was executed by a Croatian sword (Ćurčić 2015, 68-75).

Protestantism was not common in Croatian countries, except in Istria which was not exposed to the Ottoman wars. In Vojna Krajina region, Protestantism was practiced among the Austrian commanders. In Slavonia, Protestantism was present in the Hungarian nobility.

Istria contributed several prominent figures in the Protestant movement. One of the most significant was Matija Vlacic Ilirik (Croatian: Matija Vlačić Ilirik), who wrote church history in 13 books. Stjepan Konsul Istranin and Antun Dalmatin ran the Croatian Protestant printing press in Urach. Many books were printed in Glagolitic and Latin script (Kordić 2005, 215-233).

After the Thirty Years' War, the Bishop of Zagreb, Juraj Drašković, participated in the Catholic Restoration at the Council of Trent (Franković 2014, 19-38). Catholic revival in Croatia had the most success with the arrival of the Jesuits in the early 17th century. The Jesuits established a number of primary schools and high schools in Zagreb, Rijeka, and Varaždin. In 1669, Zagreb High School was elevated to the university level, so in 2019 was celebrated as the 350th anniversary of the Croatian University of Zagreb. Jesuits in Slavonia introduced new agricultural crops and the modernization of an outdated economy. One of the famous Croatian Jesuits were Bartol Kašić, author of the first Croatian grammar and Ruđer Bošković, a world-renowned philosopher, physicist and astronomer (Horvat, V. 2011, 67-132; Triplat Horvat et al. 2011, 67-74).

CROATIA IN THE EARLY MODERN PERIOD FROM 16TH TO 18TH CENTURY

The Ottoman Empire was falling behind Europe economically, technologically, and in military terms. As Europe began to introduce monetary economy based on the gold standard, the lagging Ottoman Empire continued to be based on the feudal system. Relocation of major trade routes from the Mediterranean to the Atlantic was very damaging to the Ottoman Empire. Large revenues from customs duties collected from European traders disappeared. The anti-Ottoman sentiment among the captive nations was increasing. Such occasions provoked uprisings for liberation from the Ottoman rule. At the same time, the expense of continuous warfare with the Ottomans weakened the economy and the feudal Croatian nobility. The position of peasants deteriorated significantly due to increasing taxes.

The Great Turkish War (1683-1699)

The last great Ottoman attempt to restore old glory and power was the march to Vienna in 1683 under the leadership of Great Vizier Kara Mustafa. This event marks the beginning of The Great Turkish War which lasted from 1683 to 1699. The Ottomans had been besieging the city for months and it seemed that Vienna was about to fall, the army of Polish King Jan Sobieski and German troops came to Vienna's aid. The Ottoman army was shattered. On the run after the heavy defeat at Vienna, Vizier Kara Mustafa fled to a Turkish camp near Belgrade. He was killed in Belgrade by the order of Sultan Mehmed IV. The Ottoman defeat brought European nations together, and with the Pope's blessing they formed the Holy League alliance. The goal of the Holy League was to push the Ottomans out of Europe.

Members of the Holy League were the Habsburg Monarchy, Poland, and Venice. Habsburg troops, led by Charles (Karlo) of Lorraine and Eugene of Savoy, managed to expel the Turks from Hungary and Croatia through Serbia and Macedonia. However, France, fearing increased influence of the Habsburgs in Europe, declared war on the Habsburg Monarchy. The Ottomans launched a counter-attack and regained the lost Serbian and Macedonian lands. Yet Croatian lands Slavonia, Lika, and Krbava remained liberated from Ottoman rule (Đuričić 2015, 35-55).

Croatian people organized into volunteer units, made a great contribution in the war. In Slavonia, volunteers led by Friar Luka Ibrišimović stood out. Volunteers led by priest Marko Mesić played a major role in the liberation of Lika. In Dalmatia, the struggle against the Ottomans was led by Venice. The goal of the Venetians was to reclaim its lost territories. The greatest contribution for the liberation of Dalmatia has to be attributed to the Hajduks from Ravni Kotari, led by Stojan Janković. Fearing revenge, the Muslim population fled to Bosnia. In the reverse direction, a large number of civilian Croats left Bosnia and settled in liberated areas (Skenderović 2011, 10-18).

In 1699, a peace treaty between Austria-Hungary and Ottoman Empire was concluded in Srijemski Karlovci. Most of the Croatian lands were liberated from Ottoman rule. The whole Slavonia was liberated, except eastern Srijem, and also Lika, Krbava, and the area around the river Una. The other part of the Croatian area around the Una River and the Vrbas River was retained by the Ottomans. The border of Croatia with Ottoman Bosnia established by the treaty at that time remains unchanged to this day. Contrary to what was expected by Croatians, the court in Vienna did not annex the liberated areas to Croatia. The liberated areas in Dalmatia were annexed as spoils of war by the Venetian Republic. Venice got towns of Knin, Sinj and Vrgorac and they were added to Venetian Dalmatia. It was only in 1745 that Slavonia was partially returned to the administration of the Croatian Ban and Parliament. In essence that was the deal between the Habsburgs and Venice over the booty of Croatian lands. However, the Ottoman Empire tried to reclaim their great losses and wars continued. With the Pozarevac peace treaty in 1718, the Ottomans were forced to return once conquered areas of the rest of Hungary, Srijem and part of Serbia, part of lands south of River Sava in Bosnia whereas Venice expanded its possessions in Dalmatia, with towns of Imotski and Vrgorac. On the other hand, the Habsburg Empire failed to retain Serbia. With the Belgrade peace treaty in 1739, the Habsburgs lost everything they had gained through the Požarevac treaty (Novak 2004, 24-30) but the centuries-long war with the Ottomans was finally over.

Croatian Peasants' Revolt in 1573

Although money-based economy brought some benefits to Croatian peasants their situation continued to be difficult. The nobility demanded to bring back the old economic system of in-kind taxation and barter, and to exclude peasants from the trade. In addition, peasants were obligated to build and repair fortifications which were needed because of the threat of Ottoman invasions. The overall burden of levies caused the biggest peasant revolt in Croatian and Slovenian lands. Peasant dissatisfaction peaked in January 1573 in the Susedgrad-Stubica estate owned by Franjo Tahi. The leader of the rebelled peasants was Ambroz (Matija), called Gubec. The rebellion also spread to Slovenian estates. Rebel peasants were confronted by Ban Gašpar Alapić's and captain Josip Thurn's army and the uprising was suppressed after four days. After the crucial battle at Stubičke Toplice, February 9, 1573 the defeated peasants were punished with cruel death by mutilation. The leaders of the rebellion, after trials and torture, were quartered for treason. Matija Gubec was crowned with a red-hot iron crown and quartered in front of the Church of St. Mark in Zagreb (Adamček 1968, 107).

Venetian Rule in Dalmatia and Istria

Since the mid-15th century, the Venetian Republic held under its rule almost all Dalmatian cities and the area between the Cetina and Neretva rivers. In the second half of the 16th century, the Venetians annexed Boka Kotorska to Venetian Albania. Dalmatian cities were under direct control of the Venetian government. Cities were governed by a duke, appointed by Venice from the ranks of Venetian nobility, who presided over a Grand Council of local nobility. Commoners were not involved in city government and political life. Due to these circumstances, commoners often rioted against the political dominance of the patricians. The largest public uprising broke out on the island of Hvar. The Hvar rebellion lasted from 1510 to 1514. Insurgents led by Matija Ivanić took power over the island. The Venetians sent a fleet against the rebels, and the uprising was suppressed. All surviving participants of the Hvar Rebellion were hanged on the masts of Venetian ships.

At the end of the 16th century, all Dalmatian cities were united in the province of Dalmatia, with the center in Zadar, under control of a Venetian Governor General. Venetian government in Dalmatia had a negative impact on the overall economic, cultural, and infrastructure development of Dalmatia. Venice controlled the trade and production of salt and other resources. At the same time, the Ottomans in the hinterlands caused even more damage by blocking trade with Dalmatia and damaging the already poorly developed agriculture.

Since the 14th century, Istria had been territorially divided into the Habsburg hinterland and the Venetian coast. Venice sought to maintain a dominant position at sea and superiority in maritime trade. Such Venetian policies caused frequent clashes with the Habsburgs. The Uskok war broke out in the 17th century (Gruenfelder 2003, 214-217). Apart from war devastation, Istria suffered from various epidemics and infectious diseases. Particularly devastating to the population was the plague, which appeared in 1632. In desolate Istria, the native population was decimated. Italian immigrants filled the void in the deserted coastal areas, and Croats fleeing the Ottomans settled inland.

The Republic of Dubrovnik in 16th and 17th century

The territory of the Republic of Dubrovnik (In Italian La Repubblica di Ragusa), which had been called this since the 15th century encompassed the area from the entrance to Boka Kotorska with the entire Peljesac peninsula, and the hinterland and islands of Lastovo and Mljet (Pervan and Prosperov Novak 1995, 176). The population of the Republic of Dubrovnik was approximately 20,000 - 25,000. Nobility headed by the city prince had a leading role in society. Majority of population were common citizens. Even wealthy citizens that could compare in wealth to nobility had no political rights or rights to participate in power. The foundation of Dubrovnik's power and wealth in the 16th century was maritime trade. The merchant fleet of Dubrovnik numbered about 180 ships. The maritime trade was profitable for the people of Dubrovnik. The fleet sailed all over the Mediterranean, as far as England, Portugal, and even across the Atlantic to America. According to legend, some shipwrecked people from Dubrovnik became members of the Croatan tribe in North America. After the Ottoman conquests, the brokerage trade with Bosnia's mining products collapsed. The people of Dubrovnik turned to salt production in the town of Ston. Ston's salt pans were owned by the Republic. Dubrovnik also developed manufacture of textiles and glass and made good profits in the fur and leather business and by selling local artisanal products. It minted its own money and developed a credit system. Luxury villas, still standing in neighboring Rijeka Dubrovačka and Šipan, attest to the high standard of living of Dubrovnik's aristocracy. After the golden age in the 16th century, the Republic weakened and stagnated in the 17th century.

Relocation of the trade routes from the Mediterranean to the Atlantic considerably weakened Dubrovnik's fleet. The population fled before the encroaching Venetians and Ottomans to the west, to Slovenia, Austria and Slovakia. Others migrated to Italy. The Republic of Dubrovnik suffered more than ever before in 1667 when the city was hit by a devastating earthquake and fire. The recovery took about a hundred years. Dubrovnik gradually made progress with the restoration of trade in the Mediterranean in the 18th century, until it lost its independence to Napoleon's France in 1808. Today, Dubrovnik is the most beautifully preserved UNESCO-protected urban entity and has been the largest open-air stage in Europe for 70 years, which serves as the venue of the annual Dubrovnik Summer Festival (Ivanović 2016, 79-92).

The Zrinski-Frankopan Resistance in 1671

The dissatisfaction of Croatian and Hungarian nobles over the absolutist rule of the Habsburg Empire grew more and more. The Habsburgs repeatedly violated the privileges and rights of the nobility, to which they had committed themselves by the Cetingrad Charter, signed in 1527. In addition, only Austrian officers were assigned as commanding officers in the Military Frontier. Hungarian nobility maintained that the Habsburgs had not made sufficient efforts to liberate Hungary from the Ottomans. For all these reasons, anti-court sentiment grew among the Croatian and Hungarian nobility. The pinnacle of discontent came with the shameful Peace of Vasvar, signed by the Habsburgs and the Ottomans in 1654. The provisions of the peace treaty halted the liberation of Croatian and Hungarian territories from the Ottoman rule. Croatian-Hungarian nobles decided to join a resistance organization against the Habsburg Empire (Kukuljević Sakcinski 1883, 57; Mijatović 1992, 64).

The leaders of the resistance were Croatian Ban Nikola Zrinski and his brother Petar, and Hungarian generals Franjo Vesseleny and Franjo Nadasdy. Fran Krsto Frankopan, brother-in-law of Peter Zrinski, also joined the conspiracy. The conspirators went into negotiations with France, Venice and Poland and believed that they became their allies. Katarina Zrinska, the wife of Peter Zrinski, played a large diplomatic role in the negotiations. Katarina Zrinska spoke several European languages. She belonged to the Ozalj Literary Circle of Writers (Pajur 2011, 55-60).

Her most famous work is a prayer book "Putni tuvariš" (Travel Companion). Catharine's brother, Fran Krsto Frankopan, published a collection of poems "Adrianskoga mora sirena" ("Mermaid of the Adriatic Sea") (Dukić and Lukec 2017, 273-294).

After the unfortunate death of his brother Nikola Zrinski in ta hunt, Peter Zrinski continued to organize resistance against Viennese absolutism. He entered into negotiations with the Ottomans. He requested their military assistance and recognition of the independence of Croatia and Hungary. Zrinski and Frankopans were members of high Croatian nobility. Their estates extended from the Littoral inland to Međimurje. On that route they traded in salt and ore. Trade revenue was a great source of power for both families. Their allies promised to help them and the news from Istanbul encouraged the rebels. The nobles began preparing for the uprising (Mijatović 1992, 66-89).

However, the Ottomans at the same time also informed the Habsburgs of the uprising and assured them that they would not help the conspirators. The Viennese court went into action; they took away Peter's nobility. Royal troops began to seize the possessions of Zrinski and Frankopan. As time went on, it was clear that Allies would not come to aid as promised. Peter Zrinski and Fran Krsto Frankopan headed to Vienna to negotiate. The emperor "promised" to forgive them for disobeying the court. However, after arriving in Vienna, both were accused of high treason, imprisoned, and sentenced to death. Despite the unlawful trial, the judgment was enforced on 30 April 1671 in Bečko Novo Mjesto. The consequences of the deaths of Peter Zrinski and Fran Krsto Frankopan were immense for Croatia (Mijatović, A. 1992, 90-115).

Their properties were confiscated by the Crown. Peter Zrinski's son, Adam, was killed on the battlefield. Another son, Ivan Antun, died in prison in 1703. He was the last male descendant of the Zrinski family. Wife Katherine was imprisoned in a monastery in Austria for the rest of her life. Her daughter, Aurora Veronica was also forcibly taken to a monastery in Graz. Zrinski and Frankopan were left without posterity (Vukušić 2009, 197-203).

With the death of Peter Zrinski and Fran Krsto Frankopan, high nobility who could have resisted the centralist policy of the Austrian court disappeared in Croatia. The remains of our great nobles today lie in the Croatian capital, in the Zagreb Cathedral (Pajur 2011, 57-68).

Science and Art in the Baroque Period in Croatia

The period of Baroque art began in the mid-17th century under the influence of Catholic renewal in Europe and Croatia. With the arrival of the Jesuits, development of education began. Primary and secondary schools were being opened. Among the Jesuits, Bartol Kašić (Horvat V. 2011, 67-132) and Ruđer Bošković made major contributions. Bošković (1711–1787) is a famous mathematician, physicist and astronomer born in Dubrovnik. He studied rhetoric, folozophy and mathematics. He was ordained a priest in 1744. He took over the department of mathematics at the University of Pavia until 1760 (Triplat Horvat et al. 2011, 67-74).

Ivan Gundulić (1589–1638) from Dubrovnik was particularly prominent in literature. Gundulic's most famous works, Osman, Dubravka, and Tears of the Prodigal Son, have been translated into many languages. His greatest poetic work is Ode to Freedom from the pastoral Dubravka. A cultural event Dubrovnik Summer Games opens every year with these verses (Stojan, S. 2002, 203-214). On the 50 kuna banknote there is a figure of this Croatian great.

Writer Ivan Stojković (1380–1443), a great theologian, was a university professor at the Sorbonne. Ragarding the baroque architecture in Dubrovnik, the finest exemples are the Cathedral, the Jesuit church and the sculpture of the patron Saint Blaise (Sveti Vlaho). In Boka Kotorska, a parish church on the islet in front of Perasta of Our Lady of Škrpjela with valuable Baroque frescoes and also the Kotor Cathedral which preserves the remains of Blessed Ozana Kotorska. (Prosperov Novak 2011, 155-158). On the island of Hvar, one of the oldest theaters in Europe was built in 1612. (Pavlović 2013, 495-499).

Along with the boom in literature, there was also a boom in science. Trogir's Ivan Lučić, Father of Croatian Historical Science, wrote "On the Kingdom of Dalmatia and Croatia" (Kurelac, M. 1994, 179). Marin Getaldić from Dubrovnik was a renowned mathematician and physicist, not only in Croatia but in Europe, as well as Ruđer Bošković. Unlike European castles, fortifications in Croatia were built for defense against the Ottomans. Along with the forts, the towns and the baroque palaces are being restored. The most famous Baroque palaces in Croatia are the palaces of the Patačić family in Varaždin and the Oršić Rauch family in Zagreb. Every year in Varaždin there is a music event: Varaždin Baroque Evenings (Rojnik 2010, 59-91).

The most beautiful baroque castle of that time is the Eltz castle in Vukovar. During the 1991 Homeland War, the castle was almost completely destroyed (Uzelac 2017, 53-71).

After the earthquake of 1667, Dubrovnik was renovated in the Baroque style. In Zagorje (interior of Croatia) painter Ivan Ranger painted the interior of the church of Marija Snježna in Belec and left many of his works to the Pauline church in Lepoglava and the Jesuit Church of St. Ksaver in Zagreb. Baroque sculpture and painting is associated with sacral construction. The Italian sculptor Francesco Robba made the altar of the St. Cross which was originally in Zagreb Cathedral, but now it's in Križevci. In Baroque music, Ivan Lukačić from Šibenik was a prominent composer of European rank (Stipčević 2007, 156).

Croatia at the Dawn of the Modern Age

Pragmatic Sanction of 1712

After the Zrinski-Frankopan resistance against Habsburg centralism was crushed, the Habsburg Empire was faced with problems of succession. Emperor Charles III did not have a male heir and so the Empire came to be in danger of losing the Croatian-Hungarian throne. The efforts of the Vienna court to recognize the hereditary rights by the female line of succession was first rejected by Hungary, as they saw an opportunity to break away from the Habsburg Empire. Croatia, however, sided with the court and the Croatian Parliament made a decision to accept that a Habsburg princess could become hereditary Queen of Croatia. This law came to be known as Pragmatic Sanction of 1712. With it, the Croatian Parliament officially proclaimed independence from Hungarian sovereignty (Jukić 2018, 219-237).

Croatian Lands at the Time of Englightened Absolutism

Beginning of the 18th century in Europe saw development of new enlightened ideas. The age of enlightenment resonated even in the Croatian lands at the periphery of the Habsburg Empire. Driving forces behind those ideas were members of royalty and clergy. The position of the dependant peasant farmers with feudal duties will soon be changed. The ideas of the rulers of the enlightened absolutism were to not only to serve the country but its people as well. In 1756 Empress Maria Theresa issued Urbarium by which, for the first time, the feudal obligations of peasant farmers to their lords were regulated. Limiting the rights of nobles and creating the conditions for more advanced economic developments signaled a new age – the abolishment of feudal society (Kekez 2006, 79-102).

Reforms of Maria Theresa and Joseph II

Enlightenement ideas were developing in the bigger cities in Europe and spurring national movements throughout Europe. German language thus spread from Austrian cities and Hungarian language from Hungarian cities. Croatian lands were, however, divided both teritorially and economically and so the biggest obstacle to the spread of new ideas was that there was no unified Croatian language. Croatian people spoke in different dialects and most of them were iliterate. The issue of unified Croatian language will hence become a program in the awakening of national consciousness in Croatian people.

Maria Theresa (1740–1780) was the first woman on the Austrian throne. She came to power in Croatia by Pragmatic Sanction. Rulers of other European countries did not accept a female ruler on the Habsurg throne. At the beginning of her rule, Empress Maria Theresa led wars in order to keep posession of her throne. Her biggest adversary was Prussian (German) emperor Friedrich II. The Empress managed to retain her rule for full 40 years. She was best known for, at that time, advanced reforms. In Croatia, in addition to feudal reforms proclaimed by the Urbarium, she also implemented territorial reforms. Her biggest successes were, however, reforms in administration and education. In order to repay the Croatian people for the fealty they have shown in the war of Austrian succession, the Empress returned the counties of Požega, Virovitica, and Srijem back within the borders of Banovina of Croatia (Banska Hrvatska). The Military Frontier remained separated, as the Empress wanted to use it as a training ground for Austrian officers. In the city of Varaždin, she founded the Royal Council of Dalmatia, Croatia, and Slavonia 1767. This was a Croatian Parliament (Consilium regium) presided by Ban. The Council was, however, still accountable to the Viennese court. Until the great fire of 1776, Varaždin was the capital city of Banovina of Croatia. At the end of her rule, with the use of reforms, the Empress separated education from church and introduced obligatory general education for children aged 6 to 13. In lower grades, classes were conducted in Croatian and in higher grades in German. In 1776, a Royal Academy with 3 faculties, that of philosophy, theology, and law opened in Zagreb. The Royal Academy was the foundation for modern day University of Zagreb.

Joseph II (1741-1790) was the oldest son of Empress Maria Theresa and Francis I, among 16 children. Raised in the spirit of enlightenment ideas, he succeeded his mother and continued with the reforms. He curbed power of the Church. He closed down monasteries and abolished many of religious orders. He used assets confiscated from monasteries to establish large number of foundations. In his Patent of Toleration of 1781 he equalized followers of all religions in the country and proclaimed personal freedoms of peasant farmers. This limited the power of the feudal lords. His rule was one of enlighted absolutism centralized at his court in Vienna. German language became official language of the Empire. Pressures from the nobles and clergy on one side and revolutionary events in France on the other, started to take a toll on Joseph II. At the end of his reign he abolished all of his reforms except the one for religious tolerance. Josephs rule threatened the power of Croatian nobles and so they sought help from the Hungarian nobles. In 1790 Croatian Parliament surrendered some of their political and financial affairs to the Hungarian parliament. This was the beginning of Croatia's administrative dependance on Hungary, which will last until 1848 (Katušić 2005, 151-165).

Echoes of the First Industrial Revolution in Croatia

Already at the beginning of the 18th century the Habsburg Empire tried to secure its access to the coast. For this purpose, the Vienna Court invested in the construction of roads which improved access and spurred faster growth of the Austrian market. Maritime cities of Rijeka, Bakar, and Senj started thriving. Emperor Karl's road connected the cities of Karlovac, Bosiljevo, Fužine, Bakar, and Rijeka. On the initiative of Joseph II, another road was built to connect the cities of Karlovac, Modruš, Velika Kapela and Senj. Later, at the time of the French rule in Croatia, the "Road of Louise" was built, named so after the wife of Napoleon I; this road was used as the route for the modern day highway Zagreb-Rijeka (Feletar, P. 2015, 7-273).

In the second half of the 18th century, economic growth accelerated. The introduction of machines in manufacturing led to creation of new industrial enterprises. An increasing number of foreign investors from all over the Empire started moving into Croatia, even though only smaller manufactures were opening in Croatia, so they didn't threaten Austrian companies. Most growth was in mining, textile production, food, and shipbuilding. The first industrial plants were built: sugar refineries, sawmills, and breweries. The most important centers in the Banovina of Croatia were Zagreb (cultural and political center), Osijek, Vukovar, Sisak, Karlovac and Rijeka. Those linked with river trading were Osijek on the river Drava, Vukovar on the river Danube, and Sisak at the mouth of river Kupa. Karlovac, known as the city of four rivers, served as a transhipment port for transfering goods toward Adriatic port city of Rijeka. All these cities were important transport and trade centers as well as river ports (Šidak 1990, 58-71). Other parts of Croatia did not do as well. The portion of Slavonia which was not a part of the Military Frontier was dominated by foreign noblemen who did not promote industrial development. Similarly, Dalmatia and Istria were ruled by the Venitians who were primarily interested in exploiting Dalmatia's nautral resources and hampered trade, commerce, and transport by introducing measures such as special taxes on export of wine and salt. The coastal cities of Istria and Dalmatia were notably trailing behind in their economic development.

In the 19th century Dalmatia was affected by the disease of grapevines. This led to the destruction of Dalmatian viticulture and winemaking and an economic crisis. The result was a large surge of Croatian emigration, mainly to North and South America, Australia, and New Zealand where their descendants still live today. The first mutual help society of Croatian expatriates “Zajedničar” (Commoner) in 1875 In Pittsburgh, in 1894, the Croatian People’s Community was founded, later renamed the Croatian Fraternal Community. It still operates under that name today and it has grown into the largest Croatian expat organization in the United States. Many branches of Croatian immigrant clubs are also located in Argentina, Chile, Australia and New Zealand (Telišman 1985, 69-77).

In the first half of the 19th century, the influence of the First Industrial Revolution on the development of Croatia’s economy was still hampered by remnants of the feudal society. Agriculture was still the main branch of Croatia’s economy. Peasant farmers were not landowners and were not motivated to increase their crop production or to introduce new crops and new technology. On the other hand, trade started to become an important branch of the economy. Wood and grain were traded from Hungary, Bačka, Srijem, and Slavonia. Members of the trading class became the most prominent proponents for the unification of Croatia. The slowest economic growth was still experienced in Dalmatia even though it was now part of the Habsburg Empire but remained isolated, both economically and by transport, from the rest of the Croatia and the Empire. The Vienna Court did not encourage construction of roads and railroads. Small population of Dalmatian cities consisted of merchants, ship owners, craftsmen, fishermen and farmers. Cities that were somewhat developed were Zadar, Šibenik, Split, Dubrovnik, and in Istria Poreč and Rovinj (Trogrlić and Šetić 2015, 79-87, 207-211).

Science, Education and Progress in Croatia in 18th and Middle 19th Century

Middle class in Croatia, compared to the rest of the Europe, made only a small part of the society. Most of the population was made up of iliterate peasant farmers and the trading class consisted of members of nobility and clergy. With economic development and new technological advances came the need for education of peasants. Monks and priests, who were at that time the only educated members of the society, began education of the wider portion of society. The most important Croatian enlightenment intellectuals were friar Andrija Kačić Miošić and Matija Reljković (Kožić 1979, 7-66) who laid in the 18th century foundations for subsequent creation of the uniform Croatian alphabet and language. The issue of uniform language will become the main program of the Croatian revival in the mid-19th century (Radoš 2006, 259-270).

Croatia between the Habsburgs and the French Empire

Croatian Lands under French Rule

After centuries-long rule of Venice in Dalmatia and Istria, those lands fell under the Habsburg rule from 1797 until 1805. In that year the Habsburg Empire was defeated in a war with Napoleon’s France at the battle of Austerlitz. With the peace treaty, the Empire was forced to give up western Istria, the islands of the Kvarner, Dalmatia, and the Bay of Kotor (Trogrlić and Šetić 2015, 143-149). The following year in 1806, Napoleon’s army entered the independent Republic of Dubrovnik. In 1808 Republic of Dubrovnik was formally abolished. Napoleon appointed Marshall Auguste Marmont as the military and civilian governor of

Dalmatia (Manfred 1975). The French administration wanted to develop life in Dalmatia in economic, cultural, and trading spheres. More intensive planting of tobacco and potato began. With the development of economy and trade, culture began to develop as well. In1806, the first newspaper in Croatian language, called "Kraglski Dalmatin," was published. Marshal Marmont oversaw the construction of roads with a credit of 400,000 francs from Napoleon. Those roads, which now connected all major cities in Dalmatia, significantly improved the transport of goods and passengers. Marmont also built the first road stations for passengers and mailmen (Marmont 1984, 63-64; Šidak 1990, 26-35).

Illyrian Provinces

After the new war against France in 1809, Austria had to give up the rest of Istrian lands, part of Slovenian lands and all Croatian lands south of the river Sava. Napoleon incorporated all lands conquered in two wars under the name of Illyrian Provinces. The center of administration of Illyrian provinces was the Slovenian city of Ljubljana. The governor of the provinces was Marshall Marmont. Even though the French government was trying to create and maintain a better life for the citizens of the provinces, riots were happening often due to high war taxes and the recruitment of Croatians for French soldiers. Napoleon's defeat of 1813 in the battle of Leipzig was greeted with joy. European rulers renewed the anti-French alliance. After Napoleon's final defeat at the battle of Waterloo in 1815 and the Congress of Vienna in 1814 the territory of the Illyrian Provinces became part of the Habsburg Empire. A monument to the memory of the Illyrian Provinces still stands today on the Sava River in Zagreb, at the border that once divided French and Austrian rule.

Croatian Lands under Austrian and Hungarian Administration

After the fall of Napoleon's Empire, Croatian noblemen kept pressuring the Vienna Court by demanding the return of all lands south of river Sava and Kupa under the rule of Banovina of Croatia. And, indeed, parts of the Banovina between Sava and Kupa and the Adriatic were reunited with the Banovina of Croatia and thus stayed in the Hungarian part of the Habsburg Empire. However, Dalmatia was retained by the Habsburgs and placed under direct Austrian rule from Vienna. Croatia remained disunited. Thus the efforts of Croatian noblemen were unsuccessful; nevertheless, commoners and intellectuals, even though small in number, had joined the noblemen in support of the cause for unification of Croatia, and a broad new national movement was born. And so, amid great movements in Europe and creations of new nations, a new national movement also started in Croatia, called Croatian national revival (Novak, G. 2004, 85-93).

Croatian National Revival

The progenitor of revival ideas, Maksimilijan Vrhovac, Bishop of Zagreb, advocated for unification of northern and southern Croatia in the Banovina of Croatia, and also for the creation of uniform Croatian language as the first step towards that goal. He also invested in

Croatian culture and built in 1794 a beautiful park with five lakes, first such in the southeast Europe. Today, this park is named after him and is called "Maksimilijanov mir" (Maksimilian's Peace) or short Maksimir. Bishop Vrhovac's actions announced the period of the Ilyrian movement (Macan and Holjevac 2013, 191; Tanner 2001, 68).

Croatian Language and Unification of Croatian Lands

Proponents of the Croatian national revival called themselves Illyrians. Hence, the Croatian national revival became known as the Illyrian movement. The program for the uniform Croatian language was followed by a political program for the unification of all Croatian lands. The leader of movement for a uniform Croatian language was Ljudevit Gaj, a young intellectual. In 1830 he published a program in a book called "Kratka osnova horvatsko-slavenskog pravopisanja" ("Brief basics of the Croatian-Slavonic orthography"). In it, he suggested that Shtokavian dialect in Croatian: štokavsko narječje) should become common to all Croats. In 1832, a nobleman, Count Janko Drašković published a political program in Croatian language called "Disertacija" ("Dissertation"). In it, he presented the idea of unification of Croatia, Slavonia, Dalmatia, Rijeka, and the Military Frontier into one united country, The Great Illyria. This country would be a part of the Habsburg Empire. He also suggested that Slovenia and Bosnia should also become a part of that same country. The goal of this was to gather all Croatian people under one nation with one language. As early as 1835, Gaj started a Croatian newspaper published in Croatian language and Kajkavian dialect, called "Novine Horvatszke" (The Croatian News), with the literary supplement "Danicza Horvatzka, Slavonzka y Dalmatinzka" ("The Croatian, Slavonian and Dalmatian Daystar"). A year later, the newspaper was printed in the Shtokavian dialect. Using the slogan 'Nation with no nationality is a body without bones, Gaj emphasized the unification of Croatian people through the uniform language. At that time, Latin language was used in Croatian Parliament. In 1843 Illyrian Ivan Kukuljević Sakcinski, historian, writer and politician gave the first ever parliamentary speech in Croatian language. In 1847 the Croatian language was declared as official language in the Croatian Parliament (Šidak 1990, 213-214; Vargović 2016, 117-135).

Cultural Activities of the Revivalists

Along with "Novine Horvatszke," patriotic songs, called "budnice" ("reveills") were published as well. Songs were meant to strengthen unity of the Croatian people and awaken national consciousness. In the tenth edition of the literary supplement "Danicza" of March 14, 1835, Antun Mihanović's song called "Horvatska domovina" ("Croatian Homeland") was published. Eventually, that song was set to music by Josip Runjanin and became the national anthem of Croatia, titled "Lijepa naša domovina" ("Our Beautiful Homeland"). Focal points of the revival were libraries which opened first in Zagreb, Varaždin, and Karlovac. In 1842 Croatian books started being published by Matica Ilirska, today Matica hrvatska (Aralica 2009, 447-482).

Other important institutions were established as well, such as the National Museum (1846), the Croatian Music Institute (1827) and the First Croatian Savings Bank (1846). In 1834 on St. Mark's square in Zagreb, the first theater was opened. The first ever theater production in Croatian language called "Juran i Sofija ili Turci pod Siskom" ("Juran and Sofia or Turks near Sisak"), by author Ivan Kukuljević Sakcinski, was performed in 1839. Illyrian Vatroslav Lisinski wrote and composed first ever Croatian opera called "Ljubav i zloba" ("Love and Malice") in 1846. Today, in his honor, an annual prestigious national music award called Porin is given to the best performers. The Zagreb Concert Hall carries the name of this composer today (Šidak 1990, 212-214).

Along with numerous Croatian Illyrians members of ethnic minorities also joined the Illyrian movement: Serbs, Slovakians, Germans, Hungarians, and Czechs. Dimitrije Demeter, a Croat of Greek descent was the head of the Croatian theater. Ljudevit Vukotinović, a botanist and writer, was of Hungarian descent. Two female members of the National revival should be mentioned: Countess Sidonia Erdödy Rubido and Dragojla Jarnević. Countess Erdödy sang Ljudevit Gaj's budnica in Croatian language called "Još Horvatska ni propala" ("Croatia has not yet perished") at the theater on the St. Mark's square (Frbežar, I. 2014).

Dragojla Jarnević was an active Illyrian in the city of Karlovac. She wrote songs and tales in Croatian language. On her initiative, the first all-girls school was opened in Karlovac. (Odža 2018. 87-117).

The Enemies of the Croatian National Revival

In the Banovina of Croatia, a portion of noblemen, who promoted unification of Croatian lands under Hungarian rule, stood out. Aiming to oppose the Illyrians and their program, they established in 1841 "Horvatsko-vugersku stranku" ("Croatian-Hungarian Party"). Illyirans called them "Mađaroni" ("Hungarophiles"). These were the beginnings of political conflicts between parties. Hungarophiles managed to obtain from the Vienna Court a ban of the use of the Illyrian name by the opposition party. By the decree of the Emperor, the Illyrian party had to change its name to "Narodna stranka" ("People's Party"). Constant conflicts and political contests between the two parties led to a bloodshed on July 29th, 1843. After the victory of the Hungarophiles in elections for the board of provinces, which was won by buying votes, riots broke out. Army intervened and started shooting at the members of the People's Party. Thirteen members of the party were killed, and they became the symbol of the Croatian fight for freedom. In history, this event is known as "Srpanjske žrtve" ("The July Victims"). A monument to the July victims is today located on the cemetery in Zagreb called Mirogoj. (Šidak 1990, 154).

Croatian National Revival in Dalmatia and Istria

In the second half of the 19th century revival ideas began to spread from the Banovina of Croatia to Dalmatia and Istria. Magazines and newspaper started being published and libraries were opening. In 1844 new magazine called "Zora" (Dawn) was published. In 1861 the Dalmatian Parliament convened in Zadar for the first time (Diklić 1999, 313-317).

The leaders of the People's Party in Dalmatia were Miho Klaić and Mihovil Pavlinović. Most of their opponents were members of the Autonomous Party. Their program was for an autonomous Dalmatia within the Habsburg Empire. Despite the intentions of the 'Autonomists', the 'Nationals' of the People's Party managed to win the elections in Split in

1882. Their greatest success came a year later, when in 1883 the Croatian language became official language in the Dalmatian Parliament (Šidak 1990, 164-170). Istria became part of the Habsburg Empire in the second half of the 19th century, after Austrian-Hungarian settlement. Although the Austrian administration supported the Italian minority, they could not stop the awakening of national consciousness in Istrian Croatians. The biggest merit in spreading revival ideas in Istria definitely belongs to Bishop Juraj Dobrila who toured the villages of Istria and encouraged their economic and cultural development. In 1854 he published a prayer book in Croatian language called "Oče, budi tvoja volja" ("Father, thy will be done"). The face of Juraj Dobrila is today present on the 10 kuna banknote (Dabo 2016, 186-192; Fonović Cvijanović 2016, 47-60).

By decree of the Austrian Emperor Francis Joseph I in 1861, the Istrian Parliament began convening in Poreč. But most of the members of the Parliament were members of the Italian Party, majority of whom were rich Italian traders. The Italian Party promoted the separation of Istria from the rest of the Croatian lands. Juraj Dobrila, along with a few Slovenian members, started the activities for acknowledgment of equality of the Croatian and Slovenian languages with Italian. In 1866 the first public Croatian library was opened in the town of Kastav. Newspaper "Naša Sloga" ("Our Unity") started being published in Trieste in 1870 (Dabo 2016, 186-192).

Society of Cyril and Methodius was raising money for the construction of schools in Istria. The first Croatian high school was opened in Pazin in 1887, and in Kastav the first all-boys school. In the Parliament, the number of Nationals, gathered around Matko Laginja and Vjekoslav Spinčić, was gradually increasing. In difficult conditions and under physical threats, Istrian members of the People's Party directed their activity toward connecting Istria with the rest of the Croatian lands (Šidak 1990, 164-170).

Croatians from Gradišće and Bunjevci and Šokci from Hungary (now Vojvodina in Serbia) joined the Croatian national revival. In Bosnia and Herzegovina Friar Ivan Jukić (Harni 2008. 27-50), and Friar Grga Martić actively collaborated with the Croatian revivalists and preserved the national consciousness of Croatians there (Frndić 1982. 366-379).

The Revolution of 1848 in Croatia

Revolutionary movements in Europe in 1848 known as the Spring of Nations echoed in Croatia within the Habsburg Empire.

"Demands of the People"

The Peoples Party organized a large gathering known as "Demands of the people." Resolutions of that gathering were forwarded to the Austrian emperor. The first demand was for the colonel in the Military Frontier, Josip Jelačić, to be appointed the Ban of Croatia. Next came demands for the unification of all Croatian lands and for introduction of the Croatian language in administration and education. It also demanded an independent Croatian goverment. The program envisioned civil rights as well (freedom of speech, press and religion). One of the demands was the introduction of the first elected parliament instead of the existing aristocratic one. Out of all the demands, the Emperor Ferdinand V accepted only one, which was to appoint Colonel Josip Jelačić as the Ban of Croatia. He dubbed him the general of the Military Frontier as well as the regent of Rijeka and Dalmatia. With the given titles, Ban Josip Jelačić unofficially unified the Croatian lands in his own person. It was a well thought-out move from the emperor, who by that act wanted to sway the Croatian people to fight for him against Hungarian revolutionaries. The leader of the Hungarian rebels in the Habsburg Empire in the 1848 Revolution was Lajos Kossuth, who planned the separation of Hungary from the Habsburg Empire. He fought for the rights of Hungarian people, but denied those same rights to Croatians (Marks 2004, 7-21).

Ban Jelačić and the First Citizens' Parliament in Croatia in 1848

Because of Hungarian threats to Croatia, Jelačić, as the royal general, accepted the alliance with the Habsburgs. On the eve of the war with Hungarians, Ban Jelačić severed all state and legal connections with Hungary. By decree on April 25th he abolished serfdom. After a series of unsuccessful negotiations with the Hungarians, in June of 1848 he called for elections for the first Parliament in Croatia to include citizens. Each citizen or noblemen of 24 years of age was eligible to vote. The main goals set by the parliament were: limiting the emperor's authority in Croatia, severing all connections with Hungary and, remodelling of the Empire into a union of equal nations. After the last attempt at Croatian-Hungarian negotiation fell through in July of 1848 Ban Jelačić began preparations for war (Bošnjak-Kolak 2017, 201-219).

War with Hungary

On September 7th, 1848, war was officially declared on Hungary. On September 11th general Jelačić crossed the Drava River with 40,000 troops, conquered Međimurje and moved on towards the city of Budim, the Hungarian capital. However, political circumstances were such that the Ban that he couldn't proceed to conquer Budim. In the meantime, in October of 1848, the second revolution broke out in Vienna. Revolutionaries disobeyed the Emperor and he was forced to flee the city. Jelačić was called to march towards Vienna to quash the rebellion, which he did. The revolution was put down but the Emperor Ferdinand V renounced the throne and. New ruler of the Habsburg Monarchy became the young Francis Joseph I. Since the Hungarian Parliament and the Hungarian revolutionaries didn't acknowledge Francis Joseph I as the Emperor, the war with Hungary continued. Despite the temporary conquest of Budim, the revolution escalated. The Emperor tried to end the war in favor of Austria with an imposed constitution. This constitution, which annuled Croatians' and Hungarians' political rights, enraged the Hungarian revolutionaires. In April of 1849 Hungarian leader Lajos Kossuth declared Hungary an independent nation. The war ended with the intervention of Russians who came to help fellow royalists, and Lajos Kossuth fled to the United States. Emperor Francis Joseph's rule continued to be centralistic and absolute. Hungarian and Croatian independence within the Monarchy was abolished. The Ban and royal general Jelačić had been out maneuvered. All these events took a toll on Jelačić's health. Before his death he said: "I suffered so much pain and guilt for breaking an oath by which I vowed to Croatian people to defend their rights." A statue of this great man is located on the main square in Zagreb, which also carries his name. The face of Josip Jelačić is on the 20 kuna banknote. Despite the failure of the revolutionary wave that had affected all of Europe including Croatia, it planted a seed for democracy and for the abolition of the feudal order. (Srša 2016, 117-138).

Croatia in the Twin Monarchy in the Second Half of the 19th and the Beginning of the 20th Century

After the revolution was crushed, the Emperor Francis Joseph I abolished the constitution he had imposed, and proclaimed open absolutism.

The Era of "Neo-Absolutism" or Bach's Absolutism

A special role in enforcing the Emperor's unlimited power was played by the minister of internal affairs Alexander Bach. The Emperor leaned on military institutions during his reign. Croatian people derogatorily called Bach's officers "Bach's Hussars" since they wore green uniforms which resembled those of Hungarian cavalrymen – hussars (Fernandez Andabak 2015, 1-18).

The era of neo-absolutism was characterized by strong Germanization in public life. German language was forced as official in the whole Empire. All classes in schools were taught in German. Military reign of terror was accompanied by the secret police with hired spies. Civil rights, such as freedom of press, use of Croatian flags and state emblems, were limited. Limitless power of the Emperor resulted in prosecutions of political adversaries and the exodus of dissatisfied Croats. Among the first political emigrants during that time was Eugen Kvaternik who later became a prominent Croatian politician.

Ban Jelačić performed his duties as a Ban under heavy surveillance from spies but managed despite that to carry out a series of cultural reforms. Ban Jelačić died and was buried in his family tomb on his estate Novi Dvori, near the town of Zaprešić, in 1859. In 1860 the Emperor Francis Joseph I restored the consitution with a document called The October Diploma. With this Diploma, equality of all citizens under law was proclaimed as well as the freedom of religion and the abolishment of certain taxes. After the collapse of neo-absolutism, Josip Šokčević was named as the new Ban and the Croatian language was again made official in all government offices.

Croatia within the Austro-Hungarian Monarchy

In accordance with the October Diploma, the election for the new Croatian parliament was held in early 1861. The Parliament was to make a decision on future political relations with Austria and Hungary. Members of three parties competed for seats in the Parliament: the People's Party, the Union Party, and the Party of Rights. The People's Party advocated for union of Croatia with Hungary but under condition that Hungarians acknowledge its independence, equality, and unity of Croatian lands. The Unionists promoted an unconditional union with Hungary. The Party of Rights lead by Eugen Kvaternik and Ante Starčević supported an independent Croatia, which would be connected to the Habsburg Monarchy only through the person of ruler (Personal Union) (Holjevac 1999, 289-321).

The People's Party won the election. The Parliament unanimously decided not to send representatives to the Royal Council in Vienna as the Emperor demanded. The Emperor retaliated by dismissing the Parliament again. Out of the whole program of the People's Party he accepted only the union of Croatia with Hungary. Political prosecutions of the members of the Party of Rights followed. Ante Starčević was imprisoned and Eugen Kvaternik emigrated again.

Beginning of Modernization of Croatia under Ban Ivan Mažuranić and the Settlement of 1867

After the emperor had dismissed the Parliament in 1861 one of the leaders of the People's Party, Ivan Mažuranić, urgently proposed an agreement of Croatia with Austria. He thought Austria represented a lesser threat to Croatia than Hungary. However, it was too late. Austria's defeat in the war against Prussia forced the Habsburg Monarchy to remodel. The result was the creation of a dual Austro-Hungarian Monarchy in 1867. It was a form of personal union in which Francis Joseph I was the emperor and king of the Austiran part, and was the king of the Hungarian part of the Monarchy. Austria and Hungary shared power in the administration of the Monarchy. The Dual Monarchy divided the Croatian lands. Istria and Dalmatia fell under the Austrian administration, while the Banovina of Croatia and Slavonia fell under the Hungarian administration. Although most of the members of the Parliament were dissatissfied with the Austro- Hungarian agreement, the newly elected Unionist Ban Levin Rauch supported the union with Hungary. In 1868 Rauch and his followers signed the Croatian - Hungarian Settlement. With it, Croatia gained autonomy in its internal affairs, judiciary, education, and religion. Joint arrangement included: economy, transport, trade, finance, military and foreign affairs. However, the port city of Rijeka and its surroundings were annexed by Hungary on the basis of a falsified document called "Riječka krpica" (Corpus Separatum) as a direct access to the Adriatic Sea (Polić 2010, 57-92).

The first big act of dissatisfaction with this situation in Croatia was a rebellion in 1871 in a town called Rakovica, near the city of Slunj. The leader of the rebellion was the now-returned emigrant Eugen Kvaternik, the head of the Party of Rights and a strong supporter of the idea of an independent Croatia. Due to poor organization, the rebellion was crushed in blood. Kvaternik and his followers were killed, and the Party of Rights was prohibited (Gross 1973, 191-193).

Later, in 1878, the still-prohibited Party of Rights with Ante Starčević at its helm became a strong opposition party. The political program of the Party marked the making of modern Croatia. Because of his actions and commitment to creating an independent nation of Croatia, Ante Starčević (1823 – 1896) was named "Father of the Nation." The last remains of this great man are buried in Zagreb in a cemetery in Šestine (Gross 1973, 283-308; Derossi 1996, 209-228; Barišić 2018, 437-472). Today, his face is on the 1,000 kuna banknote.

Amid all this political turmoil, Croatian politicans continued to strive for bigger political and economic autonomy. They managed to secure the appointment of the new Ban of Croatia from the Emperor, without prior consultation with the Hungarians. By this action, they managed to gain autonomy in electing Croatian representatives in the Parliament of the Monarchy. Croatian lands, however, remained divided territorially. With the appointment of Ban Ivan Mažuranić in 1873, started economic, political, and cultural modernization of Croatia (Čepulo 2000, 83-120).

Writer and politician Ivan Mažuranić (1873-1880) was called "Commoner Ban" because he was not a nobleman. During his term of office, he implemented a number of reforms and carried the title "Ban the reformer." With his reforms he built the foundations for modernization of Croatia in administration, judiciary, culture, and education. He introduced laws for obligatory four-year education, a press law, and rights of assembly. At the Ban's suggestion, many scientific, cultural, and economic institutions were founded. The pinnacle of his reforms was the opening of the University of Zagreb in 1874 with three faculties: the Faculty of Law, the Faculty of Humanities and Social Sciences, and the Faculty of Theology. He started a magazine called "Vienac" whose editor-in-chief was August Šenoa. Today, Ban the reformer's face is on the 100 kuna banknote.

Hungarization of Croatia

Due to growing political resistance of Croats to Hungary, the Hungarian government abolished the Military Frontier in July of 1881 and placed it under the administration of the Ban and the Croatian parliament. With this, they wanted to gain back the trust of dissatisfied Croatian people. Although this move was promising to Croatia's interests, the era of hungarization – forced adoption of Hungarian language and culture – followed instead. The newly appointed Ban Ladislav Pejačević started his mandate by forcing Hungarian language through joint businesses: postal, railway and tax services. In violation of the Settlement of 1868 (Banović 1987, 313-323). By putting up Croatian-Hungarian signs on public institutions he enraged Croatians. The Anti-Hungarian movement began. People destroyed illegal signs en masse and so Ban Pejačević eventually resigned in 1883.

The era of even stronger hungarization continued with the appointment of Ban of Slavic descent Károly Khuen-Hédervári (1883-1903). His term of office was marked with electoral falsifications, political violence, bribery of the members of the Parliament, and political strife between Croatians and Serbs. Serbs in Croatia were given privileged clerical positions as Hedervary used them to counter Croatian resistance. Control of railways system brought significant income to Hungarians. In high schools, the Hungarian language was imposed as an obligatory subject. Khuen's policy was opposed by the Party of Rights before and after the death of their leader and the Father of the Nation Ante Starčević (Gross 1973, 9-14).

New anti-Hungarian demonstrations arose in 1895 in Zagreb during the opening ceremony of the Croatian National Theatre. The ceremony was attended by the Emperor Francis Joseph I and the Ban Khuen-Hédervári, who wanted to show the Emperor how much he is investing in the cultural progress of Croatia. The highlight of the demonstration was the burning of the Hungarian flag on Ban Jelačić's square. That act was performed by young students of the University of Zagreb. Among them was a student of the Faculty of Law in Zagreb, Stjepan Radić (1871–1928). Radić's political activites would eventualy leave a strong mark on Croatian history. Together with fellow students, Radić was banned from the University and imprisoned. After several months, Radić was released and he continued his education in Paris. Khuen's favouritism of Serbian citizens in Croatia deepened already unstable social situation. An article published first in a Serbian literary magazine and then in a Zagreb-based Serbian newspaper "Srbobran" in 1902 triggered big anti-Serbian demonstrations, which lasted for three days (Stojanović 1902, 1149 -1159). The article was first published in a called "Serbs and Croats." The article insulted the Croatian people by denying the existence of the Croatian nation and the Croatian language. Despite a ban on public assemblies, nothing could stop the anti-Serbian demonstrations (in 1903; Biondich 2000, 59). Croatian peasants gathered on the railway station in the town of Zaprešić and burned the Hungarian flag. The military intervened and blood was shed. The situation didn't calm down until the Ban resigned. Khuen-Héderváry was awarded by Hungarians with a better position of Minister-President of Hungary. After 20 years, the era of hungarization of Croatia ended (Heka 2016, 1065-1069; Szabo 2005, 597-608).

Economic and Cultural Circumstances in Croatia in the Second Half of the 19th Century and the Beginning of the 20th Century

In the mid-19th century, faster economic growth began in Croatia. The first commercial exhibition in Zagreb opened in 1864. It continues today as an important commercial institution called Zagreb Grand Fair (Zagrebački Velesajam). Despite the lack of domestic capital and transport infrastructure, in the period from 1846 to 1914 increasing number of banks opened in Zagreb, Osijek, Rijeka, Split, and Zadar.

In the Austrian part of the Monarchy, Dalmatia was in economic distress due to the grapevine disease and a wave of emigration (Trogrlić and Šetić 2015, 80). Istria at that time was in a better position. Austria invested heavily in the city of Pula and its port and shipyards and made it the home port of the Imperial Navy. Opatija became the first tourist centre in Istria and attracted not only Austro-Hungarian nobles but also celebrities and wealthy clientele from all over Europe and the world (Trogrlić and Šetić 2015, 222-223).

Croatian literature gave birth to literary greats who contributed to the nurture of Croatian national consciousness. Those greats were: Ivan Mažuranić, August Šenoa "the Father of the Croatian novel," Vjenceslav Novak, Eugen Kumičić, Ante Kovačić, K.Š. Gjalski, and member of Party of Rights poet Silvije Strahimir Kranjčević. In 1876 Ivan Zajc composed the opera "Nikola Šubić Zrinski." Painting of that time was deeply inspired by Croatian history. The best known artists were Oton Iveković and his painting "Arrival of Croats to the Adriatic Sea," Vlaho Bukovac who painted the stage curtain of the Croatian National Theatre with revival motives (Kavazović 2007, 275-284), Celestin Medović, Emanuel Vidović, and Slava Raškaj.

In 1880 Zagreb was hit by a devastating earthquake with heavy human losses and material damage. The Zagreb Cathedral suffered damage of the main altar, the interior, and the collapse of one of the towers. The restoration in the neogothic style, designed by the Austrian architect Hermann Bolle, took from 1880-1905 (Damjanović 2005, 259-276). Bolle was also responsible for restoration and construction of many other cultural buldings and monuments in Croatia.

In the fields of inventions and discoveries, several Croatian greats stand out: Nikola Tesla (1856–1943), world renowned physicist, scientist and inventor born in the small town of Smiljan in Lika (Paar 2007, 199-2019). He gave the world over 700 inventions. Today, his last name is used by the famous American car manufacturer. A monument to Nikola Tesla is located in Smiljan and another monument by the Croatian sculptor Ivan Meštrović is located in Tesla Street in Zagreb. In the Upper Town in Zagreb, a memorial plaque on the Town Hall building commemorates Tesla's visit to Zagreb, on May 24, 1892. On that occasion, he said: "I consider it my duty, as a native son of my country, to assist the city of Zagreb by advice and help in every way I can" referring to the proposed construction of an alternating power plant.

Franjo Hanamann (1878–1941) from Slavonia, invented the lightbulb with metal wire core. Slavoljub Penkala (1871–1922), a chemical engineer and inventor from Zagreb, patented 80 inventions, from all fields, including aviation and mechanical engineering. He gave Croatia and the world his most famous invention, the mechanical pencil and the first dry-ink fountain pen (Puhlovski, B. 2000, 230-235).

World renowned explorers Dragutin Lermann (1818-1885) and brothers Mirko (1871–1913) and Stjepan (1875–1936) Seljan travelled through Africa and South America (Živković 2018, 93-95).

Along these greats we can single out the famous opera star Milka Trnina (1863–1941), known for her performances of Wagner's operas. She performed in the Metropolitan Opera House in New York. One of the falls on Plitvice Lakes is named after her. In her hometown of Vezišće in Moslavina, a monument was erected in her honor (Santo 2014, 239-254).

In the field of chemistry Lavoslav Ružička (1887–1976), who received the 1939 Nobel Prize for chemistry for his research in natural organic compounds. Ružička was born in Vukovar and did most of his scientific work in Switzerland. He held eight honorary doctorates and published 582 works in the field of natural organic compounds. Vladimir Prelog (1906–1998) received the 1975 Nobel Prize in chemistry in the field of organic natural compounds and stereochemistry. Prelog was born in Sarajevo. He finished his high school in Zagreb and and studied chemistry in Prague, where he received his Doctorate in 1929. He was an honorary citizen of Zagreb, Sarajevo, and Osijek (Sršan 2009, 75-90).

Franjo Bučar initiated development of sports in Zagreb and founded the Croatian Sports Federation in 1909. Thanks to him, many sports became popular in Zagreb and the rest of Croatia: soccer, rowing, tennis, ice skating, skiing, and fencing. The first soccer clubs in Croatia were HAŠK in Zagreb and Hajduk in Split (Škegro and Čustonja 2014, 127-133).

Creation of the Croatian People's Peasant Party and the Policy of "New Course"

Participation of Croatian peasants in anti-Hungarian movements was a strong indicator that peasants had become nationally aware and politically active. That was recognized by two brothers, Antun and Stjepan Radić who in 1899 started a magazine called "Home – educational and conversational magazine for the Croatian peasant." Soon, in 1904, they founded the Croatian People's Peasant Party (HPSS). In its program the Party emphasized the fight for civil rights and for economic progress of rural areas. They also advocated for stopping emigration and for greater independence of Croatia. Since peasants were at that time by far the most numerous population group in Croatia, brothers Radić suggested that they should be represented in the Parliament. Eventually, the leader of the Party Stjepan Radić was elected (Banac 1984, 216-245).

In the beginning of the 20th century a crisis was brewing in the Austro-Hungarian Monarchy as Hungarians started demanding more and more independence from Austria. In Dalmatia, which was in the Austrian part of the Monarchy, the idea of a "New course" policy arose among Croatian politicians who believed that Hungary was a lesser threat than Austria, and advocated for Croatia to support Hungarian demands in collaboration with Serbs and Italians living in Dalmatia. This stance was supported by the Dalmatian Party of Rights founded at the end of the 19th century by Dalmatian politicians Ante Trumbić, Frano Supilo, and Ivo Prodan. In the Banovina of Croatia this program coming from the Dalmatian politicans was adopted by politicians who supported the unification of South-Slav nations. Trumbić suggested closer connection to other nations inside the Monarchy which were facing danger from Austria. By signing a document called "Resolution of Rijeka" in 1905, followers of the "New course" policy supported the Hungarian opposition in their fight for independence of Hungary. In return, Hungary was supposed to approve the unification of Croatia and Dalmatia, civil rights and a democratic government in Croatia. Two weeks after the signing of the Resolution of Rijeka, Serbian politicians from Dalmatia and Croatia supported the "New course" policy by signing the "Resolution of Zadar." They demanded equality between the Croatian and Serbian people. Already at the end of that same year that collaboration bore fruit in the form of the newly founded Croatian-Serbian Alliance. Only the Croatian People's Peasant Party (HPSS), led by Stjepan Radić, and the Croatian Party of Rights led by Josip Frank didn't enter that alliance. The "New course" policy didn't last long. Hungarian politicians came to an agreement with the Vienna Court and they no longer needed support from Croatia. HPSS's stance proved to be forward-looking, especially in the forthcoming social circumstances which would befall Croatia leading up to the First World War. Supilo left the Croatian- Serbian alliance and his leading position was taken over by Svetozar Pribićević, a Serbian politican from Croatia. During the War, the policy of the alliance became disastrous for the Croatians, all the more since its leader Pribićević lobbied for Croatia to get closer to the Kingdom of Serbia (Novak 2004, 169-172; Matković 2003, 701-713).

Croatia in the First World War

The era of imperialism and colonialism among Europe's most powerful nations presaged worsening conflicts of interests and territorial rearrangements in Europe and the world. The "Eastern Question" and the "Great Eastern Crisis" ended with the occupation of Bosnia and Herzegovina (BH) by the Dual Monarchy and the annexation in 1908. Besides these events, the two Maroccan crises the Balkan wars presaged the First World War (Matković 1995, 24-25).

Balkan Wars – Foreplay to the World War

In such international circumstances there was increasing danger of war on a global scale, but it was averted at the Berlin Congress in 1878. The Congress authorized the Dual Monarchy to occupy Bosnia and Herzegovina. This didn't suit the Kingdom of Serbia as it thwarted its expansionist policy in Bosnia and other non-Serbian lands. However, by giving concessions at the Berlin Congress, the Kingdom of Serbia was declared an independent country along with Montenegro and Romania. With the ouster of the Obrenović dynasty by the Karađorđević dynasty in the "May Coup" in 1903 came a change in the Serbian Court. Karađorđević politically edged toward Russia. With the weakening of the Ottoman Empire Russia saw its chance to expel the Ottomans from the Balkans in alliance with the Balkan already-independent countries. On Russia's initiative and under the creed of "the Balkans to the Balkan people" in 1912, the Balkan alliance was formed between these countries: Serbia, Montenegro, Bulgaria, and Greece. The aim of this alliance was to prevent the eastern expansion of Austria and Germany alongside their own territorial expansion. The alliance waged a successful First Balkan War against the Ottomans. However, many allies were dissatisfied with their share of the conquered territories after the First Balkan War and the alliance was abolished after the Second Balkan War in 1913. The turbulent events on the Balkan Peninsula earned it a name "The Powder Keg of Europe" and intensified the military-political rivalry between Russia and other European superpowers (Kavalski 2000, 289-300).

Croatians in the First World War

The assassination of the heir to the Austro-Hungarian throne Francis Ferdinand and his wife Sofia in Sarajevo on June 28, 1914, was the proximate cause of the First World War. The assassination was planned by the members of the Serbian terrorist organization called "Young Bosnia." The assassin was Gavrilo Princip. Preparations were done with the help of the terrorist organization of the Serbian Court called the "Black Hand," led by Dragutin Dimitrijević Apis with the assistance of a secret service agent in Beograd, Rade Malobabić. The assassination in Sarajevo provoked major anti-Serbian protests in Bosnia and Herzegovina and also in Croatia. Austria-Hungary suspected the involvement of the Kingdom of Serbia and demanded an investigation from the Serbian Court. The goverment of the Kingdom of Serbia refused that demand and so Austria-Hungary declared war on Serbia on July 28, 1914. Soon almost all European countries joined the conflict.

Croatians of age started being recruited into the Austrian-Hungarian army along with other members of the countries in the Monarchy. Agricultural products and livestock were requisitioned from the peasants. Croatians mostly fought on the Balkan front against Serbia and Montenegro and on the eastern front against Russia. After Italy joined the war on the side of Allied forces with the London Accord in 1915, a new battlefield was opened on the Soča river and Croatian troops were sent to that battlefield as well. A prominent figure of the Sočan battlefield was Fieldmarshal Svetozar Boroević, of Croatian origin, also known as "The Lion of Soča" (1856–1920). He proved himself in that defensive warfare and became the only recipient of that title who wasn't of German descent. Up until the last couple of months of the war, most Croatians soldiers proved themselves to be the most loyal fighters of the Monarchy. Right before the end of the War, when a surrender of the Central powers was imminent, Croatian troops started deserting their posts and hiding in the woods and fields. They were called "Green Staff" (in Croatian: "Zeleni kadar"). Wartime requisitions of agricultural products and livestock led to extreme hunger and poverty among the civilians in Zagreb and elsewhere, humanitarian action named "Dadoh zlato za željezo" ("I traded my gold for iron") was started in order to collect money for weapons, clothing and food for Croatian troops on the battlefields. Ivan Merz (1896–1928), university professor and writer, tells about the experiences of the Great War in his diary, which experiences later strongly influenced his loyalty to the Catholic Church. Writer Miroslav Krleža (1893–1981) wrote about his experience in the War in the narrative "Bitka kod Bistrice Lesne" ("Battle of Bistrica Lesna"). The total Croatian military losses in the First World War are estimated to be around 190,000 people, although the exact number is not known (Despot et al. 2014, 33-54; Trogrlić and Šetić 2015, 225-229).

Yugoslav Committee, May Declaration, and Corfu Declaration

Several Croatian emmigrants during the war founded the Croatian Committee in Italy. Its members were: Frano Supilo, Ante Trumbić, and sculptor Ivan Meštrović. These politicians saw the solution for the Croatian issue in the cooperation with other South-Slav countries and unity with Serbia. Slovenian and Serbian politicians also joined the committee. In 1915 the Croatian Committee was renamed as the Yugoslav Committee. The headquarters of the Committee was moved to London and Trumbić was elected president. Most of the members supported the idea of the abolition of the Austro-Hungarian Monarchy as well as the union of all territories populated by Croats, Slovenians, and Serbians with the Kingdom of Serbia and Montenegro. Soon, however, disagreements arose about the structure of the new common country. Supilo proposed that internal organization of the future new country should be agreed to beforehand. The biggest opponent of this proposal was Serbian politician Nikola Pašić. As the President of the Serbian Government what he actually saw in the new Yugoslav country was an expanded Serbia. Most of the other politicians did not support Supilo's proposal either. As the War was coming to an end and the capitulation of the Central powers was becoming more and more likely, the new Austro-Hungarian Emperor Karlo I called Croatian and Slovenian representatives to the assembly of the Royal Council. They founded the Yugoslav Club in 1917 in Vienna, whose president was Slovenian Anton Korošec. In May of 1917 members of the Club issued a May Declaration proposing that Slovenians, Croatians, and Serbians should unite into a new country which would remain a part of the Monarchy. It was an attempt to change the Austro-Hungarian Empire from a dual to a triple monarchy. In reality it turned out to be actually a preparation for the creation of the future Yugoslav state. The Yugoslav Comittee in London and the Serbian Government opposed this idea. In July 1917 the refugee Serbian Government on the Greek island of Corfu together with the Yugoslav Committee signed the Corfu Declaration. This document announced the creation of a new nation after the War. This new collective nation of all Yugoslav peoples was supposed to be organized as a constitutional, democratic, and parliamentary monarchy ruled by the Serbian dynasty Karađorđević. The Corfu Declaration guaranteed national rights, right to the national flag and the alphabet to all nations in the monarchy. In reality, however, the Corfu Declaration was a dead letter as Serbia quietly continued its plans for the realization of Great Serbia.

Croatia in the First Yugoslavia

The end of the war was marked by the supremacy of the Triple Entente and the defeat of the Central Powers. Considering that the Dual Monarchy was losing the war, there was a growing tendency in Croatia to exit the Austro-Hungarian Empire and create a new state union. A People's Council of Slovenes, Croats, and Serbs was formed in October 1918 in Zagreb. On October 29, 1918, invoking the American President Wilson's right for self determination of all peoples, the Croatian Parliament cut all state and legal ties with the Austro-Hungarian Empire and proclaimed the State of Slovenes, Croats and Serbs. The People's Council became the supreme governing body of the State. Zagreb was announced as the capital (Boban 1992, 187-198).

The State of Slovenes, Croats and Serbs

However, the forces of the Triple Entente did not recognize the newly announced State. Italy demanded territory promised by the Treaty of London 1915, upon which the east Adriatic coast was to be annexed to Italy. At the same time, ever since the founding of the State of Slovenes, Croats and Serbs, there existed an idea of uniting that state with the Kingdom of Serbia. In November 1918, a meeting was held in Geneva (Switzerland) by the Yugoslav Committee, the People's Council, and the Serbian government led by Nikola Pašić. A document was drafted about the conditions of creating a united state between the State of Slovenes, Croats, and Serbs and the Kingdoms of Serbia and Montenegro. The new state was to be federal, meaning all nations would be equal. However, Nikola Pašić withheld his signature as the aforementioned document was in conflict with the goals of the Serbian government, which demanded unconditional annexation of the newly created State of Slovenes, Croats and Serbs to the Kingdom of Serbia (Horvat 1992, 19-35; Tuđman 1993, 231-236).

The Kingdom of Serbs, Croats and Slovenes

On the 23rd and 24th of November 1918, a split occurred among politicians during a session of the People's Council Central Committee. A majority of Croatian politicians, led by the leader of Serbs in Croatia Svetozar Pribićević, stood for the unconditional and immediate union with the Kingdom of Serbia. Their argument for haste was Italy's claim on Croatian coast according to the Treaty of London. However, another group of Croatian politicians, gathered around Stjepan Radić, demanded a conditional union taking into account the previous agreement about the equality of nations under one state. Stjepan Radić held his famous speech before the Central Committee of the People's Council in which he objected to sending the delegation of Croatian politicians to Serbia, saying: "Do not rush into the fog like the geese." But it was too late. Twenty eight Croatian politicians, including Pribićević, travelled to Belgrade with a document named "Naputak" ("Advisory"), meant to define the conditions of unification. However, under Serbian pressure the members of the delegation, instead the "Advisory" handed to Regent Aleksandar Karađorđević a document named "Adresa" ("Address"). In it the State of Slovenes, Croats and Serbs, together with Vojvodina, unconditionally unites with the Kingdom of Serbia and Montenegro in a Kingdom of Serbs, Croats and Slovenes. On the 1st of December 1918, Croats found themselves in the first Yugoslavia. Croatia had lost its statehood (Matković 1995, 63-71).

This marked the start of Serbian hegemony. The Croatian Parliament no longer held sessions. While the supporters of Pribićević's Serb Independent Party celebrated, opponents protested. On the 5th of December 1918, protests occurred on Jelačić Square with protesters chanting: "Long live the Republic," "Down with the Serb dynasty" and "Down with King Peter." Disarmed members of the 25th and 53rd Home Guard Regiments joined the protests. Chief of Police Grga Angjelinović gave the order to shoot the protesters. According to an official report, 13 were killed and 17 injured. A plaque still stands today on Jelačić Square, to commemorate the tragic incident (Horvat 1992, 51-53).

The Assassination of Croatian Representatives in Belgrade

The Kingdom of Serbs, Croats, and Slovenes was a multinational state. The population was approximately 12 million, with Serbs and Croats being the most numerous nations. The seat of the government was in Belgrade (Tuđman, F. 1993, 278-289). The state was centralized, with Serbian predominance in state and military services. At the time, an Austro-Hungarian currency called a crown was still in circulation in Croatia. To speed up the process of currency exchange, the state ordered overprinting the crown banknotes with the King's image and exchanging them to Yugoslav dinars at a punishing ratio of 4:1. This exchange started the destruction of Croatia's economy. With a new agrarian reform, land was taken away from Croatian landowners and given to Serbian soldiers who fought on the Thesaloniki front in World War I. The demographics of Croatia began to change in favor of Serbs (Horvat 1992, 79-82).

Following the Treaty of Rapallo and the Treaty of Rome, Italy acquired parts of the Croatian coast, but not all promised by the Treaty of London (Matković 1995, 78-85). The Croatian People's Peasant Party (HPSS) led by Radić, changed its name to Croatian Republican Peasant Party (HRSS) and started gaining strength. At first, they did not recognize the monarchy and the new Yugoslav Vidovdan Constitution of June 6, 1921 (Horvat 1990, 199-211) but changed tactic in 1925, under pressure from the government and in order to continue their growth, and accepted both. The party changed its name to Croatian Peasant Party (HSS). Soon they formed a coalition with Pribićević's Independent Democratic Party (SDS). The views of these politicans, once sworn enemies, came together by forming the Peasant-Democratic coalition (SDK). Pribićević, realizing that centralizing policies coming from Belgrade are harming even Serbs in Croatia, abandoned unitarianism and accepted federalism. Constant threats to Radić and his popular party, along with frequent arrests of Radić ordered by the Serbian regime culminated in the assasination of three members of the Croatian Peasant Party (Biondich 2000, 207-240).

The assassination of the Croatian representatives in the National Assembly in Belgrade occurred on June 28, 1928. A Serbian representative originally from Montenegro, Puniša Račić, paid by the Serbian Radical Party, killed Pavao Radić and Đuro Basariček, firing from a handgun. He also injured Stjepan Radić, Ivan Pernar, and Ivan Granđa. Stjepan Radić died of his injuries on August 8, 1928 (Horvat 1992, 388-390). Vladko Maček took over as the chairman of the Croatian Peasant Party. The King's response to this tragic incident showed his true colors. On January 6, 1929, he established open dictatorship (The Six-of-January Dictatorship). The state changed name to the Kingdom of Yugoslavia (Tuđman 1993, 7-25).

The Kingdom of Yugoslavia

The Kingdom of Yugoslavia legitimized the ideology that all Serbs, Croats, and Slovenes were one people "Yugoslavs"; legally established king's dictatorship; and abolished the constitution. The use of national symbols (flag, coat of arms, and anthem) was forbidden. Political parties that included a national name in the names of their parties were disallowed. The Kingdom was divided into nine provinces. The Croatian Parliement was abolished and the name of Croatia as a geographic term vanished from maps and official documents. Censorship of the press was conducted, and political enemies were persecuted. Singing national songs or expressing national symbols would often lead to prison time. Repression by the Serbian regime led to strengthening of the extreme political left (communists) and the right-wing (Party of Rights then gathered around Ante Pavelić). A Croatian historian Milan Šufflay lost his life during political persecutions in Zagreb in 1931. He was killed by a Serbian terorrist organization "Young Yugoslavia" by the order of King Alexander. A Serbian secret organization "Black Hand" murdered Ivo Pilar in 1933 (Horvat 1992, 506; Tuđman 1993, 53-56).

The Birth of the Ustasha Organization and Zagreb Points

The aim of Party of Rights members gathered around Pavelić was to bring down the Kingdom of Yugoslavia and create an Independent Croatian state, which would include Bosnia and Herzegovina as well (Horvat 1992, 432). In 1930 an organization called "Ustasha – Croatian Revolutionary Movement" was created. Its leader Ante Pavelić was soon forced to move to Italy (Matković 1998, 138-140).

In Pavelić's absence, the Serbian regime sentenced him to death. From Italy, Pavelić's Ustasha worked through guerrilla actions. At the same time, the Communist Party was forbidden by the king, but continued to work illegally (Koprivica-Oštrić 1984, 129-166).

To calm down the situation in the country, Alexander Karađorđević declared an octroyed "imposed constitution" (Oktroirani Ustav) in September of 1931. The constitution legitimized his absolute rule. In response, Croatian politicians signed a document called "Zagrebačke punktacije" ("Zagreb Points") in which they protested against the constitution (Matković 1998, 135). They condemned the regime that was based on Serbian dominance and Unitarianism, and asked for a solution of the Croatian Question. The King responded with new arrests. The President of the Croatian Peasant Party Vladko Maček was sentenced to three years in prison (Matković 1995, 128-137).

Resistance to Dictatorship and the Resolution of the Croatian Question

While Maček promoted settling the Croatian question by political means, Pavelić's supporters saw terrorist actions as more useful to bring down Yugoslavia. The first attempt on the life of King Alexander, in Zagreb in 1933, was unsuccessful, but the King's visit to Marseille in France in 1934 would provide another opportunity. Assassination plans were led by the Ustasha and Eugen Dido Kvaternik, alongside a Macedonian terrorist organization (VMRO). The assassin was Vlado Chernozemski, a Bulgarian revolutionary and a member of theVMRO (in North Macedonian: "Vnutarnja Makedonska Revolucionarna Organizacija," "Internal Macedonian Revolutionary Organization") (Horvat 1992, 544-545; Tuđman 1993, 126-128). The assassin was trampled on the spot to death and Italy imprisoned members of Ustasha for organizing the assassination and other terrorist acts and sequestered them on the Lipari Islands. Pavelić and his comrades were imprisoned in Turin, Italy. After the King's death, royal power was transferred to the Prince-Regent Paul, King's cousin, because the heir to the throne, Peter, was still underage (Matković 1998, 148).

The Croatian Question was still unresolved. Due to a complex international situation and the imminent war, as well as the strength of the Croatian Peasant Party, Prince-Regent Paul was forced to address the Croatian question. The Cvetković–Maček Agreement on August 26, 1939, was signed in Zagreb. This agreement established an autonomous Banovina of Croatia which included Croatia, Slavonia, Dalmatia, and territories in today's Bosnia and Herzegovina and Serbia with a Croatian majority population. Ivan Šubašić, member of the Croatian Peasant Party, was chosen as the Ban (Matković, H. 1998, 151-158). On September 1, 1939, Nazi Germany attacked Poland, marking the start of World War II.

Culture between the Two World Wars in Croatia

At the time, Zagreb became a center of culture and science. Many new university faculties opened in this period, including ones for medicine, economics, and veterinary medicine (Katić 2012. 137-168).

In the field of literature, several writers stood out, including Miroslav Krleža, Vladimir Nazor, Tin Ujević, Dobriša Cesarić, and Ivana Brlić Mažuranić, granddaughter of the famous Ban Mažuranić. She was nominated for the Nobel Prize in Literature four times. She mainly wrote short stories for children, often being called the "Croatian Andersen." Marija Jurić Zagorka, a writer and journalist, wrote many popular historic novels and was also the editor of "Ženski list" ("Woman's Magazine"). This was the first magazine for women in Croatia. A statue in her honor still stands today in Tkalčićeva Street in Zagreb (Perić 2010, 31-46).

Among sculptors, the most significant were Ivan Meštrović, who also worked in the USA, Antun Augustinčić, and Robert Frangeš Mihanović. Significant painters of that time were Ljubo Babić, Emanuel Vidović, and Krsto Hegedušić. Jakov Gotovac composed the famous opera "Ero s onoga svijeta" ("Ero from the other world").

Croatia during World War II

In September 1940, Germany, Italy, and Japan entered into a military-political alliance called the Tripartite Pact. Hungary, Romania, and Slovakia joined the Pact later the same year. At the beginning of 1941, Bulgaria and Yugoslavia joined as well. The Kingdom of Yugoslavia became a member of Tripartite Pact on March 25, 1941. Big protests ensued in Belgrade. Great Britain was unhappy as well, having lost a potential ally. The British secret service helped a group of Serbian officers led by General Dušan Simović to overthrow the Cvetković-Maček government and install him as the head of the new government. Peter was proclaimed of Age and became the new King.

The Collapse of the Kingdom of Yugoslavia

Hitler, however, did not support the new government. With no prior warning, he attacked the Kingdom of Yugoslavia on April 6, 1941, by bombing Belgrade. The so-called "April War" ended with the unconditional capitulation of the Kingdom of Yugoslavia on April 17, 1941. King Peter and the royal government fled to London. The Yugoslav regime and army collapsed. The territory of the Kingdom was divided among the members of the Tripartite Pact: Germany, Italy, Hungary, and Bulgaria (Horvat 1992, 622; Tuđman 1993, 371-372).

The Emergence of the Independent State of Croatia

Hitler wanted to appoint Maček as the leader of a new collaborationist Croatian state because his Croatian Peasant Party was very popular and strong. When Maček declined collaboration, Italian dictator Mussolini recommended Ante Pavelić, with whom he had worked during Pavelić's time in Italy. Mussolini also counted on territorial gains in Croatiaif his pick became leader. In accordance with suggestions by Italy, on April 10, 1941, the Independent State of Croatia (Nezavisna Država Hrvatska or NDH) was established. The new state was announced on the radio by Slavko Kvaternik who performed the functions of a deputy leader, Minister of Homeland Security, and Ustasha Army general (Horvat, R. 1992, 623-630). Ante Pavelić became the Poglavnik (Head) of NDH. He was the Commander-In-Chief of the regular state army called the Home Guard (Domobrani) and the Ustasha voluntary militia. The state was structured as an autocratic one-party system (Sagrak 2010, 185-200).

The state passed laws in accordance with the Nazi Third Reich and fascist Italy. All parties other than the Ustasha, including the Croatian Peasant Party, were forbidden. From the end of 1942 onwards, the Croatian Parliament did not hold sessions. Pavelić cooperated with Germany and Italy). Mussolini and Pavelić signed a treaty on May 18, 1941, in Rome. By this "Treaty of Rome," Italy gained jurisdiction over almost all Dalmatia, including the cities of Zadar, Šibenik and Split, the islands of Rab, Krk, Vis, Korčula and Mljet, as well as the Bay of Kotor; parts of the Croatian northern coast; and Gorski Kotar (Degan 2008, 265-278).

NDH had to finance complete upkeep of Italian and German troops on its land. Many Croats were taken to forced work in Germany. The Ustasha rule controlled all aspects of public life. The regime paid special attention to cultural sphere, e.g., despite the war circumstances, the "Croatian Encyclopedia" was printed. In 1941, race laws were introduced. The terror mostly affected Serbs, Jews, and Romani, but also Croats who acted as political enemies. The Archbishop of Zagreb Alojzije Stepinac fiercely criticized the Ustasha (see Chapter 5.) Prisoner concentration camps started opening up, the biggest of which were Jasenovac and Stara Gradiška. In 1942, by the orders of the Ustasha, the Jewish synagogue in Zagreb was demolished to the ground. On the other hand, as a thank you to Muslims for their loyalty, the Ustasha turned the Meštrović's Home of Croatian Artists into a mosque. The estimates for the number of victims in Jasenovac are still a controversial topic and there is an ongoing debate among historians over it (Sagrak 2010, 211-236).

The Start of the Partisan Movement in Croatia

At the start of the war a movement emerged, called the partisans, organized by the Yugoslav Communist Party. Josip Broz Tito was the chief commander of the Partisan army and a secretary general of the Party. In October 1941, the Supreme Headquarters of the National Liberation Army of Croatia (in Croatian: Narodnooslobodilačka Vojska Hrvatske) was established by the Partisans (Barić et al. 2016, 49).

By mid-1942, Partisan military actions spread to all of Croatia. While the fighting was still going on, in 1943, Vladimir Nazor, a prominent writer, was appointed as the Head of the newly-created State Antifascist Council for the National Liberation of Croatia (Croatian: "Zemaljsko antifašističko vijeće narodnog oslobođenja Hrvatske" or ZAVNOH). The ZAVNOH proclaimed the unification of Croatian land under Italian occupation with Croatia. Later, the ZAVNOH leadership appointed the government of the People's Federal State of Croatia in April 1945 in Split with the communist Vladimir Bakarić as president (Bilandžić 1983, 3-23).

On November 29, 1943, the second session of the Antifascist Council for the National Liberation of Yugoslavia (in Croatian: "Antifašističko vijeće narodnog oslobođenja Jugoslavije" or AVNOJ) was held. AVNOJ was proclaimed the supreme legislative body. The AVNOJ confirmed the decisions by the ZAVNOH. At the AVNOJ session, a provisional government was established, with Josip Broz Tito as its head. A new state union was founded, called the Democratic Federal Yugoslavia. King Peter II of Yugoslavia and the refugee government in London were forbidden from returning to the country. It was also decided that the new state would be founded as a federation of equal nationalities and ethnic groups.

The Chetnik Movement

Following the capitulation and the territorial division of the Kingdom of Yugoslavia, royal army ex-colonel Draža Mihailović had gathered the remains of the regular Serbian army and volunteers who wanted to restore the Yugoslav Kingdom and realize the ideology of Greater Serbia. The government in exile in London, dominated by the Serbs, proclaimed the Chetniks as the "Yugoslav army in the fatherland." The propaganda of Greater Serbia tried to convince the British and American public that Chetniks were leading the resistance movement against German and Italy but the Tehran Conference in 1943 exposed the reality of Chetnik activities and their cooperation with the Germans and Italians. Even though the headquarters of the Chetnik movement were in Serbia, they mostly operated in Croatia and Bosnia and Herzegovina. Chetniks committed heinous crimes in these lands, executing ethnic cleansing of Croat and Muslim civilians. They burned numerous Croatian and Muslim villages in their attacks on non-Serbian populations (Dizdar and Sobolevski 1999, 400-403).

Following the recognition of the Partisan movement as an equal partner of the Allies in the fight against Germany at the Tehran Conference in 1943, a lot of Chetniks joined the Partisans. The Chetnik and Partisan terror over the Croatian population continued until the end of the war.

Collapse of the NDH and the Bleiburg Tragedy

Following Italy's capitulation in 1943 and growing losses experienced by the Nazi Germany and Japan, it became increasingly likely that the members of the Tripartite Pact were going to lose the war. NDH ministers Mladen Lorković and Ante Vokić advised Pavelić to enter negotiations with the Allies and shift the NDH to their side (Matković 1993, 315-321). Pavelić rejected this idea and had the ministers arrested. By the end of the war they were both killed in the Lepoglava prison. To this day it is not clear who was responsible for their liquidation (Kisić-Kolanović 1998, 333-371).

In the final battles of 1944, the Red Army entered Belgrade, forcing German withdrawal to the west. At the beginning of May 1945 Partisan troops entered Zagreb. Hundreds of thousands of people tried to escape the communists and moved toward Austria in order to surrender to the Allied armies. Pavelić had fled from Zagreb a few days earlier and reached Argentina, travelling over Austria and Italy. The Partisans entered an almost empty Zagreb on May 8, 1945, and immediately started mass killings of political enemies without trial, including wounded soldiers in the hospitals. The Communists removed the Jelačić statue and the Jelačić Square was renamed the Republic Square in 1947.

Near Bleiburg in Austria, fugitives from NDH surrendered to the British army. The British army refused to accept them and handed them over to the Partisans. The Bleiburg massacre ensued. Captured Croatian soldiers and civilians were murdered enmasse, contrary to the Geneva Conventions on prisoners of war (Barić 2016, 45).

Refugees who were not killed were imprisoned and then sent on a forced march to return to the country. Some of the prisoners died along the way exhausted from hunger and thirst and others were killed. The exact number of victims during this march is unknown, but believed to be tens, most probably hundreds of thousands (Grahek Ravančić 2008, 531-550; Sagrak 2010, 347-349, see also https://www.youtube.com/watch?v=H_vUFuk MqxI#action=share).

Croatia in the Second Yugoslavia

By 1944 both Partisans and the royal government in London were preparing for the end of the war. Pressured by the Allies, Tito, representing AVNOJ, and Šubašić, the last Ban of

Croatia before the war and representing the royal government of Yugoslavia, signed an agreement on the island of Vis in 1944 and on November 2, 1944, in the liberated Belgrade. They formed a provisional government to prepare the elections for the first Constitutional Assembly. It was supposed to be balanced between the two sides, but the communists had all the power on the ground and. Šubašić couldn't achieve much. The Chetniks were discredited and the Partisan army grew into a sizeable new regular army. They also established the People's Front which included members of different groups but was completely controlled by the communists and Tito. Non-communist parties were often exposed to harassment. In the elections for the first Constitutional Assembly in 1945 voters could choose between the People's Front candidates and the opposition who could not field any candidates. For the first time, women had a right to vote. The People's Front won. The Monarchy was abolished and King Peter II was forbidden from re-entering the country (Matković 1998, 262-267).

The Federal People's Republic of Yugoslavia (FNRJ)

Human and material losses were immense in war-torn Croatia and the rest of Yugoslavia. Bridges, roads, and cities were destroyed. The land was covered with mine fields. The population faced hunger and misery. The recovery started with material help from the West. Production grew, but the standard of living stagnated. The United Nations (UN) helped Tito's Yugoslavia financially. At the end of the war in 1944 and 1945, the Communist Party of Yugoslavia set the stage for takeover of the government. The new state was named the Federal People's Republic of Yugoslavia, FNRJ in Croatian. (Federativna Narodna Republika Jugoslavija). Winning the war, FNRJ gained immense international support. The number of members in the Communist Party of Yugoslavia grew. On January 6, 1946, by the new constitution FNRJ was structured as a federal state of six republics (Slovenia, Croatia, Bosnia and Herzegovina, Serbia, Montenegro, and Macedonia) and two autonomous provinces as constituent parts of Serbia (Vojvodina and Kosovo). With the new constitution citizens were supposed to gain equality before the law, civil rights, and freedoms regardless of their religion and nationality. However, even at the beginning it was obvious what the political program of FPRY was after – all political parties except the Communist Party of Yugoslavia were abolished. The one-party system was in effect. The Communist Party strengthened its authority by controlling all parts of public life with propaganda in the media, education, and sport, all government-owned. The population was kept under control by the police, the military, and the State Security Administration (in Serbian: "Unutarnja državna bezbednost" UDBA) (Radelić 2017, 59-99).

Characteristics of Communist Rule

The Communist Party of Yugoslavia usually dealt with political opponents by arresting or persecuting via staged legal trials. Verdicts were given without concrete evidence. Arrested enemies of the state were charged with cooperating with fascists and Nazis. Religious communities were also affected by the communist rule. The Catholic Church was stripped of a majority of its assets. The Archbishop of Zagreb Alojzije Stepinac was accused of working with the Ustasha government. A staged trial sentenced him to 16 years in prison. He served his time in Lepoglava prison. Due to his deteriorated health condition he was transferred to his birthplace Krašić. He remained in house arrest until his death in 1960 (Horvat 2008, 145-230).

Political persecutions were conducted by UDBA. UDBA's agents used killings to get rid of opponents in the country and abroad (Radelić 2017, 59-99).

State borders between the Republics were still not completely defined after the war. The Allied Commission, established by the Allies to address the post-war issues but dominated by the Soviets, took away Srijem and Baranja from Croatia and gave them to Serbia. Montenegro was irretrievably given the Bay of Kotor. The demarcation negotiations with Italy began in early 1947, with the Paris Peace Treaties, and concluded with a Treaty in 1975. The SFRJ (FNRJ as renamed in 1963; "Federative" was replaced by "Socialist"), and the Republic of Italy signed a Treaty which came into effect in 1977 in an Italian town Osimo near Ancona. With this Treaty, the special status of the Free Territory of Trieste was abolished and assigned to Yugoslavia except the city of Triest and surroundings.

The law of nationalization abolished private property and introduced planned economy. With the Agrarian Reform Law in 1945, land was taken away from landowners and given to farmers. The communist government started the process of resettlement as well. Peasants from passive areas (Lika, Dalmatian Hinterland, Banovina and Kordun) were moved to fertile lands of Slavonija and Vojvodina. Under duress and threats of death, around 90 000 Slavonian Germans (so-called Volksdeutscher) left Yugoslavia after being accused of working with the occupier (Geiger 2008, 801-818). Large areas and forests previously owned by Slavonian Germans were given to Serbs.

After Stalin expelled Yugoslavia (Tito) from international communist organization Commintern (seated in Moscow) the biggest camp for Stalin supporters in the country was located on Adriatic island Goli Otok where they were tortured by brutal methods which was called "preodgajanje" (re-education) (Previšić 2013, 173-193). Croatian intellectual and communist Andrija Hebrang was jailed in 1948. A year later he was killed in prison in Belgrade without a trial. The Hebrang case remains unsolved to this day (Supek 1990, 408).

The West exploited the Tito – Stalin clash and the standstill between other communist states in Eastern Europe and Yugoslavia. The US led the way in financial and military aid. A gradual opening up to the West followed, and economic ties and tourism expanded in socialist Yugoslavia. During the 70s, tourism became the strongest economic sector in Croatia; however, more than 50% of profits went to the federal treasury in Belgrade.

The Socialist Federal Republic of Yugoslavia (SFRY)

Following the 1963 Constitution, the political leadership decided to change the name of the state. The new name was the Socialist Federal Republic of Yugoslavia (SFRY). The change occurred in the names of the Republics as well. The People's Republic of Croatia became the Socialist Republic of Croatia. The Communist Party of Croatia changed its name to the League of Communists of Croatia (Matković 1995, 226-228).

The Croatian Spring, 1971

Political conflicts over national interests of the Republics within the federation led to a political crisis in Yugoslavia during the 60s. Even though the federal state nominally advocated for brotherhood and unity of all citizens, national inequality favoring Serbs prevailed. The Croatian economy started to stagnate. Large amounts of Croatian income went to the federal treasury in Belgrade. Serbian political circles intended to create one Yugoslavian national identity and language. This kind of policy from the federal center faced open resistance in Croatia in the 1970s. Croatian intellectuals, led by the venerable cultural organization Matica Hrvatska, students, and high-ranking communist politicians in the republic, demanded federal reform and decentralization, as well as a policy called "Clean start" in financial assests distribution. They also demanded greater political freedoms and a protection of the right to express national identity. The Croatian Writers' Association, joined by 16 other institutions, published the "Declaration on the Status and Name of the Croatian Literary Language" in the "Telegram" newspaper in 1967 (Novaković 2019, 7-39).

This Declaration emphasized the inalienable right of every nation to its language. In accordance with this premise, the signers of the Declaration demanded that the Croatian language be accepted as one of four official languages in Yugoslavia inasmuch as until then the official language in Croatia was called Serbo-Croatian. What followed was persecution of the authors of the Declaration from 1967 to 1968. The communist leadership of Croatia, led by Savka Dabčević-Kučar and Miko Tripalo, requested an equitable redistribution of funds and a right to sovereignty for the republic. In 1970, Croatian aspirations to national equality turned into a movement, known as the Croatian Spring. In 1971 it became a mass movement, popularly called MASPOK ("masovni pokret," Croatian for "mass movement") (Matković 1998, 364-367).

Accusations started pouring from Serbia and some parties in Croatia that Croatian political leadership was trying to break up Yugoslavia. Many young Croatian intellectuals ended up in the prison camp on Goli Otok. Other members of the Croatian Spring movement lost their jobs. A wave of Croatian emigration ensued (Žaja et al. 2018, 102-116).

This crush of the Croatian Spring was followed by a period of "Croatian silence." Nevertheless, Tito put forth in 1974 the 3rd Yugoslav Constitution. According to it, republics and provinces were to be given a higher degree of autonomy. A right of Yugoslav nations to self-determination and a right to exit the federation were confirmed. Tito died in 1980, leaving the state in problematic conditions. The process of breaking up of the Second Yugoslavia had begun (Matković 1995, 379-385).

Croatian Diaspora and Political Emigration

The departure of Croats (so-called Gastarbeiter, German for guest workers) to work abroad during the 60s, especially to Germany, was not only the consequence of political persecutions, but also due to economic hardship. Despite the fact that Croatian emigrants abroad were politically divided, they still represented a potential threat to the Yugoslav secret service, which feared breaking up the Second Yugoslavia. In the period from 1946 to 1990, the Yugoslav state security service killed 77 Croatian emigrants and performed 24 assassinations of others within the country. For example, a renowned Croatian intellectual Bruno Bušić (1939–1978) was killed in Paris in 1978 (Mijatović 2010, 352-356).

THE RISE AND DEVELOPMENT OF AN INDEPENDENT CROATIAN STATE

Tito's death soon meant the "death" of the Second Yugoslavia as well. The country was over-indebted and by 1989 inflation reached around 2,000% (Matković 1998, 377).

The Collapse of the SFRY

In 1986 the members of the Serbian Academy of Sciences and Arts published a program called Memorandum; it advocated for Greater Serbian nationalism and accentuated "apparent" neglect of Serbs in SFRJ (Silber and Little 1996, 17-23).

When Slobodan Milošević was appointed as the leader of the Serbian Communist Party the crisis culminated. He exploited political conflicts in Kosovo and presented himself as a protector of the Serb minority in Kosoveo and other parts of the country. The goal of Serbian policy was to abolish autonomy of the Kosovo and Vojvodina provinces. Serbian dominion over the rest of SFRY was to be achieved with imposed centralism. Under the banner of communism, the idea of Greater Serbia spread beyond the borders of Serbia (Matković 1998, 386-387).

To reach that goal, the 1974 Constitution had to be revoked. A wave of meetings and mass gatherings of Serbs was organized for that purpose. Milošević had the prerequisites for overturning the Constitution as he had four votes in federal bodies: Serbia, Vojvodina, Kosovo and Montenegro. Besides, Serbs maintained a majority in the top command of the Yugoslav National Army (JNA). The head of the Yugoslav Federal (Peoples') Army supported Milošević (Silber and Little 1996, 5-35, 110-122).

However, Milošević faced resistance from the political leaders of Slovenia and Croatia. In 1989, the Croatian Social Liberal Party (Croatian: Hrvatska socijalno-liberalna stranka, HSLS) was formed, the first political party in Croatia since the war, led by Dražen Budiša, a prominent participant in the Croatian Spring. By the end of the year, the number of political parties grew. Parties collected signatures calling for free, multi-party elections. The leadership of the League of Communists of Croatia, with Ivica Račan at the helm, accepted the initiative and called for an early election in 1989. The process of creating a multi-party system was made possible by the amendments to the law by the Croatian Parliament in mid-January 1990. The new leadership of the League of Communists of Croatia and the leadership of the League of Communists of Slovenia walked out of the 14th Congress of the League of Communists of Yugoslavia in Belgrade in protest over Milošević's actions. This was the beginning of the end of SFRY and the communist system (Matković 1998, 407-408).

The First Multi-Party Elections in Croatia

A large number of non-communist parties started emerging in Croatia as soon as they were allowed: Hrvatska socijalno liberalna stranka (HSLS, Croatian Social Liberal Party), Hrvatska demokratska zajednica (HDZ, Croatian Democratic Union, led by Franjo Tuđman), along with some thirty other parties. The League of Communists of Croatia changed its name to Party of Democratic Change, under the leadership of Ivica Račan (Radelić et al. 2006). The party that continued the tradition and program of Starčević's Party of Rights was the Croatian Party of Rights 1861, with President Dobroslav Paraga. The Communist rulers had arrested him in 1980 for signing a petition for amnesty of political prisoners. He was convicted to 4 years in prison. He served his sentence in the Lepoglava prison and in the camp on Goli Otok, where he was subjected daily to torture and threats of death. During the War of Independence 1991-1995, Paraga was the founder and chief commander of the Croatian Defence Forces (HOS) from 1991-1993 (Paraga 1995, 623).

The first free multi-party elections in Croatia after World War II took place on April 22 and May 6, 1990. Winning a majority of votes, the HDZ emerged victorious. The HDZ in their program promoted sovereignty of Croatia, democracy, and pluralism, the rule of law, and a market economy (Barić et al. 2015, 31).

Following the multi-party elections in Croatia, by the end of 1990 elections were held in other republics of SFRY. In Slovenia, Bosnia and Herzegovina, and Macedonia non-communist parties also won (Gagro and Vukas 2008, 1159-1199). The elections in Serbia and Montenegro were won by communists under a new name – socialists (Silber and Little 1996, 114-121).

The Democratic Government and the Constitution of the Republic of Croatia

The first multi-party Parliament had its first session on May 30, 1990. After 45 years of communist rule in Croatia there was a peaceful handover of power. Until 2001, this day was celebrated as a public holiday, the Statehood Day. Today, it is commemorated as the day of the first multi-party Croatian Parliament. The Parliament named new bodies of the democratic government. Franjo Tuđman was appointed as the President of the Republic of Croatia. Žarko Domljan was named the President of the Parliament. The Prime Minister was Stjepan Mesić. In July of the same year, the parliament voted for amendments to the Constitution of the Socialist Republic of Croatia. Ideological terms were removed from the new Constitution. The word "socialist" was removed from the name of the Republic and Parliament. The red five-pointed star was replaced on the flag by the Croatian historic coat of arms. The new Constitution was adopted during the Parliament session on December 22, 1990 (called also the Christmas Constitution). The Constitution confirmed the trias politica system of governance: legislative, executive, and judiciary. Croatia became an indivisible democratic and social state. State rule comes from the people and belongs to the people. Sovereignty of the state is inalienable and non-negotiable. A separate Article confirmed that Republic of Croatia would remain a member of the SFRY until a new agreement by the the Yugoslav Republics and until the Croatian Parliament decided differently. By the Christmas Constitution, Croatia regained its national symbols, the coat of arms and the flag, which are still in use today (Barić et al. 2015, 32-34).

By the decision of the President of the Republic of Croatia Franjo Tuđman, the statue of Ban Jelačić was returned to Jelačić Square in Zagreb on October 16, 1990.

The propaganda of Greater Serbia was getting stronger in SFRY by the end of the 80s. This was very apparent in sporting events, where Serbian fans insulted Croatian political leadership and Croatian people. On May 13, 1990, there was a soccer match played in Zagreb between the Zagreb soccer club "Dinamo" and Belgrade's "Crvena Zvezda." The play was interrupted due to provocations from Serbian supporters who rioted in the stands and physically attacked Dinamo supporters while the police stood by. The game was cancelled and Zvezda supporters demolished the Zagreb football stadium. This was the last game held in the annual SFRY soccer championship (Barić et al. 2015, 90).

The 1990 Serb Insurrection in Croatia and the "Log Revolution"

During Croatia's negotiations for reforming SFRY, the Serbian leadership was preparing an armed insurrection of Serbs in Croatia. Following the parliamentary election in Croatia, the Yugoslav Peoples' Army (Jugoslavenska Narodna Armija, JNA) seized arms from the Croatian Territorial Defense, a backup military organization in SFRY. It was the start of preparations for a Greater Serbia war. The arming of Serbs in Croatia began. The Serb Democratic Party in Croatia, led by its president Jovan Rašković, carried out Serbian policy in accordance with the program of the Serbian Academy of Sciences and Arts Memorandum.

The greatest influence of the Greater Serbia policy was felt in the city of Knin and the surrounding area with a significant population of Serbs (Silber and Little 1996, 125-130). Armed Serbian civilians created roadblocks from fallen tree logs on August 17, 1990. It was the start of the Greater-Serbian revolution, called the "Log Revolution." Croatian police tried to establish public order and security for all citizens in that area but they were stopped by the JNA. By the end of 1990 and the start of 1991, the violence spread to other regions of Croatia: Kordun and west and east Slavonija (Matković 1998, 409).

On March 2, 1991, Serbian extremists disarmed Croatian policemen in the town of Pakrac and proclaimed the annexation of Pakrac municipality to the so-called Serbian autonomous region of Krajina (Republic of Serbian Krajina). On March 2, 1991, an intervention by special units of the Ministry of Internal Affairs Pakrac returned to Croatian control. Similar attempts of Croatian defense were stopped under threats of JNA. On March 31, 1991, in the area of the National Park Plitvice Lakes, a clash occurred between the Croatian police and the Serbian terrorists. A Croatian policeman Josip Jović lost his life. On May 2, 1991, thirteen Croatian policemen were ambushed and killed, 12 in Borovo Selo village near Vukovar, and one in Polača near Zadar (Martinić and Nazor 2019, 134-147).

This was the inception of an open Greater-Serbian war of conquest against Croatia. The Croatian government made a decision on May 28, 1991, to establish the Croatian National Guard (Croatian: Zbor narodne garde, ZNG) as the first Croatian military units. This day is still commemorated as the Armed Forces Day of the Republic of Croatia (Barić et al. 2015, 41).

The Proclamation of Croatian Independence and State Sovereignty

Unsuccessful negotiations with the SFRY leadership and the difficult life of Croats under military attack encouraged Croatian politicians to call for a referendum. Citizens of Croatia were given a right to decide whether or not Croatia should stay within the SFRY or become independent and sovereign. On the referendum held on May 19, 1991, 92.18% of citizens voted for an independent and sovereign Croatian state within a Yugoslav confederation. The Croatian government was also given an option to declare independence, should the negotiations for a confederation fail. The Parliament, led by the decision of the referendum, put forth a "Declaration on the formation of a sovereign and independent Republic of Croatia" on June 25, 1991. The decision of the Croatian people and the Parliament started the process of separation from Yugoslavia. Under pressure from Europe, Croatia and Slovenia signed the Brijuni Declaration in July 1991, by which they agreed to a three-month suspension of independence. Europe was hoping for a peaceful resolution of the Yugoslav crisis. Negotiations about a peaceful solution not only did not prevent the war, they facilitated it. JNA and paramilitary Serbian troops continued to attack Croatia (Radelić et al. 2006, 96).

JNA's Air Force attack on Banski Dvori, the official headquarters of the Croatian government in Zagreb, happened on October 7, 1991. The aim of the attack was to assassinate president Tuđman and break the Croatian political leadership but it was not successful. A memorial plaque to commemorate that event still stands on the building of the Croatian government today. After the end of the three-month suspension deadline, the Croatian Parliament issued the final decision on the termination of legal ties with SFRY on October 8, 1991. Other Republics and provinces comprising SFRY, except for Serbia and Montenegro, soon followed in doing the same. These events foreshadowed the death of Yugoslavia. Today, October 8th is celebrated as a national holiday, as the Independence Day (Barić et al. 2015, 42).

The Croatian War of Independence – Greater-Serbian Aggression towards Croatia

Being positioned all around and within Croatia, the JNA helped the Serbian paramilitary forces. In the summer of 1991, troops of the Territorial Defense of Serbia, Montenegro, and Bosnia and Herzegovina also joined the military aggression against Croatia. The enemy's intent was to capture part of the territory of Croatia with Serbian minority following the program of the Serbian Academy of Sciences and Arts Memorandum. Resistance to a superior military force was led by the limited forces of the police, Croatian National Guard (in Croatian: Zbor narodne garde, ZNG), and poorly armed Croatian voluntary units, among them units of the Croatian Party of Rights (HOS), (Barić et al. 2015, 71-74).

By forming the General Staff of the Croatian military in September 1991 and by the passage of a Bill on Defense the stage was set to develop the Armed Forces of the Republic of Croatia. Apart from the ethnic "cleansing" of non-Serbian population, Serb forces committed numerous crimes against civilians in Croatian villages and towns. The greatest atrocities happened in the baroque city of Vukovar and a place called Škabrnja in Dalmatia. With Europe and the world public watching, the city of Vukovar was leveled to the ground (Silber and Little 1996, 165-177).

The Yugoslav Navy blocked harbors and sea routes on the Adriatic. An artillery attack on the city of Dubrovnik and its UNESCO-protected city center on December 6, 1991 appalled the public worldwide (Silber and Little 1996, 178-181).

Against all military conventions, genocide, cultural genocide, and ecocide occurred in the occupied Croatian territory which was nearly a third of the country. Croatian cultural heritage was plundered and destroyed. Civilian and religious buildings were being systematically destroyed by the artillery and air strikes, land mines, and arson. Despite the assessment of most military analysts who predicted that Croatia would be beaten in a short period, the opposite happened. By the end of 1991, Croatian forces managed to liberate most of western Slavonia with a series of liberation operations: Orkan '91, Otkos '91 and Papuk '91 (Radelić et al. 2006, 132-133).

Vukovar – The City of Heroes

After they occupied Baranya, the JNA and Serbian forces started attacks on the cities of Osijek, Vinkovci, and Vukovar. The battle for Vukovar lasted from August 25 to November 18, 1991. 11,000 artillery shells were launched on the city each day. According to incomplete data, in the battle for Vukovar, the Serbian aggressor used more than 1,100 combat armoured vehicles, aircraft, and ships, hundreds of launchers of all kinds of artillery-rocket weapons, from which it systematically and without discrimination of targets fired on the city hundreds thousands of missiles. By the beginning of October 1991, the city was completely surrounded with about 50,000 well-armed enemy soldiers. The Serbian military had around 1,000 armoured vehicles and tanks at their disposal, alongside support from military ships and air force. According to a JNA source, in eastern Slavonia they had 37,613 soldiers, 676 tanks, 505 armored transporters, 428 tools of 'support artillery', 158 tools of 'anti-armour artillery' and 380 tools of 'anti-aircraft artillery', and Serbian forces 9582 'military person (Nazor 2011, 148).

The city was defended by 1,800-2,000 members of the Croatian military (Nazor 2011, 220; Nazor and Pušek 2018, 148), police, and volunteers and volunteers of Croatian and other nationalities: Hungarians, Russians, Slovaks, Germans, French, Irish, and Scots (Charuel and Besson 2011, 19-60; Barić et al. 2015, 117). Completely overrun by the enemy, the city fell on November 18, 1991. The military occupation of the city was followed by mass executions of Croatian soldiers and civilians, as well as sacking and persecution of citizens.

During the siege, around 700 shells fell daily onto the Vukovar hospital. A medical team led by Dr. Bosanac and Dr. Njavro performed over 1,000 surgeries under such conditions. Around 2,500 patients were taken care of. All wounded, regardless of their religion or nationality, were treated equally (Marušić, M. 1999, 125). On November 20th, wounded patients and medical staff from the Vukovar hospital were taken to a nearby farming estate Ovčara which was turned into a Serbian concentration camp. There they were brutally beaten, killed, and thrown into a mass grave in an excavation pit. In September 1996, 200 bodies aged 16 to 72 of those killed were exhumed from the tomb (Nazor and Pušek 2018, 150). A memorial plaque remains today in the courtyard of the rebuilt hospital in Vukovar.

Among prisoners of Ovčara was Siniša Glavašević, a journalist of Radio Vukovar, who reported daily from the city and informed the Croatian and the world public of the crimes being committed (Glavašević 2007, 7-153; Nazor and Pušek 2018, 151). Jean-Michel

Nicolier, a French volunteer soldier, was captured and killed. The site of his murder remains unknown (Nazor 2011, 333). On Trpinja road, the grave of JNA tanks, Blago Zadro, a veteran and hero, lost his life on October 16, 1991 (Dedaković et al. 1997, 78).

According to the Office for the Detained and Missing in the Ministry of Families, Veterans, and Intergenerational Solidarity of the Republic of Croatia in November 2007, during the Serbian siege in 1999 at least 1,739 people were killed in Vukovar, mostly civilians, and at least 2,500 people were wounded (data of the General Medical Staff of the Republic of Croatia (Nazor 2011, 222; Nazor and Pušek 2018, 149). Some 22,000 citizens of Vukovar were expelled, and more than 4,000 people from the Croatian side of the Danube were forcibly taken to the territory of Yugoslavia and Serbia, from where they were deported to the then-free parts of the Republic of Croatia. At least 2,796 people captured in 1991 were killed at the time in Vukovar or tortured and abused in camps and prisons in Serbia and Montenegro. The youngest detainee was 15 and the oldest was 81 years old (Nazor and Pušek 2018, 150).

The Office for Detainees and Missing Persons in Vukovar-Srijem County has uncovered 52 mass graves and hundreds of individual ones, in which the JNA and Serbian troops have buried their victims. The remains of 2,036 victims were exhumed in 2006. Since then, additional remains of 1761 Croatian combatants and civilians have been identified. According to data from the Office of Detainees and Missing as of December 2009, there are 1,030 people who were still missing and not accounted for. During an almost three-month siege of Vukovar, the heroic resistance of Vukovar, its citizens and brave soldiers were of strategic significance for the defense of Croatia. (Barić et al. 2015, 74-77). The destruction of the city revealed the truth about the conflict to the public worldwide. It became clear who was the aggressor and who the victim. The heroes of Vukovar hold a place of honor in Croatian history. A feature-length film from 2017 called "The Heart of Vukovar" from director Stipe Majić tells about the war in Croatia and the war hospital in Vukovar, which was a symbol of defense of Vukovar from Serbian aggression. In 2018 director Majić made another documentary feature-film called "Head down, hands on your back" in which he showed tortures and murders of Croatian defenders in Serbian concentration camps.

From International Recognition to Victory in the War of Independence

The Republic of Croatia was internationally recognized on January 15, 1992. Alongside the member countries of the European Community, the country was recognized by Slovenia, Lithuania, Latvia, Ukraine, Estonia, San Marino, Iceland and Vatican, Ireland, Australia, Bulgaria, Czech Republic, Slovakia, Canada, Hungary, Malta, Norway, Poland, Sweden, and Switzerland. The Members of the European Community, which collectively recognised Croatia were Austria, Belgium, Denmark, France, Greece, Italy, Luxemburg, the Netherlands, Germany, Portugal, Spain and the United Kingdom (Radelić et al. 2006, 326). Full membership in the UN was granted to Croatia on May 22, 1992.

However, the war was not over. The UN wanted to find a way for a peaceful stand-down of the parties involved in the war. The UN representative, Cyrus Vance, proposed that peacekeepers be sent to Croatia to oversee the JNA retreat and the return of exiled populations. The United Nations Security Council sent United Nations Protection Forces

(UNPROFOR) on February 21st to the so-called Pink zones for demarcation supervision (Barić et al. 2015, 78).

At the beginning of October 1991, the JNA and the Serbian paramilitary units started the aggression against Bosnia and Herzegovina. Under the command of Radovan Karadžić and Ratko Mladić, genocide was committed against 8,000 Muslims near the town of Srebrenica in July 1995. In November 1995, negotiations were held during the Dayton Agreement about ending the war in Bosnia and Herzegovina. The war ended in Bosnia and Herzegovina with the signing of the Paris Agreement in December 1995 (Barić et al. 2015, 57-58).

Despite the presence of the UNPROFOR forces, the leadership of the rebellious Serbs resisted peaceful reintegration of the Republic of Serbian Krajina to Croatia. The war in Croatia was still not finished. From May to October 1992, Croatian forces liberated Dubrovnik and all of the south of Croatia. In June 1992, the Miljevci plateau near Šibenik was liberated. By the end of January 1993, Zadar's hinterland was liberated as well. Croatian soldiers freed the area around town of Gospić in a military campaign called Operation Medak Pocket. With Operations Winter '94 and Leap 1 (in Croatian: Skok 1) in April 1995, Croatian forces liberated Livanjsko field and Dinara mountain. The Knin hinterland was under control as well (Nazor 2011, 156-166; Marijan, D. 2009, 46-47).

In only a few days from the 1st to 4th of May 1995 the west part of Slavonia was liberated with the "Operation Flash" (Bljesak in Croatian) (Marijan 2009, 48; Nazor 2011, 167). In retaliation, Serbian troops rocketed Zagreb on May 2 and 3, 1995: seven civilians were killed and 176 civilians wounded (Nazor 2011, 167-168). Among the injured was a ballet dancer Almira Osmanović and another 16 ballet dancers in the Croatian National Theatre. The attack on Zagreb was led by Milan Martić. For the war crimes he committed, he was sentenced to 35 years in prison by the International Criminal Tribunal for the former Yugoslavia (ICTY).

In the Operation Leap 2 (Skok 2) in June 1995, Croatian forces brought under their control Bosansko Grahovo and the road Bosansko Grahovo–Glamoč (Marijan 2009, 49) and came close to the territory held by the Republic of Serbian Krajina and the city of Knin. The Croatian forces aimed at liberating next the rest of Dalmatia, Lika, Kordun and Banovina. The aim of the planned Operation "Storm" (Oluja) was to defeat the Republic of Serbian Krajina and to restore the United Nations Protected Areas to the constitutional legal order of Croatia. The Croatian military and police began Operation Storm on August 4, 1995, at 5am. In the first hours of the Operation, the Croatian president Franjo Tuđman started sending every half an hour a radio message to Serbs living in Croatia. He invited them to surrender their weapons, guaranteeing amnesty to all who did not commit war crimes by Croatian laws. In the morning of August 5, 1995, members of the 4th and 7th Guard Brigades of the Croatian military liberated Knin. The day Knin was liberated was pronounced as a national holiday, the Victory and Homeland Thanksgiving Day. Around 127,000 members of the Croatian military and police participated in Operation Storm. Around 1,100 Croatian soldiers were wounded, 3 were captured and 15 went missing. In 7 days of the Operation, 18.4% of Croatian territory was liberated (Marijan 2009, 136-137).

After the Storm, on the basis of a Croatian-Bosnian agreement reached in Split 1995, Croatian forces cooperated with the Army of the Republic of Bosnia and Herzegovina in freeing Bosnian territory with "Operation Maestral." After the Dayton Agreement, negotiations were held about peaceful reintegration of the remaining occupied parts of Podunavlje: Baranja, eastern Slavonija, and western Srijem with cities Vukovar and Ilok.

Representatives of the rioting Serbs finally agreed to peacefully return Podunavlje into the legal order of Croatia. The Erdut Agreement was signed in November of 1995. The process of peaceful reintegration ended on January 15, 1998, by which date Croatia established full control over the internationally recognized borders of the Republic of Croatia (Radelić et al. 2004, 441-461; Klemenčić et al. 2013, 61-62).

Consequences of the War of Independence

The War of Independence (1991-1995) was a war of liberation from occupiers. The Republic of Croatia was attacked and forced to defend its sovereignty, independence, and territorial integrity. All military and police operations by Croatian soldiers were for defense and for liberation. By 2018 at least 150 mass graves and about 1,200 individual graves of the victims of Serbian aggression were found, from which, according to the Office for The Detained and Missing in the Ministry of Veterans of the Republic of Croatia, since November 4, 2014, 3,955 people were exhumed in 1991-1992 (for 938 people, the fate was not yet known – missing). According to the data of the aforementioned Office (situation at the end of 2017), from individual and common graves, the remains of 5,131 people were exhumed, of which 4,196 victims (81.7%) were finally identified, with additional remains of Croatian citizens (January 2017) retrieved from Serbia (108) and Bosnia and Herzegovina (62) (Nazor and Pušek 2018, 279).

Around 714 soldiers and civilians were imprisoned and abused in Serbian concentration camps Glina, Knin, Borovo Village, Manjača, Trebinje, Begejci, Belgrade, Niš, Stojić and other. The search for the detainees continues today (Barić et al. 2015, 97).

In Republic of Serbian Krajina, under the protection of UN forces until the end of 1993, about 8,000 Croats and members of other non-Serb nationalities were expelled (Nazor 2011, 304).

In 1993, the UN Security Council decided to form the International Criminal Tribunal for the former Yugoslavia, headquartered in Den Haag (Netherlands). The Serbian president Slobodan Milošević was imprisoned and tried, but he died during the trial. The majority of convicted participants in the war were Serbian politicians and generals. However, not all perpetrators were convicted. Vojislav Šešelj was released, and today he is an active politician in Belgrade. According to the incomplete data from 2016, in the Homeland War on the Croatian side (in the free region of The Republic of Croatia) about 14,000 citizens (about 40 to 50% of them civilians) were killed and about 1,000 citizens went missing (Nazor and Pušek 2018, 278).

According to data in 2013 from Andrija Hebrang, the Minister of Wartime Health, 6,891 Croatian soldiers and 7,263 civilians were killed in the Croatian War (14,154 in total) (Nazor and Pušek 2018, 278).

The war devastation in Croatia, depending on the source, consisted of between 195,000 to 217,009 residential units were destroyed or damaged, around 120 commercial buildings, and 2,423 cultural monuments, of which 495 religious objects, mainly catholic churches (Nazor and Pušek 2018, 279).

The State Commission for Census and War Damage Assessment estimated in September 1999 the total war damage in Croatia amounted to 37.1 billion US dollars.

CROATIA'S ENTRY INTO THE EUROPEAN UNION ON JULY 1, 2013

Croatia's entry into the European integration process started with membership in the Organization for Security and Co-operation in Europe (OSCE) in 1992. Croatia was declared a member of the Council of Europe in 1996. It joined the Pact for Security and Co-operation in Southeastern Europe in 1998. The first Croatian president Franjo Tuđman died on December 10, 1999. In the 2000 elections, the united opposition emerged victorious over the Croatian Democratic Union (HDZ). The new coalition government did not achieve the promised goals of democratization and economic growth. In the 2003 elections, HDZ won again, led by their president Ivo Sanader. Croatia then entered negotiations for joining the European Union. The government of the Prime Minister Jadranka Kosor successfully completed the negotiations. In February 2003, Croatia applied for full membership in the European Union. The Republic of Croatia entered NATO in 2009. The president of the country Stjepan Mesić was succeeded by Ivo Josipović in 2010. Croatian generals indicted by the ICTY, Ante Gotovina and Mladen Markač, were released on November 16, 2012. The Republic of Croatia became a full member of the European Union on the 1st of July 2013. (Barić et al. 2015, 126-129; Klemenčić et al. 2013, 62-64).

ACKNOWLEDGMENT

I thank Ana Utrobičić, MLIS., for her great help with literature sources. The kind permission of Školska knjiga Publisher, Zagreb to use and modify the figures in this chapter is acknowledged.

REFERENCES

Adamček, Josip. 1968. *Seljačka buna 1573*. Zagreb: Vjesnik. [*Peasant rebellion* 1573. Zagreb: Vjesnik].

Aralica, Višeslav. 2009. "Matica hrvatska u političkom životu Hrvatske 1935. – 1945." *Časopis za suvremenu povijest* 41(2):447-482. ["Matica Hrvatska in the political life of Croatia 1935 - 1945. *Journal of Contemporary History* 41(2):447-482].

Banac, Ivo. 1984. *Nacionalno pitanje u Jugoslaviji*. Zagreb: Globus. [*The National Question in Yugoslavia: Origins, History, Politics*. Zagreb: Globus].

Banov, Estela. 2018. "Naracija o junaštvu kao dio kolektivnog pamćenja: Nikola Zrinski u usmenim i pučkim povijesnim pjesmama." Zbornik radova Filozofskog fakulteta u Splitu 11:113-133. ["Narration about heroism as a part of collective memory: oral and popular historic songs about Nikola Zrinski." *Proceedings of the Faculty of Social Sciences and Humanities in Split* 11:113-133].

Banović, Branimir. 1987. "Emigracijska politika Austro-Ugarske i iseljavanje iz Hrvatske u razdoblju 1867 – 1914." *Migracijske i etničke teme* 3(3-4):313-323. ["The emigration policy of Austria-Hungary and emigration from Croatia in the period 1867-1914." *Migration and Ethnic Issues* 3(3-4):313-323].

Barić, Nikica et al. 2015. *Domovinski rat: Čitanka priručnik*. Zagreb: Školska knjiga. [*Homeland War: Handbook*. Zagreb: The School Book].

Barić, Nikica et al. 2016. *Drugi svjetski rat: Čitanka priručnik*. Zagreb: Školska knjiga. [*World War II: Handbook*. Zagreb: The School Book].

Barišić, Pavo. 2017. "Odnos Ivana Mažuranića i Ante Starčevića: od poredbe osoba do filozofije prava." *Prilozi za istraživanje hrvatske filozofske baštine* 43(2):437-472. ["The relationship between Ivan Mažuranić and Ante Starčević: from the comparison of persons to the philosophy of law." *Contributions to the Research of Croatian Philosophical Heritage* 43(2):437-472].

Beus, Marina. 2018. „Suradnja Dominika Mandića i Jere Jareba u svjetlu korespondencije sačuvane u Mandićevoj ostavštini." Časopis za suvremenu povijest 50(3): 503-534. [The collaboration between Dominik Mandić and Jere Jareb in light of the correspondence preserved in Mandić's legacy. *Journal of Contemporary History* 50(3): 503-534]. HYPERLINK "https://doi" doi: 10.22586/csp.v50i3.101.

Bilandžić, Dušan. 1983. "Marksistički i teoretičar i revolucionar Vladimir Bakarić." *Politička misao: časopis za politologiju*. 20(1):3-23. ["Marxist theorist and revolutionary Vladimir Bakarić." *Political Thought: Journal of Political Science*. 20(1):3-23].

Biondich, Mark. 2000. *Stjepan Radić, the Croat Peasant Party, and the Politics of Mass Mobilization, 1904-1928*. Toronto: Universitiy of Toronto.

Boban, Ljubo. 1992. "Kada je i kako nastala Država Slovenaca, Hrvata i Srba." *Radovi Zavoda za hrvatsku povijest Filozofskoga fakulteta Sveučilišta u Zagrebu*. 26(1):187-198. ["When and how the State of Slovenes, Croats and Serbs was created." *Papers of the Department of Croatian History, Faculty of Humanities and Social Sciences, University of Zagreb* 26(1):187-198].

Borovčak, Damir. 2019. *Gvozdansko: hrvatsko velejunaštvo bez svjetskog uzora. 2. dopunjeno izdanje*. Zagreb: Vlastita naklada. [*Gvozdansko: Croatian Heroism without Comparison. Second edition*. Zagreb: Author edition].

Bošnjak Kolak, Arijana. 2017. "Ratna promidžba u hrvatskim novinama 1848./1849. godine." *Zbornik Odsjeka za povijesne znanosti Zavoda za povijesne i društvene znanosti Hrvatske akademije znanosti i umjetnosti* 35:201-2019. ["War propaganda in Croatian newspapers 1848–1849." *Proceedings of the Department of Historical and Social Sciences of the Institute of Historical and Social Sciences of the Croatian Academy of Sciences and Arts* 35:201-2019].

Botica, Ivan. 2014. "Stjepan Tomašević (1461. – 1463.): slom srednjovjekovnoga Bosanskog Kraljevstva. Zbornik radova sa Znanstvenog skupa održanog 11. i 12. studenog 2011. godine u Jajcu, ur. Ante Birin, Hrvatski institut za povijest – Katolički bogoslovni fakultet u Sarajevu." *Zbornik Odsjeka za povijesne znanosti Zavoda za povijesne i društvene znanosti Hrvatske akademije znanosti i umjetnosti* 32:322-326. ["The collapse of the medieval Bosnian Kingdom. Proceedings of the Scientific Conference held on 11 and 12 November 2011 in Jajce, ed. Ante Birin, Croatian Institute of History - Catholic Theological Faculty, Sarajevo." *Proceedings of the Department of Historical and Social Sciences of the Institute of Historical and Social Sciences of the Croatian Academy of Sciences and Arts* 32:322-326].

Cattaneo, Ruggero. 2013. "L'epistola a papa Adriano VI di Marco Marulić in Italiano: versione e nota traduttologica." *Colloquia Maruliana* 22(22):145-149. ["Marko Marulić's epistle to Pope Hadrian VI in Italian: version and translation note." *Colloquia Maruliana* 22(22):145-149].

Charuel, Marc, and Gaston Besson. 2011. *Život na meti: francuski dragovoljac u Domovinskom ratu*. Zagreb: Hrvatski memorijalno-dokumentacijski centar Domovinskog rata. [*Life on a target: A French volunteer in the Homeland War. Zagreb: Croatian* Memorial and Documentation Center for the Homeland War].

Čepulo, Dalibor. 2000. "Položaj i ustroj hrvatskih gradova prema Zakonu o uređenju gradskih općina iz 1881. godine." *Hrvatska i komparativna javna uprava: časopis za teoriju i praksu javne uprave* 2(1):83-120. ["The location and organization of Croatian cities according to the Law on The Regulation of the City Municipalities from 1881." *Croatian and Comparative Public Administration: A Journal of Public Administration Theory and Practice* 2(1):83-120].

Ćurčić, Leopold. 2015. "Tridesetogodišnji rat." ["Thirty-years war"]. *Essehist* 7(7): 68-75.

Ćurić, Mijo N. 1991. *Staroiransko podrijetlo Hrvata*. Zagreb: Nezavisna autorska naklada. [*Ancient Iranian origin of Croats*. Zagreb: Independent author edition].

Čorić, Franko. 2013. "Prilog poznavanju historicističkih intervencija na dubrovačkoj Divoni 1888. – 1892." *Portal: godišnjak Hrvatskog restauratorskog* zavoda 4:37-47. ["A Contribution to the Knowledge of Historic Interventions at the Divona in Dubrovnik 1888-1892." *Portal: A Yearbook of the Croatian Conservation Institute* 4:37-47].

Dabo, Mihovil. 2016. *Sve za boga, vjeru i puk: biskup Juraj Dobrila u svom vremenu*. Pazin: Državni arhiv u Pazinu; Sveučilište Jurja Dobrile. [*All for God, Faith and People: Bishop Juraj Dobrila in his Time*. Pazin: National Archives in Pazin; University of Juraj Dobrila].

Damjanović, Dragan. 2005. "Neogotički tornjevi Zagrebačke katedrale – stil i kontekst." *Radovi Instituta za povijest umjetnosti* 29:259-276. ["Neo-Gothic towers of Zagreb Cathedral – style and context." *Papers of the Institute of Art History*. 29: 259-276].

Delić-Gozze, Vesna. 2004. "Dubrovački muzeji, dom Marina Držića: (nedovršeni) komadić dubrovačke priče." *Muzeologija* 43/44:125-133. ["Dubrovnik museums, home of Marin Držić: an (unfinished) piece of Dubrovnik story." *Museology* 43/44:125-133].

Degan, Vladimir-Đuro. 2008. "Pravni aspekti i političke posljedice Rimskih ugovora od 18. svibnja 1941. godine." *Zbornik radova Pravnog fakulteta u Splitu* 45(2):265-278. ["The legal aspects and political consequences of the Rome Treaties of 18 May 1941." *Proceedings of the Faculty of Law in Split* 45(2):265-278].

Derossi, Zlata. 1996. "Pjesme Ante Starčevića 1823. - 1896. U povodu stote obljetnice smrti "Oca domovine." *Senjski zbornik: prilozi za geografiju, etnologiju, gospodarstvo, povijest i kulturu* 23(1):209-228. ["Poems by Ante Starčević in 1823-1896. On the occasion of the 100th anniversary of the death of the "Father of the motherland." *Proceedings of Senj: Contributions to Geography, Ethnology, Economy, History and Culture* 23(1):209-228].

Despot, Igor et al. 2014. *Prvi svjetski rat: Čitanka-priručnik*. Zagreb: Školska knjiga. [*First World War: Handbook*. Zagreb: School Book].

Diklić, Marijan. 1999. "Zora Dalmatinska (1884. - 1899.)." Radovi Zavoda za povijesne znanosti HAZU u Zadru 41:313-317. ["Dalmatian Dawn (1884-1899)." *Papers of the Institute for Historical Sciences of the Croatian Academy of Sciences and Arts in Zadar* 41:313-317].

Dizdar, Zdravko, and Mihael Sobolevski. 1999. *Prešućivani četnički zločini u Hrvatskoj i u Bosni i Hercegovini 1941. - 1945.* Zagreb: Hrvatski institut za povijest; Dom i svijet. [*Concealed Chetnik Crimes in Croatia and Bosnia and Herzegovina 1941-1945.* Zagreb: Croatian Institute of History; Home and World].

Dragić, Marko. 2012. "Danak u krvi u romanu Na Drini ćuprija i u suvremenome pripovjedanju." *Hum: časopis Filozofskog fakulteta Sveučilišta u Mostaru* 8:123-139. ["A tribute in blood in the novel The bridge on the Drina and in modern narrative." *Hum: Journal of the Faculty of Humanities and Social Sciences,* University of Mostar 8:123-139].

Dukić, Davor, and Jasmina Lukec. 2017. "Pjesme Ane Katarine Zrinski – poetika i kontekst." *Croatica: časopis za hrvatski jezik, književnost i kulturu* 41(61):273-294. ["The poems of Ana Katarina Zrinski – poetics and context." *Croatica: Journal of Croatian Language, Literature and Culture* 41(61):273-294].

Đuričić, Siniša. 2015. "Princ Eugen Savojski u Velikom bečkom ratu do oslobođenja Beograda (1683. – 1688.)." *Scrinia Slavonica: Godišnjak Podružnice za povijest Slavonije, Srijema i Baranje Hrvatskog instituta za povijest* 15(1):35-55. ["Prince Eugene of Savoy in the Great Vienna War until the liberation of Belgrade (1683-1688)." *Scrinia Slavonica: Yearbook of the History Institute of Slavonia, Srijem and Baranja of the Croatian Institute of History* 15(1):35-55].

Fabijanić Gagro, Sandra, and Budislav Vukas, ml. 2008. "Pravna priroda i politička pozadina oružanih sukoba u Hrvatskoj i Bosni i Hercegovini." *Zbornik Pravnog fakulteta u Zagrebu* 58(5):1159-1199. ["Legal nature and political background of armed conflicts in Croatia and Bosnia and Herzegovina." *Proceedings of the Faculty of Law in Zagreb* 58(5):1159-1199].

Feletar, Petar. 2015. *Hrvatske povijesne ceste – Karolina, Jozefina i Lujzijana: prometno-geografska studija o povezivanju kontinentalne i jadranske Hrvatske.* Samobor: Meridijani. [*Croatian Historic Roads – Carolina, Josephine and Louisiana: a traffic and geographical study on the connection between continental and Adriatic Croatia.* Samobor: Meridians].

Fernandez Andabak, Katarina. 2015. *Bachov apsolutizam.* Osijek: Filozofski fakultet. [*Bach's absolutism.* Osijek: Faculty of Social Sciences and Humanities].

Fonović Cvijanović, Teodora. 2016. "Jezik četiriju izdanja molitvenika Otče, budi volja tvoja biskupa Jurja Dobrile." *Croatica Christiana periodica* 41(79):47-60. ["The language of the four editions of the prayer book Father, thy will be done by Bishop Juraj Dobrila." *Croatica Christiana Periodica* 41(79):47-60].

Franković, Đuro. 2014. "Hrvatski prinosi protestantizmu i katoličkoj duhovnoj obnovi s osobitim osvrtom na djelatnost kardinala Jurja Draškovića." *Zbornik Janković* I(1):19-38. ["Croatian Contributions to Protestantism and Catholic Spiritual Renewal with Special Reference to Cardinal Juraj Draskovic's Activity." *Proceedings Janković* I(1):19-38].

Frbežar, Igor. 2014. Sidonija Rubido Erdödy. *Hrvatski povijesni portal: elektronički časopis za povijest i srodne znanosti.* [*Croatian Historical Portal: Electronic Journal for History and Related Sciences*]. Accessed April 11 2020. http://povijest.net/2018/?p=612http://povijest.net/2018/?p=612.

Galović, Tomislav. 2018. "Milan Moguš i Bašćanska ploča." *Senjski zbornik: prilozi za geografiju, etnologiju, gospodarstvo, povijest i kulturu* 45(1):265-285. [Milan Moguš and the Baška Tablet." *Proceedings of Senj: Contributions to Geography, Ethnology, Economy, History and Culture* 45(1):265-285].

Galović, Tomislav. 2019. "Suzbijanje korupcije u Hrvatskoj u srednjem vijeku: na primjeru pravnih spomenika na hrvatskom jeziku – Vinodolski zakon (1288.) i Krčki-vrbnički statut (1388.)." *Zbornik Pravnog fakulteta Sveučilišta u Rijeci* 40(2):869-894. ["Combating Corruption in Croatia in the Middle Ages: The Case of Legal Monuments in the Croatian Language – Vinodol Law (1288) and the Statute of Krk (1388)." *Proceedings of the Faculty of Law*, University of Rijeka 40(2):869-894].

Geiger, Vladimir. 2008. "Josip Broz Tito i sudbina jugoslavenskih Nijemaca." *Časopis za suvremenu povijest* 40(3):789-818. ["Josip Broz Tito and the fate of the Yugoslav Germans." *Journal of Contemporary History* 40(3):789-818].

Glavašević, Siniša. 2007. *Priče iz Vukovara*. Zagreb: Matica hrvatska. [*Tales from Vukovar*. Zagreb: Matica Hrvatska].

Gračanin, Hrvoje. 2008. "Od Hrvata pak koji su stigli u Dalmaciju odvojio se jedan dio i zavladao Ilirikom i Panonijom." *Povijest u nastavi* VI(11):67-69. ["One part of the Croats, who arrived in Dalmatia, separated and took over the Illyiria and Panonia." *History in Teaching* VI(11):67-69].

Grahek Ravančić, Martina. 2008. "Na križnom putu kroz Slavoniju." *Scrinia Slavonica: Godišnjak Podružnice za povijest Slavonije, Srijema i Baranje Hrvatskog instituta za povijest* 8(1):301-316. ["On the Way of the Cross through Slavonia." *Scrinia Slavonica: Yearbook of the History Institute of Slavonia, Srijem and Baranja of the Croatian Institute of History* 8(1):301-316].

Gross, Mirjana. 1973. *Povijest pravaške ideologije*. Zagreb: Institut za hrvatsku povijest. [*History of the ideology of Croatian Party of Rights*. Zagreb: Institute for Croatian history].

Gruenfelder, Anna Marija 2003. "Uskočki rat: međunarodni aspekti." *Senjski zbornik: prilozi za geografiju, etnologiju, gospodarstvo, povijest i kulturu* 30(1):211-257. ["The Uskok war: international aspects." *Proceedings of Senj: Contributions to Geography, Ethnology, Economy, History and Culture* 30(1):211-257].

Harni, Slavko. 2008. "Bibliografski rad Ivana Franje Jukića i kraj kulturne povijesti. Bibliografije kao izvor za povijest knjige i kulturnu povijest." *Libellarium: časopis za povijest pisane riječi, knjige i baštinskih ustanova* 1(1):27-50. ["Bibliographic work by Ivan Franjo Jukić and the end of cultural history. Bibliography as a source for book history and cultural history." *Libellarium: Journal for the History of the Written Word, Book and Heritage Institutions* 1(1):27-50].

Heka, Laszlo. 2016. "Analiza Austro-ugarske i Hrvatsko-ugarske nagodbe (u povodu 150. obljetnice Austro-ugarske nagodbe)." *Zbornik Pravnog fakulteta Sveučilišta u Rijeci* 38(2):855-880. ["Analysis of the Austro-Hungarian and Croatian-Hungarian Settlements (on the occasion of the 150th anniversary of the Austro-Hungarian Settlement)." *Proceedings of the Faculty of Law*, University of Rijeka 38(2):855-880].

Heka, Vladimir. 2019. "Vlaški statuti i njihova usporedba s povlasticama mađarskih hajduka." *Podravina: časopis za multidisciplinarna istraživanja* 18(35):26-45. "Vlach statutes and their comparison with the privileges of the Hungarian Hajduks." *Podravina: Journal for Multidisciplinary Research* 18(35):26-45].

Holjevac, Željko. 1999. "Jezik i nacija u hrvatskim i srpskim nacionalnim ideologijama: Starčevićeva polemika iz 1852. godine." *Migracijske i etničke teme* 15(3):289-321.

["Language and nation in Croatian and Serbian national ideologies: Starčević's polemics from 1852." *Migration and Ethnic Themes* 15(3):289-321].

Horvat, Rudolf. 1992. *Hrvatska na mučilištu*. Zagreb: Školska knjiga. [*Croatia in torture*. Zagreb: School Book].

Horvat, Vladimir. 2008. *Kardinal Alojzije Stepinac, mučenik za ljudska prava*. Zagreb-Samobor-Krašić: Meridijani [*Cardinal Alojzije Stepinac, human rights martyr*. Zagreb-Samobor-Krašić: Meridians].

Hrvatska enciklopedija, mrežno izdanje. 2020. Klović, Julije. Zagreb: Leksikografski zavod Miroslav Krleža. [*Croatian Encyclopedia, internet edition*. 2020. Klović, Julije. Zagreb: Lexicographic Institute Miroslav Krleža]. Accessed April 4 2020. http://www.enciklopedija.hr/Natuknica.aspx?ID=32010.

Hrvatska enciklopedija, mrežno izdanje. 2020. Kőszeg. Zagreb: Leksikografski zavod Miroslav Krleža. [*Croatian Encyclopedia, internet edition*. 2020. Kőszeg. Zagreb: Lexicographic Institute Miroslav Krleža]. Accessed April 4 2020. http://www.enciklopedija.hr/Natuknica.aspx?ID=33406.

Hrvatska enciklopedija, mrežno izdanje. 2020. Stećci. Leksikografski zavod Miroslav Krleža. [*Croatian Encyclopedia, internet edition*. 2020. Stećci. Zagreb: Lexicographic Institute Miroslav Krleža]. Accessed April 4 2020. http://www.enciklopedija.hr/Natuknica.aspx?ID=57932.

Huzjan, Vladimir. 2008. "Pokušaj otkrivanja nastanka i razvoja kravate kao riječi i odjevnoga predmeta." *Povijesni prilozi* 27(34):103-120. ["An attempt to detect the emergence and development of a tie as a word and a garment." *Historical Contributions* 27(34):103-120].

Ivanović, Marin. 2016. "Obnova Kneževa dvora u Dubrovniku nakon potresa 1979. godine u svjetlu novih spoznaja." *Mostariensia: časopis za društvene i humanističke znanosti* 20(1-2):79-92. ["The restoration of the Rector's Palace in Dubrovnik after the 1979 earthquake in light of the new findings." *Mostariensia: Journal of Social Sciences and Humanities* 20(1-2):79-92].

Ivančević, Radoslav. 1986. *Umjetničko blago Hrvatske*. Beograd: Jugoslovenska revija. [*Croatian Art Treasure*. Belgrade: Yugoslav Magazine].

Jakšić, Nikola. 2014. "Od hagiografskog obrasca do političkog elaborata – škrinja Sv. Šimuna, zadarska arca d'oro." *Ars Adriatica* 4:125-154. ["From the hagiographic pattern to the political elaboration – the chest of St. Simon, Zadar arca d'oro." Ars Adriatica 4:125-154].

Jarak, Mirja. 1998. "O karolinškim i bizantskim utjecajima u karolinškoj arhitekturi Trpimirova doba." *Opuscula archaeologica* 22:119-128. ["On Carolingian and Byzantine influences in Carolingian architecture of the Trpimir era." *Opuscula Archaeologica* 22:119-128].

Jukić, Ivana. 2018. "Why Was the Habsburg Princess Granted the Right to Rule the Kingdom of Croatia in 1712?" *Povijesni prilozi* 37(54):219-236.

Jurković, Miljenko. 1995. "Sv. Spas na vrelu Cetine i problem westwerka u hrvatskoj predromanici." *Starohrvatska prosvjeta* III(22):55-80. ["St. Spas at the spring of Cetina and the problem of westwerk in the Croatian pre-Romanesque history." *Old Croatian Education* III(22):55-80].

Josipović, Ivan. 2018. "Tri nova posvetna natpisa s imenima hrvatskih vladara iz karolinškog perioda." *Starohrvatska prosvjeta* III(44-45):137-151. ["Three New Votive Inscriptions with the Names of Croatian Rulers from the Carolingian Period." *Old Croatian Education* III(44-45):137-151].

Katušić, Maja. 2005. "Usmene predaje o caru Josipu II." *Povijesni prilozi* 24(29):151-165. ["Oral Tradition on Emperor Joseph II." *Historical Contributions* 24(29):151-165].

Karbić, Damir. 2004. "Šubići Bribirski do gubitka nasljedne banske časti (1322.)." *Zbornik Odsjeka za povijesne znanosti Zavoda za povijesne i društvene znanosti Hrvatske akademije znanosti i umjetnosti* 22:1-26. ["Šubići of Bribir until the loss of hereditary Ban's honor." *Proceedings of the Department of Historical Sciences of the Institute of Historical and Social Sciences of the Croatian Academy of Sciences and Arts* 22:1-26].

Karbić, Damir. 2008. "Odnosi gradskog plemstva i bribirskih knezova Šubića: Prilog poznavanju međusobnih odnosa hrvatskih velikaša i srednjovjekovnih dalmatinskih komuna." *Povijesni prilozi* 27(35):43-58. ["Relations between the City Nobility and the Bribir Princes Šubić: A Contribution to the Knowledge of the Interrelationships between Croatian Princes and Medieval Dalmatian Communes." *Historical Contributions* 27(35):43-58].

Katić, Ivan. 2012. "Pioneer female veterinarians." *Rad 511 Hrvatske akademije znanosti i umjetnosti. Medicinske znanosti* 37:137-168. ["Pioneer female veterinarians." *Paper 511 of the Croatian Academy of Sciences and Arts. Medical Sciences* 37:137-168].

Katičić, Radoslav. 2007. *Litterarum studia: književnost i naobrazba ranoga hrvatskog srednjovjekovlja. Drugo izdanje*. Zagreb: Matica hrvatska. [*Litterarum studia: literature and education of the early Croatian Middle Ages*. 2nd edition. Zagreb: Matica Hrvatska].

Kavalski, Emilian. 2000. "The Balkan way to regional conflict solving." *Migracijske i etničke teme* 16(3):289-300. [*Migration and Ethnic Themes* 16(3):289-300].

Kavazović, Robert. 2007. "Majka i dijete – još jedno nepoznato Bukovčevo djelo." *Peristil: zbornik radova za povijest umjetnosti* 50(1):275-284. [Kavazović, Robert. 2007. "Mother and child - another unknown work of Bukovac." *Peristyle: Proceedings for the History of Art* 50(1):275-284].

Kisić-Kolanović, Nada. 1998. *Mladen Lorković – ministar urotnik*. Zagreb: Golden marketing. [*Mladen Lorković – Minister Conspirator*. Zagreb: Golden Marketing].

Kekez, Hrvoje. 2006. "Urbarijalni nameti i katastarski popis kmetskih selišta na vlastelinstvu Brlog u 18. stoljeću." *Povijesni prilozi* 25(30):79-102. ["Urbars' levies and cadastral census of agricultural settlements on the Brlog estate in the 18th century." *Historical Contributions* 25(30):79-102].

Klaić, Nada. 1975. *Povijest Hrvata u ranom srednjem vijeku*. Zagreb: Školska knjiga. [*History of Croats in the early Middle Ages*. Zagreb: School Book].

Klaić, Nada. 1976. *Povijest Hrvata u razvijenom srednjem vijeku*. Zagreb: Školska knjiga. [History of Croats in the developed Middle Ages. Zagreb: School Book].

Klemenčić et al. 2013. *Hrvatska: zemlja i ljudi*. Zagreb: Leksikografski zavod Miroslav Krleža. [*Croatia: country and people*. Zagreb: Lexicographic Institute Miroslav Krleža].

Kolanović, Josip. 1993. "Hrvatsko običajno pravo prema ispravama XIV. i XV. stoljeća." *Arhivski vjesnik* 36:85-98. ["Croatian common law according to the documents from XIV and XV century." *Archival Newsletter* 36:85-98].

Kordić, Ivan. 2005. "Croatian Philosophers IV: Matija Vlačić Ilirik – Mathias Flacius Illyricus (1520–1575)." *Prolegomena: Časopis za filozofiju* 4(2):219-233. ["Croatian Philosophers IV: Matija Vlačić Ilirik – Mathias Flacius Illyricus (1520–1575)." *Prolegomena: Journal of Philosophy* 4(2):219-233].

Kožić, Maja. 1979. "Narodni život i običaji u Reljkovićevu Satiru: uz dvjestotu obljetnicu drugoga izdanja." *Etnološka tribina: Godišnjak Hrvatskog etnološkog društva* 9(2):7-66. ["Folk life and customs in Reljković's Satire: At the Occasion of the 200th Anniversary of the Second Edition." *Ethnological Panel: Yearbook of the Croatian Ethnological Society* 9(2):7-66].

Kukuljević Sakcinski, Ivan. 1883. *Zrin Grad i njegovi gospodari*. Zagreb: Tiskara narodnih novinah. [*Zrin Grad and its masters*. Zagreb: National Newspapers Press].

Kunčević, Lovro. 2008. "No harm in hearing it all: medicean attitude to the conspiracy of Marin Držić." *Dubrovnik Annals* 12:7-44.

Latinčić, Ivan and Paula Vuković. 2018. "Znanstveni kolokvij Sisačka bitka 1593. – 2018." *Povijesni prilozi* 37(55):384-387. ["Scientific colloquium Sisak Battle 1593–2018." *Historical Contributions* 37(55):384-387].

Lisac, Josip. 2012. "Hrvatski jezik Vrančićeva rječnika i njegove proze." *Filologija* 59:37-47. ["Croatian language in Vrančić's vocabulary and his prose." *Filology* 59:37-47].

Lokmer, Juraj. 2004. „Europska sastavnica hrvatske obrane od Turaka: Družba Svetoga Mauricija u opisu krbavske bitke popa Martinca". [European component of the Croatian defence against Turks: Society of Saint Mauritius in description of the battle of Krbava by priest Martinac]. *Croatica Christiana periodica* 28(54):19-28.

Lokös, Istvan. 2008. "Još jednom o alegorijskom tumačenju Judite." *Colloquia Maruliana* 17(17):189-197. ["Once again on the allegorical interpretation of Judita." *Colloquia Maruliana* 17(17):189-197].

Macan, Trpimir, and Željko Holjevac. 2013. *Povijest hrvatskoga naroda*. Zagreb: Školska knjiga. [*History of the Croatian people*, Zagreb: School Book].

Manfred, Albert Zaharovič. 1975. *Napoleon Bonaparta I-III*. Subotica: Minerva. [*Napoleon Bonaparte I-III*. Subotica: Minerva].

Margaritoni, Marko. 2003. *Nasljedne i rodbinske veze hrvatskih vladara*. Dubrovnik: Državni arhiv u Dubrovniku. [*Hereditary and family ties of Croatian rulers*. Dubrovnik: State Archives in Dubrovnik].

Marijan, Davor. 2009. *Oluja*. Zagreb: Hrvatski memorijalno-dokumentacijski centar Domovinskog rata. [*Storm*. Zagreb: Croatian Homeland War Memorial and Documentation Center].

Marks, Ljiljana. 2004. "Ban Josip Jelačić in Croatian oral legends: between history and myth." *Narodna umjetnost: hrvatski časopis za etnologiju i folkloristiku* 41(1):7-21. [Folk Art: *Croatian Journal of Ethnology and Folklore Research* 41(1):7-21].

Maršal Marmont. 1984. *Memoari*. Split: Logos. [Marshal Marmont. 1984. *Memoirs*. Split: Logos].

Martinić Jerčić, Natko, and Ante Nazor. 2019. "Ubojstva hrvatskih policajaca 2. svibnja 1991. – najava velikosrpske agresije na Hrvatsku." *Časopis za suvremenu povijest* 51(1):123-150. ["Murders of Croatian policemen on May 2, 1991 – Announcement of the Greater-Serbia Aggression against Croatia." *Journal of Contemporary History* 51(1):123-150].

Martinović, Ivica. 2002. "Optička rasprava Marka Antuna de Dominisa: geneza, metodologija, značenje." *Prilozi za istraživanje hrvatske filozofske baštine* 28(1-2):67-145. ["Optical discussion of Mark Antun de Dominis: Genesis, methodology, meaning." *Contributions to the Research of Croatian Philosophical Heritage* 28(1-2):67-145].

Marušić, Matko, editor. 1991. *Medical Testimony of the Vukovar Tragedy*. Croatian Medical Journal, separate edition.

Matasović, Ranko. 2019. "Ime Hrvata." *Jezik: časopis za kulturu hrvatskoga književnog jezika* 66(3):81-94. ["The Name of the Croats." *Language: Journal for the Culture of Croatian Standard Language* 66(3):81-94].

Matković, Hrvoje. 1995. *Suvremena politička povijest Hrvatske*. Zagreb: Ministarstvo unutarnjih poslova Republike Hrvatske. [*Contemporary political history of Croatia. Zagreb: Ministry of Internal Affairs of the Republic of Croatia*].

Matković, Hrvoje. 1998. *Povijest Jugoslavije (1918.-1991.): hrvatski pogled*. Zagreb: Naklada Pavičić. [*History of Yugoslavia (1918-1991): Croatian view*. Zagreb: Pavičić Press].

Mijatović, Anđelko. 1992. *Zrinsko-Frankopanska urota*. Zagreb: Alfa [*Zrinski-Frankopan conspiracy*. Zagreb: Alfa].

Mijatović Anđelko. 2010. Bruno Bušić: prilog istraživanju života i djelovanja (1939. –1978.). Zagreb: Školska knjiga. [*Bruno Bušić: Contribution to the Research on Life and Action* (1939–1978). Zagreb: School Book].

Matković, Stjepan. 2003. *"Novi Kurs" Srba u Hrvatskoj*. Zagreb: Hrvatski institut za povijest. [*"New Course" of Serbs in Croatia*. Zagreb: Croatian Institute for History].

Milošević, Ante. 2016. "Doseljenje Hrvata u Dalmaciju krajem 8. stoljeća: mač K-tipa iz Koljana kao mogući dokaz. *Starohrvatska prosvjeta* III(43):239-262. ["The Migration of the Croats to Dalmatia at the end of 8th century: The K-type sword from Koljane as possible evidence." *Old Croatian Education* III(43):239-262].

Mužić, Ivo. 1989. *Podrijetlo Hrvata*. Zagreb: Nakladni zavod Matice hrvatske. [Origin of Croats. Zagreb: The Publishing Institute of Matica Hrvatska].

Mužić, Ivan. 2007. *Hrvatska povijest devetoga stoljeća. Drugo dopunjeno izdanje*. Split: Naklada Bošković. [*Croatian history of the ninth century. Second updated edition*. Split: Bošković Press].

Mužić, Ivo. 2010. "Bijeli Hrvati u banskoj Hrvatskoj i županijska Hrvatska." *Starohrvatska prosvjeta* III(37):265-298. ["White Croats in Banska Croatia and Cantonian Croatia." *Old Croatian Education* III(37):265-298].

Nazor, Anica. 2008. *Knjiga o hrvatskoj glagoljici: "Ja slovo znajući govorim…"*.Zagreb: Erasmus naklada. [*The book about Croatian glagolitic: "I have a letter knowingly speaking…"*. Zagreb: Erasmus publishing.].nazor

Nazor, Ante. 2011. *Velikosrpska agresija na Hrvatsku 1990-ih godina*. Zagreb: Hrvatski memorijalni i dokumentacijski centar Domovinskog rata. [*Greater-Serbian aggression on Croatia in the 1990s*. Zagreb: Croatian Homeland War Memorial and Documentation Center].

Nazor, Ante, and Tomislav Pušek, editors. 2018. *Domovinski rat: pregled političke i diplomatske povijesti*. Zagreb: Nakladni zavod Globus; Hrvatski memorijalno-dokumentacijski centar Domovinskog rata. [*Homeland War: a review of political and diplomatic history*. Zagreb: Globus Publishing Institute; Croatian Homeland War Memorial and Documentation Center].

Nemet, Dražen. 2006. "Smrt hrvatskog kralja Zvonimira - problem, izvori i tumačenja." *Radovi: Radovi Zavoda za hrvatsku povijest Filozofskoga fakulteta Sveučilišta u Zagrebu* 38(1):73-92. ["The death of Croatian King Zvonimir - problem, sources and interpretations." *Papers: Papers of the Institute of Croatian History, Faculty of Humanities and Social Sciences, University of Zagreb* 38(1):73-92].

Novak, Grga. 2004. *Prošlost Dalmacije: knjiga druga.* Split: Marijan tisak. [*History of Dalmatia: book second.* Split: Marijan Press].

Novaković, Šimun. 2019. "Reakcije partijskih organa na pojavu Deklaracije o nazivu i položaju hrvatskog jezika prema pisanju nekih srbijanskih tiskovina." *Mostariensia: časopis za društvene i humanističke znanosti* 23(1):7-39. ["Reactions of the party organs to the emergence of the Declaration on the Name and Position of the Croatian Language according to the writings of some Serbian printed newspapers." *Mostariensia: Journal of Social Sciences and Humanities* 23(1):7-39].

Odža, Ivana. 2018. "Pedagoško djelovanje Dragojle Jarnević u kontekstu idejnoga svijeta Dnevnika." *Metodički ogledi: časopis za filozofiju odgoja* 25(1):87-117. ["Pedagogical activity of Dragojla Jarnević in the context of the ideological world of Diary." *Methodical Reviews: Journal for Philosophy of Education* 25(1):87-117].

Paar, Vladimir. 2007. "Tesla: vizionar 21. stoljeća." *Radovi Zavoda za znanstveni rad Varaždin* 18:199-219. ["Tesla: visionary of the 21st century." *Papers of the Institute for Scientific Research in Varaždin* 18:199-219].

Pajur, Franjo. 2011. "O Zrinsko-Frankopanskoj uroti: uz 340. obljetnicu." *Kaj: časopis za književnost, umjetnost i kulturu* 44(5):57-67. ["On the Zrinski-Frankopans conspiracy: on the occasion of the 340th anniversary." *Kaj: Journal of Literature, Art and Culture* 44(5):57-67].

Paraga, Dobroslav. 1995. *Goli otok: istočni grijeh Zapada.* Zagreb: Vlastita naklada autora. [*Goli otok: The Eastern Sin of the West.* Zagreb: Author edition].

Paro, Frane. 1984. "Tipografska analiza hrvatskog glagoljskog prvotiska Misala po zakonu rimskog dvora iz 1483. godine." *Slovo: časopis Staroslavenskoga instituta u Zagrebu* 34:91-110. ["Typographic analysis of the Croatian Glagolitic first printed edition of the Missal by the law of the Roman Court from 1483." *Letter: Journal of the Old Church Slavonic Institute in Zagreb* 34:91-110].

Pavlović, Cvijeta. 2013. "Pozornica kulture – kapital kulture. O 400 godina Hvarskoga kazališta." *Croatica et Slavica Iadertina* 9/2(9):459-499. ["The stage of culture – capital of culture. On 400 years of Hvar Theatre." *Croatica and Slavica Iadertina* 9/2(9):459-499].

Perić, Martina. 2010. "Problematizacija ženskog roda i identiteta u Zagorkinom romanu Kamen na cesti." *Kaj: časopis za književnost, umjetnost i kulturu* 43(4):31-46. ["Problematization of the female gender and identity in Zagorka's novel The Stone on the Road." *Kaj: Journal of Literature, Art and Culture* 43(4):31-46].

Peričić, Eduard. 1971. "Ban Petar Berislavić." *Crkva u svijetu* 6(3):258-266. ["Ban Petar Berislavić." *Church in the World* 6(3):258-266].

Pervan, Ivo, and Slobodan Prosperov Novak. 1995. *Dubrovnik.* Split: Croil, Nova grafika [*Dubrovnik.* Split: Croil, New Graphic].

Previšić, Martin. 2013. "Broj kažnjenika na Golom otoku i drugim logorima za informbiroovce u vrijeme sukoba sa SSSR-om (1948. - 1956.)." *Historijski zbornik* 61(1):173-193. ["The number of convicts on Goli otok and other internment camps during the Informbiro period and the conflict with the USSR (1948-56)." *Historical Proceedings Papers* 61(1):173-193].

Prosperov Novak, Slobodan. 2011. *Boka Kotorska: od kampanela do kampanela*. Zagreb: AGM. [*Boka Kotorska: from bell tower to bell tower*. Zagreb: AGM].

Polić, Maja. 2010. "Riječka Krpica 1868. godine i uvjeti za njezino naljepljivanje na Hrvatsko-ugarsku nagodbu." *Rijeka* 15(1):57-92. "The 'Rijeka Patch' from 1868 and the preconditions for its attachment to the Croatian-Hungarian settlement." *Rijeka* 15(1):57-92].

Puhlovski, Boris. 2000. "Patenti ing. Slavoljuba Penkale." *Acta stomatologica Croatica* 34(2):230-235. ["The Patents of Slavoljub Penkala." *Acta Stomatologica Croatica* 34(2):236-239].

Radelić, Zdenko et al. 2006. *Stvaranje hrvatske države i Domovinski rat*. Zagreb: Školska knjiga [Creation of the Croatian state and the Homeland War. Zagreb: School Book].

Radelić, Zdenko. 2017. "Ozna / Udba: popisi neprijatelja i njihova kategorizacija (1940-ih i 1950-ih)." *Časopis za suvremenu povijest* 49(1):59-99. ["Ozna / Udba: lists of enemies and their categorization (1940s and 1950s)." *Journal of Contemporary History* 49(1):59-99].

Radoš, Zvjezdana. 2006. "Recepcija Andrije Kačića Miošića u zadarskoj periodici na hrvatskom jeziku u 19. stoljeću." *Croatica et Slavica Iadertina* 2(2):259-270. ["Reception of Andrija Kačić Miošić in Zadar periodicals published in Croatian language during the 19th century." *Croatica and Slavica Iadertina* 2(2):259-270].

Raguž, Jakša. 2003. "Osnivački skup SDS-a za Dubrovnik – Otvorena najava agresije na dubrovačko područje." *Časopis za suvremenu povijest* 35(1):37-77. ["Inaugural gathering of the Serb Democratic Party (SDS) in Dubrovnik – An open announcement of aggresion on Dubrovnik Region." *Journal of Contemporary History* 35(1):37-77].

Rojnik, Raymond. 2010. "Diskografija 40 godina Varaždinskih baroknih večeri i njezin značaj za promicanje i očuvanje hrvatske i europske glazbene baštine." *Radovi Zavoda za znanstveni rad Varaždin* 21:59-91. ["The discography of 40 years of Varaždin Baroque Evenings and its importance for the promotion and preservation of Croatian and European musical heritage." *Papers of the Institute for Scientific Research in Varaždin* 21:59-91].

Sagrak, Darko, editor. 2010. *Nezavisna Država Hrvatska: prijepori i mitovi*. Zagreb: vlastita naklada. [*Independent State of Croatia: Controversies and myths*. Zagreb: Author edition].

Santo, Renata. 2014. "Ostavština Milke Trnine u Zbirci izvaneuropskih kultura Etnografskog muzeja." *Etnološka istraživanja* 18/19:239-254. ["Legacy of Milka Trnina in the Collection of Non-European Cultures of the Ethnographic Museum." *Ethnological Research* 18/19:239-254].

Silber, Laura and Allan Little. 1996. *Smrt Jugoslavije*. Opatija: Otokar Keršovani. [*The death of Yugoslavia*. Opatija: Otokar Keršovani].

Sikirić, Zvjezdana. 1992. *Bitka kod Siska 1593*. Zagreb: Zavod za hrvatsku povijest. [*Battle of Sisak* 1593. Zagreb: Institute for Croatian History].

Skenderović, Robert. 2011. "Ivan Andrija Makar i fra Luka Ibrišimović u službi zagrebačkog biskupa." *Cris: Časopis Povijesnog društva Križevci* XIII(1):10-18. ["Ivan Andrija Makar and Father Luka Ibrišimović in service of Zagreb Archbishop." *Cris: Journal of the Historical Society of Križevci* XIII(1):10-18].

Srša, Ivan. 2016. "Spomenik banu Josipu Jelačiću u Zagrebu: uz 150. obljetnicu podignuća spomenika i 215. obljetnicu rođenja bana Josipa Jelačića." *Kaj: časopis za književnost, umjetnost i kulturu* 49(3-4):117-138. ["The Ban Josip Jelačić monument in Zagreb: Commemorating the 150th anniversary of the monument's erection and 215 years since Jelačić was born." *Zagreb. Kaj: Journal of Literature, Art and Culture* 49(3-4):117-138].

Sršan, Stjepan. 2009. "Nobelovci Leopold Lavoslav Ružička (1887.-1976.) i Vladimir Prelog (1906.-1998.)." *Medicinski vjesnik* 41(3-4):75-90. ["Nobel Laureates Leopold Lavoslav Ružička (1887-1976) and Vladimir Prelog (1906-1998)." *Medical Journal* 41(3-4):75-90].

Stipčević, Ennio. 2007. *Ivan Lukačić*. Zagreb: Muzički informativni centar KDZ. [*Ivan Lukačić*. Zagreb: Music Information Centre KDZ].

Stojan, Slavica. 2002. "Ivan Gundulić (1589-1638) u zapisnicima kaznenog suda u Dubrovniku." *Anali Zavoda za povijesne znanosti Hrvatske akademije znanosti i umjetnosti u Dubrovniku* 40:203-214. ["Ivan Gundulić (1589-1638) in the minutes of the Criminal Court in Dubrovnik." *Annals of the Institute of Historical Sciences of the Croatian Academy of Sciences and Arts in Dubrovnik* 40:203-214].

Stojanović, Nikola. 1902. "Srbi i Hrvati." *Srpski književni glasnik* 2(6):1149-59. ["Serbs and Croats." *Serbian Literary Gazette* 2(6):1149-59].

Szabo, Agneza. 2005. "Uzroci i posljedice političkih demonstracija u Hrvatskoj 1903. godine." *Časopis za suvremenu povijest* 37(3):597-608. ["Causes and consequences of political demonstrations in Croatia in 1903." *Journal of Contemporary History* 37(3):597-608].

Supek, Ivan. 1990. *Krunski svjedok u Hebrangovu slučaju*. Zagreb: Globus. [*Crown witness in Hebrang's case*. Zagreb: Globus].

Šidak, Jaroslav. 1990. *Hrvatski narodni preporod: Ilirski pokret.* Drugo izdanje. Zagreb: Stvarnost. [*Croatian National Revival: Illyrian Movement.* Second edition. Zagreb: Stvarnost].

Škegro, Dario, and Zrinko Čustonja. 2014. "The beginnings of education and training for delivering physical education classes in Croatia – 140 years of tradition." *Kinesiology* 46(Suppl. 1):127-133.

Tanner, Marcus. 2001. *Croatia: a nation forged in war.* Second edition. New Haven: Yale Nota Bene.

Telišman, Tihomir. 1985. "Hrvatska bratska zajednica kao socijalna organizacija hrvatskih iseljenika u SAD." *Migracijske i etničke teme* 1(2):69-77. ["The Croatian Fraternal Union as a social organization of Croatian immigrants in the United States of America." *Migration and Ethnic Issues* 1(2):69-77].

Tomorad, Mladen. 2011. "Europska politika Matijaša Korvina: Matijaševa vanjska politika prvih godina vladavine (1458–1464)." *Kroatologija: časopis za hrvatsku kulturu* 2(1):165-191. ["European politics of Matijaš Korvin: Matijaš's foreign policy in the first years of his rule (1458–1464)." *Croatology: Journal of Croatian Culture* 2(1):165-191].

Triplat et al. 2011. "Application of Boškovic's Geometric Adjustment Method on Five Meridian Degrees." *KoG* 15(15):67-74.

Trogrlić, Marko and Nevio Šetić. 2015. *Dalmacija i Istra u 19. st.* Zagreb: Leykam international. [*Dalmatia and Istria in 19th century*. Zagreb: Leykam International].

Tuđman, Franjo. 1993. *Hrvatska u Monarhističkoj Jugoslaviji 1918. – 1941.: knjiga prva i knjiga druga*. Zagreb: Hrvatska sveučilišna naklada. [*Croatia in Monarchist Yugoslavia 1918-1941: Book first and book second*. Zagreb: Croatian University Press].

Vargović, Eduard. 2016. "Ivan Kukuljević Sakcinski u časopisu Radovi Zavoda za znanstveni rad Hrvatske akademije znanosti i umjetnosti u Varaždinu." *Radovi Zavoda za znanstveni rad Varaždin* 28:117-135. ["Ivan Kukuljević Sakcinski in the journal Papers of the Institute for Scientific Research of the Croatian Academy of Sciences and Arts in Varaždin." *Papers of the Institute for Scientific Research in Varaždin* 28:117-135].

Vrana, Josip. 1955. "Da li je sačuvan original isprave Kulina bana: paleografijsko-jezična studija o primjercima isprave iz g. 1189." *Radovi Staroslavenskog instituta* 2(2):5-57. ["Is the original document of Kulin Ban preserved: A palaeographic-linguistic study of copies of the document from 1189." *Papers of the Old Church Slavonic Institute* 2(2):5-57].

Vukušić, Luka. 2009. "Uzničko pismo Katarine Zrinske od 26. lipnja 1671." *Arhivski vjesnik* 52(1):197-203. ["Letter from Katarina Zrinska from 26 June 1671." *Archival Newsletter* 52(1):197-203].

Yriarte, Charles. 1999. *Istra & Dalmacija: putopis*. Zagreb: Antibarbarus. [*Istria & Dalmatia: Itinerary*, Zagreb: Antibarbarus].

Žaja et al. 2018. "Život na Golom otoku kroz tetovaže." *Socijalna psihijatrija* 46(1):102-117. ["Life on Goli otok through tattoos." *Social Psychiatry* 46(1):102-117].

Živković, Marija. 2018. *The Seljan Brothers in Wilderness and Desert*. Zagreb: The Ethnographic Museum.

BIOGRAPHICAL SKETCH

Karmen Perković

Affiliation: Primary School Ivan Goran Kovačić, Zagreb, Croatia

Education: Professor of History, Czech language and literature.

Business Address: Primary School, Ivan Goran Kovačić, Mesićeva Street 35, Zagreb, Croatia.

Email: Karmen.p62@gmail.com

Research and Professional Experience: Works in methodical research.

Since year 2000 I have been working at the primary school Ivan Goran Kovačić. With gifted students, on the occasion of 50th anniversary of the School in 2005, I launched historical drama group "Agram." The student play "The famous Illyrians and their contribution to the awakening of the national consciousness" was presented as an innovative example of teaching practice on the 3rd Symposium of Teaching History 25-28 March 2008 in Poreč. The screenplay was published in the Proceedings of the Symposium on the topic "National Movement in Croatia in the 19th century."

From year 2010 I head the Historical Glagolitic Group "Zagrebački glagoljaši." Project "Open doors of the Zagreb Glagolitic Treasury" I presented at the County Expert Councils of the Teachers of History 2015 and 2016. According to the Law on Protection and Preservation of cultural goods, on 7 April 2014. "Zagrebački glagoljaši" and our school were included in the list of institutions of cultural intangible heritage.

The project "Vukovar Time Machine" was presented in 2013 at 6th Symposium the State Expert Gathering of Teachers of History on the Homeland War in Zadar, organized by the Education and Training Agency or Croatia.

Project "Living History – History and Culture of Knighthood" was organized by the Knights of the city of Zagreb and our school, on my initiative and implemented as a pilot project in 2013/2014. Knights, dressed in authentic medieval clothes, conducted students through a medieval past. I presented the project in the Cantonal Council for Teachers of history in 2014.

In March 2015 I created and realized the project "The time capsule: My School in the Future."

I am the author of the history exam in 5th and 6th primary school class. The exams were published in 2008, by the Alfa publishing house, Zagreb.

From 2006 I mentored the students of the Department of History for the subject "Methodical teaching of history," University of Zagreb Faculty of Humanities and Social Sciences.

Professional Appointments: History teacher, Mentor to students of history at the Faculty of Humanities and Social Sciences, University of Zagreb.

Honors: Teacher mentor, 2012; Teacher advisor, 2017.

Publications from the Last 3 Years:

1) Perković, Karmen. 2019. *Recenzija. Udžbenik Klio 5, za eksperimentalni program u povijesti, za 5. razred Osnovne škole*. Zagreb: Školska knjiga. [Perković Karmen. 2019. *Review. Tutorial Klio 5, for experimental Program in History for 5th Grade Primary School class*].
2) Perković, Karmen. 2019. *Recenzija. Udžbenik Klio 6, za eksperimentalni program u povijesti, za 6. razred Osnovne škole*. Zagreb: Školska knjiga. [*Review. Tutorial Klio 6, for experimental Program in History for 6th Grade Primary School class*].
3) Perković, Karmen. 2019. *Recenzija. Zadatci Klio 5, za ocjenjivanje postignuća učenika u povijesti za 5. razred osnovne škole*. Zagreb: Školska knjiga. [*Review. Tasks Klio 5, for evaluation of student achievements in history for 5th Primary School class*].
4) Perković, Karmen. 2019. *Recenzija. Nastavni listići Klio 5, iz povijesti za pomoć u učenju za 5. razred osnovne škole*. Zagreb: Školska knjiga. [*Review. History instructional ballots Klio 5, teaching aid for the 5th primary School class*].
5) Perković, Karmen. 2019. *Radionice. "Rješavanje problema kao pristup poučavanja" projektna i istraživačka metoda u povijesti i geografiji*. Zagreb: Školska knjiga. [Perković Karmen. 2019. *Workshops. "Solving problems as a teaching approach" project and research teaching method in history and geography*].

6) Perković, Karmen. 2020. Projekt *"Povijest u slikama," radionice za učenike 6. razreda Osnovne škole u suradnji s vitezovima Reda Čuvara grada Zagreba*. Zagreb: Školska knjiga. [*Project "History in pictures," workshops for pupils in the 6th grade of primary school in cooperation with the Association of Knights of the city of Zagreb*].

In: Croatia: Past, Present and Future Perspectives
Editor: Matko Marušić

ISBN: 978-1-53618-300-9

Chapter 2

THE CROATIAN LANGUAGE

Sanda Ham*

Department of Croatian Language and Literature,
Faculty of Humanities and Social Sciences,
Josip Juraj Strossmayer University, Osijek, Croatia

ABSTRACT

The history of the Croatian standard (literary) language is presented in the paper. Knowing the history of the Croatian language is needed to comprehend its current state not only as a linguistic phenomenon but also as a crucial component of the Croatian national identity. To Croats, language is its expression and the manifestation of intellectual and political freedom. It is a sensitive subject even nowadays. Croats' sensitivity about Croatian emerges from their permanent resistance to attempted De-Croatization aiming at demonstrating that Croatian is not a distinct (socio)linguistic phenomenon. Battles for the Croatian language – many were fought – were also battles for Croatian freedom.

A concise overview of the standardization of the Croatian language is presented, from the first Croatian grammar (1604) to the first Vukovian grammar (1899). The concept of *vukovština* [Vukovianism] and its devastating impact on Croatian is explained. The ideology of Vukovianism is based on a misapprehension that Shtokavian, the Croatian standard prestige dialect, is exclusively Serbian, so Croatian must be a constituent of the Serbian language.

The Croatian literary language was developing independently until the state union with Serbs in 1918. From that moment till the formation of Banovina of Croatia (1939) and Independent State of Croatia (1941-1945), Croatian was subjected to unitaristic pressures and severe De-Croatization that peaked in *Pravopisna uputstva* (1929). These orthography directives erased the Croatian language characteristics, substituting them with Serbian ones. Ever since, the orthography has been a crucial linguistic and Croatian national issue.

Yugoslavian language policy and planning after World War II (1945–1991) was a continuation of the policy of unitarism and De-Croatization, now within the framework of communist ideology. The *Novi Sad Agreement* (1954) postulated that Croats and Serbs

* Corresponding Author's Email: sanda.ham@gmail.com.

are one nation with one language (circular reasoning: they are one nation because they speak one language/they speak one language because they are one nation). Accordingly, a common orthography manual was published in 1960 followed by efforts to produce a (never finished) common dictionary. Simultaneously, to the world, an image was projected of the Serbian language being the sole public communication means. Croatian was ignored as well as Bosnian and Montenegrin – all three were presented as mere vernaculars, which was the source of contemporary foreign contestations of the Croatian language and related misconceptions.

Croats responded to the pressure with the *Declaration on the Status and Name of the Croatian Literary Language* (1967) and a liberation movement called the Croatian Spring (1971). After the movement had been politically decapitated, the period of involuntary Croatian silence begun. Finally, in 1991, Croats won national sovereignty and the language, after one century, could develop independently again. However, the legacy of the past is still strong, especially widespread prejudices about Croatian—it is still internationally treated as the Serbo-Croatian, Shtokavian, or Western Variant of the Common Literary language.

Unfortunately, politics still casts shadow on the Croatian language. In 2012, the successor of the former Communist Party came to power in Croatia, dismissed the Council for the Croatian Standard Language Codification, and, in 2013, made a political decision on orthography.

Keywords: Croatian as a Slavic language; Croatian language, history; Croatian dialects; Croatian scripts and orthography; De-Croatization; Croatian Spring, language; language, differences between Croatian and Serbian; Yugoslavia, unitaristic language policy

INTRODUCTION

The history of Croatia is inherently the history of the Croatian language since in it and by it every foreign presence has been remembered—the language remembers by its vocabulary, by its system, by the totality of all documents and written works ever created in it.

> "The earliest testimony of mentioning the name *Croat* can be found in Duke Trpimir's Deed of Donation (March 4, 852), where Duke's title was cited as *dux Chroatorum*, 'the ruler of Croats.' That charter has been preserved as the 16th century transcript, but no doubt has been raised regarding its authenticity. A somewhat younger testimony is the Branimir inscription (Branimir ruled 879–892), found in Crkvina (village Šopot), whereby Branimir was named *dux Cruatorum*." (Matasović 2019)

The Croatian language had many names during history—Slovic (*slovinski*), Slavic (*slavjanski*), Dalmatian (*dalmatinski*), Slavonic (*slavonski*), Bosnian (*bosanski*), Illyrian (*ilirski*), Croatian (*hrvatski*)—but it was never, until the end of the 19th century, put in a compound with Serbian. (Grčević 2019) It was written in Latin, Croatian Glagolitic, and Croatian Cyrillic—the scripts adjusted to the Croatian phonology system.

The development of the Croatian language received an extraordinary impetus after the Catholic Church Council of Trent (1545–1563), during the Catholic revival. Many colleges (named Illyrian after the name of a Roman province encompassing today's Croatia) were founded aiming at educating young clergy in the Croatian language in Italy, in Loreto, Rome,

Fermi, S. Giovanni Rotondo, but also in the then Croatia, in Split and Zadar. The Catholic Church encouraged publications in Croatian (Bezina, 1994), thus considerably enhancing the number of books in Croatian (Horvat 2001, Krasić, 2009).

The Catholic revival, or Counter-Reformation, also stimulated a young Jesuit clergyman Bartul Kašić to produce his books, including the first Croatian grammar. Namely, Bartul Kašić received a commission from Pope Clement VIII and general Aquaviva to produce the grammar of the Croatian (Illyrian) language. Along with the grammar, printed in 1604, Bartul Kašić authored the dictionary in 1599 and a translation of the Bible in 1625. Both manuscripts remained unpublished, so we had to wait until 1831 for the first Croatian printed translation of the Bible by Matija Petar Katančić, which was published posthumously (Babić Nada 2018). The translation by Kašić was at last published in 1999 (Kašić 1999). Croatian linguistic literature has its roots far back in the past—Croatian orthographic manuals have been known since 1639: *Nauk za dobro pisati latinskijem slovima riječi jezika slovinskoga* [Guidelines How to Write Well the Slovic Language Words in Latin Letters] by Rajmund Džamanjić, grammars since 1604: *Osnove ilirskoga jezika* [Fundamentals of the Illyrian Language] by Bartul Kašić, and dictionaries since 1595: *Rječnik pet najplemenitijih europskih jezika latinskoga, talijanskoga, njemačkoga hrvatskoga i mađarskoga* [Dictionary of the Five Noblest Languages Latin, Italian, German, Dalmatian, and Hungarian] by Faust Vrančić. These works substantiate a very early inclusion of Croats and their Croatian language in the West-European culture. The language with orthography, grammar, dictionaries, liturgy in the national language, and developed sacral and profane literature—it is a language that testifies to the unique national culture.

The Croatian language is different from any other language. It is unique as Croats are nationally unique and different from any other nation. Yet, that uniqueness must be emphasized again and again even nowadays because there are still people who do not recognize the Croatian language and call it Serbo-Croatian, denying the uniqueness of it. For example, numerous world university centers still offer Serbo-Croatian study programs, which do not, or do not want to, recognize differences between the two languages.

Outside Croatia, the study programs of Croatian language and literature (Croatistics) are offered only in Sydney and Toronto, whereas in Europe, out of all the universities that have study programs of Slavic languages, Croatian included, the Croatian language study is separated from the Serbian one only in Hungary and the United Kingdom. In Bosnia and Herzegovina, the study of Croatistics was established at the University of Mostar in 1994, where Croatian is the language of instruction.

In Germany, 36 universities offer study programs in Serbo-Croatistics and just a few of them have Croatian lectors. Bosnia-Serbo-Croatistics, that is the Bosnian-Serbian-Croatian language, has being studied even at the well-known Viennese Slavistics Department, although, during the last hundred years and more, the most distinguished professors of the Department were Croats: great names of the Croatian philology or linguistics like Vatroslav Jagić, Josip Hamm, and Radoslav Katičić (Kovačec 2006).

The Croatian public was dismayed by the events at the World Slavic Congress in Cracow in Poland in 1998, where Serbian linguists distributed leaflets expressing strong anti-Croatian attitudes – *Slovo o srpskom jeziku* [Word on the Serbian language], printed in Belgrade in 1998. (Babić 1998) It was emphasized in the leaflet that no differences existed between Croatian and Serbian since it was just one language, consequently just one literature – only the Serbian language and Serbian literature existed. The following was the principal thesis: "All Shtokavians are Serbs and all Serbs are Shtokavians." Similarly, at the Slavistics Congress in Belgrade in 2018 Serbian minister Ivica Dačić delivered a speech at the Congress' opening ceremony; what was said was totally inappropriate as regarded his status among the attending scholars, not to mention that it was adverse to scientific truth:

> "The situation in Balkans has additionally been complicated by the continuous process of the Serbian language fragmentation; various political and state-forming reasons were used to justify the creation of new language variations from the common and single language corpus although these variations do not differ from each other; however, at the level of politics, they assume features of being different and national-state-building, and very often their identity is based on the denial of their language original."

Misunderstanding of the past and present of the Croatian language is not immanent to just Serbian politicians and linguists; it is shared by general public all over the world. Robert D. Greenberg (2004) also advocates the opinion that the Croatian language originated from Serbo-Croatian only after the political breakup of Yugoslavia; Snježana Kordić leads the linguists of Croatian origin who also endorse that opinion (2010). Fortunately, world-prominent linguists like Leopold Auburger (1999) or Artur Bagdasarov (2010) approach the study of the Croatian language with knowledge, understanding and arguments, thus unmasking Great-Serbian pretensions.

Genesis of the Croatian Language and Script

Croatian and Serbian languages are undisputedly Slavic languages; they are very close, genetically kindred and the level of intelligibility among them is high. And yet, intelligibility level among all Slavic languages is high, but nobody considers Serbian and Bulgari.

Croatian among the Slavic (Slavonic) Languages

The Croatian language belongs to the group of Slavic languages. They are conventionally classified into three big subgroups. The group of East Slavic languages consists of Russian, Belarusian, and Ukrainian; the Western group embraces Czech, Slovak, Polish, Kashubian, Polabian, Upper Sorbian (Lusatian) and Lower Sorbian (Lusatian); and the Southern group consists of Old Slavic, Bulgarian, Macedonian, Slovenian, Croatian, Serbian, Bosnian and Montenegrin. The Western South Slavic idioms are Slovenian, Kaykavian, Chakavian, Shtokavian, and Torlakian. The Shtokavian idiom can be divided into Western Shtokavian and Eastern Shtokavian. Croats utilized the former for the stylization of the Croatian standard language (Moguš 1993, Matasović 2009), whereas the latter was used to build up the Serbian standard language. (Language stylization refers to the prevailing language components of vernaculars recognized in the literary language.)

For the sake of clarity, the vernaculars (languages or dialects spoken by the ordinary people in a particular country or region) are not in focus here; we are speaking about the standard language—and Croatian and Serbian standard languages are different. Every standard language is a reflection of culture and a result of deliberate, planned efforts to achieve particular language expression; in their formation and development, Croatian and Serbian took different paths. Their language-codifying superstructures are different.

The First Slavic and the First Croatian Literary Language

A literary language is a language used in literary works, but also in writings related to liturgy, law, administration, economy and education. The first Slavic literary language is nowadays called Old Church Slavonic, or Old Slavonic, or Old Slavic, or Church Slavonic. It was created in the period of Pan-Slavic unity. The facts related to the origin of the language and its script, Glagolitic, nowadays appear almost mythical, assuming almost a fairy-tale tone. And yet, the facts have been historically verified:

> "The origin of the first Slavic literary language is usually dated to the mid-9th century and put in relation to the mission of the Holy Brothers Cyril (Constantine) and Methodius. Prince Rastislav of Great Moravia sent emissaries to Constantinople to the Byzantine Emperor Michael in 862 with the request for a missionary who would 'explain the true Christian religion' to his people in their language. The Emperor considered Constantine Cyril to be most suitable and appointed him for that mission. Cyril created a new, Glagolitic script and started to translate books in the Slavic language. That act and later Holy Brothers' mission among Slavs are the cornerstones of the first Slavic literary language." (Mihaljević 2009, 283)

That Proto-Slavic literary language started to disintegrate at the end of the 11th century under the influence of regional dialects (regiolects). It was open to their forms and many were assimilated into it over time. Thus, several recensions were developed, out of which national languages would develop later: Macedonian-Bulgarian, Serbian, Croatian, Czech, Russian, Romanian. The Croatian recension of the Church Slavonic language is the Croatized Church Slavonic language. In that language one can find Croatian components and specificities. The year 1561 is considered to denote the end of the Croatian Church Slavonic language period. In that year, the last book in Church Slavonic language of the Croatian recension was printed – Nikola Brozić, a pastor, notary and rector in Omišalj, island Krk, printed the breviary in Venice (Mihaljević 2009, 286).

Bečki listići [Fragmenta Vindobonensia or Vienna Fragments] are considered the oldest monuments of the Croatian recension of Old Slavic; they are dated to the end of the 11th or beginning of the 12th century.

CROATIAN SCRIPTS

Croats wrote their language using three scripts: Latin, Glagolitic, and Croatian Cyrillic. The Latin script is the oldest script Croats became familiar with and the Latin language was also their first literary language.

Latin

"When Croats arrived to the areas of Pannonia and Dalmatia, i.e., ancient Illyria, or the territory of contemporary Croatia, during the great migration in the Early Middle Ages, they came into contact with Christianity and Christians … as well as with the script; Christianity is a religion of script, Holy Scripture … interest in the script went hand in hand with interest in the Christian faith, which was first adopted by the representatives of authority—*knezovi*, and only later by common people. The first monuments of Latin literacy were dukes' deeds, documents and inscriptions on churches…" (Bratulić 2009, 20) (*Knez*, plural *knezovi*, is a historical Slavic title, both royal and noble. *Knez* was a chieftain of a Slavic tribe prior to the feudal statehood. *Knez* may be translated as: prince, duke, count; author's note.)

The Latin alphabet is a contemporary Croatian script (Moguš and Vončina 1969). During history, Croatian literacy was characterized by two types of Latin script. One type prevailed in the territory along the Adriatic coast, whereas the other type prevailed in the inland and is known as the continental Latin script, developed according to the German and Hungarian models. (Moguš and Vončina 1969). It was reformed twice during the 19th century in order to make it generally acceptable across Croatia. Both times the reformer was Ljudevit Gaj, after whom it was named "Gajica." (Vončina 1986) The first Latin alphabet reform was done in 1830 (Gaj 1830), and the second in 1835 (Gaj 1835). The Croatian Latin alphabet is also called *abeceda* according to the first letters [Croats pronounce letters a, b, c and d like: ɑ-be-tse-de]. The oldest Croatian work in Latin script is from the year 1345: *Red i zakon sestara dominikanki* [The Order and Law of the Dominican Sisters].

Glagolitic

The genesis of the first Slavic and Croatian script assumed the shape of a legend in Croatian history. We can imagine a saint, inspired by the Divinity, who walks across the land and spreads his Christian teachings: he "glagolja" [speaks]. According to the name of the script and their mission, the clergymen who disseminated Glagolitic script and copied scriptures into Glagolitic were named "glagoljaši" [Glagolitic scribes].

"Glagolitic is the first Slavic script made up by Constantine Cyril in the year 836, before his journey to Moravia's Slavs. The biography of Saint Cyril, *Žitje Konstantina Ćirila* (Chapter 14) reports: "Upon his departure, Philosopher(e), respecting his original custom, commit himself to praying with his disciples. Soon, the God, who listens to the prayers of His servants, spoke to him, and he promptly created letters and started to write down Gospel words: 'In the beginning was the Word, and the Word was with God, and the Word was God.' "Constantine Cyril is the first man in the world of Christianity who created the whole alphabet system according to his understanding of religion, culture, and visual art. And, actually, he composed his script, Glagolitic, as a closed, compact system" (Bratulić, 2009, 36–37).

Glagolitic is a unique alphabet. The first version comprised 38 symbols that represented 40 letters. Glagolitic may be round and angular. Croatian was the angular one. Croats used the Glagolitic script for almost a millennium—from the 9th until the 19th century— and most extensively from the 13th until the 15th century. Its idiosyncrasy stemmed from the fact that each letter had its name and numerical value.

The oldest Croatian Glagolitic monument is *Baščanska ploča* [Baška Tablet] dated to the beginning of the 11th century. The inscription was chiseled in a stone partition between the altar and the rest of the Church of St. Lucy in Jurandvor near Baška on the island Krk. It was discovered on September 15, 1851. Among its Glagolitic letters there are several Cyrillic and Latin letters.

Croatian Cyrillic (Bosančica)

The third Croatian script is Croatian Cyrillic, commonly known as Bosančica or Western Cyrillic. It is basically a Greek alphabet to which certain Glagolitic letters were added. In Croatia, both the Glagolitic and Croatian Cyrillic scripts were simultaneously used. The oldest verification of Bosančica is dated to the 11th century. *Povaljski prag* [Povlja Threshold], the oldest Croatian Cyrillic monument, is dated to the year 1184; it is an inscription on the stone lintel (transom) above the door of the Benedictine abbey in Povlja on the island Brač. This old Croatian Cyrillic, nowadays extinct, is different from the contemporary Serbian Cyrillic alphabet, which originated from the script reform conducted by the Serbian philologist Vuk Stefanović Karadžić in the 19th century.

CROATIAN TRIDIALECTISM—CHAKAVIAN, KAYKAVIAN, SHTOKAVIAN

The Croatian language is based on three dialects: Chakavian, Kaykavian, and Shtokavian. A dialect is, in general terms, a particular group of local, regional vernaculars that has common linguistic characteristics. The standard language, which is the official, public, state language, is superior to a dialect.

Croatian Dialects and Standard Croatian

Croatia has only one standard language and three main dialects. They are named by the interrogative-relative pronoun "what": *ča* [tʃʌ] or cha in English, *kaj* [kʌi] or kay, and *što* [ʃtɔ] or shto. Each of the dialects has its specific features that distinguishes it from the others and from the standard language as well. However, all three dialects contributed to the stylization of the Croatian language throughout Croatian history. The term stylization refers to the predominant, prestigious language components in the literary (standard) language. The Croatian standard language is a stylized language in which Shtokavian language components prevail. We must emphasize here that these are not components of any concrete, actual Shtokavian vernacular; we are speaking here about the Shtokavian stylization that embraces the most pronounced features of the entirety of Shtokavian vernaculars. In that sense, it is superordinate to dialects. (Katičić 2013, Štambuk 2016) Croatian Shtokavian stylization has been predominant throughout Croatian history, therefore, nowadays, the Croatian standard language has been codified as Shtokavian. Croats use their standard language in official and public communication, whereas they sometimes use their respective dialect in everyday, less formal situations. Moreover, a rich dialectal literature exists, especially poetry; the Kaykavian dialect has even got the status of a literary language in the ISO categorization since 2015 (ISO 639–3).

Chakavian Literary-Language Stylization

The expression “a tridialectal standard language” refers to the fact that all the three Croatian dialects contributed evenly to the development of the Croatian literary language; the tridialectism is the heart of the oneness of the Croatian literary language making it uniquely Croatian and distinguishing it from the genetically kindred Serbian. The Serbian language does not have such a tridialectal feature.

Croatian Chakavian, Kaykavian, and Shtokavian words are closely interwoven thus enriching each other. In certain time periods, one will become more powerful due to its prevalence in literary language, but the other two will always follow it in use. Since the very beginnings of Croatian literacy

> “The Croatian Glagolitic scribes... cherished the first Slavic literary language... they participated in the continuous process that aimed to build up an acceptable common literary idiom composed of elements belonging to several language systems.” (Damjanović 1995)

It means that components first of Chakavian and then of Kaykavian and Shtokavian dialects were gradually incorporated in the Glagolitic language foundations. In order to facilitate getting a clear insight into the Croatian medieval literacy, its triscript nature and tridialect Croatian stylization, Table 1 has been created according to Damjanović, Kuzmić, Mihaljević, and Žagar (2009, 457–540). It displays names of the Croatian written monuments, scripts with which they were written, and their general literary-language stylization.

Literary Chakavian blossomed in the 16th century in the works of famous Croatian writers like Petar Hektorović, Hanibal Lucić, Petar Zoranić and others. The Venetian sources from the year 1553 described the Chakavian language used in Split, in which Marko Marulić wrote, in the following manner:

> “All citizens of Split live by Slavic customs and orders, and their mother tongue is so sweet and charming that it holds primacy in Dalmatia as the Tuscan dialect does in Italy…” (Vince 1990, 28).

Venetians considered literary Chakavian equal in beauty and utility to the language of their best literary works.

The already mentioned Vrančić’s dictionary (1595) appeared some forty years later. The Chakavian recorded in it is the Croatian literary language of high quality. It should be emphasized again that the very same Chakavian was just a foundation, like it would be the case with Kaykavian and Shtokavian later, in which the components of the other two dialects were built in as well (Vigato 2013). Such a standard-language building procedure is understandable in Croatian history. Written texts, especially liturgy ones, must be intelligible and for that practical reason authors reached for dialectal variety, thus deliberately creating a literary-language hybrid. Furthermore, Croatian political reality throughout history has underpinned the people's mindset that standard language is a constituent part of the Croatian national being—language connects the scattered parts of homeland; and it has been a shield against national alienation, estrangement. Therefore, the literary language was expected to be comprehensible to all Croats and they all should use it regardless of variegated dialects and local vernaculars. Therefore, it must take at least something from every dialect to be accepted as appertaining to all Croats, thus being the constituent of national identity. That connection between the language and national identity has always been and is very strong in Croats' minds.

Table 1. The script and literary-language stylization of the Croatian written monuments and documents up to the year 1500

Monuments and documents	Dated	Script	Literary-language stylization
Bašćanska ploča	around 1100	Glagolitic	Church Slavonic, Chakavian
Povaljski prag	1184	Cyrillic	Church Slavonic, Chakavian
Povelja Kulina bana	1189	Cyrillic	Shtokavian
Bečki listići	11th/12thcent.	Glagolitic	Church Slavonic, Chakavian
Grškovićev odlomak apostola	12th cent.	Glagolitic	Church Slavonic, Shtokavian
Mihanovićev odlomak apostola	12th cent.	Glagolitic	Church Slavonic, Shtokavian
Kukuljevićev odlomak misala	13th cent.	Glagolitic	Church Slavonic, Chakavian
Povaljska listina	1250	Cyrillic	Church Slavonic, Chakavian
Vinodolski zakon (16th cent. transcript)	1288	Glagolitic	Chakavian
Istarski razvod	13th cent.	Glagolitic	Chakavian
Prvi vrbnički brevijar	13th/14th cent.	Glagolitic	Church Slavonic, Chakavian
Red i zakon (sestara dominikanki)	13th/14th cent.	Latin	Chakavian
Krčki statut (16th cent. transcript)	14th cent.	Glagolitic	Church Slavonic, Chakavian
Misal kneza Novaka	1368	Glagolitic	Church Slavonic, Chakavian
Brevijar Vida Omišljanina	1396	Glagolitic	Church Slavonic, Chakavian
Pariška pjesmarica	14th cent.	Glagolitic	Chakavian
Regula sv. Benedikta	14th cent.	Glagolitic	Chakavian
Šibenska molitva	14th cent.	Latin	Chakavian
Cantilena pro sabatho	14th cent.	Latin	Chakavian
Ivančićev zbornik	14th/15th cent.	Glagolitic	Church Slavonic, Chakavian
Hrvojev misal	around 1404	Glagolitic	Church Slavonic, Chakavian
Hvalov zbornik	1404	Cyrillic	Church Slavonic, Chakavian
Prvi vrbnički misal	1456	Glagolitic	Church Slavonic
Drugi vrbnički misal	1462	Glagolitic	Church Slavonic
Petrisov zbornik	1468	Glagolitic	Chakavian, Kaykavian, Church Slavonic
Misal po zakonu rimskoga dvora	1483	Glagolitic	Church Slavonic, Chakavian
Kolunićev zbornik	1486	Glagolitic	Chakavian, Kaykavian, Church Slavonic
Brevijar po zakonu rimskoga dvora	1491	Glagolitic	Church Slavonic, Chakavian
Baromićev brevijar	1493	Glagolitic	Church Slavonic, Chakavian
Senjski misal	1494	Glagolitic	Church Slavonic
Drugi novljanski brevijar	1494	Glagolitic	Church Slavonic, Chakavian
Spovid općena	1496	Glagolitic	Chakavian
Žića svetih otaca	14th/15th cent.	Latin	Chakavian
Poljički statut	15th cent.	Cyrillic	Chakavian, Shtokavian
Prvi hrvatski vatikanski molitvenik	around 1400	Latin	Shtokavian
Akademijin dubrovački molitvenik	around 1450	Latin	Shtokavian
Lekcionar Bernardina Splićanina	1495	Latin	Chakavian

Kaykavian Literary-Language Stylization

The Chakavian literary language disappeared almost entirely by the mid-18th century literature being substituted by the Kaykavian and Shtokavian regiolects in the process of literary language stylization. The golden age of Kaykavian was the 18th century, but traces of the Kaykavian written language are much older—they can be tracked back to the end of the 16th century, to the very period of flourishing Chakavian. Naturally, in that old Kaykavian one can find the same components as in literary Chakavian. In the 17th century, vivid Kaykavian, based predominantly on the Zagreb actual speech, lives in the works by Juraj Habdelić, but the components from the other two dialects can also be recognized—a continuous Croatian-specific language development tendency. In the 17th century, the established name for Kaykavian language was *slovenski* [Slovenian] and for Chakavian *horvatski* [Croatian] language.

Later, Kaykavian was called *horvatski jezik* [Croatian language], but all the time it was standing on the shoulders of the other two dialects. The Ozalj Literary Circle is characteristic in that sense. It was named after the Croatian noble estate Ozalj that was the center of a kind of literary academy and where its most prominent members, Croatian noblemen Petar Zrinski and Fran Krsto Frankopan as well as a noblewoman Katarina Zrinska resided. They created a unique Croatian tridialect literary koine. The term koine stands here for a language that emerged from the generalization of features characterizing three dialects. Such a koine played a role of literary language. The language of the Ozalj circle mirrored the then common people's environment – the multiethnic mixture of the Croatian population in the region is reflected in the multivernacular characteristics of their language—from the Ikavian Chakavian speakers and Shtokavian Bunjevac people to Kaykavian Ekavian and Shtokavian Yekavian speakers. (Ikavian, Ekavian and Yekavian speeches refer to the three ways in which old Church Slavonic semivowel "yat" was reflected in pronunciation and writing: *pisma*, *pesma*, *pjesma* [song]; author's note). All mentioned make the Ozalj circle's language a supradialect, the then actual literary language (Vončina 1968). Even the 18th century Kaykavian writers, being deeply devoted and loyal to the Kaykavian dialect, wrote certain works in Shtokavian, thus preparing a path, a fertile ground for its final appearance on the stage of language standardization. Tituš Brezovački, for example, the most prolific Kaykavian author of the 18th century, wrote his books in the Slavonian Shtokavian dialect, for "Slavince" – Slavonians! It should be mentioned also that the Kaykavian grammar handbooks were used for a century and more across Croatia; the last one being written in the first half of the 19th century (Jembrih 1977, Ham 2013, Štebih 2013).

Croatian Shtokavian Literary-Language Stylization

If we consider the detrimental influence of the Greater-Serbia politics and Serbian language, especially those from the end of the 19th and during the 20th century, answering the questions about the Shtokavian stylization of the Croatian language becomes of utmost importance (Vulić 2013). For a century and half, a politicized untruth has been imposed on Croats saying that we do not have our own language; in that interpretation Croatian is just a variant of the Serbian language. A falsehood has been spread that in the 19th century the

Croatian language was created by Vuk Stefanović Karadžić, Serbian public worker, philologist, and reformer of the Serbian language and script.

Generally speaking, language becomes the literary one when it has been accepted by the entire language community for their public communication – when it has assumed the features of omni applicability and omni acceptance, thus becoming elevated above all local speeches and narrow borders from where it has emerged (Brozović 1991). Specifically speaking, Shtokavian became the literary language when it had been adopted across the entire national realm.

It is of outmost importance to emphasize that Croatian Shtokavian reached the literary-language level in the mid-18th century (Moguš 1991, 17–16). Katičić even claimed that the rudiments of the Croatian language standardization were associated with the 16th century Counter-Reformation activities (Katičić 1999). The 18th century Croatian Shtokavian was so developed and polished that it could serve in each and every domain of life – in poetry, liturgy, and science alike. Shtokavian reached its full polyfunctionality.

As explained below, Croatian Shtokavian became a literary language in the moment when it became the translation language of the Bible, since "the translation of the Holy Scripture into the language of any ethnic or national group is a typical example of inclusion into the international civilization" (Babić 1990, 76). And that moment was the appearance of *Ritual rimski* [Roman Rite] in 1613, the translation by Bartol Kašić. *Ritual rimski* was in use for 289 years in all Croatian lands; its resemblance to the contemporary Croatian language is such that even after three centuries, *Ritual rimski* is still recognizable and familiar to us (Babić 1994, 97).

Also, at the end of the 15th century, Shtokavian poets of Dubrovnik created their verses using the Shtokavian dialect that we, contemporary Croats, recognize and understand as the Croatian language. They were poets of *Ranjinin zbornik* [Nikša Ranjina's Miscellany], dated back to the 14th–15th century.

> "The Štokavian Croatian literary language of the 17th century is primarily based on the extensive Dubrovnik Baroque literature and works by Croatian writers of the Catholic Reformation, which had started in the late 1500s and early 1600s, and gradually developed in the 17th century." (Vulić 2013, 637)

Industrious Shtokavian literary artists, Andrija Kačić Miošić, Antun Kanižlić, Matija Antun Reljković, played a prominent role in the history of the standard language. They wrote grammars as successfully as they did liturgy and literary texts. Their literary works – *Razgovor ugodni naroda slovinskoga* [Pleasant Conversation of Slavic People] (1756) by Kačić, Reljković's *Satir iliti divlji čovik* [Satir or Savage Man] (1762), or *Sveta Rožalija* [Saint Rose] (1780) by Kanižlić – were very popular at the time, even among common people who read them, or listen them being read, for decades. They followed the already established Shtokavian tradition, primarily the one created by Dubrovnik poets. However, they conscientiously reached out for numerous Chakavian elements as well, since, in their opinion, the literary language should play the role of a uniting not a separating factor; if a broad reading audience was desired, then the language must be acceptable to all.

> "The most significant writers in this development include Andrija Kačić Miošić, from the Makarska region, and Matija Antun Relković, from the Slavonia region around the river Sava. This clearly indicates that Croatian lands were unified by a single literary language. Since the 1750s, the dialectally stylized literary language spread to the northern Adriatic region. Chakavian stylizations of the literary language have since disappeared from regular use in writing, remaining only in diaspora, in what is today the Austrian state of Burgenland and the surrounding regions." (Katičić 2013a, 635)

Regardless of which point in time is to be considered as the starting point of the Stokavian stylization of the Croatian literary language, the following is more than obvious: origins of the Croatian literary Shtokavian reach so far back in the past that its antiquity alone affirms Croatian as a distinct national language (Pederin 1970).

Croatian Shtokavian Stylization in the Final Stages of Standardization at the Beginning of the 19th Century

Shtokavian was selected by the Illyrians (see the next section) in the final stages of the standardization of Croatian because it was spread and accepted across most of the Croatian territory. The Croatian language has the Western Shtokavian stylization. At the same time, the Eastern Neo-Shtokavian lect, the one advocated by Karadžić, was just a local lect; it still did not get features of the developed literary language – it was not widely accepted nor was it multifunctional. What it was like, can be revealed through the well-known (and so eagerly imposed on Croats) Karadžić's Serbian dictionary (Srpski Rječnik) from 1818. In that dictionary, for example, *struja* [current] is a female personal name, or *nagon* [impulse] means driving a herd of cattle across a river. There were plenty of reasons for the dictionary to be called, according to the words of Karadžić's contemporaries in Serbia, the dictionary of swineherds and cowherds. The totality of its vocabulary fund indicates it was useful exclusively to village people, i.e., a rural folklore community. No scientist or artist could have used it for their purposes; it was not functional in those domains. In the dictionary, one cannot find words to express scientific abstractions, or subtle artist's emotions. On the other hand, there are numerous words that could be used in detailed descriptions of agricultural tools. It means that the Serbian Dictionary was created on the basis of a particular rural culture lect. Brozović named it Neo-Shtokavian Folklore koine (Brozović 1970).

In the period when Croatian culture had been an acknowledged constituent of European culture for several centuries, all that was known about Serbian culture were Karadžić and folk lyrics and epics; at the time the polished Croatian literary Shtokavian flourished, the Serbian one just started to emerge. In Croatia, the Yekavian Shtokavian stylization had already been generally accepted, so August Šenoa could elevate that language to the highest artistic level in the second part of the 19th century in his novels. In Serbia, until the mid-19th century, a vivid controversy was caused by the topic should Serbs use Serbian at all or should they further nurture Slavic-Serbian (*slavjanoserpski*), the mixture of Russian, Old Church Slavonic and Serbian languages (Stojanović 1924, 579–591).

Croatian Language Status in the Austrian and Austrian-Hungarian Monarchy

The 19th century Europe was overflowed with national movements, political as well as cultural and linguistic ones. Croatia, then being under the wing of Austria, did not lag behind the European movements. Croatia was politically a constituent of the Austrian Monarchy and later of the Austrian-Hungarian Monarchy, therefore a part the Western European culture. In line with national and cultural awakening among many peoples in many Western European countries, Croatian national revival blossomed in Croatia in the first half of the 19th century. Within the framework of the Croatian national revival, the Illyrian movement was born. It was a political movement based on both the political and language-development program.

The Illyrian movement brought many good things to Croats and left a valuable legacy. First, it was a *reveille* of Croatian national awareness and then a powerful driving force for the standardization of the Croatian language. The movement and its legacy played a crucial role in the acknowledgement of the Croatian language as an official language within, first, the Austrian and then Austrian-Hungarian Monarchy.

Croatian as the Language of Politics, Administration, Journalism, and Teaching

Croatia of the 19th century was not an independent state and the Croatian language was not the official language of Croatian Parliament, *Hrvatski Sabor* (Sabor), administration, or education system until the second half of the century. That struggle was yet to be won.

Croatia was on the verge of national language alienation. This was especially pronounced in Dalmatia and Slavonia. Nothern Croatia was Kaykavian.

> "Prior to our national awakening, educated Chakavians and educated Shtokavians in Croatia, apart from the narrow Dubrovnik area, used their mother tongue only in their communication with servants or common people. Among educated persons, they spoke foreign languages. Among Croatian Kaykavians, however, the domestic Kaykavian language was spoken and written even in the most respectable salons, so German newcomers had to learn Croatian…" (Gjalski 1926, 8)

In the Sabor Latin was spoken; German was the language of state administration. Nevertheless, the Sabor passed the famous Article LVIII in 1861, by which the Croatian language was declared the official language in diplomacy. In Istria and Dalmatia, Italian played the role of the official language. In the aftermath of the Austro-Hungarian Compromise of 1867, Hungarians worked aggressively to introduce the Hungarian language. The Croatian language was declared official just at the very end of the 19th century (see Table 2 and Table 3), whereas in Istria, Italian was the official language until the moment of its union with Yugoslavia in 1945. (Samardžija 2004, 128–134) The first secondary (grammar) school with instruction in Croatian was opened in a small Istrian city of Pazin only in 1899.

Table 2. Chronology of the most important developments in the process of accepting the Croatian language as a political and administrative language in the 19th century Austrian Monarchy and Austrian-Hungarian Monarchy

Year, date	Persons, events and works relevant to the recognition of the Croatian language as the political and administrative language in the 19th century
1832	Rukavina Vidovgradski spoke out in the national language in the Sabor (Parliament). It was not the speech of a representative, but a speech of appreciation. "Juraj Rukavina, being appointed the Vice-Lieutenant Field Marshal of the Kingdom of Croatia, expressed his gratitude to the Croatian Sabor, contrary to custom, in Croatian." (Moguš 1996, 283) (Lieutenant Field Marshal was the supreme commander of the army of the Kingdom of Croatia, Austrian troops included, in the 19th cent. The position was inherent to the political title of Ban; author's note.)
1833	Herman Bužan announced in the Hungarian-Croatian Diet in Bratislava (Croatian: Požun) that Croats were going to substitute the Latin language with Croatian.
1839, 1842	Antun Mažuranić, Croatian philologist and grammarian, published the first Croatian differential grammar: Temelji ilirskoga i latinskoga jezika za početnike [Fundamentals of the Illyrian and Latin Language for Beginners]. The grammar paved the way for Croatian. In it, he demonstrated that the Croatian language has the same, if not greater, expression potential as the Latin language. (Moguš 1978, Ham 2006)
May 2, 1843	Ivan Kukuljević Sakcinski, Croatian nobleman, politician, and writer, gave the first representative speech in the Croatian Sabor in the Croatian language. He undertook to "speak ardently about the homeland and his nation! It must be heard." (Deželić 1861) This important, crucial speech could not be published in Croatia then. It was printed in Branislav, illegal Illyrian journal (Branislav 1844), and was distributed across Croatia in the form of transcripts. As soon as political circumstances became favorable, the speech was printed in Zagreb in 1861 as a part of the book Ivan Kukuljević Sakcinski by Deželić. It should be highlighted that it was written in the language of the Zagreb philology school. (Ham 2011a)
October 23, 1847	After Kukuljević's Croatian speech in Sabor, a proposition was submitted to declare Croatian the official language of diplomacy. (Samardžija 2004)
October 18, 1848	The act on Croatian becoming the language of diplomacy and the official language in the Sabor was passed. (Samardžija 2004)
1850	Vienna Literary Agreement—The Austrian attempt to compose common legislative terminology for Serbs and Croats in the Monarchy was encouraged by Alexander von Bach, an Austrian minister. The objective was also the creation of common political and administrative language. The Agreement failed to reach its goals in its time but was a germ of future unitaristic efforts. (See chapter: Political attempts to unite the Croatian and Serbian language, Vienna Literary Agreement)
June 19, 1860	Croatian became the official language of the inferior administrative bodies in Croatia, i.e., of municipalities, districts and counties. At the higher administrative levels German remained the official language of authorities. (Samardžija 2004)
1861	The famous Article LVIII was passed in Hrvatski Sabor, the parliamentary decision requesting the introduction of Croatian as the official language. (Kušan and Šuhaj 1862, 69–71) Yugoslav Academy of Sciences and Arts was founded. (Kušan and Šuhaj 1862, Moguš et al. 2011). (Nowadays, it is the Croatian Academy of Sciences and Arts; acronym: HAZU; author's note.)
November 8, 1868	The Croatian-Hungarian Settlement defined Croatian as the official language "within the borders of the Kingdoms of Croatia, Slavonia and Dalmatia." (Samardžija 2004)
July 20, 1883	The Croatian language was declared official in the Sabor of Dalmatia.

Table 3. Chronology of developments in the process of acknowledging Croatian as the language of teaching/instruction in the 19th century Austrian Monarchy*

Year, date	Persons, events and works relevant to the recognition of the Croatian language as the official language of instruction in the 19th century
November 6, 1832	Matija Smodek started to teach in Croatian during "free classes" at the Zagreb Pravoslovna akademija [Law Academy]. Instruction was mandatory delivered in Latin. Smodek taught in the Kaykavian stylization of Croatian. Namely, Shtokavian stylization had not yet been adopted by the members of the Illyrian movement. Kaykavian and Shtokavian are still rivals.
1835	Antun Mažuranić took over teaching at the Zagreb Law Academy. At that moment, the Shtokavian stylization had already been chosen for the literary language. Mažuranić delivered lectures, especially on Dubrovnik literature, in the Shtokavian stylization of the Croatian language. Dubrovnik literature, being Shtokavian, was deeply appreciated by Illyrians.
August 10, 1840	Hrvatski Sabor, under Ban Juraj Haulik, reached the decision that the Croatian language should be introduced in grammar schools, "chairs of a pure people's language." The decision was not implemented until 1845.
1845	In January, Stolica za hrvatsko-slavonski jezik i književnost [Chair in Croatian-Slavonic Language and Literature] was established at the Zagreb Royal Academy. A call was open for the professorship candidature at the Chair in Croatian-Slavonic Language and Literature.
June 16, 1846	Vjekoslav Babukić, a prominent Croatian philologist, public worker and grammatist, was chosen for the position of professor of the Croatian-Slavonic language at the Royal Academy in Zagreb. He was already famous at the time since his grammar (1836) was very popular throughout Croatia.
October 5, 1846, at 4 p.m.	Vjekoslav Babukić delivered the first lecture in the official Croatian language. Two days later, Narodne novine described that important event as "a supremely important moment when the national language, firstly spoken from the chair, resounded, thundered publicly through our Royal Academy." (Samardžija 2004, 92)

*According to data published in Samardžija 2004.

Croatian journalism played an important role in spreading the Croatian language. The first newspaper in Croatian was published in Zadar in 1806, Kraljski Dalmatin (*Il Regio Dalmata=Kraglski Dalmatin*). Several newspapers were published in Croatia before Kraljski Dalmatin, but not in Croatian. During the 18th century, three newspapers were read in Croatia – first, in 1771, a newspaper in Latin appeared: *Ephemerides Zagrebiensis*, followed by two newspapers in German: *Agramer deutsche Zeitung* in 1784 and *Kroatischer Korrespondent* in 1789.

The first issue of the bilingual Kraljski Dalmatin was printed in 500 copies on July 12, 1806. Eight two-column pages were published every week. The left column was in Italian under the title *Il Regio Dalmata*, and the right one, in Croatian, was titled *Kraglski Dalmatin*. After 176 issues, the newspaper was discontinued in 1810.

Ignjac Kristijanović initiated publishing the *Danica zagrebačka* in Zagreb in 1834. The newspaper was written in Kaykavian stylization.

In 1835, Ljudevit Gaj started publishing *Novine horvatske* [Croatian newspaper] on January 6, 1835. The literary magazin *Danica horvatska, slavonska i dalmatinska*, attached to *Novine horvatske*, debuted on January 10. (Danica is the Croatian name for Venus – Jutrenjica or Morning Star is the other name – from the 14th century. Ancient observers of the sky connected its appearance with dawn. It is a symbol of revival, the beginning of a new day; author's note.)

Although *Novine horvatske* aka *Narodne novine* is the longest-lived Croatian newspaper because it is still published, *Danica* is a true champion as the first literary magazine in the Croatian language. It was published during three periods: 1835–1849, 1853, and 1863–1868 under different names. *Novine* and *Danica* were frequently forced to change their names under political pressure. In 1843, when the name Illyrian had been banned, it became *Narodne novine* with *Danica Horvatska, Slavonska i Dalmatinska*; the name was changed again in 1845 into *Novine Horvatsko-Slavonsko-Dalmatinske*, whereas *Danica* changed its name into *Danica ilirska* in 1848. In 1849 readers read again *Narodne novine*, but without *Danica*; in 1852 it became *Carsko-kraljevske Narodne Novine*. Since 1861 it has had the title *Narodne novine*. The two following editions of *Danica* (1853, 1863–1867) had the title *Danica ilirska* (Ham 2006a).

Narodne novine and *Danica* were crucial in spreading the Croatian language.

> "The appearance of *Novine Horvatzke* in 1835 and, even more, the appearance of its cultural appendix *Danica*, which was a literary laboratory to Illyrians and a blacksmith workshop where the Croatain Shtokavian discourse was made, ... enabled, due to the number of subscribers, for the first time in history of Croatian literature an adequate readers' reception of domestic literary texts..." (Prosperov Novak 2003, 177)

After Gaj's *Danica*, many Croatian literary magazines followed: *Kolo*, Zagreb, in 1842; *Zora dalmatinska*, Zadar, in 1844; *Branislav*, Belgrade, in 1844 (an illegal Illyrian newspapers), *Glasnik dalmatinski*, Zadar, in 1849; *Arkiv za povjestnicu jugoslavensku*, Zagreb, in 1851; *Neven*, Zagreb-Rijeka, in 1852; *Jadranske vile*, Rijeka, in 1859; *Pozor* (*Novi Pozor*, *Zatočnik*, *Obzor*), Zagreb, in 1860; *Glasonoša*, in 1861; *Naše gore list*, Zagreb, in 1861; *Narodni list*, Zadar, in 1862; *Književnik*, Zagreb, in 1864; and *Vienac*, Zagreb, in 1869.

Zagreb Philology School

Diverse philological schools, aiming to codify the Croatian language, started to develop in Croatia after 1830; the most famous among them was the Zagreb philology school. It stemmed directly form the Illyrian movement and was, in the linguistic sense, its continuation. Its rich legacy consists of orthography manuals, several dozens grammars, and Croatian dictionaries. (Vince 1990, Ham 1998). The most prominent and meritorius Croatian philologists, members of the Zagreb philology school, were: Ljudevit Gaj (1830, 1835), Vjekoslav Babukić (1836, 1854), Adolfo Veber (1859, 1871, 1887), Antun Mažuranić (1839, 1859), and Bogoslav Šulek (1860, 1874). Besides the Zagreb philology school, the Zadar philology school (Vince 1990, 1998) and the Rijeka philology school (Stolac 2006) were active. The activity of the latter two faded away little by little in the second half of the 19th century with no relevant influence on the standardization of Croatian.

Adolfo Veber Tkalčević expressed the philological principles of the Zagreb philological school in 1887:

> "Zagreb philological school's mission was to attract, bring Kaykavians and Chakavians to the Shtokavian circle, thus extending the field of literature. Illyrians, among whom there were Shtokavians as well, knew that it would not have been wise to immediately adopt exclusive Shtokavian because many fine words and phrases, not present in the Shtokavian lect, would have been sacrificed and discarded as well as many word forms, which appeared to be more correct than the Shtokavian word forms recently developed; Shtokavian exclusivity would have jeopardized, if not completely blocked, the endaveor of unification. Therefore, after a thorough study of all the three dialects, they adopted those Shtokavian word forms that were most specific to it and kept those Kaykavian and Chakavian word forms that had not yet been forgotten among Shtokavians and appeared to be more correct, in that way brothers could well understand each other, which was the principal aim of language unity. In that manner Illyrians succeeded to include Kaykavians and Chakavians in the Shtokavian community in a very short time period, to the astonishment of the world." (Veber 1887, 458).

The Zagreb philology school continued with the language codification outlined back in the time of Kašić (16th/17th cent.) – the foundation to the literary language was Shtokavian, which was being clarified and polished through time, thus assuming ever newer forms. The older morphonological and morphological features were chosen due to being common to all three Croatian dialects – these features were not yet extinct in (Old)Shtokavian, and for Kaykavians and Chakavians they were genuinely vivid, as opposed to the extreme Shtokavian that did not recognize those features. That extreme Shtokavian was the one chosen by Vukovians for their type of literary-language stylization, which was in opposition to the Zagreb philology school principles. It was Shtokavian of new forms – Neo-Shtokavian that had no support in the Croatian tridialectism. In Veber's words:

> "From everything already mentioned, it is obvious that the Zagreb school, which, through many years of its work, attained respect that should not be undermined, works wisely and correctly when utilizing certain older word forms, quite in accordance with its mission. When the objective will be reached, only then a question can be put forward:

should the Zagreb school be assimilated completely into the Daničić (i.e., Vukovian, author's note) school. If people will decide so, I do not care..." (Veber 1887, 462).

The linguistic skills of Croatian grammatists appeared to be excellent—not only that they were competent to build up a superstructure of their linguistic concept on the already existent foundations but they did not break the development of literary language; on the contrary, they listened carefully to that developmental flow and adjusted all language changes and their own lingusitic concepts to comply with it in harmony.

Vukovians

Croats who adopted Vuk's unitaristic approach to the Croatian language are called Croatian Vukovians. They were followers of Serbian philologist and quasi-politician Vuk Stefanović Karadžić and Serbian grammatist Đuro Daničić. Vukovianism got its name after Vuk Karadžić; Serbians call him Vuk in accordance with their cultural habits.

Croatian Vukovians aimed at creating the common, single language of Croats and Serbs, therefore, their works were linguistic promoters of the unity of all South Slavs (*jugoslavenska ideja* or Yugoslavism). Yugoslavism appeared in the 19th century also among certain Croatian intellectuals, philologists and writers included.

It is said that history is written by winners, and political winners in the last decade of the 19th century were Croatian Vukovians—in the history written by Vukovians, the Zagreb school's language was lifeless, obsolete, enclosed within grammars (*slovnica*) and far away from actual utilization. However, reality was not quite like that; evidence can be found in the comparison of grammars and literary works of the time. Literary texts of the 19th century reveal that Croatian writers were writing in a manner prescribed by the Croatian grammars and vice versa: Croatian grammars codified language in line with the Croatian authors' texts. Permeation was complete (Ham 1998).

Zagreb Philology School and Vukovian Language Principles

The fundamental difference between the Zagreb school and Vukovians' normative principles was in the following: Zagreb grammatists codified with the awareness that the literary language was above local lects and dialects, and that it should not be sought there. Their principle was: Write as good writers do. Namely, their starting point in codification was in the Croatian written literary art and literary-language tradition. Croatian Vukovians codified literary language by leaning on an actual, concrete vivid idiom; their principle was: Speak as good Shtokavians speak. Namely, in language codification their starting point was the spoken Shtokavian idiom. There was also another relevant principal difference: good Croatian Shtokavian writers were careful not to burden their art with Kaykavianisms and Chakavianisms but to adorn their literary works with easy-wearing ornaments. The good Shtokavian in the Vukovian principle does not know any Kaykavian or Chakavian; the Vukovian norm is pure Shtokavian and directed against any Kaykavianisms or Chakavianisms.

Croatian grammars produced by the advocates of the Zagreb philology school were agents and conveyors of Croatdom (Croatian national identity). Such perception of grammars was shared at the time by both their supporters and antagonists. Here is what J. Miškatović, an adversary to the Zagreb philology school, wrote in 1864 in his letter to V. Jagić, Croatian Slavist recognized in the world, who already considered himself a member of the Croatian Vukovians and a conveyor of the idea of South-Slavic unity:

> "Our people, who are in the position of authority, fear that something evil, bad for us will come from Serbs; they think that if we adopt Serbian orthography, as required by science and logic, then Srbianism will overwhelm Croatianism. Those are people who still think that our entire struggle should focus on the perservation of language ... they hope we can repel Srbianism only under the condition that the Croatian orthography and grammar are kept separate from the Serbian ones." (Jagić 1930, 62)

In short and most simply said, with no analysis of complex political and national relationships, the Vukovians' starting point is an idea that Croats and Serbs are one nation and, given one nation, they should have a single language.

Since no shared language, or language community of Croats and Serbs existed before or at the time of Croatian Vukovians, a common language was artificially being built according to the language model that Vuk S. Karadžić lexically defined and recorded in his *Srpski rječnik* [Serbian Dictionary] in 1818 and grammatically systematized in a short grammar annexed to the Dictionary; the language model described by his close associate Đuro Daničić at the levels of phonology, phonetics, and morphology in his *Mala srpska gramatika* [Little Serbian Grammar] in 1850 and *Oblici srpskoga jezika* [Morphemes in the Serbian Language] in 1863 (Ham 2006, 125–159).

Open Usurpation of the Croatian Language

The first two editions of Daničić's *Morphemes* were published in Cyrillic, whereas the third edition was in Latin and had a dedication: *To Serbs of the West Church—a Serb of the East Church*. "Serbs of the West Church" was his name for Croats. In the fifth edition in 1869 (and seventh in 1874), Daničić changed the title from *Oblici srpskoga jezika* into *Oblici srpskoga ili hrvatskoga jezika* [Morphemes in the Serbian or Croatian Language], although there were no differences in contents between the pure Serbian edition and the one with the added Croatian name in the title. Literary stylization was Shtokavian, but it was the lect of common people, peasants and herdsmen, the idiom the Croatian Vukovians wanted to elevate to the literary language level and keep it pure Shtokavian. It is the East-Shtokavian lect. That choice was acceptable to Serbs since they just started to seek a dialectal basis for their future literary language. To Croats the choice was unacceptable. Croatian Shtokavian is West Shtokavian. Croats chose the Shtokavian stylization as the grammar stylization back in the 17th century, as was presented in the grammar by B. Kašić (1604); the Croatian Shtokavian was founded on Croatian literary works. Croatian literary texts, on which language description Kašić's grammar was based, are evidence that the Croatian literary-language Shtokavian was even older than the Croatian first grammar. Until the appearance of Vukovians in the 19th century, that Shtokavian has already been filtered, amply upgraded, enriched, and adjusted to the Croatian tridialectal language reality.

Table 4. The most pronounced differences in grammar norms between the Zagreb philology school and Croatian Vukovians*

	Zagreb Philology School	**Croatian Vukovians**
Grammar model	Noun declensions types are classified according to the suffix in the genitive case singular. The locative case is the 6th and instrumental is the 7th case.	Noun declensions types are classified according to the noun gender. The locative case is the 7th and instrumental is the 6th case.
Terminology	*Slovnica, samostavnik, pridavnik, brojnik, zaime, spol, osobno zaime, glagolj, glagoljna osoba, prošlo vrieme, predlog, veznik, uzkličnik* or *umetak, prislov.*	*Gramatika, imenica, pridjev, broj, zamjenica, rod, lična zamjenica, glagol, glagolsko lice, pređašnje vrijeme, predlog, savez, usklik, prilog.*
Spelling	*tj, ć* = ć; *dj, gj* = đ Up to 1876 a long reflex of the Old Church Slavonic *jat* was recorded as *ĕ*; *syllabic r* as er. Since 1876 jat has been recorded as *ie, je*; *syllabic r* as r.	ć, đ, dž (newly introduced letters) A long reflex of the Old Church Slavonic *jat* is recorded as ije, whereas a short reflex is recorded je; *syllabic r* is recorded without accompanying e.
Orthography	Morphonological, korienski [root spelling] according to the principle expressed by Babukić: Write for the eyes, read for the ears.	Phonological, according to the principle expressed by Karadžić: Write as you speak.
Phonology and Phonetics	A long reflex of jat is a phoneme, a diphthong and one syllable. The system of four accents (only Babukić had three accents). The long rising accent is recorded as ˆ, and short falling accent as ′.	A long reflex of jat is a phoneme, a monophthong and one syllable. The system of four accents. The long rising accent is recorded as ′, and the long falling accent as ˆ.
Morphology	In noun declension in the genitive case plural ending *-h* is recorded: jelen-*ah*, konj-*ah*, sel-*ah*, žen-*ah*, stvar-*ih*. In the noun dative, locative, and instrumental cases plural endings are non-syncretized: Dative plural: jelen-*om*, žen-*am*, stvar-*im* Locative plural: jeleni-*ih*, žena-*ah*,stvar-*ih* Instrumental plural: jelen-*i*, žen-*ami*, stvar-*mi.* Dative and instrumental dual in all nouns with suffixes *-ima, -ama*: jelen-*ima*, žen-*ama*, stvar-*ima*. Enclitic accusative singular of pronoun ona reads *ju*. Enclitic dative of pronoun sebe reads *si*.	In noun declension in the genitive case plural, ending *-h* is not recorded: jelen-*a*, konj-*a*, sel-*a*, žen-*a*, stvar-*i*. In the noun dative, locative, and instrumental cases plural endings are syncretized: Dative plural: jelen-*ima*, žen-*ama*, stvar-*ima* Locative plural: jeleni-*ima*, žena-*ama*, stvar-*ima* Instrumental plural: jelen-*ima*, žen-*ama*, stvar-*ima.* No dual exists. Enclitic accusative singular of pronoun ona reads *je*. Enclitic dative of pronoun sebe does not exist.

	Zagreb Philology School	**Croatian Vukovians**
	Regular arrangement of extensions in the pronoun-adjective declension: Genitive singular: žut-*oga* Dative singular: žut-*omu* Locative singular: žut-om Instrumental singular: žut-*im*.	Irregular arrangement of extensions in the pronoun-adjective declension: Genitive singular: žut-*oga* i žut-*og* Dative singular: žut-*omu*, žut-*om*, žut-*ome* Locative singular: žut-*omu*, žut-*om*, žut-*ome* Instrumental singular: žut-*im*.
	The recommendation on the application of declension to numerals *dva, oba tri, četiri*; in numerals *dva* and *oba, dvije* i *obje* genders are differed: *dvaju* and *dviju, dvama* and *dvjema*. Transgressives (present and past verbal adverbs) are a separate type of inflective participles (declension): *prikazujuća* slika, *prikazujuće* slike. Futur II: *bit ću kopao*.	The recommendation not to inflect numerals *dva, oba tri, četiri*; in numerals *dva* i *oba*, *dvije* i *obje* genders are not differed: *dvaju* i *dviju, dvama*. Transgressives (present and past verbal adverbs) do not exist. Futur II does not exist.
Syntax	*Prema* and *protiv* are congruent with the dative case. *Mimo* is congruent with the accusative case.	*Prema* is congruent with the dative case, whereas *protiv* with the genitive case. *Mimo* is congruent with the genitive case.

*Ham 2006.

This fundamental difference in the stylization of literary language, though both are Shtokavian, leads to different codification procedures and different concrete codifying solutions (see Table 4). Vukovians relied on common people's idiom recorded in folk poetry and narratives, folktales, brought to the world primarily by Karadžić and other collectors of folklore verbal artifacts. Out of that corpus, alive, currently existing rural populace's discourse, the most widespread characteristics were selected. The Vukovian literary-language stylization was supposed to be recorded using phonological orthography and reformed Cyrillic, whereas among Croats Latin alphabet should be used. Namely, not even Croatian Vukovians would have been prepared to waive Latin script and accept Cyrillic, not even in the name of two *peoples' unity*.

Here we must emphasize that Karadžić's endeavors were outrageously aggressive – at the time when the development of the Croatian Latin script, named "Gajica" was in full swing, he tried to impose Cyrillic letters on Croats as substitutes for Croatian palatals. He even had letters cast in Vienna for that Latin-Cyrillic patchwork with the intention of printing books for Croats despite their rejection. (Ham 2011) Apart from the proposed eight new letters (ђ, ж, љ, њ, ћ, ч, ш, џ), by which he wanted to replace Croatian *dj*, *ž*, *lj*, *nj*, *ć*, *č*, *š*, *dž*, he wanted also to omit close-mid unvocalized *è* before *r* (so to delete letter *è* in *èr* in *pèrst* and write the word *prst*) and "rogato ě," by which the reflex of *yat* was recorded in "Gajica," because he was irritated by its four-way pronunciation (*ě* = *i*, *e*, *je*, *ije*). Karadžić spoke derogatorily about the Croatian "diacritic letters" (č, ć, š, ž, dž, đ, lj, nj): "... when, according to Gaj's orthography, a word, for example, *pisati* is written and then a fly leaves its 'trace' above the letter *s*, then that *s* will be read *š*." (Stojanović 1987, 682) ("Pi*s*ati" means to write, whereas "pi*š*ati" means to urinate; author's note.)

Karadžić's, and later generally accepted Vukovians', orthographic principle: Write as you speak, it would be advisable to cite a judgement expressed by Zlatko Vince, an excellent expert on the 19th century language-related issues and events. Namely, the citation picturesquely summarizes the nature of the Vukovians' approach to language and, consequently, the nature of turmoils the Croatian literary language was forced to sustain due to the Vukovian intrusion into its codification space:

> "The principle 'Write as you speak', i.e. its aspect related to a phonological pronunciation, could be born only in the mind of a simple, unsophisticated man, the person not preocupied with historical language issues who cannot other than write words as he hears them … In line with the other meaning of the principle, Karadžić requested that in writing one should use people's simple language, the language used by peasants, herdsmen, and not the educated slavenosrpski [Slavonic-Serbian] language, which was predominantly used in Serbian literature." (Vince 1990, 274)

Greater Serbian and Unitaristic Vukovians' Language Principles

Karadžić's language efforts in the beginning were aimed primarily at Serbs. However, Karadžić considered and explicitly said in the paper *Srbi i Hrvati* [Serbs and Croats] in 1861: "Name 'Croat' can justifiably be attributed to: 1) All Chakavians; 2) *Kekavci* [Kaykavians] in the kingdom of Croatia, who have already adapted to the name. Name 'Serb' refers justifiably to all Shtokavians regardless of their faith and place of residence; they differ from Croats, apart from other irrelevant differences, in the following: 1) they do not say *ča* or *kaj* but *što* or *šta*; and 2) they transform *l* into *o* at the end of syllables, i.e., instead of *kotal*, *kazal*, *žetelci*, they say *kotao*, *kazao*, *žeteoci*, etc." (Vince 1990, 301). Simply, Karadžić contended that all Shtokavians were Serbs (regardless of their religion), Kaykavians were Slovenians, only Chakavians were Croats.

Karadžić's activity spread among Croats; it spread its roots among the Croatian followers and advocates of Yugoslav idea of brotherhood of Croats and Serbs, primarily via language – grammar.

Today, we clearly see the unsustainability and quasi-scientific nature of the postulate that all Shtokavians are Serbs. The hypothesis was scientific in its time and in line with the standpoints of European Slavistics that distinguished and acknowledged peoples according to the criterion of language. Karadžić skillfully used that to create thesis published in the paper *Srbi svi i svuda* [Serbs Everyone and Everywhere]. The paper was publicized within *Kovčežić za istoriju, jezik i običaje Srba sva tri zakona*, 1849 [A Small Suitcase for the History, Language and Customs of the Serbs of all Three Religions], but it was written in 1836. In it, Karadžić invoked philological authorities of the time to prove that Serbs were everyone and everywhere: "Dobrovski and Šafařik demonstrated that name 'Serbs' was used for all Slavic people and that the name is older than names Slavs or Slovs." We should not forget either the aforementioned dedication in the third edition of Daničić's *Oblici srpskoga jezika* [Morphemes of the Serbian Language] (1850): "To Serbs of the West Church – a Serb of the East Church" because the dedication clearly revealed what it was all about in that dedication and grammar—for Karadžić, all Shtokavians were Serbs; the only difference between them was their faith, so Croats were nothing else than Catholic Serbs. Unfortunately, this idea is still alive today in the Serbian nationalistic circles. For example, in 2005, Serbian linguist Miloš Kovačević ascertained that: all Shtokavians were Serbs, all Shtokavianism was Serbian, and Croats were merely Vuk's Serbs (Kovačević 2005).

The Zagreb philology school, contrary to the Great-Serbia ideology, was deeply, firmly rooted in the Croatian soil. It defended itself with the same weapon it had been attacked with – language: the Zagreb philology school's Croatian codification was different from the one of Vukovians; its rationale was the awareness that it was standing on the Croatian language barricades.

Political Attempts to Unify the Croatian and Serbian Language: The Vienna Literary Agreement in 1850

The Austrian court was interested in bringing Croats and Serbs closer together because of the Serbian population that had been colonized by the Monarchy in its Croatian part. In order to reduce administrative costs and reinforce political safety in the Monarchy Austrian politicians supported Vukovian ideas because Vukovians wanted to make an amalgam out of the two languages, thus eventualy creating one nation; Austria did not care at all that Croats would be suffocated linguistically and nationally by Vukovianism. Political encouragement to Vukovians was provided by Austria when the Vienna Literary Agreement was convened in 1850. Historically, it was the first of the two agreements that attempted to unify, to blend the Serbian and Croatian languages. The Vienna Agreement did not bear any fruit in its time;

however, since it was incorporated into the foundations of the Yugoslav Novi Sad Agreement from the year 1954, we should pay an appropriate amount of attention to it.

A seemingly simple practical reason can be found in the background of the Vienna Agreement convocation—the creation of a common legislative terminology. Under management by Austrian minister Bach, participants were supposed to create new legislative-political terminology that would be common and intelligible to the Slovene and Croato-Serbian dialects. Since Croatian and Serbian were at the time so much different, it was necessary to reach an agreement among the parties about the terminology. The agreement was called the Vienna Literary Agreement. Although its contemporary influence was insignificant, in the mid-20th century, in communist Yugoslavia, it assumed mythical significance and proportions, and became a cornerstone of the Great-Serbia policy. The first sentence of the Vienna Agreement reveals reasons for it:

> "We, the undersigned, being aware of the need that one nation should have one literature and watching in grief our poor fragmented literature … have met these days to talk about how to, as far as possible for the moment, agree and unite in literature." (Vince 1990, 279)

Vukovians did not believe there was any national difference between Croats and Serbs. By emphasizing the concept of one nation (people), they were, in fact, emphasizing the notion that it was Serbian nation. That inferrence was not explicitly stated in the text of Agreement; however, evidence of Karadžić's works and activities before and after the Agreement undoubtedly indicate what it was about. Karadžić wrote in 1836, fourteen years before the Agreement:

> "The name is also one of the big obstacles: it is very difficult to persuade them (Illyrians/Croats) to acknowledge that they are Serbs; on the other hand, only crazy people would comply with the proposal to abandon our glorious name." (Stanojević 1924, 681)

After having determined, on the basis of the Shtokavian dialect, and attributed Serbian nationality to Croats, Karadžić cannot admit that the Croatian literary language differs from the Srbian one, therefore he committed himself to language unification, which would erase most of the Croatian specificities. Ljudevit Gaj commented on the Agreement in *Narodne novine*, and used the following words:

> "Time will soon show whether this proposition is practical and would it lead, under the contemporary circumstanes, to the yearned concord and equality, or to an even greater separation and literary discord." (Vince 1990, 281)

At this point it would be advisable to investigate why did the Croatian representatives – Kukuljević, Demeter, Mažuranić, Pacel and Pejaković, sign the Agreement? To get an answer, we must recall that in the first half of the 19th century, in the time of national revival movements, state and national borders in Croatian territory were different from the borders in modern sense; at that time clear comprehension of and clear criteria for the sovereign determination of national affiliation did not exist. Judgements were still based on the romantically based cognitions, swinging between the South-Slavic and Pan-Slavic ideas; what did exist was a powerful national enthusiasm. Croats did not live in their sovereign state. Given a small nation, Croats hoped for benefiting nationally from the union with other Slavic peoples, even if the union with Serbs was just spiritual or 'fraternal', or of any other nature, like political. Moreover, at the time of the Agreement, once captivating Illyrian ideas had already faded away. The great romantic Pan-Slavism went to pieces, so Yugoslavism arose as the Pan-Slavic idea in miniature. This was the context in which the Agreement must be understood; it was an attempt of just a lingual, spiritual, and fraternal union and no political union was implied, so there was no implementation liability either.

Most of the Croatian intellectuals at that time clearly understood that the acceptance of Karadžić' ideas would lead to neglect, if not abandonment, of their own language, of the identity of own literary heritage, and even of national identity. Their judgement was reflected in fierce polemics about language and national question that were published in both Croatian and Serbian newspapers, written by prominent cultural and political figures: Vjekoslav Babukić, Šime Starčević, Adolfo Veber, Bogoslav Šulek, Franjo Rački, Vatroslav Jagić, Vinko Pacel, Stjepan Ivićević, Mihovil Pavlinović, Mirko Bogović. These ferocious discussions were put together in four books of *Polemics in Croatian Literature* (1982) consisting of over 3,000 pages!

Political Victory of Croatian Vukovians at the Turn of the Century

Three works were crucial for the Vukovians' success in overwhelming the language of the Zagreb philology school at the turn of the century; these works were instrumental in breaking and transforming the up-till-then predominant Croatian literary-language norms: *Hrvatski pravopis* [Croatian Orthography or Croatian Normative Guide] by Ivan Broz in 1892; *Gramatika i stilistika hrvatskoga ili srpskoga književnog jezika* [Grammar and Stylistics of the Croatian or Serbian Literary Language] by Tomo Maretić in 1899; and *Rječnik hrvatskoga jezika* [Dictionary of Croatian Language] by Franjo Iveković and Ivan Broz in 1901. In the last decade of the 19th century, the Croatian literary language assumed a new shape. This period is known under the name 'the turn of the century'; metaphorically speaking, it was 'the turn of the Croatian language'.

Orthography by Broz introduced phonological orthography into schools and public communication with considerable changes in spelling: *ije/je* (instead of *ie/je*), *đ* (instead of *dj*, *gj*), *ć* (instead of *tj*), and introduced *dž*. (Broz 1892) Grammar by Maretić, completely supporting Broz's orthography, introduced considerable changes into the former phonological and morphological design of literary language. (Maretić 1899) Dictionary by Broz and Iveković subjected the tridialectal literary-language dictionary basis to strict Shtokavian purism (Broz and Iveković 1901). These three codifying handbooks complemented each other, thus forming an unbreakable triune entirety. Therefore, if language-normative changes at the turn of the century are to be comprehended thoroughly, all three works need to be well known.

One should also know the political circumstances in which these books originated, because those very circumstances enabled the creation of these particular codifying manuals. The orthography manual by Broz and Maretić's grammar were written by the order of the Royal Croatian-Slavonian-Dalmatian Government and its Department of Worship and

Teaching, during the rule of hated Viceroy (Ban) Khuen Hédervåry, based on a proposition submitted by an expert committee composed of the followers of the Vukovian linguistic views. The committee acted in line with the unionistic (Croatian-Hungarian Party) politics. Unionists eagerly adopted Vukovianism as the party members were both Croats and Serbs. It should be known that Croatian Vukovian Tomo Maretić was loyal to both philology and politics—in two five-year mandates, he was a representative of Unionists in the Croatian Parliament (Hrvatski Sabor). No coincidence in that the orthography reform in Croatian schools, based on the Vukovian principles, was implemented in the same year T. Maretić became a representative in the Parliament and the orthography manual by Broz was published – in the same year: 1892! Croatian Vukovians overpowered the Zagreb philology school as political champions not linguistic champions! Maretić's grammar should be considered in that light as well. Many of its contemporaries shared the same perspective in their observations, the two most important among them were political champion Antun Radić, as a bitter adversary of the Yugoslav idea and consequently of Vukovianism, and linguistic champion Vatroslav Jagić, as an emphatic supporter of Yugoslavism and, especially, Vukovianism. Although they were on the opposite political and linguistic sides, their critiques of Maretić's grammar shared principally the same idea. Radić's critique was sharper, blunter and fiercer, whereas Jagić expressed his thoughts in a softer, meeker, and more reconcilable manner.

> "Let us imagine the grammar had already been translated into whichever foreign language … A foreign reader might easily presume that the Croatian literary language did not exist before Vuk and, further, if no literary language existed, then there was no literature … The Croatian literary language is not and cannot be anything else but the language of Croatian literature for four hundred years now. Who ignores that literature, cannot and must not write Croatian literary language grammar." (Radić 1937, 7–24)

> "I would not mind if he had clearly revealed his aim in advance that his aim was to write the grammar of Vuk and Daničić' language … Maretić's grammar gives ammunition for an unfounded contention, already frequently repeated by even sensible people, that Croats took away language from Serbs. However, the truth is that literary Shtokavian, which among Croats has lived long before Vuk under different names (Croatian, Bosnian, Dalmatian, Slavonian), under Vuk's influence assumed a more consistent, more people-friendly form." (Jagić 1948, 532–537)

Both critics were right: Maretić wrote his grammar exclusively on the basis of works by V. S. Karadžić and Đ. Daničić, whereby he completely ignored contemporary literature and declared that contemporary writers who wrote in the Zagreb philology school language were obsolete. In that way, the previously valid literary-language codification was pushed into obscurity, and the weapons used in attacking the Croatian language were made out of Maretić's linguistic indifference to Croatian literature. Deleterious effects of Maretić's grammar can be felt even today because the works of the 19th century Croatian writers were subjected to language changes – they were falsified in the process of language editing to comply with this grammar in order to create the illusion of the unified, integral language.

From Maretić's time onwards, readers usually read lingually forged Croatian classics of Romantism and Realism; their original language was presented to a broad reading audience as obsolete and regional. (Brozović 1985) In that way, all language characteristics and directions that existed before Vukovians' victory, i.e., before Vukovian literary-language codifying solutions, have been erased, thus creating the impression that no Croatian-specific lingusitic foundations existed in the 19th century to be included in the common literary language construction.

Maretić was blind to the entire Croatian linguistic tradition not only to contemporary concrete linguistic solutions of the Zagreb philology school; he did not notice any of the 19th century grammatists, not to mention the older ones, and their contribution to the development of the Croatian literary language. Due to the political circumstances of the time and his impeccable, undisputed scientific reputation of European proportions, Maretić managed to secure the position of his grammar at the very top of Croatian linguistics, where it stayed untouched deeply in the 20th century. For decades, his grammar was an ideal of language correctness and standard into which the Croatian language must be molded, no objections permitted. It has left a deep trace in the Croatian literary language. By enforcing itself, politically for the most part, as an undisputed methodological model and an ideal of language correctness and purity, the grammar determined and fortified the Croatian language codified standard up to the mid-second half of the 20th century (Piškorec 2015). Only then did methodologically and normatively more modern grammars manage to upstage it.

Skerlić's Survey in 1912

Not being in the joined state with Serbs up until 1918 allowed Croats to quite freely maintain, to a certain extent, their original, Pre-Vukovian Croatian literary language for some time despite many open and sometimes powerful attempts from the Serbian side to exert political pressure on the Croatian language to change it according to the Vukovian principles—a never-ending Great-Serbian hunger for subjugating Croatia in full operation. In linguistic sense, Karadžić's ideas of Serbs and Croats being one nation that must have one literature only, as well as one language, were very alive in Serbia at that time. In the architecture of that one language, it was necessary to overcome apparent discrepancies between the two languages: Croatian is Yekavian and uses the Croatian Latin script, whereas Serbian is Ekavian and uses the Serbian Cyrillic script. The Croatian Latin alphabet was a script adjusted to the Croatian language (see Table 5). Ljudevit Gaj reformed it in 1835 and it was immediately widely accepted. (Gaj, 1830, 1835) The Serbian Cyrillic was reformed by Karadžić in 1811, but his reformed Cyrillic was adopted in Serbia just in 1868 (Stanojević 1924).

Jovan Skerlić, a Serbian cultural figure, politician, and writer, and an extreme Serbian nationalist, offered a solution by which the Yekavian/Ekavian and Latin/Cyrillic discrepancy should have been overcome. He proposed that Croats should accept the Serbian language, whereas Serbs should accept the Latin alphabet. To be precise, we must say that Skerlić spoke only about the Ekavian, Eastern dialect; however, Ekavianism brings Serbian lingual features with itself, as has been demonstrated through the years, especially the lexical ones as well as morphological and syntactical features. Consequently, Croats were supposed not only to abandon Yekavianism but their entire language as well, whereas Serbs were expected just to shift from Cyrillic to the Latin script – one nation would have had only one language: Serbian written in Latin. In Skerlić's words: "Besides the Eastern dialect the Latin script will become a general literary *azbuka* [alphabet]." (Jonke 1971, 201) Skerlić attempted to scientifically justify his proposal – he conductet a survey among prominent cultural workers, authors and scientists, Serbs and Croats alike; how much of science was there in his arguments, we leave to readers to judge about:

> "1) A greater in numbers and culturally stronger part of the Serbian-Croatian people speaks the Eastern dialect;
>
> 2) The Ekavian dialect has been and is a literary dialect;
>
> 3) The Ekavian dialect is more innocent, simpler, easier; it provides tools for effortless writing to both Ekavians and Ikavians;
>
> 4) The Eastern dialect is most appropriate for poetry writing;
>
> 5) The Eastern dialect is expansive; it has so many things that support it; it is a winner in itself over the South dialect." (Jonke 1971, 201).

The renunciation of own language, consequently of own nationality, the enforced acknowledgment of alleged shortcomings, faults of the Croatian language – all that should have been a part of the brotherly Serbian hug, 'grappling embrace'. Yet, galvanized by the idea of one, brotherly, nation with two names, certain Croatian authors would naively adopt Ekavian idiom, even the Serbian language. Very soon, however, Croats forsook all that as the proclaimed brotherhood turned out to be false (Jonke 1971, Samardžija 2012).

Croatian Language Up Until the Foundation of the Republic of Croatia: 1918-1991

Due to the beginning of World War I (the Great War) the realization of Skerlić's ideas was put to a halt. In the aftermath of the War, however, the Great- Serbian pressure became ever stronger. For example, newspaper *Narodne novine*, launched during the Illyrian movement, was published in the Croatian language, linguistically and orthographycall aligned with the principles of the Zagreb philology school language stylization from 1835 to 1918. *Narodne novine* has been, and is to this day, a daily state-owned newspaper and the official gazette with a large readership. In the past, *Narodne novine* was widely read and rather influential, and fitted well in the general language image according to which Croats were using their Zagreb language stylization without restriction until they joined the State of Slovenes, Croats and Serbs. *Narodne novine* shifted to the Vukovian language stylization as soon as Croatia entered the newly unified Kingdom of Serbs, Croats and Slovenes in 1918; the first text edited and published in the so stylized language was the Constitution of the Kingdom of SHS (Ham 2006a).

Croatian Language in the Kingdom of Serbs, Croats and Slovenes, and in the Kingdom of Yugoslavia

The multinational Austrian-Hungarian Monarchy disintegrated in 1918 into several smaller states and Croatia entered into a political union with Serbs. The Kingdom (Kraljevstvo) of Serbs, Croats and Slovenes was their first common state, which changed its name twice until 1941: the Kingdom (Kraljevina) of Serbs, Croats and Slovenes, and the Kingdom of Yugoslavia. (The Croatian language has two words for the English word "kingdom": "kraljevina" indicates primarily state or social organization or interior organization – like: republic, kingdom, empire, federation, confederation, etc.; whereas "kraljevstvo" indicates space over which king rules, realm. Author's note according to Bašić, 2017.) Nevertheless, whichever name the new state formation might have, the status of Croats and the Croatian language in it was always the same—markedly to the detriment of the Croatian national identity and language (Samardžija 2012).

With no protection from anyone or anywhere, Croats and their language were subjected to the policy of Great Serbia and unitarism. Belgrade, the capital of Serbia, was also the capital and administrative center of the new state. In regard to language, it meant that all laws, decrees, decisions as well as text-books were in the Serbian language and printed in Belgrade. Language used in diplomacy, public service, police, and military without restrictions because state institutions—state administration, military and police forces, the judiciary, and the education system, managed by Serbs, made it possible. Consistent attempts were taken to introduce Ekavianism and Cyrillic script in the entire territory of the joined state—common language was constructed so that Serbian was enforced everywhere. The common language imposed on Croats had various names: Croatian-Serbian-Slovenic, Serbian-Croatian-Slovene, SerboCroatian, CroatoSerbian, Yugoslav.

Although grammar, vocabulary, and orthography based on the Vukovian language principles were installed in Croatia two decades ago, within the Austrian-Hungarian Monarchy, now they were imposed on Croats by the Yugoslav government with no administrative limits or interference. We must keep in mind one thing: although an adjective "Vukovian" is easily associated with Serbian, the adjective regards Croatian Vukovians. That means that the mentioned codifying works did not depart too far from the critical Croatian features, especially in the grammar and orthography, therefore they could grow roots among Croats. The Croatian orthography was especially different from the Serbian and was an obstacle to a thorough Serbianization of the Croatian languge. Being aware of that fact, the Belgrade state administration attempted to overcome obstacles to the Serbian language expansion – *Pravopisno uputstvo* [Orthography Guidelines] was prescribed in 1929 for all elementary, secondary, and vocational schools in The Kingdom of SHS. Since the unitaristic principles from *Pravopisna uputstva* had strong impact on the Croatian language in Tito's Yugoslavia and later until the foundation of the Republic of Croatia, here the introduction to the guidelines is cited in full length (the original was in Serbian and Serbian Cyrillic):

> "In all schools of the Monarchy one orthography has been used, the one based on the Vuk Karadžić's great language and orthography reform. Nevertheless, in different parts of our country certain disparities have occurred in spite of the fact that the said orthography complied always with the same fundamental principles; these discrepancies prevent school instruction from being completely leveled. At the same time, even teachers frequently do not know which othography variant is better and which one should be preferred and applied. In the interest of uniform instruction, better and more correct student grading, and improved literacy in our school, here is the list of all wavers regarding the orthography and directives which variant should be utilized in the future. On rare occassions two variants are permitted. In these cases, it will be teachers' responsibility to provide consistency, i.e., that in a particular school or with a particular

> student always the same permitted variant is used. The same way of writing, presented in this book of regulations, should be implemented in all new editions of textbooks. Not a single textbook, regardless of whether it is a new edition of a previously published book, or its first edition, can be approved as a school textbook if not prepared in compliance with the regulations presented here. What is not mentioned in this book of regulations is either already unified or is by its essence out of the scope of this kind of directives. Of course, our school instruction will be completely uniform only when its terminology will become uniform as well; this aspect of school instruction uniformity has not been discussed here." (Maksimović 1929, 5–6)

It did not take long for the common school terminology to appear: *Srednjoškolska terminologija i nomenklatura* [Secondary School Terminology and Nomenclature] was published by the Ministry of Education of the Kingdom of Yugoslavia in 1933. Under the pretense of developing the common language, Croatian scientific terminology was also subjected to Serbianization.

Croatian Language in the Independent State of Croatia 1941 – 1945

The foundation of the Banovina of Croatia (the autonomous province of Croatia in the Kingdom of Yugoslavia) in 1939 and later of the Independent State of Croatia (known by the acronym NDH from the Croatian name: *Nezavisna država Hrvatska*) in 1941, created favorable circumstances for Croats to to alleviate the detrimental cultural and linguistic effects of Serbianization. On the eve of the NDH foundation, in 1940, Croatian linguists Petar Guberina and Kruno Krstić published their famous *Razlike između hrvatskoga i srpskoga jezika* [Differences between the Croatian and Serbian Language] with the supplemented differential Serbian-Croatian dictionary. The Croatian State Office for Language (*Hrvatski državni ured za jezik*), a department of the NDH Government, was responsible for planning and care of the Croatian language. Legislative provisions stipulated the use of the Croatian language, orthography and script; the use of Cyrillic script was banned on April 25, 1941. The *Law Decree on the Croatian Language, on its Purity and its Orthography* is well known from that period. (Samardžija 2008, 129-155). Croats returned to the traditional pre-Vukovian orthography; it was then called *korienski* [etymological] orthography or spelling like in the time of the Zagreb philological school. The whole period was characterized by linguistic purism.

As a lingustic movement, purism originated in the 19th century Europe as a component of ethnic-national movements. In principle, the Croatian language benefited from purism in the 19th century – Croatian general and scientific vocabulary was being developed on the basis of puristic principles that resulted in the lexis appropriate for any Croatian language style. Famous lexicographer Bogoslav Šulek (1860, 1874) was the champion of Croatian vocabulary development; he was a creator of Croatian scientific and military terminology as well as of many entries in general vocabulary.-This means neologisms were not anything new or rear in the Croatian language architecture, neither did NDH bring anything essentially new in that sense. What was new was the language law and strictness by which it was implemented. Today, we clearly understand that language, as a component of personal freedom of every speaker, cannot be *enforced* through laws and legislative means. However, publicly used language, language of public communacation needs to be protected; it is especially important nowadays when the Croatian language must struggle for its distinct identity and recognition in the world. A shadow cast on NDH was its Nazism with racial laws and the shadow was cast also on its language planning. Up until today and especially in the period of Tito's Yugoslavia that shadow was used against the Croatian language; every attempt to separate Croatian from Serbian got an Ustasha label. Tito used Ustasha epithet whenever he wanted to supress any Croatian liberation act or movement. Persecuting supporters of the famous *Declaration on the Status and Name of the Croatian Literary Language* (1967), Tito used Ustashadom and Chetnikdom to frighten advocates of any Croatian demand, thus denying it. Namely, any Croatian invocation of the Croatian language was interpreted by Communists as a call to overthrow the state:

> "But they worked in secrecy, preparing the 'Declaration' and suddenly stab in the back. Such a way of doing things cannot be allowed here any more. Entire Yugoslavia is embittered by such acts, especially Croats. Because Serbs also live in Croatia, not in small numbers, and both know that brotherhood and unity are of vital importance to them. They have experienced well the Ustasha and Chetnik knives..." (excerpted from the speech by Josip Broz Tito "Nećemo nikome dozvoliti da narušava bratstvo i jedinstvo." [We will not allow anybody to ruin our brotherhood and unity]) (Vjesnik XXVII, no. 7211: 4; March 3, 1967)

Croatian Language in Communist Yugoslavia

With the end of NDH its Croatian language policy was repudiated, and Croats and their language were caught again in the Serbian "brotherly" choke hold. History repeated itself – namely, everything regarding the orthography manual published in the Kingdom of SHS was repeated in 1954 with the Novi Sad Agreement. When the unification of terminology is considered, the project of writing the common dictionary was launched, in which the Serbian lexis predominated. It was just a recycled concept of the Serbianization of Croatian vocabulary from the time of the Kingdom of Yugoslavia.

Croatia was a part of the totalitarian communist state of Yugoslavia when the Novi Sad Agreement took place. The supreme power in the state was the Communist Party of Yugoslavia (Komunistička partija Jugaslavije, KPJ), from 1952 known as SKJ (Savez komunista Jugoslavije [League of Communists of Yugoslavia]) with the majority of membership being Serbian and managed from Belgrade. Every Croatian attempt to break the ideological communist shackles (since it was impossible to break the state ones peacefully, as was demonstrated in 1991) would end in vilification emphasizing "the facist legacy of NDH." That legacy was a constant companion of the Croatian liberation idea; it followed everything Croatian like a shadow of death and choked it for half a century. It particularly followed every, even the smallest, attempt to introduce language changes that would be in favor of Croatian.

Novi Sad Agreement in 1954

The Novi Sad Agreement was organized in accord with the principles of the Viennese Literary Language Agreement and Skerlić's survey. A new survey on the following issues of the Serbo-Croatian language was published in Letopis Matice srpske [Matica Srpska Chronicle] in 1953: unification of orthography, unification of script, unification of dialect, unification of vocabulary, especially the professional and scientific terminology, with the aim to reinforce brotherhood and unity (Jonke 1971). The Serbian party decided on the topics, or issues, because in Croatia no one had any objections to language differences. In the next year, carefully selected writers and linguists from Zagreb, Beograd, Novi Sad, and Sarajevo were summoned to Novi Sad to participate in the meeting where the results of the survey would be discussed. No one in Croatia had a clue where would the discussion lead to, so only seven participants, out of the twelve invited, appeared in the meeting. And where did the discussion actually lead to was perfectly summarized by Ljudevit Jonke, university professor and prominent Croatian linguist. At the Zagreb railway terminal, exiting the train from Novi Sad, he exclaimed: "We saved Ijekavianism!" Indeed, in the whole affair, Croatian participants could not do anything else but to try to save what was left of the Croatian language! The conclusions of the Novi Sad Agreement were designed in advance. Participants were allowed to talk about everything, but only the premeditated thougths were recorded in the minutes of the meeting. Thus, the Croatian proposal on the stylization of the name of the language was left out of the minutes and Agreement – instead, the language was called Croato-Serbian; the same happened with the Croatian proposal on equal use of both languages in state administration services – the role was assigned to Serbian. The pre-conceived destiny, or should we call it impending doom, of the Croatian language was disguised by a seemingly democratic and tolerant conclusion about the equality of languages, scripts, Yekavian and Ekavian pronunciations. The principle of equality of languages, as elaborated in the conclusions of the Novi Sad Agreement, enabled the Serbian language to appear in Croatia in newspapers and in radio and television shows; it opened way for the Serbian language to schools and to teaching; however, the Serbian language was installed as the exclusive language in the army and the only state official language. It gradually suppressed Croatian by pushing it out of public and educational use; the Croatian language should have become just a regional dialect of the Western variant (Jonke, 1971). Any resistance to that Agreement was qualified as a menace to brotherhood and unity, as an Ustashadom revival, an act against the state.

The conclusions of the Novi Sad Agreement seemingly, theoretically, provided equality to languages, but in practice Serbian was imposed on all, and in 1960 it was confirmed by the Novi Sad orthography manual published in two variants: *Pravopis hrvatskosrpskoga jezika* [Orthography of the Croato-Serbian Language], in Latin and Yekavian, published by Matica hrvatska, Zagreb; *Pravopis srpskohrvatskoga jezika* [Orthography of the Serbian-Croatian], in Cyrillic and Ekavian, published by Matica Srpska, Novi Sad (Pravopisna komisija 1960). The orthographies differed only in scripts and Yekavian/Ekavian duality. This unitaristic orthography manual erased not only spelling differences between the two languages; when we open it today, we can clearly see how it was possible that so many loanwords, aliens, and Serbisms had been introduced into the Croatian language in recent times (Brodnjak's Differential Dictionary from 1992 recorded as many as 30,000! of them; Samardžija's Explanatory Dictionary from 2015 had about the same number). Numerous Serbisms can be found in the examples that illustrate orthography rules. These Serbisms occurred in the Novi Sad orthography manual due to the implementation of the 'equality' principle; namely, the 'equality' principle was implemented in such a way, recommended by the authorities, that between two posible words the one should be used which was common to both Croatian and Serbian. Thus many Croatian words were erased from the common lexis. The name of language was also changed not only in the titles of language codifying works but also as the name of a school subject: the Croatian language existed no more; instead, some other "languages" were the subject core of instruction: CroatoSerbian, Croato-Serbian, Croatian-Serbian, Croatian or Serbian. Linguistic works with the Croatian name in the title were prohibited or withdrawn from sale (Auburger 2011).

At the time of the Novi Sad Agreement, the theory of variants was conceived. It proclaimed that Croatian and Serbian are only variants of the same, one common language. Croatian is only the Western version of Serbian – Serbian is the only representative language used in diplomacy. Although this theory has been proven unfounded thus unsustainable (Pavletić 1969), it still has its supporters even nowadays. In Europe, this is how Croatian is viewed, and all the efforts aside, it is difficult to convince slow and obstinate European diplomacy that Croatian is not Serbo-Croatian, not even as a variant of it. The consequences are still felt. TheCroatian public was rightly outraged when a spokeswoman for The Hague Tribunal, Florence Hartmann, addressed the Croatian public in an almost perfect Serbian—namely, that language was taught in diplomatic schools in Belgrade and was the official diplomatic language used to represent Yugoslavia. The first conviction by the Tribunal of Croatian generals was read to them in a mixture of Croatian and Serbian in 2011, which was devastating and deeply offensive to Croats, adding insult to injury. (Reading of the verdict was broadcast by the Croatian state television live on April 15 at 10:30 a.m.). Paradoxically enough, only a Serbian, Vojislav Šešelj, publicly protested against the language policy of the Tribunal, demanding his documents be submitted in Serbian. Šešelj's demand was denied in 2004 with the following reasoning, signed by Hildegard Uertz Retzlaff on behalf of the Hague prosecution on November 23, 2004:

> "[..]. "The insisting of the accused on the existence of Serbian as a separate language has no roots in reality. Linguistically speaking, Serbo-Croatian cannot be separated into two or more languages. Although nationalists, such as the accused, may insist on the use of 'Serbian' or 'Croatian' or 'Bosnian' language, these are just different designations given to the same member of the South Slavic branch of the Indo-European language family. Differences in writing, syntax and pronunciation are not significant enough to treat 'Serbian', 'Croatian' and 'Bosnian' as separate languages. Any possible autonomy that exists between the so-called 'different languages' comes from ideological and political values that are worthless from the scientific, linguistic point of view. "Therefore, those who understand Croatian and Serbian as two languages or two literary languages are 'nationalists' in The Hague Tribunal's interpretation." (Grčević 2008, 191)

If for no other reason than just for these facts, the recent history of the Croatian language should continuously be proven.

Declaration on the Status and Name of the Croatian Literary Language in 1967

A response to the implementation of the Novi Sad Agreement's orthography manual and Yugoslav language planning, in which Croatian was repressed, appeared in the form of the famous *Deklaracija o nazivu i položaju hrvatskoga književnog jezika [Declaration on the Status and Name of the Croatian Literary Language]*. It did not appear immediately – the Novi Sad Agreement took place in 1954, *Novi Sad Orthography Manual* occurred in 1960, and *Declaration* in 1967. The described language planning was being implemented slowly and for a decade or so. Step by step the Croatian language was driven to be assimilated by the Serbian language. Individual resistance existed, but did not bear any significant fruit. One person, two, or three persons could not stop the flood of Serbianization (also known as Serbification; in Croatian: *posrbljavanje*) caused by the Novi Sad Agreement. Therefore, *Matica hrvatska* in Zagreb discussed the issues of the Croatian language equality and independence after which seven experts met on March 13, 1967 and created the text today known under the title *Declaration on the Status and Name of the Croatian Literary Language* and published it in the Zagreb magazin Telegram. (Matica hrvatska, in Latin: Matrix Croatorum, is the oldest independent, non-profit and non-government Croatian national institution, founded in 1842. Its principal mission is to promote Croatian national and cultural identity primarily in the fields of art, science, and public life. "Matica hrvatska" may be literally translated as "Parent body of Croats" from "matica" meaning center, queen bee or parent body; author's note.)

It has always been emphasized that the *Declaration* was a collective work with many contributors, but its actual writers were: Miroslav Brandt, Dalibor Brozović, Radoslav Katičić, Tomislav Ladan, Slavko Mihalić, Slavko Pavešić, and Vlatko Pavletić. The Declaration was signed by the most prominent Croatian cultural and scientific institutions; in a word, by the entire Croatian *intelligentsia*. The *Declaration* was based on the demand for equality of the Croatian and Serbian languages, a true and full equality, which meant that the Croatian literary language should be used as the official language in Croatia. The same equality was sought for all the other languages of other Yugoslav peoples. However, SKJ's interpretation was that the *Declaration* was a gunshot aimed at the very foundations of the Yugoslav idea. Therefore the counterattack on the *Declaration* was fierce and immediate; the condemnations started to appear as early as March 17, 1967, the very day the Declaration was published in Telegram. The entire communist public and huggers rose to fiercely persecute the signatories and supporters of the *Declaration*; only after April 20, 1967 the persecution slightly subsided.

To commemorate these events, Croatian Parliament decided in 1997 that "the days of March 11-17, each year, are proclaimed the Croatian Language Days on the occasion of the anniversary of the *Declaration on the Status and Name of the Croatian Literary Language* (1967)." Each year, thereafter, different cultural programs commemorating the *Declaration* are organized in Croatia at that time.

The *Declaration* demonstrated that resistance was possible. In the years following the Novi Sad Agreement, it had lost its original suppressive power. The illusions about equality in the fraternal communist union were abandoned. It is worth mentioning here that we witnessed a great cultural event in 1968 – the Croatian translation of the Bible, written in pure Croatian, was presented *urbi et orbi*. Today, we know it under the name the Zagreb Bible and it is an ideal of biblical style. Language advisors in the translation projects were eminent Croatian linguists (Šuljić 2018).

Croatian linguists discontinued working on the common *Dictionary of Serbo-Croatian* in 1967 that was supposed to be the lexical and lexicographical crown of language unitarism. This was an additional blow to the common language construction because in Croatia only first two volumes were published, from A to K. Because in Croatian A to K is pronounced ɑ:dɔk), the dictionary is popularly called *Adok* even today. Croatians, recognizing the attempts to annihilate the Croatian language, said a decisive NO to the unitaristic language planning and policy (Pavletić 1969).

The Serbian lobby abroad did a great damage to the Croatian language and systematically worked on the suppression of its recognition even beyond the borders of Yugoslavia. Pavle Ivić was among the most eager lobbyist (Babić 1992). In 1970, as a result of Serbian endeavors, the Croatian language was deleted from the ISO standard of the International Organization for Standardization, and was returned only in 1988 with the ISO number 862 and abbreviation *hr*. However, a complete international affirmation of the Croatian language came ten years later when the existing three-letter Croatian and Serbian designation was deleted from the ISO 639-2 norm for bibliographic description. The point was that in the international standardization organizations, all Latin literature was recorded as Croatian and Cyrillic literature as Serbian (Maštrović and Machala 2011).

Croatian Spring, 1971

Croatian resistance broke out in 1971 in the form of a movement for political liberty called the Croatian Spring, but it was suppressed mercilessly and participants were persecuted and imprisoned (Kratofil 2005). From the linguistic point of view, the valuable legacy of the Croatian Spring was the public renunciation of the Novi Sad Agreement and the appearance of the *Croatian Orthography* by Stjepan Babić, Božidar Finka and Milan Moguš. Due to the collapse of the Croatian Spring, the orthography manual could not be published in Croatia. The entire print run was confiscated and destroyed in the Zagreb Paper Mill (Babić 2005, 76). "The Orthography Manual by Babić, Finka and Moguš was withdrawn from the printing press, the printed copies were withdrawn and destroyed, and the printing plates were destroyed as well. The rescued copies were kept in hiding, the police raided and seized the copies they found; possession alone was considered a punishable act." (Brozović 2005, 60). It was published by the Croatian Expatriates in London. Hence its popular name *Londoner*. The *Londoner* denoted a return to the tradition of the Croatian orthography legacy prior to the Novi Sad Agreement; the principles and spelling solutions of the Agreement orthography were rejected. Croats used the *Londoner* for years; it was circulated under the table because it was not publicly allowed. The official orthography was still the one of the Novi Sad Agreement. A new *Review of the Grammar of the Croatian Literary Language* from 1973 was withdrawn from sale because of the monomial Croatian name in the title; this codifying work was, like the *Croatian Orthography*, printed in London in 1974 (Ham 2006, 219–215). However, according to the testimony of one of the participants in these events, Stjepan Babić, printing abroad also caused a collateral damage to the cause of the Croatian language:

> "The *Orthography* was printed in fifty thousand copies and, in the form of loose quires, it was awaiting approval, whereas one copy of eight hundred quires bound, without preface and introduction, was brought by Zlatko Markus to London to Jakša Kušan, editor of *New Croatia*. We found out about it shortly afterwards, and Z. Markus recently boasted about it (Focus, November 2, 207; author's note), although he had nothing to boaast about because he had obviously done so at the initiative of Stanko Pekeč, KOS captain. (KOS – Kontraobaveštajna služba [Counter-intelligence Service; author's note]. Jakša Kušan advertised the *Croatian Orthography* for six months and the Yugoslav embassy was in a position to somehow prevent its printing because, under the Berne Convention, nothing was allowed to be printed in the signatory countries without copyright, and Yugoslavia and Britain were signatories, but the embassy remained silent to achieve one goal – to provide that for the *Croatian Orthography* the door to Croatia would be closed and remained closed; namely, the following political rule prevailed: what was printed by the extreme emigration, can by no means be printed in the homeland; and *Nova Hrvatska* was considered an institution of the Croatian extreme emigration, as well as all Croatian institutions abroad." (Babić 2008, 57)

This was the case with all works that originated in the Croatian emigration; even today these works are almost anonymous to the Croatian public; for example, the orthography manual by Pero Tutavac was printed in Buenos Aires (1971), however, only few people in Croatia know about it.

"Croatian Silence"

With the collapse of the Croatian Spring, the fifteen-year-long Croatian silence began. Croatian intellectuals and linguists were under the particular control of the notorious secret service Uprava državne bezbednosti (UDBA) [State Security Administration] (Kratofil 2005). Work of Matica hrvatska, a reputable Croatian national cultural institution, founded in 1842, was forbidden. Violence against Croats because of their language did not subside. The case of Ivan Šreter, a doctor at Pakrac Hospital, is well known. He wrote a diagnosis for a patient in the Croatian language (not in Croato-Serbian) and was therefore subjected to public media lynching and sentenced to prison. Serbian Chetniks abducted and killed him in 1991; the location of his grave is still not known. In memory of him and as a symbol of all Croatian tribulations and victims who suffered because they supported the Croatian language, the award for the best new Croatian word bears his name (Ham, 2019).

In linguistic terms, *Jezik*, kept the flame of the Croatian language alive. The magazine was launched in 1952 with the mission to promote the Croatian language. *Jezik* has been published 68 years without interruption and remained dedicated to its original mission. The League of Communists of Yugoslavia (*Savez komunista Jugoslavije,* acronym *SKJ*; author's note) knew that *Jezik* promoted the distinctive features of the Croatian language and closely monitored it. In 1985, the Central Committee of the League of Communists of Yugoslavi issued a directive (No. 03/S-4094/1-85, Zagreb, December 3, 1985) to the lower-level party branches regarding the language policy implementation. Obviously, the language policy was the Yugoslav, unitaristic one, the one proclaimed by the Novi Sad Agreement. On page 6, items 11–13, the following was explicitly written:

"11. It is necessary to publish the *Orthography of the Croatian or Serbian Language* as soon as possible (in Latin and Cyrillic).

Responsible for the task execution: the president of the Republic Committee for Education, Culture, Physical and Technical Culture.

Deadline: immediately.

12. Investigate again whether it would be possible to continue the work on the completion of the *Dictionary of the Croato-Serbian Language*, which work Matica hrvatska terminated in 1970 and discontinued its cooperation with Matica srpska; in the meantime, the second Cyrillic edition of the Dictionary was published in Novi Sad.

Responsible for the task execution: the president of the Republic Committee for Education, Culture, Physical and Technical Culture.

Deadline: up to the end of January 1986.

13. Provide that journal "Jezik" operates in the spirit of the socially proclaimed language policy and, accordingly, take necessary appropriate actions regarding the Editorial Board membership and its financing.

Responsible for the task execution: Republic Committee for Technology and Informatics, and Republic *SIZ* for Scientific Work with the journal's publisher and Editorial Council. (SIZ stands for Samoupravna interesna zajednica [Self-governing Interest Union]; author's note.)

Deadline: up to the end of January 1986."

Items 11 and 12 were realized. According to party documents available to the public and interpreted (Selak 1992, Babić 1990a), party linguists Josip Silić and Vladimir Anić wrote the orthography manual (1986, 2001) and Vladimir Anić prepared the dictionary (1991). The dictionary turned out to be a kind of publishing ruse; namely, it had originated as the project of the Croato-Serbian dictionary, but its title was changed from 'Croato-Serbian' to 'Croatian' and as such was presented to the Croatian public in Zagreb in 1991, in the swing of the Homeland War. It is obvious from the dictionary contents that it is not a normative Croatian dictionary since it comprises words regardless of whether they are Croatian or Serbian. The dictionary was inspired by unitarism, regardless of its Croatian name.

Item 13 was not realized. The publication of journal *Jezik* has been continued, firmly on the Croatian linguistic and national path.

Regardless of the party pressure exerted by SKJ (League of Communists of Yugoslavia) and the party's efforts to overshadow the Croatian language with Serbian in Yugoslavia and in the world, to portray it merely as the Western variant of Serbian, the Croatian linguists did not give up. In 1986, the Croatian Academy of Sciences and Arts (HAZU), in cooperation with the private publishing house *Globus*, published two capital books—the syntax (Katičić 1986) and word formation/morphology (Babić 1986) of the Croatian language, which were prepared within the project of the publication of comprehensive Croatian grammar. These works had only the Croatian language name in their title (and not 'Croatian or Serbian') and provoked a lot of criticism at the time. Katicic's *Syntax of the Croatian Literary Language* was particularly exposed to attacks because it brought, along with the syntax descriptions of the Croatian language, examples of the Croatian language from the 18th century. This was contrary to the official Yugoslav language policy that claimed the Croatian language did not exist before the Illyrians and Vuk Stefanović Karadžić in the 19th century. Katičić thus demolished and devalued Karadžić's claim to primacy by the syntactic examples taken from the Croatian literature of the 18th century.

In 1990, the long-awaited *Croatian Orthography*, the reprint of the *Londoner*, was finally published in Croatia.

CROATIAN IN THE REPUBLIC OF CROATIA 1991–2020

The Republic of Croatia declared its independence in 1991. However, for almost a decade, from the first multi-party elections in 1990 until the process of reintegration was completed in 1998, Croatia was struggling to fully implement its sovereignity during the severe Homeland War, the defensive war she was forced to wage against Serbia. The war was accompanied by numerous war and civilian victims, crimes committed against Croats, and destruction of Croatian properties. Nevertheless, at last, the long desired and dreamed sovereignty was realized.

Encouragement of Language Freedom

A new page of Croatian history was turned on, and the Croats were finally free to decide on their political fate by themselves. Croatian linguists immediately became very active; they were involved in the creation of a modern Croatian military terminology. Namely, Croatia did not have its own army; in Yugoslavia there was common 'Jugoslavenska narodna armija' [Yugoslav Peoples' Army] (JNA). JNA was usurped by Serbs at the beginning of the Homeland War, so Croats were forced to constitute their own armed forces out of almost nothing. The Croatian military terminology had to be established as well, because the terminology in army use was the one prescribed by Serbs. That terminology was strange to Croats. A new Croatian military terminology was created with reliance on tradition and older Croatian military terms (Šulek 1870–1912, Toth 1900). Of course, not only military terminology was reconsidered; Croatian linguists revised terminology, previously imposed on Croats, for all areas of public life, including police force, legislation, education, and administration. The Croatian language had a long-standing lexical tradition; it was utilized as the basis for the creation of the vocabulary that could serve the Croatian public life (Mamić 1992).

The Croatian Academy of Sciences and Arts continued to work on its project of comprehensive Croatian grammar and in 1991 part three was published (Babić et al. 1991). In 1994, after a public hearing, the *Croatian Orthography* was published (authored by Babić, Finka and Moguš). It has been in open public use since then. In 2005, *Hrvatski školski pravopis* [Croatian Orthography for Schools], authored by Babić, Ham and Moguš, was published. The grammatical and spelling norm thus became Croatian at last. Lexicographic activity was not lagging behind either – in 1992 *Razlikovni rječnik srpskog i hrvatskog jezika* [Differential Dictionary between Serbian and Croatian] (Brodnjak 1992) was published; on 600 pages it brought numerous non-Croatian lexemes and offered Croatian lexemes or translations instead of Serbianisms that had been imprinted into Croatian by a century-long pressure of the Serbian language. At last, two monolingual general dictionaries, the first one in 2000 (Šonje ed. 2000) and the second in 2015 (Katičić ed. 2015), filled the century-old void and met the need for a monolingual Croatian dictionary. Prominent Croatian linguists have written histories of the Croatian language that represent the development of Croatian in a credible way from the beginning of literacy to the present (Vince 1990, Moguš 1993, Ham 2006, Auburger 2009, Katičić 2013). The Croatian language was slowly returning to its natural course of development.

Today, Croatia does not have a law on the Croatian language, and there is no government office to look after the Croatian language in public use and advance its standardization. An attempt was made to remedy the situation with the establishment of two councils for the Croatian language standardization. Prominent Croatian linguists from respected Croatian cultural and scientific institutions were members of both councils. Council for the Croatian Standard Language Codification was founded by the Ministry of Science and Technology on March 16, 1998 and it operated until the year 2000 (Editorial Board 2017). The second Council was founded by the Ministry of Science, Education and Sport on April 14, 2005. It was scandalously and aggressively dismissed on May 8, 2012 by a decree, in a manner adversary to democratic procedure: council members received a letter informing them they were disengaged from any further duty, with no explanation or any opportunity for discussion (Katičić and Editorial Board 2013).

Political Shadow Cast over the Croatian Language

Besides the information on the forced dissolution of the Council for the Croatian Standard Language Codification, the author feels obliged to give information about another apparent fact of Croatian society and the young Croatian state that is a strong alignment of political parties with language policies. With no intention to open any discussion about politics, the position of certain political parties regarding the Croatian language should be explained here.

In 1989, in the year of democratic changes in the eve of its independence, new political parties were founded. Hrvatska demokratska zajednica (HDZ) [Croatian Democratic Union] stands out due to its large membership and its mission to be an agent of democratic changes. It won the first democratic elections. During its first electoral mandate, the independent Republic of Croatia was founded. Its member and first president was also the first democratically elected Croatian President Franjo Tuđman. Croats have bestowed their trust on it on several occassions, and HDZ ruled Croatia in several mandates, 22 years in total. All the afore-mentioned important Croatian linguistic works were published when HDZ was in power.

As it turned out, the reformed communist party emerged as the second largest party, by both influence and membership. It changed its name in 1990 from SKJ [League of Communists of Yugoslavia] into Socijaldemokratska partija Hrvatske (SDP) [Social Democratic Party of Croatia], but retained its old communist members and a significant portion of its old ideological values. Unfortunately, it retained its non-affirmative position on the Croatian language as well. The SDP's position is rather close to the unitaristic conception of the Croatian language, although such a position was overcome on the eve of the foundation of the Republic of Croatia. Croats elected SDP twice to rule Croatia; each time SDP came into power, the Croatian language was in a way trampled over (Bašić 2005).

On the first arrival of the SDP to power the Anić and Silić's orthography manual (2001) was introduced again; the manual comprised most of the Novi Sad orthography (1960) rules. It was a first-class publishing ruse of Novi Liber and a return to linguistic unitarism. Namely, Novi Liber was a publishing house that published the last orthography manual of the Croato-Serbian language in 1986 (Anić and Silić 1986); now, in 2001, they published it again under the name Croatian Orthography (Anić and Silić 2001). The same contents got a different title. The manual was promoted as a modern Croatian orthography manual, which "adapts the spelling rules to the actual pronunciation of the modern Croatian spoken language ..." (Anić and Silić 2001). That sentence could have been appealing to the general public, but linguistic experts know that the orthography manual is not written for spoken language but for the written one; therefore, that sentence actually meant a turn back to the Vukovian rule: Write as you speak. (Ham 2001) At that time, the work of the Council for the Croatian Standard Language Codification came to an end as the SDP's Ministry no longer needed their expertise.

The change of government and the re-installation of the HDZ in power in 2003 meant the revitalization of the Croatian language. A new Croatian language council was established that adopted Croatian orthography principles and the recommended spelling manuals were aligned with those principles (Babić, Ham, and Moguš 2012, Babić and Moguš, 2010).

The second coming of the SDP in power was characterized by a markedly destructive actions. The new SDP minister abolished the Council forcibly and without discussion, revoking its decisions. Top Croatian linguists were dismissed and humiliated; the Croatian language was handed over to the then unknown and not established linguist Željko Jozić. He was appointed a director of the Institute of Croatian Language and Linguistics. Complying with SDP wishes, a newly appointed director initiated work on a new *Croatian Orthography Manual* (Jozić ed. 2013). It was presented as a collective work of the Institute's linguists. This orthography manual ignored Croatian spelling tradition and muddled again the Croatian language, its history and its present. The manual was accompanied by an unprecedented media campaign and aggressive advertising. Tensions and resistance against such a treatment rose in public, so that the Ministry did not feel strong enough to approve the orthography manual for school use; the manual has only been recommended. By that, SDP realized one agenda point of the old party program from the year 1985 (See section: Croatian silence)—orthography. The second realized agenda point was cessation of funding for the journal *Jezik*—for the first time in its history *Jezik* did not receive any financial support from the state (Hebrang 2015, 215–232).

Kinship and Differences between the Croatian and Serbian Standard Languages

The Croatian language and the Serbian language are undoubtedly kindred. That cognation was explained long ago (Brozović 1970) and Croats do not deny it. However, the standard languages of Croats and Serbs were taking different paths during history. They are differently stylized. Croatian, along with its tridialectal stylization, has its stylization stronghold in the West Shtokavian lect. Codifying superstructures of the two languages are different. Croats justifiably experience and consider their language to be distinct from Serbian. A century and half long coexistence and language coercion in Croatia did not manage to fuse the Croatian language with Serbian. Papers on the differences between these two languages were publicized whenever political conditions were favorable. The first systematic scientifically-based description of the differences was made by Guberina and Krstić (1940). They described the differences between the two languages at all levels, lexical differences being the richest. Since lexical differences are most conspicuous, the dissimilarity between Croatian and Serbian is best discerned in vocabulary. Brodnjak's differential dictionary (1992) originated from that idea. However, the differences are numerous at other levels as well. The best description of the differences was made by Stjepan Babić (2009), so the differences presented here have been excerpted predominantly from his description. In order to be as precise as possible, we must emphasize here again: the differences we are speaking about are the differences between the two standard languages.

The differences are noticeable even to laymen who are just listening to Croatian and Serbian speakers: Croats speak Yekavian (*svijet*), Serbians Ekavian (*svet*) [world]. A written Serbian text is nowadays unintelligible to the majority of Croats since Serbs use Serbian Cyrillic, a script that is not taught any more in Croatian schools. (The exception is, of course, the curriculum of the minority schools; namely, Serbian is a minority language in Croatia. As such, it has all minority rights as all other minority languages. Cyrillic was compulsorily taught in former Yugoslavia. Serbs, on the other hand, nowadays use the Latin script as well).

Common, nonexpert comprehension of the differences between the two languages is usully reduced to *shtakanje* and *dakanje*. *Shtakanje* is a popular name that describes the usage of the Serbian relative pronoun *šta* (*nešta*) versus the Croatian *što* (*nešto*) [what]. *Dakanje* is a popular name for the Serbian frequent usage of the clause construction *da*+present tense: *Volim da pišem pesme*, versus the Croatian construction with infinitive: *Volim pisati pjesme*. Naturally, it is not as simple as it might seem if only the presented simple examples are considered. Numerous lexical differences should be added to these simple and easily observable examples. Similarities between two languages may feasibly be estimated at up to 85% of language totality; however, the differences in the rest of 15% of language totality are so great that they may present difficulties in communication (Babić 2008, 184).

A sentence: *I'm going to the market to buy green beans and carrots*, is translated in Serbian as: *Idem na pijacu da kupim boranije i šargarepe*, whereas in Croatian it reads: *Idem na tržnicu kupiti mahune i mrkvu*.

A sentence: *A dozen young men competed for the post of a secretary in a large company* is translated into the Croatian language like: *Desetak mladića konkuriralo je za mjesto tajnika u velikom poduzeću* or *Desetak mladića natjecalo se za mjesto tajnika u velikoj tvrtki*, whereas in Serbian it would be: *Desetak mladića konkurisalo je za mesto sekretara u velikom preduzeću*. (Babić 2008,163).

The train will depart at 11 a.m. is translated in Serbian like: *Voz će da krene u 11 časova*, whereas the Croatian translation will be: *Vlak će krenuti u 11 sati*.

Although Croatian and Serbian are genetically kindred and although both standard languages are Shtokavian, there are systemic differences between them. These differences are not emerging only from cultural superstructures; their origin is rooted in the system. In Table 5 these differences, according to Babić (2008), are presented; however, certain spelling and orthographic differences have been added. The presentation has been simplified, reduced to the most pronounced differences, and adjusted to a wider reading audience.

Table 5. Differences between the Croatian and Serbian standard languages

Language	Croatian standard language	Serbian standard language
Script	Latin (abeceda, Gajica)	Cyrillic (azbuka – азбука)
Orthograpy See Brozović (2005, 41–46) for different orthographic principles.	Phonemic-morphophonemic spelling. Tendency to write words down separately (*pisat ću, ne ću, na žalost, gurnuti pod nos, govoriti u ime*). The principle of writing names (proper nouns) and from them derived adjectives according to the original orthography (*Bleiburg, bleiburški Shakespeare, Shakespeareov*). Orthographic handbooks do not have rules on how to pronounce certain foreign names. Period is always put after the ordinal number (regardless of the following punctuation mark) (*Zar je na cilju 5.?* It reads: *Zar je na cilju peti?*)	Phonemic spelling. Tendency to couple words together when writing (*pisaću, neću, nažalost, gurnuti podnos, govoriti uime*). The principle of writing names (proper nouns) and from them derived adjectives according to the pronunciation (*Blajburg, blajburški; Šekspir, Šekspirov*). Orthographic handbooks have rules on how to pronounce certain foreign names. Period is not put after the ordinal number if any punctuation mark follows (*Zar je na cilju 5*? It reads: *Zar je na cilju pet?*)
Phonemes	Diphthong (*svijet, pjesma*). Yekavian speech, yekavian monosyllabic pronunciation Use of *h* (*hrđav, hrđa; suh*). Distribution of *ć* v. *št* (*opći, općina, sveopći, svećenik*).	Long and short *e* (*svet, pesma*). Ekavian speech. Seldom use of *h* (*rđav, rđa; suv*). Distribution of *št* v. *ć* (*opšti, opština, sveopšti, sveštenik*)
Accent	Proclitic words take over an accent from a pronoun in prepositional phrases (*nà mene, nà tebe, nà sebe*). Accent is short in the genitive plural of masculine gender nouns (*Mnogi brȁkovi završavaju sretno., Sȁtovi su skupi.*). In present tense, the short accent is on the first syllable (*čȉtāmo, čȉtāte*).	No transfer of accents on proclitic words (*na mȅne, na tȅbe, na sȅbe*). Accent is long in the genitive plural of masculine gender nouns (*Mnogi brákovi završavaju sretno., Sátovi su skupi.*). In present tense, the long accent is on the second syllable (*čitámo, čitáte*).
Morphology	Pronoun *što* (*nešto*). In pronouns, *t* is used (*tko, netko, svatko*). Enclitic *ju* (Vidim *ju*), enclitic *si* (Operi *si* ruke). Masculine names finishing in *-o* (*Pajo, Bajo, Cigo*); in declension of masculine names like *Mile, Đorđe* no t is inserted (*Mile, Mili, Milom; Đorđa, Đorđu, Đorđem)*. Use of suffixes *-i* and *-ju* in the instrumental singular of feminine gender nouns: *ljubavi, ljubavlju; radosti, radošću.* Use of the conditional second (*bila bih pisala*).	Pronoun *šta* (*nešta*). No *t* in pronouns (*ko, neko, svako*). Enclitic *je* (Vidim *je*); no enclitic *si* (Operi ruke). Masculine names finishing in *-a* (*Paja, Baja, Ciga*); in declension of masculine names like *Mile, Đorđe* t is inserted (*Mileta, Miletu, Miletom; Đorđeta, Đorđetu, Đorđetom*). Use of suffix *-ju* in the instrumental singular of feminine gender nouns: *ljubavlju; radošću.* The conditional second is not used

Table 5. (Continued)

Language	Croatian standard language	Serbian standard language
Word formation Lexical differences are thoroughly described in two Croatian contemporary prominent differential dictionaries (Brodnjak 1992, Samardžija 2015). Together, they comprise over 50,000 dictionary entries.	Suffixes *-ist* (*biciklist*), *-ni* (*jezični*), *-ski* (*akumulacijski*), *-ica* (*profesorica*), *-telj* (*čitatelj*). Diminutive formation from the nouns denoting sth. inanimate using suffix *-čić* (*lončić, prozorčić*). Words loaned from Latin and Greek without the original suffix (*kurikul, aluminij, atrij, Herkul*). Verb formation using suffix *-irati* (*definirati, regulirati*) Word formation using prefix *su-* (*sučesnik, sučenik*), *protu-* (*protunapad*). Tendency to substitute loanwords (aliens) with the Croatian ones.	Sufixes *-ista* (*biciklista*), *-čki* (*jezički*), *-ioni* (akomulacioni), *-ka* (*profesorka*), *-lac* (*čitalac*). Diminutive formation from the nouns denoting sth. inanimate using suffix *-če* (*lonče, prozorče*). Words loaned from Latin and Greek with the original suffix (*kurikulum, aluminijum, atrijum, Herkulus*) Verb formation using suffix *-isati* (*definisati, regulisati*) Word formation using prefix *sa-* (*saučesnik, saučenik*), *protiv-* (*protivnapad*). Openness to loanwords.
Syntax	The use of infinitive instead of present tense (*Pođimo se prošetati.*) Use of conjunctions *iako, makar, premda* in permissible clauses (*Iako je teško, ipak radim.*). Use of *pošto* in temporal clauses (*Pošto je pao mrak, pošli smo kući.*). Use of prepositions *unatoč, usprkos* with the dative case (*usprkos odluci, unatoč odluci*).	Extensive use of the expression da + present tense (*Pođimo da se prošetamo.*). Use of a conjunction *mada* in permissible clauses (*Mada je teško, ipak radim.*). Use of *pošto* in conditional clauses (*Pošto naučiš, možeš da pođeš u kino.*). Use of prepositions *unatoč, usprkos* with the genitive case (*usprkos odluke, unatoč odluke*).

Maybe several specificities from some other language have crept into this recital of the Croatian language specificities; however, that cannot have any influence on the entirety of specificity. All specificities mentioned so far are interlinked into the whole, into a system; that means that if any of them would be chosen, then all the other will immediately follow together with it because they are all associated by the link *and-and*: so, when one chooses one specificity, he/she inevitably chooses all the other specificities linked with the chosen one; for example if *točan* [punctual], then *općina* [municipality], *kemija* [chemistry], etc. When we first meet with any of the specificities, we are immediately aware that we are dealing with the Croatian language.

When, for example, it is heard in a radio or TV broadcast:

> *Sada je* ***točno*** *pet* ***sati*** [It is five o'clock].,

then a listener knows that he/she is listening to the Croatian language and that he/she will also hear *mlijeko, bilješka, juha, netko, opći, kršten, kemija, Cígo, suučenik, protuotrov, deportirati, siječanj, časnik, glazba, skladatelj, kazalište, sveučilište...*" (Babić 2008, 179). However, if it is heard: *Sada je* ***tačno*** *pet* ***časova***, then the listener knows it is Serbian and he/she will expect *mleko, beleška, supa, neko, opšti, kršćen, hemija, Ciga, saučenik, protivotrov, deportovati, januar, oficir, muzika, kompozitor, pozorište, univerzitet…*

CONCLUSION

The Croatian language was often suppressed and denied during its long history due to the supremacy of various Non-, even Anti-Croatian politics. A political shadow still lingers over it; a better care by the state and more effort invested in its recognition in the world are lacking. It is especially important nowadays when the languages with a smaller number of speakers are subjected to neglect and suppression in the European Union, as evident from the examples described below.

In the year 2013, the year in which Croatia became an EU member state, the Croatian language also became the 24th official language of EU. However, even in the middle of negotiations between Croatia and EU, the following could be read coming from the European Parliament:

> "The European Parliament points out that now, when the original Serbo-Croatian language has been fragmented into several official languages in probable future state candidates from that area; it also emphasizes that interpretation costs have a considerable influence on the budget of European institutions; therefore, the European Commission is called upon to find out, together with the Croatian authorities and before the association process would be completed, an appropriate solution regarding the Croatian language that would not in advance prevent later comprehensive agreement on language with Bosnia and Herzegovina, Montenegro and Serbia, when these states will become EU member states." (https://m.vecernji.hr/vijesti/zeleni-mastaju-o-izvornome-srpsko-hrvatskom-jeziku-82580).

The starting premise is, of course, thoroughly incorrect—Croatian was not born when "the original Serbian language" split; Croatian was independently and under its own name included in the European cultural community several centuries ago.

Let me remind you, dear reader, that the same formal reasons inspired Austrian minister Alexander Bach to summon Croatians, Serbians, and Slovenians to Vienna in order to design the Vienna Agreement on common language in 1850. (See section: Vienna Literary Agreement.)

EU reduced translation services to Croatian, Irish, and Maltese in the beginning of 2019. There are few Croatian translators and not all EU documents are translated into Croatian. Croatia objected strongly to the Croatian language sidelining in the European Parliament at the end of 2019 and demanded equal rights for Croatian: a complete affirmation was demanded for one of the EU acknowledged official languages. Nothing has changed as of this writing.

There is no doubt in Croatia that the Croatian and Serbian languages are genetically kindred, but they are also distinct languages, especially the standard ones. The languages developed in different cultural and political environments and under different conditions. Although the Croatian language was forced into the co-existence with Serbian in two former states (first in the Kingdom of Serbs, Croats and Slovenes that became the Kingdom of Yugoslavia in the period 1918-1941, and later in Tito's Yugoslavia 1945-1991), it managed to preserve its integrity. During times of great threats of disaster, the Croatian people identified themselves with their language; defending and protecting language meant to defend and protect the nation.

Language superstructures of Croatian and Serbian are different. Each standard language has its own phonological inventory, its own features of morphological structure and syntactic characteristics. Lexical differences are, especially in the domain of scientific terminology, insurmountable. Each language is written with its own script and orthography.

Standards achieved in the protection of the Croatian language are inviolable. It is the official language of the Republic of Croatia, as stated in the Croatian Constitution, which came into force on December 22, 1990. Due to the date of its passing, this Constitution is also known as the Christmas Constitution. Mentioning Christmas in relation with the *Constitution* and the *official standard Croatian language* is by no means irrelevant here – on the contrary, during the long Croatian history, Catholicism frequently played the role of a crucial factor in the survival of Croats and their language.

The Croatian contemporary literary language is characterized by the Shtokavian stylization. Shtokavian is one of the three dialects Croats use in their everyday communication. Together with the Shtokavian, there are the Kaykavian and the Chakavian dialects. Shtokavian, being the fundamental stylization of the Croatian literary language, has ages ago surpassed its dialectal framework; nowadays, it is a distinctive koine that Croats have created for centuries. The Shtokavian koine was being created spontaneously from the very beginnings of the Croatian literacy in the Croatian language through the Croatian liturgy and works of the Croatian writers. However, the koine was later in history deliberately created through Croatian grammars and dictionaries. Shtokavian koine is not exclusive—it is open to both the Kaykavian and Chakavian dialects; it is not pure Shtokavian, more often it is a tridialect one. That linguistic fact, which has been a crucial factor in the development of the Croatian language, has legally been protected by the state of Croatia on November 29, 2019 through the act that declared the Croatian dialects as the Croatian protected intangible heritage (Katičić 2014, Štambuk 2016). Thus, the Croatian language has become protected by the law as cultural heritage of the Croatian people and Croats can never again be deprived of their Croatian language.

References and Sources

Anić, Vladimir. 1991. *Rječnik hrvatskoga jezika*. Zagreb: Novi Liber. [*Dictionary of the Croatian language*].

Anić, Vladimir, and Josip Silić. 1986. 1990. *Pravopisni priručnik hrvatskoga ili srpskoga jezika*. Zagreb: Novi Liber. [*Orthographic Handbook of Croatian or Serbian Language*].

Anić, Vladimir, and Josip Silić. 2001. *Pravopis hrvatskoga jezika*. Zagreb: Novi Liber, Školska knjiga. [*Orthography of the Croatian Language*].

Auburger, Leopold. 2011. "O serbokroatističkom degradiranju glotonima hrvatski." *Jezik* 58, no. 1: 1–6. [*About the Serbo-Croatian Degradation of the Glottonym Croatian*].

Auburger, Leopold. 1999. *Die Kroatische Sprache und der Serbokroatismus*. Ulm/Donau: Gerhard Hess Verlag. [*The Croatian Language and Serbo-Croatism*].

Auburger, Leopold. 2009. *Hrvatski jezik i serbokroatizam*. Translated by Nikolina Pašić and Leopold Auburger. Rijeka: Maveda, Hrvatsko filološko društvo. [*The Croatian Language and Serbo-Croatism*].

Babić, Nada. 2018. *Hrvatski prijevodi Novoga zavjeta od 20. st*. Zagreb: Kršćanska sadašnjost. [*Croatian Translations of the New Testament from the 20th Century*].

Babić, Stjepan. 1986. *Tvorba riječi u hrvatskom književnom jeziku*. Zagreb: Hrvatska akademija znanosti i umjetnosti, NZ Globus. [*Word Formation in the Croatian Literary Language*].

Babić, Stjepan. 1990. "Jezik Rituala rimskoga – važna sastavnica u razvoju hrvatskoga književnoga jezika." *Filologija* 18, no. 1: 75–81. ["The Language of the *Ritual rimski* [Roman Rite] – an Important Component of the Development of the Croatian Literary Language"].

Babić, Stjepan. 1990a. *Hrvatski jezik u političkom vrtlogu*. Zagreb: Naklada Pelivan [*The Croatian Language in the Political Vortex*].

Babić, Stjepan, Dalibor Brozović, Milan Moguš, Slavko Pavešić, Ivo Škarić, and Stjepko Težak. 1991. *Povijesni pregled, glasovi i oblici hrvatskoga književnog jezika*. Zagreb: Hrvatska akademija znanosti i umjetsnosti, NZ Globus. [*Historical Overview, Phonetics and Morphology of the Croatian Literary Language*].

Babić, Stjepan. 1992. "Pravo lice Pavla Ivića." *Jezik* 39, no. 3: 96. ["The Real Face of Pavle Ivić."]

Babić, Stjepan, Božidar Finka, and Milan Moguš. 1994. *Hrvatski pravopis*. Zagreb: Školska knjiga. [*Croatian Orthography*].

Babić, Stjepan. 1998. "Sumrak srpske filologije." *Jezik* 46, no. 1: 36–40. ["Twilight of Serbian Philology"].

Babić, Stjepan. 2005. *Temelji hrvatskomu pravopisu*. Zagreb: Školska knjiga. [*The Groundwork of the Croatian Orthography*].

Babić, Stjepan, Sanda Ham, and Milan Moguš. 2012. *Hrvatski školski pravopis*. Zagreb: Školska knjiga. [*Croatian Orthography for Students*].

Babić, Stjepan, Dalibor Brozović, Ivo Škarić, and Stjepko Težak. 2007. *Glasovi i oblici hrvatskoga književnog jezika*. Zagreb: Hrvatska akademija znanosti I umjetnosti, NZ Globus. [*Phonetics and Morphology of the Croatian Literary Language*].

Babić, Stjepan. 2008. "Hrvatski pravopis – vrući kesten u ministarskim rukama." *Jezik* 55, no. 2: 54–64. ["Croatian Orthography – A Hot Potato in Ministerial Hands"].

Babić, Stjepan. 2009. "Hrvatski književni jezik, ponajprije njim samim." *Jezik* 56, no. 5: 161–189. ["Standard Croatian Language Described Primarily by Itself"].

Babić, Stjepan, and Milan Moguš. 2010. *Hrvatski pravops*. Zagreb: Školska knjiga. [*Croatian Orthography*].

Babukić, Vjekoslav. 1836. *Osnova slovnice slavjanske narěčja ilirskoga*. Zagreb. [The Fundamentals of the Slavic Grammar of the Illyrian Language].

Babukić, Vjekoslav. 1854. *Ilirska slovnica*. Zagreb: Tiskarnica Ljudevita Gaja. [*Illyrian Grammar*].

Bagdasarov, Artur R. 2010. *Hrvatski književni jezik*. Rijeka: Maveda. [*The Croatian Literary Language*].

Banac, Ivo. 1991. *Croatian Language Question*. Zagreb: Društvo hrvatskih književnika.

Bašić, Nataša. 2005. "Jezična politika kao razgradnja hrvatskih jezičnih norma." *Jezik* 52, no. 1: 7-21. ["Language Politics as the Deconstruction of the Croatian Language Norms"].

Bašić, Nataša. 2017. "Višečlana imena država u imenima trgova i ulica." *Jezik* 64, no. 5: 194–195. ["Multisegmental Names of States in Square and Street Names"].

Bezina, Petar. 1994. *Kulturni djelatnici franjevačke Provincije Presvetoga otkupitelja u 18. i 19. stoljeću*. Zagreb: Kršćanska sadašnjost. [*Cultural Workers of the Franciscan Province of the Most Holy Redeemer in the 18th and 19th Centuries*].

Bratulić, Josip. 2009. "Hrvatski jezik, hrvatska pisma i hrvatska književost – svjedoci identiteta vremena." In *Povijest hrvatskoga jezika, srednji vijek*, edited by Ante Bičanić, 9-57. Zagreb: Croatica. ["The Croatian Language, Croatian Scripts and Croatian Literature – Witnesses to Time Identity". In *History of the Croatian Language*, Middle Ages].

Brešić, Vinko. 2014. "Časopis 'Neven' i 'Jadranske vile'." *Kronika Zavoda za povijest hrvatske književnosti, kazališta i glazbe Hrvatske akademije znanosti i umjetnosti.* VI, no. 13–15: 7-114. ["The Periodical 'Neven' and 'Jadranske vile'"].

Brodnjak, Vladimir. 1992. *Razlikovni rječnik srpskog i hrvatskog jezika*. Zagreb: Školske novine. [*A Differential Dictionary of the Serbian and Croatian Language*].

Broz, Ivan. 1892. *Hrvatski pravopis*. Zagreb: s.n. [*Croatian Orthography*].

Broz, Ivan, and Franjo Iveković. 1901. *Rječnik hrvatskoga jezika*. Zagreb: Štamparija Karl Albrecht (Jos. Wittasek). [*Dictionary of the Croatian Language*].

Brozović, Dalibor. 1970. *Standardni jezik*. Zagreb: Matica hrvatska. [*Standard Language*].

Brozović, Dalibor. 1985. "Jezična i pravopisna previranja u Hrvatskoj na prijelazu iz 19. u 20. stoljeće." *Jezik* 33, no. 1: 1-15. ["Linguistic and Orthographic Turbulence in Fin-de-Siecle Croatia"].

Brozović, Dalibor. 2005. *Prvo lice jednine*. Zagreb: Matica hrvatska. [*First Person Singular*].

Damjanović, Stjepan. 1995. *Jezik otačaski*. Zagreb: Matica hrvatska. [*The Language of the Fatherland*].

Damjanović, Stjepan. 2009. "Staroslavenski i starohrvatski u hrvatskim srednjovjekovnim tekstovima." In *Povijest hrvatskoga jezika, srednji vijek*, edited by Ante Bičanić, 351–

403. Zagreb: Croatica. ["Old Slavic and Old Croatian in Croatian Medevial Texts". In *History of the Croatian Language, Middle Ages*].

Damjanović, Stjepan, Boris Kuzmić, Milan Mihaljević, and Mateo Žagar. 2009. "Antologija hrvatskih srednjovjekovnih djela." In *Povijest hrvatskoga jezika, srednji vijek*, edited by Ante Bičanić, 357–54. Zagreb: Croatica. ["The Anthology of Medevial Croatian Texts. In History of the Croatian Language in the Middle Ages"].

Daničić, Gjuro. 1850. *Mala srpska gramatika*. Beč: Štamparija Jermenskog manastira. [*Small Serbian Grammar*].

Daničić, Gjuro. 1850. *Oblici srpskoga jezika*. Beograd. [Morphology of the Serbian Language].

"Deklaracija o nazivu i položaju hrvatskoga književnog jezika." *Telegram* 8, no. 359: 1 (March 17, 1967). [The Declaration of the Name and Status of *The Croatian Literary Language*].

Deželić, Stjepan. 1861. *Ivan Kukuljević Sakcinski*. Zagreb: Brzotisak Dragutina Albrechta. [Ivan Kukuljević Sakcinski].

Duda, Bonaventura, and Jure Kaštelan, editors. 1968. *Biblija*. Translated by Antun Sović, Silvije Grubišić, Filibert Gass, and Ljudevit Rupčić. Zagreb: Stvarnost [Bible].

Džamanjić, Rajmund. 1639. *Nauk za dobro pisati latinskijem slovima riječi jezika slovinskoga*. Venecija: Marko Ginammi. [Guidelines How to Spell Well the Slovic Language Words in Latin Letters].

Editorial Board. 2017. "Spisi Vijeća za normu hrvatskoga jezika." *Jezik* 64, no. 2: 60–76. [Records of the Council for the Croatian Standard Language Codification].

Gaj, Ljudevit. 1830. *Kratka osnova horvatsko-slavenskoga pravopisaňa, poleg mudroľubneh, narodneh i prigospodarneh temeľov i zrokov=Kurzer Entwurf einer kroatisch = slavischen Orthographie nach philosophischen, nazionälen und ökonomischen Grundsätzen*. Budim: Tiskara Kralevskog Vseučilišta. [A Concise Basis of the Croatian-Slavic Orthography by the Philosophical, National and Economic Foundations and Samples].

Gaj, Ljudevit. 1835. "Pravopisz." *Danica Horvatzka, Slavonska y Dalmatinska* 1, no. 10–12: 41–43, 12: 46–48. [Orthography].

Gjalski, Ksaver Šandor. "O hrvatskoj kajkavštini." *Obzor* 67, no. 91: 8 (April 3, 1926). [About Croatian Kaykavianism].

Grčević, Mario. 2008. "Poteškoće u priznavanju hrvatskoga jezika u inozemstvu." *Jezik* 55, no. 5: 189–192. [Difficulties in the Recognition of the Croatian Language Abroad].

Grčević, Mario. 2019. *Ime "Hrvat« u etnogenezi južnih Slavena*. Zagreb, Dubrovnik: Hrvatski studiji, Matica hrvatska. [Name 'Croat' in the Ethnogenesis of the South Slavs].

Greenberg, Robert D. 2004. *Language and Identity in the Balkans. Serbo-Croatian and its Disintegration*. New York: Oxford University Press.

Guberina, Petar, and Kruno Krstić. 1940. *Razlike između hrvatskoga i srpskoga književnog jezika*. Zagreb: Matica hrvatska. [Differences Between the Croatian and Serbian Literary Language].

Ham, Sanda. 1988. *Jezik zagrebačke filološke škole*. Osijek: Matica hrvatska. [Zagreb School of Philology].

Ham, Sanda. 2006. *Povijest hrvatskih gramatika*. Zagreb: NZ Globus. [The History of Croatian Grammar Books].

Ham, Sanda. 2006a. "Uloga Narodnih novina u oblikovanju hrvatskoga književnog jezika u 19. st." In *Narodne novine. Zbornik uz 170. obljetnicu neprekinutoga izlaženja 1835-2005*, edited by Ivan Bekavac, 165–179. Zagreb: Narodne novine. [The Role of the National Newspapers in the Formation of the Croatian Language in the 19th Century. In National newspapers. Proceedings Marking the 170th Anniversary of Continuous Publication 1835–2005].

Ham, Sanda. 2011. "I abeceda ima svoju filozofiju." In *Hrvatski bez kompleksa, Jubilarni zbornik posvećen Ernestu Bariću*, edited by Timea Bockovac, 111–118. Pečuh, Mađarska: FF Pečuh. [Alphabet Has its Philosophy Too. In Croatian Without Complex, Jubilee Proceedings Dedicated to Ernest Barić].

Ham, Sanda. 2011. "Kukuljevićev saborski govor iz 1843." In *Ivan Kukuljević Sakcinski*, edited by Tihomil Maštrović, 157–182. Zagreb: Hrvatski studiji [Linguistic Characteristics of Kukuljevic's 1843 Parliamentary Speech. In Ivan Kukuljević Sakcinski].

Ham, Sanda. 2013. "Hrvatske gramatike u 17. i 18. stoljeću." In *Povijest hrvatskoga jezika*, 17. i 18. stoljeće, edited by Ante Bičanić, 371-427. Zagreb: Croatica. [Croatian Grammar Books in the 17th and 18th Century. In History of the Croatian Language, 17th and 18th Century].

Ham, Sanda. 2019. "Natječaj za najbolju novu hrvatsku riječ." *Jezik* 66, no. 4–5: 165–173. [Contest for the Best New Croatian Word].

Hebrang, Ivana, editor. 2015. *Hrvatski znanstveni časopisi*. Zagreb: Školska knjiga. [Croatian Scientific Journals].

Horvat, Vladimir. 2001. "Četiri stoljeća od početka visokoškolske nastave hrvatskog jezika." *Jezik* 48, no. 1: 1–10. [Four Centuries of Teaching of Croatian at the Academic Leve l].

Jagić, Vatroslav. 1948. "Gramatika i stilistika hrvatskoga ili srpskoga književnog jezika. Napisao Dr. T. Maretić, Zagreb, 1899." In *Vatroslav Jagić, Izabrani kraći spisi*, edited by Mihovil Kombol, 532–547. Zagreb: MH. [Grammar and Stylistics of Croatian or Serbian Language. Written by Dr. T. Maretić 1899. Vatroslav Jagić, Selected shorter papers].

Jagić, Vatroslav. 1930. *Spomeni mojega života*. Beograd: Mlada Srbija. [Memories of My Life].

Jembrih, Alojz. 1997. *Na izvorima hrvatske kajkavske književne riječi*. Čakovec: Zrinski. [On the Fountains of the Croatian Kaykavian Literary Words].

Jonke, Ljudevit, editor. 1967. *Rječnik hrvatskosrpskoga književnog jezika*. Zagreb, Novi Sad: Matica hrvatska, Matica Srpska. [Dictionary of the Croatian-Serbian Literary Language].

Jonke, Ljudevit. 1971. *Hrvatski književni jezik 19. i 20. Stoljeća*. Zagreb: Matica hrvatska. [*Croatian Literary Language of the 19th and 20th Centuries*].

Jozić, Željko, ed. 2013. *Hrvatski pravopis*. Zagreb: Institut za hrvatski jezik I jezikoslovlje. [*Croatian Orthography*].

Karadžić, Vuk Stefanović. 1818. *Srpski rječnik*. Beč. [Serbian Dictionary].

Karadžić, Vuk Stefanović. 1849. *Kovčežić za istoriju, jezik i običaje Srba sva tri zakona*. Beč. [A Small Suitcase for the History, Language and Customs of Serbs of all Three Religion].

Kašić, Bartol. 1604. *Institutiones linguae Illyricae libri duo*. Rim. [Fundamentals of the Illyrian Language in Two Books].

Kašić, Bartul. 1999. *Biblia Sacra*, Versio Illyrica Selecta, seu Declaratio Vulgatae Editionis Latinae, Bartholomaei Cassij Curictensis e Societate Iesu Professi, ac Sacerdotis

Theologi. Ex mandato Sacrae Congregataionis de propag: Fide. Anno 1625. Edited by Reinhold Olesch, and Hans Rothe. Paderborn: Ferdinand Schoningh (Biblia Slavica).

Katičić, Radoslav. 1986. *Sintaksa hrvatskoga književnog jezika*. Zagreb: Hrvatska akademija znanosti i umjetnosti, NZ Globus. [Syntax of the Croatian Literary Language].

Katičić, Radoslav. 1987. "Vuk Stefanović Karadžić i književni jezik u Hrvata." *Jezik* 35, no. 2: 38–48. [Vuk Stefanović Karadžić and Croatian Literary Language].

Katičić, Radoslav. 1999. *Na kroatističkim raskrižjima*. Zagreb: Hrvatski studiji. [At the Croatists' Crossroads].

Katičić, Radoslav. 2013. *Hrvatski jezik*. Zagreb: Školska knjiga. [Croatian Language].

Katičić, Radoslav. 2013a. "Hrvatski jezik u 17. i 18. stoljeću obuhvaćen jednim pogledom." In *Povijest hrvatskoga jezika, 17. i 18. stoljeće*, edited by Ante Bičanić, 9-75. Zagreb: Croatica. [A Unifed View of the Croatian Language in the 17th and 18th Century. In History of the Croatian Language in the 17th and 18th Century]..

Katičić, Radoslav. 2014. "Zlatna formula hrvatskoga jezika: ča-kaj-što." *Kolo* 4. [The Golden Formula of the Croatian Language: ča-kaj-što].

Katičić, Radoslav, editor. 2015. *Veliki rječnik hrvatskoga standardnog jezika*. Zagreb: Školska knjiga. [Great Dictionary of the Croatian Standard Language].

Katičić, Radoslav, and Editorial Board. 2013. "Vijeće za normu hrvatskoga standardnog jezika." *Jezik* 60, no. 2–4: 41–160. [The Council for the Croatian Standard Language Codification].

Kordić, Snježana. 2010. *Jezik i nacionalizam*. Zagreb: Durieux [Language and Nationalism].

Kovačec, August. 2006. "Hrvatski jezik i Europa." *Jezik* 53, no. 3: 87–96. [Croatian Language and Europe].

Kovačević, Miloš. 2005. "Sudbina srpskog jezika. Govor Vukovih Srba." *Politika*. March 11, 2005. [The Fate of the Serbian Language. Speech of Vuk's Serbs].

Krasić, Stjepan. 2009. *Počelo je u Rimu*. Zagreb: Matica hrvatska. [It All Started in Rome].

Kratofil, Mirko. 2005. *Politički procesi Vlade Gotovca*. Zagreb: Institut „Vlado Gotovac." [Political Processes against Vlado Gotovac].

Kušan, Dragojlo, and Mirko Šuhaj, editors. 1962. Spisi saborski. Zagreb. [Parliamentary Records].

Majetić, Alojz, editor. 1982. *Polemike u hrvatskoj književnosti*. Kolo I; Knjiga I-IV. Prepared by Ivan Krtalić. Zagreb: Mladost. [Polemics in the Croatian Literature].

Mamić, Mile. 1992. *Temelji hrvatskoga pravnog nazivlja*. Zagreb: Hrvatska sveučilišna naklada. [The Foundations of the Croatian Legal Terminology].

Mamić, Mile. 2007. "Hrvatsko vojno nazivlje u rječniku Juridisch-politische Terminologie." *Jezik* 54, no. 2: 55–60. [Croatian Military Terminology in the Dictionary Juridisch-politische Terminologie].

Maretić, Tomo. 1899, 1931, 1963. *Gramatika i stilistika hrvatskoga ili srpskoga književnog jezika*. [Grammar and Stylistics of the Croatian or Serbian Language].

Maštrović, Tihomil, and Lobel Machala, eds. 2008. *Međunarodno priznanje hrvatskoga jezika*. Zagreb: Nacionalna i sveučilišna knjižnica. [International Recognition of the Croatian language].

Matasović, Ranko. 2009. "Od praslavenskoga do hrvatskoga jezika." In *Povijest hrvatskoga jezika, srednji vijek*, edited by Ante Bičanić, 59–105. Zagreb: Croatica. [From Proto-Slavic to the Croatian Language. History of the Croatian Language, Middle Ages].

Matasović, Ranko. 2019. "Ime Hrvata." *Jezik* 66, no. 3: 81–97. [The Name of Croats].

Mažuranić, Antun, 1839, 1842. *Temelji ilirskoga i latinskoga jezika za početnike*. Zagreb. [The Foundations of the Illyrian and Latin Language for Beginners].

Mažuranić, Antun. 1859, 1861, 1866, 1869. *Slovnica Hèrvatska, Dio I: Rěčoslovje*. Zagreb. [Croatian Grammar, Part 1, Morphology].

Mihaljević, Milan. 2009. "Hrvatski crkvenoslavenski jezik." In *Povijest hrvatskoga jezika, srednji vijek*, edited by Ante Bičanić, 283–349. Zagreb: Croatica. [Croatian Church Slavonic Language. In History of the Croatian Language, Middle Ages].

Moguš, Milan, and Josip Vončina. 1969. "Latinica u Hrvata." *Radovi zavoda za slavensku filologiju* 11: 61–81. [Latin script of Croats].

Moguš, Milan. 1993. *Povijest hrvatskoga književnoga jezika*. Zagreb: NZ Globus. [History of the Croatian Literary Language].

Moguš, Milan. 1978. *Antun Mažuranić*. Zagreb: Zavod za znanost o književnosti, Sveučilišna naklada Liber. [Antun Mažuranić].

Moguš, Milan et al., editors. 2011. *150 HAZU 1861-2011*. Zagreb: Hrvatska akademija znanosti i umjetnosti. [150 HAZU 1861–2011].

Novak, Slobodan Prosperov. 2003. *Povijest hrvatske književnosti*. Zagreb: Golden marketing. [History of the Croatian Literature].

Pavletić, Vlatko, editor. 1969. Hrvatski književni jezik i pitanje varijanata. *Kritika*. Special Issue. [Croatian Literary Language and the Question of Variations].

Pavletić, Vlatko, editor. 1971. Preporod hrvatskih sveučilištaraca. *Kritika*. Special Issue. [Croatian students' Revival].

Pederin, Ivan. 1970. "Pretvorba hrvatskoga iz crkvenog u književni jezik." *Crkva u svijetu* 5, no. 1: 65–71. [Transformation of Croatian from the Liturgical to the Literary Language].

Piškorec, Velimir. 2015. *Tomo Maretić na raskrižju filologije i jezične politike*. Zagreb: Udruga zagrebačkih esperantisa. [Tomo Maretić at the Crossroads of Philology and Linguistic Politics].

Pravopisna komisija [Orthography Commission]. 1960. *Pravopis hrvatskosrpskoga jezika*. Zagreb: Matica hrvatska. [Orthography of the Croatian-Serbian Language].

Radić, Antun. 1937. *Sabrana djela Dra Antuna Radića*. Zagreb: Seljačka sloga. [The Collected Works of Dr. Ante Radić].

Sakcinski, Ivan Kukuljević. 1844. "Govor za uvedenje narodnoga jezika, dàržan od Ivana Kukuljevića Sakc. na saboru kraljevinah Hàrvatske, Slavonie i Dalmacie od 12. Svibnja 1843." *Branislav* 1: 17–19. [Corrigo: U Branislavu je tiskarska pogrješka, piše 12. Svibnja, a treba 2. svibnja.=There is a typo in Branislav, it says May 12th instead of correct May 2nd]. [Speech Advocating for the Introduction of the National language Delivered by Ivan Kukuljević Sakcinski in the Parliament of the Kingdoms of Croatia, Dalmatia and Slavonia, May 12th, 1843].

Samardžija, Marko. 2004. *Iz triju stoljeća hrvatskoga standardnoga jezika*. Zagreb: Hrvatska sveučilišna naklada. [From Three Centuries of the Croatian Standard Language].

Samardžija, Marko. 2008. *Hrvatski jezik, pravopis i jezična politika u Nezavisnoj Državi Hrvatskoj*. Zagreb: Hrvatska sveučilišna naklada. [Croatian Language, Orthography and Language Politics in the Independent State of Croatia].

Samardžija, Marko. 2012. *Hrvatski jezik i pravopis od ujedinjenja do kraja Banovine Hrvatske (1918-1941)*. Zagreb: Školska knjiga. [The Croatian Language and Orthography from the Unification until the end of the Croatian Banovina (1918-1941)].

Samardžija Marko. 2015. *Srpsko-hrvatski objasnidbeni rječnik*. Zagreb: Matica hrvatska. [Serbo-Croatian Explanatory Dictionary].

Selak, Ante. 1992. *Taj hrvatski*. Zagreb: Školske novine. [That Croatian].

Stojanović, Ljubomir. 1924. *Život i rad Vuka Stefanovića Karadžića*. Beograd: BIGZ. [The Life and Work of Vuk Stefanović Karadžić.]

Stolac, Diana. 2006. *Riječki filološki portreti*. Rijeka: Filozofski fakultet. [Portraits of the Philologists of Rijeka].

Šonje, Jure, ed. 2000. *Rječnik hrvatskoga jezika*. Zagreb: Leksikografski zavod, Školska knjiga. [Dictionary of the Croatian Language].

Štebih Golub, Barbara. 2013. "Kajkavski hrvatski književni jezik u 17. i 18. Stoljeću." In *Povijest hrvatskoga jezika*, 17. i 18. stoljeće, edited by Ante Bičanić, 221–461. Zagreb: Croatica. [The Kaykavian Croatian Literary Language in the 17th and 18th Century. In History of the Croatian Language, 17th and 18th Century].

Štambuk, Drago. 2016. *Maslinov vijenac 5*. Zagreb: Croatia Rediviva. [Olive Wreath 5].

Šulek, Bogoslav. 1860. Němačko-hrvatski rěčnik. Zagreb. [German-Croatian Dictionary].

Šulek, Bogoslav. 1874. *Hrvatsko-njemačko-talijanski rječnik znanstvenoga nazivlja*. Zagreb. [Croatian-German-Italian Dictionary of Scientific Terminology].

Šulek, Bogoslav. 1870-1912. *Naredbenik za kraljevsko hrvatsko-ugarsko domobranstvo*. Zagreb. [Service Rules for the Royal Croatian-Hungarian Home-Guard Army].

Šuljić, Anton. 2018. *Zagrebačka Biblija. Uz 50. obljetnicu zagrebačke Biblije*. Zagreb: Kršćanska sadašnjost. [Zagreb Bible. Marking the 50th Anniversary of the Zagreb Bible].

Težak, Stjepko, and Stjepan Babić. 1966, 1969, 1970, 1971, 1972. *Pregled gramatike hrvatskosrpskog jezika za osnovne i druge škole*. Zagreb: Školska knjiga. [An Overview of Grammar of the Croatian-Serbian Language for Elementary and Other Schools].

Težak, Stjepko, and Stjepan Babić. 1973. *Pregled gramatike hrvatskoga književnog jezika*. Zagreb: Školska knjiga [An Overview of the Grammar of the Croatian Literary Language]. In London, a phototypic reprint was published by the New Croatia in 1974; however, a reprint of the London edition was published without the publisher's name, or year and place of the publication.

Težak, Stjepko, and Stjepan Babić. 1992, 1992, 1994, 1995, 1996, 2000, 2003, 2004, 2009. Gramatika hrvatskoga jezika – Priručnik za osnovno jezično obrazovanje. Zagreb: Školska knjiga. [Grammar of the Croatian Language – A Handbook for the Basic Language Education].

Tóth, Teodor, Dragutin Schweitzer, Šandor Pandić, and Mavro Spicer. 1900. Vojnički rječnik. Magjarsko-hrvatski dio. Budimpešta: Pallas. [Military Dictionary. The Hungarian-Croatian Part].

Tutavac, Pero. 1971. *Pravopis hrvatskoga jezika*. Buenos Aires: Naklada Svitlenik. [Orthography of the Croatian Language].

Veber, Adolfo. 1859. Skladnja ilirskoga jezika. Beč. [Syntax of the Illyrian Language].

Veber, Adolfo. 1871, 1873. *Slovnica hèrvatska*. Zagreb. [Grammar of the Croatian Language].

Veber, Adolfo. 1876. *Slovnica hrvatska*. Zagreb. [Grammar of the Croatian Language].

Veber, Adolfo. 1887. *Djela Adolfa Vebera, svezak III*. Zagreb. [Works by Adolf Weber, Volume III].

Vigato, Ivica. 2013. "Čakavski hrvatski književni jezik u 17. i 18. stoljeću." In Povijest hrvatskoga jezika, 17. i 18. stoljeće, edited by Ante Bičanić, 263-297. Zagreb: Croatica.

[The Chakavian Croatian Literary Language in the 17th and 18th Century. In History of the Croatian Language, 17th and 18th Century].

Vince, Zlatko. 1990. *Putovima hrvatskog književnog jezika*. Zagreb: Matica hrvatska. [Along the Paths of the Croatian Language].

Vince, Zlatko. 1998. *Ikavica u hrvatskoj jezičnoj povijesti*. Zagreb: Matica hrvatska. [Ikavian in the Croatian Linguistic History].

Vončina, Josip. 1968. "Ozaljski jezično-književni krug." *Radovi zavoda za slavensku filologiju* 10: 195–205. [The Ozalj Literary and Linguistic Circle].

Vončina, Josip. 1986. "Temelji i putovi Gajeve grafijske reforme." *Filologija* 13, no. 1: 7-88. [The Foundations and Ways of the Orthographic Reform by Gaj].

Vrančić, Faust. 1595. *Rječnik pet najplemenitijih europskih jezika latinskoga, talijanskoga, njemačkoga hrvatskoga i mađarskoga*. Venecija. [Dictionary of the Five Noblest European Languages Latin, Italian, German, Croatian, and Hungarian].

Vukušić, Stjepan, Ivan Zoričić, and Marija Grasselli-Vukušić. 2007. *Naglasak u hrvatskome književnom jeziku*. Zagreb: Hrvatska akademija znanosti i umjetnosti, GZ Globus. [The Accent in the Croatian Literary language].

Vulić, Sanja. 2013. "Štokavski hrvatski književni jezik u 17. stoljeću." In Povijest hrvatskoga jezika, 17. i 18. stoljeće, edited by Ante Bičanić, 95–161. Zagreb: Croatica. [The Štokavian Croatian Literary Language in the 17th Century. In History of the Croatian Language, 17th and 18th Century].

Biographical Sketch

Sanda Ham, PhD

Affiliation: PhD, Full Professor, Faculty of Humanities and Social Sciences, Josip Juraj Strossmayer University of Osijek, Osijek, Croatia

Education: Finished her elementary and grammar school education in Osijek where she graduated from the Faculty of Education Sciences, Department of the Croatian Language and Literature in 1982. Attained her Master of Science and Philosophy Doctor degrees in the field of linguistics (Croatistics) at the Faculty of Humanities and Social Sciences, University of Zagreb and in 1988 defended her MSc thesis: *Pasivna rečenica u suvremenom hrvatskom književnom jeziku*, [Passive Clause in the Croatian Contemporary Literary Language], supervisor Prof. S. Babić, PhD, and co-supervisor Prof. Jasna Melvineger, PhD; in 1994 defended her PhD thesis: *Jezik Josipa Kozarca, sklonidbeni sustav* [Language of Josip Kozarac, Declension System], supervisor Prof. S. Babić, PhD).

Speaks English and Russian; passive knowledge of German (B1).

Business Address:

Faculty of Humanities and Social Sciences, Jagerova 9, 31 000 Osijek, Croatia
Phone +385-31-211-263 sanda.ham@gmail.com

Research and Professional Experience:

- Started her professional research and scholarly career in 1983 as a research and teaching Assistant appointed to the university course Croatian Contemporary Literary Language at the Department of the Croatian Language and Literature of the Faculty of Education Sciences in Osijek, Croatia (nowadays it is the Faculty of Humanities and Social Sciences, Josip Juraj Strossmayer University of Osijek, Croatia).
- Research and Scholarly advancements: appointed Assistant Professor in 1997, Associate Professor in 2000, Full Professor in 2005. Since 2009 Tenured Full Professor.

Graduate University Program Courses:

- At her resident faculty lectures in: *Hrvatska morfologija* [Croatian Morphology], *Hrvatska sintaksa* [Croatian Syntax], *Hrvatski jezik u 19. st.* [Croatian Language in 19th Century]
- At the University of Zagreb Croatian Studies for nine years lectures in *Jezik hrvatske književnosti 19. i 20. st.* [Language of the 19th and 20th Century Croatian Literature]

Academy Graduate Program Courses:

- At the Academy of Teacher Education in Slavonski Brod for seven years lectures in *Hrvatski jezik i jezična kultura* [Croatian Language and Language Culture]
- At the Academy of Teacher Education in Osijek lectures in *Hrvatski jezik i jezična kultura* [Croatian Language and Language Culture]
- At the Academy of Vukovar gave lectures in *Hrvatski jezik i jezična kultura* [Croatian Language and Language Culture]
- At the University of Mostar Faculty of Education Sciences lectured in *Hrvatski jezik* [Croatian Language] in academic years 1997/1998 and 1998/1999
- Visiting professor at the University of Budapest in 1999.

Post-Graduate University Program Courses (PhD Programs):

- At the University of Zagreb Faculty of Humanities and Social Sciences lectured in *Hrvatski književni jezik u doba realizma* [Croatian Literary Language in Realism] in 2000 and 2002
- At the J.J. Strossmayer University of Osijek Faculty of Humanities and Social Sciences lectures in *Jezik zagrebačke filološke škole* [Language of the Zagreb philology School]
- At the University of Zagreb Croatian Studies lectures in *Jezik hrvatske književnosti 19. i 20. st.* [Language of the 19th and 20th Century Croatian Literature]

Research Projects:

- A researcher in the projects: *Hrvatska leksikologija i frazeologija* [Croatian Lexicology and Phraseology] (1990–2003), and *Gramatizacija u suvremenom hrvatskom standardnom jeziku* [Grammatization in the Croatian Contemporary Standard Language] from 2003 to 2006.

Editorships:

- *Jezik:* Editor-in-Chief since 2004; an Editorial Board member since 1996
- Editor: Language Library of Matica hrvatska; Department of the Croatian Language with the Osijek Branch of Matica hrvatska (2004–2010); Language Phone, language counselling service
- Editorial Board member: *Strani jezici*, *Jezikoslovlje* (in a two-year mandate)
- Publishes in Croatian and international scientific proceeding, and in the following journals: *Jezik* (Zagreb), *Filologija* (Zagreb), *Književna revija* (Osijek), *Jezikoslovlje* (Osijek), *Kolo* (Varaždin), *Fluminensia* (Rijeka), *Dometi* (Rijeka), *Riječ* (Rijeka), *Riječ* (Budapest).
- Has participated in more than 30 national and international scientific meetings; has delivered numerous invited lectures on codification issues of contemporary language in Croatia, Hungary, Poland, and Bosnia and Herzegovina.

Professional Appointments:

Presidencies

- Department of Croatian language and Literature of the Faculty of Education Sciences in Osijek (1995–1997)
- Chair of Croatian Language of the Faculty of Education Sciences in Osijek (1999–2001)
- Matica hrvatska Osijek, Department of Croatian Language (2004–2010)
- City of Osijek, Cultural Council (2006–2009)
- National Commission, XI. National Competition in the Croatian Language Proficiency (2006–2007)
- Chair of Croatian Contemporary Language of the Faculty of Humanities and Social Sciences in Osijek (2007–2009)
- Governing Council of the Institute of Croatian Language and Linguistics (2016–2017)

Memberships

- Council of the Croatian Literary Language Codification with the Ministry of Science (1998–2000)
- National Commission, IX. National Competition in the Croatian Language Proficiency (2003–2004)
- City of Osijek, Book and Publishing Committee (2006–2009)
- Expert Work Group for National Exams with the National Center for External Evaluation of Education (2007–2008)
- Humanities Scientific Field Committee—field Philology (2009–2013)

- Evaluation Committee of the Croatian Foundation for Science, Higher Education and technological Development (2009)
- Croatian Academy of Sciences and Arts (HAZU), Scientific Council for Education (2016–2018)
- Work-Groups of the HAZU Scientific Council for Education for the Croatian language: (a) for the restitution of the Council for the Croatian Standard language Codification; (b) for the Croatian language teaching (2017–2018)

Honors:
University of Mostar Letter of Gratitude (1998)
Charter of the Vukovar-Srijem County (2010)

Publications from the Last 3 Years:

1. *Školska gramatika hrvatskoga jezika.* 5th revised edition. 2017. Zagreb: Školska knjiga. [*School Grammar of the Croatian Language*]
2. "Hrvatski jezikoslovci u Povjesti književnosti hrvatske i srpske Đure Šurmina." 2017. *Zbornik o Đuri Šurminu, Zbornik radova znanstvenoga skupa Zagreb – Varaždin – Čazma, April 21st and 22nd 2016.*, edited by Tihomil Maštrović, 255-270. Zagreb: Hrvatski studiji. ["Croatian Grammatists in Đuro Šurmin's History of Croatian and Serbian Literature"].
3. "Morfo(no)loška obilježja imena i prezimena u hrvatskom književnom jeziku." 2018. *U jezik uronjeni Zbornik posvećen Ireni Vodopiji,* edited by Dubravka Smajić, Irena Krumes and Nina Mance, 237-256. Osijek: Fakultet za odgojne i obrazovne znanosti, ["Morpho(no)logical Characteristics of Names and Surnames in Standard Croatian Language". *A collection dedicated to Irena Vodopija immersed in language*].
4. "O nekim nejasnoćama oko Škarićeva Prijevoda Svetoga pisma." 2018. *Jezik* 65, no. 4-5: 121-134. ["On Some Ambiguities Relating to Škarić's Translation of the Holy Script"].
5. "Natječaj za najbolju novu hrvatsku riječ." 2019. *Jezik* 66, no. 4-5: 165-173. ["Contest for the Best New Croatian Word"].
6. "Radoslav Katičić i časopis Kritika." 2019. *Kolo* 4: 250-260. ["Radoslav Katicic and the Journal Kritika."]

In: Croatia: Past, Present and Future Perspectives
Editor: Matko Marušić
ISBN: 978-1-53618-300-9

Chapter 3

THE CROATIAN QUESTION IN AUSTRIA-HUNGARY AT THE BEGINNING OF THE TWENTIETH CENTURY: BETWEEN FEDERALISM AND TRIALISM

Željko Holjevac**[*]**
Ivo Pilar Institute of Social Sciences, Zagreb, Croatia

ABSTRACT

This chapter presents the Croatian question in Austria-Hungary at the beginning of the twentieth century between federalism and trialism. The author deals with Aurel C. Popovici's political study of the United States of Greater Austria and the contributions of some Croatian intellectuals such as Nikola Zvonimir Bjelovučić about the Croatian state in the Trialist or Federalist Monarchy. Federalism and trialism as concepts for the reorganization of Austria-Hungary resulted from the demands of the time and the activities of engaged intellectuals. Their insights stemmed from their interest in politics, but their hopes for change failed due to conflict with efforts to preserve the existing structure of dualism. Although the Yugoslav idea at that time was by no means the only answer to the Croatian question, it triumphed as a result of the dissolution of Austria-Hungary and the creation of the Yugoslav state at the end of the World War I.

Keywords: Austria-Hungary, Croatia; Austria-Hungary, federalism; Austria-Hungary, trialism; Bjelovučić, Nikola Zvonimir; Greater Austria; Popovici, Aurel C.

INTRODUCTION

The Austro-Hungarian Compromise of 1867 provided that the lands of the Hungarian crown on one hand and other Habsburg hereditary and crown provinces on the other were two separate Central European states in a multinational empire called Austria-Hungary (see Kann 1964). The medieval Kingdom of Croatia, from the twelfth century in the state union with the

[*] Corresponding Author's Email: Zeljko.Holjevac@pilar.hr.

Kingdom of Hungary, was divided in the sixteenth century between the Habsburg Monarchy, the Ottoman Empire, and the Venetian Republic. After the Austro-Hungarian Compromise of 1867, the Triune Kingdom of Croatia, Slavonia, and Dalmatia, which existed since the Napoleonic Wars only in the Habsburg Monarchy, was divided between the lands of the Hungarian crown (Croatia and Slavonia) and other Habsburg territories (Istria and Dalmatia) represented in the Imperial Council in Vienna. The Croatian-Hungarian Compromise which followed in 1868 regulated the position of Croatia and Slavonia as an autonomous state within the Hungarian half of Austria-Hungary with authority in judiciary, education, internal administration, and religious affairs. Habsburg dualism was a compromise not only for the emperor and king Franz Joseph I, who gave up absolutism and became a constitutional monarch, but also for the Hungarian elite, who abandoned the idea of full state independence in order to gain political parity in the dual state of a reorganized Habsburg Monarchy. In 1871, a Croatian law journal stated the following: "The Habsburg Monarchy, by its constitution today, is neither a unitary state nor a federal state or an alliance of states; neither is it organized on the basis of the principle of nationality nor is it strictly constitutional or strictly absolutist" (Holjevac 2018, 62). Even though there was some progress in the period of dualism (for example, the opening of the University of Zagreb, initial development of tourism etc.) the economic conditions worsened and a significant number of Croatians emigrated to the United States of America and other overseas countries in search of better living conditions. In the era of the formation of modern nations and the creation of national states, Austria-Hungary was not a national state of any nation that lived in that dual state. Dualism also remained a key obstacle to the political unification of Croatian regions and territorial integration of the Croatian nation.

The United States of Greater Austria

The influence of politicians who opposed the dualism increased in Hungary at the beginning of the twentieth century. They were seeking independent customs, trade and foreign policy as well as an independent Hungarian army. At the same time, in Austria, a circle of people gathered around the heir to the Habsburg throne, Archduke Franz Ferdinand (Gross 1970, 9-72). The Archduke wished to weaken Austro-Hungarian dualism and strengthen Austrian domination in Austria-Hungary. In 1905, Croatian politicians demanded independent political, cultural, financial, and economic survival and progress. At the same time, Serbian politicians in Croatia demanded that the equality of the Serbian minority in Croatia with the Croatian nation must be recognized (Cipek and Matković 2006, 495-498). In 1906, in search of a solution to the national question and the state crisis as central problems in Austria-Hungary, Aurel C. Popovici, a Romanian politician from Transylvania, published a political study in Leipzig entitled *Die Vereinigten Staaten von Groß-Österreich* (The United States of Greater Austria) (Karpowicz-Toševa 1994, 65-80). Popovici proposed the transformation of the Habsburg state into a federal union of 15 national states with autonomous enclaves as a possible form of state for the Habsburg Empire.

According to Popovici's vision of a federal organization, the entire Austro-Hungarian state area, with the exception of Bosnia and Herzegovina, would be divided into the following national-political entities: (1) German Austria, (2) German Bohemia, (3) German Moravia

(Silesia), (4) Bohemia, (5) Hungary, (6) Transylvania, (7) Croatia, (8) Western Galicia, (9) Eastern Galicia, (10) Slovakia, (11) Carniola, (12) Vojvodina, (13) Székely Land, (14) Trento, and (15) Trieste. These fifteen national states would together form a monarchist federal state under the name "The United States of Greater Austria" and under the crown of the emperor Franz Joseph I. Every citizen of a national state would also be an Austrian citizen. No one would be able to practice political rights in more than one national state. The United States of Greater Austria would form a common customs territory (Popovici 1906, 317-318).

This federal empire would practice the right of legislation, law enforcement and justice according to a unified constitution for its entire territory. The authority of the federal empire and its organs would extend to the issues common to all member states of the federation: (1) the state budget for the crown; (2) all foreign affairs including the representation vis-à-vis foreign countries as well as the necessary decrees in relation to international contracts; (3) a single army and navy with a legislation governing recruiting as well as the manner in which military service would be performed including ordinances relating to the deployment and provision of the army and navy; (4) customs legislation; (5) legislation regarding all civil law, criminal law, and judicial proceedings; (6) legislation and administration of an empire-wide railroad network including the lines necessary to defend the empire; (7) provisions regarding citizenship and permanent residence; (8) legislation regarding maritime law, commercial law, and promissory note law; (9) issuance of passports, and medical and veterinary policies; (10) determination of the coinage and the money; (11) measurement and weight system; (12) hallmark, trademark, and design protection including invention patents; (13) jurisdiction over the legal disputes in the areas listed above (14) the administration of Bosnia and Herzegovina; and (15) finance including federal revenue and expenditures. The federal imperial government would be composed of representatives of the national states. It would be headed by the imperial chancellor appointed by the emperor. The federal imperial parliament would consist of the House of Deputies and the House of Nobles (Popovici 1906, 318-319).

The legislative power of the federal empire would be jointly exercised by the emperor, the House of Deputies, and the House of Nobles. The House of Deputies would be formed by the deputies elected from the entire people of the empire or federation in general, direct and secret elections. Members of the House of Nobles would be adult princes of the imperial house by birth. Members of this house by right would be archbishops and bishops of various churches, rectors of various universities, heads of various academies of science, and heads of chambers of commerce and crafts from the provincial capitals. Members of the House of Nobles by election from each state would be from each of the classes of doctors, lawyers, engineers, architects, bank directors, farmers, middle and elementary school teachers, civil servants, and the class of the press, each of whom would send one representative to the House of Nobles for a period of five years. The emperor would have the right to appoint members to the House of Nobles for life from the men in the national states who had distinguished themselves through their contribution to the state or church, to science, army, navy, trade and industry or art, etc. The House of Deputies and the House of Nobles would meet in Vienna (Popovici 1906, 319-320).

The emperor would exercise the executive power of the federal empire together with the imperial government. The governments of the national states would send their authorized representatives to the imperial government according to the following voting ratios: German Austria 7, Hungary 7, Bohemia 5, Transylvania 4, Croatia 3, Western Galicia 3, Eastern

Galicia 3, German Bohemia 2, Slovakia 2, German Moravia (Silesia) 1, Carniola 1, Vojvodina 1, Trento 1, Trieste 1, and Székely Land 1, or a total of 42 votes. The government would form the following committees from its members: (1) home affairs, (2) foreign affairs, (3) army and navy, (4) finance, and (5) administration of Bosnia and Herzegovina. At least three national states would be represented in each of these committees. Each state would have one vote within each committee (Popovici 1906, 320-321).

The person of the emperor would be sanctified, inviolable, and not answerable to any authority. He would exercise his authority through the government and its subordinate officials. Responsibility for the imperial government would rest with the chancellor of the same. The emperor would appoint and dismiss the chancellor of the imperial government as well as staff all offices in all branches of the imperial service at the request of the chancellor of the government, unless the law would provide otherwise. The emperor would appoint the governors of the individual national states and their senior officials. He would award titles, medals, and other state awards. The emperor would exercise supreme command over the armed forces. He would conclude international treaties as well as authenticate and receive emissaries. The consent of both houses, the House of Deputies and the House of Nobles, would be obligatory for the validity of the commercial and those major contracts which would burden the empire or parts thereof or which would oblige individual citizens of the same. The emperor would have power to coin money. Laws would be published on behalf of the emperor, relying on the approval of the constitutional representatives and signed by the chancellor of the imperial government or the relevant governor. The emperor would represent the whole empire under international law. He would have the right, with the consent of the imperial government, to declare war on behalf of the empire, and to make peace. The emperor would call, open, adjourn and close the House of the Deputies and the House of Nobles. Both legislative bodies would have to be convened at least once a year (Popovici 1906, 322-323).

An imperial supreme court would be established, which would have to decide regarding the following matters: (1) legal disputes in which the empire was a party; (2) legal disputes between individual national states, between these and the empire, between one national state and the citizens or corporations of another, and between the citizens of different national states; (3) charges against imperial officials; (4) treason against the security of the empire; (5) insults and acts of violence against the imperial authorities; (6) crimes and offenses against international laws; and (7) acts of the press against the dynasty, the empire and its organs (Popovici 1906, 323-324).

All matters that would not be expressly reserved for the competence of the empire would belong to the competence of the individual national states. A parliament, a national government and judicial system would be established in each national state. For each national state, the emperor would appoint an imperial governor to head the government. The governor had to be a citizen of the concerned national state. The emperor would appoint the members of the government of the national state at the suggestion of the governor. Every national state would enact its own constitution subject to the approval of the empire (Popovici 1906, 324).

Every national state would determine its own language. The international language of communication within the federal empire would be German. As such, it would be the official language of all imperial authorities residing in Vienna, the imperial government, parliament, the army and the navy, and it would be the official language between the individual national states on one hand as well as between them and the empire on the other. In the imperial parliament, however, each member could also use its own language. All imperial authorities, except the military ones, would officiate in the national language of the concerned national state. For this reason, every federal official had to provide evidence that he completely mastered both the national language of his state and the German language. All laws, ordinances, and announcements of the imperial authorities would be required to be written and published not only in German as the international language of communication within the empire but also in the national language of the respective state. All inscriptions from the side of the imperial authorities, including the military ones, could only be written in the national language of the respective state. All national languages had to be used equally on the coins and banknotes (Popovici 1906, 325-326).

Austria – Hungary – Croatia

Popovici deliberately borrowed many provisions almost literally from the Austrian December Constitution of 1867 as well as from the constitution of the German Empire from 1871 in order to reduce any fear of change (Popovici 1906, 322). But his federalist proposal to resolve the national question and the crisis of dualism in Austria-Hungary did not gain any wider support. Therefore, at the beginning of the twentieth century, there were more and more Croats who had come to believe that the Croatian question could not be resolved in Austria-Hungary and that the Triune Kingdom of Croatia, Slavonia, and Dalmatia should seek its future outside the Habsburg Empire, above all in unity with Serbs and the rest of the Southern Slavs (Holjevac 2018, 65). The ultimate aim of the efforts around the Croatian-Serbian unity was to create an "independent and free, national and state union of Yugoslavia," as envisioned by the National Party in Croatia in 1874 (Korunić 1989, 245-247). At the same time, some of Archduke Franz Ferdinand's plans for reforms, although he was rather enigmatic about them (Hannig 2013, 99-104, 236-243), raised hopes among many individuals for the overthrow of dualism and the transformation of the Habsburg Empire into a triple state. The third state would be Croatian or South Slavic with a nucleus in Croatia and Slavonia as the only Slavic country that enjoyed a degree of political autonomy in Austria-Hungary.

So, the Croatian Party of Rights, having in mind the Croatian state law and national principle, promoted by all legal means the idea of unification of the Croatian people living in Croatia, Slavonia and Dalmatia, Rijeka and Međimurje, as well as in Bosnia and Herzegovina and Istria, into an independent state within Austria-Hungary. It also supported the efforts of Slovenes to join the Slovene territories to that state. The Croatian Party of Rights also tried to affirm the Kingdom of Croatia as a constitutional state with the rule of law, in which the people, through its representatives in all branches of life, would freely exercise in the Croatian Parliament legislative power in agreement with the crown. It considered that the Croatian viceroy should be at the head of the parliamentary government and that the Kingdom of Croatia should participate in the joint affairs of the whole monarchy on an equal basis with the Kingdom of Hungary and other Habsburg provinces. The Croatian Party of Rights worked to ensure that the constitution, freedom, and legal independence of the Kingdom of Croatia were enshrined and guaranteed by all legitimate guarantees, in particular by free election rules, the right to assemble and meet, as well as freedom of conscience, speech, and the press (Cipek and Matković 2006, 540-541).

In 1911, a Croatian historian, N. Kovačević, published in Zagreb a brochure entitled *Put do trijalizma* (The Road to Trialism). The author claimed that permanent peace with the Hungarians is not possible because of their aspirations as well as the turbulent relations between the Austrian and Hungarian parts of Austria-Hungary. He saw trialism between Austria, Hungary, and Croatia as the only way out of this situation. Kovačević was convinced that there was a possibility of sympathy from the crown and the Austrian half of Austria-Hungary for trialist solution. He claimed that the interests of Croatians and the Habsburgs were alike (Holjevac 2018, 65). The author criticized some Croatian parties, attributing to them excessive aspirations combined with an unrealistic understanding of the historical development of Austria-Hungary and an anachronistic fear of Austria, a negation of the existence of Serbs in Croatia, as well as other unenforceable programs. Kovačević believed that the trialist program would be as profitable for the Monarchy as for Croatia. According to him, the only connection between three sides (Austria, Hungary and Croatia) would be "a common army, a joint representation abroad, a single customs area, and the same money" (Kovačević 1911, 33).

In 1911, a Croatian historian and writer, Nikola Zvonimir Bjelovučić, published in Dubrovnik a study entitled *Trializam i hrvatska država* (Trialism and the Croatian State). According to him, the Croatian state would extend from Trieste to Zemun near Belgrade. It would cover not only the Triune Kingdom of Croatia, Slavonia, and Dalmatia, including Međimurje and Rijeka, but also new territories of Istria, Trieste and Gorizia (both today in Italy), Carniola (today in Slovenia), southern (Slovenian) Styria, southern (Slovenian) Carinthia, Syrmia (today in Serbia), as well as Bosnia and Herzegovina. The imagined Croatian state from Trieste to Zemun would be called the "Kingdom of Croatia" (Holjevac 2018, 66). It would be divided into 25 counties, of which the County of Trieste would have autonomous status. The Croatian Parliament and the Croatian Government in Zagreb would be in charge of all the mentioned territories and would be an equal member of the imperial triad as the Austrian provinces of the imperial crown and the Hungarian lands of St. Stephen's Crown. The right to rule this Croatian state would belong to the Habsburg dynasty.

In his study Bjelovučić wrote that joint affairs of the imagined Austrian-Hungarian-Croatian Monarchy (with the Latin abbreviation A-H-C) would be the joint Naval Ministry in Pula, the joint Ministry of the Army, the joint Foreign Ministry, and three parliamentary delegations that would discuss and decide on common affairs. Special branches of the Croatian Government headed by the viceroy would be the Ministry of the Interior, the Ministry of Finance, the Ministry of Justice, the Ministry of Commerce, and the Croatian Colonies (actually the Croatian emigration abroad), the Ministry of Agriculture, the Ministry of Home Guard, the Ministry of Railways and Transport, as well as the Ministry of Education. There would be the Croatian citizenship, the Croatian political nation, the Croatian national flag, the Croatian national coat of arms, and the Croatian nobility. Autonomous municipalities would have their own flags and individual counties would have their own coats of arms. The official language would be Croatian, and the names of towns and villages would be written in Croatian. There would be Croatian banknotes and coins, Croatian marks, and Croatian colonies, i.e., the Croatian emigration. The higher educational institutions would be the Franz Joseph I University of Zagreb, the University of Trieste, the University of Sarajevo, the Technical College in Zagreb, and the Veterinary School in Zagreb. High schools would be trade academies, maritime schools, lower trade schools, real high schools, mining and agricultural schools. The lower schools would be crafts, vocational, fishing, and elementary schools. There would also be private schools. The Catholic Church would have both the Slavic-Catholic rite in Old Slavic language and Glagolitic script as well as the Roman Catholic rite in Latin language and script. The Serbian Orthodox Church would have its ecclesiastical council in Srijemski Karlovci, while the Muslim religion would have its confessional assembly in Sarajevo. A new Croatian Orthodox Church was also planned, while Protestants and Jews would practice their religion in the Croatian language (Bjelovučić 1911, 3-20).

In 1912, the Croatian author and poet Miho Jerinić published a booklet in the German language entitled *Selbständiger Südslavischer Armeebereich* (The Independent South-Slavic Military Area), which was printed in Vienna and devoted to the imagined separate military area for the South Slavs in Austria-Hungary. "They wish to follow their own flags, their own generals and their own officers and then they will storm from victory to victory for their own king, for their own country and for the emperor and the empire," wrote the author (M. Jerinić 1912, 27).

In the summer of 1912, a magazine entitled *Trializam* (Trialism) was published in Trieste. The magazine was writing in favor of the need for cooperation of Croatian, Slovenian, and Serbian representatives in the struggle for trialism in Austria-Hungary. "We southern Slavs, infected with the flames of independence of the homeland under the ruling house, must dance together, and inspired by that ideal celebrate the victory" was the motto of the magazine (Holjevac 2018, 68). Indeed, on 20 October 1912, some Slovene Catholic populists and delegates of temporarily united parties of rights from Croatia, Slavonia, Dalmatia, Istria, and Bosnia and Herzegovina met at the "first Croatian-Slovenian assembly" in Ljubljana, which was an important manifestation of the trialist dreams (Rahten 2008, 161-169). "We want what all true Croats want, we want a great and united Christian Croatia that will be fair to all religions and in which all Croatian and Slovenian countries will be represented," proclaimed some supporters of the Croatian Catholic movement (Cipek and Matković 2006, 663). However, the alternative program of the National Party in Croatia from 1874 for the unification of the South Slavs and the creation of the Yugoslav state became more popular in the wider Croatian public, evolving from social solidarity and cultural cooperation to radical unitarity in political terms under the influence of the sudden military successes of Serbs and Montenegrins in the Balkan wars (1912-1913) (Despot 2013, 260-268). "Our goal is to create a young, modern, free-thinking, revolutionary Yugoslavia in our Croatian and Serbian regions," claimed those Croatian and Serbian young people who shared the belief that Croats and Serbs were one nation with two equal names (Cipek and Matković 2006, 647).

In 1913, the previously mentioned Nikola Zvonimir Bjelovučić published a pamphlet in Dubrovnik entitled *Federalistička Monarhija i hrvatsko pitanje* (The Federalist Monarchy and the Croatian Question). Having in mind the many different nations of Austria-Hungary, he proposed that dualism should be replaced by federalism based on the internal division of the Monarchy into seven political units: (1) German-Austrian countries, (2) Czech countries, (3) Polish countries, (4) Ukraine, (5) Romanian-Austrian countries, (6) Hungary, and (7) Croatia. According to him, the Kingdom of Croatia would have to be created through unification of the Kingdom of Croatia with Dalmatia, Rijeka, Međimurje, Vojvodina, Bosnia and Herzegovina, as well as Istria. Slovenia, consisting of Carniola, the Slovenian part of Styria, the Slovenian part of Carinthia, Gorizia and Trieste, would have to be annexed to the Kingdom of Croatia. Croats, Serbs and Slovenes would use their language, and the same right would be granted to the Italians in Trieste. "The Kingdom of Croatia and all its separate parts shall fight by all lawful means for their unification," wrote the author (Bjelovučić 1913, 15).

A couple of years before World War I, imagining "our Empire as a federal state," the Croatian politician Stjepan Radić wrote: "Dualism weakens our Empire, and the Slavs, especially the Croats, being just ruined" (Radić [1910], 2-5). However, Austria-Hungary entered the Great War without any kind of reform that would resolve the national question and the state crisis. In the bloody vortex of World War I, on 30 May 1917, Croatian representatives from Dalmatia and Istria together with Slovenian representatives created the Yugoslav Club in the Imperial Council in Vienna and issued the Declaration pleading for the unification of all Slovenes, Croats and Serbs in Austria-Hungary on the basis of the "national principle and the Croatian state law" under the Habsburg crown (Šišić 1920, 94). Despite the fact that this Declaration was not a negation of Croatian statehood such as another Declaration signed on 20 July 1917 by representatives of the Yugoslav Committee and the Council of Ministers of the Kingdom of Serbia in exile on the Greek island of Corfu, it was seen by the Croatian Party of Rights rather as a step towards the Yugoslav state than as an attempt to introduce trialism in Austria-Hungary (Matijević 2016, 79-106).

Going into the opposite direction, the Croatian lawyer and author Ivo Pilar (alias L. v. Südland) published a book in early 1918 in the German language entitled *Die südslawische Frage und der Weltkrieg* (The South Slavic Question and the World War) in Vienna. After analysing the history of Slavs in the Balkans, the creation of Croatian, Serbian, and Bosnian states, as well as comparing Catholicism and Eastern Orthodoxy, Pilar found that the essence of the South Slavic problem was precisely in the efforts to achieve Croatian-Serbian unity. He believed that the idea of the Greater Serbia rather than the idea of the Yugoslav state was the authentic guiding force of Serbian state policy. After US President Thomas Woodrow Wilson had proclaimed in January 1918 that "the peoples of Austria-Hungary, whose place among the nations we wish to see safeguarded and assured, should be accorded freest opportunity of autonomous development" (Šišić 1920, 111), Pilar proposed as the very urgent solution for the South Slavic question the unification of Croatia, Slavonia, and Dalmatia with Bosnia and Herzegovina into a Croatian state within Austria-Hungary: "We must begin our remarks with the categorical assertion that the Monarchy, if it maintains its previous southern policy, must inevitably and irretrievably lose the South Slavic provinces" (Südland 1918, 717).

At the top of the dual monarchy for a long time there was no will to do anything, so the new emperor Karl I embraced change of the political system only in the waning days of the empire. In the end, on 6 October 1918, the National Council of Slovenes, Croats and Serbs was established in Zagreb. Two days later, the Croatian-Serbian Coalition, which had a majority in the Croatian Parliament of that time, joined the National Council. On 19 October 1918, the National Council proclaimed itself a political representative of the South Slavs in Austria-Hungary and called for their unification into a single and fully sovereign state. On 21 and 22 October 1918, a group of politicians from the oppositional Croatian Party of Rights received the consent of the Emperor Karl I in Vienna and the Hungarian Government in Budapest to proclaim the trialist Austro-Hungarian-Croatian Monarchy under the Habsburg crown (Matijević 2016, 107-119). However, it was too late for that. On 29 October 1918, just a day after the proclamation of Czechoslovakia in Prague, the Croatian Parliament met in Zagreb and declared secession of the Triune Kingdom of Croatia, Slavonia, and Dalmatia with Rijeka from Austria-Hungary. The Parliament actually proclaimed that Croatia, Slavonia, and Dalmatia with Rijeka had become an independent state, which entered the provisional State of Slovenes, Croats and Serbs. Austria-Hungary collapsed, and the National Council in Zagreb conducted an urgent unification with the Kingdom of Serbia because of the Italian expansion into the Eastern Adriatic. Finally, in Belgrade, on 1 December 1918, the unification of the State of Slovenes, Croats, and Serbs with the Kingdom of Serbia into the Kingdom of Serbs, Croats and Slovenes was officially proclaimed.

So none of the many ideas and proposals for a federalist or trialist Habsburg Empire ever came even remotely close to being realized because of the collapse of Austria-Hungary at the end of the World War I in late 1918 and the subsequent creation of the Kingdom of Serbs, Croats and Slovenes, which was in 1929 renamed into the Kingdom of Yugoslavia.

Conclusion

This chapter is an attempt to present the Croatian question in Austria-Hungary at the beginning of the twentieth century through the lens of attempts for a reform of the Empire along the federalist and trialist lines. The Austro-Hungarian Compromise of 1867 provided that the lands of the Hungarian crown and other Habsburg hereditary and crown provinces were two separate states that formed a multinational empire called Austria-Hungary. Dalmatia and Istria belonged to the Austrian and Croatia with Slavonia to the Hungarian half of the dual state, of which the Croat-Slavonic part gained political autonomy through the Croatian-Hungarian compromise of 1868. At the beginning of the twentieth century, the influence of politicians who opposed the Austro-Hungarian dualism increased in the Hungarian half of Austro-Hungary. They asked for independent customs, trade, and foreign policy, as well as a Hungarian army. At the same time, a circle of people gathered around Crown Prince Franz Ferdinand in the Austrian half of Austria-Hungary. The heir to the throne wished to replace Austro-Hungarian dualism with Austrian dominance in Austria-Hungary. In 1906, the Romanian politician Aurel Popovici proposed the "United States of Greater Austria" as a federation composed of 15 national states with autonomous enclaves. The exit from the turbulent relations between the lands of the Hungarian crown and other Habsburg provinces was seen by some politicians and authors in trialism, i.e., in creation of a third political unit in the Habsburg Empire. This would be the Croatian or the South Slavic unit with a nucleus in Croatia and Slavonia as the only Slavic country with political autonomy in Austria-Hungary. After the Croatian historian N. Kovačević had claimed that the interests of Croatians and the Habsburgs were alike, the Croatian historian and publicist Nikola Zvonimir Bjelovučić advocated trialism in form of the united Croatian state under the Habsburg sceptre. It would extend from Trieste to Zemun near Belgrade as one of seven units in the imagined Federalist Monarchy. The Croatian publicist and poet Miho Jerinić proposed the imagined separate military area for South Slavs in Austria-Hungary. In 1912, a monthly *Trializam* (Trialism) was launched in Trieste. This magazine was writing in favour of cooperation of Croatian, Slovenian, and Serbian national representatives in a struggle for the trialism in Austria-Hungary. Writing during the World War I on the South Slav question, the Croatian jurist and publicist Ivo Pilar suggested that this question would be resolved by the unification of Croatia, Slavonia, Dalmatia, and Bosnia and Herzegovina into a Croatian state within Austria-Hungary. However, in the vortex of the Great War, Austria-Hungary ceased to exist, and in 1918 the Croatian nation entered the Yugoslav state.

References

B.[jelovučić], N.[ikola] Z. 1913. *Federalistička Monarhija i hrvatsko pitanje*. Dubrovnik: Štamparija de Giulli i dr. [*Federalist Monarchy and the Croatian Question*].

B.[jelovučić], N.[ikola Zvonimir]. 1911. *Trializam i hrvatska država*. Dubrovnik: Štamparija de Giulli i dr. [*Trialism and the Croatian State*].

Cipek, T., and Matković, S. 2006. *Programatski dokumenti hrvatskih političkih stranaka i skupina 1842.-1914*. Zagreb: Disput. [*Programatic Documents of Croatian Political Parties and Groups 1842-1914*].

Despot, Igor. 2013. *Balkanski ratovi 1912. – 1913. i njihov odjek u Hrvatskoj*. Zagreb: Plejada. [*Balkan Wars 1912-1913 and their Echo in Croatia*].

Gross, Mirjana. 1970. "Hrvatska politika velikoaustrijskog kruga oko prijestolonasljednika Franje Ferdinanda." *Časopis za suvremenu povijest* 2:9–72. [*Croatian Policy of the Great Austrian Circle around the Heir of the Throne Frant Ferdinand*].

Hanning, Alma. 2013. *Franz Ferdinand: Die Biographie*. Wien: Amalthea. [*Franz Ferdinand: A Biography*].

Holjevac, Željko. 2018. "Horvát javaslatok a Habsburg birodalom átalakítására (1832-1918)." In *Megosztó kompromisszum. Az 1867. évi kiegyezés 150 év távlatából*, edited by Róbert Hermann and Dávid Ligeti, 53-70. Budapest: Országház könyvkiadó. ["Croatian Proposals for Reform of the Habsburg Empire (1832-1918)"].

J.[erinić], S.[tagnita] M.[ihajlo]. 1912. *Selbständiger Südslavischer Armeebereich*. Wien: Kroatische Korrespondenz. [Independent South-Slavic Military Area].

Kann, Robert A. 1964. *The Multinational Empire: Nationalism and National Reform in the Habsburg Monarchy, 1848-1918*. New York: Octagon Books.

Karpowicz-Toševa, Ljubinka. 1994. "Program Velikoaustrijske federacije Aurela C. Popovicija." *Časopis za suvremenu povijest* 26:65–80. ["Program of the Great Austrian Federation by Aurel C. Popovici"].

Korunić, Petar. 1989. *Jugoslavizam i federalizam u hrvatskom nacionalnom preporodu 1835-1875: Studija o političkoj teoriji i ideologiji*. Zagreb: Globus. [*Yugoslavism and Federalism in the Croatian National Revival 1835-1875: A Study of Political Theory and Ideology*].

Kovačević, N. 1911. *Put do trializma*. Zagreb: Kovačević N. [*The Road to Trialism*].

Matijević, Z. 2016. *Između sna i jave. Rasprave o hrvatskoj političkoj povijesti 20. stoljeća*. Zagreb: Golden marketing – Tehnička knjiga. [*Between Dream and Reality. Debates on the 20th Century Croatian Political History*].

Popovici, Aurel. 1906. *Die Vereinigten Staaten von Groß-Österreich: Politische Studie zur Lösung der nationalen Fragen und staatsrechtlichen Krisen in Österreich-Ungarn*. Leipzig: Verlag von B. Elischer Nachfolger. [*The United States of Greater Austria. A Political Study for Resolving National Question and State Crisis in Austria-Hungary*].

Radić, Stjepan. [1910]. "Naša carevina kao federalistička ili savezna država." In *Federalizam naše carevine i narodno oslobođenje*, edited by Stjepan Radić, Josip Predavec and Ante Radić, 1-10. Zagreb: Izdanje Slavenske knjižare St. i M. Radić. ["Our Empire as a Federal State"].

Rahten, Andrej. 2008. *Savezništva i diobe: Razvoj slovensko-hrvatskih političkih odnosa u Habsburškoj Monarhiji 1848.-1918*. Zagreb: Golden marketing-Tehnička knjiga.

[*Alliances and Divisions. The Development of Slovenian-Croatian Political Relations in the Habsburg Monarchy* 1848-1918].

Südland, L. v. 1918. *Die südslawische Frage und der Weltkrieg: Übersichtliche Darstellung des Gesamt-Problems*. Wien: Manzsche K. u. K. Hof-, Verlags- u. Universitäts-Buchhandlung. [*The South-Slavic Question and the World War I: Clear Presentation of the Total-Problem*].

Šišić, Ferdo. 1920. *Dokumenti o postanku Kraljevine Srba, Hrvata i Slovenaca 1914.-1919.* Zagreb: Matica hrvatska. [*Documents on the Creation of the Kingdom of Serbs, Croats and Slovenes 1914-1919*].

Biographical Sketch

Željko Holjevac, PhD

Affiliation: Ivo Pilar Institute of Social Sciences

Education: PhD in history (University of Zagreb, Croatia, 2006)

Business Address: Ivo Pilar Institute of Social Sciences, [Zeljko.Holjevac@pilar.hr], Zagreb, Croatia

Research and Professional Experience: Croatian history of the Early Modern Period and the nineteenth century in the Central European context

Professional Appointments: former Interim Dean of the Faculty of Humanities and Social Sciences of the University of Zagreb, current Director of the Ivo Pilar Institute of Social Sciences

Publications from the Last 3 Years:

1) Holjevac, Željko. 2017. "Reports by the Croatian Press Regarding Slovaks in the Period of Dualism: Some Examples." In *Croatia and Slovakia. Historical Parallels and Connections (from 1780 to the Present Day)*, edited by Željko Holjevac, Martin Homza and Martin Vašš, 65-73. Zagreb-Bratislava: FF press.
2) Holjevac, Željko. 2017. "Franz Vaniček i zapadna Hrvatska." In *Franz Vaniček i vojnokrajiška historiografija*, edited by Robert Skenderović and Stanko Andrić, 301-310. Slavonski Brod: Hrvatski institut za povijest – Podružnica za povijest Slavonije, Srijema i Baranje ["Franz Vaniček and Western Croatia. "].
3) Holjevac, Željko. 2018. "Horvát javaslatok a Habsburg birodalom átalakítására (1832-1918)." In: *Megosztó kompromisszum. Az 1867. évi kiegyezés 150 év távlatából*, edited by Róbert Hermann and Dávid Ligeti, 53-70. Budapest: Országház könyvkiadó ["Croatian Proposals for the Transformation of the Habsburg Empire (1832-1918) "].
4) Holjevac, Željko. 2018. "'Vječni rob' u habsburškoj i južnoslavenskoj monarhiji ili o tranzicijskom iskustvu Miha Jerinića." *Radovi Zavoda za hrvatsku povijest*

Filozofskog fakulteta Sveučilišta u Zagrebu 50:185–203 [The 'Eternal Slave' in the Habsburg and South Slavic Monarchies or on the Transitional Experience of Miha Jerinić].

5) Holjevac, Željko. 2019. "Croatia-Slavonia in the Year 2014 from a Cultural Perspective." *Orpheus noster. Journal of Károli Gáspár University of the Reformed Church in Hungary* 11:7–33.

In: Croatia: Past, Present and Future Perspectives
Editor: Matko Marušić
ISBN: 978-1-53618-300-9

Chapter 4

FIELD MARSHAL SVETOZAR BOROEVIĆ AND THE WAY TO CROATIAN NATIONAL UNIFICATION

*Darko Richter**
Department of Pediatrics, University of Zagreb School of Medicine and University Hospital Center, Zagreb, Croatia

ABSTRACT

Svetozar Boroević was the only Croat and the only Slav who rose to the rank of Field Marshal in the Austro-Hungarian Monarchy. He was born in Croatia in 1856, christened in Greek-Eastern Orthodox faith and joined the military school at the age of 9. He ran a typical military career of the time. At the beginning of World War I, he was engaged on the Eastern Front where he was able to frustrate the Russian offensive after a series of Austro-Hungarian defeats. With Italy switching sides after the Treaty of London in 1915, and Croatian and Slovenian territories promised to Italy in reward, he was hastily transferred to the Italian front. He stood his ground until the end of the war with his 5th (later 1st and 2nd) Army, consisting mainly of Croats and Slovenes. At the same time the Yugoslav Committee formed principally by Croatian politicians in emigration from the Austro-Hungarian Monarchy, managed to lobby in Paris and London for the idea of a broader South Slav state that later became Yugoslavia, thus preventing Italy and Serbia from establishing a common Italo-Serbian frontier on the Adriatic at the expense of Croatia and Slovenia. These efforts were later supported by the 14-point declaration of the American President W. Wilson, at the Peace Conference in Paris, affirming the right of nations to self-determination. The physical presence of Boroević's Army and the political maneuvering of the Yugoslav Committee prevented Italian occupation of Dalmatia. Nevertheless further political development led to the dissoltion of the 150,000 strong Boroević's Army and rejection of Boroević for political reasons. He was a Croat born in the Orthodox faith and, having become an icon of the Croatian struggle for freedom, would have been an obstruction to Serbian intentions to dominate the new Yugoslav state and to impose Serbian national identity on the whole Orthodox population. He died in exile in Klagenfurt, Austria, in 1920. Less than three decades later, in 1945, the communist Yugoslav Army under another Croat, Marshal Tito, captured

* Professor of Pediatrics (retired). Corresponding Author's Email: darkorichter@gmail.com; darko.richter@zg.t-com.hr.

again the territories of Istria, Western Slovenia, and Trieste aiming to spread the communist revolution as far as possible. It took two years to negotiate the Treaty of Paris in 1947 and achieve the reintegration of all Croatian territories occupied by Italy in 1918. The case of one of these territories, Istria, was decided in favor of Croatia on the extraordinary testimony of Croatian Istrian Catholic clergy, led by Msgr. Božo Milanović, before the Paris Peace Conference in 1946 about the Croatian identity of their Istrian congregations, despite full awareness that this meant political incorporation into the communist system. Small nations often do not have a chance to carve out their states by the rule of self-determination, but in the long run, resilient national awareness across all religious, political and ideological differences, and sometimes incompatible intentions and interests can result in the fulfillment of justified national aims.

Keywords: Svetozar Boroević; Austria-Hungary, Croatia; Italy, World War I; Soča battlefront; Woodrow Wilson, Yugoslavia; World War II, Tito; Istria, Božo Milanović

INTRODUCTION

Field Marshal Svetozar Baron Boroević von Bojna is possibly one of the most significant and well referenced military commanders of World War I, yet he was left in an uneasy historical position even a full century after the Great War. Using ample material already published, his life and his military achievements will be recapitulated, and his merits placed into the historical and political perspective that will shed light on how he influenced the shaping of the modern Croatia: a country that has been emerging slowly and painfully following the disintegration of the Austro-Hungarian Empire in 1918, the wipe-out of the Kingdom of Yugoslavia in 1941, the annihilation of Croatian striving for independence in 1945, and the resurrection of a free and independent democratic Croatian state following the bloody breakup of communist Yugoslavia and Serbian aggression in 1991-1995. It will become clear that it was Field Marshal Boroević who prevailed within an all-Austrian General Staff in setting up defense against Italy on Soča river (Ital. Isonzo), and who successfully conducted its defense through 12 Soča battles (1915-1917). Thus, he prevented Italian forces from setting foot on large parts of Croatian territory before the end of World War I, and that denied Italy some of the gains promised by the Triple Entente in the Treaty of London in 1915.

However, the old world and values that he was loyal to died with the end of World War I. He was exhausted by the strains and labors of the war, and even more by political intrigues around the General Staff and the Emperor (Kaiser) Karl IV of Austria (in Croatia and Hungary: King Karl I) and back home in Zagreb, and personally crushed by the death of his only son in 1918. Furthermore, he was rejected by all sides that emerged from the ruins of the war. He was not allowed to return to Croatia, and died in exile in Klagenfurt in Austria. He was probably not himself aware of the far-reaching consequences of his military exploits. Now that we can delve into the events that preceded the creation of the modern Croatian state it becomes possible at long last to bring Field Marshal Boroević out of the oblivion that has surrounded him for so long.

It appears appropriate to first get a brief glimpse of his origins. Although the genealogy of Svetozar Boroević has been described with some differences between the authors (Tatić 2017, 11-15; Tatić 2020; Roksandić 2007, 17-20), it is tempting to add here the family tree reconstructed by his descendants (Richter and Boroević, 1967) and laid out to the public for the first time in this study (Figure 1).

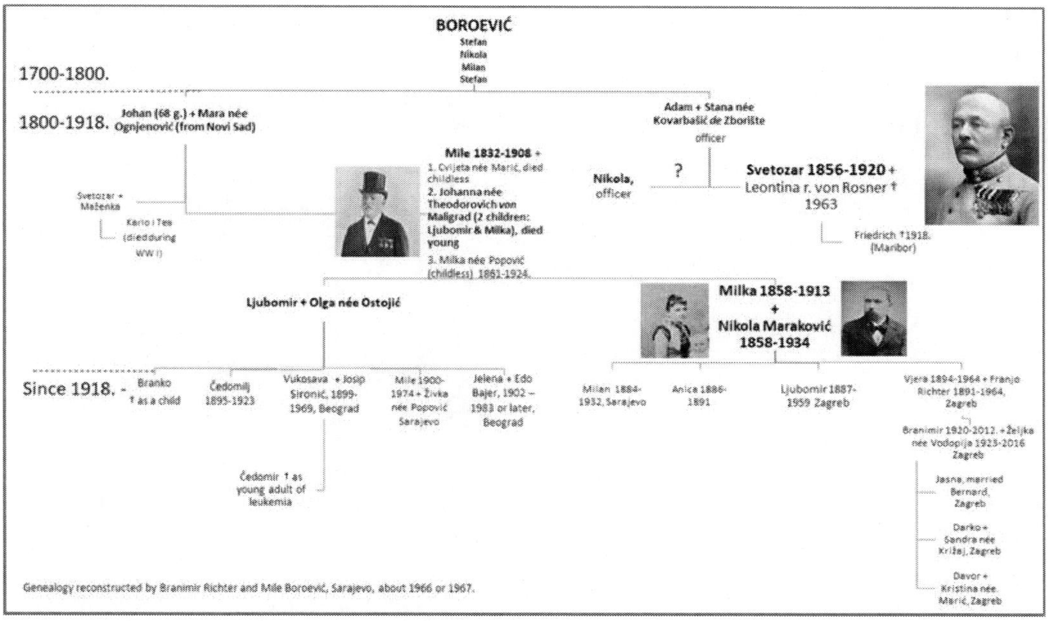

Figure 1. Genealogy of the Boroević family.

The Boroevićs had been a Vlach clan that originated from the southern part of Sandžak, which today is the northern part of Montenegro, and which, at the time, was a province of the Ottoman Empire. Family tradition had it that at the end of the 17th century they moved to Bihać, the westernmost post of the Ottoman Empire (Lončarević 2003, 22). Following the Treaty of Karlowitz in 1699, many of the Vlachs moved across the border into the Habsburg Monarchy to become frontier guards at which time they appear to have been largely slavicized (Winnifrith 1987, 129). The Boroevićs crossed the border a short distance into the region of Banovina, in Croatia, which was part of the Military Frontier (Croat. Vojna Krajina; Germ. Militärgrenze; Fr. Confins Militaires), a militarily organized buffer zone of the Habsburg Monarchy against the Turks. This zone was gradually set up from the mid-16th century during the heaviest fighting in Hundred-Year Croatian-Turkish War and was formally reintegrated into the Croatian civilian order in 1881. For generations, the Boroevićs served as officers in the Military Frontier. They were of Greek-Eastern Orthodox confession under the Patriarchate of Srijemski Karlovci (Hung. Karlóca, Germ. Karlowitz, Serb. Sremski Karlovci) (Hrvatska enciklopedija 2020). It was first founded as Metropolitanate of Srijemski Karlovci in 1713, and became Patriarchate in 1848. It was independent of any Patriarch under the Ottoman rule (Radoev Ivanov 2018, 26-27).

With time the Boroevićs assumed either a Croatian or Serbian national identity (Richter 2018a, 165; Richter 2018b, 32-39).

Svetozar Boroević was, by all evidence, born into the Orthodox family in an Orthodox environment (Tatić 2019, 14 and 146-147), but documents of the place and date of his baptism are not available (Tatić 2019, 206-207). Later, he once stated he was Greek-Catholic (Tatić 2019, 30), although the formal evidence from a Greek-Catholic source is, again, missing. He was buried in Catholic cemetery in Klagenfurt with the local bishop Hefter leading the ceremony, and shortly thereafter was transferred to the Arcades of the Central Cemetery in Vienna.

Svetozar Boroević's niece, Milka Boroević (Figure 1), of the Orthodox, Greek-Eastern faith, revealed her Croatian identity on the cover of her scrapbook (Figure 2). The bottom two lines on the cover state her motto: “A birdsong reveals the bird, and the Croatian girl is revealed by her word.” The scrapbook is dated 27 December 1873 when she was 15 years old.

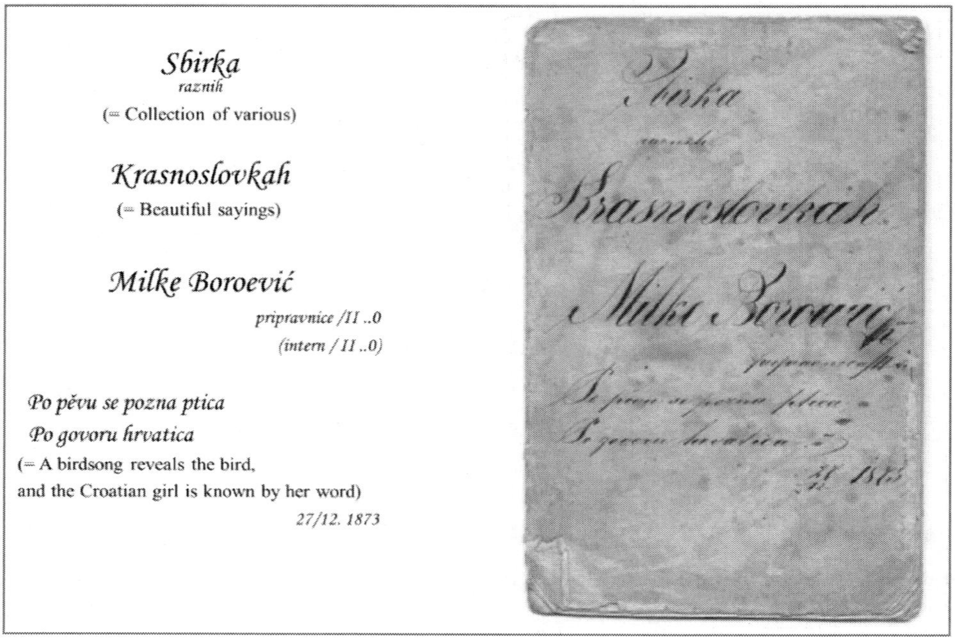

Figure 2. The cover of the scrapbook of Milka Boroević with Croatian transcript and subtitles in English (family possession).

LIFE AND MILITARY CAREER BEFORE THE GREAT WAR

The life course of Svetozar Boroević (Umetić December 2, 1856 – Klagenfurt May 20, 1920) is well described by many authors whose sources will be used here to briefly lay out his life and military career (Bauer 1985; Pojić 2006; Roksandić 2007; Tatić 2017).

Svetozar Boroević was born in Umetić in Croatian Military Frontier, in Banovina, close to a small town of Kostajnica. He is presumed to have been christened in the local parochial Orthodox church, possibly on 13 December 1856, but written proof of the time and place is missing. His father was Adam Boroević and his mother was Stana née Kovarbašić of noble descent. He attended the elementary school in Zrin where his father Adam served as a military commander. After that, at age nine years, he was admitted to the lower military gymnasium in Srijemska Kamenica (Germ. Kamenitz) and graduated in 1869. The same year he entered the higher gymnasium in Kiseg (Hung. Köszeg, Germ. Güns), and graduated in 1872 in the rank of corporal. From 1882-1883 he served in the 52nd Regiment in Pečuh (Hung. Pécs), continuing his military education: from 1872-1874 he attended and graduated from the military cadet school in Liebenau near Graz, and from 1881-1883 he attended and graduated from the Military Academy (Germ. Kriegsschule) in Vienna.

Simultaneously he rose in the military hierarchy: sergeant (Germ. Feldwebel) - 1873, a cadet (Germ. Kadett) - 1874., sergeant major (Germ. Kadett-Offizier-Stellvertreter) - 1875. The same year he was promoted to the rank of lieutenant.

With the 52nd Hungarian Regiment from Pečuh (Hung. Pécs), he took part in the occupation of Bosnia-Herzegovina (1878) for which he was decorated with the Cross For Military Service (Germ. Militärverdienstkreuz). He was promoted into the rank of the first lieutenant on 1 May 1880. In 1881 he became battalion adjutant in the 52nd Hungarian Regiment. After graduating from the Military Academy in Vienna (1883) he was dispatched to the Command of the 15th Corps in Sarajevo, where he was promoted to the rank of staff captain (Germ. Hauptmann 1. Klasse). From 1887-1891 he was a lecturer in tactics, military organization and military history at the Military Academy "Theresianum" in Wiener Neustadt, the highest military school in the Austro-Hungarian Empire. Although a lecturer, he never attended the Theresianum Academy. He became major in 1892. Thereafter he became chief of staff of the 19th Infantry Division in Plzeň (Germ. Pilsen), then of the 18th Division in Mostar and of the 27th Division in Košice (Hung. Kassa, Germ. Kaschau), where he was promoted to the rank of lieutenant-colonel and lecturer at the military officer school. Since 1896 he was the second staff officer of the 6th Division in Košice. Shortly thereafter he was appointed commander of the 3rd battalion of the 17th Infantry Regiment. As of 1897, he became a colonel and in 1898 was appointed head of staff of the 8th Division in Prague.

As was often the case with Austro-Hungarian professional soldiers, he married quite late to a significantly younger spouse. In 1899, aged 43, he married the 22-year old Leontine von Rosner (July 7, 1877 - February 12, 1963). They had one son, Friedrich (Fritz) (February 15, 1901 - September 28, 1918), who died young in a drowning accident while in a cadet school in Maribor (Mirnik 2011, 163).

On May 15, 1904, he was promoted to the rank of major-general. In 1905. he became commander of the 14th infantry brigade in Petrovaradin (Germ. Peterwardein). The same year (May 2) he was ennobled with the title "de Bojna" (Nečak 2015, 176). On July 17, 1907, he was appointed commander of the 7th Croatian-Slavonic District command in Zagreb. On May 8, 1908, he was promoted to the rank of lieutenant-field-marshal. From 1912 he was back in Košice as commander of the 6th Corps, the position he held at the promotion to the rank of general of the infantry in 1913.

During World War I, he was promoted to the rank of colonel-general on 10 May 1916 and finally to the rank of field marshal on 1 February 1918. He was the only Croat and the only Slav in the Austro-Hungarian Monarchy who had ever been promoted to this highest military rank. This promotion was based on his victorious campaign on Soča (the 12th battle of Soča), which was so impressive that the Emperor Karl IV did not care about the fact that Boroević had not graduated from the military Academy of "Theresianum," a previously indispensable qualification for this rank.

Boroević was the next-to-last Austro-Hungarian field marshal. Despite his merits and loyalty to the Emperor and King Franz Josef I and Karl IV his promotion was delayed by two days to allow Hungarian-born Baron Franz Rohr von Denta and Austrian-born Baron Eduard von Böhm-Ermolli to be promoted first (January 30 and 31, 1918, respectively). The last Austro-Hungarian field marshal, Archduke Josef from the royal family was promoted on October 24, 1918 shortly before the collapse of the Monarchy. The other royals bearing the rank of field marshal were Archdukes Friedrich (1914) and Eugen (1916). Professional soldiers in the rank of field marshal, besides Boroević, Rohr von Denta and von Böhm-Ermolli were: Earl Franz Conrad von Hötzendorf (1916), chief of staff of the Austro-Hungarian armed forces during most of WWI, Baron Hermann Kövess von Kövesshaza (1917) and Baron Alexander von Krobatin (1917) (Pollak 2013).

World War I

At the beginning of World War I, General of the Infantry Svetozar Boroević found himself with the 6th Infantry Corps in Košice wherefrom he advanced to the Eastern Front in Galicia. On September 12, 1914, he took command of the 3rd Army that had already been retreating under the Russian offensive. He managed to hold the Russians, then at Limanova push them back and lift the siege of Przemysl on October 10, 1914. This earned him the decoration of the Cross of the Leopold Order on 4 November 1914. In the spring of 1915 at the Dukla canyon, he frustrated Russian intention to invade Hungary. At that time Boroević was already hailed as an invincible hero by the Austro-Hungarian press. (Tatić 2019, 53-56).

With Italy entering the war on the side of the Entente, on May 23, 1915, Boroević was quickly dispatched to the Italian front where he took command of the 5th Army on May 27, 1915. His was heavily outnumbered by Italian forces: 5:1 in infantry and 10:1 in artillery (Rahten 2019, 300). In August 1917, the 5th Army was transformed into the 1st and 2nd Army. At first, the Austrian members of the General Staff lead by the Chief of Staff Conrad von Hötzendorf kept proposing the defense line deep within the borders of the Monarchy, as far inside as the river Sava (Bjaželj 2019, 5-6), hoping that this would blunt further Italian ambitions, as Italy would have with this scheme already gained most of the territories promised to it by the terms of the Treaty of London (April 26, 1915) (Rudolf 2008, 61), Boroević opposed that strategy and insisted on putting up the defense right on the border with Italy on the river Soča (Ital. Isonzo) (Tatić 2019, 167-168; Antolčič and Svoljšak 2018, 180), relying on the motivation of his Croatian and Slovenian soldiers in the defense of their homes (Figure 3).

His army consisted mostly of Croats, Slovenes, Serbs and members of other Slavic nations from the Monarchy (44 %), while the rest was made up of Austrians (28 %), Hungarians (18 %), Romanians (8 %) and even Italians (2 %) (Volkar 2012, 9). His resoluteness brought him significant popularity among Croats and Slovenes, and he was supported by Emperor Franz Joseph I who considered Boroević's arguments persuasive and gave him the command over the 5th Army which held the 80-100 km long battlefront on the river Soča. During the first 11 battles that took place between 6 June 1915 – 27 October 1917 (Tatić 2017, 260-270), Boroević commanded over an average of 160,000 men (varying from 78,000 – 255,000 per battle) and an average of 752 artillery pieces (varying from 356 – 2,200 per battle), against the 2nd and 3rd Italian Armies of some 310,000 men and an average of 1,750 artillery pieces per battle (varying from 225,000-400,000, and 700-2,200, respectively) under the command of General Luigi Cadorna (Tatić 2017, 18-21; Marjanić 2015, 62-64).

Total casualties, from June 1915 - November 1917, were 950,000 on the Italian side, and 520,000 on the Austro-Hungarian side (Marjanić 2015, 62-65).

Figure 3. The Soča (Isonzo) front (dashed line).

Boroević at times shared the command over the Soča front with several other commanders, including Field Marshal Conrad von Hötzendorf (Chief of Staff until 1917), Archduke Eugen of Austria, Field Marshal Franz Rohr von Denta, and the German General Otto von Below, but he was the only one to have commanded in all 12 battles. The Isonzo front has truly become synonymous with Boroević. Thus, he was successful in repulsing 11 Italian offensives, a feat for which he was hailed as the Lion of Soča (Germ. Der Löwe von Isonzo). His tenacity, stubbornness and self-confidence earned him, among his opponents in the military hierarchy, the derisory nickname of "Croatian big-head" (Germ. kroatischer Dickkopf) (Gračanin 2010).

He was resolute in defending every inch of the territory, but not reckless, avoiding to incur unnecessary human losses. His Croatian, Slovenian and Serbian soldiers gave him the name of endearment "naš Sveto" ("our Sveto"; Sveto is a familiar name for Svetozar) out of appreciation for his military ability and dedication to his soldiers.

On May 1, 1916, he was promoted to the rank of colonel-general (Germ. Generaloberst). In June of 1917, immediately after the 10th battle of Soča, he was decorated with the Military Order of Maria Theresa – the Commander's Cross (Kommandeurkreuz des Militär-Maria-Theresien-Ordens) - the highest military honor of the Habsburg Monarchy, second only to the Grand Cross (Grosskreuz) which was reserved for high aristocracy (Bauer 1985, 158). This decoration would automatically be accompanied by the title of "baron," which had to be requested, but Boroević never did it or never cared to do (Nečak 2015, 177; Richter 2020). Although formally not a baron, he is, nevertheless, widely known as "Baron Svetozar

Boroević von Bojna". The article "von" was used more currently than "de," which is the form that had been in use in the Kingdom of Croatia and Hungary (Richter 2020).

Although his dynamism would have predisposed him to command offensive operations, the circumstances, especially at the beginning of the operations on the Italian front, made him excel in defensive strategy and made him one of the greatest defensive commanders of the Great War. Nevertheless, he was in a position to demonstrate his offensive instinct in the last, 12th battle of Soča (known as the Battle of Kobarid - Ital. Caporetto) when he, together with the German General Otto von Below, was the architect and commander in the routing victory over the Italian forces.

A gramophone recording of his speech in German to his soldiers of the Soča Army, held probably between the 11th and the 12th battle, i.e between September 12, and October 24, 1917, has been preserved and is available in the audio archives of the Croatian Radio-Television (HRT) and in *mp3* format from the author. The transcript in the German original and the translation are as follows:

> "Kameraden der Isonzo-Armee,
>
> An Euch richte ich auch bei diesem Anlaß das Wort um Euch zu sagen wie stolz und glücklich ich darüber bin an euerer Spitze zu Stehen.
>
> Viele von Euch begrüße ich als meine alten Kriegskameraden aus der galizischen- und Karpaten-Schlacht, alle aber als die Helden von den Kämpfen am Isonzo deren Ruhm durch die Welt hallt.
>
> Solange es Kulturmenschen geben wird, wird man Euch als Muster von Vaterlandsliebe, von Gehorsam und Pflichtgefühl, und blendender Tapferkeit und unvergleichicher Zähigkeit preisen.
>
> Den Namen Doberdob, Monte Michele, Görz, Podgora, Sevna, Oslavia, Monte Sabattino, Monte Sancto, Zagora, Plava, Santa Lucia, Dolje, Mrzli und Vodil Vrh, Krn, die durch euere Taten Weltklang gewonnen, werdet Ihr gewiss viele neue hinzufügen wenn ich Eueren heißesten Wunsch erfüllen und das Signal geben darf: Vorwärts!"

> "Comrades of the Isonzo-Army,
>
> I am turning to you also on this occasion to tell you how proud and happy I am to be at your head.
>
> I greet many of you as my old companions of war in the battles of Galicia and the Carpathians, but all of you as the heroes of the battles on Isonzo whose glory resounds throughout the world.
>
> As long as there will be civilized people, you will be praised as the exemplary model of patriotism, obedience, and sense of duty, of shining courage and insuperable tenacity.
>
> To the names of Doberdob, Monte Michele, Görz, Podgora, Sevna, Oslavia, Monte Sabattino, Monte Sancto, Zagora, Plava, Santa Lucia, Dolje, Mrzli and Vodil Vrh, Krn, which, thanks to your exploits have acquired world fame, you will, for sure, add many new ones when I shall be in a position to fulfill your desire and hoist the signal "Forward!"

The 12th battle (The battle of Kobarid – Ital. Caporetto) took place October 24 – November 19, 1917. Some 350,000 strong Army Group Boroević and some 50,000 men strong 14th German Army under general Otto von Below, with 2,200 artillery pieces, faced the 856,000 strong Italian force, with 6,900 artillery pieces (Marjanić 2015, 65). After the initial German surprise breakthrough at Kobarid (Ital. Caporetto), the combined Army Group Boroević and the 14th German Army advanced deep into Italy to the left bank of the Piave river, some 20 km from Venice. This victory was accompanied by a spontaneous outburst of enthusiasm of Boroević's Croatian, especially Dalmatian, and Slovenian soldiers who felt that it put an end to aggressive Italian aspirations to their homeland on the eastern coast of the Adriatic Sea. Multiple testimonies of enthusiasm of simple soldiers serving under Boroević in the "Piave battle" have been remembered (Richter 2016) and some recorded (Roksandić 2007, 13), indicating that the speech held by Boroević between the 11th and the 12th Battle of the Soča was in fact a much awaited hint at the following offensive operations.

It is worth remembering that coincidentally with land operations, there was the intact Austro-Hungarian fleet in Northern Adriatic under the command of Vice-Admiral Maximilian Njegovan (1858-1930), another high ranking Croatian officer in the Austro-Hungarian Army. As of February 2, 1917, he was the chief in command over the whole Austro-Hungarian Navy. He was patrolling the Northern Adriatic Sector thus preventing possible Italian attempts to start naval operations against Trieste, Istria, and Dalmatia. Both the German and the Austro-Hungarian Emperor pressed him to start bombarding Venice when Boroević reached Piave. Njegovan refused and Venice was never bombarded. He was, however, not immediately sacked. This happened on March 27, 1918, following the mutiny of Cattaro, February 1-2, 1918 (Halpern 2004), although Njegovan had no direct resposibility in the evetns. (Bauer 1985, 7). It is grotesque that in 1920 Italy demanded the extradition of the top military leaders of Austria-Hungary, including Boroević and Njegovan, to try them on the count of war crimes. The Austrian press described it as an attempt to take revenge "characteristic only of the Antique, because in more recent history there has been nothing of the sort" (Tatić 2019, 168-169).

The 12th battle of Soča entered history as the greatest defeat of the Italian armed forces ever. The Italian casualties amounted to 305,000 killed or wounded, compared to 70,000 on the Austro-Hungarian and German side. Almost all of the Italian artillery was captured. As the immediate consequence, and even before the operations were halted, a new Italian government was instituted under Prime Minister Vittorio Emanuele Orlando, and General Cadorna, having fled to Padua some 100 km behind the front lines, was sacked. Cadorna was known to have been a rather harsh and reckless commander, a proponent of vehement frontal attacks, and who, on warnings that his military plans might cause disproportionate human losses, allegedly replied that in that case, the war reparations would be so much higher. He was quick to mete out severe punishments of common soldiers and massive dismissals of higher officers for not attaining the preset goals: he sacked 217 generals and colonels and 355 battalion commanders (Keegan 1999, 375-376). Despite that, in 1923, within a year of his accession to power, Mussolini promoted him to the rank of Marshal of Italy (Ital. Maresciallo d'Italia) (Pavičić 1942, 571).

Boroević was promoted to the rank of Field Marshal on February 1, 1918.

Until the end of the war, Boroević was the "Kaiserlicher und königlicher" (Imperial and Royal) commander of the group of armies (Germ.: K.u.k. Heeresgruppenkommando Generaloberst/Feldmarschall Boroević von Bojna). He held his positions on the Piave river until the end of October 1918 but eventually was forced to retreat due to the chaotic circumstances in the Empire which impacted the supply lines and moral of his armies. Emperor Karl IV was trying to engage in negotiations with Italy, but the response was the Italian offensive of Veneto on October 24, 1918 (the name was later changed to Vittorio

Veneto). As general dissatisfaction in the Monarchy was mounting, Czech, Hungarian, Croatian, Slovenian and Serbian soldiers in increasing numbers were refusing to continue to fight (Boroević 1923, 13-14). By mid-October, the Empire was starting to fall apart, as the Emperor's offer to reorganize the country on federalist principles (October 16, 1918) was outright rejected, including by the National Council of Slovenes, Croats and Serbs in Zagreb (Oct 19, 1918). (Hauptmann 1941, 780; Matijević 2008a, 42-47).

The Emperor issued the order to the army on October 29, 1918 to retreat from the region of Veneto hoping to appease the Italian animosity and obtain better conditions for the upcoming negotiations. While he was still in control of what remained of his armies, Boroević wrote on 1 November 1918 to the National Council of Slovenes, Croats, and Serbs in Zagreb imploring them not to sever his supply lines and pledging to keep the army at their disposition – he was still in command of 150,000 strong formation. (Pojić 2006, 9). He was, however, refused. Of course, the Serbs within the leadership of the National Council (primarily Svetozar Pribićević) were openly opposed to the Boroević's offer (Kovač 2003, 141-172). The immediate consequence was that the Italian troops, after military failures throughout the war, were able to occupy without any resistance the lands promised by the Treaty of London, adjacent to the positions they held at the end of the war, including Trieste, Western Slovenia as far as 25-30 km to the east of the river Soča, and the whole of Istria. Another consequence was that the National Council placed the South Slav lands and peoples of Austria-Hungary in a weak position in the negotiations with the Kingdom of Serbia. The responsible for the defense within the National Council, Dr. Mate Drinković, was, in his own words, "finally relieved of heavy burden of organizing and leading the army of the State of SHS" (Matijević 2008b, 81). The day following the proclamation of unification (December 1, 1918), Drinković sent a telegram to the president of the Yugoslav Committee, Dr. Ante Trumbić: "Here everything is arranged as best it could be" (Krizman 1963, 57). This inferior position continued throughout the interwar period and was dearly paid by the Croatian people who felt oppressed in the Serbian dominated Kingdom of Yugoslavia. Boroević, reportedly, similarly offered his Army to Emperor Karl IV to help his precarious position in Vienna, but the Emperor declined, because he did not want to use force against the tumultuous socialist movement already shaking the capital. (Bauer 1985, 126-127). Cease-fire with Italy was signed on November 3, 1918 in Villa Giusti near Padua. Karl IV abdicated on November 11, 1918, the same day when the cease-fire between Germany and the Entente was signed (Tatić 2017b, 270).

Aftermath and Death

Boroević was retired by the new Austrian government on 1 December 1918. In the turbulent events that followed the dissolution of the Austro-Hungarian Empire and the formation of national states, Svetozar Boroević found himself rejected by all: the Slovenes confiscated his savings of 120,000 Crowns, the National Council in Zagreb forbade him to return to Croatia, the King of Serbia Peter I Karađorđević, soon to be the monarch of the Kingdom of Serbs, Croats and Slovenes, refused his services, and socialist Austria denied him the citizenship, allegedly because he was considered Yugoslav (Tatić 2019, 163-168).

His only source of income was an allowance he was entitled to as the bearer of the Military Order of Maria Theresa. He spent the last years of his life in a hotel room in Klagenfurt with his wife Leontine von Rosner. To make the tragedy worse his only son Friedrich died by accident in Maribor on 28 September 1918 (Tatić 2019, 159).

Boroević has during his lifetime on all occasions declared his Croatian national identity as, for example, on the Soča front when he exclaimed to his Dalmatian soldiers: "You are Croats, and I was born by a Croatian mother!" as reported by *Narodni list* (Ital. *Il Nazionale*), the first newspaper in Croatian language, published in Zadar since 1862 (Oršolić 2011, 95). Because of the omnipresent fear of Italian Irredenta, nurtured by the terms of the Treaty of London, the newspapers in Dalmatia were closely following Boroević's campaigns on the Italian front (Oršolić 2011, 91-100). After his death, with the growing appreciation of his merits and historical significance, there have emerged sweeping assertions and contrived constructions to make him Serbian, or, at least "less" Croatian, i.e., reduce him to a "political" Croat (Tatić 2019, 203-208), or "adopted" Croat (Nečak 2015, 175), all based on the Orthodox confession of his native social environment (Roksandić 2007, 7-17). The identification of religious confession with national allegiance is absurd. The Field Marshal's niece, Milka Maraković née Boroević (Figure 1 and 2) was of Orthodox faith, and, according to the testimony of her son, Dr. Ljubomir Maraković, "a convinced Croat till the end of her life" (Lončarević 2003, 22). At the time Svetozar and Milka Boroević had been born the Patriarchate of Srijemski Karlovci in Croatia wielded authority over the whole of the Orthodox population of the Monarchy, including Romanians, Rusyns, Ukrainians, Croats, and Serbs. The Autocephalous United Serbian Orthodox Church of the Kingdom of Serbs, Croats, and Slovenes was founded by a political decree issued by the Crown Prince Alexander (later King Alexander I) on June 17, 1920 with the intention to assimilate the Orthodox population of the new state into the Serbian nation. It was a forced integration of the Patriarchate of Srijemski Karlovci, the Metropolitanate of Belgrade and the Metropolitanate of Montenegro to which the Patriarchate of Karlovci did not consent. The new Church's canonical recognition was secured by paying 1,500,000 golden Francs in three installments to the Patriarchate of Constantinople. Some church historians see it as an act incompatible with the Apostolic Canon no. 29, which warns against trading church offices, roles and sacred things (simony) (Radoev Ivanov 2018, 28).

Boroević made every possible effort to return to Croatia. However, all was in vain. He died on May 23, 1920 of a cerebrovascular cause in the Klagenfurt hospital. He was buried in Klagenfurt three days later and the funeral was led by the local bishop Hefter who had befriended Boroević during his last years.

Because of his loyalty, the exiled Emperor Karl IV had his coffin transferred from Klagenfurt and reburied in the Arcades of the Vienna Central Cemetery on October 21, 1920. On that occasion, several thousand Boroević's fellow soldiers gathered to salute him one last time. Colonel Stevo Duić held eulogy over the grave (Tatić 2019, 191-192). Duić was later assassinated in exile (Karlsbad, Chechoslovakia 1934) by the Yugoslav secret police.

During the war, Boroević was, in gratitude for his exploits declared honorary citizen of many Croatian and Slovenian towns. In Slovenia, he became the honorary citizen of Ljubljana, Sežana, Renče, Goče na Vipavskem, Osek-Vitovlje, Šempas, Kamenj pri Ajdovščini.

In Croatia, the University of Zagreb awarded him an honorary doctorate. On Feb 1, 1916 Rector Fran Barac, professor at the Catholic Faculty of Theology, Milorad Stražnicki, Dean of the Law School, sculptor Robert Frangeš Mihanović and a janitor at the University, Ivan Kišur, representing as a group the reverence and affection for the intelligentsia, the artists and common workers of the Croatian population, visited him on the battlefront to award him the doctoral diploma in person. That same year he was made an honorary citizen of Zagreb, and Pazin in Istria (at that time formally in Austria). Other towns that gave him the status of an honorary citizen were: Bakar, Koprivnica, Kostajnica, Petrinja Karlovac, Varaždin, Slavonski Brod and Požega (Tatić 2017a).

Sadly, the honors bestowed upon him during the war were withdrawn one-by-one during the post-war political uncertainties and pressures.

Despite initial rejection by all South Slav and Austrian political actors, the Slovenes were, after a full century, the first to come around and to appreciate the significance of Field Marshal Boroević in the defense of their national territory. On December 10, 2016, a monument with his image was erected on Preval near Nova Gorica by the Slovenian society "The Isonzo front 1915-1917" which keeps the memory alive of the Great War and the defense of Slovenia and Slovenians. On that occasion, the president of the Society, Tadej Munih, said: "Whoever was defending the Monarchy, defended also the Slovenian lands and population against the apocalypse. That is the sole reason for which this General deserves a monument. All other stuff are speculations and insinuations which are better left to the historians and military analysts." (Močnik 2016).

In Serbia, there is one street named since 2008 after "Svetozar Borojević od Bojne" in Ugrinovci, on the outskirts of Zemun in Srijem (Serb. Srem). The Serbian media wrote on that occasion: "So now will one of the streets ... carry the name of the greatest Austro-Hungarian military commander who defeated the Italians on the Soča (Svetozar Borojević od Bojne)... " (Tatić 2017a).

Croatia has so far remained silent. There is only a small street in the town of Bjelovar named after Svetozar Boroević.

Political Background

Field Marshal Boroević's military activity took place within a historical and political framework that would make his achievements not only a case study of military exploits, but would bear far-reaching consequences on the fate of the Croatian and Slovenian nations in the 20th century.

Italy was a junior member of the Triple Alliance with Germany and Austria-Hungary. At the beginning of World War I Italy at first remained neutral because the Triple Alliance was an essentially defensive pact. Weighing what would be better in terms of territorial gains, Italy decided to join the Triple Entente (Great Britain, France, and Russia) and signed the Treaty of London on April 26, 1915.

In return for opening a front in the Austro-Hungarian south-west flank, Italy would be rewarded with significant territorial gains (Figure 4).

These included: Slovenia west of the Ljubljana basin, Trieste, and the following Croatian lands and cities: Istria, the Kvarner (Ital. Quarnero) islands, Northern Dalmatia (including cities of Zadar and Šibenik) and most of the Dalmatian islands.

Figure 4. Croatian and Slovenian territories promised to Italy and Serbia by the Treaty of London 26 April 1915. (Italy: full line; Serbia: dashed line). For South Tyrol, see Figure 5.

There were several other terms including the annexation of South Tyrol, the protectorate over Albania, and some conditional terms regarding the redistribution of Turkish and German colonies. Less attention has so far been paid to the fact that the same Treaty provided for Serbian territorial claims (Serbia was not present at negotiations in London), which were even more sizeable: the whole of Bosnia-Herzegovina, central and south Dalmatia with the cities of Split and Dubrovnik and the island of Brač (Ital. Brazza), all of Slavonia and Srijem (area between the rivers Danube and Sava in Croatia), and parts of Southern Hungary along the Danube river.

The territorially mutilated Croatia would retain only the city of Rijeka (Ital. Fiume) as its access to the sea.

The main terms of the Treaty were leaked almost as soon as it was signed, possibly due to disagreements among the allies, primarily regarding Italian objections over unwanted Serbian gains on the Adriatic littoral. Although not the signatory, the text of the Treaty was officially provided to Serbia. The full text was published amid the revolutionary upheavals in Russia in November 1917 by the Soviet journal *Izvestia* (Holger 2014, 153).

Italy declared war on Austria-Hungary on May 24, 1915, and Boroević was in position as early as May 27, 1915.

Having learned of the Treaty, Croatian politicians in exile headed by Ante Trumbić, Fran Supilo, and Ivan Meštrović hastened the formation of the Yugoslav Committee in Paris on May 30, 1915 (Matković and Trogrlić 2019, 7-35). The Committee included Croatian, Slovenian and Serbian politicians in exile from the Austro-Hungarian Empire. This body was to represent the interests of all South Slav nations within the Austro-Hungarian Empire and its original goal was to secure the right of Slovenes, Croats, and Serbs to unify in one state with Serbia and Montenegro. However, in the practical circumstances of the moment, the Committee found itself preoccupied with the urgent need to overcome the damage to Croatia and Slovenia from both Italy and Serbia which was planned by the Treaty. The Committee presumed that Austria-Hungary first had to be dissolved. This at first was not welcomed by the Triple Entente, and particularly not Italy, which feared that the new Yugoslav state would dominate the Eastern Adriatic coast. Serbia, on the other hand, worked with the Committee, but covertly hoped to put through the realization of Greater Serbia along the Treaty terms. The Yugoslav Committee was not in a particularly strong position with the Entente, as the South Slav nations within the Monarchy, unlike the Czechs and Poles, were not recognized as allies by the Triple Entente, nor was the Committee considered their official representative. Some members abandoned the Committee in 1916 due to the Committee's failure to take a firm negotiating stand against some of Serbian demands. However, the dismal developments on the front forced the Serbian army and government to retreat to Greece in 1915, and gradually brought about a more supple Serbian position. Eventually the Declaration of Corfu was signed on July 20, 1917 between the Serbian Government and the Yugoslav Committee laying down the broad egalitarian and democratic principles of future unification. Except for being a milestone in the process of South Slav unification, the Corfu declaration was not able to guarantee a reconciliation of the Serbian unitarist and the Yugoslav Committee federalist approach to this matter.

On October 5, 1918, the National Council of Slovenes, Serbs, and Croats was formed in Zagreb from most major political parties, organizations and representatives of all three nations of the Austro-Hungarian Empire. The Yugoslav Committee thereafter slowly ceased to play a practical role and was dismantled in March 1919. The National Council on October 19, 1918, rejected the offer of the Emperor Karl IV for a federalist organization of the Monarchy, proclaimed independence from the Monarchy on October 29, and adopted the decision to enter the unification process with the Kingdom of Serbia on November 24. The regent and later king Alexander I Karađorđević proclaimed the new Kingdom of Serbs, Croats, and Slovenes on December 1, 1918.

As already mentioned, in the weeks leading up to the unification, Boroević was pledging to keep the rest of his army at the disposition of the National Council. His proposal was, however, flatly rejected, probably for fear of provoking Serbian ire, but stripped the National Council of significant leverage in negotiations (Tatić 2019, 163-168).

It should be noted that not all Croatian political parties participated in this project: The Croatian Peasant Party (Croat. Hrvatska seljačka stranka, HSS) and The Croatian Party of Rights (Croat. Hrvatska stranka prava, HSP) were opposed (Nazor and Ladić 2003, 332). The Croatian Peasant Party later evolved into the main opposition party in Yugoslavia between the two world wars.

On the battlefront, the breakup of the Monarchy became obvious in mid-October when Boroević noted that the fighting moral of his soldiers was crumbling in paralell to each nations' rejection of the Emperor's offer for a federalist constitution of the Monarchy. The High Command issued orders on October 29, 1918, for armies to abandon their positions and allowed soldiers to return home (Tatić 2017b, 270). The Peace terms were agreed upon with Italy on 3 November, and the Emperor abdicated on 11 November (Tatić 2019, 158).

It appears that Boroević had been well informed of what was going on in the political background, but kept his absolute loyalty to the Emperor and the idea of Austria as a home for all the diverse nations that he so successfully brought together on the battlefield (Schalek

1920). He was often forced to fight for his ideas against the prevailing opinions of the Austrian-dominated General Staff. Despite the obstacles he faced, he made it: not only did he have his way, but he did not lose a single battle during the Great War.

However, Boroević had not nurtured close connections with local Croatian politicians, or, perhaps, they did not want these connections, which placed him in a precarious position when the Monarchy fell apart. As already mentioned, Boroević was abandoned by everyone and was not allowed to return to the Kingdom of Serbs, Croats, and Slovenes. Who would want a Habsburg Field Marshal who fought so loyally for the fallen Monarchy? How could one have expected the Serbian side to put up with such a personality? How could one have hoped to be accepted by the Yugoslav Committee or the National Council who have lobbied with the Triple Entente for the dissolution of the Austro-Hungarian Monarchy and for detaching the South Slav lands from the Monarchy? In Austria, he was considered "Yugoslav," and lived under constant pressure by the press and various extradition threats (the Entente and Italy demanded his extradition) (Tatić 2019, 168). He was in an impossible position.

Not having relevant political connections in the newly arisen circumstances after the war, Boroević turned for help to his former *aide de camp*, Slavko Kvaternik in Zagreb. In a letter in 1919, he wrote:

> "Dear Slavko! … I thank you for your efforts in rehabilitation. Since I have scant information about the present Croatian circumstances, I leave everything up to you. I would be sorry to see any rehabilitation provided to me in front of my Croatian compatriots only at the request of Serbia. Is there a chance to publish the whole record, translated, of course, in "Obzor" with my commentary on my point of view as a Croat and my influence during the war in favor of the South Slavs? Would "Obzor" stand up to my defense concerning Kranjska? ... Cordially, Your old Boroević, Field Marshal." (Pojić 2006, 10). *Obzor* (Engl. Horizon) was the most influential Croatian daily newspaper at the time.

It was, of course, in vain. It is startling to note how Boroević could have for a minute entertained the idea that Serbs would request any rehabilitation of his name from the National Council in Zagreb. It shows either extreme despair or extreme naivete of the great Field Marshal.

Borders with Italy

The Kingdom of Serbs, Croats, and Slovenes was established on December 1, 1918.

The borders were by and large settled by the multilateral Paris Peace Conference (the Versailles Peace Conference) convened on July 18, 1919, and by two bilateral treaties: the Treaty of Rapallo of November 12, 1920, and the Treaty of Rome of January 27, 1924. (Rudolf 2005, 65-66) (Figure 5).

Briefly, the Versailles Conference acknowledged the Italian occupation of Western Slovenia, Istria, and the Kvarner islands. The border ran some 25-30 kilometers inside the left bank of Soča river and included Trieste and all of Istria. Rijeka (Ital. Fiume) was declared free territory. Dalmatia (except for the city of Zadar and the islands of Lastovo and

Palagruža), that was promised to Italy by the Treaty of London, was, however, saved. How was that possible?

The Conference was dominated by various narrow national interests, but it did also consider the Fourteen Points laid out by the American president Woodrow Wilson (January 8, 1918), of which, the points 9., 10., and 11. addressed the South Slav problem (Throntveit 2011, 465):

> "9. A readjustment of the frontiers of Italy should be effected along clearly recognizable lines of nationality.
>
> 10. The people of Austria-Hungary, whose place among the nations we wish to see safeguarded and assured, should be accorded the freest opportunity to autonomous development.
>
> 11. Romania, Serbia, and Montenegro should be evacuated; occupied territories restored; Serbia accorded free and secure access to the sea; and the relations of the several Balkan states to one another determined by friendly counsel along historically established lines of allegiance and nationality; and international guarantees of the political and economic independence and territorial integrity of the several Balkan states should be entered into."

Figure 5. The disintegration of the Austro-Hungarian Empire. Croatia, by joining The Kingdom of Serbs, Croats, and Slovenes, avoided the loss of Dalmatia; Istria, the cities of Rijeka (Fiume) and Zadar (Zara), the Kvarner islands and the island of Lastovo, as well as part of Western Slovenia, went to Italy. Austria lost all of South Tyrol.

Wilson defended Point 9. trying to reconcile Italian aspirations with the just aspirations of nations on the Eastern Adriatic, stating that "everywhere a poll has been taken the result has been unfavorable to Italy" (Throntveit 2011, 465).

At the time of the Conference, Dalmatia was already incorporated into the newly formed Kingdom of Serbs, Croats, and Slovenes, and the Italian troops were not able to set foot in Dalmatia, as they did in Western Slovenia when the Austro-Hungarian army was recalled on October 29, 1918.

Therefore, the Treaty of Rapallo signed on November 12, 1920, sought to regulate the border that could no more follow the lines of the Treaty of London.

With Dalmatia saved, the Treaty of Rapallo still contained significant ethnic imbalances. According to the Austrian population census of 1910, the disputed territory that was given to Italy had a Croatian and Slovenian majority (480,000 *vs.* about 350,000 ethnic Italians) (Hehn 2005, 45). In Dalmatia, there were but 13,000 ethnic Italians, compared with the Croatian population of 646,000 (Lačen and Bašić 1943, 113-122). On the basis of indirect criteria (confession and language) the proportion of Croats in Dalmatia could be estimated at 80.56 %, Serbs 16.46 % and Italians 2.79 % (Bralić 2014, 188).

From the history presented here it is evident that the fact that Dalmatia, with other core Croatian lands, joined the new South Slav state, is to a large extent thanks to Field Marshal Boroević who devised the successful strategy to defend the Monarchy on the river Soča, instead of Sava. This proved to be the necessary prerequisite to frustrate the full implementation of the terms of the Treaty of London, and to create a more favorable position in the ensuing diplomatic negotiations (Rudolf 2008, 65). The primacy of the situation on the ground over written agreements is best appreciated when Dalmatia is compared to South Tyrol. South Tyrol, promised to Italy by the Treaty of London, was occupied in November 1918, following the signing of cease-fire on November 3, and in subsequent peace talks went to Italy (Steininger 2004, 14-15). There were voices of lamentation in Austrian media that South Tyrol would not have been lost had there been someone like Boroević on that front (Schalek 1920, 1-4). At least, the German speaking part could have been saved, by peace negotiations or referendum as it happened in the partition of Carinthia between Austria and The Kingdom of Serbs, Croats, and Slovenes in 1920 (Barth-Scalmani 2010, 228).

By the Treaty of Rome, the Kingdom of Serbs, Croats, and Slovenes ceded the free territory of Rijeka (Ital. Fiume) to Italy (though it was not promised by the Treaty of London), and retained the city of Sušak, across the river Rječina, with joint control of its estuary and the port facilities (Rudolf 2008, 66).

The border of the new Yugoslav State with Italy was principally the accomplishment of Field Marshal Boroević, who found the way to combine his military competence, high rank, and the Emperor's trust to defend the Slovenian and Croatian lands within the Monarchy against the Italian irredentistic aspirations. His 11 successful defensive stands on the Soča river and the victorious 12th battle of Kobarid (Ital. Caporetto) and break-through to Piave, to within 20 km of Venice, prevented Italian occupation of Dalmatia despite the abrupt collapse of the Monarchy. Thus, time was bought during which the political unification of the Slovenian and Croatian lands with the Kingdom of Serbia was completed, and Dalmatia integrated into the new state. Dr. Ante Trumbić as president of the Yugoslav Committee and the foreign affairs minister in the newly formed Kingdom od Serbs, Croats and Slovenes, earned himself a significant political and diplomatic credit in securing Dalmatia from further

Italian encroachement in the negotiations leading up to the Treaty of Rapallo (Matković and Trogrlić 2019, 7-35; Rudolf 2008, 65).

1941-1995

World War II came to Yugoslavia in 1941. German Army crushed the state that was brimming with internal strife in less than a fortnight (April 6-18, 1941).

Immediately, satellite regimes were created in Serbia (Government of National Salvation) and Croatia (The Independent State of Croatia). Slovenia was partitioned between Germany and Italy, Dalmatia was annexed by Italy, Vojvodina was added to Hungary, Kosovo and Western Macedonia were annexed to Albania, and Central and Eastern Macedonia and South-East Serbia were annexed by Bulgaria. Montenegro and Albania were placed under Italian protectorate.

The ensuing four-year war between regular and irregular military units of the satellite states, and royalist and communist guerillas ended only within the larger framework of the resolution of World War II. The communist guerilla led by Croat Josip Broz Tito was the only one to maintain operations across the whole territory of the former Kingdom of Yugoslavia (although not all the time in all the places), and to claim to reconstitute the Yugoslav state on republican, federalist and democratic principles. However, the democratic principles were only the communist propaganda cover to disguise real plans to realize a bolshevik-style revolution, once they would prevail as the single real power on the ground. Tito was personally obsessed with both: the bolshevik revolution and with the recreation of Yugoslavia.

Tito entered Belgrade on October 20, 1944, after Germans evacuated in response to broader maneuvers of the Soviet Red Army, and marched into Zagreb on May 8, 1945. The city had been abandoned by the regime forces and many civilians who were fleeing toward Carinthia. In the meantime, the 4th Yugoslav Army, advancing from Dalmatia, entered Rijeka, Istria and Trieste by May 3, 1945. The 4th Army was 48,000 soldiers strong, of whom 69 % were Croats, 14 % Serbs, 10 % Slovenes and 4 % Italians (Nazor and Ladić 2003, 372).

Tito now stood on the ground that 30 years previously had been defended by Field Marshal Boroević, leading again troops with a similar ethnic composition (to that of Boroević's Army) that could guarantee their high motivation to fight in this area.

However, while Boroević fought for his Croatian homeland and the Habsburg Dynasty with equal loyalty, Tito, as Stalin's agent at that time, was preoccupied with broadening Yugoslav territory and communist rule by manipulating the Croatian national sentiment. Boroević's military exploits and subsequent diplomatic activities by Dr. Ante Trumbić (Rudolf 2008, 65) were instrumental in securing Dalmatia for the ensuing phase of Croatian history. Tito added Istria, Zadar and the Kvarner islands at the cost of imposing the bolshevik-style revolution.

The occupation of Trieste was, however, more than the Western Allies could swallow. Decided to prevent the spill-over of communist influence into Italy, they forced an agreement with Tito to pull out of Trieste and declared the formation of "zone A" incorporating Trieste and surroundings, under allied control, and "zone B" incorporating the north-western corner of Istria under Yugoslav control. Tito was instructed by Stalin to comply. The agreement was signed in Belgrade on June 9, 1945.

Thus, the issue of final boundaries with Italy was not resolved but postponed.

There ensued intense diplomatic and lobbying activity with the Allies by both Italy and Yugoslavia. Various criteria were invoked: historical right, spoken language, ethnic allegiance, population censuses. The Austrian one of 1910 lacked the national identification, and the Italian (1921), and Yugoslav (1945) were considered unreliable due to repressive circumstances they were conducted in: the forcible Italianization during the Italian control (1919-1943) when almost the entire Croatian Istrian intelligentsia had to emigrate, mainly to Zagreb, and, in 1945 the atrocities of the invading Yugoslav communist army performing mass executions and ousting of Italians and ideological enemies as "enemies of the people". The idea of a referendum was rejected on the same grounds.

In this situation, the Allies formed a Committee to address the problem. The Committee wanted to hear from Istrian Catholic clergy about the issue. A meeting was set up during the Committee's visit to Pazin (central Istria), on March 15, 1946. Istrian priests were represented by Reverend (later Monsignor) Božo Milanović, Tomo Benko and Leopold Jurc. They brought with them a memorandum with testimonies of 55 Croatian Istrian priests to the Croatian character of Istria. Msgr. Milanović was able to prove to the Allies that 75 % of Istrian parishes were Croatian or Slovenian, 12 % Italian, and 13 % mixed. This document was at once translated into English, French, and Russian, and proved decisive in the future negotiations (Trogrlić 2011, 135). Msgr. Milanović continued to lobby for the annexation of Istria to Croatia and Yugoslavia during the preparations for the Paris Peace Conference which convened on July 29, 1946 – October 15, 1946. When in May 1946, in Paris, asked by Catholic journalist Walter Eberhard: "Why do you, priests, prefer to come under communist Yugoslavia, rather than Catholic Italy?", Milanović responded: "State boundaries are determined for centuries while regimes change, and, under Italy, the life of our people is in danger." (Richter 2011a; Trogrlić 2017). He managed to convince French and Belgian Catholic circles, lead by Archbishop of Paris, Cardinal Souhard, who was trusted by the Allies on such questions, of the righteous claim to the Croatian identity of Istria. The intervention of Italian bishops of Rijeka (Ital. Fiume), and Trieste, Msgr. Santin and Msgr. Radossi, in favor of the Italian cause, were not accepted (Trogrlić 2017).

Finally, a peace accord was signed in Paris, on February 10, 1947, between Italy on one side, and Yugoslavia, USA, Great Britan, France, and Soviet Union , on the other, confirming the Yugoslav sovereignty over the upper Soča valley which went to Slovenia, and Istria (outside the zones A and B), the cities of Zadar and Rijeka, The Kvarner Islands and the islands of Lastovo and Palagruža, which were added to Croatia.

Zones A and B were initially declared to be "The Free Territory of Trieste," under international oversight, but this was eventually resolved by the Memorandum On Agreement between Yugoslavia, Italy, Great Britain, and the USA in London, October 5, 1954. It recognized the actual control each side had on the ground: zone A went to Italy and zone B to Yugoslavia, where the part north of the river Dragonja was added to Slovenia, and south of it to Croatia (Vukas 2007, 1056-1057) (Figure 6).

Figure 6. The internal and external borders of Yugoslavia following the Memorandum on Agreement (London 1954) and the resolution of the Free Territory of Trieste issue, confirmed by the Treaty of Osimo (1975). The borders did not change after the breakup of Yugoslavia in 1991-1999. (Dashed line: the former Soča front).

Italy did not ratify the terms of the Memorandum until the Treaty of Osimo (full title of the document: Treaty on the delimitation of the frontier for the part not indicated as such in the Peace Treaty of 10 February 1947), signed October 10, 1975, whereby all bilateral questions regarding boundaries, citizenship, private property and social insurance were resolved (Nazor and Ladić 2003, 392). The Treaty was recognized by the Vatican which modified the limits of ecclesiastical jurisdiction zones accordingly.

Communist Yugoslavia fell apart in 1991. Serbia seemed convinced of the continuing viability of the terms of the Treaty of London (1915), and sought to annex all of Bosnia-Herzegovina and to carve out of Croatia almost the exact territory promised in 1915. The war ended with the Dayton Peace Conference November 1-21, 1995. Dayton Peace Accords were signed in Paris, December 14, 1995, with the borders of the new states following the interrepublic borders of the communist Yugoslavia.

PRESENT

The Treaty of Osimo was not questioned by Italy or Croatia following the international recognition of Croatia as an independent state in 1992. However, Italy did not provide the bank account for the indemnification of the Italian property remaining from the Yugoslav succession.

Moreover, occasional incidents continue to indicate that various forces in Italy have not accepted the present state of the borders.

Speaking to a rally of Dalmatian "esuli" (Ital. for exiled) and irredentists, October 14, 2004, Gianfranco Fini, the vice-president of the government of Silvio Berlusconi, exclaimed: "Istria, Rijeka and Dalmatia have always been Italian lands!" (Rudolf 2008, 79). Italian president Giorgio Napolitano on 10 February 2007, the "Memorial Day of Foibe Massacres and Istrian-Dalmatian exodus", spoke about "... Slavic annexationist design, which prevailed above all in the peace treaty of 1947, and assumed the sinister shape of 'ethnic cleansing'..." (Napolitano, 2007). In 2019, on the same occasion, Italian president of the EU Parliament, Antonio Tajani, exclaimed: "Long live Italian Istria, long live Italian Dalmatia" (Euractiv, 2019). These escapades were followed-up by the usual apologetic diplomatic notes which, however, could not obfuscate the premeditated nature of those statements. In 2011 there was an attempt maneuvred by an irredentistic lobby in Vatican to enable the Benedictine Abbey of Praglia in Italy to take control of Dajla, a previous Benedictine real estate property in Istria that was reimbursed by the Treaty of Osimo and given by the Croatian Government to the Istrian Bishopric of Poreč and Pula. This caused an uproar in Croatia, and the row ended where it began: in returning Dajla to the Croatian state (Richter 2011a; Richter 2011b). It is interesting that, following the Dajla affair, the cause of Reverend Miroslav Bulešić (May 13, 1920 – August 24, 1947), a young Istrian priest who was a close collaborator of Msgr. Milanović, but who was stabbed to death *in odium fidei* (in hatred of the faith) by communists, was hurriedly moved forward to beatification by the then-Pope Benedict XVI, on September 28, 2013. The cause had been initiated in 1956 and completed in 2004, but it was left waiting indefinitely in the drawer of the Congregation for the Causes of Saints.

Conclusion and Future Perspective

The past 100 years have seen the breakup of the Austro-Hungarian Empire (1867-1918), the Kingdom o Yugoslavia (1918-1941), the Independent State of Croatia (1941-1945), and communist Yugoslavia (1945-1990). In each phase the Croatian nation was forced to fight against external disintegrative forces, coming mainly from Serbia and Italy, and ideological claims of fascism and communism. This study centered on the disputes with Italy, starting with World War I. It did not seek to provide major new historical facts, but rather to shed light on the continuum of the struggle on the western Croatian borders for national integration that was fought by such confessionally and ideologically disparate Croatian personalities as exemplified by Field Marshal Svetozar Boroević of Austria-Hungary, Marshal Tito of Yugoslavia and Msgr. Milanović of the Croatian Istrian Catholic clergy.

Without a resolute and successful military defense of the Soča (Ital. Isozno) front, Croatia would have lost Dalmatia after World War I. After the breakup of the Kingdom of Yugoslavia in World War II, Dalmatia was the cradle of the antifascist movement against the Italian occupation. World War II was won by the Yugoslav communist forces under Tito who worked together with the Croatian Istrian clergy under Msgr. Milanović to join Istria to

Yugoslavia. The Dalmatian question in 1945 was off the table altogether and there was no risk of it surfacing as a significant issue in the ensuing peace talks.

Small nations often do not have chance nor the privilege to carve out their states by the rule of self-determination, but in the long run, the resilient national awareness across all religious, political and ideological differences can result in the fulfillment of justified national aims. The concept of a well-organized nation should be the path forward in the world of ever-changing circumstances and never-changing greed.

REFERENCES

Antolčič, Gregor, and Petra Svoljšak. 2018. *Leta strahote. Slovenci in prva svetovna vojna.* [*Years of Disaster: Slovenians in the First World War*]. Ljubljana: Cankarjeva založba.

Barth-Scalmani, Gunda. 2010. "Memory-Landscapes of the First World War: The Southwestern Front in Present-Day Italy, Austria and Slovenia." In *From Empire to Republic: Post-World War I Austria*, edited by Günter Bischof and Fritz Plasser, 222-253. New Orleans: New Orleans University Press.

Bauer, Ernest. 1985. *Der Löwe von Isonzo.* [*The Lion of Isonzo*. Book in German]. Graz: Verlag Styria.

Bjaželj, Anja. 2019. *Maršal Boroević: zamolčani Soški vitez.* [*Marshal Boroević: Untold Knight of the Soča River*]. Ljubljana: Univerza v Ljubljani https://repozitorij.uni-lj.si/Dokument.php?id=121428&lang=slv.

Boroević, Svetozar. 1923. *O vojni proti Ialiji* [*On The War Against Italy*, Book in Slovenian]. Ljubljana: Delniška tiskara.

Bralić, A. 2014. "Scope and Limitations of Dalmatian Politics Regarding the Balkan Wars [1912-1913]". In *Balkan Nationalism(s) and the Ottoman Empire*, Vol. II, edited by Dimitris Stamatopoulos, 187-212. Istanbul: ISIS Press.

Euractiv. 2019. *Slovenia accuses Tajani, Salvini of World War II revisionism.* https://www.euractiv.com/section/eu-elections-2019/news/slovenia-accuses-tajani-salvini-of-world-war-ii-revisionism/. Last modified March 14, 2019. Accessed February 5, 2020.

Gračanin, Hrvoje. 2010. "'Hrvatski glavonja' Svetozar Borojević – Žuto-crni general". ["Croatian Big-Head" Svetozar Boreović – The Yellow-Black General". Article in Croatian]. *Večernji list*, June 26. https://www.vecernji.hr/vijesti/hrvatski-glavonja-svetozar-borojevic-zuto-crni-general-158724. Accessed Jan 25, 2020.

Halpern, Paul. 2004. "The Cattaro Mutiny, 1918". In *Naval Mutinies of the Twentieth Century: An International Perspective,* edited by Christopher M. Bell and Bruce Elleman, 45-65. London: Frank Cass.

Hauptmann, Ljudmil. 1941. "Povijest Austrije". Hrvatska enciklopedija svezak 1 [History of Austria", *Encyclopaedia Croatica Volume 1*], edited by Mate Ujević, 765-781. Zagreb: Naklada Konzorcija Hrvatske enciklopedije.

Hehn, Paul N. *A Low, Dishonest Decade: The Great Powers, Eastern Europe and the Economic Origins of World War II, 1930-1941*. New York: The Continuum nternational Publishing Group.

Holger, Herwig H. 2014. *The First world War. Germany and Austria-Hungary 1914-1918.* [2nd Edition]. London: Bloomsbury Academic.

Hrvatska enciklopedija [*Croatian Encyclopedia*]. 2020. "Karlovačka mitropolija". [The Metropolitanate of Karlowitz. Article in Croatian]. Zagreb: The Miroslav Krleža Institue of Lexicography. http://www.enciklopedija.hr/natuknica.aspx?ID=30590. Accessed 25 January.

Keegan, John. 1999. *The First World War.* New York: Alfred A. Knopf.

Kovač Miro. 2003. "Raspadanje Austro-Ugarske i rađanje Kraljevine SHS u svjetlu francuske politike (od listopada do prosinca 1918.)" ["The Fall of the Austro-Hungarian Empire and Creation Of The Kingdom of Serbs, Croats and Slovenians from the French Perspective (October – December 1918)". Summary in English]. *Časopis za suvremenu povijest* 35:141-172.

Krizman, Bogdan. 1963. "Korespondencija A. Trumbić – M. Drinković – J. Gazzari (1918-1919)" ["Correspondence A. Trumbić-M. Drinković – J. Gazzari"]. *Historijski pregled* 9:56-70.

Lačen, Franjo, and Petar Bašić. 1943. "Demografija" ["Demography"]. In *Naša domovina,* edited by Filip Lukas, 113-122. Zagreb: Izdanje Glavnog ustaškog stana.

Lončarević, Vladimir. 2003. *Luči Ljubomira Marakovića*, [*The Shedlights of Ljubomir Maraković*. Book in Croatian]. Zagreb: Filozofsko-teološki institut Družbe Isusove u Zagrebu.

Marjanić, Danijela. 2015. "Svetozar Borojević od Bojne – zapovjednik austrougarskih postrojbi na Jugozapadnom (talijanskom) bojištu u prvom svjetskom ratu 1915-1918." ["Svetozar Borojević de Bojna – The Commander of the Austro-Hungarian Formations on the South-Western (Italian) Battlefield in the First World War". Article in Croatian]. *Fontes* 21:51-68.

Matijević, Zlatko. 2008a. "Narodno vijeće Slovenaca, Hrvata i Srba u Zagrebu. Osnutak, djelovanje i nestanak (1918./1919.)" ["The National Council of Slovenes, Croats and Serbs in Zagreb. Establishment, Operation and Disappearance (1918/1919)". Article in Croatian]. *Fontes* 14:35-66.

Matijević, Zlatko. 2008b. "The creation and activity of the National Council of Slovenes, Croats and Serbs in Zagreb from the Zagreb resolution to the cessation of state-legal relations with the Austro-Hungarian monarchy (from 2/3 March to 29 October 1918)." *Review of Croatian History* 4:49-84.

Matković, Stjepan, and Marko Trogrlić. 2019. "Trumbićevo povijesno značenje i objavljivanje njegovih bilježaka." [Trumbić's Historical Significance and the Publication of His Notes." Article in Croatian]. In *Političke bilješke Ante Trumbića, 1930.-1938* [Political Annotations of Ante Trumbić], edited by Stjepan Matković and Marko Trogrlić, 7-35. Zagreb-Split: Hrvatski institut za povijest & Odsjek za povijest Filozofskog fakulteta u Splitu.

Mirnik, Ivan. 2011. "Feldmaršal Svetozar barun Boroević od Bojne na medaljama" [Field Marshal Svetozar Borojević de Bojna on Medals]. In: *Feldmaršal Svetozar barun Borojević od Bojne (1856.-1920.) – Zbornik radova* [*Field Marshal Svetozar baron Boroević de Bojna (1856-1920) – Proceedings Book*], edited by Marino Manin. 161-178. Zagreb: Hrvatski institut za povijest.

Močnik, Blaž. 2016. "Soški lev vendarle dobil spomenik." [The Lion of Isozno nonetheless gets the monument. Article in Slovenian]. *Delo*, December 10.

https://www.delo.si/novice/slovenija/soski-lev-vendarle-dobil-spomenik.html. Accessed January 31, 2020.

Napolitano, Giorgio. 2007. “Presidenza della Repubblica, official speech for the celebration of ‘Giorno del Ricordo’, Quirinal on 10 February 2007.” Available at: https://en.wikipedia.org/wiki/Foibe_massacres#cite_note-48. Last modified January 3, 2020. Accessed February 5, 2020.

Nazor, Ante, and Zoran Ladić. 2003. *History of Croatians – Illustrated Chronology*. Zagreb: Multigraf d.o.o.

Nečak, Dušan. 2015. “Nekaj premislekov, dilem in popravkov o življenjepisu feldmaršala Boroevića: junak ali uživač?” [A Few Considerations, Dilemmas and Rectifications about the Biography of Field Marshall Boroević. Abstract in English]. *Prispevki za novejšo zgodovino* 60:173-183.

Oršolić, Tado. 2011. “Jugozapadno talijansko bojište i maršal Borojević u dalmatinskim novinama *Narodni list* i *Smotra Dalmatinska* [1915.-1918]..” [The South-Western Italian Battlefield and Marshal Borojević in the Dalmatian Newspapers *Narodni list* and *Smotra Dalmatinska*. Article in Croatian]. In: *Feldmaršal Svetozar barun Borojević od Bojne [1856.-1920]. - Zbornik radova*, edited by Marino Manin, 91-100. Zagreb: Hrvatski institut za povijest.

Pavičić, Slavko. 1942. “Cadorna, Luigi.” In *Hrvatska enciklopedija, svezak 1* [Encyclopaedia Croatica, Volume 1], edited by Mate Ujević, 571. Zagreb: Naklada Konzorcija Hrvatske enciklopedije.

Pojić, Milan. 2006. *Vojskovođa Svetozar Boroević 1856-1920. Povodom 150. obljetnice rođenja*. [Field Marshal Svetozar Boroević 1856-1923. On the occasion of his 150th anniversary. Book in Croatian].. Zagreb: Hrvatski državni arhiv.

Pollak, Karl. 2013. “Die Österreichisch-Ungarische Armee 1914 – 1918. Feldmarschälle der k.u.k. Armee.” [The Austro-Hungarian Army 1914-1918. Field marshals of the k. u. k. Army]. Last modified March 10. http://www.weltkriege.at/index.htm. Accessed February 17, 2020.

Radoev Ivanov, Alexander. 2018. *The Croatian Orthodox Church Was, Is And Shall Be*. Zagreb: self-published. [ISBN 978-953-59546-4-4].

Rahten, Andrej. 2019. “Častniki stare monarhije in meje nove države.” [Officers of the Old Monarchy and Borders of the new state. Summary in English]. *Kronika* 67:293-306.

Richter, Branimir and Mile Boroević. 1967. Rodoslovlje porodice Boroević. Rukopisna skica u porodičnom vlasništvu [autor]. [The genealogy of the family Boroević. A handwritten sketch in family posession (author)].

Richter, Darko. 2011a. “Tko ima pravo na Dajlu?”. [Who Holds the Right To Dajla? Article in Croatian]. Portal Hrvatskog kulturnog vijeća. Published online September 4. Accessed January 25, 2020. https://www.hkv.hr/izdvojeno/nae-teme/inicijative/8976-darko-richter-tko-ima-pravo-na-dajlu.html.

Richter, Darko. 2011b. “Dajla je crkveno, povijesno, pravno i političko pitanje.” [Dajla Is Church, Historical, Juridical and Political Affair. Article in Croatian]. Published online September 11. Accessed January 25, 2020. http://www.hkv.hr/razgovori/8999-o-dajli-intelektualcima-politici-i-zdravstvu-s-dr-sc-darkom-richterom.html

Richter, Darko. 2018a. “Rascjep pravoslavne porodice između hrvatstva i srpstva.” [The Tear Within the Orthodox Family Between Croatian and Serbian Allegiance]. International Conference “Migrations and Identity”], Zagreb, Croatia, December 6-8. Knjiga sažetaka

[Abstract Book in Croatian]. Zagreb: Institute for Migration and Ethnic Studies. http://www.imin.hr/en/c/document_library/get_file?uuid=561c7207-f856-4fe5-8c48-d736673e40df&groupId=10156.

Richter, Darko. 2018b. "Hrvatski su pravoslavci Hrvati, a ne Srbi." [Croatian Orthodox Are Croats, Not Serbs. Article in Croatian]. *Hrvatski tjednik*, July 12.

Richter, Davor. 2020. Personal e-mail communication.

Richter, Željka [née Vodopija]. [13 Mar 1923 - 7 Aug 2016]. Personal communication of the testimony of Josip Vodopija [6 Mar 1893 – 3 Dec 1963].

Roksandić, Drago. 2007. *Svetozar Borojević od Bojne. Lav ili Lisica od Soče?* [Svetozar Borojević de Bojna. The Lion or The fox of the Isonzo? Book in Croatian]. Zagreb: Vijeće srpske nacionalne manjine Grada Zagreba.

Rudolf, Davorin. 2008. *Granice s Italijom u mirovnim ugovorima nakon Prvoga i Drugog svjetskog rata*. [Borders with Italy in Peace Treaties Following World War II. Summary in English]. *Adrias* 15:61-80.

Schalek, Alice. 1920. "Ein Mann. Persönliches von Boroevic." [A Man. Boroević Personally. Article in German]. Neue Freie Presse, June 12.

Steininger, Rolf. 2004. *Südtirol im 20. Jahrhundert: Vom Leben und Überleben einer Minderheit*. [South Tyrol in the 20th Century. On Life and Survival of a Minority]. Innsbruck: Studeinverlag GSMBH.

Tatić, Danijel. 2017a. "Beograd hrvatskom velikanu Borojeviću odaje počast, Zagreb ništa". [Belgrade Honours the Great Croatian, Zagreb Not]. *Večernji list – blogosfera*. January 31. https://blog.vecernji.hr/danijel-tatic/beograd-hrvatskom-velikanu-borojevicu-odaje-pocast-zagreb-nista-9112 . Last accessed February 15, 2020.

Tatić, Danijel. 2017b. *Prvi svjetski rat – talijansko bojište*. [The First World War – the Italian battleground. Book in Croatian]. Zagreb: Despot Infinitus d.o.o.

Tatić, Danijel. 2019. *Feldmaršal Svetozar Borojević – Životopis prešućenoga velikana*. [Field Marshal Svetozar Boroević – The Biography Of A Great Man Kept in Silence. Book in Croatian]. Zagreb: Despot infinitus d.o.o.

Tatić Danijel. 2020. Personal e-mail communication, January 22.

Trogrlić, Stipan. 2011. *Mons. Božo Milanović, istarski svećenik (1890. – 1980.); crkveno-vjersko i javno-političko djelovanje*. [Msgr. Božo Milanović, Istrian Priest, 1890-1980; Ecclesiastic-Religious and Public-Political Activity. Book in Croatian]. Zagreb – Pazin: Kršćanska sadašnjost and Državni arhiv Pazin.

Trogrlić, Stjepan. 2017. "Vlč. Božo Milanović i istarsko svećenstvo bili su među najzaslužnijima za pripojenje Istre Jugoslaviji." [Rev. Božo Milanović and Istrian Clergy Were Among Those Deserving the Most Credit for Joining Istria to Yugoslavia]. https://www.bitno.net/academicus/znanost/bozo-milanovic-stipan-trogrlic/ Last modified February 12, 2019. Accessed January 25, 2020.

Volkar Miha. 2012. *Soška fronta. Logistično inženirstvo - Vojaška logistika*. Diplomsko delo. [The Isonzo Front. Logistical Engineering – Military Logistics. Bachelor's thesis. Abstract in English]. Ljubljana: B&B Višja strokovna šola. Available at: https://docplayer.net/21000434-Soska-fronta-diplomsko-delo-visjesolskega-strokovnega-studija-b-b-visja-strokovna-sola-program-logisticno-inzenirstvo-modul-vojaska-logistika.html. Last accessed January 25, 2020.

Vukas, Budislav ml. 2007. "Tršćanska kriza u prijelomnom vremenu prve polovice 50-ih godina XX. Stoljeća." [Triest crisis in pivotal period of the first half of 1950's.

Diplomatic, political and legal discussion. Smmary in English, German and Italian]. *Zbornik Pravnog fakulteta Sveučilišta u Rijeci* 28:1017-1065.

Throntveit, Trygve. 2011. "The Fable of the Fourteen Points: Woodrow Wilson and National Self-Determination." *Diplomatic History* 35:445-481.

Winnifrith, Tom J. 1995. *The Vlachs – The History of a Balkan People*.

Biographical Sketch

Darko Richter, MD, PhD

Affiliation: Department of Pediatrics, University Hospital Center Zagreb, Zagreb, Croatia (retired)

Education:

1979	MD, Zagreb, Croatia
1986	Specialist in pediatrics
2000	Senior consultant in pediatrics
2007	Subspecialist in pediatric allergy and clinical immunology
2008	PhD, Medical Faculty, Osijek, Croatia [Thesis: Diagnostic Interpretation Of The Results Of The Dosimetric Methacholine Bronchial Challenge Test In Childhood Asthma]

Business Address: University Hospital Center Zagreb, Kišpatićeva 12, 10000 Zagreb, Croatia

Research and Professional Experience:

1980 - 2003	Dept. of Pediatrics, University Hospital Center Zagreb, resident, specialist: gastroenterology, allergy, immunology & critical care
1985 - 1986	Fellow, Pediatric and Neonatal intensive care, Grenoble, France
1989 - 2000	Physician for the American Embassy, Zagreb
1993 - 2000	Assistant Director, University Hospital Center, Zagreb.
2003 - 2008	Children's Hospital 'Srebrnjak', Zagreb [Special hospital for pediatric respiratory disease and tuberculosis] Chief, Department of Pediatrics, Allergy, Immunology & Critical Care
2008 - now	Department of Pediatrics, University Hospital Center Zagreb, Croatia. Chief, Division of Day Care and Outpatient Services; Senior Consultant: allergy, immunology & critical Care

Honors:

1979, 1990	Member, Croatian Medical Chamber, Croatian Medical Association
2009 - 2013	President, Croatian Pediatric Society of Zagreb
2013 - now	Executive Board Member, Croatian Pediatric Society,
2010 - now	President, Section of Allergy and Clinical Immunology of the Croatian

Pediatric Society
2001 - now Member, European Academy of Allergy and Clinical Immunology
2009 - now Member, Central European Vaccination Advisory Group [CEVAG]
1990 - 2018 Member, Editorial Board, *Liječnički Vjesnik*
1993 - 2018 Member, Editorial Board, *Paediatria Croatica*
2003 - now Reviewer, *Pediatric Allergy and Immunology*

Publications from the Last 3 Years:

Medicine:

1. De la Morena MT, Leonard D, Torgerson TR, Cabral-Marques O, Slatter M, Aghamohammadi A, Chandra S, Murguia-Favela L, Bonilla F, Kanariou M, Damrongwatanasuk R, MD, Kuo CY, Dvorak CC, Meyts I, Chen K, Kobrynski L, Kapoor N, Richter D, et al. [46 others]. 2017. "Long term outcomes of 176 patients with X-linked hyper IgM syndrome treated with or without hematopoietic cell transplantation." *Journal of Allergy and Clinical Immunology* 139:1282–1292. http://dx.doi.org/10.1016/j.jaci.2016.07.039.
2. Santrić, Lena, Darko Richter, Ivan Begovac. 2017. "Klinička slika konverzivnog poremećaja u hitnoj pedijatrijskoj službi: prikaz triju bolesnica." [Clinical Presentation of Conversion Disorder in Pediatric Emergency Service: Three Case Reports. Summary in English]. *Paediatria Croatica* 2016;60:117-20.
3. Richter, Darko. 2017. "Allergies to vaccines in children." *Central European Journal of PLaediatrics* 13:24-29. http://cejpaediatrics.com/index.php/cejp/article/view/15/pdf.
4. Richter, Darko. 2017. "Cjepivo kao lijek." [The Drug Properties of a Vaccine. Summary in English]. Croatian Pediatric Spring School. Split, 24-28 Apr 2017. *Paediatria Croatica* 2017; 61(Suppl 1):199-205.
5. Ivković-Jureković Irena, marta Navratil, TamaraVoskresensky-Baričić, Blaženka Kljaić-Bukvić, Alenka Gagro, Darko Richter, Biserka Čičak, Jadranka Kelečić. 2018. "Alergija na hranu." [Allergy to food. Summary in English]. *Paediatria Croatica* 62(Suppl 2):20-37.
6. Richter, Darko. 2018. "Gripa – mikrobiologija, imunologija i epidemiologija za liječnika koji razmišlja o cijepljenju." [Influenza – Microbiology, Immunology and Epidemiology for the Physician Contemplating Immunization. Summary in English]. *Liječniki Vjesnik* 140:321-327. https://doi.org/10.26800/LV-140-11-12-44.
7. Mészner, Zsófia, Jacek Wysocki, Darko Richter, Dace Zavadska, Inga Ivaskeviciene, Vytautas Usonis, Marko Pokorn, Atanas Mangarov, Ligita Jancoriene, Sorin C. Man, Zuzana Kristufkova, Milos Jesenak, Goran Tešović, Justyna Pluta and Lara J. Wolfson. 2019. "Burden of varicella in Central and Eastern Europe: findings from a systematic literature review". *Expert Review of Vaccines* 18:281–293. https://doi.org/10.1080/14760584.2019.1573145.
8. Ivković Jureković, Irena, Darko Richter. 2019. "Anafilaksija." [Anaphylaxis. Summary in English]. Croatian Pediatric Spring School. Split, 8-12 Apr 2019. *Paediatria Croatica* 63 (Suppl 1): 141-147.
9. Richter, Darko. 2019. "Hiper-IgE u primarnim imunodeficijencijama: dijagnoz ai terapija." [Hyper-IgE In Primary immunodeficiency Diseases: A diagnostic And

Therapeutic Challenge. Summary in English]. Croatian Pediatric Spring School. Split, 8-12 Apr 2019. *Paediatria Croatica* 63(Supl 1): 160-163.

10. Richter, Darko. 2019. "Neobični oblik anafilaksije, desenzitizacija i provokacija lijekom." [Unusual Form Of Anaphylaxis, Drug Desensitization And Drug Provocation. Summary in English]. Croatian Pediatric Spring School. Split, 8-12 Apr 2019. *Paediatria Croatica* 63(Suppl 1): 173-177.
11. Richter, Darko. 2019. "Kontraindikacije, nuspojave i mjere opreza prilikom cijepljenja djece." [Contraindications, Undesirable Effects, Special Warnings and Precautions for Chidlhood Immunization. Summary in English]. Croatian Pediatric Spring School. Split, 8-12 Apr 2019. *Paediatria Croatica* 63(Suppl 1): 229-235.

Other:

1. Richter, Darko. 2011. "Tko ima pravo na Dajlu?" [Who Holds the Right to Dajla? Article in Croatian] Hrvatskog kulturnog vijeća. Published online September 4. https://www.hkv.hr/izdvojeno/nae-teme/inicijative/8976-darko-richter-tko-ima-pravo-na-dajlu.html . Accessed January 25, 2020.
2. Richter, Darko. 2011. "Dajla je crkveno, povijesno, pravno i političko pitanje." [Dajla Is a Church, Historical, Juridical, and Political Affair. Article in Croatian]. [Article in Croatian]. Published online September 11. http://www.hkv.hr/razgovori/8999-o-dajli-intelektualcima-politici-i-zdravstvu-s-dr-sc-darkom-richterom.html. Accessed January 25, 2020.
3. Richter, Darko. 2018. "Hrvatski su pravoslavci Hrvati, a ne Srbi." [The Croatian Orthodox are Croats, not Serbs. Article in Croatian]. *Hrvatski tjednik*, July 12.
4. Richter, Darko. 2018. "Rascjep pravoslvane obitelji između hrvatstva i srpstva." [The Tear Within the Orthodox Family Between Croatian and Serbian Allegiance. Abstract in Croatian]. Paper presented at the International Conference "Migrations and Identity"], Zagreb, Croatia, December 6-8. Abstract Book [Croatian only]. Zagreb: Institute for Migration and Ethnic Studies, 165. Availabe at: http://www.imin.hr/en/c/document_library/get_file?uuid=561c7207-f856-4fe5-8c48-d736673e40df&groupId=10156.

In: Croatia: Past, Present and Future Perspectives
Editor: Matko Marušić

ISBN: 978-1-53618-300-9

Chapter 5

ALOJZIJE STEPINAC: PROFILE IN COURAGE

Esther Gitman*
Independent Historian, New York, NY, US

ABSTRACT

Alojzije Viktor Stepinac was born on May 8, 1898, in Krašić, Croatia, to a family of farmers. From this humble formative background arose a Croatian hero, who was to stand as firm as a rock against the various catastrophes which later besieged him and his beloved Croatian nation. In World War I he was decorated for bravery. In 1934, the then archbishop of Zagreb, Antun Bauer, was asked: "Why did you choose such an inexperienced and unknown priest to be a successor to one of the largest dioceses in the world?" Bauer's reply was: "The future archbishop of Zagreb will have to suffer and die for the faith and Croatia. Stepinac will do that!" On December 7, 1937, Alojzije Stepinac, at the age of 36, succeeded Bauer to the See of Zagreb and became Metropolitan of Croatia and the youngest Archbishop in the world.

After the end of World War II, Milovan Djilas, one of the most powerful men in Tito's communist Yugoslavia, was asked in 1949 whether Stepinac was guilty of crimes attributed to him, and he replied: "I do not think, nor does any other intelligent communist think, that Stepinac is guilty. He is a man of integrity and a firm character, not to be subdued. I acknowledge that he was unjustly convicted, out of political necessity! Had he only been a firm Croat, that is natural and it would not have bothered us, but when he remained firm in his loyalty to Catholicism and to the Papacy that was an intolerable problem with the system and Roman Catholicism." From Djilas's testimony it is clear that Stepinac's trial and conviction were a political necessity for the Yugoslav communist regime and it had nothing to do with his, so-called, "collaboration" with the Nazi occupiers and their Ustasha collaborators.

Throughout the war years, Stepinac provided shelter to individuals and groups, and when he realized that more could be done, he sent a message throughout the country that stated:

"When you are visited by people of the Jewish or Eastern Orthodox faith, whose lives are in danger and who wish to convert to Catholicism, accept them… Do not question them on any religious facts, the Eastern Orthodox are Christians like us, and the

* Corresponding Author's Email: estherg2039@gmail.com.

Jewish faith is the source from which Christianity draws its roots. The role and duty of Christians is to save human lives. And, when this time of madness and of savagery passes, those who converted out of conviction will remain in our Church, while the others, after the danger passes, will return to their Church."

This is the story of Archbishop Stepinac in a nutshell.

Keywords: Croatian church; Holocaust; Croatia, Jewish-Catholic relations; Stepinac Alojzije, Cardinal; communism, trials; Yad Vashem, Stepinac; Yugoslavia, prosecutions

LIFE OF ALOJZIJE STEPINAC

Alojzije Viktor Stepinac grew in Krašić, Croatia, to a family of farmers, who earned their livelihood cultivating the land from morning to evening, never knowing what the outcome would be. In their anxiety they turned to God in prayer. As a youth, Stepinac experienced the Croatian peasant's hardships and endless struggle for livelihood and shared with his people the desire for harmony and justice. From this humble, formative background arose a Croatian hero who decided never to be separated from his people and who was determined to stand as firm as a rock against those who wished to harm his beloved Croatian nation and the Catholic Church. He served in the military during World War I and was decorated twice for bravery.

Alojzije Stepinac was ordained in 1930 and upon his return from Rome as a priest having obtained his Ph.D., he rejoined the Archdiocese of Zagreb. He had a keen desire to serve ordinary people. In 1934, the then archbishop of Zagreb, Antun Bauer, was asked: "Why did you choose such a young, inexperienced and unknown priest to be your successor to one of the largest dioceses in the world?" Bauer replied:

> "The future archbishop of Zagreb will have to suffer and die for the faith and Croatia. Stepinac will do that." (Vraneković 2011).

Stepinac's Caritas was established in 1934 when the war did not yet begin in Croatia. This Croatian charity organization was helping Croatia's poor and subsequently thousands of refugees flocking to Croatian shores from the war-stricken Europe. Bauer's predictions about what the future would hold in store for Stepinac and Croatia turned out to be true (Benigar 1993, 22).

Years later Stepinac described his reaction upon hearing the news of his appointment:

> "When the late Archbishop informed me that he had chosen me as his successor, I knelt in front of him, joined my hands together, and begged him not to do it. It shocked me so much that at first I thought the old man had lost his reason. On the occasion of the consecration everyone cheered and rejoiced, but my heart bled" (Gitman 2011, 2019).

Like an Old Testament prophet Stepinac remained relentlessly true to his Church and the natural laws. He became the voice of conscience during three successive and contrasting dictatorial regimes: the Serbian monarchy's dictatorship (1929-1941); in the Ustasha (Ustaša) Independent State of Croatia (Nezavisna država Hrvatska, NDH) under Nazi occupation (1941-1945), and finally under Tito's communist regime (1945-1960, the year he died).

Stepinac defended the teachings of the Church and demonstrated in this manner how a religious man attuned to the universal laws comprehended the unity of the world in its diversity. In his sermons and letters, in his whole life and up to his death, Stepinac paved the way out of the crisis created by Nazi Germany, which divided the world into races, and by communists into a political theocracy, it is to say that communist ideology replaced religion as was known prior to the arrival of communism. Stepinac stood for Christian values and the values of Western civilization by his continual defense of freedom and value of the individual as an independent entity; freedom and respect for religion; freedom and respect for all races and nations; freedom and respect for private property as the basis of freedom of the individual and family; and freedom and respect for the rights of every nation to its full development and independence in its national life (Gitman 2005, 2011).

Trial and Confinement

In 1946, under Tito's communist regime, Stepinac was accused of collaborating with occupying Nazi Germany and their collaborators, the Ustasha. This accusation came only after it was established that he had no intention of establishing an independent Croatian Church unaffiliated with the Pope and the Holy See (Benigar 1993; Gitman 2019). On June 2, 1945, Tito himself met with a Catholic delegation aiming to influence them or, better yet, "twist their arm" to establish a new type of Catholic Church in Yugoslavia. Specifically, he declared, "I would like if the Catholic Church in Croatia would be national and independent." (NARA a). Archbishop Stepinac was noticeably absent from these discussions, in which Tito requested that the Croatian clergy break away from the Universal Church in Rome (Randall 1963, 18).

Despite the talks between Tito and the clergy, Stepinac continued protesting and criticizing the regime on a daily basis. It became clear that he had no intention of leading an independent Catholic Church. Tito decided: Stepinac was either to leave the country or be eliminated. Consequently, the decision was made to launch a prolonged negative propaganda campaign against Stepinac to the extent that even his coreligionists began questioning his conduct and some believed that he was guilty. Consequently, Tito initiated massive negative propaganda against Stepinac in the local and foreign media, highlighting his treasonous assistance to Nazi occupiers and their collaborators, the Ustasha. The media daily concocted new crimes that Stepinac had allegedly committed. Once Stepinac's character was discredited, his arrest, indictment, and conviction followed and were publicized in Yugoslavia and abroad. One of Tito's closest collaborators, Milovan Djilas, stated many years later that Tito's communists had issues not with Stepinac's conduct during the war years, but with his post-World War II refusal to separate the Croatian Catholic Church from the Pope and the Vatican (Djilas 1985). Stepinac repudiated the idea of leading an independent church and thus rejected Tito's request, even at the cost of his own life.

On September 18, 1946, Stepinac was arrested (together with 16 Ustasha) and was tried on six charges: 1) support and collaboration with German, Italian, and Ustasha authorities during World War II, i.e., from 1941 to 1945 in Croatia; 2) support of Ustasha through Catholic organizations and the press; 3) approval of forced conversions of people of Orthodox and other faiths to Catholicism; 4) crimes of the clergy and military because of his designation as the Croatian Army (Ustasha and Home Guard) Apostolic Vicar; 5) collaboration with the Ustasha in 1945 to overthrow the peoples' government; 6) plan to initiate the political overthrow of the regime. On October 11, 1946 he was sentenced to 16 years' imprisonment and forced labor. The USA put pressure on Tito, and Tito agreed to allow Stepinac to leave the country. But Stepinac refused to abandon his people; he spent in Lepoglava 1864 days, i.e., 5 years. (Source: the Biography of Cardinal Stepinac on the website of the Archdiocese of Zagreb, http://stepinac.zg-nadbiskupija.hr/hr/o-stepincu/zivotopis/100). After the prison term Stepinac was placed under house arrest in his birthplace Krašić. He died there in 1960 (United American Croatians 1961, 9).

The charges leveled against Stepinac by Tito's regime, as well as by contemporary postwar historians and Serbian politicians, are still best refuted by reports sent by the American Consulate in Zagreb to the U.S. Secretary of State in Washington, D.C., in 1946, where they recounted the strong defense of the Archbishop against the accusations of the Peoples' Court in the People's Republic of Croatia by Ivo Politeo, Stepinac's defense lawyer.

The following is a triumphant vindication of Archbishop Stepinac, summed up by the U.S. diplomats after the trial:

> "The prosecution was unable to prove any wrong-doing by him. His innocence became more obvious as the trial progressed. Their cunningly devised structure of falsehood and distortion collapsed under the weight of documentation and testimony, which, though strictly limited in quantity, had the evident hallmark of truth. Whatever doubt might have remained was dissipated by the magnificent statement uttered by the Archbishop himself on the fourth day of the trial. He was guilty only of having attacked injustice and tyranny, not only under the Ustasha State but also under the present communist regime. Archbishop Stepinac emerged from the trial, not as an evildoer, but as his people's distinguished benefactor. His courageous and dignified bearing, his indomitable spirit, his ready acceptance of responsibility for his own acts and his steady refusal to utter a word which might have compromised others, or pass judgement upon other, made a striking impression not only in Croatia but even in Serbia." (NARA b).

Officials in Tito's government later admitted that the accusations were bogus, because the Ustasha had violated every precept of the Church and that Stepinac was not their supporter. For example, Milovan Djilas, Tito's former secretary for propaganda and the media, stated, first:

> "The problem Tito had with Stepinac was not his politics vis-à-vis the Ustasha, but his politics vis-à-vis the communists and mostly his loyalty to Rome." (Benigar 1993, 428). Second, when Djilas was asked why Stepinac had been punished so severely, he replied:
>
> "To tell you truthfully, I think, and not only is me, that Stepinac a man of integrity, a strong and unbreakable character. Although in fact innocent he was convicted; but then history frequently tells of innocent people being convicted for political necessity." (Barnett 2006, 79).

In Tito's own words:

> "It is not true that we persecute the Church, we simply do not tolerate that certain people serve with impunity foreign interests instead of the interests of their own people." (Meštrović 1956).

In 1950, a group of American Senators made freedom for Archbishop Stepinac a condition for American aid to Yugoslavia. Tito, whose state was in a dire economic situation, wanted to improve relations with the West and agreed to the deal with one stipulation that Stepinac must leave the country. (Similar requests had also been made by the Serbian Kings and Pavelić, but in both cases Stepinac refused to leave, arguing that he would remain with his people unless they took him by force.) Finally, in December 1951, Josip Broz Tito ordered Stepinac's release, but placed him under house arrest in his native village of Krašić. In 1953, when he was elevated to Cardinal by Pope Pius XII, reporters asked him whether he would leave for that occasion (Skertić 1961). He replied:

> "As long as Croatia is not free, the whole country is my prison. My place is in Croatia with my people, not in the Vatican." (Skertić 1961, 9).

International Response to Communist Conviction of Stepinac

Historian Michael Phayer maintained that Tito's attack against Stepinac was possible because The Vatican failed to come to his aid:

> "Unfortunately, the Holy See let no one know that Archbishop Stepinac had dared to speak out against racism and genocide or whether it approved of his conduct. Based on Stepinac's words, the Holy See might have established guidelines for the bishops to follow regarding genocide and based on Stepinac's actions – he gave refuge to endangered Jews and Serbs – the papacy might have held him up as a model for Catholics to emulate. His words were courageous and principled; because he – a Croat – denounced Croatian nationals, Stepinac had no illusions about his fate should Marshall Tito's communists come to power." (Phayer 2000, 84).

Ernest Pezet, (1887-1966), was a French National Representative and Senator. During World War II he was vice president of the French society of journalists. He served as an official reporter covering the problem of Central and Eastern Europe, for the Commission for French Foreign Affairs, in the French Parliament. On his first visit to Yugoslavia he focused on political, religious and economic conditions under the dictatorship of King Alexander Karađorđević. In 1933, as a result of his visit, a book entitled *Yugoslavia in Danger* was published. Years later, in 1959, Pezet published his study entitled *Stepinac – Tito.* Understanding the region and the people, he examined the totalitarian communist Yugoslavia. It was clear to him that it was essential to reveal the background and the causes of the trial against, by then, Cardinal Stepinac. In his study Pezet sets forth well confirmed facts and cites original documents which substantiate Stepinac's persistent, courageous assistance to people of all faiths, nations, and political affiliations, especially the Jews (Pezet 1959, 32, 44). Also, Stepinac defended, without reservations, the rights and dignity of all oppressed people from the Serbian reign of discrimination and terror, from all sorts of Nazis and fascists, from the Anglo-American bombing of civilian populations, and finally, from atheistic communist totalitarianism. Hundreds of original documents and living witnesses testified to this fact. Pezet asks a rhetorical question: "If that is accurate and known proven and irrefutable and it is, why then the arrest, the trial, the imprisonment and the detention of Archbishop Stepinac?" (Pezet 1959, 149-159).

The New York Times Editorial (The New York Times 1946) wrote: ... "Archbishop Stepinatz has been tried and convicted in Tito's slave press. No one outside Yugoslavia doubts that the verdict of the four-man court, is already signed and sealed. But the churchman, dragged to the bar, is proving more formidable than he was when free. He is unafraid, careless of the fate reserved for him. He refuses to defend himself as an individual but defends his right to exercise his ecclesiastical functions among his flock and bestow the blessings of the church on all its faithful. Not since cardinal Mercier, Roman prelate of Belgium in the First World War, and pastor Niemoeller in Hitler's protestant Germany, has any churchman so boldly faced entrenched tyranny, shielded only in the armor of his conscience. The communist dictatorship will not tolerate among the masses any influence it cannot digest and use for its own nutriment. It will acknowledge no control over men's minds other than its own. The secret police was aware that the Catholic Church, especially powerful among the Croats, is the strongest bulwark against communism in Yugoslavia today. Therefore, it must be crushed. Murders of priests by the secret police have failed to crush it. The trial of Archbishop Stepinatz is the heaviest weapon against the church Tito has yet rolled out. If the lessons of religious history mean anything, he is merely making a martyr, whose spirit and influence he cannot kill."

Winston Churchill, Prime Minister of Great Britain, in the British House of Commons, on November 1, 1946, stated: "The circumstances of the trial and condemnation of Archbishop Stepinac have created widespread regret ... The Catholic Church and clergy in Croatia are being persecuted with the greatest severity, and the strictest measures of a police government are being applied against political dissension." (The New York Times 1946).

A strong affirmation of Stepinac's role in saving Jews during the war came just two days after Stepinac was sentenced by the court in October 1946. The president of the American Jewish Union, Louis Breier, said at a gathering at the Bronx, New York: "Next to Pius XII, Archbishop Stepinac was the greatest defender of the persecuted Jews in Europe. This great churchman has been charged with being a collaborator with the Nazis. We Jews deny that. We know from his record since 1934, that he was a true friend of the Jews, who were beaten into the earth by Hitler and his henchmen. Stepinac was one of the very few men in Europe who stood up against Nazi tyranny when it was difficult and dangerous for him to do so. This man, now the victim of a sham trial, all during the Nazi regime spoke out openly, unafraid, against the dreadful Nuremberg Laws, and his opposition to the Nazi terrorism was never relaxed. He also cried out against the infamous yellow tag' system, contending it violated the dignity of man and he is credited with being the main force in having it abandoned...." (Breier 1946).

Bishop Dionisije Milivojević, Head of the Serb Orthodox Church in the United States and Canada, stated: "The trial was prepared in the political sphere. It was for the purpose of dividing the Catholic Church in Croatia from its leadership at the Vatican. Tito has openly expressed this purpose. The strategy, which comes definitely from the Kremlin Russia, is to break the leadership of religion. It should be noted that opposition to atheism is stronger when there is an outside leadership of religion. The trial was not based on justice, but was an outrage on justice. Tito's regime has no interest in justice. It seeks only to stifle opposition ...His parishioners fervently prayed, telling each other: "May God help him to keep his spirit high and to endure the hardship with courage, Christianity may win!" (O'Brien 1947, 81-82).

The editorial of *New York Times* of December 10, 1946, New York, included the following statement:

"The petition of the Catholic War Veterans and of the National Conference of Christians and Jews filed with the United Nations on behalf of Archbishop Stepinac and of the thousands of victims of Soviet persecution, provides the test of the ability of the United Nations' to function according to the good will and high principles of the overwhelming majority of its members. If the United Nations hopes to have the good opinion of the civilized world, or aspires to be a force for humanity and justice in international affairs, it cannot evade or ignore these appeals."

Professor Christopher Spalatin, Marquette University, WI, U.S.A, stated:

"Aloysius Stepinac is a Catholic by religion, a Croatian by nationality. As Archbishop of Zagreb he had to come to grips with two burning issues that had faced the Croatians since 1918: the opposition within Yugoslavia of the dominant Serbian group to the aspirations for national freedom of the Croatians, and the even more important life and death struggle between communism and Christianity. Defeat of the Yugoslav armed forces in spring 1941, when Croatian nationalists went overboard, the Archbishop of Zagreb stood like a rock and opposed the Pavelić Government in their racial policy. When the communists assailed the Church after their victory in 1945, the same Archbishop raised his energetic voice to protect the right of free man. Cardinal Stepinac is a great man because in a period of general confusion about human values, in a time of mass delirium, he dared to risk his own position and his own life to tell his fold what the real scale of values is. When the crowds [Croatian people] lost their direction following false prophets [communists], when the majority of men bent their heads in fear, he raised his head and spoke above the multitudes with authority and wisdom and courage…" (Spalatin 1959, 8).

The Montreal Gazette of February 11, 1960, pp. 99-100 reacted to the arrest and conviction of Archbishop Stepinac on his death, stating:

"Cardinal Stepinac was a symbol of faith and protest, a symbol of the refusal of Christian clergyman to bow before scythe blade of totalitarian persecution and intolerance. When the trial became a farce, his imprisonment became embarrassment for his jailers. Attempts were made to remove the embarrassment by promising him release if he would leave Yugoslavia. Archbishop Stepinac refused such a compromise. Resisting all temptations that might, even in the smallest degree, sully his and his Church's name; he remained in prison…Yesterday his suffering ended. But his name will endure. Wherever in this world of so much cruelty and hate, a Christian of any denomination seeks courage; he will only have to recall the example of His Eminence."

Norman F. Lent, Member of the United States Congress from New York, stated: "On the 20th anniversary of the death of the martyred Cardinal Aloysius Stepinac it is appropriate that we commemorate his most courageous struggle against persecution, oppression and discrimination with the designation of West 41st Street as Cardinal Stepinac Place. May this revered name serve as proud symbol of the magnificent spirit of the Croatian people in their efforts to win freedom and independence?" (cf. O'Brian 1999, 117).

Count O'Brien of Thomond, a churchman of Irish origins, traveled around Europe. While in Prague he witnessed the development of the Sudeten crisis. The Czechs' firm determination was to resist Hitler's threats but they were betrayed by England and France. O'Brien arrived in Zagreb, on December 1, 1938. Later, he summed up his visit as follows:

> "During the past twenty years I had visited many countries and had met, especially at the various International Eucharistic Congresses, the majority of the world's greatest churchmen, Cardinals, Archbishops and Bishops. Most of them I had come to esteem, others to admire. But two of them have made upon me an impression which shall last as long as I live. And I shall always consider myself fortunate for having had the opportunity of meeting these two whose great part in the history of the Church was then unforeseen; in 1923, the then Apostolic Nuncio in Germany, Msgr. Eugenio Pacelli, the present Holy Father; and in 1938, Msgr. Aloysius Stepinac."

For two years once a week, Stepinac and O'Brien had lunch together, sharing experiences and discussing the bleak future of Europe. O'Brien described Stepinac's contempt for the German and Italian occupiers and for Croatia's puppet regime. In his book, *Archbishop Stepinac, The Man and His Case,* he wrote:

> "Mgr. Stepinac has taught the whole world a lesson: he has taught us to despise all forms of totalitarian government, be they of the Left or of the Right; all forms of government which crush the souls and bodies of men; all forms of government which degrade free men to the level of slaves; in a word, all forms of government which are not based on the moral law." (O'Brien 1947, 83).

All of the above individuals and entities considered Stepinac a holy man who has fought for human rights and dignity of every human being regardless of the person's religion, ethnicity, color or political affiliation. This opinion is not shared by the current Jewish leadership and the past and current Serbian regimes.

CRITICISM OF STEPINAC

Serbian historians, past and current Serbian regimes accused Stepinac of "failing to raise his voice against the Nazi occupiers and the Ustasha." The five fiercest critical opponents were those who wrote at the time of the communist regime in Yugoslavia and after its demise. The first accuser was Vladimir Dedijer who wrote in the early 1950s. His charges were: "The Catholic Archbishop of Croatia openly sided with the Germans and their quislings in Croatia. On April 11, 1941, while fighting between the German and the Yugoslav army was still going on in the Bosnian Mountains. Archbishop Stepinac openly called on Pavelić's deputy, Slavko Kvaternik, and congratulated him on the formation of the Quisling State of Croatia. At the same time Stepinac sent a pastoral letter to all clergy in Croatia calling on them to help the Quisling State of Croatia. At a Church conference held later, he as chairman urged a resolution in favor of collaboration. Stepinac himself, also accepted appointment as arch-vicar of Pavelić's army, although he never had an active role." (Dedijer 1953, 139)

Dedijer, like many Serbian historians, demonstrates blatant ignorance of what was required of a man in Stepinac position. As a Roman Catholic prelate, Stepinac was bound by the apostolic Constitution *Sollicitudo Ecclesiarum* issued by Pope Gregory XVI in 1831. This document was consistent with provisions of the 1907 Hague and 1929 Geneva Conventions, which affirm that, during a state of war, all legal power passes into the hands of the occupier, who is authorized and obligated to maintain public order and public life by demanding obedience of the inhabitants, with specified exceptions. The conventions required of the Church's representatives to enter into relations with persons who actually controlled the country. The objective was to ensure uninterrupted spiritual welfare and rights of their parishioners. By following the same instructions throughout Europe, the prelates in fact defended the rights of the Roman Catholic Church in almost the same format that existed prior to the occupation. Bound by the aforementioned obligations Stepinac who served under the three regimes acted as was expected of him by the aforementioned entities (NARA c).

The second accuser, Srdja Trifković, most likely knew that Stepinac had lacked all-encompassing authority over priests from other dioceses. He wrote: "After more than two years of Ustasha rule, on October 31, 1943, Stepinac stated in a sermon: 'There are people who accuse us of not having taken action against the crimes committed in different regions of our country. Our reply is: we cannot sound the alarm, for every man is endowed with his own free will and is alone responsible for his acts. It is for this reason that we cannot be held responsible." (Trifković 2016). Nevertheless, Trifković's conclusion as to Stepinac's actions seems to be based first on his personal opinion of what he thought was right or wrong for Stepinac to do; second, his accusations were based on an erroneous understanding regarding the Catholic canon law, since under canon 273 an archbishop, like any other priest, was responsible primarily for his own conduct (NARA c).

The third accuser, Lazo M. Kostich, like other pro-Serbian historians, without a single reference as proof stated: "Stepinac lacked the qualities required of a spiritual and moral leader at a time when countless atrocities were committed in the name of his Church. He was not a direct accomplice, but he did not vigorously oppose them either. He may have sinned more by omission than by commission, but he sinned nevertheless: "…Stepinac's primary fault was in his failure to take an open stand against the bloodbath and terror. By not doing so, he has betrayed not only his universal duty to the victims, but also his own people. His silence had facilitated the descent into mortal sin. Stepinac's failing was also in his timid and reluctant attitude to those members of the Croatian clergy who openly identified with the Ustasha regime, or even became supporters of, and active participants in the genocide." (Kostich 1981, 22).

Other critics came from Israel. The former Director of the Israel office of the Simon Wiesenthal Center Efraim Zuroff was on a visit to Serbia in 2015. On that occasion, he was asked what his thoughts were on Stepinac being declared a saint. He stated: "Although Pavelić was one of the biggest mass murderers during World War II, Cardinal Stepinac was his spiritual advisor…. What does it say about the Catholic Church?"

I wonder why Zuroff would degrade himself by concocting a historical event! It is widely known and proven that Pavelić and Stepinac met only once in the Zagreb Cathedral and on official function. Most other contacts were conducted through Andrija Artuković, the Minister of the Interior. Furthermore, Zuroff's ignorance is surprising: it is quite hard to imagine that Pavelić would ask Stepinac to become his confessor when Stepinac had proclaimed:

"The Catholic Church cannot accept that one race or one nation, because it is more numerous or better armed, may commit violence against a smaller nation. We cannot accept that innocent people may be killed. The system of shooting hundreds of hostages for a crime, when the person guilty of the crime cannot be found? It is a pagan system which only results in evil! We condemn all forms of injustice; all killings of innocent people; all burning of peaceful villages. We sorrow for the miseries and the sadness of all who today suffer unjustly; the Catholic Church upholds that order which is as old as the Ten Commandments." (Pattee 1953, 285-286.)

The fifth accuser is Ronen Shnidman, a journalist from *The Times of Israel*. He pretended that he was interested in publishing an article on my book *Alojzije Stepinac - Pillar of Human Rights*. One of the five questions he sent to me on September 4, 2019 was: "The vast majority of the Jewish Community of Zagreb believes that all the Croatian Jews were killed by the Ustasha during the war. Why did Stepinac not publicly oppose the Holocaust as a man of conscience?" The accusations against the Archbishop are biased and yet readily accepted considering the catastrophe that befell Jews, Serbs, Roma and other dissidents in the NDH. It is also clear that some individuals in the Zagreb Jewish Community were blinded by Serbian-communist propaganda against Stepinac. Stepinac had worked tirelessly to save all those who asked him for help, most specifically the Chief Rabbi of Croatia, Dr. Miroslav Shalom Freiberger. Also, it is of importance to put the questions into the historical context of World War II in the countries of the former Yugoslavia. Stepinac opposed Nazi ideology and the one promulgated by the Ustasha collaborators. The venerable historian Raul Hilberg stated:

> "...Hitler was the supreme architect of the Jewish catastrophe. It is he who transformed the liquid ideas of 1940 into the hard reality of 1941. Hitler made his final steps in the inexorable outcome of all the anti-Jewish measures taken over the years, and he forged Germany's diverse centralized administrative apparatus into a network of organizations acting in unison to the end so that shooting operations and gassings could be implemented simultaneously. It is clear that nowhere was the determination to implement the final solution so deeply rooted as in Germany; nowhere was the issue so fundamental." (Hilberg 1993, 16-17).

To confront the accusations leveled against Stepinac, one has to acquaint oneself with the history of the period. In his memoirs, Ernst von Weizsäcker, the German ambassador to the Holy See from 1943-1945, wrote:

> "Even institutions of worldwide importance such as the International Red Cross or the Roman Catholic Church did not see fit to appeal to Hitler in a general way on behalf of the Jews or to call openly on the sympathies of the world. It was precisely because they wanted to help the Jews that these organizations refrained from making any general and public appeals, for they were afraid that they would thereby injure, rather than help, the Jews." (Gitman 2012, 200).

Various Vatican documents contain clear instructions to clergy on how to conduct themselves. For example, on June 2, 1943, like on many previous occasions, Pius XII sent a letter to the Sacred College of Cardinals advising that:

> "Every word that we address to the responsible authorities and every one of our public declarations has to be seriously weighed and considered in the interest of the persecuted themselves in order not to make their situation unwittingly even more difficult and unbearable." (Randall 1963, 18).

The Pope had emphasized that one best assisted the oppressed by quietly and persistently performing acts of rescue. Stepinac recognized the validity of these instructions. He had to act prudently and without ostentatious protests, especially in order to prevent his replacement by a fervent Ustasha supporter such as Sarajevo Archbishop Sarić (Tomasevich 2002, 552). Yet, often he raised his voice and, as seen above, he also risked being replaced.

Few archbishops, and never any Serbian bishop, were confronted with the following question: "Why did they fail to raise their voices against the Nazis and their collaborators in their own countries?" "Was Stepinac that different from all the other religious leaders or is it the desire and the need of Croatia's enemies to 'destroy' Stepinac's stature in the eyes of his people and all others around the world?" The following will demonstrate that, despite the instructions received from the Vatican not to raise his voice, Stepinac raised his and his life was often in danger. As demonstrated throughout this chapter, while quoting many references, it was confirmed that he had raised his voice and that he had saved the lives of thousands. One of the most encompassing works on the rescue activities of Archbishop Stepinac was written by Anthony Henry Count O'Brien of Thomond. O'Brien personally visited Stepinac and after the war he conducted thorough research on the rescue activities of Archbishop Stepinac:

> "Thousands and thousands of Austrian, German, Czech and Polish Catholics of Jewish origin owe perpetual gratitude to Mgr. Stepinac. They asked for his help and received it. Within his Caritas in Zagreb he organized a special Relief Committee for Refugees. For over two years I was allowed to help him in this work. From what I have seen with my own eyes I can testify that he did all in his power to find shelter for these people in Croatia and to enable them to live an honest and decent life; that he helped those who wished to leave Yugoslavia, mostly for England, the United States or South America; that in most of these cases he paid out of his own pocket the major part of the travelling expenses, which were far beyond the means at the disposal of the Relief Committee." (O'Brien 1947, 10).

The reply to the question raised by Shnidman should be, and I quote: "Yes, many Jews perished at the hands of the Ustasha. The data and the various statistical analyses confirm the conclusion that the brutality and savagery of the Ustaše surpassed even that of Nazi Germany. On the eve of World War II, the Jewish population in the territories of the NDH which included Bosnia-Herzegovina was 39,500. In Croatia, there were 25,000 Jews and in Bosnia-Herzegovina 14,500. In total, approximately 9,500 Jews survived and 30,000 perished" (Romano 1980, 5-14). The differences among historians in presenting figures and percentages regarding the prewar population, number of casualties and survival rate may reach as much as 20 percent. For a detailed discussion of how and why these differences occurred see also Ivo

Goldstein (Goldstein and Goldstein 2001, 632-648). However, it is known that not all perished at the hands of the Ustasha. Some died while serving in the Partisans. Some were murdered by the Serbian Chetniks and Milan Nedić's Serbian army, still others died in various Nazi concentration camps, such as: Auschwitz and Dachau, Sobibor, Majdanek and still others starved and died of diseases while running for shelter. This is not to suggest that the Ustasha did not murder, however, historians and journalists owe it to posterity and for the sake of clarity to provide an accurate portrayal based on documents and oral histories. Historians and others should at all times refrain from making broad-brush accusations.

No power in Europe and beyond was mightier than Nazi Germany. In this configuration, Stepinac was nothing but a cog in this great conglomerate called Nazi Germany. It is evident that the Nazi occupiers had the power, the determination and the plan, first to conquer the entire world and simultaneously to eliminate the Jews. Why then does the current Jewish leadership in Zagreb - to mention Ivo Goldstein, who in his books and his many writings on the subject incriminates Stepinac for most of the catastrophes that befell the Jews of NDH - fail to mention all the good and positive he has done? Often it seems that some historians ignore facts and use Stepinac as a pawn in a very dangerous game.

Stepinac was and still is a *persona non grata* by for the Serbian Karađorđević kingship, the Nazi occupier, the Ustasha, the communists, the current Jewish Community in Zagreb, and the current Serbian regime. Yes, it is problematic to include so many entities and periods in one sentence, but it is clear that Stepinac's spirit is alive and a unification of the South Slavs will not take place. This is undoubtedly controversial. The following text reveals Stepinac's character and work showing that all criticism has its roots in issues at variance with reason, objectivity and honesty.

The People in the South Slavs within the Historical Context

To try to understand the Balkans and its people, one has to identify some of the underlying causes that created an extreme heterogeneity in a relatively small parcel of land of the South Slavs. The Slavic tribes arrived in the sixth or seventh century and settled in the west, the present-day Slovenes and the Croats fell under the influence of Rome, whereas the Serbs, who settled in the east, came under the aegis of Byzantium. The split between East and West was established early in the history of this region (Auty 1965; Tomasevich 1955). In the middle of this territory the inhabitants were known as Bosnians who in time partly became Bogumils, followers of a medieval Manichaean sect that had also penetrated Bulgaria. During Ottoman rule a high percentage of them converted to Islam (Obolensky 1946). Thus, in this relatively small parcel of land often referred to as the "Balkan Quagmire" three major religions of the European world found home in the South Slavic lands.

It is clear that throughout the centuries, the South Slavs have demonstrated a wide spectrum of ethnic and religious diversity. The native nationalities included: Serbs, Croats, Slovenes, Macedonians, and Montenegrins. Among them settled ethnic minorities: Hungarians, Germans, Slovaks, Romanians, Albanians, Turks, and Jews. They differed in many ways, but two major difficult issues separated them: religion and political affiliation.

Owing to varied historical circumstances, no two South Slavic regions developed in a similar fashion. In the Habsburg lands the Slovenian territories became part of the Austro-Hungarian Empire. After centuries of Venetian domination, Dalmatia in the nineteenth century also came under Austrian rule; and Croatia, which had formerly been an independent kingdom, in 1102 accepted a union with Hungary. The Croats in 1519 received recognition by Pope Leo X and the country was defined as the *Antemurale Christianitatis* (Bulwark of Christendom), for their bravery in keeping the Ottomans at bay; Croatia saved the Catholic Church in the Balkans. Under the Hungarian Crown of St. Stephen, one encounters also the lands of Banat, Bačka, and Baranya, collectively later known as Vojvodina. The Austro-Hungarian final expansion was the annexation of Bosnia and Herzegovina in the second half of the nineteenth century (Banac 1984).

The Serbian Empire reached its peak in the mid-fourteenth century under the leadership of Tsar Stefan Dušan. Thereafter Serbia, Macedonia and Bosnia succumbed to Turkish conquest. Throughout the years, the condition of the South Slavs under Ottoman rule deteriorated greatly. In the seventeenth and eighteenth centuries, many tribes that settled in the region in time migrated to Habsburg territory, later to become Orthodox Serbs. Serbia, by the end of the nineteenth century, managed to free itself from Ottoman rule – by 1830 Serbia had gained autonomy under its own prince becoming a kingdom in 1881. With the end of World War I in 1918, a totally new entity emerged from the collapse of the Austro-Hungarian Empire: the Kingdom of Serbs, Croats and Slovenes (Banac 1984).

The London-based Committee of Croats and Serbs was aimed at promoting the creation of the South Slavic State composed of Serbs, Croats and Slovenes (SHS). Politicians of all three nation-states identified themselves with the idea of creating a unified entity, although they were aware that the concept of South Slavism was promoted and influenced by Serbian historical ambition to spread to the West. The Serbs had the largest state and were those who aspired to unification albeit without any intentions to become Yugoslavs, in the sense of developing a new national consciousness, either political or cultural. Historians, including Aleksa Djilas, argued that the Serbian desire to form a centralized government under the banner of the Serbian monarch Aleksander Karađorđević, a strong military and political leader, was motivated by selfish reason thus failing to consider the needs and desires of the Croats and Slovenes (Djilas 1991, 59).

It is of essence to put the South Slavs into historical context in which, despite a great degree of heterogeneity, the Serbs desired vehemently to absorb the Croats. Thus, the conflicts between the Serbs who aspire to prevail over the Croats, while the latter struggle to preserve their unique identity. It can be safely suggested that the contentious relationships between these two nation-states extend to medieval times. From their early history, it was manifested that Serbs and Croats were not the same people. The dominant difference between them is religion and belonging to different civilization circles. The Croats predominantly had developed an organic link with the universal Catholic Church, which led to the formation of its unique character, influenced by the Pope and the Vatican. The regime in Belgrade aimed to sever the bond between the Croats and the Holy See and thus eradicate Croatia's distinctiveness. This was demonstrated in 1902 when Nikola Stojanović (1880-1965), a lawyer, politician, and newspaper publisher, wrote:

> "The Croats are not and cannot be a separate nation, but they are on their way to becoming Serbs. By taking Serbian as their literary language, they have taken the most

important step towards unification. Also, the process of merging continues apart from the language. By reading every single Serbian book, any folk song, by singing any Serbian song, an atom of fresh Serbian democratic culture is passing into their organism. This struggle must be fought until extermination, yours or ours. One party must succumb." (Stojanović 1902).

With several abortive attempts to assimilate the Croats, some historians today acknowledge that Yugoslavia was more an ideal than a reality; it was only a vision, along with Pan-Slavism. But as matters stand today, it seems that Serbia still holds that unification is possible, provided Cardinal Stepinac's philosophy, teachings and image are obliterated from the minds and hearts of his Croatian people. This is the reason why the Serbs, with the collaboration of other ethnic groups, continue unabatedly character assassination of Stepinac.

On October 31, 1918, the National Council of the State of Slovenes, Croats and Serbs, informed the Allied Powers of its decision to create a permanent and officially recognized unified state, the State of Slovenes, Croats and Serbs in the South-Slavic lands that had been part of Austro-Hungary. The Allies, weary of a succession of Balkan wars, agreed to the Council's proposal to unify the South Slavs, with clear expectations to prevent future wars by demonstrating to neighboring countries, mostly to Italy, Bulgaria and Hungary, that new wars in the region would be costly for all sides (Auty 1965; Banac 1984).

The Croats' main objective was to secure their culture, religious heritage and territorial rights as a means of protecting their national integrity from being "obliterated" by either Serbia or Italy. Slovenia, the smallest entity, also aspired to retain its unique characteristics. Thus, despite the mutually exclusive objectives held by each entity prior to their unification, the Kingdom of Serbs, Croats, and Slovenes (SHS) was proclaimed on December 1, 1918. The unified entity included the prewar kingdoms of Montenegro and Serbia and the South Slavic parts of Austria-Hungary (Slovenia, Croatia, Dalmatia, Bosnia and Herzegovina, and Vojvodina). What was difficult for Croats and Slovenes to comprehend was the fact that their lands were far more developed than Serbian and Bosnian ones. The Croats recognized that they were numerically smaller than the Serbs, yet they succeeded in fending off the Ottoman Empire while the Serbs, for five centuries were an occupied nation, yet they wished to be the leader. Thus, even before their unification, there was reason to be concerned about the success and longevity of such a union. Not only did economic disparity exacerbate the tensions and animosity between Serbs and Croats, it reverberated also to other ethnic groups (Banac 1984).

The illiterate and uneducated peasants did not easily adapt to the use of modern technologies or new agricultural practices, and agriculture continued to stagnate, making the country constantly dependent on imports (Šišić 1920, 201, 216-217, 275, 309; Djilas 1991, 108-109). This major necessity to rely on other countries for basic needs had created daunting economic problems. Although the agricultural sector, which employed 75% of the population, underwent radical pressure to modernize as Yugoslavia opened its borders to European markets, it failed to master the new technologies and implements. Thus, the Kingdom of Serbs, Croats and Slovenes remained underdeveloped, making the country reliant on foreign capital, much of which eventually came from Germany (Djilas 1991, 15-150).

Once the funds from France and Great Britain dried up, poverty and hardship were the outcome. The government, without much thought, sold mining rights to foreign companies but the proceeds from the sales, money, food, agricultural implements, failed to alleviate poverty and hunger. The heterogeneity and divergent interests among the constituent states also affected the national economy (Nazor and Ladić 2003, 325-376). Thus, due to persistent economic and political internal frictions and violence, on January 6, 1929, King Alexander dissolved the legislature, abolished the constitution, declared a royal dictatorship, and few months later renamed the country the Kingdom of Yugoslavia (Tomasevich 1955).

The declaration of a Serbian dictatorship blocked all hope of democratic solutions to Yugoslavia's problems. The Serb-Croat conflict was probably the most important single reason for the breakdown of the post-1918 Yugoslav state and for the escalation of brutalities during World War II – genocide and internecine massacres and counter-massacres by extremist Croatian, Serbian, and Muslim nationalists (Kolanović 1996). It is clear that the decision to unite with the Kingdom of Serbia demonstrated both Serbian strength and the Croatian Parliament's (Sabor) weakness.

After Unification the Croats Felt Betrayed and Cheated

Croatian discontent grew to dangerous proportions, as expressed in the "Memorandum" composed and written by Croats living in the Diaspora, as a petition for the "Croatian Right to Self-Determination." This document was sent to the League of Nations on behalf of Croatia and its citizens. The signatories included 250,000 American, Canadian, South American, and West European citizens of Croatian ancestry (HR-HDA a). In the document, the Croatian leadership enumerated in detail the ideals and aspirations of the Croatian people based on the principles expressed by Woodrow Wilson in his address at Mount Vernon on July 4, 1918. The grievances of the Croats came to a head following the assassination of Stjepan Radić, the Croatian Peasant Party leader (in 1928), two other Croatian deputies, and the wounding of other deputies in the Belgrade Parliament. It is clear that in 1918 the Croats entered the union of the South Slavs as a completely independent and free people with the objective to remain free and independent. The Memorandum delineates, on one hand, their aspirations on the eve of unification and, on the other, the consequences of that unification. Their aspirations were to achieve a united front of the South Slavs, but with the retention of Croatian Statehood. The Memorandum enumerates the intrigues in the Geneva protocols, the beginning of terrorism, and the Croats' refusal to accept the arrangement of December 1, 1918. The Croats also described how the pledge of national independence was broken, and the Constitution adopted was contrary to the parliamentary provisions. After King Alexander had dissolved the Parliament in 1929 and declared a personal dictatorship, the Croats in ever larger numbers began flocking towards the radical nationalist movement, the Ustasha. Their leader Ante Pavelić escaped from the country fearing retribution from the King's government. He was supported by the fascist Italian leader Benito Mussolini who had aimed to annex parts of the Adriatic. Pavelić's conception of the Jews was that they were an economic power in Croatia. He stated: "All financial businesses and all trade are in Jewish hands; and communism and Judaism work together against the national liberation of Croatia." (Curtis 1992, 29).

The Croats argued that, instead of obtaining better security, they suffered annihilation and a betrayal of Croatian interests in all spheres of life, particularly in the economic sphere. "The truth, as it unfolds is the matter-of-fact, official Serbian statistics for the year 1932. Contrary to the supposed demographic equality between the Serbs on one hand, and the Croats and Slovenians on the other, there are the following inequalities:

- Military Academy: 1,300 Serbs, 140 Croats, 50 Slovenians;
- Supreme Court: 30 Serbs, 1 Croat;
- The Presidential Council: 13 Serbs, 0 Croats;
- Foreign Affairs: 180 Serbs, 38 Croats;
- Army Generals: 115 Serbs, 1 Croat.

This is but one example out of many that are available to demonstrate the gross inequalities in all administrative offices, which were 80%, 95%, and up to 99% occupied by Serbs. Such was Serbian domination and its administrative anti-Croatianism." (HR-HAD b, c).

Most Croats attributed their predicament to the manipulation and exploitation of the economy by the government. It has been suggested that failure was structurally unavoidable and demonstrates how the governance of the Kingdom of Yugoslavia always depended on coercion. It was evident to the writers of the "Memorandum" that the Serbian monarch engaged in manipulative acts with the Croatian Treasury, which was "robbed" of more than two-thirds of its savings (HR-HAD b, c). The Croatian citizens also believed that the rate of taxation was not only unfair and exorbitant but also ruinous. The Croatian deputies accused Serbia of encouraging the relocation of business enterprises to Serbia; the Belgrade authorities refused to issue business licenses to Croatian firms unless their headquarters were relocated from Croatia to Serbia (Maček 1957, 113-117). On January 7, 1935, the American Citizens of Croatian Ancestry sent another "Protest to the League of Nations" against the Yugoslav Monarchy that had inflicted undue pain and suffering on the Croatian people (HR-HDA b, c).

Deep Discontent Leading to Establishment of the Ustasha Movement

As mentioned earlier, ever since the unification of the South Slavs in 1918, Croatian nationalists aimed to nullify the union with Serbia. In 1931, the world economic crisis had a major impact on Yugoslavia. Foreign trade plummeted, and the trade deficit skyrocketed. The exhaustion of credit sources to the South Slavs resulted in unemployment; mines closed, bankruptcies increased, and severe weather conditions caused rural starvation. Employment of Croatian workers was also a critical issue, particularly when Croatian government employees in Zagreb were replaced by Serbian manpower. Croatian discontent manifested itself primarily in the rising membership of right-wing nationalist parties. Heightened ethnic tensions thus provided a fertile climate for the Ustasha movement, which burgeoned in the mountainous regions of Croatia and Bosnia and Herzegovina where Catholic and Orthodox populations were intermixed and where the pressure against the Croats was most brutal. The combative spirit of poor Croatian villagers often led to their arrest and torture by the Yugoslav police. The issues of their protests included high taxes, a corrupt administration, and the harsh conditions of military service. They mistrusted the Serbian political and military elite and by extension all the Serbs (Djilas 1991, 110-120). In general, the Croatian peasant lived in the hope that at some future date an independent Croatian state would emerge, and the peasantry would be better off.

The majority of Croats wanted a way out of the union with Serbia, while the intellectuals still hoped to sustain it. It is interesting to note that both sides of the Croatian conflict gravitated towards authoritarian regimes: one to the right-wing ideologies of the highly nationalistic Croatian Peasant Party (Hrvatska seljačka stranka, HSS), including certain fascist elements, and the second, towards the left-wing ideology of communism and "brotherhood of all working men" (Maček 1936, see also Krizman 1986, 564-573).

It is evident that the basic characteristic of the Ustasha regime was appalling to many Croats. Therefore, the regime had limited popular support among ordinary people. The Ustasha were a small political group who were installed and maintained in power by the traditional enemies of the Croatian nation and who accepted international treaties that were injurious and degrading to the Croatian people. They inaugurated genocidal policies against the Serbian and Jewish populations and introduced drastic measures against the remaining Croatian population. In the 1930s, the population of nationalistic political prisoners and the peasants recognized Ante Pavelić as their leader since he expressed his determination to free the country from Serbian bondage. Among the discontented peasants, proto-fascist sentiment sprouted on the fertile ground of hatred. (Kolanović 1996; Goldstein and Goldstein 2001, 68-69). Even though many peasants considered Pavelić as their leader, nevertheless an Ustasha comprehensive ideology did not exist in Croatia prior to the beginning of World War II. However, from the inception, the Ustasha declared that they would resort to violence, if necessary, to obtain freedom from Serbia. Ante Pavelić, who signed his letters as Poglavnik (The Leader), stated:

> "The dagger, revolver, machine gun and bomb, those are the bells that will ring the dawn and the Resurrection of the Independent State of Croatia."
>
> In 1934 Pavelić was a co-conspirator in the successful plot to assassinate King Alexander of Yugoslavia and French Foreign Minister Barthou (NARA a).

From all that had transpired during the 23 years under the unified South Slavs it is apparent that the co-mingling of peoples in a political structure by itself is not sufficient to achieve true unification that creates a "nation." The South Slavs demonstrably lacked the cultural attributes and the sense of a common history that together could provide a strong foundation for political unity. It is not surprising that ethnic distrust, religious rivalry, language barriers, and cultural conflicts plagued the political entity that began as the Kingdom of Serbs, Croats, and Slovenes, and after 1929 was known as the Kingdom of Yugoslavia (Đodan 1970, 50-51).

The Emergence of Anti-Semitism

In 1940, Prince Pavle (Paul) of the Kingdom of Yugoslavia, visited Nazi Germany's leader Adolf Hitler, and *Numerus Clausus* (closed number) was applied to Jews in Yugoslavia. This most specifically referred to their admission to institutions of higher learning, their admission to positions carrying a special status, like the military. The new law also affected the livelihood of many Jewish businesses specializing in the trade of certain food items and products which they imported. By April 1941, most of Yugoslavia was occupied but no longer as a unified country. It was dismembered among the Axis partners. Each received a part of the territories they held as being theirs. Serbia was under Nazi control but in practice Milan Nedić, a former general, gained control. (For Serbian Nazi past and the Holocaust of-Jews see: Helsinki Committee for Human Rights in Serbia. http://http:// holocaust-of-Jews-in-serbia.blogspot.hr).

Those who had introduced anti-Semitic ideology in Yugoslavia were not the Ustasha but the Serbian elite; the publishers of books such as *Protocols of the Elders of Zion* translated and published in Serbia from 1929 to 1945. Although the book was banned for distribution, nevertheless from 1933 to 1940 (Lazar Prokić's pamphlete dates from 1941) more than ten anti-Semitic brochures were published. In 1941, Lazar Prokić published the article "Naši problemi – Jevreji u Srbiji" ["Our Problems: Jews in Serbia"] in the newspaper *Obnova* (*Renewal*), on November 15, 1941. *Zbor* (*Assembly*) published a brochure titled: "Srpski narod u kandžama Jevreja" ["Serb People in the Claws of Jews"] written by Milorad Mojić. The founder of *Obnova,* Dimitrije Ljotić, modeled his work after *Mein Kampf*. In *Obnova* and *Naša borba* (*Our Struggle*) Milorad Mojić advocated: "An energetic liquidation of Jews unless we want to witness the destruction of the Christian civilization." (See Appendix 1 for a comprehensive list of anti-Semitic literature in Serbia.)

Historians should search Google and eBay among many other sources in which they will find hundreds of anti-Semitic posters and stamps issued by Serbia. No other occupied country had such a privilege to carry its own country name on posters and stamps! From 1941-45, fifty-one (51) anti-Semitic brochures were published in Serbia (United States Holocaust Memorial Museum, https://collections.ushmm.org/search/catalog/pa1102421).

On October 22, 1941, the Grand Anti-Masonic Exhibition opened in Belgrade. The exhibition focused on an alleged Jewish-Masonic, communist conspiracy for world domination and contained a vicious setup. One of the directors of the exhibition declared that the Serbs would have little compassion for Jewish suffering since "Zionists" - those who dream and hope to rebuild their ancient homeland in Palestine - cannot be loyal citizens and that they are a foreign element in Yugoslavia. It is possible that Serbian Prime Minister Milan Nedić had borrowed the Serbian propaganda from the Tsarist Secret Police before the Russian Revolution in the well-known forgeries of *Protocols of the Elders of Zion*. Besides the exhibits, the visitors encountered vast amounts of propaganda material at the exhibition. This material was aimed at arousing in ordinary Serbs even greater hatred than they already felt towards the Jews. The exhibition organizers advertised that "this concept of exhibition will be unique not only in Serbia and the Balkans, not only in southeastern Europe and Europe, but in the world." (United States Holocaust Memorial Museum, (https://collections.ushmm.org/search/ catalog/pa1102421). On the grounds of the exhibition there were over 200 thousand various brochures, 60 thousand posters, 100 thousand flyers, 108 thousand samples of 9 different types of envelopes, 176 propaganda movie clips, four different postage stamps etc. (United States Holocaust Memorial Museum, (https://collections.ushmm.org/search/catalog/pa1102421https://collections.ushmm.org/search /catalog/pa1102421) (see Appendix 1).

Anton Korošec was a Slovene Catholic priest and politician. From 1935 to1938 he was Minister of the Interior supporting the introduction of fascism into Yugoslavia and collaborating with Nazi Germany and fascist Italy. In September 1938, he stated:

"The Jewish issue did not exist in Yugoslavia." Yet at the same time he refused to accept Jews fleeing from war-stricken Europe. (AMHI, doc. 16, file 1'"4, box 2.7; doc·2.6, file 1"'6, box 27, cited in Philip Cohen 1996; See also p. 72. See also, *Obnova* and *Naša borba,* Appendix 1). A year later he proclaimed: "Jewish refugees from Nazi Germany are not welcome here."

While Stepinac, the archbishop of Zagreb, grieved for the lost lives and assisted in the conversion of Jews and others, it is noted that Jews and Roma were not permitted to convert to Serbian Orthodox religion in order to save their lives. Thus, Belgrade became the first city in Europe free of Jews or *Judenfrei* (Gitman 2019, p.80). Serbian Bishop Nikolaj Velimirović, who had spent two months as the "honorary prisoner" in Dachau, wrote:

> "Europe is presently the main battlefield of the Jew and his father, the devil, against the heavenly Father and his only begotten Son… (Jews) first need to become legally equal with Christians in order to repress Christianity, next turn Christians into atheists, and step on their necks. All the modern European slogans have been made up by Jews, the crucifiers of Christ: democracy, strikes, socialism and atheism, tolerance of all religions, pacifism, universal revolution, capitalism and communism… All this has been done with the intention to eliminate Christ. You should think about this, my Serbian brethren, and correspondingly correct your thoughts, desires and acts." (Velimirović 1985, 161-162).

Despite widespread animosity towards the regime in Belgrade, a comprehensive Ustasha ideology of plunder and annihilation of Serbs, Jews and Gypsies was not formulated before World War II (Goldstein and Goldstein 2001, 68-69). While in Italy, Pavelić absorbed the basic tenets of the fascist philosophy although he had not formulated a coherent policy on how to treat the three ethnic groups. It took Hitler to tell him what and how to do it. Pavelić was aware that, despite the disappearance of capital and credit during the Depression years, Jews managed to establish national and international personal connections, which allowed them to conduct trade without interruption and develop their enterprises. Except in Bosnia and Macedonia, Jews throughout Yugoslavia, and especially those in Serbia and Croatia, prospered during this period, which was one of hardship for the rest of the country. Aided by Nazi propaganda, Jewish success and envy of their prosperity fed some contentious reactions, but not yet physical and violent anti-Semitism (Gitman 2019, 71-76).

The Third Reich's plans for Europe were modeled after the success in consolidating the entire German nation: industry, bureaucracy, the party, and the military around one purpose – conquest. This "impressive" integration of the four pillars of social structure also included countrymen living abroad. In Yugoslavia they relied on 500,000 Volksdeutsche (Yugoslav citizens of German origin). In this new system, the citizens of the Third Reich and those collaborating with them were indoctrinated with the idea that change in the political, economic, social, and religious structures was of the essence and the price to pay for social progress (Neumann 1942). Their ideology was characterized by the slogan: "Today Germany belongs to us, tomorrow the entire world." (Colville 2002, 154).

The means for achieving this goal were summed up by Heinrich Himmler: "The only way to solve the social problem is for one lot to kill the others and take their land." (Goetz and Heim 2002, 25-26). Nazi ideology intended to trample the Judeo-Christian ethic (Talmon

1973). Coming to power on April 10, 1941, with the support of Nazi Germany and fascist Italian sponsors, Pavelić was installed as a leader by the Axis partners. Prior to this, the Croatian Peasant Party (HSS) leader Vladko Maček declined the German offer to assume the post of head of an independent Croatian state. For Pavelić, Hitler's choice, his Bosnian birth, and his ten years in exile, most of it in Italy, were political liabilities in nationalist Croatia.

From the beginning, most of the Croatian intelligentsia was hostile to the Ustasha regime and its policies. Pavelić often took note of this and was quoted as saying that "in Croatia, the Zagreb intelligentsia above all was against the government." Thus, Pavelić was obliging and malleable for Germany. In return for Croatian territorial gains and "independence" from Serbia, Nazi Germany demanded that Pavelić's regime implements the Nazi-like ideology enshrined in legislation for the "Protection of the Croatian (Aryan) People" (Ciano 1946, 341).

With Germany's indulgence, Pavelić and his associates developed a somewhat idiosyncratic notion of racial purity that encompassed not just the Volksdeutsche and the 6.3 million nominally Slavic Croats but also the 750,000 Bosnian Muslims in Bosnia and Herzegovina, who were deemed by the new state as "the flower of the Croatian people," and thus "honorary Aryans" (NARA f).

Under Axis occupation, Yugoslavia reverted to a collection of disparate states, all of them plagued by chaos and civil war (Matković 1994, 242).

STEPINAC AND THE INDEPENDENT STATE OF CROATIA (NDH)

Nazi Germany occupied the entire country and partitioned it among the Axis Partners. The Croats gained freedom from Serbia only to come under the control and tutelage of Nazi Germany. In return for Germany's financial and military assistance, Pavelić made ideological concessions, one of them being the vigorous implementation of the Final Solution to the Jewish Question in the NDH. To expedite the process of annihilation of Jews and others, Nazi Germany provided a template to accomplish this task: first, confiscate all Jewish assets and use them to rebuild the NDH and expel Jews from all public posts. Second, destroy their religious and cultural symbols and finally exterminate them (Gitman 2015).

Already in May 1941, Stepinac realized that Nazi Germany was in control and that Pavelić was a puppet executing their commands. He voiced concern to the NDH leaders warning them that their inhumane policies against the Jews and others embraced a totalitarian character, which threatened to inflict great harm to the Croatian people and the Catholic Church, for years to come. He stated:

> "The Ustasha would be a liability to the humanitarian fabric of the Croatian society for years to come... The Croatian government would have to bear full responsibility for the growth of the Communist partisan movement... because of severe and unlawful measures employed against Orthodox Serbs, Jews and Gypsies, in imitation of German methods." (Gitman 2019, 54).

The loss in human lives during the war was disturbing and morally repugnant to many Croats. They began writing petitions to their new government explaining that the hunted Jews were good, honest, and hardworking people and that it was a mistake to persecute them. In the Croatian State Archives, I uncovered 520 petitions on behalf of Jews, signed by thousands, which indicated that concerned citizens expected an answer from their government (Gitman 2005).

Stepinac was bound by the Church Constitution, the Hague and Geneva Conventions to interact with the forces of occupation for the sake of public peace and order. Stepinac had to remain on speaking terms with Pavelić because he was the only controlling authority that was in a position to alleviate the terror and the killings. Stepinac's letters, like those of his parishioners, were sent to both Ante Pavelić and Interior Minister Andrija Artuković, in which he expressed his distress with the conduct of the government. Stepinac denounced Nazism, fascism, communism, and the inhumanity of the Ustasha and throughout the war years he followed one maxim: '*only one race exists and that is the human race created by God.*' Nevertheless, Stepinac recognized that his holiest duty as a representative of the Catholic Church was to raise his voice against the conduct of the Ustasha. Ivo Politeo, his trial defense lawyer, let the people know that:

> "...They [Stepinac's sermons] were attended in masses not only by the Catholics but even by those who otherwise did not go to Church. Those sermons were spread, recounted, copied and distributed in thousands and thousands of copies among the people and even penetrated to the liberated territory. They became an underground press, a means of successful propaganda against the Ustasha, a partial substitute for an opposition press." (NARA c).

Stepinac's efforts to prevent the annihilation of innocent people angered the Nazis who served in Zagreb and in one of their daily reports they informed Germany of the Archbishop's continued sermons stating:

> "Only one race really exists and that is the Divine race. Its birth certificate is found in the Book of Genesis. All of them without one exception, whether they belong to the race of Gypsies or to another, whether they are Negroes or civilized Europeans, whether they are detested Jews or proud Aryans, have the same right to say 'Our Father who Art in Heaven'" (HR-HDA d; O'Brien 1947, 19).

Fearless, Stepinac went on to say: "The system of shooting hundreds of hostages for a crime, when the person guilty of the crime cannot be found, is a pagan system which only results in evil." (Pattee 1953, 285-286). Stepinac often emphasized: "It can bring us no glory if it is said about us that we have solved the Jewish problem in the most radical way that is to say, the cruelest." (Štambuk-Škalić et al. 1997, 162, document 6.23.1).

During his trial in 1946, Stepinac indicated that the Serbs ascribed to him the guilt for the rebaptism of Serbs. He said that this was a misleading expression for who is once baptized, need not be re-baptized.

In one of his conversations with Stanislaw Rapotetz, a Slovene who was in the service of the Royal Serbian family in London and was sent on a mission to inquire how to transfer funds for the starving Serbian population, Stepinac acknowledged:

> "The Germans and Ustasha destroyed our people's souls and bodies. Their gory work was made easier by those in our midst who are false of heart. Among the false, to

our shame, were Catholic priests in isolated localities, who as individuals used their holy robes for treacherous political purposes. They were no longer men of God acting under the authority of the Church. They represented nothing, no one, but their own warped desires, whetted by what they saw with their diseased eyes of German power and glory." (NARA e; Phayer 2001, 38).

The Archbishop was stigmatized by Pavelić's Minister Julije Makanec, for his failure to grasp the sign of the times and the significance of the issues. He was directly accused of meddling in politics:

"…that high ecclesiastical dignitary who has recently, in his sermons, passed beyond the limits of his vocation and begun to meddle in affairs in which he is not competent. He who does not understand the meaning of political struggle, who has no comprehension of political values, and who does not know how to weigh and evaluate them, will always do best to keep himself aloof from the political sphere, leaving these affairs to those more competent." (Makanec 1943).

It is to be noted that with the declassification of U.S. Intelligence Records under the Nazi War Crimes Disclosure Act of 1998, many one-sided perspectives were replaced by more nuanced versions of the role Alojzije Stepinac played in the drama of World War II. My own research demonstrates that Stepinac forcefully denounced the violation of human rights through legislation directed against Jews, Serbs and Roma, and that at every opportunity he demanded a return to the Law of God. In 1941, when two of his priests and six nuns whose origin was Jewish were absolved from wearing the yellow Star of David intended by the Nazis as a badge of shame, Stepinac solemnly declared:

"I have requested that these priests and nuns continue wearing this sign of belonging to the people from which Our Savior was born as long as others will have to do so." (O'Brien 1947, 20).

During the first month e Stepinac tried to work with the Ustasha government (Žubrinić 1997). This might have been in part because Pavelić portrayed himself as a "good Catholic" who would enforce "Christian values" neglected in the previously heterogeneous society. Cooperation between Stepinac and Pavelić was short-lived; after one month Stepinac distanced himself from the regime and began criticizing the Ustasha's barbarous racial activities. Tomasevich states that the ire of the Croats towards Pavelić is not surprising. First, the Ustasha as a political group was corrupt on a large scale. Second, for many people, the arbitrary nature of justice in the NDH resulted in arrests, jail, concentration camps, death or disappearance. People in authority with good contacts, such as Stepinac and others, intervened with powerful individuals and state authorities on behalf of those victimized by the regime. In the NDH, such intervention became part of the system (Krišto 2007, 59; Tomasevich 2002, 349).

Writer Evelyn Waugh, then a captain affiliated with the British Mission in Yugoslavia, on June 17, 1945 sent the following testimony about Stepinac's protests against Pavelić and the deportations of Jews, stating:

> "Thus, in June 1941 Archbishop Stepinac led a deputation to Pavelić to protest against the persecution of the Jews; many of the clergy of Zagreb wore the yellow star in the streets to ridicule Pavelić's attempt to mark Jews in the Nazi manner. Recently Archbishop Stepinac issued a condemnation of the acts of cruelty committed by both sides. The Archbishop also expelled some people from the University for their criticism of the anti-Ustasha activities of the clergy." (Waugh 1979, 17-26).

This highlights the proactive role that Stepinac played in saving human lives.

On May 17, 1941, Pavelić went on a mission to Rome in order to seek recognition from the Holy See. The Pope agreed to see him, but only as a private individual, not as head of state, thus dashing Pavelić's hopes of gaining legitimacy for himself and the Ustasha regime. But Stepinac resolutely refused to join the delegation to Rome. Bishop Salis-Seewis explained:

> "The Archbishop chose not to be part of Pavelić's delegation. I was selected. I objected, arguing that I didn't like the idea of being mixed up in this business... I knew that the people from the (Croatian) Peasant Party were against it; those people were already sympathizing with the English and the French. The Archbishop, however, just said: that's the way it's got to be' "Kaj je, je" [What is, is]...at that moment we couldn't all withdraw, I went" (Glas Koncila 1967).

The most painful issue for Pavelić was the Vatican's refusal to recognize the NDH, citing its established custom that it did not recognize states created during war until peace treaties were concluded and the new states were accepted into the community of nations after the hostilities ended. Abbot Giuseppe Ramiro Marcone was assigned to the NDH as the Apostolic Visitor with the Croatian episcopate, and the Croatian state had an unofficial representative in the Vatican. Viewing Stepinac's failure to sway the Vatican to the side of the NDH, Pavelić blamed Stepinac for the setback for the new so-called "Catholic state" (Krizman 1983, 140).

The files of Hans Helm demonstrate that Archbishop Stepinac was often identified as a "traitor" by the Nazis and the extreme Ustasha. Helm, who was a Third Reich police attaché in Zagreb, sent daily documents to Berlin informing the authorities also that the life of the Archbishop was in danger (HR-HAD e). From the testimonies given by Hinko Mann to the National Commission in 1945, as well as Amiel Shomrony and other survivors, it is clear that Stepinac was called to act on behalf of the Jews with the Ustasha on many occasions. He always responded favorably, but often his interventions were unsuccessful since he was considered a "Jew lover" by the regime. Obviously, the regime had no interest in assisting him, particularly when the cause involved helping the Jews. Stepinac's efforts were often unanswered because of a conflict of interest between his requests and the goals of the Ustasha and the Gestapo (HR-HAD f; File 365; Shelah 1990, 292-293).

Every year, the bishops of Croatia gathered in Zagreb for a meeting. The bishops had to resolve the delicate situation of converted Jews. The bishops requested that the NDH government give the Jews who had converted to Catholicism and their family members all the rights and privileges granted to Croatian citizens (at that time there were thousands of converts). Furthermore, the bishops demanded that all the properties and assets of the converted Jewish be protected (HR-HAD g).

Refuting the Stands That Stepinac Did Too Little to Save Jews during the Holocaust

There are ample examples available to demonstrate Stepinac's unending efforts to rescue people, regardless of their religious, ethnic, or political affiliation. He was a young energetic man with great compassion. In contrast to Korošec, Stepinac already in 1936 appealed to his wealthier parishioners, stating:

> "Dear Sir, due to violent and inhuman persecution, a large number of people have had to leave their homeland. They were left without means for a normal life; they wander throughout the world... Every day, a large number of emigrants contact us asking for intervention, for help in money and goods. It is our Christian duty to help them... I ask you to write your monthly contribution in the enclosed leaflet." Signature: Alojzije Stepinac, the Archbishop of Zagreb (HR-HDA h).

This letter attests to the fact that Archbishop Stepinac was not a Germanophile, fond of the Germans, but on the contrary, he did everything to shield the Jews and all others whom the Germans for whatever reason wanted to persecute. The letter was found among the documents of the NDH government in exile in 1945. Information most relevant to Stepinac's rescue of Jews includes the documented testimonies by individuals whom he rescued and by those who witnessed such occurrences, and by those who learned about them from primary sources (Krišto 2007; see also, *Fontes*, 2/1996, https://hrcak.srce.hr/fontes).

Anthony O'Brien count of Thomond, a British citizen, stayed in Zagreb for over two years. He developed a close relationship with Stepinac during this period. In 1941, O'Brien escaped from Zagreb and ended up on the Croatian island of Korčula. He related that, for safety reasons, approximately 1,000 NDH Jews were corralled on that island, which was referred to as the "Island of the Jews." O'Brien stated:

"What the Jews on the Island of Korčula reported, while I waited for a transport to Ireland, made me feel proud of belonging to the Catholic Church. I was prouder than I have ever felt in my whole life. His [Stepinac's] was a particularly high conception of authority and the rule of law. He was the most outspoken opponent of mob rule. And yet, it was to be his fate to live in two periods when mob rule, in its two worst possible forms, was rampant in his own country: first the National Socialist and fascist regimes and then the communist regime." (O'Brien 1947, 12-13).

Judge Srećko Bujas, although appointed by the Ustasha as a commissioner to oversee the Sephardic Jews in Sarajevo, was a fair and dedicated public servant. He cooperated with the Zagreb and Osijek Jewish communities in their effort to alleviate the hardship of the inmates. In his postwar testimony, to the National Commission for the Verification of Crimes committed against the Jews, he informed the Commission about the unique relationship that existed between Zagreb Rabbi Freiberger and Archbishop Stepinac:

> "Whenever I visited the Jewish Community in Zagreb, I met the chief Rabbi, Dr. Freiberger, and the President, Dr. Hugo Kon, and presented to them the current situation of the Jews of Sarajevo. At those meetings, I heard both of them give high praise to the

manly and heroic stand of the Archbishop of Zagreb and the help and the assistance provided by the nuns in this period of the deportation of Jews. He also related to the Commission that the Rabbi read many of Stepinac's uplifting sermons." (HR-HDA i).

Over 60 personal testimonies were submitted to Yad Vashem on behalf of Archbishop Alojzije Stepinac and sent twice to Jerusalem, in the 1970s and again in the 1990s, with the objective to include Archbishop Alojzije Stepinac among the *Righteous among the Nations*. It is impossible to make reference to all the testimonies. Therefore, I will mention here just a few.

Ljudevit Stein, born in Zagreb in 1935, described how in 1943 Archbishop Stepinac saved him from the detention center on Savska Street. He stated that on June 14-15, there were mass deportations of Jews. Margita Stilinović, his father's sister, was married to a Catholic and was desperate to save Stein, her only surviving relative. After everything failed, she approached Stepinac, whom she begged to intervene on behalf of her eight-year-old nephew. In his letter to Yad Vashem, Ljudevit states that he, his wife, and their children are eternally grateful to Stepinac who rescued him (Stein 1999, 1-2).

Olga Rajšek-Neumann, a Catholic, described how with the assistance of Archbishop Stepinac she became, in 1942, the rescuer of Danko Stockhammer. Dr. Danko Stockhammer and his wife Lea Kon Stockhammer, residents of Chicago, wrote to Yad Vashem on behalf of Archbishop Stepinac, they are grateful for having rescued them from the Ustasha and shielding them in his orphanage till the end of the war. I had an opportunity to interview Olga Rajšek-Neumann on December 26, 2002, in Zagreb.

Dan Baram's testimony describes how Stepinac saved his life.

Dr. Teodor Gruner stated that his father, Bernard Gruner, the chief Cantor of the Jewish Community in Zagreb, was captured and sent to the city's central detention center. Gruner stated that Stepinac had pressured the authorities to release the cantor on the grounds that his son was a physician in the service of the government on a medical mission in Bosnia.

Major General Dr. Stjepan Steiner described with respect and admiration the efforts exerted on behalf of Jews by Stepinac and Dr. Ante Vuletić, whom he defined as "two extraordinary Croats" who rescued a large number of Jews during the war (Gitman 2005, 2009, 2011). When I asked him for a number, he suggested that Stepinac had saved at least 400 Jews, besides those from mixed marriages, and those in the Italian zones (Gitman 2003, 2005).

Dr. Amiel Shomrony, who relocated to Israel after the war, was a former secretary of Rabbi Miroslav Shalom Freiberger, the chief rabbi of Croatia. He knew Archbishop Stepinac well and he was eager to tell me everything he knew about him and what he had done to protect and rescue Jews. His hope was that one of his many visitors who heard his story would be willing and able to convince the authorities at Yad Vashem to grant the Stepinac the award of the title *Righteous among the Nations* (Gitman 2003, 172, 190).

During Tito's regime only a few historians loyal to him had access to archival documents. These individuals failed to publish material on serious philosophical conflicts between the Church and the Ustasha regime regarding the duty of Christians. On several occasions, the Vatican offered Stepinac a choice to lead a different kind of life, but his conscience and his strong belief in the inalienable rights of each person to live the life given to them by the Creator motivated him to stay in Zagreb and care for thousands of victims who totally depended on him – first and foremost his parishioners, and also many others who were rejected by the Nazi and the Ustasha regimes. Stepinac was motivated to act in accordance with his conscience and the tenets of the Catholic Church, relative to saving the lives of those who were in danger and who sought his assistance. He was fully devoted to this task.

One of Stepinac's biggest actions to save Jews and Serbs in the NDH was his acceptance and defense of "mixed marriages." However, on May 3, 1943, the newspaper *Narodne novine* in a bold caption declared:

> "Statutory Orders given by Pavelić [the Poglavnik], state that as of today, all the customary and legal practices of conversion from one religion to another are abolished. For a conversion to be legal, a person desiring to change his religious denomination must first notify the local authority and receive an official receipt that the notification was registered. At the same time, a declaration has to be made from which religion a person desires to convert. Only after approval is granted by the Minister of Religion can a person approach a local church." (*Narodne novine* 1941).

However, Stepinac vigorously defended mixed marriages, and the news reverberated throughout the NDH. Many Croatian women, whose husbands were Jewish, were advised by their priests to seek help from Archbishop Stepinac. Women from Osijek, Zagreb, Sarajevo and other locations wrote heart-wrenching letters to Stepinac begging and pleading with him to act on behalf of their husbands, which he did. In March 1943, Nazi agent Hubner wrote to Hans Helms, the Nazi police attaché in Zagreb, that he had received the following information from his agents, code names Mravunac and Gošnjak:

> "As a result of the registration of Jews in mixed marriages some of them turned to Archbishop Stepinac requesting his protection. It is also said that the Archbishop promised protection and that he sent a letter to the Pope in Rome. According to the 'dogmas' of the Catholic Church, a couple in a mixed marriage cannot be separated. And if the Croatian government undertakes action against mixed marriages, then in protest against such acts the Archbishop will close all the Catholic Churches for a certain period. Stepinac considers such acts as an interference in the internal affairs of the Church."

Furthermore, there were rumors circulating in Zagreb that the Pope personally approached Hitler to obtain assurances that no actions would be taken against mixed marriages (HR-HAD j).

During World War II, Amiel Shomrony, was personal secretary to the Chief Rabbi of Zagreb, Dr. Freiberger. Since Amiel's father had special protection known as "Honorary Aryan" even as late as 1943, he was free to roam the streets of Zagreb without having to identify himself as a Jew. On one such errand for the Rabbi, he went to the Archdiocese where he was informed that, in the following few days, there would be new roundups of Jews and that on this occasion all Jews, including those who enjoyed special protection, will be captured and sent to concentration camps. On this last occasion, Amiel was told that Archbishop Stepinac wishes to invite the Rabbi, his wife Irena, his parents and his sister Ljubica to relocate for safety reasons to his palace in the Archdiocese of Zagreb (Bilten 1996, interview). In this interview Amiel Shomrony was asked: "If Archbishop Stepinac helped so many Jews, why, then, have such a small number of Jews spoken on his behalf?" He replied:

> "The Jews are neither united nor do they hold one opinion in their own country or in the world. I, for example, never favored the communist regime, this is one of the reasons that I never chose to return to Zagreb, yet many Jews favored communism."

When Rabbi Freiberger heard that the plan of deportation included all the Jews of Zagreb, he graciously declined Stepinac's offer to stay with him, choosing instead to be deported with his community. However, the Rabbi wanted to know if he could send his library for safekeeping to the Archdiocese. Stepinac gladly fulfilled the Rabbi's wish. After the war, Amiel Shomrony confirmed that the entire library was saved and returned intact to the newly reopened Jewish Community. Archbishop Stepinac served as a role model for many other clerics as well as his own parishioners because of his assistance and conduct (Bilten 1996; interview; Shomrony, interview, October 10, 2003, Nathania, near Tel-Aviv, Israel).

Shomrony's testimony is not unique in emphasizing the close working relationship that existed between the Archbishop and the Jewish Community. The letters of the Chief Rabbi of Croatia, Rabbi Miroslav Šalom Freiberger, attest to their positive relationship. The Rabbi frequently turned to the Church for assistance; on July 4, 1942 he wrote a letter of thanks to Pius XII. The Rabbi indicated that the remaining Jews had lost almost all hope and had no more energy to fight the daily hardships. They placed their destiny in the hands of God who had saved his Jewish people for 2,000 years. The Rabbi ended his letter to Pius XII by saying that he would like to confirm his eternal gratitude to the Church and Archbishop Stepinac (Krišto 2007, documents 287, 298, 198, 209).

On December 15, 1942, Rabbi Freiberger, through the Apostolic Visitor to Croatia, Monsignor Giuseppe Ramiro Marcone, asked the Holy See for help in transferring 50 to 60 orphan children from Zagreb to any of the three places, Florence, Livorno, and Padua, where Jews were waiting for them. Another letter from the Rabbi asked Stepinac to speak on behalf of 200 Jewish orphan boys aged 7-17 who needed to be evacuated to Italy. On January 9, 1942, the Archbishop sent a letter to Cardinal Maglione requesting his assistance and intervention in sending 200 boys to the Jewish community in Florence – or to any other community that would care for them and enable them to attend regular school (Krišto 2007, 231, 242). (A reply was received whereby the Minister of Interior did not approve the relocation of the children from Zagreb to Italy).

One of the most heroic acts of both Archbishop Stepinac and Abbot Marcone occurred in mid-May 1942. A problem emerged when the Governor of Dalmatia, Giuseppe Bastianini, reported that the number of Jews entering the annexed territories had escalated to alarming levels. He issued orders to repel the refugees, despite the traumatic scenes of frantic Jews trying to escape. Nevertheless, Bastianini requested military intervention to end the exodus to Dalmatia (Shelah 1986, 257). When news of Bastianini's planned extradition of Jews from the Italian zones to the NDH – with fateful consequences – reached Stepinac, he, in concert with Abbot Marcone, decided to act. An urgent message was sent to Cardinal Luigi Maglione, the Vatican's Secretary of State, to request that the Italian authorities reconsider Bastianini's request and allow Jews to remain in the Italian annexed territories on the Adriatic (Shelah 1986, 258). Permission was granted (Shelah 1986, 281; Phayer 2001, 84). The grounds for this permit were the argument that by 1942 about 30 percent of the Jews of Zagreb had converted. Because some were baptized, Maglione obtained permission from the Italian government to allow all Yugoslav Jewish refugees to remain in the Italian zones (Shelah

1986, 281). Approximately 5,000 Jews survived there – 1,000 in Korčula, 3,600 on the Island of Rab, and some were spread all over. For all these undertakings Stepinac's life was in danger and on several occasions, he was kept locked. He was spared only thanks to the love, admiration and the loyalty of his people.

The Jews survived in the Italian zones of occupation thanks to Stepinac and the Vatican until September 1943. Once Italy capitulated, over 5,000 Jews had survived there (Shelah 1990, 277-308).

On April 8, 1943, Archbishop Stepinac arranged work permits for the Jewish Community in Zagreb that remained open even after the Rabbi's deportation. He also wrote a letter to Interior Minister Andrija Artuković:

> "Mr. Minister, I feel free to present to you a request from the Jewish Community in Zagreb to release from detention some of their employees so as to resume work for the welfare of their members. Minister, I hope you will accommodate their request and instruct your people to free some of their workers. I am thankful to you for all you have done and for the things you will do in the future so that the ethical and Christian character of our people may be saved. Respectfully, Dr. Alojzije Stepinac." (HR-HAD k; Štambuk-Škalić et al. 1997, 64).

On December 6, 1943, the German authorities in Zagreb entered the home for the Jewish elderly "Lavoslav Schwarz" and ordered the residents to vacate the building within ten days. The Nazis warned them that if they would not leave, they would be deported to Auschwitz. Josipa Schulhof, a former employee of the Jewish community testified that when a demand to vacate the home for the elderly came, in their desperation the head of the Jewish Community turned to Archbishop Stepinac who immediately agreed to provide a building and a permission to renovate it so as to accommodate 58 elderly. Alojzije Stepinac, organized the transfer of all the elderly, about 58 people, to the archbishopric's building in Brezovica near Zagreb (Gitman 2005, Appendix 6.1.8; HR-HAD l). The former residents of "Lavoslav Schwarz" lived on Catholic premises for four years, from 1943-1947 (Goldstein 1991). During their stay from 1943 to 1947, the elderly received regular financial assistance from a humanitarian organization in Switzerland. Archbishop Stepinac cared for them and attended to their needs. Because they were under the protection of the Church, all survived only five residents died, all of natural causes (HR-HDA m).

On October 16, 1944, two individuals Jakica Gaon and Moric Katan who managed to escape from the Island of Rab, reached the Jewish Community in Zagreb. Despite warnings not to leave the premises, they left and were captured. The Ustasha entered the premises of the Jewish Community and arrested all eight employees. With the assistance of Archbishop Stepinac, Dr. Robert Glücksthal, the official representative of the Jewish Community and his assistant Asher Kišicki were released due to the intervention by representatives of the International Red Cross. Archbishop Stepinac made it possible for the Jewish Community of Zagreb to function to the end of World War II (HR-HDA m).

Many acknowledged with gratitude and praise the Archbishop's work on behalf of the Jews. After the burial of Sabina Steiner, the Jews made a collection to honor the dead. The sum collected was donated to an orphanage in gratitude and honor of Archbishop Stepinac (HR-HDA n).

Dr. Meir Tuval Weltmann represented the Jews in Palestine and was stationed in Istanbul in order to assist in the rescue of European Jews. On June 11, 1943, he wrote two letters of thanks, one to apostolic legate Monsignor Angelo Roncalli (later Pope John XXIII) and the second to Archbishop Stepinac. Weltmann wrote:

> "With deep gratitude, recognition and appreciation to the Holy See and to Archbishop of Zagreb Stepinac for his conduct and assistance to the Jews of Croatia and especially for assisting Dr. Hugo Kon and the Chief Rabbi Dr. Freiberger. A specific request was made to Archbishop Stepinac to use his power to convince the regime to allow the Jews to transfer peacefully to Hungary and Italy and, from there, to Palestine." (Krišto 2007, 300, documents 291, 292).

In February 1944, Chief Rabbi Herzog wrote two letters from Ankara on the eve of his departure for Eretz Israel (Palestine). One letter is addressed to the apostolic legate, Monsignor Angelo Roncalli, and the second to Archbishop Stepinac:

> "Before my departure, God willing tonight, I wish to extend my deepest gratitude for your energetic efforts to rescue our unfortunate, innocent victims from unimaginable fear and forceful conduct. This inhuman conduct with which our people are confronted is contrary to all religious and moral behavior. Please convey my appreciations to the Holy See from the bottom of my heart. May God bless you with the blessings of Zion and Jerusalem? The Jewish people will never forget the help of His Holiness and his high officials."
>
> His letter addressed to Archbishop Stepinac:
>
> "Here I am, for some time now, making an effort to assist our unfortunate brethren and sisters who face tremendous persecutions.... I beg of you, do all you can to save the sons of Abraham, Isaac, and Jacob in our most tragic moment in history, one that is still living proof of God's providence in this world." (Krišto 2007, 343-344, documents 329, 330).

I challenge the widespread perception given by some historians, among them two Israelis, Dr. Efraim Zuroff (HINA 2015) and Dr. Gideon Greif (Kosanović 2019), and the Serbian regime that the entire Croatian population then and now is guilty of the crimes committed by the Ustasha. Stepinac's accusers fail to mention that 150,000 Croats were partisans, including Stepinac's family members. At this point I would seriously ask some historians to provide documents when criticizing Alojzije Stepinac and demonstrate to the readers the grounds for their criticism.

Alojzije Stepinac, Pillar of Human Rights

My research in Zagreb archives revealed that Archbishop Stepinac helped not only Jews; he helped Serbs, Roma, representatives of the Yugoslav monarchy in London and many others. Stepinac was unique – he held strong views that all human beings are God's creation and as such have a right to a life with dignity. The paragraphs below were uttered by Stepinac and they illustrate how and why he has been the pillar of human rights (Gitman 2019):

> "The Catholic Church cannot accept that one race or one nation, because it is more numerous or better armed, may commit violence against a smaller nation. We cannot accept that innocent people may be killed; that the system of shooting hundreds of hostages for a crime, when the person guilty of the crime cannot be found, is a pagan system which only results in evil. It is absolutely certain that if order is sought through such measures, many people who till now have obeyed the voice of the Church, will, finally, attempt to seek safety in the forests. We condemn all injustice; all killings of innocent people; all burning of peaceful villages. We sorrow for the miseries and the sadness of all who today suffer unjustly; the Catholic Church upholds that order which is as old as the Ten Commandments." (Pattee 1953, 285-286).

The message to convert all those who asked for it, regardless who they were, was passed from one parish to another. Although Stepinac's position was that Serbs were already baptized and thus did not require a formal process of conversion, he recognized that more Serbs are likely to survive if they just went through this process.

In June 1941, when the persecutions of Jews and Serbs were relentless, Stepinac took a bold step by writing to the Interior Minister:

> "… I take the liberty, Mr. Minister, [Interior Minister Artuković], to ask you to prevent, through your power, all unjust proceedings against citizens who individually can be accused of no wrongdoing. I do not think it can bring us any glory if it is said of us that we have solved the Jewish problem in the most radical way, that is to say, the cruelest. The solution to this question should provide only for the punishment of Jews who committed crimes, but not for the persecution of innocent people…" (Randall 1963, 18).

Considering the situation on October 26, 1941, Stepinac told his parishioners:

> "I would like to draw your attention today to one thing if you really want to be true subjects of Christ the King, and that is to love for your neighbor, love for man himself regardless of his name. A danger exists that even those who glory in the name of Catholicism, not even to speak of those who glory in a spiritual vocation, may become victims of passion, hatred or forgetfulness of the law that is the most beautiful characteristic trait of Christianity, the law of love." (Pattee 1953, 258-260).

Already on December 29, 1941, Hans Helm, German police attaché in Zagreb, wrote to the office of SS Sturmbahnführer Hanke, Einsatzgruppen Sipo:

> "We were informed all along about the political meddling of the Cleric [Stepinac] in the internal affairs of the country. He has connections in every department, most specifically education and he controls the media. The most significant news is that the Church in Croatia has contacts with London and the Government in exile. This approach undertaken by the Church could be viewed as contrary to the interests of the Third Reich

and of the NDH. Our objective is to eliminate the influence of the Cleric [Stepinac]." (HR-HAD f, Book VII).

In late May 1942, Stepinac informed his congregation as follows:

> "It is absurd to speak of a new world order, as demonstrated in communist and Nazi ideologies, because, if in their orders the human personality was not valued... Each soul has its inalienable rights which no human power can or ought to limit." (Štambuk-Škalić et al. 1997, 264-266).

On October 25, 1942, Stepinac asked his parishioners a laconic question:

> "How then must we judge individuals who arrogantly behave as if God no longer exists on earth?"

He answered his own question:

> "Only one race really exists and that is the Divine race. Its birth certificate is found in the Book of Genesis... All of them without exception, whether they belong to the race of Gypsies or to another, whether they are Negroes or civilized Europeans, whether they are detested Jews or proud Aryans, have the same right to say 'Our Father who Art in Heaven!'" (HR-HAD d, k; O'Brien 1947, 19; Phayer 2001, 85).

O'Brien suggests that Stepinac strongly condemned anti-Semitism; he also stated that he has heard many times about the assistance Stepinac gave the Jewish people (O'Brien 1947).

Under the circumstances it is no surprise that Ante Pavelić detested Stepinac, called him "balavac" ("wet-nose" derogatory term for somebody too young for the issue in question). Pavelić recognized from the start that he would find no comforting words from Stepinac.

Stepinac's sermons reached an increasingly wide audience, a fact that angered the Nazis and the Ustasha. As time went on, rumors circulated in the country and abroad that he was dead. Stepinac's followers feared for his life; many in fact, predicted that Stepinac's days of freedom were numbered, as was seen when he was under house arrest by the Ustasha and years later under Tito (HR-HDA o).

In October 1942, Glaise von Horstenau, the German Plenipotentiary in Zagreb, recorded in his diary:

> "Archbishop Stepinac [of Croatia] and his entourage are friendly to the Jews, (Judenfreundlich), and therefore enemies of National Socialism. The same Archbishop had been the protector of Jewish émigrés under the Yugoslav regime, although he paid no attention to the misery of his own people." (Steinberg 1990, 80).

It is obvious that Stepinac's words were directed to the Fuehrer, to the Duce, and to the Poglavnik Pavelić, it was they who had behaved so arrogantly. He continues:

> "That is why the Catholic Church has always condemned and condemns today all injustice and all violence whether committed in the name of theories of class, race, or nationality." (Pattee 1953, 205).

Despite his struggle against the Ustasha regime, Stepinac's critics argued that his joy with the creation of the NDH suggests that he failed to oppose the Ustasha and Aryan ideology. However, it was propaganda concocted by his opponents. Stepinac fought Pavelić from his arrival in the country.

On July 7, 1943, BBC Radio via the Vatican broadcast two excerpts from the sermons Stepinac delivered to his parishioners, in the Croatian language, explaining Stepinac's defiance despite German threats:

> "The Archbishop of Zagreb has strongly and sharply condemned the deportations of Jews and other ethnic groups that were based on Nazi theories and Nuremberg Laws. Radio Vatican announced that Archbishop Stepinac stated that every people and every race on earth has a right to exist and to humane treatment. If God gave this right to mankind, there is no government on earth that can take it away." The speech was published in *The New York Times*, July 8, 1943 under the title "Croat Attacks Germans: Archbishop of Zagreb Denounces Their Theories of Race" (Figure 1, HR-HDA o).

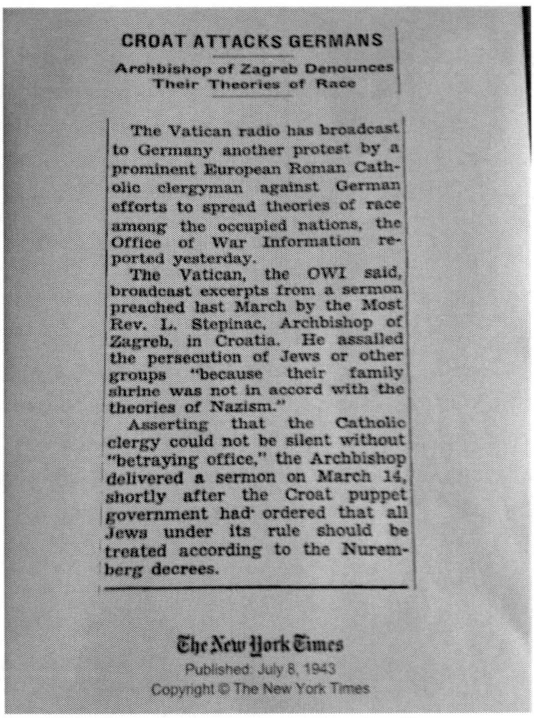

CROAT ATTACKS GERMANS

Archbishop of Zagreb Denounces Their Theories of Race

The Vatican radio has broadcast to Germany another protest by a prominent European Roman Catholic clergyman against German efforts to spread theories of race among the occupied nations, the Office of War Information reported yesterday.

The Vatican, the OWI said, broadcast excerpts from a sermon preached last March by the Most Rev. L. Stepinac, Archbishop of Zagreb, in Croatia. He assailed the persecution of Jews or other groups "because their family shrine was not in accord with the theories of Nazism."

Asserting that the Catholic clergy could not be silent without "betraying office," the Archbishop delivered a sermon on March 14, shortly after the Croat puppet government had ordered that all Jews under its rule should be treated according to the Nuremberg decrees.

The New York Times

Published: July 8, 1943

Copyright © The New York Times

Figure 1. The photocopy of The New York Times, article published on July 8, 1943 under the title "Croat Attacks Germans: Archbishop of Zagreb Denounces Their Theories of Race" (HR-HDA o).

Stepinac acknowledged that the Ustasha would be a liability to the humanitarian fabric of the Croatian society for years to come, and he equally detested the Nazis, the Ustasha and the communists. Hans Helm described the conduct of Stepinac as treasonous because he acted forcefully and threatened Pavelić:

> "The Croatian People would have to bear full responsibility for the growth of the Communist partisan movement… because of severe and unlawful measures used against

Orthodox Serbs, Jews and Gypsies, in imitation of German methods." (Shelah 1990, 277-308).

Living under Nazi occupation and the Ustasha collaborators, Stepinac identified the universal values that were lacking in the world in general and in Croatian society in particular and stated that their absence posed a threat to the Catholic way of life and possibly to life itself:

> "...We should shed light on the questions that trouble the world today, and on the chaos of war, a war that would not be had the voice of the Teacher been heeded. The issues that must be resolved are:
>
> (a) Freedom and value of the individual as an independent entity;
>
> (b) Freedom and respect for religion;
>
> (c) Freedom and respect for every race and nationality;
>
> (d) Freedom and respect for private property as the basis of freedom of the individual and independence of the family;
>
> (e) Freedom and respect for the right of every nation to its full development and to independence in its national life." (HR-HDA p, r, s).

Shomrony left Yugoslavia before Stepinac's trial in 1946, but he volunteered to come to Zagreb as a witness for the defense. Those who were aware that the trial was only symbolic urged him not to come, fearing that the Communist government would arrest him, and his testimony would not be heard. Other émigrés who wished to give their testimonies were given similar advice (Bilten 1996).

On March 3, 1943, Stepinac emphasized that no one had the right to dissolve a marriage consecrated by the Roman Catholic Church (Hilberg 1993, 45, 261). Since the Church's position was that marriage and baptism were holy sacraments, the principled position of the Catholic Church was that they must protect baptized Jews and Jews involved in sanctified mixed marriages. Thus, they could not remain silent about the dissolution of such a union because one of the partners was unable to demonstrate that all four of his or her grandparents were Christians (Krasić 1999; HR-HAD g).

During the years 1941 to 1945, Archbishop Stepinac stood unequivocally for the rule of law and for the God-given right of every people and every race to exist. This is the main reason why countless individuals and newspapers around the world protested against his prosecution by Tito's government.

On July 9, 1943, Radio Vatican, in its BBC radio broadcast from London, program "Free Yugoslavia," portrayed Stepinac as a:

> "Resolute soldier advocating moral justice and freedom."

Some of those who heard him speak sent letters of thanks and gratitude, his voice was heard throughout the free world. On the same date, it was broadcast on Radio XTW, in the Croatian language, radio broadcast Slobodna (Free) Yugoslavia:

> "The Catholic Church has been right and that it cannot act otherwise. We do not profess these principles from one day to the next; we do not profess them, through fear or out of personal interests. The Catholic Church recognizes races and nations only as God's creatures." (Batelja and Tomić 1996, 176-180).

Throughout the war years Stepinac's statements and acts of rescue were so powerful, so sincere and could not be compared to any other leader, religious or otherwise. Stepinac was sincere and resolute in his efforts to protect human beings and distance himself from the ideologies that threatened Judeo-Christian ethics. He had no tolerance for arbitrary and undeserved pain and suffering of innocent people. Stepinac condemned all acts of cruelty committed by all sides - Hitler's, Pavelić's and Serbian Nedić's - while fighting for the right to life of all innocent people. And this is how Stepinac emerged as a Pillar of Human Rights (Gitman 2005, Gitman 2019).

He instructed his clergy: The role and duty of Christians is in the first place to save people. (Labor Weekly 1946.).

Due to Stepinac's instructions to save all those who asked for help, many Serbs survived the war, and most returned to their own religion, as can be seen from the interview of Archpriest Dušan Kašić, an Orthodox Serb. In 1975 he attested that ascertaining the number of wartime converts was difficult, since all such conversions were deemed acts of political violence and annulled by the postwar civilian authorities. Of the converts from that period, only a few remained Catholic. They were mostly Orthodox Serbs who had married Catholic women and chose to remain of that faith. (Tomasevich 2002, 571). Despite threats from the local SS agents and Ustasha authorities who admonished Stepinac for his meddling on behalf of Jews, Serbs and other dissidents, Ivo Politeo, his defense lawyer, was mentioned in the U.S. diplomatic mail as quoting Stepinac during the 1946 trial:

> "As an Archbishop and representative of the Catholic Church, I am free to call to your attention some events that are painful to me. I am sure hardly anyone has the courage to point them out, so it is my duty to do so. From many various sides I hear about the inhuman and cruel treatment of the so-called non-Aryans." (HR-HDA k, file 301681).

On October 16, 1941, Stepinac addressed the Ustasha authorities:

> "But to take away all possibility of existence from members of another nation or race and to mark them with the stamp of shame is already a question of humanity and of morals. And moral laws are applicable not only to the lives of individuals but also to those who rule the states. These days, general morality does not brand as ill-reputed those criminals who have been released from prisons and who have been sentenced as murderers. ... Why treat in this way those who are members of another race through no fault of their own? Do we have the right to commit this outrage against the human being?... I ask you, Mr. Minister, to issue appropriate orders so that the laws against Jews and others similar to them (the measures against the Serbs) are executed in such a way that the human dignity and personality of every man is respected." (HR-HDA t; see also, Krišto 2007, 17).

Conclusion

Although one can fill several books with information about the Cardinal and now Blessed Alojzije Stepinac, no side will be fully satisfied with the outcome. I know for a fact that Stepinac sent the Vatican every bit of information about events in Croatia and how he handled them! In fact, he wrote so much that Maglione, the Secretary of State in Vatican, asked him to reduce the details. We will have to wait a few more months for the 2020 opening of the Vatican Archives of the period of World War II in order to verify and uncover the truth of what happened in Nazi occupied former Yugoslavia.

The Vatican's approval of the very young Stepinac as coadjutor was in part because of his total devotion to the Church and his ascetic life during his years of study in Rome. The Vatican may also have felt that a young priest without any special ties to local clerical or political parties could be more easily directed than a man with local and political allegiances. Accordingly, as archbishop coadjutor from 1934 to 1937 and then as archbishop until the partition and occupation of Yugoslavia, in April 1941, Stepinac stated a number of revealing things about himself, some fundamental religious and political matters in his daily sermons regarding his views on Protestantism, Eastern Orthodoxy, communism and Freemasonry (Meštrović 1956, 203). Nevertheless, the Ustasha hard-liners had always regarded Stepinac as Yugoslav in orientation. Stepinac was unwavering in his principles regardless of the circumstances. He was honest to himself and the Church. He refused to tell a different story even to his jailers:

> "Because my conscience is clear I'm ready to die at any moment." (Zagreb daily newspaper *Vjesnik*, October 9, 1946.)

> During the trial the newspaper posted this caricature under the caption: "Moja savjest je čista" [My Conscience is clean!]).

Stepinac's claim that all human beings, including Serbs, are God's creation angered the "Catholic Ustasha Youth." The letter was composed in German and Croatian languages, by Stepinac's enemies:

> "You have to know that you are 'our greatest enemy,' but we are letting you know that if you go on speaking against us as you have been doing till now, and despite your red Roman sash, we will kill you in the street like a dog." (Meštrović 1993, p. 324).

All along, Alojzije Stepinac truly believed that the Catholic Church in general was the greatest civilizing force in the history of mankind and the leader in developing a superb civilization worthy of praise by all those who loved the truth. But while the Church was engaged in its beneficial work, the "gates of hell" of which Jesus spoke did not stay closed. … Humanity, which had believed in these false prophets, can truly sigh today with the Jews of old:

> "We expected light and we got darkness. Instead of blessing we have damnation, instead of paradise we have hell in which society suffers today." (Stepinac 1980).

Stepinac was bitterly critical of Eastern Orthodoxy. To him, as to many other Croats, Orthodoxy and Serbia represented a great threat to the Catholic Church in Croatia and to the Croatian nation:

> "All in all, Croats and Serbs are two worlds, the north and south poles, which will never become close except through a miracle of God. The schism is the greatest curse of Europe, almost greater than Protestantism. In it, there is no morality, no principle, no truth, no justice, no honesty." (Blažević 1980, 161).

Historians who followed his postwar trial treated it as an isolated historical event never trying to put it in the historical context of the period. While Stepinac chose to be silent and not defend himself, nevertheless he let the prosecution know that he will not compromise, stating:

> "To those of you who consider me a collaborator with the Ustasha, I state: When there is peace, when it is possible to publish documents, and when everyone can say his own words without fear, then there will be no one who will say a word against me." (O'Brien 1947, p. 62, a statement made during his trial).

References

Auty, Phyllis. 1965. *Yugoslavia*: London: Walker and Co.

Banac, Ivo. 1988. *The National Question in Yugoslavia*: Ithaca: Cornell University Press.

Barnett, Neil. 2006. *Tito*. London: Haus Publishing.

Batelja, Juraj, and Celestin Tomić. 1996. *Propovijedi, govori, poruke, 1941 – 1946 Alojzije Stepinac* [Sermons, Speeches, Messages, 1941 – 1946 Alojzije Stepinac]. Zagreb: AGM.

Benigar, Aleksa. 1993. *Alojzije Stepinac, hrvatski kardinal* [Alojzije Stepinac, Croatian Cardinal]. Zagreb: Hrvatska franjevačka provincija sv. Ćirila i Metoda.

Bilten 44-45, June 1996. In an interview with the journalist of the Croatian Catholic weekly *Glas Koncila* [*The Voice of the Council*] Amiel Shomrony.

Blažević, Jakov. 1980. *Mač, a ne mir: za pravnu sigurnost građana* [The Sword but not Peace: For Legal Security of Citizens]. Zagreb: Mladost.

Breier, Louis S., Program Director. 1946. "*The National Conference of Christians and Jews*." Bronx, NY, Round Table, NCCJ, October 13.

Ciano, Galeazzo 1946. *The Ciano Diaries 1939-1943*. Garden City; New York: Doubleday and Company.

Cohen, Philip J. 1996. *Serbia's Secret War: Propaganda and the Deceit of History*. College Station: Texas A&M University Press.

Colville, John 2002. *The Fringes of Power. The Incredible Inside Story of Winston Churchill during World War II*. Guilford, CT: Lyons Press.

Curtis, Glenn E. 1992. *Yugoslavia: A Country Study*. Washington, DC: Federal Research Division, Library of Congress.

Dedijer, Vladimir 1953. *Tito Speaks: His Self Portrait and Struggle with Stalin*. London: Weidenfeld and Nicolson.

Djilas, Aleksa. 1991. *The Contested Country, Yugoslav Unity and Communist Revolution, 1919-1953*. London: Harvard University Press; Cambridge, Massachusetts.

Djilas, Milovan. 1985. *Rise and Fall*. London: Macmillan.

Đodan, Šime. 1970. *Ekonomska politika Jugoslavije* [Economic Policy of Yugoslavia]. Zagreb: Školska knjiga.

Gitman, Esther. 2003. Intervju s Teodorom Grunerom [Gitman, Interview with Teodor Gruner], Zagreb: Croatia, January 14.

Gitman, Esther. 2005. *Rescue of Jews in the Independent State of Croatia, 1941–1945*, Ph.D. diss. GC of the City University New York.

Gitman, Esther. 2009. "The Rescue of Jewish Physicians in the Independent State of Croatia (NDH), 1941-1945." *Holocaust and Genocide Studies* 23(1):76-91.

Gitman, Esther. 2011. *When Courage Prevailed, The Rescue and Survival of Jews in the Independent State of Croatia, 1941-1945*. St. Paul: MN, Paragon House.

Gitman, Esther. 2012. *Kad hrabrost prevlada. Spašavanje i preživljavanje Židova u Nezavisnoj Državi Hrvatskoj 1941.-1945*. [When Courage Prevailed, The Rescue and Survival of Jews in the Independent State of Croatia, 1941-1945]. Zagreb: Kršćanska sadašnjost.

Gitman, Esther. 2015. "Archbishop Alojzije Stepinac of Zagreb and the Rescue of Jews, 1941–45." *The Catholic Historical Review*, 10(3), 488-500.

Gitman, Esther. 2019. *Alojzije Stepinac--Pillar of Human Rights*. Zagreb: Croatia, Kršćanska sadašnjost and Hrvatsko katoličko sveučilište.

Goetz, Aly, and Susanne Heim. 2002. *Architects of Annihilation: Auschwitz and the Logic of Destruction*. Princeton: New York, Princeton University Press.

Glas Koncila. 1967. "Interview with Bishop Salis-Seewis," Zagreb, September 16, 1967.

Goldstein, Slavko. 1991. "Intervju." *Globus* (Zagreb), July 23.

Goldstein, Ivo, and Goldstein, Slavko. 2001. *Holokaust u Zagrebu* [Holocaust in Zagreb]. Zagreb: Novi Liber and Židovska općina.

Hilberg, Raul. 1993. *Perpetrators, Victims, Bystanders. The Jewish Catastrophe 1933-1945*. New York: Harper Perennial.

Hina. 2015. "Zuroff o genocidu u NDH: Stepinac je bio Pavelićev duhovni savjetnik. [Zuroff on Genocide in the NDH: Stepinac was Pavelić's Spiritual Advisor]." Index reporting what Zuroff said for the Belgrade daily *Politika*, Belgrade, July 14, 2015. Accessed January 6, 2020. https://www.index.hr/vijesti/clanak/Zuroff-o-genocidu-u-NDH-Stepinac-je-bio-Pavelicev-duhovni-savjetnik/830695.aspx.

HR-HDA a. Hrvatski državni arhiv [Croatian State Archives]-416-Ivo Politeo File. "Memorandum of the National Council Youngstown, Ohio," United States of America, October 5, 1933, sent to the League of Nations under 'the terrible cost of liberation." Zagreb: Hrvatski državni arhiv [Croatia: Croatian State Archives].

HR-HDA b. *Hrvatski državni arhiv* [*Croatian State Archives*]-416-Ivo Politeo File. Copy of a 'Memorandum' sent to the League of Nations by the Croatian National Council Youngstown, Ohio, United States of America. March 9, 1935. Zagreb: Hrvatski državni arhiv [Croatia: Croatian State Archives].

HR-HDA c. Hrvatski državni arhiv [*Croatian State Archives*]-416-Ivo Politeo File. Manifesto: By order of the Second Croatian National Congress, in Chicago Illinois, (United States of North America, the 30th day of November, 1935).

HR-HDA d. Hrvatski državni arhiv [*Croatian State Archives*]-416-Ivo Politeo File. "File sent to Yad Vashem with the material of Cardinal Stepinac."

HR-HDA e. Hrvatski državni arhiv [*Croatian State Archives*]-1521-Hans Helm File. Hrvatska: Hrvatski državni arhiv [Croatia: Croatian State Archives], Zagreb, fond 1521 [pool 1521], Hans Helm File.

HR-HDA f. Hrvatski državni arhiv [*Croatian State Archives*]-1521-Hans Helm File. Box 33, book XIII, p. 5-7. (BVA-I521, Hans Helm File, box 33. p. S.7, book XIII, in Box 33.

HR-HDA g. Hrvatski državni arhiv [*Croatian State Archives*]-416-Ivo Politeo File. Rezolucija Hrvatske biskupske konferencije o Židovima [Resolution of the Croatian Bishops' Conference about Jews], Vrhovni Sud NRH, stup [pile] 6/1946, 863.

HR-HDA h. Hrvatski državni arhiv [*Croatian State Archives*], AP, vol. C, p. 711, photocopy; Translation: A general letter from Archbishop Stepinac at the beginning of WWII. (The document was found among the documents of the NDH exile government in Leibnitzen, 1945).

HR-HDA i. Hrvatski državni arhiv [*Croatian State Archives*], 306-ZKRZ -2235/2-45, Box 10, Srećko Bujas, Sarajevo, February 27, 1945, 243 (40).

HR-HDA j. Hrvatski državni arhiv [*Croatian State Archives*]-1521-Hans Helm File. Subject Mixed Marriages, March 24, 1943, 267.

HR-HDA k. Hrvatski državni arhiv [*Croatian State Archives*]-416-Ivo Politeo File. Subject A. Stepinac, 1175.

HR-HDA l. Hrvatski državni arhiv [*Croatian State Archives*], 306-ZKZR.2235/45-2. box 10, Zapisnik [Record] br. [No]. 1771, testimony given by Josipa Schulhof on June 9, 1945, 2-21).

HR-HDA m. Hrvatski državni arhiv [*Croatian State Archives*], 306-ZKZR.2235/2-45, Box 10, Zapisnik [Record], June 9, 1945, 14.

HR-HDA n. Hrvatski državni arhiv [*Croatian State Archives*]-416-Ivo Politeo File. A. Stepinac, 204.

HR-HDA o. Hrvatski državni arhiv [*Croatian State Archives*]-1549-ZIG NDH. MUP RH 1-25, 426-428.

HR-HDA p. Hrvatski državni arhiv [*Croatian State Archives*]-416-Ivo Politeo File. File A. Stepinac, document 1026, October 26, 1941.

HR-HDA r. Hrvatski državni arhiv [*Croatian State Archives*]-416-Ivo PoliteoFile. File of A. Stepinac. Amiel Shomrony's testimony.

HR-HDA s. Hrvatski državni arhiv [*Croatian State Archives*]-416, Ivo Politeo File, A. Stepinac, file 301681, jacket 12, box 1, pp. 21, 22. A personal letter sent from the Archbishop of Zagreb to the Minister of Internal Affairs, Artuković, on May 22, 1941. The original letter found in the Archives of the Archbishopric. Also in Optužnica Pavelić-Artuković, box 118.

Kolanović, Josip. 1996. *Holocaust in Croatia, Documentation and Research Perspectives*. Zagreb: Hrvatski državni arhiv.

Kosanović, Saša. 2019. "*Štampači Jasenovca*." *Novosti* (Zagreb), October 6. Accessed January 22, 209. https://www.portalnovosti.com/stampaci-jasenovca.

Kostich, Lazo M. 1981. *The Holocaust in the Independent State of Croatia*. Chicago: Liberty.

Krasić, Ljubo, ed. 1999. *Croatian Almanac, Stepinac the Man for this Time*. Chicago: Croatian Franciscan Publications.

Krišto, Jure. 2007. "The Catholic Church in Croatia and Bosnia-Herzegovina in the Face of Totalitarian Ideologies and Regimes" in *Religion Under Siege: The Roman Catholic Church in Occupied Europe 1939-1950*, eds. J. Bank and L. Gevera. Leuven: Belgium, Peeters Publishers.

Krizman, Bogdan. 1983. *Pavelić između Hitlera i Mussolinija* [Pavelić between Hitler and Mussolini]. Zagreb: Globus.

Krizman, Bogdan. 1986. *Ante Pavelić i Ustaše* [Ante Pavelić and Ustasha]. Zagreb: Globus.

Labor Weekly. 1946. Editorial. "*The New Leader, the Self-Described Liberal*," October 11.

Maček, Vladko. 1957. *In the Struggle for Freedom*. University Park: Pennsylvania University Press.

Makanec, Julije. 1943. Pozvani i nepozvani." [Called and Uncalled] *Hrvatski narod, br. 879, 7. XI. 1943, 1-2.* [*Croatian People*, No. 879, December 7, 1943, pp. 1-2].

Matković, Hrvoje. 1994. *Povijest Nezavisne Države Hrvatske* [The History of the Independent State of Croatia]. Zagreb: Naklada P. I. P. Pavičić.

Meštrović, Ivan. 1956. "Stepinac, the Spiritual Hero." *Hrvatska revija*, 6, no. 3.

Meštrović, Ivan. 1993. *Uspomene na političke ljude i događaje*. Zagreb: Matica hrvatska.

Narodne novine. 1941. [Official Gazette], Zagreb, May 3.

NARA a. United States of America (USA), National Archives and Records Administration *(NARA), D-2005526.* State Department, Central files, Microcopy 860.00/10.1446, To: The Secretary of State, The Foreign Service of the U.S.A. From: T. J. Hohenthal, American Consul, Zagreb, October 31, 1946, *Trial of Archbishop Aloysius Stepinac of Zagreb and others.*

NARA b. United States of America (USA), National Archives and Records Administration (NARA), 860H.00/10.1446, 10, Dispatch 536, November 9, 1946, (Belgrade: American Embassy. A prominent political personality in Yugoslavia for security reasons his name was not revealed, only the statement is known: "Archbishop Stepinac went into the trial as the spiritual Shepherd of the Croatians; he left the courtroom as the universally acknowledged national hero of his people").

NARA c. United States of America (USA), *National Archives and Records Administration* (NARA), RG 59, [U.S. State Dept]., Lot file no. 61 D33. Legal Adviser Relating to War Crimes. Box 33, Enclosure no. 1 to Dispatch no. 4, American Consulate, Zagreb, October 31, 1946. 5.

NARA d. United States of America (USA), National Archives and Records Administration (NARA). Edmund Glaise von Horstenau, Germany's plenipotentiary general in Croatia, November 26, 1941 to Colonel Friedrich von Mellenthin, Wehrmacht High Command (OKW). *U.S. Department of State, Documents on German Foreign Policy*, 1918-1945 (DGFP). Washington, D.C.: 1960-64, Series D, 12:515-17.

NARA e. United States of America (USA), *National Archives and Records Administration* (NARA). Microfilm Roll 25, 806H. 404/79, enclosure 181, 2.

NARA f. 1960-64, Series D.

Nazor, Ante, and Zoran Ladić. 2003. *History of Croatians, Illustrated Chronology*. Zagreb: Multigraf.

Neumann, Franz. 1942. *Behemoth: The Structure and Practice of National Socialism*. Oxford: Oxford University Press.

Obolensky, Dimitry. 1946. *The Bogumils: A Study in Balkan Neo-Manichaeism*. London: Cambridge.

O'Brien, Anthony Henry. 1947. *Archbishop Stepinac, The Man and His Case*. Dublin: Standard House, Pearse Street.

O'Brien, Anthony Henry. 1999. "The Man for this Time" In Croatian Almanac, edited by Ljubo Krasić, 117. Chicago: Croatian Franciscan Publications.

Pattee, Richard. 1953. *The Case of Cardinal Aloysius Stepinac*. Milwaukee: The Bruce Publishing Company.

Pezet, Ernest. 1959. *Stepinac – Tito*. Pariz: Nouvelles Éditions Latines.

Phayer, Michael. 2001. *The Catholic Church and the Holocaust*. Bloomington: Indiana University Press.

Randall, Alec. 1963. *The Pope, the Jews, and the Nazis*. London: Catholic Truth Society.

Romano, Jaša. 1980. *Jevreji Jugoslavije 1941-1945. žrtve genocida i učesnici narodnooslobodilačkog rata* [Jews of Yugoslavia, 1941-1945, Victims of Genocide and Freedom Fighters]. Belgrade: Savez jevrejskih opština Jugoslavije [The Federation of Jewish Communities in Yugoslavia].

Shelah, Menahem. 1986. "The Italian Rescue of Yugoslav Jews 1941-1943." In *The Italian Refugee: Rescue of Jews during the Holocaust*, edited by Ivo Herzer. Washington, DC: The Catholic University of America Press.

Shelah, Menachem, editor. 1990. *History of the Holocaust: Yugoslavia*. Jerusalem: Yad Vashem Jerusalem.

Shomrony, Amiel. 1996. "*Prenosimo, Glas Koncila: Razgovor s Dr. Amielom Shomronyom*" [Interview with Dr. Amiel Shomrony], Bilten 44-45, June 1996.

Skertić, S. W. 1961. "The Man of God and His People." Cleveland: *United American Croatians of Cleveland*. February 12.

Spalatin, Christopher. 1959. *Aloysius Cardinal Stepinac*. Chicago: Croatian Franciscan Press.

Stein, Ljudevit. 1999. ["Testimony of Rescue by Stepinac"]. *Glasnik Postulature*, 6.

Steinberg, Jonathan. 1990. *All or Nothing. The Axis and the Holocaust 1941-1943*. New York: Rutledge Taylor and Francis Group.

Stepinac, Alojzije. 1980. "*By Their Fruits You Shall Know Them*." Reprinted in *Danica*, Chicago, April 4, 1980.

Stojanović, Nikola. 1902. "*Srbi i Hrvati*." Srpski književni glasnik 2(6):1149-59.

Šišić, Ferdo. 1920. *Dokumenti o postanku Kraljevine Srba, Hrvata i Slovenaca 1914-1919*. [Documents on establishment of Kingdom of Serbs, Croats and Slovenians 1914-1919]. Zagreb: Matica hrvatska.

Štambuk-Škalić, Marina, Stjepan Razum, and Josip Kolanović, editors. 1997. *Proces Alojziju Stepincu – dokumenti*. [*The Trial of Alojzije Stepinac – documents*]. Zagreb: Kršćanska sadašnjost.

Talmon, Jacob Leib. 1973. *European History as the Seedbed of the Holocaust*. New York: Theodor Herzl Foundation.

Tomasevich, Jozo. 1955. *Peasants, Politics, and Economic Change in Yugoslavia*. Stanford: Stanford University Press.

Tomasevich, Jozo. 2002. *War and Revolution in Yugoslavia*. Stanford: Stanford University Press.

The New York Times. 1946. Editorial: "*The Stepinatz Trial*," October 3.

Trifković, Srđa. 2016. *Ustaše – Balkansko srce tame*. Belgrade: Catena Mundi.

Velimirović, Nikolaj. 1985. *Kroz tamnički prozor – reči srpskom narodu iz logora Dahau.* [*From dark window-tell the Serbian people from the Dahau*]. Himelstir: Srpska pravoslavna eparhija za zapadnu Evropu.

Vraneković, Josip. 2011. Dnevnik: Život u Krašiću zasužnjenog nadbiskupa i kardinala Alojzija Stepinca [*Diary: Life in Krašić of Convicted Archbishop and Cardinak Alojizije Stepinac*]. Zagreb: Postulatura blaženoga Alojzija Stepinca.

Waugh, Evelyn. 1979."Testimony about the rescue of Jews." *South Slav Journal* 2 no. 4;17-26.

Žubrinić, Darko. 1997. *Cardinal Alojzije Stepinac and saving the Jews in Croatia during the WW2*. Accessed December 19, 2019. http://www.croatianhistory.net/etf/jews.html.

Appendix 1. Some of the Serbian Newspaper Articles Published in Belgrade, during WWII, 1941-1945 (The Cyrillic Titles Transcribed to Latin Letters, Roman Numerals Are Months, Modifications by Esther Gitman)*

Newspaper	Date	Title [English translation]
1941, Belgrade		
JIM	1941	Komanda mesta Beograd. Jevrejima. (Jevrejski Historički Muzej). [The Belgrade Command Post: "To Jews"]
Naša borba	02. X.	Jazbina iz kojega su potekla sva zla i sve nesreće [The Burrow where All Evils and Calamities Began]
Obnova	22. VIII.	Rasnopolitičke pretpostavke za rešenje jevrejskog pitanja [Racial and-Political Postulates for the Solution of the Jewish Question]
Naša borba	02. XI.	Jevrejski metodi [Jewish Methods]
Novo vreme	07. VIII	Jevreji u Srbiji [Jews in Serbia]
Obnova	03. XI.	Jevreji nikad više neće biti ljekari, apotekari, sudije u Srbiji [Jews Will Never Again Be Physicians, Pharmacists, Judges in Serbia]
Novo vreme	19. X.	Jevreji financiraju komunističke bande [Jews Finance Communist Bands]
Naša borba	26. X.	Sa skorašnog velikog Jevrejskog sabora u Moskvi [From the Recent Jewish Assembly in Moscow]
Obnova	01. X.	Jevrejski rat [The Jewish War]
Novo vreme	25. VII.	Tri Internacionale [Three Internationales]
Novo vreme	11. V.	Rat je posao Jevreja [War is the Business of Jews]
Obnova	11. VII.	Jevreji ne mogu da se naviknu na red [Jews Are Unable to Get Used to Order]
Obnova	01. X.	Nagomilavanje hrane u Jevrejskoj sinagozi [Amassing Food in the Jewish Synagogue]
Obnova	04. XII.	Engleska vodi Judin rat [England Is Waging Juda's War]
Novo vreme	29. VII.	Stroge mere [Strict Measures]
Novo vreme	25. XII.	Priznanje komunističkog komesara Dr. Levia [Confession of Communist Commissar Dr. Levi]
Obnova	17. X.	Ariziranje hrvatske privrede [Aryanization of the Croatian Economy]
Obnova	22. IX	Zločini Jevreja, naša nacionalna sramota [Crimes of the Jews, Our National Disgrace]
Obnova	01. X.	Tamne sile [Dark Forces]
Naša borba	21. XII.	Svedočanstva, Jevreji prema hrišćanstvu [Testimonies, Jews to Christianity].
Obnova	09. V.	Naredba koja se odnosi na Jevreje i Cigane [Order that Applies to Jews and Gypsies]
Obnova	20. X.	Nasi seljaci i radnici robovi Jevrejski [Our Peasants and Workers Jewish Slaves]
Novo vreme	31. X.	Srbi su najtolerantniji narod na svetu. [Serbs Are the Most Tolerant People in the World]
Vojna komanda IV.		Naredba [Order]
Novo vreme	11. XII.	Poziv, AUFFORDERUNG [Invitation, AUFFORDERUNG]
Obnova	18. IX	Jevreji protiv nas i protiv kolektivnih interesa [Jews against Us and against Collective Interests]
Obnova	09. IX.	Nevidljivi crv [Invisible Worm]
Novo vreme	28. VII.	Stroge mere protiv Jevreja i komunista u Beogradu [Strict Measures against Jews and Communists in Belgrade]

Appendix 1. (Continued)

Newspaper	Date	Title [English translation]
Novo vreme	29. VII.	Uredba o predaji oružja [Ordinance on Handover of Arms]
Obnova	28. VII.	Mi i Jevreji [We and the Jews]
Novo vreme	17. VIII.	U Zemunu je Jevrejima zabranjeno kupovanje pre devet sati [In Zemun Jews are Forbidden to Shop Before Nine O'clock]
Obnova	12. XII.	Pred historijom, Rusvelt će ostati glavni krivac novog svetskog Rata [History Will Remember Roosevelt as the Main Culprit of a New World War]
1942, Belgrade		
Naša borba	15. II.	Poštovati samo svoju veru i zakone, a sve druge vere i zakone rušiti [(We should) Respect only Own Faith and Laws, and Destroy all Other Faiths and Laws]
Naša borba	28. VI.	Jevrejski bog i Jevrejski moral [Jewish God and Jewish Morality]
Obnova	08. IX.	Loža Jevrejska osnovana 1911. u Beogradu dobila je ime Srbija, čime je osvojena još jedna Država [Jewish Lodge Constituted 1911 in Belgrade was Named Serbia, thus Another State Was Conquered]
Novo vreme	03. I.	Uredba koja se odnosi na primanje na konak Jevreja [Decree on Providing Shelter to Jews]
Nova borba	22. III.	Jevreji i izbeglice, novac - glavna snaga i oružje Jevrejstva [Jews and Refugees, Money – Key Power and Weapon of Jewry]
Novo vreme		Obavezna prijava Jevrejske imovine [Mandatory Registration of Jewish Property]
Obnova	17. XI.	Boljševička zemlja domovina Jevreja [Bolshevik Country Homeland of the Jews]
Obnova	15. XII.	Kompolt međunarodnog Jevrejstva [Compolt of International Jewry]
Srpski narod	19. XII.	Jevrejski rat [The Jewish War]
Obnova	20. III.	Navala Slovačkih Jevreja na krštenje [Onrush of Slovak Jews to Get Baptized]
Obnova	04. X.	Jevejsko vršenje u Rumuniji [Jewish Roaming in Romania]
Obnova	26. III.	Uloga Jevreja u životu naše zemlje pre rata [The Role of Jews in the Prewar Life of our Country]
Novo vreme	30. VIII.	Uredba o pripadanju imovine Jevreja Srbiji [Decree on Jews' Property Belonging to Serbia]
Naša borba	15. VIII.	Misli Jevreja i njegovih agenata [Thoughts of Jews and Their Agents]
Srpski narod	27. XI	Hrišćanski narodi u službi Jevrejstva [Christian Nations in the Service of the Jews]
Naša borba	26. IV	Istervanje Jevreja – spas Evrope [Expulsion of Jews – Salvation of Europe]
Novo vreme	14. IX.	Rusvelt predaje američku privredu Jevrejima [Rosevelt Hands Over the American Economy to the Jews]
Obnova	19. XII.	Jevreji kuju osvetu [Jews Plan a Revenge]
1943, Belgrade		
Novo vreme	21. XI.	Nova Entanta u životu srpskoga naroda [New Entente in the Life of Serbian People]
Obnova	20. VIII.	Strast uništenja [A Passion for Destruction]
Obnova	10. V.	Golgota po drugi put [A Second Calvary]
Novo vreme	11. II.	Našu su otadžbinu razarali paraziti [Our Homeland Was Ravaged by Parasites]
Novo vreme	21. IX.	Nova etapa u životu srpskog naroda [A New Stage in the Life of the Serbian People]
Srpski narod	18. XII.	Nesrbi i Jevreji treba da oslobode Srbe [Non-Serbs and Jews Should Liberate the Serbs]
Novo vreme	17. IV.	Nalog ubistva [Warrant for Murder]
Obnova	15. IV.	Jevreji – đelati poljskih oficira [Jews – Butchers of Polish Officers]
Newspaper	Date	Title [English translation]
Novo vreme	06. VIII.	Evropski narodi protiv Jevrejskog boljševizma [European Nations against Jewish Bolshevism]
Srpski narod	06. III.	Američka štampa u rukama Jevreja [American Press in the Hands of the Jews]
Obnova	03. XI.	Oni mrze mir [They Hate Peace]
Novo vreme	08. V.	Rat i Jevreji [War and the Jews]
Obnova	23. I.	Jevreji su svuda – Jevreji [Jews are Everywhere – Jews]
Srpski narod	29. V.	Juda podnosi račun [Judas Gives an Account]
1944, Belgrade		
Novo vreme	24. II.	Jevrejski vek [The Jewish Age]
Obnova	13. IV.	Kobna uloga Jevreja u našem javnom životu [The Fatal Role of the Jews in our Public Life]

*See United States Holocaust Memorial Museum, (https://collections.ushmm.org/search/catalog/pa1102421).

Biographical Sketch

Esther Gitman, PhD

Affiliation: Retired.

Education:

PhD in Jewish history from City University of New York, 1999- 2005; Dissertation title: Rescue and survival of Jews in the Independent State of Croatia, 1941-1945.

MPS (Master of Professional Studies); Criminal Justice, Long Island University, C. W. Post, Long Island, 1975. Dissertation: Is the family responsible for the deviant behavior of its children.

BA History and Sociology, Carleton University, Ottawa, Canada, 1972. Teachers' College, 1960-1962, 1962-1967. Taught biology grades 6th to 9th.

Research and Professional Experience:

In 2002 I arrived in Zagreb, Croatia, on year Fulbright Fellowship. My objective was to fill the historiographic gap on the rescue of Croatian and Bosnian Jews during the Second World War.

The collapse of communism in the 1990s, the publication of new materials, and the opening of archives in the former countries of Yugoslavia paved a way in the pursuit of serious and nuanced historical investigations—as did the Nazi War Crimes Disclosure Act of 1998, which declassified U.S. Intelligence records from the 1930s and 1940s. I also had a "last moment" opportunities to interview survivors and rescuers who although advanced in years were in a position to provide me with the best oral history of the war years. I followed these survivors from Croatia, Bosnia, Serbia, Israel, Canada and the United States.

Although initially motivated by a personal quest to find out who helped my mother and me but even beyond that I recognized that even in the darkest hours in the history of the world, there had been bright sparks of light emanating from those who were determined to defy such dictators as Hitler, Mussolini, Croatian Ante Pavelić and Serbian Milan Nedić. Subconsciously I knew that there were people to whom I wished to say thank you. The best way I knew how to accomplish it was to uncover and publish their humanity and heroism.

In June 2016I I was a keynote speaker presented in the European Parliament; the title of my presentation was: "The importance of Archbishop Dr. Stepinac and his work for the understanding of contemporary Europe." It was the first time Stepinac's deeds and actions during WWII were presented to such important international body. It was the greatest moment for Croatia and for me. A booklet was published in English and in in Croatian.

Professional Appointments:

Served in the Israeli Navy 1958-1960, honorable discharged with a rank of sergeant.

1981-1999 owner and president of IEG Sales Company, Inc., a successful Jewelry company which sold its products in the major department stores of the likes of Macy's, Saks Fifth Avenue, Lord and Taylor and many others.

Honors:

- Marquis, Who is Who in American Women, 15th edition, 1987/88.
- Fulbright fellowship, 2002-3. Focus: research of original documents and on oral histories of Holocaust survivors and rescuers. This research revealed the significant impact the social and political environment had on the conditions of rescue.
- Postdoctoral fellowship 2007-08, granted by Barbara and Richard Rosenberg at the Center for Advanced Holocaust Studies of the United States Holocaust Memorial Museum, (USHMM).
- Croatian Women of Influence & Future Leaders Award, Zagreb, March 8, 2017.
- President of Croatia Madam Kolinda Grabar Kitarović Award "Medal Knez Branimir," for promoting Croatia in the World.
- Honorary Doctorate by the University of Split (Split, Croatia) for importance of my scientific research about Archbishop Stepinac.

Publications from the Last 3 Years:

Gitman, Esther. 2019. *Alojzije Stepinac, Pillar of Human Rights*. Zagreb: Kršćanska sadašnjost.

In: Croatia: Past, Present and Future Perspectives
Editor: Matko Marušić

ISBN: 978-1-53618-300-9

Chapter 6

Can Communism Have a Human Face? The Testimony of a Prominent Croatian Catholic Intellectual Smiljana Rendić from the Mid-Sixties in Yugoslavia

*Marino Erceg**
Journalist, Glas Koncila [The Voice of the Council], Zagreb, Croatia

Abstract

The chapter presents the everyday life of Croatian Catholic laypeople during the period of pivotal ecclesiastical and socio-political changes during the mid-1960s in Yugoslavia. The topic is approached through content analysis of the written legacy of Smiljana Rendić, Catholic laywoman, prominent intellectual, and one of the most important figures of Catholic journalism in Croatia during the communist regime. Catholic laypeople were aggressively driven to the margins of society starting soon after 1945, when communists rose to power, and continued in the following years. However, during the 1960s, circumstances have changed, and the first dialogue was established between the representatives of the Holy See and the communist government of Yugoslavia. Further development was put on hold after Yugoslav dictator Tito purged reformist groups from the ranks of the ruling League of Communists [Savez komunista] in December 1971.

This chapter aims to determine, from the perspective of the letters of Smiljana Rendić, what the real impact was of this dialogue and changes in everyday life of Croatian Catholic laypeople in the period between 1966 and the end of 1971. Rendić points out that the dialogue and a certain accommodation between the Catholic Church and the communist regime took place only on a practical level and not in the sphere of ideas, due to the fact that Catholicism is a religion, and Marxism is an antitheist ideology. Her letters show that Catholic laypeople in Yugoslavian society continued to be endangered, which created many existential fears among them, including a possibility of losing a job and remaining jobless. Although certain guarantees of the freedom of speech and the freedom of religions were included in Yugoslavian legal documents at the time,

* Corresponding Author's Email: marinoerceg3@gmail.com.

Catholic laypeople were generally unable to engage in any sort of public activities as Catholics. Laypeople were thus driven into an "inner emigration" in their own homeland and the only way they could leave this position was by betraying or hiding their religious convictions. Rendić's correspondence shows that the position of the Catholic laypeople in Croatia under the communist regime in the second half of the 1960s had not essentially changed much in comparison with previous historical periods after 1945.

Keywords: Catholic laypeople, Croatia; religion, communism; Catholic Church, Rendic, Smiljana; Yugoslavia, liberalization

INTRODUCTION

After the end of the Second World War in 1945, the Yugoslavian communists were the first among other communist parties under the Soviet influence to abolish monarchy, first to adopt a Soviet-style constitution in January 1946, first to institute legal procedures against the Catholic Church dignitaries of episcopal rank (with a staged trial of Archbishop of Zagreb Alojzije Stepinac in October 1946), first to introduce a Soviet-style planning in economy, and first to establish the system of collective farms by the end of 1948 (Banac 2017, 576). But despite its initial harshness, the communist regime was unable to impose its control over the Catholic Church as it did with all other opposing groups, such as the pre-war political parties (Radelić 2006, 99). Yugoslavian communists were constrained in their actions due to some factors, unfavorable to them, such as the mood of the general population and the international situation. The Catholic Church had a great reputation and influence among the Croats, not just as a religious institution but also as an institution present in the spheres of education and charitable work (Radelić 2006, 99). It had highly educated priesthood and support from abroad as well. The Catholic Church soon became the major ideological opponent to the communists and a potential focal point for gathering of all social groups opposed to communist rule (Radelić 2006, 99).

After their split with Stalin in 1948, Yugoslavian communists tried to make a "theoretical break" from the communist block and formulate their version of the same ideology, by which they tried to reconcile the communist ideology with some principles of liberalism (Mihaljević 2016, 543). This version of a more humane socialism was an outgrowth of the economic model of "workers self-management," a variant that became one of the most recognizable characteristics of socialist Yugoslavia (Radelić 2006, 284). Some limited fruits of the Yugoslavian way into communism were felt by the Catholic Church in Croatia, but not up until the 1960s when the first unofficial and official contacts were established between the representatives of the Holy See and the Yugoslavian regime. New contacts were made possible by the new orientation of the Catholic Church after the Second Vatican Council (1962-1965) and its readiness for dialogue with communists, and by Yugoslavia's special position as a "non-aligned" state in the context of the Cold War partition of the world into two political blocks (Cvrlje 1992, 116).

The dialogue between the Church and the regime was accelerated during the second half of the 1960s, leading to the full restoration of diplomatic relations in 1970, and Tito's official visit to Pope Paul VI in 1971 (Radelić 2006, 376). At the same time, Aleksandar Ranković, who was the chief of the Yugoslavian secret police "Udba," the vice president of Yugoslavia, and the leader of the block of hardline communists in the Yugoslav communist party, was ousted from power in 1966 (Banac 2013, 119-121). Yugoslavian society after the fall of Ranković witnessed a period of reduced political repression and more freedom in everyday life (Supek 1992, 161). But, in contrast to this reformist reaches, unsolved problem remained for Catholic laypeople concerning their everyday life.

THE YUGOSLAVIAN VISION OF A DIFFERENT SOCIALISM

Although the workers self-management model brought communist Yugoslavia a higher degree of individual responsibility and independence in business decision-making (Spehnjak and Cipek 2007, 259), the Yugoslavian communists faced an obvious paradox from the beginning. The workers self-management was supposed to become the backbone of a relentless criticism toward USSR and repudiation of their methods but, at the same time, some key elements of a socialist state, such as the dictatorship of the Communist Party, state ownership of property, and planned economy were not abolished (Radelić 2006, 287). But, despite the appearance of self-management, as Ivo Banac (2017, 579) stressed, the Yugoslav workers self-management system, "depended on the invisible hand of the Party." Therefore, the Yugoslavian self-management model could be described as a "quasi-real" denial of state socialism (Calic 2010, 194, quoted in: Bing, Mihaljević and Nießer 2018, 99). However, in the eyes of the West from the end of the1950s, the Yugoslavian variant of socialism enjoyed the reputation of a different and a more humane version of socialism in comparison with other communist countries. For example, one British tourist guidebook from 1958 presented Yugoslavia as a "unique communist country in the world that allows everyone to stick their nose inside its borders and see how Marx functions in practice" (Duda 2003, 816). During the 1950s and 1960s some reformist politics toward a more humane socialism were also present in the other European communist countries. Notably, the reforms of the "Prague Spring" earned overwhelming popular support in Czechoslovakia, and a demand for a "socialism with a human face" became a slogan identified with that entire reformist process (Kramer 2017, 159). As the "Croatian Spring" was crushed in 1971 by Tito (see Chapter 7), the "Prague Spring" was crushed by the Soviet military intervention in 1968 (Kramer 2017, 159).

Among the current Croatian research community and the general public there is still no clear consensus about the historical period between 1945 and 1990. Josip Mihaljević (2016, 22) notes that the period of communist rule is often observed in a Manichaean way and from extreme points of view, meaning that the Yugoslavian communist history is regarded strictly negatively or strictly positively. Therefore, for some authors Yugoslavia was a tyranny, a totalitarian state that did not respect basic democratic principles, a state that tried to destroy traditional and national identity, and used terror and ideological propaganda (Mihaljević 2016, 22-23). For others, Yugoslavian communist authorities fought for the interests of the working class and cared about social security, national equality, and the spirit of brotherhood and unity (Mihaljević 2016, 23). It is difficult to decipher who is right only from historical documents – these answers lie in people's everyday life in communist Yugoslavia. Who has not lived under communism cannot fully understand its character. Some answers from the perspective of everyday life in communist societies, in general and in particular in Central Europe, may be found in the literary works, for example in the Czech writer Milan Kundera's novels “The Joke” (1967/2006) and “The Unbearable Lightness of Being” (1984/2006). For the case of Croatia this chapter utilizes the letters of a prominent Croatian journalist, the late Ms. Smiljana Rendić, which are available in the Archive of the Archdiocese of Zagreb. Kundera’s depiction of everyday life in communism shown in art is comparable to Rendić’s testimony in life. Although Rendić’s letters are not historic documents in a strict sense, they are an ideal source to form a picture of the life of Croatian Catholic laypeople in the pivotal political changes in the mid-sixties (1966–1972).

THE FIRST 15 YEARS OF COMMUNIST POLITICS TOWARD THE CATHOLIC CHURCH IN CROATIA

Historian Zdenko Radelić (2006, 98-99) explains three key motives of communist politics toward the churches and believers in Yugoslavia.

The first motive is connected to the ideology of Marxism, which claims that religion is the main ideological tool of the exploiters in subjugating the exploited masses and acting against the freedom of the people. From that perspective, any participation of religious communities in activities concerning politics is denied (Radelić 2006, 98-99).

The second motive is connected with the historical memory, in which religions and churches are part of the overthrown political order. In the communist interpretation, religious and national differences generate conflicts that result in civil or religious wars, and only atheism could be an integrative “religion” (Radelić 2006, 99). Considering the context of national, religious, and cultural differences in Yugoslavia, this integrative potential of atheism was especially important to Yugoslavian communists.

The third motive is connected with the totalitarian character of the communist regimes. The communist parties claimed to be the only ideological and political authority and consequently every authority outside the Party had to be destroyed (Radelić 2006, 99).

Beside the motives pointed out by Radelić, two additional motives of communist regime’s rigidness may be identified in case of Croatia in communist Yugoslavia. There were strong connections of Catholic Church in Croatia with numerous Croatian Catholic congregations in the world, which had been established along with the mass emigration of Croats at the beginning of the 20th century (see Chapter 11). The Croatian emigration became a true guardian of the Croatian spirit and a carrier of a credible historical narrative (Krišto 2019, 430-432). The Catholic Church in Croatia also has strong connections with the Holy See in Vatican and the Yugoslavian communists could hardly influence it (Lučić 2008, 42). The reason for this Croatian loyalty to the Holy See lies in Rome’s long historical support of Croats, even going back to the fact that pope John VIII recognized in the ninth century Croatian medieval statehood and the rule of Duke Branimir (Cvrlje 1992, 1; see also Chapter 1).

The implications of these motives were evident even before the Communists took power in Yugoslavia. Numerous imprisonments and killings happened against Catholic priests and laypeople during World War II and especially at the end of the war. Some coherent data about its extents is offered by Stjepan Kožul (1998, 222-229 quoted in: Radelić 2006, 102). For the wartime period and the first years of the postwar period, Kožul reported 458 killed priests, 73 killed seminarians, and 30 killed nuns (Kožul 1998, 222-229 quoted in: Radelić 2006, 102).

Anto Baković (2007: 963) estimated 663 priests, monks, and nuns as victims of atrocities during World War II and in the first years after it. Although some of these victims during wartime were killed by the Axis forces or by Allied bombings, it is clear from the research data offered by Radelić (2006, 100-103) that most of these crimes were committed by the communist partisan forces, and that the Catholic Church was religious institution affected the most by these atrocities in comparison with other religious communities, as well as other Catholic states in Europe.

All interwar organizations of Catholic laypeople were disbanded after the war (Polegubić 2007, 29), and the entire Catholic press in Croatia was shut down (Miklenić 2012, 159). The political activities of Croatian emigrants also bothered the Yugoslavian authorities, so the communists waged a sort of a "secret international war" against them, resulting in killings of many emigres living in different countries (Vukušić, 2001). In addition to the trial of archbishop Stepinac in 1946 (see Chapter 5), the culmination of communist rigid politics towards the Catholic Church in Croatia in the first postwar years came in December 1952, when the Yugoslavian authorities broke diplomatic ties with Vatican (Cvrlje 1992, 116-117).

A Short Biography of Smiljana Rendić

Smiljana Rendić was a long time and prolific contributor to *The Voice of the Council* [*Glas Koncila*] (Čutura 2011 b, 7), the official newspaper of the Archdiocese of Zagreb. *The Voice of the Council* was established at the time of the first session of the Second Vatican Council; it soon became the most important religious publication of the Catholic Church (Novak 2005, 598). Following are two testimonials about the importance of Rendić's work:

> "I think that without her (Smiljana Rendić), the longtime journalistic stance of *The Voice of the Council* cannot be understood, and neither this entire part of our (Croatian) history. Therefore, she must never be forgotten" (Živko Kustić, Croatian priest and longtime editor in chief of *The Voice of the Council*; quoted in: Burilović 2019, 472).
>
> "She deserves a critical publication of her collected works. It is an exceptional work. When all of her original texts would be published, then it could be seen that she in quantity exceeded the work of Miroslav Krleža. We do not have a proper insight into her works, so we can only speculate about treasures we could find there. Thousands and thousands of pages of her texts exist because she was an exceptional writer, and it is extremely valuable that her information is credible. That was the fruit of her massive knowledge. When we would not know something, we would just ask Smiljana" (Ivan Miklenić, Catholic priest and current editor in chief of *The Voice of the Council*; quoted in: Burilović 2019, 466).

Smiljana Rendić was a prominent Catholic intellectual, Vatican expert, Judaist, translator, and author of many critiques and polemics. She was born in Split in 1926, where she finished primary and high school and joined the organization of Catholic laypeople "Domagoj" while still in her teenage years. The engagement in that organization became problematic for Rendić in the first months of communist rule: she was prevented from enrolling to the eighth grade of the high school in Split in 1944/1945 school year on account of her Catholic activities, and she had to repeat the seventh grade (Burilović 2016, 36). In 1948, the communist authorities confiscated her family's private property and evicted them from their apartment in Split; Rendić then lived with her mother in a government-owned apartment shared with another family in the same city (Čutura 2011 a, 284).

The next experience of communist repression for Rendić came in 1955, when she was terminated from her job because she was marked as "clerical," as she explained in the letter to the priest Stanko Romac in March 1965, stored in the Archdiocesan Archive in Zagreb, (HR.NAZG 1965). The reason for her loss of job was the fact that she publicly opposed the idea of identifying her Catholicism with fascism (Burilović 2019, 38). In 1961, she got a job in the administration of the magazine *Seamanship* [*Pomorstvo*]. When communist authorities allowed the renewal of the Catholic press at the beginning of the 1960s, she started to write for *The Herald of Saint Anthony of Padua* [*Glasnik svetog Antuna Padovanskog*] in 1963, and she signed her works with a pseudonym "Vjera Marini" (Čutura 2011 a, 284). In the same year, she started to write for *The Voice of the Council* and became a regular part-time contributor. Rendić published unsigned texts and texts signed with her pseudonym "Berith" (Čutura 2011 a, 284). The first text by "Berith" was published in *The Voice of the Council* on January 26, 1964 (Krišto 2019, 542). Her pseudonym did not have a direct political connotation; it was primarily connected with her vast interest in Judaism (Čutura 2011 b, 37-39). In Hebrew, word "berith" means covenant, an alliance between God and man, which is mentioned many times in Bible, such as the alliance between God and Abraham (Gen 17, 2-27). Her texts signed with "Berith" brought the stories from everyday life of Catholics in officially atheistic Yugoslavia, and her articles were very popular (Čutura 2011 b, 33). Bishop Petar Čule gave Rendić the "Medal of the Council" for her contribution in spreading the ideas of the Second Vatican Council by her writing in *The Voice of the Council* (Čutura 2011 a, 284).

At the peak of the Croatian Spring in 1971, Rendić published a notable article "A Departure from Genitive or the Second Croatian Revival" [Izlazak iz genitiva ili drugi hrvatski preporod] in the magazine *Critique* [*Kritika*]." She was persecuted for this in 1971 in a staged trial in Rijeka and sentenced to one year of strict prison and one year of prohibition of public engagement. This sentence was reduced in 1973 by the Supreme Court to probation, but she was also punished by the loss of her job and forced retirement (Čutura 2011 a, 285). Since 1973 she lived in Trsat in Rijeka. In 1988 she was awarded by *The Voice of the Council* with a unique reward "Golden Quill of The Voice of the Council." She died in May 1994 (Čutura 2011 a, 285).

General Observations about Rendić's Correspondence

When communists came to power in Yugoslavia in 1945, any public role of the Church was prohibited and Christianity in general was pushed onto the margins of society, into "catacombs." But in these "catacombs" only the most faithful believers were ready to descend (Burilović 2019, 29-30). On the heels of persecution of numerous Croatian Catholic intellectuals (many of whom were forced to emigration), and in the context of the ban on participation in public life for Catholics, the circle of people communicating with Rendić in the letters analyzed in this chapter can be described as a sort of social "underground" (COURAGE Registry, 2020). There are numerous letters that Rendić exchanged during mid-sixties with Catholic priests, monks, laypeople, and intellectuals; they are all stored in the Archive of the Archdiocese of Zagreb. For the purposes of this chapter 17 letters were analyzed. Rendić's most frequent correspondent was Ivan Mužić (in 8 letters), a lawyer and a historian from Split. The analyzed letters are voluminous material because Rendić's average letter consists of a dozen of pages of densely typed texts. Therefore, a simple estimate is that approximately 200 pages of letters were analyzed in this chapter.

Rendić and her correspondents did not plan to form a political party or a political organization that would formally challenge the communist monopoly on power. The correspondence with numerous Catholic laypeople was an important source of information and subjects for Rendić's popular articles.

Political questions that impacted everyday life of Catholic laypeople were discussed, in fact, very rarely. A reader may notice a certain dose of auto-censorship in these texts because there was a fear that some government office could secretly open and read these letters. This fear is expressed in two letters that were exchanged between Rendić and Majda Slivar in 1970. Slivar wrote to Rendić in a letter on August 13, 1970 that she suspected that someone had opened one of her letters with "some kind of small machine" and she asked Rendić if something like that was still possible (HR.NAZG 1970 a). Two days later, on August 15, Rendić replied by saying that something so obvious is hardly possible and that this type of highhandedness is, in fact, an unlawful act, but she pointed out that someone who opens a letter does that by using stealthier methods (HR.NAZG 1970 b).

Some remarks about the regime's oppressive politics present in Rendić's letters, were also publicly emphasized by archbishop of Zagreb Franjo Kuharić, making Rendić's private letters a stronger historical testimony. When Tito officially visited pope Paul VI in March 1971 – giving a symbolic nod to the process of renewal of diplomatic ties that begun in 1966 – archbishop Kuharić wrote in April 1971 in *The Voice of Council* about some discrepancies between regime's constitutional and legal guarantees and the reality of everyday life in Yugoslavia. Kuharić warned that religious people face difficulties because of their faith and emphasized the necessity of ensuring enough space for them to live a life of religious unity (Erceg 2019, 65).

THE DIALOGUE BETWEEN THE CATHOLIC CHURCH AND THE YUGOSLAVIAN REGIME

The dialogue between the Catholic Church and the Yugoslavian communist regime is the most frequently discussed subject in the Rendić's letters. The aim of dialogue between the regime and the Catholic Church was the effort to renew diplomatic relations between Yugoslavia and the Vatican, which had been broken off by the Yugoslavian regime on December 17, 1952 (Akmadža 2003, 184). One of the reasons for this break was that the Archbishop of Zagreb Alojzije Stepinac, who was sentenced in a staged trial in 1946 to 16 years of prison, had been proclaimed a Cardinal of the Catholic Church just two weeks earlier, on November 29, 1952 (Akmadža 2013, 145). This was The Day of the Republic, one of the most important state holidays in communist Yugoslavia (Banac 2013, 112), so the communist regime interpreted this act as a provocation and interference by the Holy See in the internal affairs of Yugoslavia (Akmadža 2003, 171). The key problem in the relations between the Catholic Church in Croatia and the regime from 1945 to the end of the communist reign in 1990 was the refusal of the regime to acknowledge that the Holy See is the supreme authority for the Catholic Church in Croatia (Krišto 2019, 529).

But, as Agostino Casaroli, a distinguished long-time Vatican diplomat who served in the Holy See's "Eastern Politics" of dialogue with the European communist regimes, points out in his memoirs *The Martyrdoom of Patience*, the Catholic Church in Croatia was in some sense in a better position than the Church in other communist states, like Hungary or Czechoslovakia. Casaroli (2001, 319) notes that the Yugoslavian communist regime did not adopt the Soviet approach of deep interference with Church's internal operation, such as appointments of priests or bishops, which limited the life of the Church elsewhere in Eastern Europe from 1949 on. The reason for this difference in Yugoslavian policy, in Casaroli's (2001, 319) opinion, was Tito's split from Stalin in 1948.

New Dynamics in the 1960s

During the 1960s, Yugoslavian willingness to reestablish diplomatic relations with the Holy See did not mean that Yugoslavia was giving up its attempt of establishing control over the Catholic Church in Croatia. But some improvements in their relations were made. For example, the regime allowed the renewal of the Catholic press. After the Catholic biweekly *The Voice of the Council* was founded in 1963, many other religious media followed this example (Krišto 2019, 541-543). In 1966, 8.5 million copies of religious newspapers were sold in Croatia (Banac 2017, 587). But both sides, the Catholic Church and the regime, interpreted their agreement and the process it opened in their own way (Radelić 2006, 376).

Rendić's Stance toward the Dialogue between the Church and the Regime

Rendić addressed this dialogue in a letter with a high-ranking churchman, Frane Franić, Archbishop of Split and Makarska on June 31, 1970. She referred to the canonization of Nikola Tavelić and warns Franić that Marxism remains a kind of new barbarianism. She also criticized Croatian theologian Tomislav Janko Šagi-Bunić for his naïve approach to the dialogue with communists (HR.NAZG 1970 c). But Rendić's harshest critiques were aimed at Franić and other Church representatives for their participation in the dialogue with the regime. In a letter to Ivan Mužić, on October 22, 1969, Rendić explained that Archbishop Franić knew from the beginning that true dialogue with the communists was impossible, but the Archbishop indulged in such a thing because he expected to profit in some practical way, such as freer life in his archdiocese. In the same letter she also criticized Franić for trying to combine theological conservatism with pastoral progressivism and adds that "Jesus warned not to pour new wine into old bellows" (HR.NAZG 1969 a).

The essence of Rendić's stance toward the dialogue between the Catholic Church and the communist regime was in differentiating between the *possibility* of cooperating with Marxism on the material plane and the *impossibility* of collaboration in the sphere of ideas. Rendić explains in aforementioned letter to Mužić from October 1969 that Catholics could cooperate with Marxists in a sphere of the common good, in actions such as humanitarian initiatives. The possibility of cooperating with Marxism in the sphere of ideas Rendić calls "throwing dust in the face." She criticizes "Christomarxists" harshly for their belief that Christians can take over many ideas from Marxism except its atheism. On the other hand, if a Marxist would accept anything from Christianity, he would become a dissenter from the official ideology (HR.NAZG 1969 a). She added that some forms of ideological dialogue could be held with Marxist dissenters, but pointed out that they are nowhere in power, including Yugoslavia: "The Catholic 'exaltados' (fanatics) of dialogue in our country try to talk with Marxists in power but it is futile because they are not talking with Roger Garaudy or Ernst Bloch" (HR.NAZG 1969 a). In another part of the same letter to Mužić, Rendić offers a broader explanation of her stance:

> "Most Catholic intellectuals in our country are ready for a 'dialogue,' but they do not have anyone to talk with and if they would have then they would realize that they do not have anything to talk about because our Marxist intellectuals, including the Marxist dissenters, although they may be against 'administrative measures,' did not give up old ideological militancy. On the contrary, they still hold outdated positions of anticlericalism from the last century, which is even more rigid because Marxist opening toward the Church still does not forget that, even subconsciously, it is in power at this moment." (HR.NAZG 1969 a).

In a letter to Mužić on November 3, 1969, Rendić also points out the possibilities of manipulation of the dialogue by the communist regime from which even the most conservative circles of the Church are not safe:

> "Enthusiasm about the cooperation [in efforts to] (sic) eliminate hunger in the Third World, and cooperation toward peace in the world, sounds attractive only to those who were up until yesterday firmly forgotten in their bunkers. This enthusiasm is instrumentalized because the Catholics could only be 'poputčiks' (bystanders, see Radčenko 2006, 153) in this cooperation. Catholics also do not have enough courage on that way to say that they fight for the welfare and progress of the Third World in the Name of God, not just in the name of human solidarity…" (HR.NAZG 1969 b).

Rendić and the Idea of the Concordat

The dialogue between the Catholic Church in Croatia and the communist regime could be seen by the Catholics and general public in Yugoslavia as leading to a sort of a concordat. A concordat is, in simple terms, a treaty that is signed by the Holy See and a sovereign state to regulate the position of Catholics in that state, and the relations of the local Catholic Church with the state authorities (Šentija 2003, 494). This type of solution had a negative connotation for many Catholics in Yugoslavia because it was associated with the attempts at a concordat arrangement between the Vatican and the Kingdom of Yugoslavia during the 1930s. Although this concordat was almost signed in July 1937, its withdrawal was forced a few months later by the protests organized by the Serbian Orthodox Church (Ninčević and Brčić 2016, 305).

However, Rendić saw in a concordat between communist Yugoslavia and the Holy See a potential solution for the future development of relations between the Catholic Church and the communist regime. In a letter to Ivan Mužić on February 19, 1970, Rendić argued that a concordat or a similar type of accord in countries that have antireligious regimes could solve the question of relations between the state and religious communities (HR.NAZG 1970 d). In her opinion, this type of solution should not only apply to the Catholic Church in Yugoslavia, but similar type of agreement with the state could also be made by other religious communities, thus not making the Catholic Church a privileged religious community in the country (HR.NAZG 1970 d). But most importantly, Rendić pointed out that a concordat would ensure respect for the fact that the Holy See is a supreme authority for the Church in Croatia. She explains that Jesus Christ is the founder of the Church and that because of it, the power to administer in the Church comes from God only and does not come from the people, as is the case in parliamentary democracies (HR.NAZG 1970 d).

The Reality of a "Humane" Communism in the Social Life of Catholics in Yugoslavia

Some concrete results of political liberalization by the Yugoslavian communists, like much wider possibilities of traveling abroad and reduced border controls (Goldstein 2008, 509), which was a very untypical phenomenon for a communist state, were presumably felt by many individuals in everyday life. Some of these achievements may create a more humane image of Yugoslavian socialism in comparison with other countries governed by communist dictatorships. But the episodes from everyday life described by Rendić give a contrasting image.

The Impossibility of Public Work and Existential Fears

In a letter from October 7, 1970, to a parish priest Luka Vincetić from Vinkovci, who asked Rendić to give a public lecture to young Catholics in that town, Rendić explained that such an act could still be very dangerous for her. She wrote that the period of martyrs oppressed by the regime had passed, but that there were still many possibilities for harassment (HR.NAZG 1970 i). She explained that in communist regime the position of Catholic laymen is much more delicate than that of a priest or monk. When layman loses a job as a result of his or her public Catholic engagement, official Church structures often cannot guarantee that the culprit will not die from hunger. On the other hand, a priest, Rendić explains, would have something to eat even if he were imprisoned (HR.NAZG 1970 i).

One of the key causes of the precarious position of Catholic laypeople in the Croatian society under communist rule during the second half of the 1960s for Rendić was in the fact that the dialogue between the Church and the communist authorities was held predominantly between the clerical representatives of the Church and the representatives of the regime (HR.NAZG 1970 i). This led to the identification of the Catholic Church only with its priests, although in the spirit of the changes brought up by the Second Vatican Council laypeople had a stronger position in the Church, alongside with the priests in the hierarchy (Polegubić 2007, 51). Rendić thought that the laymen were still perceived by the regime only as privately religious persons, and that this tendency significantly limited the possibilities of their public engagement (HR.NAZG 1970 i). This was the key deficiency of The Protocol from 1966 for the everyday life of Croatian Catholics. Rendić explained to Vincetić that the possibility of public engagement was provided to only a small number of Catholics who were in workplaces directly connected with the Catholic Church and not employed in the state sector. For other Catholics, a threat remained that their work organization could dismiss them from their jobs, as would likely happen in the state-controlled economy (HR.NAZG 1970 i).

In a letter to the Franciscan Ljubo Hrgić on October 16, 1970 Rendić explained that she was forced to publish all of her articles in the Catholic press under a pseudonym because she was employed in the state sector and feared repercussions (HR.NAZG 1970 j). By this Rendić implied that the economy was still firmly controlled by the communist regime, but, more importantly, her position was paradoxical because she was employed in a sector which was a part of the state-controlled economy on one hand, and on the other hand she was publishing her works in Catholic newspapers, working in that manner for the benefits of a religion and a religious institution (Catholic Church) that was despised by the same regime. In the same letter, Rendić expressed her uncertainties about the state repressive apparatus and secret police reacting to her open engagement in the Catholic press (HR.NAZG 1970 j). Although there was no law in Yugoslavia or Croatia that could prohibit such an activity, Rendić pointed out that there were many ways by which a worker in a government sector could be prevented from writing in Catholic media (HR.NAZG 1970 j). She referred to her own experience of near starvation during the time she was unemployed between 1955 and 1958. This is how Rendić described her devastating experience of hunger in a letter to priest Stanko Romac on March 31, 1965:

> "I suffered in Split from harsh hunger, a hunger that made me search for food leftovers in trash cans of my neighbors in 1956. Sometimes I would not eat anything except water with some salt for four days, I repeat, for four days. It was the time when I was, as an 'enemy of the people, poisoned by religion,' how the 'comrades' formulated it, unemployed for three years, without any means of subsistence. The only money I could make was 2,500 dinars from donating a quarter liter of my blood in a transfusion station every two months (…) My nail polish and my lipstick were at the time representing my desperate struggle for my dignity, it was a struggle not to sink into moral misery and disorderliness, although I sank into a material one, into hunger from which it was foggy in my eyes, and I felt like hovering, not walking (…) By this, I was doing the same thing as lady in a concentration camp was doing, a few meters from the gas chamber, when she duly and decisively cleaned her only shoes every day" (HR.NAZG 1965).

Consequences of Speaking Publicly

In a letter to Ivan Mužić on January 14, 1970 Rendić directed her attention to the opinion expressed in public by a well-known Croatian writer Petar Šegedin and by economist Šime Đodan (HR.NAZG 1970 g). Šegedin was publicly fighting for greater respect and distinctiveness of the Croatian language (Radelić 2006, 444). In the book *We are All Responsible* [Svi smo odgovorni] published in 1971, he also warned that Croatia and Pakistan were the only countries in the world that were divided in two parts, referring to the fact that Bosnia and Herzegovina had an access to the Adriatic see through the town of Neum, splitting the Croatian Dalmatian coast in two parts (Radelić 2006, 442). On the other hand, Đodan was a prominent critic of the Yugoslavian regime's unfair economic policy, arguing about how Croatia was lagging behind, and the irrational investments into undeveloped Yugoslavian republics, pointing out their poor productivity and poor utilization of industrial capacity (Radelić 2006, 443).

Rendić pointed out that although Đodan and Šegedin were allowed to express their opinions in public and to "speak loudly" the public arena also "loudly crucified them," which also explains the real atmosphere in society (HR.NAZG 1970 g). Rendić judged that a far greater problem would emerge for them if their writings would achieve a higher profile in the general public, writing in the same letter: "If you go over that line, defined by their circles (she refers to governing communists), someone will soon show you who the real authority in this country is" (HR.NAZG 1970 g).

In a letter to Mužić from January 20, 1970, Rendić referred again to Đodan's and Šegedin's public activities, noting that the possibility of expression of their opinions was a sign of progress in comparison with the times after 1945, when they would probably be imprisoned for their public criticism (HR.NAZG 1970 f). Indeed, Šegedin and Đodan did continue their public appearances. After the crush of Croatian Spring in 1971, they were among intellectuals who were expelled from public life, marginalized, or imprisoned (Radelić 2006, 457).

The State of Permanent Fear and "Inner Emigration"

In a letter to Luka Vincetić on October 7,1970 Rendić noted that even real liberalization is not by itself a sufficient guaranty for laypeople who would want to be public promoters of the Catholic faith (HR.NAZG 1970 i). In an unsent letter to Mužić, dated on April 27, 1970, Rendić stated that her engagement in the 1960s was much easier because she was unmarried and did not have a family, but many prominent Catholic laypeople who were engaged in prewar organizations of Catholic laypeople in Croatia did have families and they could not risk their welfare by public engagement in a communist country (HR.NAZG 1970 k). She felt that this was the reason why the movement and organizations of Catholic laypeople remained unexplored by historians: revealing the names of people active in that movement before 1945 would only create problems for them (HR.NAZG 1970 k). In the same letter Rendić argued that a state of permanent fear remained in the consciousness of many Catholics and that it was hard to get rid of it even after objective reasons for those fears were no more present in everyday life (HR.NAZG 1970 k). It was, in Rendić's words, "a fear in which one lives, a fear in which one breathes, a fear for one's safety, and one's piece of bread, for one's place under the sun, and for one's own and unrepeatable life, in a homeland that was taken away by forcing one into an inner emigration" (HR.NAZG 1970 k).

In an unpublished article "The Church in a Ghetto" from April 2, 1969 (preserved in Archdiocesan Archive in Zagreb) Rendić explained the concept of an "inner emigration." She insisted that a distinction between the separation of the Church from society and the separation of the Church from the state should be made clear because these two phenomena are not the same thing. She argued that the Catholic Church and Catholic laypeople during the "liberal" 1960s remained isolated in a sort of mental ghetto on the margins of society (HR.NAZG 1969 c). This thesis is also mentioned in her letters. In a letter to Ivan Mužić on

September 5, 1969, Rendić explained that the departure from this "inner emigration" was possible only to those people who were willing to publicly abandon the Church at the cost of betraying their deepest beliefs (HR.NAZG 1969 d). In the aforementioned unsent letter to Mužić from April 27, 1970, Rendić said that many people chose this betrayal because they thought it was more productive in the long run, although many of them were proclaiming their "full loyalty to Christ" up until 1945 (HR.NAZG 1970 k). She pointed out that for most of the true Catholics this conformism was morally unacceptable, and that they would rather chose a life on the margins of the socialist society in an "inner emigration in their homeland" (HR.NAZG 1970 k).

Public Antagonism toward the Catholic Church

Although some progress was made in the sphere of diplomatic relations between Vatican and Yugoslavia, Rendić's letters also reveal that public antagonism toward the Catholic Church during mid-1960s was still strong. Rendić's letters show that this antagonism was not catalyzed by the opinion of common people, but by the state-controlled media and intellectuals favored by the Yugoslavian regime.

In a letter to Ivan Merlak, the editor in chief of the Slovenian Catholic newspaper *The Family* [Družina], in August 24, 1970 Rendić explained that the Catholic press in Croatia avoided writing about delicate problems in the life of the Church (HR.NAZG 1970 e). For example, some of these problems were the "Church cases" in which some priests and laymen groups openly showed their disagreement with the Church authorities (Mikić 2016, 124). She explained that Catholics still got most of the information about those cases only from articles published in the state-controlled media (HR.NAZG 1970 e). This can be interpreted as Rendić's general mistrust toward the intentions of the Yugoslavian state-controlled media, because it would not be wrong to assume that the media could manipulate some facts about this delicate issues in order to weaken the position of the Catholic Church. But some other controversial topics from the history of the Catholic Church, in Rendić's opinion, could not be discussed in Yugoslavia publicly even by Catholic intellectuals. Using the example of medieval inquisition, Rendić warned Ivan Mužić in a letter from January 20, 1970 about the widely present antagonism of the public:

> "Just because atheists and the enemies of the Church would gladly publish such things, I do not want to write about them. Writing about those issues would be a contribution to the struggle against the Church in these parts of the state and our homeland. By showing *hic et nunc* to the public the ugly face of inquisition, I would contribute to the understanding, which is already widely spread, that this is the exclusive face of the Church" (HR.NAZG 1970 f).

Rendić also added that some of the articles she meant to publish would be promptly exploited in atheistic media and literature, and by some prominent Yugoslavian Marxist intellectuals. As an example she mentioned Branko Bošnjak, a prominent philosopher of the Yugoslavian Marxist *Praxis* group, and a critic of the Church. She emphasized that Bošnjak and his colleagues would eagerly accept that type of work "as cheese on their macaroni" (HR.NAZG 1970 f). In the same letter to Mužić, Rendić stressed that the public sphere in

Yugoslavia is still contaminated with the communist ideology and hostility toward the Catholic Church, but she also emphasized that some cracks in that "wall of vulgar hatred" were present, although they were "still very thin and soft" (HR.NAZG 1970 f).

The Croatian National Question in Everyday Life

Yugoslavia was a strange political entity, somewhat like a platypus, a conglomerate of nations and a unique geopolitical synthesis emerged from the ruins of two multicultural polities, the Austro-Hungarian Monarchy and the Ottoman Empire (Bing, Mihaljević and Nießer 2018, 97). Therefore, Tito's Yugoslavia was often described as a country consisting of "six republics, five peoples, four languages, three religions, two scripts, and one Tito" (Ahtisaari 2002, 23, quoted in: Bing, Mihaljević and Nießer 2018, 97). In the context of polyethnic, polylinguistic, and polycultural diversity of Yugoslavia, religious tensions would often intertwine with the problems of national relations within the state. Religion was an important attribute of Yugoslavian nations, and churches were also important guardians of national identities (Spehnjak and Cipek 2007, 266). Therefore, for Yugoslavian communists atheism was, in a manner of speaking, the only "religion" that could work as a strong enough integrative factor in overcoming such differences (Radelić 2006, 99).

Religion and National Identity

The fact that Catholicism was at the core of the Croatian identity (see Chapter 11) was not important only to devout believers but also in the wider population, which respected the Catholic Church as a guardian of Croatian nation (Spehnjak and Cipek 2007, 257). The combination of national and religious motives in opposition to the communist ideology has had a much longer intellectual tradition in Croatia than the communist rule itself. Communism and its atheism opposed the very idea of Catholicism, but to the Croatians communism was also unacceptable from the perspective of the Croatian national question in Yugoslavia. It should be emphasized that the Communist party had first taken the course of the unitaristic position during the period of the Kingdom of Yugoslavia (Kljaić 2016, 255). This means that the communists were eager to create an integral Yugoslavian, not Croatian, nation. During the Second World War, the Communist party accepted the idea of federal Yugoslavia, which was again a negation of an independent Croatian nation (Kljaić 2016, 255). Liberals opposed communism and the communists for many reasons, including their negation of nationalism (as opposed to their proletarian internationalism) (Kljaić 2016, 255). However, public opposition to communism was led mainly from conservative and nationalist intellectuals, as liberalism has been rather weak in Croatia (Kljaić 2016, 231-232).

Croats and Communist Partisans

In a letter to Mužić from January 14, 1970, Rendić wrote that the high percentage of Croatians in the partisan movement could not stop the tragedies of the mass slaughter of

Croats in the months following the end of the Second World War (HR.NAZG 1970 g; see also Chapters 9 and 11). She argued that the preservation of Croatian consciousness was for Croats the only type of humanity needed, although in communist Yugoslavia the term "Croat" became nearly taboo. She maintained that partisans were changing the texts of some famous Dalmatian songs that were sung against the Italian fascist occupation and that were calling for the liberation of the Croatian people. The communists would, she explained, simply cut out the parts where Croatian name or identity was mentioned, and insert a term related to communism or Soviet Russia or the Yugoslavian communist idea of "brotherhood and unity", which again negated the special identity of the Croatian nation (HR.NAZG 1970 g). Although many Croatians from Dalmatia joined the partisan movement, they, explained Rendić, were not Croatian fighters but they became "people's fighters" (HR.NAZG 1970 g). This meant that the communists stripped the Dalmatian Croatian partisans of their original national identity, trying to place them in a broader identity of "Yugoslavian peoples," that could be understood as a sort of supranational identity which integrated all of Yugoslavian nations under the same name.

Rendić expanded this thesis in the same letter to Mužić, explaining that the Croatian people did not have a name in the "Yugoslavian Partisan Dictionary" related to the wartime struggle against fascism, and, more importantly, she stressed that this tendency was still present in the actual political moment (HR.NAZG 1970 g). This meant that in a drive to integrate all Yugoslavian nations under the identity of "Yugoslavian people" the original national identity was negated. To support this thesis, Rendić described the speech that the president of Yugoslavian Academy of Arts and Science Grgo Novak gave on the occasion of the opening of an exhibition of Croatian medieval Glagolitic script in 1970. Novak referred only to "peoples," not Croatians, and he explained that the exhibition represented the heritage of, again, "peoples" and not the Croatian people. Rendić then asks a rhetorical question: "Why does the president of the Academy from Zagreb still think that it is advisable to omit the name of the Croatian people?" (HR.NAZG 1970 g). This example is emblematic of many aspects of the aggressive suppression of the Croatian language and identity in Yugoslavia. Rendić also argued that the Croatian nation is a part of the Western civilization and that the fact that the Croats were on the margins of this civilization during different historical periods does not mean that they are not, in fact, a part of the West (HR.NAZG 1970 h). She presented that opinion in the letter to Mužić on January 30, 1970.

The Role and the Destiny of the Croatian Peasant Party

Rendić also took a positive stance toward the politics of Vladko Maček, the leader of Croatian Peasant Party, a party that during the interwar years became a sort of a Croatian national movement against the repression of Croats in the Kingdom of Yugoslavia (Supek 1992, 22-24), but its functioning was terminated by the Yugoslavian communists during the first postwar years (Radelić 2006, 97). As its leader, Maček was forced to emigrate from Yugoslavia in 1945, and subsequently was regularly depicted by the regime as a traitor of the Croatian people (Radelić 2006, 40-42). In a letter to Ivan Mužić in January 1970, Rendić wrote very positively about Maček, comparing the role he and his Croatian Peasant Party had in the Kingdom of Yugoslavia with Mahatma Gandhi and his Indian National Congress (HR.NAZG 1970 h). She also compared Maček with Alexander Dubček (Czechoslovakian leader who spearheaded the aforementioned reformist process of the “Prague Spring”) saying that Maček had been as popular in Croatia before Second World War as Dubček was in Czechoslovakia during the peak of the 1968 Prague Spring (HR.NAZG 1970 h).

The Rise and Fall of the Croatian Spring in 1971

During the 1960s, the national question in European communist states was brought back into the public space by the new elites in communist governments who tried to legitimize their position by addressing it (Mihaljević 2016, 48). The 1960s brought back discussions about the national question in Yugoslavia as well, although it had never quite gone away. The harshness of the communists’ centralist policy before the 1960s and permanent campaigns against nationalism made this phenomenon a controversial topic of political discussions (Banac 2017, 584-585).

The second half of the 1960s in Croatia was especially marked by the national question, and the reformist movement, called the “Croatian Spring,” which became in a way a national movement (Mihaljević 2016, 48-49, see also Chapter 7). The “Croatian Spring” was a very complex political and social phenomenon that opened up discussion about many problems in the Yugoslavian economy, federalism, freedom, rule of law, and most importantly, it articulated the need for equality in inter-ethnic relations within the country (Mihaljević 2016, 49).

In a letter to Mužić on January 14, 1970, Rendić commented that Catholic laypeople should not be so confident about the reach of this reformist politics in the ranks of the Croatian communist elite (HR.NAZG 1970 g). She made a distinction between the support for specific political and economic reforms and the support for the Marxist ideology on which the League of Communists of Croatia was based (HR.NAZG 1970 g). Rendić also pointed out that many people were not aware of this distinction (HR.NAZG 1970 g). In the same letter, Rendić warned Mužić about the real reach and limits of these reformist orientations of communists:

> “Anyway, what does this support of non-communists mean to the Central Committee of Croatia? This body is an authority and it is deciding what to do on its own. It is not a parliamentarian government that counts on what is in parliamentarism called the ‘outer support of the opposition’ [i.e., bipartisan support, author’s note]. The opposition does not exist in our country” (HR.NAZG 1970 g).

Rendić’s phrase “outer support of opposition” can be understood in this context as a situations of “minority governments” or “governments of national unity,” that are formed in parliamentary democracies during major social crisis or in societies with deep social divisions (Hrvatska enciklopedija 2020 a).

The key observation from Rendić was in the fact that she understood that the Church could still be persecuted, despite the reformist tendencies of the leading Croatian communists. In the letter to Mužić from January 20, 1970, she pointed out that Vladimir Bakarić, the Croatian Communist leader since wartime, announced the possibility of organizing a special session of the Croatian Central Committee that would discuss the position of “The Voice of the Council” (HR.NAZG 1970 f). She maintained that the ruling communists still perceived the Catholic Church as an organization that only "services private religiosity." She also said that the Catholic Church in Croatia "is people, consisting of a few millions of individuals that do not want to be squeezed into the sacristy" (HR.NAZG 1970 f). It was a common statement by the communists in Yugoslavia, in attempts to limit the Church's activities, to say that they want to push the Church into the sacristy, which meant, in fact, a tendency to radically limit any possibility of public activity or influence by the Catholic Church. Rendić concluded that the Catholic Church could still be persecuted (HR.NAZG 1970 f).

Rendić's thoughts on the limits of the liberalization movement were confirmed by Tito's termination of reformist activities at the end of 1971. The communist regime realized that increased individual freedom would threaten the communist monopoly in power (Mihaljević 2016, 550). When the Yugoslavian leader Josip Broz Tito realized that further reformist activities could radically endanger the supreme position of the League of Communists in the Yugoslavian society and create a deep political crisis, he shut down the reformist initiatives (Radelić 2006, 451). He called a meeting of communists at the end of November 1971 in Karađorđevo, a small town in western Serbia, (Radelić 2006, 451) and, backed by the army and hard-line communists, begun a major party purge, which devastated Croatia's reformist leadership (Banac 2017, 590). In a manner of a traditional authoritarian dictator, Tito extended this purge onto reformists in other Yugoslavian states (Spehnjak and Cipek 2007, 260). In Croatia itself, more than 2,000 people were arrested and several thousand members of the League of Communists of Yugoslavia were expelled from the Party. The members of a select group of intellectuals and student leaders were tried and sentenced (Banac 2017, 590).

Rendić was amongst intellectuals imprisoned or marginalized from public life, because of her article "The Departure from Genitive or Second Croatia Reviwal" (Novak 2005, 765). Paradoxically, Rendić was accused of disseminating enemy propaganda with her article although it was published in a public journal, which was legal. As her lawyer Milan Vuković (1995, 45-46) recollects, Rendić wrote to him that this accusation was surreal because enemy propaganda is usually distributed by illegal means and channels, not via a public magazine. She implied that the criminal offense was not the act of publishing such an article, but her very person, primarily because of her previous public engagements in the Catholic press (Vuković 1995, 45-46).

Systematic Negation of the Croatian Language

In her article "The Departure from the Genitive or the Second Croatian Revival" Rendić made public her opinions about the negation of the Croatian identity by the Yugoslavian regime's linguistic policies (Čutura 2011 b, 17-19). In a letter to Ivan Mužić on January 14, 1970, Rendić said that partisan propaganda materials, publications, and newspapers distributed to Croats during the Second World War were full of Serbian and Russian words, and that the same practice continued with the main Yugoslavian news agency Tanjug (HR.NAZG 1970 g). She assumed that the Communist party considered the Croatian language just a western accent of the Serbo-Croatian language, which was in fact the Serbian position (see Chapter 2). Rendić also wrote to Mužić that many key partisans' documents during the war were written by the people who did not know the Croatian language. She also emphasized that the fact that a great number of Croatians from Dalmatia who participated in the partisan movement could not stop the fact that their main newspaper "Free Dalmatia"

[Slobodna Dalmacija] was using a kind of Serbianized Croatian language (HR.NAZG 1970 g).

In the letter to Mužić from January 30, 1970, Rendić also talked about many methods by which reviewers, editors, and other media workers were systematically negating the Croatian language in newspapers and literature (HR.NAZG 1970 h). Rendić shared her personal experience from the beginning of the 1960s when a publishing house gave the task to a professor of Serbian nationality to translate a book into Croatian. He did not want to do it and gave Rendić his assignment. Her translation was evaluated as sounding too much Croatian, and the final version of the text was filled with Serbian words and phrases borrowed from Tanjug (HR.NAZG 1970 h). She also quoted an example of a high school mathematical teacher of Serbian nationality, who forced students to use Serbian terms. From that Rendić concluded that the existence of Croatian language had not been threatened so strongly even during the Kingdom of Yugoslavia (HR.NAZG 1970 h). It is important to note that these practices occurred in socialist Yugoslavia, a state that proclaimed the federal principle that should have protected the national identities of all Yugoslavian nations.

But some limited and careful attempts to protect the Croatian language could be made even in such circumstances. In the same letter to Mužić from January 30, 1970, Rendić revealed that *The Voice of the Council* managed to use some original Croatian words that were forbidden after 1945 because of their usage in the Independent State of Croatia. She added that, after some words were used by *The Voice of the Council*, other media in Croatia, including those controlled by the communist authorities, followed this example (HR.NAZG 1970 h). Still, this type of practice was frequently limited because typesetters and correctors would make changes minutes before printing the newspapers. Rendić explained to Mužić that it was not a rare phenomenon for those media workers to "insert some catchy words from 'Tanjug' or smuggle some words in the Serbian form" before printing new issue of *The Voice of the Council* (HR.NAZG 1970 h).

Attempts to Blame the Entire Croatian Nation for the Fascist War Crimes against Serbs in the Second World War

In the letter to Mužić from January 20, 1970, Rendić said that the request for German war reparations could be used as an explanation for the exaggerated reports of the number of people killed on the territory controlled by the regime of the Independent State of Croatia, but she also referred to different opinions about this matter (HR.NAZG 1970 f). She said that there was still a tendency of blaming the entire Croatian people for all killings during the war as a result of atrocities committed by the regime of the Independent State of Croatia (HR.NAZG 1970 f). The Independent State of Croatia was an Axis ally based in those parts of the territory of the Kingdom of Yugoslavia (which capitulated to the Germans on April 17, 1941) with a Croat majority that were not annexed by other Axis countries (Banac 1988, 4). The Independent State of Croatia was, in fact, an Italo-German condominium, under their occupation, and ruled by the nationalist insurgents Ustasha (Ustaše, Croatian word for insurgents) who were a minuscule Croatian nationalist organization headed by Ante Pavelić (Banac 1988, 4).

In Rendić's opinion, stated in the letter to Mužić from January 20, 1970, the Serbian Orthodox Church was one of the key proponents of connecting the Ustasha war crimes with all Croatian people. As an example of the strength of this tendency, even in the international context, Rendić quotes a Frenchman (whose name she did not mention) who publicly stated that all 1,700,000 victims of war in Yugoslavia were exclusively of Serbian nationality and Orthodox faith (HR.NAZG f). She warned that such a statement can lead to the conclusion that all those victims were killed by Croats only (HR.NAZG 1970 f).

The claim about this alleged genocide committed by the Croatian people on Serbs who were living in the territory of the Independent State of Croatia during the Second World War, was also the backbone of the Yugoslavian regime's allegations of the Catholic Church's "clerofascism." By linking the entire Catholic Church in Croatia with the regime of the Independent State of Croatia and by pointing out the Church's collaboration with the Ustasha and by stressing the Church's alleged fascist sins during the wartime, the communist regime was expanding its attacks on the Church as its main ideological enemy that was thoroughly irreconcilable with the socialist political order (Tuđman 1989, 416).

In the context of Croatian-Serbian relations, Rendić showed a remarkable historical knowledge when she traced the beginning of all hostilities between the Croats and the Serbs on the territory of the present-day Republic of Croatia to the reign of Count Khuen Hédervàry, a Hungarian politician and nobleman who administered the Kingdom of Croatia and Slavonia at the end of the 19th century (see also Chapter 9). In the letter to Mužić from January 20, 1970, she explained that Hédervàry was the first important politician to manipulate the Serbs living in the Croatian lands and pit them against the Croats, with tragic historical consequences. The important thing for Rendić was finding a solution by which these Serbian people would accept that Croatia is also their homeland because they have been living in those areas for hundreds of years (HR.NAZG 1970 f).

CONCLUSION

The position of Catholic laypeople in Croatian society during the second half of the 1960s had not changed in its substance in comparison with the previous periods of communist rule after 1945, although the Yugoslavian Communists were willing to make certain compromises in relations with the Catholic Church, as they were also pragmatic in their easing of hard pressure and repression on society in general. The absence of harsh repressive methods during the mid-sixties in Croatia does not support any argument that Yugoslavia was not a totalitarian country. Rendić's letters show that the regime was still prone to impose a wide range of formal and informal pressures by which the ruling communists were able to neutralize their opponents and maintain full control over the society. Some of those pressures were even worse than physical repression. These insights demonstrate that the reforms of 1960s in Yugoslavia were just "one of the stages in the cyclical repressive activities by the totalitarian authority," as has been phrased by Mihaljević (2016, 544). Therefore, the widely accepted image of Yugoslavia as a more humane communist state functioned only on a superficial level as a façade that covered the inherently inhuman nature of communist regime. Rendić's letters show us that any idea of a democratic society is incompatible with the idea of communism.

ACKNOWLEDGMENTS

The author of this chapter expresses his gratitude to Vlado Čutura, journalist of *The Voice of the Council* [*Glas Koncila*] and a close associate of Smiljana Rendić during the final years of her work in 1990s, for sharing information about personal experiences with Rendić.

REFERENCES

Ahtisaari, Martti. 2002. *Beogradska zadaća: Kako je slaman Milošević* [Mission in Belgrade: How Milošević was Toppled]. Zagreb: Naklada Szabó.

Akmadža, Miroslav. 2003. "Uzroci prekida diplomatskih odnosa između Vatikana i Jugoslavije" [The Causes of Termination of the Diplomatic relations Between the Vatican and Yugoslavia], in: *Croatica Christiana periodica*. 27(52), p. 171-202.

Akmadža, Miroslav. 2013. *Katolička Crkva u komunističkoj Hrvatskoj 1945. – 1980.*[The Catholic Church in Croatia 1945. – 1980]. Zagreb-Slavonski Brod: Despot Infinitus-Hrvatski institut za povijest – Podružnica za povijest Slavonije, Srijema i Baranje.

Baković, Anto. 2007. *Hrvatski martirologij XX. stoljeća: 1 Svećenici-mučenici Crkve u Hrvata* [Croatian Martyrology of the Twentieth Century: 1 Priest martyrs of Church in Croatia]. Zagreb: Martyrium Croatiae.

Banac, Ivo. 1988. *With Stalin against Tito*. Ithaca-London: Cornell University Press.

Banac, Ivo. 2013. *Hrvati i Crkva: Kratka povijest hrvatskog katoličanstva u modernosti* [The Croats and the Church: The Short History of Croatian Catholicism in the age of modernity]. Zagreb-Sarajevo: Profil Knjiga-Svjetlo Riječi.

Banac, Ivo. 2017. "Yugoslav Communism and the Yugoslav State," in: *The Cambridge History of Communism: The Socialist Camp and World Power 1941-1960-s; Volume II.*, edited by Norman Naimark, Silvio Pons i Sophie Quinn-Judge, 570-596. Cambridge: Cambridge University Press.

Bing, Albert; Mihaljević, Josip and Nießer Jacqueline. 2018. "Yugoslavia," in: *The Handbook of COURAGE: Cultural Opposition and Its Heritage in Eastern Europe*, edited by Balázs Apor, Péter Apor and Sándor Horváth, 97-116. Budapest: Institute of History-Research Centre for Humanities-Hungarian Academy of Sciences.

Burilović, Silvana. 2019. *Smiljana Rendić: katolička novinarka i pratiteljica Drugoga vatikanskog koncila* [Smiljana Rendić: The Catholic journalist and a Reporter on Second Vatican Council]. Split: Katolički bogoslovni fakultet.

Calic, Marie-Janine. 2010. *Geschichte Jugoslawiens im 20. Jahrhundert* [The History of Yugoslavia in 20th Century]. Munich: C. H. Beck.

Casaroli, Agostino. 2001. *Mučeništvo strpljivosti: Sveta Stolica i komunističke zemlje 1963. – 1989.* [The Martyrdom of Patience: The Holy See and the Communist States 1963 – 1989]. Zagreb: Kršćanska sadašnjost.

COURAGE Registry. 2018. "*Smiljana Rendić Collection*" by Stipe Kljaić (http://cultural-opposition.eu/registry/?lang=en&uri=http://courage.btk.mta.hu/courage/individual/n33248&type=collections). Date of access: May 5, 2020.

Cvrlje, Vjekoslav. 1992. *Vatikanska diplomacija: Pokoncilski Vatikan u međunarodnim odnosima* [The Vatican's Diplomacy: Post-council Vatican in international relations]. Zagreb: Školska knjiga-Kršćanska sadašnjost.

Duda, Igor. 2003. "Dokono mnoštvo otkriva Hrvatsku. Engleski turistički vodiči kao izvor za povijest putovanja na istočnu jadransku obalu od 1958. do 1969." [The Leisured Masses Discover Croatia: English Travel Guidebooks as a Source for the History of Travelling to the Eastern Adriatic Coast in the 1950s and 1960s], in: *Časopis za suvremenu povijest* [Journal of Contemorary History], 35(3): 803-821.

Čutura Vlado, 2011 a. "Napomena priređivača" [Editor's Note], in: *Katolički identitet i hrvatski preporod* [The Catholic Identity and Croatian Revival], 292-293, edited by Vlado Čutura. Zagreb: Glas Koncila.

Čutura, Vlado. 2011 b. "Smilje Zlatnog pera" [The Immortelle of the Golden Pen], in: *Katolički identitet i hrvatski preporod* [The Catholic Identity and Croatian Revival], 7-40, edited by Vlado Čutura. Zagreb: Glas Koncila.

Erceg, Marino. 2019. Glas Koncila *i obnova diplomatskih odnosa Svete Stolice i socijalističke Jugoslavije (1966. – 1971.): Između izazova dijaloga i opozicije komunističkim vlastima* [The Voice of the Council and the Renewal of the Diplomatic Relations Between the Holy See and Socialist Yugoslavia (1966 – 1971): Between the Challenge of the Dialogue and the Opposition to the Communist Authorities]. Master Thesis. Zagreb: Sveučilište u Zagrebu-Hrvatski studiji.

Goldstein, Ivo. 2008. *Hrvatska 1918. – 2008.* [Croatia: 1918 – 2008].. Zagreb: Europapres holding – Novi Liber.

Hrvatska enciklopedija [Croatian Encyclopedia]. 2020 a. "Vlada" [The Governement]. Leksikografski zavod Miroslav Krleža (https://www.enciklopedija.hr/Natuknica.aspx?ID=65016). Date of access: May 4, 2020.

Kljaić, Stipe. 2017. *Nikada više Jugoslavija: Intelektualci i hrvatsko nacionalno pitanje (1929 – 1945)* [Never again Yugoslavia: The Intellectuals and the Croatian National Question (1929 – 1945)]. Zagreb: Hrvatski institut za povijest.

Kožul, Stjepan. 1998. *Martirologij Crkve zagrebačke: spomenica žrtvama ljubavi Zagrebačke nadbiskupije* [Martyrology of Church of Zagreb: Memorial to the Victims of Love of Archdiocese of Zagreb]. Zagreb: Prometej-Zagrebačka nadbiskupija.

Kramer, Mark. 2017. "The Changing Pattern of Soviet-East European Relations 1953-1968," in: *The Cambridge History of Communism: The Socialist Camp and World Power 1941-1960-s*; Volume II., edited by Norman Naimark, Silvio Pons i Sophie Quinn-Judge, 139-169. Cambridge: Cambridge University Press.

Krišto, Jure. 2019. *Stoljeće naroda i Crkve: Povijest Katoličke Crkve u Hrvatskoj i Bosni i Hercegovini u 20. stoljeću* [The Century of the People and the Church: The History of Catholic Church in Croatia and Bosnia and Herzegovina in 20th Century]. Zagreb: Školska knjiga.

Kundera, Milan. 1967./2006. *Šala* [The Joke]. Zagreb: Meandar.

Kundera, Milan 1984./2006. *Nepodnošljiva lakoća postojanja* [The Unbearable lightness of being]. Zagreb: Meandar.

Lučić, Ivica. 2008. "Komunistički progoni Katoličke crkve u Bosni i Hercegovini 1945. – 1990. [The Communist Persecutions of Catholic Church in Bosnia and Herzegovina 1945. – 1990]., in: *National security and the future*, 9(3): 41-72.

Mihaljević, Josip. 2016. *Komunizam i čovjek: Odnos vlasti i pojedinca u Hrvatskoj (1958. – 1972.)* [The Communism and Man: The Relationship Between the authorities and individuals in Croatia 1958 – 1972]. Zagreb: Hrvatski institut za povijest.

Mikić, Anto. 2016. *Crkveno i društveno značenje Glasa Koncila od 1963. do 1972.* [The Ecclesiastical and social role of The Voice of the Council from 1963 until 1972]. PhD diss. Zagreb: Sveučilište u Zagrebu – Hrvatski studiji.

Miklenić, Ivan. 2012. "Doprinos 'Glasa Koncila' u borbi za oslobođenje od komunizma" [The Contribution of The Voice of the Council in Struggle for the Liberation from Communism], in: *Represija i zločini komunističkog režima u Hrvatskoj* [The Repression and Crimes of the Communist Regime in Croatia], 159-172, edited by Romana Horvat. Zagreb: Matica hrvatska.

Ninčević, Marino and Brčić, Filip. 2016. "Diplomatski odnosi Vatikana i Kraljevine Jugoslavije: konkordat iz 1935. godine" [The Diplomatic Relations of the Vatican and the Kingdom of Yugoslavia: The Concordate from 1935]., in: *Nova prisutnost* [The New Presence], 15(2):299-307.

Novak, Božidar. 2005. *Hrvatsko novinarstvo u 20. Stoljeću* [The Croatian Journalism in 20th Century]. Zagreb: Golden marketing – Tehnička knjiga.

Polegubić, Adolf. 2007. *Stoljeće katoličkog laikata u Hrvatskoj* [The Century of Catholic Laypeople in Croatia]. Zagreb: Glas Koncila.

Radčenko, Marina. 2006. "Semantička adaptacija ruskih posuđenica u hrvatskom jeziku od 1945. do 2000. godine" [Semantical adaptation of Russian loanwords in Croatian between 1945. and 2000]., in: *Croatica et Slavica Iadertina* 2(2): 145-160.

Radelić, Zdenko. 2006. *Hrvatska u Jugoslaviji 1945. – 1991.: od zajedništva do razlaza* [Croatia in Yugoslavia 1945 – 1991: From the Communion to the Departure]. Zagreb: Školska knjiga.

Spehnjak, Katarina and Cipek, Tihomir. 2007. "Disidenti, opozicija i otpor – Hrvatska i Jugoslavija 1945.-1990." [Dissidents, opposition and resistance – Croatia and Yugoslavia 1945. – 1990]., in: *Časopis za suvremenu povijest* [Journal of Contemporary History] 39(2): 255-297.

Supek, Ivan. 1992. *Krivovjernik na ljevici* [The Heretic on the Left]. Zagreb: Nakladni zavod Globus.

Šentija, Josip. 2003. *Veliki školski leksikon* [The Great School Lexicon]. Zagreb: Školska knjiga.

Tuđman, Franjo. 1989. *Bespuća povijesne zbiljnosti* [Wastelands of Historical Reality]. Zagreb: Nakladni zavod Matice hrvatske.

Vuković, Milan. 1995. *Sudski progoni hrvatstva: dokumenti vremena* [The Judicial Persecutions of Croathood: The Documents of Time]. Zagreb: Narodne novine.

Vukušić, Bože. 2001. *Tajni rat Udbe protiv hrvatskih iseljeništva* [Udba's Secret War Against Croatian Emigration]. Zagreb: Klub hrvatskih povratnika iz iseljeništva.

Archival Sources

HR NAZG 1965. Nadbiskupijski arhiv u Zagrebu [*Archdiocesan Archive in Zagreb*]. Smiljana Rendić's letter to Stanko Romac on March 31, 1965. Zagreb: Nadbiskupijski arhiv [Zagreb: Archdiocesan Archive].

HR NAZG 1966. Nadbiskupijski arhiv u Zagrebu [*Archdiocesan Archive in Zagreb*]. Smiljana Rendić's letter to Frane Franić on February 18, 1966. Zagreb: Nadbiskupijski arhiv [Zagreb: Archdiocesan Archive].

HR NAZG 1969 a. Nadbiskupijski arhiv u Zagrebu [*Archdiocesan Archive in Zagreb*]. Smiljana Rendić's letter to Ivan Mužić on October 22, 1969. Zagreb: Nadbiskupijski arhiv [Zagreb: Archdiocesan Archive].

HR NAZG 1969 b. Nadbiskupijski arhiv u Zagrebu [*Archdiocesan Archive in Zagreb*]. Smiljana Rendić's letter to Ivan Mužić on November 3, 1969. Zagreb: Nadbiskupijski arhiv [Zagreb: Archdiocesan Archive].

HR NAZG 1969 c. Nadbiskupijski arhiv u Zagrebu [*Archdiocesan Archive in Zagreb*]. Smiljana Rendić's unpublished manuscript Crkva u getu [*The Church in a Ghetto*] dated on April 2 1969. Zagreb: Nadbiskupijski arhiv [Zagreb: Archdiocesan archive].

HR NAZG 1969 d. Nadbiskupijski arhiv u Zagrebu [*Archdiocesan Archive in Zagreb*]. Smiljana Rendić's letter to Ivan Mužić on September 5, 1969. Zagreb: Nadbiskupijski arhiv [Zagreb: Archdiocesan Archive].

HR NAZG 1970 a. Nadbiskupijski arhiv u Zagrebu [*Archdiocesan Archive in Zagreb*]. Majda Slivar's letter to Smiljana Rendić on August 13, 1970. Zagreb: Nadbiskupijski arhiv [Zagreb: Archdiocesan Archive].

HR NAZG 1970 b. Nadbiskupijski arhiv u Zagrebu [*Archdiocesan Archive in Zagreb*]. Smiljana Rendić's letter to Majda Slivar on August 15, 1970. Zagreb: Nadbiskupijski arhiv [Zagreb: Archdiocesan Archive].

HR NAZG 1970 c. Nadbiskupijski arhiv u Zagrebu [*Archdiocesan Archive in Zagreb*]. Smiljana Rendić's letter to Frane Franić on June 31, 1970. Zagreb: Nadbiskupijski arhiv [Zagreb: Archdiocesan Archive].

HR NAZG 1970 d. Nadbiskupijski arhiv u Zagrebu [*Archdiocesan Archive in Zagreb*]. Smiljana Rendić's letter to Ivan Mužić on February 19, 1970. Zagreb: Nadbiskupijski arhiv [Zagreb: Archdiocesan Archive].

HR NAZG 1970 e. Nadbiskupijski arhiv u Zagrebu [*Archdiocesan Archive in Zagreb*]. Smiljana Rendić's letter to Ivan Merlak on August 24, 1970. Zagreb: Nadbiskupijski arhiv[Zagreb: Archdiocesan Archive].

HR NAZG 1970 f. Nadbiskupijski arhiv u Zagrebu [*Archdiocesan Archive in Zagreb*]. Smiljana Rendić's letter to Ivan Mužić on January 20, 1970. Zagreb: Nadbiskupijski arhiv [Zagreb: Archdiocesan Archive].

HR NAZG 1970 g. Nadbiskupijski arhiv u Zagrebu [*Archdiocesan Archive in Zagreb*]. Smiljana Rendić's letter to Ivan Mužić on January 14, 1970. Zagreb: Nadbiskupijski arhiv [Zagreb: Archdiocesan Archive].

HR NAZG 1970 h. Nadbiskupijski arhiv u Zagrebu [*Archdiocesan Archive in Zagreb*]. Smiljana Rendić's letter to Ivan Mužić on January 30, 1970. Zagreb: Nadbiskupijski arhiv [Zagreb: Archdiocesan Archive].

HR NAZG 1970 i. Nadbiskupijski arhiv u Zagrebu [*Archdiocesan Archive in Zagreb*]. Smiljana Rendić's letter to Luka Vincetić on October 7, 1970. Zagreb: Nadbiskupijski arhiv [Zagreb: Archdiocesan Archive].

HR NAZG 1970 j. Nadbiskupijski arhiv u Zagrebu [*Archdiocesan Archive in Zagreb*]. Smiljana Rendić's letter to Ljubo Hrgić on October 16, 1970. Zagreb: Nadbiskupijski arhiv [Zagreb: Archdiocesan Archive].

HR NAZG 1970 k. Nadbiskupijski arhiv u Zagrebu [*Archdiocesan Archive in Zagreb*]. Smiljana Rendić's unsent letter to Ivan Mužić on April 27, 1970. Zagreb: Nadbiskupijski arhiv [Zagreb: Archdiocesan Archive].

Biographical Sketch

Marino Erceg

Affiliation: Journalist in Croatian Catholic weekly Glas Koncila [The Voice of the Council] Zagreb, Republic of Croatia.

Education:
Master of Communication Sciences (Centre for Croatian Studies – University of Zagreb, 2017-2019)
University Bachelor of History and University Bachelor of Communication Sciences (Centre for Croatian Studies – University of Zagreb, 2014–2017).

Business Address: Kaptol 8, Zagreb, Republic of Croatia.

Research and Professional Experience:

Work for Croatian Catholic weekly Glas Koncila [The Voice of the Council] covering themes related to the history of the Catholic Church in communist Yugoslavia: doing interviews, reportages or special coverages.

Project "COURAGE – Connecting Collections" – As a student volunteer participated in international project "COURAGE – Connecting Collections" (October 2016 – October 2018): Presenting the project to the student population and wider scientific community through lectures and through posts on social media; several presentation of the "COURAGE" internet site and online database of archival collections of cultural opposition and dissent in Communist regimes in Europe; engagement in entering bibliographic data related to the project COURAGE into the reference management software "Zotero"; writing reports from exhibitions or cultural events related to the project "COURAGE."

As a student demonstrator assisted in teaching and conducting seminars in compulsory and elective courses that is part of undergraduate and graduate studies on Division of Communication Studies in Centre for Croatian Studies (University of Zagreb)

Experience in researching history of Catholic Church in Yugoslavia between 1945 and 1990; and history of media and communication in communist Yugoslavia between 1945 and 1990; and history of formal and informal oppositional activities under the Communist regimes in Europe.

Professional Appointments:
Journalist in *Glas Koncila* [The Voice of the Council] (August 2019 – present)
Journalist in Croatian News Agency HINA (June 2018 – June 2019).

Honors:

- Rectors' Award (University of Zagreb) in academic year 2018/2019 for individual scientific paper
- Dean's Award (Centre for Croatian Studies – University of Zagreb) for excellence in Master Studies (2019)
- Dean's Award (Centre for Croatian Studies – University of Zagreb) for excellence in Bachelor Studies (2017).

Publications from the Last 3 Years:

Erceg, Marino. 2019. *Proizvodnja zločina humorom: političke karikature satiričkoga tjednika Kerempuh u pripremi i prezentaciji sudskoga procesa zagrebačkomu nadbiskupu Alojziju Stepincu (1945.–1946.).* Zagreb: Sveučilište u Zagrebu. [Manufacturing Crime with Humor: Political Cartoons of Satirical Weekly *Kerempuh* in Preparation and Presentation of the Trial of the Archbishop of Zagreb Aloysius Stepinac (1945 -1946). Zagreb: University of Zagreb].

Erceg, Marino. 2019. Glas Koncila i obnova diplomatskih odnosa Svete Stoliuce i socijalističke Jugoslavije (1966. – 1971.): Između izazova dijaloga i opozicije komunističkim vlastima. Zagreb: Sveučilište u Zagrebu. [*The Voice of the Council* and the Renewal of the Diplomatic Relations between the Holy See and Socialist Yugoslavia (1966 – 1971): Between the Challenges of Dialogue and Opposition to the Communist Authorities. Zagreb: University of Zagreb].

In: Croatia: Past, Present and Future Perspectives
Editor: Matko Marušić
ISBN: 978-1-53618-300-9

Chapter 7

CROATIAN SPRING: THE CROATIAN NATIONAL REFORM MOVEMENT IN SOCIALIST YUGOSLAVIA (1967 – 1972)

Josip Mihaljević*
Croatian Institute of History, Zagreb, Croatia

ABSTRACT

This chapter gives a historical overview of the Croatian Spring, a socio-political movement from the second half of the 1960s to the early 1970s in the Socialist Republic of Croatia, which was one of six republics of the Socialist Federal Republic of Yugoslavia. The movement emerged in the 1960s as a wave of heterogeneous processes, usually called liberalization in Croatian historiography. The emergence of the movement was facilitated by a conflict within the ruling League of Communists of Yugoslavia that split into two wings. The reform wing advocated for the decentralization of Yugoslavia and a greater autonomy of its republics, and the dogmatic wing of the party which sought to preserve a rigid and centralized model of governance. The movement gained mass support from the Croatian people and was in opposition to the centralist policy of the federal authorities in Belgrade. In addition to the reform-oriented wing of the ruling party, the movement included two different social circles. The first one included Croatian intellectuals gathered around the most prominent cultural institution of the Croatian people, called Matica hrvatska (Matica in further text). The second circle of the movement were students of the University of Zagreb whose participation ensured the movement's growth in size. The Croatian Spring was a struggle against centralism and unitarism. The actors of the Spring criticized the socialist regime because of its economic, political, demographic, and cultural failures. They advocated Croatian cultural integration, political and administrative decentralization of Yugoslavia, a fairer distribution of state revenues, and the liberalization and democratization of political and economic life. The Croatian Spring represented a trend to introduce a wider circle of citizens into politics, which was contrary to the Stalinist view of the role of the party. The liberalization of the system would call the communist political monopoly into question. At the end of 1971, a political coup overthrew the reformist leadership in Croatia,

* Corresponding Author's Email: josip@isp.hr.

followed by repression against the most prominent Croatian Spring figures. The liberal wing of the party was crushed, and numerous intellectuals and students ended up imprisoned for long-terms. The destruction of the Croatian national movement will also mark the ultimate failure of democratization in the Yugoslav communist system.

Keywords: Croatian Spring; reform movement, Croatia; Yugoslavia, League of Communists of Yugoslavia; League of Communist of Croatia; Croatian intellectuals, student protest

Introduction - The Sixties in Croatia

Many authors consider that the 1960s in Yugoslavia, and especially in Croatia, was a decade of liberalization (Mihaljević 2017). In those years, a period of accelerated reforms began, manifesting in almost every field of social life (Pavličević 2007, 485). A key event that paved the way for this strongest liberalization to date was the political fall of Aleksandar Ranković in 1966. Ranković (1909-1983) was Vice President of the Socialist Federal Republic of Yugoslavia (SFRY) and a symbol of the Yugoslav communist repressive apparatus. At the Fourth Plenum of the Central Committee (CC) of the League of Communists of Yugoslavia (LCY) that was held on the island Brijuni on 1 July 1966, he was dismissed from office and expelled from the LCY (Kovač, Dimitrijević, and Popović 2016). A direct outcome of Ranković's removal was not only a reform of the secret police (*Uprava državne bezbednosti* – Udba) but also a new organizational reform of the party and a constitutional reform (Batović 2017, 85). From 1967 until 1971, the Constitution of Yugoslavia (1963) was significantly amended many times. In debates about these changes, critical voices could be heard regarding problems with the economy, society, and national issues that were pressing Yugoslavia and that had become more and more visible to ordinary citizens. The fall of Ranković and the loosening of the party discipline influenced the spread of freedom, especially from the point of view of its political and psychological impact in public. The method of governance in the federation began to change. Sharp criticism of centralism and bureaucracy, and the weakening of the power of the secret police, caused a more democratic atmosphere in the Yugoslav public (Klasić 2006, 42). Compared to other communist countries at the time, political conditions in Yugoslavia were less restrictive. The centralized state apparatus was reduced, although lower levels of bureaucracy had grown. The role of the secret police was somewhat diminished but was certainly not eliminated (Oleszczuk 1981b, 825).

In the 1960s, there was a partial shift in economic policy towards the adoption of market economy. The economic reform that began in 1965 sought to develop a market-based economy with workers self-governing, with a particular focus on increasing openness to the world. This development of market relations, as well as the strengthening of decentralization in decision-making, suggested general pluralization and democratization in Yugoslavia (Vojnić 2006, 408). However, it should also be emphasized that the economic reform also had significant negative economic and social effects, above all in the sharp increase in unemployment. Also, many disputes around the economic reform were directly related to the national question. Economically, there were major differences between the Yugoslav republics - the northwestern republics (Slovenia and Croatia) were richer than the southeastern ones. The distribution of scarce resources was one of the main causes of the division between Croats, Serbs, and other nations in the 1960s and the 1970s. This was particularly evident in the policies of faster development of less developed federal republics and of foreign exchange; both policies shortchanged Croatia and Slovenia which contributed the most to the federal budget (Vojnić 2006, 409; Radelić 2006, 412-423).

Attitudes towards Croatian emigration started to change. Under the chair of Većeslav Holjevac from 1964 to 1968, the Emigrant Foundation of Croatia connected with Croats abroad more actively (Spehnjak 2001, 34; Kraljević 2009). Along with developing tourism (mostly in Croatia), traveling abroad was legalized for Yugoslav citizens. This had multiple positive and negative effects on the overall economic and social situation in Yugoslavia. With the increase in unemployment, the most significant negative social impact was the migration of a large number of citizens abroad, and this was especially true for Croatia and the Croats from Bosnia and Herzegovina, as they emigrated the most (Radelić 2006, 424-428).

Popular culture and western patterns of behavior penetrated the Yugoslav media and public sphere. This process led to increased familiarity with the West in the eyes of Yugoslav citizens. Western values were getting closer and closer, including an awareness of the values of democracy, political pluralism, and freedom of the media (Spehnjak and Cipek 2007, 265). This partial opening up of the political system allowed civil society to engage more politically (Spehnjak and Cipek 2007, 260).

National culture flourished. Many new branches of Matica hrvatska opened, as well as linguistic, historical, cultural, and other organizations (Pavličević 2007, 485). There was also a significant development in social sciences and humanities, with an increasing number of students at universities.

Global Cold War tensions in the 1960s influenced the countries under communist rule. The emergence of student movements around the world also had an impact on Yugoslavia. The ideas of freedom of speech and the ideas of freedom of political activity spread across the country (Marković 2003). An even more significant development was that the nations and their republics in Yugoslavia began to voice their demands for greater independence more and more clearly (Dukovski 2007, 16). Such demands erupted in Croatia first.

The Roots of the Croatian Spring

The reforms of the 1960s led to limited decentralization and other changes that would encourage the expression of national dissatisfaction of the Croatian people. In the 1960s, a movement called the Croatian Spring emerged: ironically, the term 'Croatian Spring' (Hrvatsko proljeće) was coined only after it was suppressed in December 1971 – and would be banned from Yugoslav discourse until 1989 (Batović 2017, 236). There is another term – "Mass movement" (Maspok) - that was used by the authorities who wanted to defame the Croatian national movement after the December 1971 purges.

In Croatian historiography, various authors have defined differently the period of the Croatian Spring, but the most accepted variant is the period from the publication of the "Declaration on the Name and Status of the Croatian Literary Language" in 1967 until the arrest of intellectuals in January 1972 (Dukovski 2007, 28). The Croatian Spring was a complex social phenomenon in Croatia that articulated many problems such as the issues of economy, federalism and statehood of the republics, equality in national relations, rule of law, freedom, etc.

Economic liberalization in Yugoslavia had a significant impact on the rise of the Croatian Spring. That is evident in one of the most talked about demands of the actors of the Croatian Spring - the demand for the change of the system of foreign currency distribution under the motto, "Croatian foreign currency for Croatia." This demand was first formulated by Šime Đodan, who was then an assistant professor at the Faculty of Law in Zagreb and the business secretary of Matica (Pavličević 2007, 490).

By the mid-1960s, the model of socialist development was already outdated and lagging behind modern developments in the West, and the communists needed to formulate a new program and solve many social problems (Tripalo 1990, 8-9). The Croatian Spring initially did not imply any organization or activity outside the constitutional framework but meant a political awakening of the population that wanted to participate not only in the implementation of the party policy but also in the policy-making (Tripalo 1990, 23). However, this awakening did not come about overnight, rather it was a culmination of a process that started much earlier and was originally initiated by the party in power (Oleszczuk 1981a, 171-174). The 8th Congress of LCY in December 1964 was a key event and a prerequisite for the initiation of economic reform in 1965, for the initiation of numerous other liberalization steps, and eventually for addressing national issues in Yugoslavia. That congress also defined a policy that made it possible to overthrow Ranković and initiate partial liberalization of Yugoslav society (Ponoš 2007, 17).

However, the emergence of liberalization and the fact that the communists themselves initiated it should still be put in a wider context. Namely, the communist authorities could not ignore the processes on the international scene that had their echoes in Yugoslavia as well. So, the question is to what extent the communist government itself wanted these reforms, and to what extent it was forced to do them. A good example of external influences on developments in Yugoslavia is the student movement, which could more easily articulate its tendency to organize and speak publicly by relying on student activities around the world.

In the turbulent 1960s, the European communist countries were faced a resurgence of questions about national identities which had been suppressed after 1945. Many of the political elites of those countries attempted to address national issues while also bolstering their legitimacy (Spehnjak 1998, 319; Spehnjak and Cipek 2007, 272). The suppressed national identities of each nation in Yugoslavia did not disappear in federal Yugoslavia either, and the party sought to neutralize national issues by strengthening the position of national republics and by conducting top-down reforms in the 1960s (Oleszczuck 1981b, 821). Communist authorities in several European countries, including Yugoslavia, attempted to reform socialism by combining nationalism and liberalism (Spehnjak and Cipek 2007, 273).

The Croatian Spring was also marked with Croatian aspirations for national affirmation. One of the problems, very painful for Croatian and other nations, was Serbian overrepresentation on federal bodies and in general administration. The Serbs made up 66.6% in the general administration and Croats for example only 8.9% of civil servants (Batović 2017, 94-95), although according to the census in 1971 Croats made up 22.1% of the population and Serbs 39.7%. Namely, due to the long-standing personnel policy in Croatia, which directly or indirectly favored Serbs in certain state and public services, especially in the police and the Yugoslav People's Army (*Jugoslavenska narodna armija* - JNA), Croats increasingly felt that the Socialist Republic (SR) of Croatia was becoming more a homeland of Serbs than of Croats (Radelić 2006, 390). According to some data, in 1971 in Croatia, in Udba there were only around 20% Croats, and about 30% Croats in the police, while around 76% and 80% of the staff were Serbs. In Zagreb, the capital of Croatia, of the 13 police station chiefs only three were Croats. In the state bodies of the SR of Croatia, about 24% of the employed were Serbs. This was quite disproportionate to their share in the population of SR Croatia, where they made up 14.16%, while Croats were 79.38% (Radelić 2006, 393-395).

Feelings of discontent spread within the Croatian people, and in the second half of the 1960s, the reformist wing of the League of Communists of Croatia (LCC), the Croatian branch of the party, took that standpoint. However, those Croatian intellectuals who were outside party structures, or had fallen out of those structures before and had become dissidents, articulated this problem most clearly.

THREE CIRCLES OF THE CROATIAN SPRING

The actors at the center of the Croatian Spring can be analyzed through three different social circles. Each of those circles had its specificities and impacts on the Croatian Spring, although they often intertwined with each other. The first circle/group was the reform wing within the Croatian party, the second were intellectuals gathered around the Matica, and the third group were Croatian students of the University of Zagreb.

Reformists within the Party

If we try to simplify this complex phenomenon, we can say that in many aspects at the very beginning, the Croatian Spring was an expression of the struggle between centralists and liberals (decentralists) in the leadership of Yugoslavia (Spehnjak 1998, 318). The majority of the Croatian political elite in the League of Communists advocated radical reforms, decentralization, and a liberalization of social life. In a time of crisis, when the old communist model was losing its credibility, this wing of the Croatian Communists believed that such reforms would give new legitimacy to their rule. This circle was dominated mainly by younger politicians, the most prominent being Savka Dabčević-Kučar and Miko Tripalo, with Pero Pirker, Dragutin Haramija, Srećko Bijelić and others. These politicians were making efforts to modernize Yugoslavia in the late 1960s (Batović 2017, 3).

Dabčević-Kučar had been a full professor of political economy at the University of Zagreb since 1965, a president of the Central Committee of the League of Communists of Croatia (CC LCC) since 1968 and a member of its Executive Committee since 1963. From 1967 to 1968 she was the president of the Executive Council of the Parliament of the SR of Croatia. As an economist and politician, she demanded changes in the economic system, advocating for more free-market-oriented principles, as well as a reform of the federation in the direction of greater independence of republics. Miko Tripalo was the president of the Executive Committee of the CC LCC from 1966 and since 1969 a member of the Executive Bureau of the LCY Presidency and the SFRY Presidency (Radelić 2006, 430). In some high political circles, Tripalo was considered even one of the potential successors of Josip Broz Tito.

Their high positions and the support initially given to them by Josip Broz Tito enabled them to steer the Croatian party onto a strong reform course. Their policies were accepted by the LCC in January 1970 at the 10th meeting of the CC LCC. In conflict with Miloš Žanko, the foremost proponent of centralism among Croatian communists, the majority of the CC condemned Yugoslav unitarism as a threat to the stability of the system. This was almost a kind of political revolution in Croatian politics and was seen live because the 10th meeting was the first party meeting that was broadcast live on television (Bilandžić 1999, 557). After the meeting, it became possible to publicly criticize Yugoslav unitarism more strongly, and thus to affirm an independent Croatian political direction. The 10th meeting was, in a way, "an indirect attack on Belgrade's federal structures and perceived Serbian dominance" (Batović 2017, 135). The Croatian public and the media also widely accepted the conclusions of that meeting. In the public sphere, Croatia was regarded more and more as a separate political community, and that standpoint was boosted during the debates on the amendments to the constitution of Yugoslavia in 1971. The constitutional amendments adopted in June 1971 affirmed the federalist principles in the Yugoslav state and substantially reduced the powers of the federation. Federation powers were restricted to areas of defense, foreign policy, and regulation of the common market, while all other powers came under the control of the republics (Batović 2012, 85; Smerdel 2007, Sunajko 2012). From the perspective of the Croatian reformist, it was a huge success.

Intellectuals

The second circle of the Croatian Spring is the circle of intellectuals gathered around Matica, a Croatian cultural institution that was founded in the first half of the 19th century. During the Croatian Spring, Matica became the central Croatian cultural and publishing institution around which many other Croatian cultural and academic institutions and intellectuals gathered. Matica gathered Croatian intelligentsia that was dissatisfied with Croatia's position within the Yugoslav federation at the time, and especially with the federal government's attitude towards Croatian national identity. In November 1970, Matica adopted a program that addressed various political and economic questions earlier formulated by the reformist wing of the party and started to broaden their membership. In a single year (November 1970 – November 1971) their membership increased from 2,323 to 41,000 members (Irvine 2008, 161-162). Matica helped the creation of wide support for reform ideas of the Croatian Spring through many old and newly-established branches around the country. Although the policy of the reform wing of the LCC created the conditions for the emergence of the Croatian Spring, only the activity of this circle on the cultural, and especially on the linguistic field, marked the real beginning of a new Croatian national movement. As mentioned before, the act of publication of the Declaration on the Name and Status of the Croatian Literary Language is considered by many the beginning of the Croatian Spring.

The Declaration was a manifesto of Croatian linguists. Eighteen Croatian scholarly and cultural institutions signed the document. Besides Matica, the signatories were the Society of Writers of Croatia, the Croatian center of the PEN–club, the Croatian Philological Society, various departments of the Yugoslav Academy of Sciences and Arts (JAZU), and departments and chairs of Croatian language at universities in Zagreb and Zadar ("Deklaracija o nazivu i položaju hrvatskog književnog jezika" 1967). It was published on March 17, 1967 in Zagreb, in the weekly *Telegram*, the magazine of the Society of Writers of Croatia. Croatian writers and linguists were dissatisfied with the official dictionaries and orthographies in which Serbian and Croatian were considered one language, called Serbo-Croatian. That name of the language was officially adopted when prominent linguists and writers from four Yugoslav republics signed the Novi Sad Agreement in 1954. Since the mid-1960s, Croatian writers and linguists wanted to change that unitaristic practice, and they decided to produce an amendment to the 1963 Constitution of SR Croatia in late 1966 and early 1967. That was the prime motive for writing the Declaration. The text of the Declaration was drafted on Matica's premises by a group of academics and literary and cultural workers (Miroslav Brandt, Dalibor Brozović, Radoslav Katičić, Tomislav Ladan, Slavko Mihalić, Slavko Pavešić, Vlatko Pavletić). The Steering Committee of Matica approved the content of the Declaration on March 13, 1967 and sent it to other Croatian cultural and academic institutions (Mihaljević 2018a). Along with eighteen Croatian academic and cultural institutions, a significant number of prominent intellectuals also signed the Declaration. "The declaration spoke openly and boldly about the difficulties of everyday use of the Croatian language, which was being discriminated against in public institutions in comparison to the Serbian variant of the joint language" (Batović 2017, 72).

The signatories of the Declaration found that the Croatian language was put at an unequal position because the Serbian variant was implemented as the state language throughout the federal Yugoslav administrative apparatus and as the language of public and mass communication. They stood up openly against the practice that spread through diplomacy, administration and legislation, and federal institutions especially in the army (JNA), Central News Agency (TANJUG), Yugoslav Radio Television (JRT), Postal, Telegraph, and Telephone Service (PTT), Yugoslav Railways (JŽ) where Serbian was *de facto* used as the state language (Radelić 2006, 405; Kovačec 2017, Samardžija 2017). The signatories took a stand that each nation in the federation has the right to name and use its own language, and they demanded equal status for the Croatian language. The dominance of the Serbian language revealed the overall economic, political, and cultural subordination of Croatia within Yugoslavia (Mihaljević 2018a; Kovačec 2017).

The publication of the Declaration was not only a cultural but also a political affair. It had additional significance because Miroslav Krleža, probably the most prominent left-wing intellectual not only in Croatia but also in all of Yugoslavia, signed the document together with other intellectuals. Although the writers of the Declaration were cautious and attempted not to breach any boundaries set by the League of Communists (they used the usual communist phraseology and the style of "self-managing socialism" and the Yugoslav slogan of "fraternity and unity"), the publication of the Declaration triggered strong political reactions and set the repressive apparatus in motion (Mihaljević 2018a).

The 'conservative' wing of the LCC leadership led by Miloš Žanko, a member of the CC LCC and vice-president of the Parliament of the SR of Croatia, and since 1967, vice-president of the Federal Assembly of the SFRY, attacked the Declaration and its signatories. There were even some suggestions in the media to prosecute the signatories. However, Vladimir Bakarić, "the old guard Croatian communist leader and a serial opportunist" (Harris 2017, ix), stopped the attacks and the demands for prosecution, saying in a meeting of the executive committee of the CC of the Croatian party that if someone were to be put on a trial, he would probably be released and that would not be good for the image of the party (Radelić 2006, 406).

A special plenary session of the CC LCC in April 1967 was dedicated to the Declaration. Većeslav Holjevac, one of the most popular Croatian politicians at the time, was dismissed from the CC, and Franjo Tuđman, who will later become the first post-Communist president of Croatia, was dismissed from the position of Director of the Institute of the History of the Labor Movement of Croatia and expelled from the party. Miroslav Krleža had agreed to resign from the CC (Batović 2017, 75). Out of seventy members of the party who supported the Declaration, 24 of them were censured and 10 were expelled from the party (Radelić 2006, 406). Although many of the initiators of the Declaration were punished, federal authorities accepted some of the demands from the Declaration: thus, at the end of 1967, the Executive Council of Parliament of the SFRY decided that from 1968 all federal regulations should be published in the languages of all nations, including separate Serbian and Croatian versions (Radelić 2006, 407).

From 1967 until 1971, new constitutional amendments to the SFRY Constitution were adopted. These amendments introduced some confederal elements in the Yugoslav Constitution, including proportional representation of all republics and autonomous provinces in federal administration, and consensual decision making with veto power at the highest level of the federal government (Radelić 2006, 383-388; Jonjić 2017).

In the debates outside the high-level party forums, most Croatian intellectuals started expressing, first privately and then publicly, the conviction that the sovereignty of Croatia is indivisible and demanding a clear definition of the position of Croatia and Croats in the SFRY. Croatian journalists of that time also played a significant role. Although they were still limited by the communist party directives, in the period of the Croatian Spring they increasingly turned towards the examples and principles of Western journalism (Novak 2010, 165). The majority of Croatian media experienced a limited liberalization and advocated public debate and political pluralism. They supported Croatian interests as opposed to the federal center. *Vjesnik*, the most important daily newspaper in Croatia that was under party control since the 1940s, as well as Radio Television Zagreb (RTZ), had become increasingly nationalistic media and reflected the political atmosphere of that time as well as the situation in Croatian society (Novak 1997; Novak 2005, 561). The journalists who carried on the liberalization process were connected with the reform-oriented wing of the LCC and they shared the same fate after the demise of the Croatian Spring.

In addition to *Vjesnik*, *Vjesnik u srijedu* (VUS) was a political weekly newspaper that developed investigative journalism and was heavily engaged in writing against unitarism (Novak 2005, 557). These newspapers also published articles written by pro Croatian intellectuals, especially economists such as Marko Veselica, Vladimir Veselica, Hrvoje Šošić, Šime Đodan, and others who wrote about the economic and political issues that caused the rise of the Croatian Spring. These economists also supported the Croatian Spring with their writing in other publications and by public speeches. Most of their findings were published in 1971 in magazines not directly controlled by the party, the *Hrvatski gospodarski glasnik* (Croatian Economic Herald: Journal for Economic and Political Issues) and the *Hrvatski tjednik: novine za kulturna i društvena pitanja* (Croatian Weekly: Newspaper for Cultural and Social Issues). *Hrvatski tjednik* was published by Matica in 1971 (April 16 - December 3). It was the primary media through which Matica and a circle of intellectuals gathered around it spread the ideas of Croatian national movement. “In advocating for Croatian cultural integration and equality within the Yugoslav federation, the paper openly criticized the socialist regime due to its economic-political, demographic and cultural failures. It was the most vocal media of the Croatian Spring that shared the destiny of the movement. After a precipitous ascent, the government extinguished it" (Mihaljević 2018b). *Hrvatski tjednik* was able to penetrate all sections of Croatian society and thus provoked negative reactions from the regime. The regime considered Matica and *Hrvatski tjednik* a platform of the Croatian political opposition. Although it was primarily devoted to economic issues, the *Hrvatski gospodarski glasnik,* which was published by the Society of Economists of Croatia, supported views similar to those in the *Hrvatski tjednik* (Šajnović 2019). These media advocated the need for systematic economic reforms and raised the issues of introducing a free market system and controlling the republic's share of the federal revenue. During the Croatian Spring, there were many other magazines advocating reform ideas such as the *Hrvatsko sveučilište*, *Kritika*, *Kolo*, *Encyclopaedia Moderna*, *Omladinski tjednik*, *Studentski list* etc.

In addition to the issues of organization of the federation, linguistic, and economic issues, the Croatian Spring put a great emphasis on issues of Croatian history and national symbols. By increasing usage of national symbols, such as the use of the Croatian flag without a communist five-pointed star, Croatian national identity was emphasized. The increased freedom allowed the writers and historians to speak and write more freely about some of the previously taboo historical topics. Thus, Croatian historians began to study some of the national heroes of the past that had been neglected until then, such as the Croatian ban Josip Jelačić, the noble families of Zrinski and Frankapan, as well as some more recent figures of Croatian history such as Stjepan Radić, a former leader of the Croatian Peasant Party that was politically opposed to the Communist Party. For the first time in Croatia, the inaccurate, but official and prevalent claim that over 700,000 people were killed in the Ustasha concentration camp Jasenovac during the Second World War was called into question. One of the historians who stood out the most was Franjo Tuđman, a communist dissident who, through his works and public appearances, questioned inaccurate historical assessments. He became involved in a broad national reform movement as a historian. In 1970, he became a member of the Society of Writers of Croatia, a member of the Executive Board and the Steering Board of Matica, and the President of its Commission for Croatian History since 1971. In 1971, he wrote in magazines (*Dubrovnik*, *Kritika*, *Riječi*, *Hrvatski tjednik*) and spoke publicly about the right of peoples to self-determination and the necessity of building Croatian state sovereignty (Knežević and Mihaljević 2018, 362).

Students

University students were the third critical social circle of the Croatian Spring. In the 1960s, the number of university students in Croatia grew. At the time, the University of Zagreb was the only university in Croatia with additional faculties of the university in some major Croatian cities like Split, Zadar, and Rijeka. With the increasing number of students coming from all over Croatia, including Croats from Bosnia and Herzegovina and other parts of Yugoslavia, the University of Zagreb was the meeting place for the entire young Croatian intelligentsia. Through its activities, the university significantly influenced national integration (Sučić 2017, 401). Students participated in social life in various university facilities and attended the events organized by the Society of Writers of Croatia and Matica.

Students broadly accepted the key reformist standpoints of Croatian intellectuals and politicians, supporting demands they could read in the pages of the reform-oriented magazines, radio, and television (Sučić 2017, 401-402). Analytical articles of Croatian intellectuals who wrote about the neglect of Croatia, as well as numerous scientific conferences, roundtables, and student forums with similar topic received a positive reception among Croatian students (Sučić 2017, 404). They began to participate more and more in the Croatian reform movement and to support leaders of the reform wing of the Croatian branch of the party (Bukvić 2018c).

As early as the late 1960s, university reform began. One of the reforms was a new statute of the University of Zagreb, which ensured that one-third of the members of the University Assembly must be students, and that a Student Vice Chancellor should be elected from their ranks in addition to the Chancellor and two Vice Chancellors that were elected from among the professors. In December 1970, Ivan Supek was elected Chancellor, Hrvoje Požar, and Nikša Alegretti Vice Chancellors, and Ivan Zvonimir Čičak a Student Vice Chancellor. Čičak was a student of comparative literature and law and a student at the Institute for the Theological Culture of Laypersons at the Faculty of Theology in Zagreb. Following his election, the leadership of the Student Union of Zagreb, a student organization that was controlled by the party, began a campaign to dismiss Čičak, saying he was a nationalist and a clericalist (Sučić 2017, 408). In spite of that, at the official student meetings which subsequently took place, most students supported Čičak and the democratically elected bodies of the University. They also supported the reform policy defined at the 10th meeting of the CC LCC and supported Croatian political leaders Savka Dabčević-Kučar and Miko Tripalo.

Soon, on April 4, 1971, new elections were held for the Assembly of the Student Union of Zagreb, where Dražen Budiša became the new president (Sučić 2017, 409-410; Ponoš 2012, 339). At the same time, Ante Paradžik was elected president of the Student Union of Croatia, which brought together representatives of all Croatian university faculties (Veselinović 2015, 135). Thus, Čičak, Budiša, and Paradžik became the undisputed leaders of the student movement in Zagreb and Croatia.

Through speeches, student newspapers and pamphlets distributed at the University and other places, and by scrawling graffiti with slogans at public places, students promoted ideas of equality of Yugoslav nations and greater Croatian autonomy (Bukvić 2018b). They expressed rebellion against undemocratic practices, as well as against unitarism. On this wave, the student movement was shaped and spread across all faculties and became a political factor with which the government needed to deal (Sučić 2017, 408-409).

The regime press from Belgrade reacted vehemently against the rise of the student movement. A more serious attack on the student movement occurred in July 1971, when the party organization in Zagreb expelled Šime Đodan and Marko Veselica. As students admired and supported those two new party dissidents, the centralist wing within the CC LCC started to publicly speak against the Student Union of Zagreb and the Student Union of Croatia. However, the vast majority of students remained committed to the reform policy (Sučić 2017, 411-412). In support of reformist political leadership in Croatia, students organized mass rallies during 1971 and ultimately a strike. On November 22, 1971, a gathering of Croatian university students began in the large hall of the Student Center in Zagreb, at which a vice-president of the Student Union of Croatia Goran Dodig spoke of the delay of the federal authorities in solving problems with foreign exchange, banking, and foreign trade, and urged students to strike. About three thousand students who attended the rally agreed and launched the strike. Soon, meetings were held at many colleges, and strike committees and strike guards were formed. The next day, student organizations began to receive messages of support from factory workers from all over Croatia. On the second day of the strike, a plenum of the Student Union of Croatia decided to strike at all higher education institutions in Croatia. The deans of the faculties based in Zagreb supported the strike and students' demands (Bušić 1983, 244).

The student movement in 1971 was also significant in Split (Mužić 2017, 638-639). The Plenum of the Student Union of Split was held on November 25, bringing together more than a thousand students who gave their full support to the conclusions of the plenum in Zagreb. Students in Zadar also stopped attending classes (Bušić 1983, 244). However, on the same day, Miko Tripalo gave a speech on television in which he said that the student strike endangered the position of the Croatian reform leadership and he urged students to end the strike (Ponoš 2007, 186-187). This speech caused a schism in the Presidency of the Student Union of Zagreb but did not result in the end of the strike (Ponoš 2012, 340-341). At that point, Tito decided to break the Croatian Spring and to remove the Croatian party reformists. Opinions differ whether Tito made that decision before the strike broke out, and used the strike merely as a pretext, or whether the strike actually precipitated it (Ponoš 2012, 340; Hrvatska enciklopedija Online 2020).

The End of the Croatian Spring

The Croatian reform movement initiated the process of social and national emancipation and in a very short time it spread through almost all sections of Croatian society - from political and intellectual elites, through students, to ordinary workers who were increasingly supporting the movement and attending various rallies. The reform movement created an unprecedented national euphoria that spread even outside Croatian borders, and reached Croatian emigration as well. The period of the Croatian Spring was the period of the strongest communication between Croatian political emigrants with individuals and institutions in their homeland. This was a unique period of relations between Croats in the homeland and Croatian emigration because the liberal wing of the Croatian communist party sought to implement a slightly different policy towards the Croatian emigrants, including political emigrants. Until then, the communist authorities in Croatia, as well as the authorities at the federal level, considered Croatian political emigration extremely hostile, labelling it generally as Ustasha leftovers and making no distinction between numerous currents that existed in the divided Croatian emigration (Krašić 2018, 436-437). Many Croatian emigrants hoped that the Croatian Spring would set Croatia free from communist dictatorship. Those hopes were dashed at the end of 1971.

The movement was opposed to those trends and policies in Yugoslavia that advocated for continuing centralism, unitarism, and one-party rule. Proponents of these policies were primarily in Serbia, although they were in other republics as well. Powerful groups within the army and the Serb community in Croatia also opposed the Croatian reform movement.

Tito's attitude towards the Croatian Spring changed with time. At first, he supported the reformists within the Croatian leadership in their critique of unitarism and foreign exchange policy. Tripalo believed that Tito was giving his full support to the Croatian leadership until the 7th meeting of the Presidency of the Executive Bureau of LCY, held in late April 1971 (Jakovina 2005, 168-173). However, Tito also called a meeting of the CC LCC on July 4, 1971 to warn Croatian leadership of the danger that the "eruption of nationalism" might cause Soviet intervention and requested measures against it. According to some CIA reports, Tito emphasized in that meeting, "that he was ready to become a dictator if that is what it took to resolve this situation" (Batović 2017, 183). But in September 1971 it seemed that Tito was still supporting the Croatian leadership: during his trip to Croatia Tito said that claims of chauvinism in Croatia were absurd. This statement was received with great relief in Croatia and many contemporaries interpreted Tito's words as an expression of support to the Croatian leadership (Novak 2005, 686- 687; Klasić 2006, 162-166). Nevertheless, Tito's subsequent moves showed that the Croatian leadership had lost his support. At the end of September, Leonid Brezhnev arrived in Belgrade, after which Yugoslavia began to strengthen its economic and military ties with the USSR (National Foreign Assessment Center 1980; Rusinow 1978, 320). In early October 1971, the military maneuvers of the SFRY armed forces called "Freedom '71" was carried out only on Croatian soil. Many contemporaries interpreted this military exercise as Tito's indirect threat to the Croatian political leadership (Batović 2017, 259-260; Godić and Knežević 2016). It was supposed to intimidate Croatia, because of its demands for renegotiation of national relations within Yugoslavia (Godić and Knežević 2016, 187).

At the end, President Josip Broz Tito must have concluded that the Croatian reform movement was threatening the stability of the country and his influence, and he suppressed the Croatian Spring at the end of 1971. At the 21st meeting of the Presidency of the LCY held at Tito's country residence in Karađorđevo (November 31 – December 2, 1971), Tito condemned the Croatian national movement as a restoration of Croatian nationalism and criticized Croatian political leaders Tripalo and Dabčević-Kučar. They were forced to resign from their political functions at the CC LCC session (December 12, 1971). It was a classic party purge (Mihaljević 2016, 356-357).

Certainly, one of the deciding factors that Tito must have considered was the international political constellation. Namely, neither the West nor the Soviets wanted the destabilization of Yugoslavia, which played a role as a buffer zone in the Cold War world order. Any destabilization of Yugoslavia could have caused significant movements in international relations.

Ivan Supek explains Tito's vacillation with a difficult international situation at that time. Supek believes that Leonid Brezhnev's visit to Belgrade in September 1971 (just one week after Tito expressed his support for the Croatian leadership) caused that change. Brezhnev was extremely critical of "anti-socialist forces" in Yugoslavia and, allegedly, demanded the suppression of liberal tendencies in Croatia and Yugoslavia. Afterwards, Tito visited the United States to ask for help, but the timing was bad because there were presidential elections then, and Richard Nixon and Henry Kissinger had other priorities (Supek 1992, 192). Many historians also find the international position of Yugoslavia as one of the critical reasons for Tito's decision (Bilandžić 1999, 645; Jakovina 2005, 168-173; Banac 2011). On the other hand, Jasper Ridley believes that the main reason for Tito's decision to stifle the Croatian Spring was his talk with army general Nikola Ljubičić, who warned him that the Partisan War Veterans' Association (SUBNOR) was very concerned that Tito had not reacted against Croatian nationalists (Ridley 2000, 435).

After the fall of the Croatian Spring, Savka Dabčević-Kučar, Miko Tripalo, and several other leaders were excluded from political and public life. Besides the high officials, all politicians and government officials who openly advocated demands of the Croatian national movement were forced to resign in the coming months, totaling around 2,000 people. The liberal reform wing within the League of Communists of Croatia was replaced with those who obediently implemented the policy defined in the federal center. Milka Planinc became the new president of the Croatia's CC, and Vladimir Bakarić continued to steer the Croatian party behind the scenes.

The other two circles of the Croatian Spring were subject to worse repression. Many intellectuals and students were arrested and sentenced to prison. The students were the first who experienced the repression. On December 11, 1971, Public Security Secretariat in Zagreb filed criminal charges with the District Public Prosecutor in Zagreb against student leaders Ivan Zvonimir Čičak, Dražen Budiša, Ante Paradžik, and Goran Dodig on the grounds of enemy propaganda and "criminal offences against the people and state by a counter-revolutionary attack on the state and social order" (Bukvić 2018a). Dražen Budiša was convicted to four years in prison, Ivan Zvonimir Čičak and Ante Paradžik to three and Goran Dodig to one year.

One of the main targets of repression was Matica. The Communist government perceived Matica as a source of oppositional political ideas, and in 1972 Matica was practically abolished. The members of the Executive Board and the Steering Board of Matica were forced to resign in 1972. Many of its prominent members came under attack and were accused of "Croatian nationalism." (Mihaljević 2018c). Following a political decision in Karađorđevo in December 1971, Republic Internal Affairs Secretariat (RSUP) of the SR of Croatia, compiled a report on oversight of the legality of the work of Matica, which was a basis for future indictments and the court prosecution of Matica's members. The report concluded that Matica "has grown into an association for achieving counter-revolutionary goals" (Mihaljević 2018c). Due to this report, many Croatian intellectuals were sentenced to long-term prison sentences.

One consequence of this was that the publications of Matica ceased to be printed. After issue no. 33 of *Hrvatski tjednik*, which was published on December 3, 1971, the regime shut down the magazine and launched persecution of its editors. Many of them faced harassment, dismissal, political trials, and imprisonment. Vladimir (Vlado) Gotovac, who had been editor-in-chief since July 1971, was indicted on January 6, 1972, for "counter-revolutionary assault on the state and the social system" and sentenced to a four-year imprisonment with an additional three-year loss of civil rights. Ten other Croatian intellectuals were charged and sentenced in the same process with Gotovac: Marko Veselica, Šime Đodan, Ante Bruno Bušić, Hrvoje Šošić, Jozo Ivičević-Bakulić, Zvonimir Komarica, Ante Glibota, Ante Bačić, Vlatko Pavletić and Franjo Tuđman (Knezević and Mihaljević 2018, 362-363). Marko Veselica received the highest sentence – seven years of imprisonment in a high-security prison (Artuković and Antić 2013).

The collapse of the Croatian Spring had multiple effects. A return of the "firm hand" rule resulted in a period of so-called "Croatian silence" in which Croatia was practically pacified until the breakup of Yugoslavia, and was on a political defensive in relation to the federal center and other Yugoslav republics, primarily SR Serbia, although its own reform leadership was also purged in 1972. "To try to avoid the appearance of anti-Croatian oppression, liberal and religious leaders in Slovenia and Serbia were also targeted and removed" (Batović 2017,

233). The arrests and convictions of student leaders and prominent Matica members, along with the purges within the LCC, traumatized the Croatian republic and ultimately weakened pro-Yugoslav tendencies in Croatian society (Hrvatska enciklopedija Online 2020). At the same time, a new wave of Croatian political emigration emerged with some emigrants becoming radicalized and starting to take even terrorist actions against the Yugoslav communist regime.

CONCLUSION

We can analyze the Croatian Spring from several different perspectives. However, it is primarily a story of a Croatian national revival during the communist rule. It is a massive national movement and a tempestuous political reform period of national affirmation of Croatia and Croats, a fight for equality, democracy, and civil liberties.

The Croatian national movement was analyzed through three different social circles: the liberal wing of the party, Croatian intellectuals gathered around Matica and Croatian university students. Each of those social groups had their standpoints regarding the position of Croatia within the SFRY that were not always unanimous, and each of the groups put their distinctive impact on the Croatian Spring. Croatian intellectuals and especially Croatian students were far more radical in their reform demands than the liberal wing of the party. However, these impacts often intertwined with each other and that produced the Croatian national movement. Although the movement was politically and socially heterogeneous, those three social groups found unity in the struggle for general Croatian national interests (Dukovski 2007, 37).

The movement initially emerged as a reaction of the Croatian communists and intelligentsia to the dismissal in 1966 of Aleksandar Ranković who was a symbol of the Yugoslav communist repressive apparatus and its centralist and unitarist ideology. Conditions for some kind of political liberalization in Yugoslavia were more favorable after that time. A reduction of political repression had great influence on the emergence of the Croatian Spring, and separately on the new Croatian emigration wave in the 1960s when many Croats tried to find better living conditions abroad, mostly in the Western European democracies. However, the Croatian Spring is at the same time a story of the failed liberalization and democratization of Yugoslavia. At first, liberalization of society was promulgated from above, but once it began to spread, the government could not control it, and this fact would ultimately spell the doom of the reformist wing in the LCC and the end of the Spring. The 1960s brought some softening of the totalitarian Yugoslav system, but the hoped-for social reform and real liberalization did not happen.

There are several causes for this failure and for the fall of the Croatian Spring. Different cultural and historical traditions of national and ethnic groups, as well as different economic conditions, were a significant impediment to liberalization because the communist government feared that growing freedom could cause Yugoslavia's disintegration along national lines. Another political cause of the failure of the liberal reforms in Yugoslavia were Soviet roots of the Yugoslav communist leadership and the never-abandoned Stalinist techniques of rule that included party purges, arrests of "class enemies," etc. (Oleszczuk 1981b, 826-828). One-party system limited the scope of reforms. Rigid communist leadership had mechanisms to avoid liberalization. Repression and prisons were always there for those who would go "too far" (Oleszczuk 1981b, 829). We must also not forget external political context – Cold War balance of power between the Eastern and the Western Block. Both blocs feared to disrupt that balance in Yugoslavia (Spehnjak 1998, 320).

In economic terms, the League of Communists wanted to make the Yugoslav system more effective by introducing a measure of market economy, but such an economy entailed free movement of capital, goods, services, labor, and ideas, which was incompatible with a one-party dictatorship (Spehnjak and Cipek 2007, 273). Most of the party leadership was afraid of democratic development, as broad sections of the population began to challenge many areas of social and political life, and warning of shortcomings and irregularities in the work of the leadership which was untouchable up to that moment (Tripalo 1990, 26).

The Croatian Spring brought a wider circle of citizens into politics, which was contrary to Stalinist perceptions of the role of the party in the state (Tripalo 1990, 27). Demands for national rights in the nationally heterogeneous Yugoslav state shook the traditional communist ideological ties and endangered the totalitarian power of the party. The liberalization of the system was a threat to the political monopoly that the hardline communists and the *nomenklatura* did not want to give up. The dogma of the communist leadership could not be questioned and that was an insurmountable obstacle to the real reforms Yugoslavia needed (Bilandžić 1999, 553-554; Spehnjak and Cipek 2007, 273). The fall of the liberal faction of leadership in Yugoslavia in the early 1970s, especially those in Croatia and Serbia, meant the return of the old dogmatic cadres (Mihaljević 2017, 275; Spehnjak and Cipek 2007, 275; Dukovski 2007, 22-23).

The Croatian Spring was a struggle for political and administrative decentralization of Yugoslavia and a struggle against centralism and unitarism, and, to a lesser extent, for the liberalization and democratization of political and economic life (Mihaljević 2017). The national issue was primary, while democracy and liberalism were secondary goals of the Croatian Spring (Radelić 2006, 462-466). Besides, within a totalitarian system, it was not even possible to invoke liberalism or nationalism openly, because it was an ideology opposite to communism, as high-ranked communists including Tito emphasized many times (Mihaljević 2016, 372-373). In such a context, the demands for a multi-party system also could not be demanded openly, although some of the actors of the Croatian Spring had such hopes.

To calm the discontent in Croatia after the collapse of the Croatian Spring, the central government made some concessions and even implemented some of the demands that had been formulated within the Croatian Spring (Hrvatska enciklopedija Online 2020). However, the disappointment experienced by Croats in 1971 was so great that new reforms of Yugoslavia were no longer sufficient. The vast majority of Croatian people then "gave up" on Yugoslavia, and the idea of Croatian independence would ultimately prevail. The conditions to realize that idea will ripen twenty years later when the actors of the Croatian Spring led democratic political initiatives and new democratic political parties that would overthrow the communist dictatorship in the first free multiparty elections in 1990. Nowadays, the Croatian Spring is seen as a period that played a pivotal role in the historic development of Croatia (Batović 2017, 1; Šute 2006).

REFERENCES

Artuković, Mato and Ljubomir Antić. 2013. *Sudski progoni dr. Marka Veselice: Dokumenti.* Zagreb: Hrvatski institut za povijest. [Judicial Persecutions of Dr. Marko Veselica: *Documents.* Zagreb: Croatian Institute of History].

Banac, Ivo. 2011. "Kako su Rusi lomili Tita i slomili Hrvatsku" [How the Russians tried to Break Tito, and Broke Croatia]. *Večernji list* (on-line), November 20, 2011. Accessed January 13, 2020. http://www.vecernji.hr/hrvatska/kako-su-rusi-lomili-tita-i-slomili-hrvatsku-347999.

Batović, Ante. 2017. *The Croatian Spring: Nationalism, Repression and Foreign Policy under Tito*. London: Bloomsbury Publishing.

Bilandžić, Dušan. 1999. *Hrvatska moderna povijest* [Croatian Modern History]. Zagreb: Golden marketing.

Bukvić, Nenad. 2018a. "Copy of a criminal indictment against student leaders. 11 December 1971. Archival document." COURAGE Registry. Accessed January 13, 2020. "http://cultural-opposition.eu/registry/?uri=http://courage.btk.mta.hu/courage/individual/n25295&type=masterpieces.

Bukvić, Nenad. 2018b. "Operation Tuškanac in the Croatian State Security Service Collection (1971)." COURAGE Registry. Accessed January 13, 2020. http://cultural-opposition.eu/registry/?uri=http://courage.btk.mta.hu/courage/individual/n43250&type=collections.

Bukvić, Nenad. 2018c. "Pamphlet of support for Croatian reformist and nationally-oriented political leaders. 1971. Archival document." COURAGE Registry. Accessed January 13, 2020. http://cultural-opposition.eu/registry/?uri=http://courage.btk.mta.hu/courage/individual/n123763&type=masterpieces.

Bušić, Bruno. 1983. *Jedino Hrvatska! Sabrani spisi* [Only Croatia! Collected Writings]. Toronto / Chicago: ZIRAL.

"Deklaracija o nazivu i položaju hrvatskog književnog jezika" [Declaration on the Name and Status of the Croatian Literary Language]. 1967. *Telegram: jugoslavenske novine za društvena i kulturna pitanja* 8, no. 359, March 17, 1967: 1.

Dukovski, Darko. 2007. *Istra i Rijeka u Hrvatskome proljeću* [Istria and Rijeka in Croatian Spring]. Zagreb / Pula: Alinea; Ogranak Matice hrvatske Pula.

Godić, Darjan and Domagoj Knežević. 2016. "Vojni manevar 'Sloboda 71'. Prilog istraživanju" [The Military Maneuver "Freedom '71. Contribution to Research]. *Historijski zbornik* 69(1):165-187.

Harris. Robin. 2017. Foreword to *The Croatian Spring: Nationalism, Repression and Foreign Policy Under Tito* by Ante Batović, viii-xiii. London: Bloomsbury Publishing.

Hrvatska enciklopedija Online. 2020. S. v. "Hrvatsko proljeće" [Croatian Spring]. Accessed January 13, 2020. http://www.enciklopedija.hr/natuknica.aspx?ID=26516.

Irvine, Jill. 2008. "The Croatian Spring and the Dissolution of Yugoslavia." In *State Collapse in South-Eastern Europe: New Perspectives on Yugoslavia's Disintegration*, edited by Lenard J. Cohen, and Jasna Dragović-Soso, 149-178. West Lafayette: Purdue University Press.

Jakovina, Tvrtko. 2005. "Jugoslavija, Hrvatsko proljeće i Sovjeti u detantu" [Yugoslavia, the Croatian Spring and the Soviets in detente]. *Kolo* 15(4):173-183.

Jonjić, Tomislav. 2017. "Ustavni amandmani (1971) i Ustav iz 1974.: pokušaj spašavanja države osuđene na propast" [Constitutional Amendments (1971) and the 1974 Constitution: an Attempt to Save a Doomed State]. In *Hrvatska i Hrvatsko proljeće 1971.: Zbornik radova* [Croatia and the Croatian Spring 1971: proceedings], edited by Igor Zidić, 415-501. Zagreb: Matica hrvatska.

Klasić, Hrvoje. 2006. *Hrvatsko proljeće u Sisku* [Croatian Spring in Sisak]. Zagreb: Srednja Europa.

Knežević, Domagoj and Josip Mihaljević. 2018. "Political Trials against Franjo Tuđman in Socialist Federal Republic of Yugoslavia." *Review of Croatian history* 14(1):353-381.

Kovač, Svetko, Bojan Dimitrijević, and Irena Popović. 2016. *Slučaj Ranković: iz arhiva KOS-a* [The Ranković Case: From the Counterintelligence Service Archives] Zagreb: Despot Infinitus, 2016.

Kovačec, August. 2017. "Deklaracija o nazivu i položaju hrvatskoga jezika u povijesnom kontekstu" [Declaration on the Name and Status of the Croatian Language in Historical Context]. *Hrvatska revija* 1. Matica hrvatska. Accessed October 4, 2018. http://www.matica.hr/hr/511/deklaracija-o-nazivu-i-polozaju-hrvatskoga-jezika-u-povijesnom-kontekstu-26706/.

Kraljević, Iva. 2009. "Matica iseljenika Hrvatske 1964. – 1968." *Časopis za suvremenu povijest* 41, No. 1: 71–92. [Emigrant Foundation of Croatia 1964 -1968. *Journal of Contemporary History*, 41(1):71–92.].

Krašić, Wollfy. 2018. *Hrvatsko proljeće i hrvatska politička emigracija* [Croatian Spring and Croatian Political Emigration]. Zagreb: Školska knjiga.

Marković, Predrag J. 2003. "Studentski pokret u Jugoslaviji 60-tih godina 20. veka: između nacionalizma i internacionalizma, između reformizma i dogmatizma" [Student Movement in Yugoslavia in the 1960s: Between Nationalism and Internationalism, Between Reformism and Dogmatism]. In *Dijalog povjesničara/istoričara 7* [*Dialogue of historians* 7], edited by Hans-Georg Fleck and Igor Graovac, 393-412. Zagreb: Friedrich Naumann Stiftung.

Mihaljević, Josip. 2016. *Komunizam i čovjek: odnos vlasti i pojedinca u Hrvatskoj od 1958. do 1972.* [Communism and Man: The Relationship between the Government and the Individual in Croatia (1958 – 1972)]. Zagreb: Hrvatski institut za povijest.

Mihaljević, Josip. 2017. "Liberalizacija 1960-ih - podloga Hrvatskog proljeća" [The Liberalization of the 1960s - The Basis of the Croatian Spring]. In *Hrvatska i Hrvatsko proljeće 1971.: Zbornik radova* [Croatia and the Croatian Spring 1971: Proceedings], edited by Igor Zidić, 263-277. Zagreb: Matica hrvatska.

Mihaljević, Josip. 2018a. "Declaration on the Name and Status of the Croatian Literary Language, 1967. Typescript." COURAGE Registry. Accessed January 13, 2020. http://cultural-opposition.eu/registry/?lang=en&uri=http://courage.btk.mta.hu/courage/individual/n247666&type=masterpieces.

Mihaljević, Josip. 2018b. "Gotovac, Vlado, ed. Hrvatski tjednik (Croatian weekly), 1971. Journal." COURAGE Registry. Accessed January 13, 2020. http://cultural-opposition.eu/registry/?uri=http://courage.btk.mta.hu/courage/individual/n14543&type=masterpieces.

Mihaljević, Josip. 2018c. "Report on oversight of the legality of the work of Matica hrvatska, 1972. Typescript." COURAGE Registry. Accessed January 13, 2020. http://cultural-opposition.eu/registry/?search=matica%20hrvatska&lang=en&uri=http://courage.btk.mta.hu/courage/individual/n130852&type=masterpieces.

Mužić, Ivan. 2017. "O hrvatskom masovnom pokretu u Splitu" [About the Croatian Mass Movement in Split]. In *Hrvatska i Hrvatsko proljeće 1971.: Zbornik radova* [Croatia and the Croatian Spring 1971: Proceedings], edited by Igor Zidić, 635-643. Zagreb: Matica hrvatska.

National Foreign Assessment Center (U.S.). 1980. *Key Soviet-Yugoslav Documents: A Reference Aid*. Washington, D.C.: Central Intelligence Agency.

Novak, Božidar. 1997. "Doprinos medija Hrvatskom proljeću" [Contribution of the Media to the Croatian Spring]. In *25. obljetnica boljševičkog udara i sjećanje na Hrvatsko proljeće: Zbornik radova* [25th Anniversary of the Bolshevik Strike and Remembering the Croatian Spring: Proceedings], edited by Slobodan Kaštela, Božidar Novak, and Vladimir Veselica, 159-180. Zagreb: HAZU.

Novak, Božidar. 2005. *Hrvatsko novinarstvo u 20. stoljeću* [Croatian Journalism in the 20th Century]. Zagreb: Golden marketing-Tehnička knjiga.

Novak, Božidar. 2010. "Doba reformi: Sedam povijesnih godina" [The Era of Reforms: Seven Historical Years]. In *HND – prvo stoljeće: Hrvatsko novinarsko društvo 1910. – 2010.* [The First Century of the Croatian Journalists' Association, 1910-2010], edited by Mario Bošnjak, 165–197. Zagreb: Medijska agencija Hrvatskog novinarskog društva.

Oleszczuk, Thomas. 1981a. "The Commanding Heights and Liberalization: The Case of Yugoslavia." *Comparative Politics* 13, no. 2: 171-185.

Oleszczuk, Thomas. 1981b. "The Liberalization of Dictatorship: the Titoist Lesson to the Third World." *The Journal of Politics* 43(3):818-830.

Pavličević, Dragutin. 2007. *Povijest Hrvatske* [History of Croatia]. Zagreb: Naklada Pavičić.

Ponoš, Tihomir. 2007. *Na rubu revolucije – studenti'71.* [On the Edge of Revolution – Students in 1971]. Zagreb: Profil international.

Ponoš, Tihomir. 2012. "Studentski pokret u Hrvatskom proljeću – zametci političkog pluralizma" [Student Movement in the Croatian Spring – The Embryos of Political Pluralism]. In *Hrvatsko proljeće 40 godina poslije* [Croatian Spring 40 Years Later], edited by Tvrtko Jakovina, 333-341. Zagreb: Centar za demokraciju i pravo Miko Tripalo / Filozofski fakultet / Fakultet političkih znanosti / Pravni fakultet.

Radelić, Zdenko. 2006. *Hrvatska u Jugoslaviji 1945.-1991.: od zajedništva do razlaza* [Croatia in Yugoslavia, 1945-1991: From Unity to Dissolution]. Zagreb: Školska knjiga/ Hrvatski institut za povijest.

Ridley, Jasper. 2000. *Tito: biografija* [Tito: Biography]. Zagreb: Prometej.

Rusinow, Dennison. 1978. *The Yugoslav Experiment 1948-1974*. Oakland: University of California Press.

Samardžija, Marko, ed. 2017. *Deklaracija o nazivu i položaju hrvatskog književnog jezika 1967.-2017.: vijesti, komentari, osude, zaključci* [Declaration on the Name and Status of the Croatian Literary Language 1967-2017: News, Comments, Judgements, Conclusions]. Zagreb: Matica hrvatska.

Smerdel, Branko. 2007. "Primjena federalnog načela i pouke ustavne reforme 1971. godine" [Application of the Federal Principle and the Lessons of the Constitutional Reform in 1971]. In *Primjena federalnog načela i pouke ustavne reforme 1971* [Application of the Federal Principle and the Lessons of the Constitutional Reform in 1971], edited by Branko

Smerdel, 17-38. Zagreb: Pravni fakultet Sveučilišta u Zagrebu / Centar za demokraciju i pravo Miko Tripalo.

Spehnjak, Katarina, and Tihomir Cipek. 2007. "Disidenti, opozicija i otpor – Hrvatska i Jugoslavija 1945.-1990." *Časopis za suvremenu povijest* 39, No. 2: 255-297. [Dissidents, Opposition and Resistance – Croatia and Yugoslavia, 1945-1990. *Journal of Contemporary History*, 39(2):255-297].

Spehnjak, Katarina. 1998. "Izbori u Hrvatskoj 1967. i 1969." [Elections in Croatia in 1967 and 1969]. *Časopis za suvremenu povijest* 30 (2):317-346.

Spehnjak, Katarina. 2001. "Preteča Hrvatskoga proljeća" [Forerunner of Croatian Spring]. *Matica: mjesečna revija za hrvatske zajednice u svijetu* 51 (2):31-34.

Sučić, Stjepan. 2017. "Hrvatski sveučilištarci od studentskog pokreta do političke organizacije" [Croatian University Students from Student Movement to Political Organization]. In *Hrvatska i Hrvatsko proljeće 1971.: Zbornik radova* [Croatia and the Croatian Spring 1971: Proceedings], edited by Igor Zidić, 401-413. Zagreb: Matica hrvatska.

Sunajko, Goran. 2012. "Hrvatsko proljeće i načela ustavnih reformi" [The Croatian Spring and the Principles of Constitutional Reform]. In *Hrvatsko proljeće 40 godina poslije* [Croatian Spring 40 Years Later], edited by Tvrtko Jakovina, 205-223. Zagreb: Centar za demokraciju i pravo Miko Tripalo / Filozofski fakultet / Fakultet političkih znanosti / Pravni fakultet.

Supek, Ivan. 1992. *Krivovjernik na ljevici* [Heretic on the Left]. Zagreb: Globus.

Šajnović, Luka. 2019. "Gospodarska pozadina Hrvatskog proljeća: Zajedničko nastupanje hrvatskog političkog rukovodstva i suvremenog tiska" [The Economic Background of the Croatian Spring: The Joint Action of the Croatian Political Leadership and the Contemporary Press]. Ma thesis, University of Zagreb.

Šute, Ivica. 2006. "1971. kao uvod u 1991." [1971 as Introduction to 1991]. In *Hrvatska politika u XX. stoljeću* [Croatian Politics in 20th Century], edited by Ljubomir Antić, Ljubomir, 457-469. Zagreb: Matica hrvatska.

Tripalo, Miko. 1990. *Hrvatsko proljeće* [Croatian Spring], 2nd edition. Zagreb: Globus.

Veselinović, Velimir. 2015. "Politička djelatnost Ante Paradžika." *Anali Hrvatskog politološkog društva: časopis za politologiju* 12(1):133-155. [The Political Activites of Ante Paradžik. *Annals of Croatian Politology Society: Journal for Politics*, 12(1):133-155].

Vojnić, Dragomir. 2006. "Reforma i tranzicija. Kritički osvrt na događanja u prijelomnim vremenskim razdobljima." *Ekonomski pregled* 57(5-6):393-4. [Transition and Reform. Critical Review of the Events in the Crucial Time Periods. *Economy Review*, 57(5-6):393-4].

Biographical Sketch

Josip Mihaljević, PhD

Affiliation: Croatian Institute of History, Zagreb, Croatia

Education:

2001-2008: Faculty of Humanities and Social Sciences University of Zagreb, Department of History (MA in history)

2008-2014: Faculty of Humanities and Social Sciences University of Zagreb, Postgraduate doctoral studies of Modern and Contemporary Croatian History in European and World Context (PhD in history)

Business Address: Opatička 10, 10000 Zagreb, Croatia

Research and Professional Experience:

2008-2009: Croatian State Archives

2009- : Croatian Institute of History

Professional Appointments:

2010-2015: Secretary of the scientific journal *Časopis za suvremenu povijest* [Journal of Contemporary History]

2016: Assistant Editor in Chief of the scientific journal *Časopis za suvremenu povijest*

2016-2019: Deputy National Task Manager in Horizon 2020 project "Cultural Opposition: Understanding the Cultural Heritage of Dissent in the Former Socialist Countries (COURAGE)"

Honors:

2017: National Science Award of Republic of Croatia

2017: Annual Science Award of the Society of University Teachers, Scholars and Other Scientists of Zagreb

2019: "Vjekoslav Klaić" Award (Croatian National Committee for Historical Sciences) for Popularization of History

Publications from the Last 3 Years: 2017-2019

Mihaljević, Josip. 2017a. "Deal with the Devil: Intellectuals and Their Support of Tito's Rule in Yugoslavia (1945–80)." In *Secret Agents and the Memory of Everyday Collaboration in Communist Eastern Europe*, edited by Péter Apor, Sándor Horváth, and James Mark, 191-206. London/New York: Anthem Press.

Mihaljević, Josip. 2017b. "Liberalizacija 1960-ih - podloga Hrvatskog proljeća" [The Liberalization of the 1960s - The Basis of the Croatian Spring]. In *Hrvatska i Hrvatsko proljeće* 1971. Zbornik radova [Croatia and the Croatian Spring 1971: Proceedings], edited by Igor Zidić, 263-277. Zagreb: Matica hrvatska.

Mihaljević, Josip. 2017c. "Povjesničarsko razbijanje dogmi u partijskoj državi – slučaj Ljube Bobana 1964." [Historians Breaking Dogmas in a Party State - Ljubo Boban's Case in 1964]. In *Ljubo Boban i istraživanje suvremene povijesti* [Ljubo Boban and the Research of Contemporary History], edited by Damir Agičić and Marica Karakaš Obradov, 115-129. Zagreb: FF press.

Mihaljević, Josip. 2018a. "Kako su se kalili partijski kadrovi: osnivanje, koncepcija i djelatnost Političke škole SKJ 'Josip Broz Tito' u Kumrovcu [How Were the Party Cadres Tempered: the Founding, Conception and Activity of the Political School of SKJ "Josip Broz Tito" in Kumrovec]." *Historijski zbornik* 71, No. 2: 367-399.

Mihaljević, Josip. 2018b. "Većeslav Holjevac - zaboravljeni dissident" [Većeslav Holjevac - Forgotten Dissident]. *Prispevki za novejšo zgodovino* 58, No. 3: 128-147.

Mihaljević, Josip. 2019a. "Doprinos akademika Dušana Bilandžića suvremenoj povijesnoj znanosti" [Academician Dušan Bilandžić's contribution to contemporary historical science]. In *Dušan Bilandžić: 1924. - 2015.*, edited by Zvonko Posavec, 45-63. Zagreb, Hrvatska akademija znanosti i umjetnosti.

Mihaljević, Josip. 2019b. "Ekonomska povijest u Časopisu za suvremenu povijest (1969. – 2018.) [Economic History in the Journal of Contemporary History (1969–2018)]." *Časopis za suvremenu povijest* 51, No. 3: 741-784.

Mihaljević, Josip. 2019c. "Social Inequalities from Workers' Perspective in 1960s Socialist Yugoslavia." *Revue d'études comparatives Est-Ouest* 50, No. 1 (5): 25-51.

Co-author

Apor, Péter, Josip Mihaljević, and Cristina Petrescu. 2018. "Collections of Intellectual Dissent: Historians and Sociologists in post-1968 Hungary, Romania and Yugoslavia." In *The Handbook of COURAGE: Cultural Opposition and its Heritage in Eastern Europe*, edited by Balazs Apor, Peter Apor, and Sándor Horváth, 369-390. Budapest: Research Centre for the Humanities, Institute of History, Hungarian Academy of Sciences.

Bing, Albert, Josip Mihaljević, and Jacqueline Nießer. 2018. "Yugoslavia." In *The Handbook of COURAGE: Cultural Opposition and its Heritage in Eastern Europe*, edited by Balazs Apor, Peter Apor, and Sándor Horváth, 97-115. Budapest: Research Centre for the Humanities, Institute of History, Hungarian Academy of Sciences.

Knežević, Domagoj and Josip Mihaljević. 2018. "Political trials against Franjo Tuđman in Socialist Federal Republic of Yugoslavia." *Review of Croatian History* 14, No. 1: 353-381.

In: Croatia: Past, Present and Future Perspectives
Editor: Matko Marušić
ISBN: 978-1-53618-300-9

Chapter 8

THE CROATIAN WAR OF INDEPENDENCE (1991 – 1995)

Andrijana Perković Paloš*

Independent Historian, Split, Croatia

ABSTRACT

This chapter will discuss the war that followed dissolution of the multinational communist Yugoslavia and the creation of new national states, among them Croatia. More commonly used terms for "Croatian War of Independence", which lasted from 1991 to 1995 in Croatia, are "Homeland War" and "Greater-Serbian aggression". During this four-year aggression, Croatia was subjected to ruthless destruction and occupation of almost one third of its territory. It had immense human losses and war damage: nevertheless, it gained its independence, achieved international recognition, and liberated its occupied territories. This chapter will briefly present causes of the Greater-Serbian aggression, main events and consequences of the war, and recent findings of Croatian scholars. It will also address certain sensationalist theses presented by some authors regarding controversial questions from that period and present evidence that contradict it, for example the question of the culprit for Serbian insurgency and the outbreak of war and the attitude of Croatian leadership toward Serbs in that period.

Keywords: Memorandum SANU; Serbian propaganda; Croatian leadership; JNA, Greater-Serbian aggression; Operation Storm

INTRODUCTION

In an attempt to comprehend the causes of the war in Croatia that occurred during the disintegration of communist Yugoslavia, we often find simplistic interpretations. In other words, a complex set of causes that led to the bloody collapse of the multinational country, famous for its slogan "brotherhood and unity", is often muddled by sensationalist and

* Corresponding Author's Email: ppalos.andrijana@gmail.com.

simplistic approach of some authors who suggest that ethnic hatred between Balkan tribes ignited and escalated the war. Silber and Little (1996, 371) in their famous book dramatically entitled "The Death of Yugoslavia" claim that ethnic segregation was the purpose of the war, while Denich (1994, 368) saw the conflict as a civil war that "restored the Balkan peninsula to its historic reputation as a zone of endemic ethnic conflict and international intervention." Ignoring primary sources and chronology of events, some authors relativize culpability for the war by equalizing the policies of Croatian President Franjo Tuđman and Serbian President Slobodan Milošević (Nation 2002, 188), while others claim that "nationalist leaders succeeded in manipulating ethnicity by spreading fear, insecurity, and hatred, which advanced their political agenda of separate national states" (Oberschall 2000, 998). Authors proposing opposite theses suggest that either ethnic hatred between nations in communist Yugoslavia did not exist or that communists successfully overcame it by nurturing good relations between nations, but that these relations were severely aggravated exclusively by the policies of the new nationalist leaders.

Contrary to these theses, the chapter presents evidence from recent findings which show that Serbian leadership with Slobodan Milošević caused the violent dissolution of Yugoslavia with their attempts to centralize Yugoslavia and if that failed, to create Greater Serbia that would include large parts of Croatia. The consequence was brutal Greater Serbian aggression on Croatia. On the other hand, the Croatian leadership with Franjo Tuđman strived to preserve Croatian sovereignty in Yugoslavia and avoid the war, which is why on numerous occasions, even after the final military victory in the Operation Storm, which liberated most occupied parts of Croatia, they gave priority to peaceful negotiations.

Causes of the Greater-Serbian Aggression on Croatia

Relations of Croats and Serbs at the end of the 20th century were significantly marked with their experiences from two Yugoslav states – Kingdom of SHS (1918-1941, from 1929 Kingdom of Yugoslavia) and communist Yugoslavia (1945-1991). Contrary to theses that "ethnic hatred" caused the war, it is important to stress that before entering the common state in 1918, Croatia and Serbia had no legal ties and had been developing in different political and cultural frameworks. Although this chapter does not present analysis of different political, historical, cultural, and religious background of nations in Yugoslavia, it should be noted that the main problem of two Yugoslav states was the unsolved national question. Both oppressive regimes, especially the communist, prevented non-Serbian nations, in particular Croatian, to achieve their autonomy and sovereignty (Radelić 2006, 24, 338, 379-383).

Serbian Memorandum and Rise of Slobodan Milošević

The death of communist dictator Josip Broz Tito in 1980 was a turning point for Socialist Federative Republic of Yugoslavia (SFRY) which consisted of six republics (Slovenia, Croatia, Bosnia-Herzegovina, Serbia, Montenegro, and Macedonia), and two autonomous provinces in Serbia (Voivodina and Kosovo). The period after Tito's death was marked by economic crisis with high unemployment rate, inflation, and enormous foreign debt. Such conditions exacerbated differences between Yugoslav republics and provinces and led to different views of their leaderships regarding the country's future (Barić 2005, 25).

A majority of republics and provinces wanted to preserve and expand their powers and rights given to them by the Constitution of 1974, whereas Serbia, with the support of the Yugoslav People's Army (Jugoslavenska narodna armija: JNA), advocated for strengthening the powers of federal institutions. Furthermore, Serbia strived to gain more control over its two autonomous provinces that had become almost equal in their rights to the republics (Barić 2005, 26). At the same time, in the spring of 1981 riots broke out in Kosovo. Kosovo Albanians, who formed the majority of province's population, advocated for Kosovo to become a republic separate from Serbia, but police and JNA intervened and suppressed Albanian dissent (Barić 2005, 28). The intervention did not, however, settle down the situation; moreover, it led to further deterioration of relations between Albanians and Serbs in Kosovo.

Also, some Serbian academics created a document entitled "Memorandum of The Serbian Academy of Science and Arts" (SANU) published in the newspaper "Večernje novosti" in Belgrade in September 1986. In the "Memorandum" they expressed discontent with the fact that 1974 Constitution had increased autonomy of Serbian provinces of Voivodina and Kosovo. The Memorandum also alleged endangerment of Serbs in Kosovo. Part of the leadership of the Serbian Orthodox Church and many authors of books of chauvinistic content also joined in support (Nazor 2011, 20; Nazor and Pušek 2018, 19-20; Antić 2007, 225). One of the most common slogans from that time was "Serbian borders are where Serbian graves and pits are" (Antić 2007, 225). This left no room for doubt that ethnocentric tendencies were present in influential Serbian circles.

The rise of new Serbian leader Slobodan Milošević in 1986 occurred in such conditions. His centralistic policy contributed to a deepening divide between the leaderships of the Yugoslav republics and provinces and to deteriorating relations between the nations in Yugoslavia. Serbian media already depicted Albanians as people who threatened the existence of Serbs, so Milošević imposed himself as a protector of Kosovo Serbs (Barić 2005, 29). During the commemoration of the 600th anniversary of the Battle of Kosovo in 1989, at the Gazimestan monument on the Kosovo field, Milošević openly threatened non-Serbian nations in Yugoslavia with a possibility of addressing the political crisis with violence (Barić 2005, 30).

By the beginning of the 1990s, in order to centralize Yugoslavia and secure dominant position for Serbia in a new political framework, Milošević installed a puppet government in the Socialist Republic of Montenegro and abolished the autonomy of the provinces of Voivodina and Kosovo. With four votes, he gained control over half of members in the Yugoslav Presidency, a collective governing body established after Tito's death with six representatives from the republics and two from the provinces (Barić 2005, 30). However, his attempt to gain control over the League of Communists of Yugoslavia at the 14th (extraordinary) Congress held in January 1990 was unsuccessful. Slovene and Croatian delegates left the Congress, in protest over the Serbian policy (Barić 2005, 32-33). The breakdown of the League of Communists of Yugoslavia, one of the country's pillars, signaled that the end of the communist regime was near. By the end of the year free multiparty elections were held in all Yugoslav republics (Barić 2005, 33).

Serbs in Croatia Accept Milošević's Policy

The situation of Serbs in Kosovo and Milošević's infamous Gazimestan speech made a significant impact on Serbs in the Socialist Republic (SR) of Croatia. At the time, the Serbian minority in Croatia was substantial with approximately 12% of population, and their status was also a topic of discussions among Serbian academics in Serbia. One part of the previously mentioned "Memorandum" addressed the position of Serbs in Croatia and introduced a claim about their alleged forced assimilation. In particular, it mentioned that founding Serbian associations and cultural institutions in Croatia was prohibited. However, they did not mention that communist authorities in Croatia opposed any form of nationalism and that Croatian associations and cultural institutions were banned as well (Barić 2005, 27-28). Furthermore, it was claimed in the "Memorandum" that "except in the period of NDH, Serbs in Croatia in the past have never been endangered as they are today" (Memorandum SANU 1986). This assertion shaped the narrative of propaganda from Serbia to Serbs in Croatia. The claims from "Memorandum" were not supported by any relevant evidence. In reality, according to data presented by Barić (2005, 41), Serbs enjoyed full civil rights and were significantly represented in many civil services in Croatia. In fact, they were represented disproportionally more than Croats in municipal authorities, judiciary, police, school system, and commercial enterprises. Such situation caused frustrations among Croats because they tended to view this as privileges given to Serbs.

After the "Memorandum" was published, Serbs in Croatia were subjected to aggressive propaganda from Serbia that constantly reminded them of Ustasha crimes committed against Serbian people in the NDH (Barić 2005, 577) with a goal of inciting their fears. The assertion that Croats were enemies of Serbs with whom life was no longer possible, was increasingly accepted among the Serbian minority (Žunec 2008, 45). Accordingly, they responded positively to Milošević's policy. In 1989, nationalistic mass Serbian meetings were organized in SR Croatia with participants chanting Milošević's name and wearing symbols of Chetniks, chauvinist Serbian fighters who during World War II collaborated with Nazis and Fascists and committed crimes against Croats and Muslims (Barić 2005, 44-45). As Nazor (2011, 25) pointed out, these meetings were in fact the beginning of Serbian insurgency in Croatia.

Serbian Reactions to Croatian Democratic Leadership

In such an environment, the communist party in Croatia, under some pressure from democratic changes elsewhere in Europe, allowed the establishment of opposition political parties that advocated for democracy and urged Croatian communist leadership to call free multi-party elections. This marked the end of the period from 1972 to 1989 known as "Croatian Silence" when every public advocacy for Croatian national interests in Yugoslavia was punishable by law as nationalism. At the end of the "Croatian Silence", various communist dissidents and patriots entered public life again and engaged in the elections.

The winner of the elections, held in April and May 1990, was Croatian Democratic Union (Hrvatska Demokratska Zajednica: HDZ) led by a communist dissident and historian Franjo Tuđman, who was proclaimed president of the Presidency of the SR Croatia by the Croatian Parliament (Sabor) at the end of May 1990. HDZ gained the confidence of the Croatian people with its anticommunist rhetoric, and by stressing importance of the preservation of Croatian sovereignty in Yugoslavia. HDZ also enjoyed the support of Roman Catholic Church and had a strong financial backing by Croatian diaspora. It was perceived as a party that would manage to resist Milošević's policy and aggressive Serbian nationalism in Croatia, which had already induced fear among Croats (Ramljak 1990; Marić 1990).

Although the HDZ did not include any idea of "ethnically pure Croatia" in its program, Serbs in Croatia perceived it as the revival of the Ustasha regime, encouraged as they were by propaganda from Serbia. Sometimes rough and explicit rhetoric made by some HDZ members did strengthen these perceptions (see Barić 2005, 60; Nazor and Pušek 2018, 47). Some authors even interpret one part of Tuđman's speech in February 1990 as his attempt to open the door to the revival of the NDH (Pavlaković 2009, 168; I. and S. Goldstein 2011, 206). In fact, Tuđman in his speech called the NDH not only "a 'quisling' formation and a 'fascist crime' but also an expression of the historical aspirations of Croatian people for its independent state." He proceeded to address antifascism and its contribution to the Croatian cause. Tuđman emphasized that at the end of World War II Croats found themselves "on the side of victorious democratic forces," and that SR Croatia existed within SFRY "as the national state of Croatian people", and that provided a basis "for the realization of the full-state sovereignty of Croatian people" (Programske zasade i ciljevi HDZ 1990, 9-13). Regardless of the fact that he was talking about Croatian sovereignty and Croatian state as a legitimate aspiration of Croatian people, not about the Ustasha regime, and that he stressed the importance of Croatian antifascist struggle, Serbs in Croatia had already been roused by propaganda from Serbia and fearful for their future. In reality, that fear had no solid basis and was not supported by any evidence other than statements that at the time may have seemed ambiguous.

On the other hand, the new democratic government provided wide range of freedoms for all nations and ethnic groups living in Croatia. It enabled foundation of political parties for national minorities and various national cultural institutions and organizations, something that was not possible during communist Yugoslavia (Barić 2005, 54-57). For example, in February 1990 the Serbian Democratic Party was formed and five of its members entered the Sabor (Barić 2005, 61).

Serbian propaganda was built on lies in the absence of evidence and that was demonstrated by "the Mlinar case". Miroslav Mlinar, one of the members of Serbian Democratic Party, was allegedly attacked and found stabbed on May 18, 1990 in Benkovac, a town in Croatia with a majority Serbian population. The leadership of the Serbian Democratic Party and Serbian press used the incident to show the alleged genocidal character of Croatian people and the HDZ and to proclaim it as "attack on all Serbs in Croatia" (Barić 2005, 63). The purpose of the propaganda was to reinforce Serbs' mistrust in Croatian authorities and to depict the HDZ as an Ustasha revival party aiming to destroy Serbian people (Barić 2005, 63). According to official police and medical findings, however, Mlinar's injuries were self-inflicted and falsely used as a propaganda tool (Nazor and Pušek 2018, 46; Martinić Jerčić and Nazor 2019, 128).

Nevertheless, Serbian Democratic Party suspended relations with the Sabor (Martinić Jerčić and Nazor 2019, 126). That clearly showed that it rejected efforts for peaceful negotiations offered by the Croatian leadership. The leader of the Serbian Democratic Party Jovan Rašković used this incident as an excuse to refuse the position of Vice President of the Sabor and to call on members of his party to boycott the Sabor; he also rejected an offer by Tuđman for the establishment of cultural autonomy for Serbs in those areas in Croatia with the highest Serbian population (Barić 2005, 63; Ramet 2005, 80; 2008, 36). The unwillingness of the Serbian Democratic Party to cooperate with Croatian leadership was lying in its close connections with Milošević and his policy and plans to create Greater Serbia. As Barić (2005, 55) noted, the program of the party anticipated the formation of an autonomous Serbian territory in Croatia. The unilateral realization of the plan by Serbian Democratic Party to form this territory began in June 1990 with redrawing of the territorial-administrative boundaries of Croatia and creating a separate territory populated predominantly by Serbs (Nazor 2011, 35; Nazor and Pušek 2018, 47).

In July 1990 Sabor adopted amendments to the Constitution of the SR Croatia that removed the adjective "socialist" from the name of the state and installed traditional national symbols more suitable for the new political framework (Nazor 2011, 35). Historical Croatian flag with a red and white "checkerboard" Croatian coat of arms, dating back to at least the 15th century, was brought back, whereas the communist five-pointed red star was dismissed from official use (Nazor 2011, 35). Serbs perceived this as a restoration of the NDH which also used the "checkerboard" as a state symbol even though the same "checkerboard" was also used in the communist period, although always next to the red star. As Ramet (2008, 35) pointed out, if the use of the "checkerboard" by the Ustasha regime delegitimized it for any other political framework, the same rule should be applied to the Serbian double-headed eagle and the Cyrillic markings "C C C C", used by the quisling government of Milan Nedić during World War II in Serbia, use of which in the late 1980s and 1990s no one questioned.

Serbian Insurgency in Croatia

Atmosphere of hostility at the mass meetings of Serbs in Croatia from 1989 on, their reactions to the new Croatian leadership, and their refusal to use Croatian national emblems (Barić 2005, 68-69) showed that they would not obey Croatian laws and would not accept peaceful coexistence with their Croatian neighbors in the Republic of Croatia, regardless of attempts by Croatian authorities to negotiate (Nazor and Pušek 2018, 46; Ramet 2008, 36; Sekula Gibač and Vučur 2018, 15-18).

Influenced by Milošević's propaganda and the idea that all Serbs must live in one country, Serbs in the Croatian regions of Northern Dalmatia and Lika announced "plebiscite of the Serbian people in the Republic of Croatia on Serbian autonomy", aiming to separate from Croatia and later to rejoin Yugoslavia under Serbian domination (Barić 2005, 75). The Croatian constitutional Court proclaimed the announced plebiscite, set on August 19 to September 2, illegal (Narodne novine 1990; Šmidt 1990, 3).

Due to the fact that Serbian civilians had armed themselves and organized "guards" near Knin with an excuse that they were threatened by Croats, right before the illegal plebiscite, Croatian Ministry of Interior decided to seize the weapons from the police stations in Dalmatia and Lika in order to prevent the insurgency (Barić 2005, 78; Nazor 2011, 40). It was the exact area where the insurgency had been preparing. Said decision of Croatian authorities to seize the weapons only served to Serbian extremists as "a direct motive for proclaiming a 'state of war'" (Nazor 2011, 40). Therefore, August 17, 1990, Serbian police officers and civilians from Knin put barricades on roads and cut off traffic connections between Northern and Southern Croatia, thus ruining the ongoing tourist season and causing significant damage to the Croatian economy. It was the beginning of an armed Serbian insurgency against Croatia. In order to settle down the situation, Croatian Ministry of Interior sent officials to Knin, the center of the insurgency, to negotiate but their helicopters were forced to return to Zagreb under JNA's threat of intervention. This act demonstrated that the JNA sided with the insurgents.

With regard to stated chronology of events and evidence which show that Serbian insurgency was orchestrated by the Milošević regime, conclusion of R. Craig Nation (2002, 104), that the insurgency "was in part a spontaneous reaction to the provocations of the Tudjman regime" is not accurate. Silber's and Little's claim that Croatian leadership's "insensitivity to Serbian's legitimate worries" pushed Serbs in Croatia even further to extremism (1996, 88) also is not accurate and not evidence-based. Their viewpoint on their position in Croatia, Croatian leadership and their future relations had already been shaped by the Serbian propaganda. As Marijan (2016, 24) stressed "Serbs acted upon the construction about Croats which they had set up by themselves, and not according to moves of the Croatian leadership."

JNA as Serbian Army

Serbian policy from the mid-1980s also involved centralizing the country's Army. The Armed Forces of the SFRY were reorganized so that Territorial Defense (TD), a kind of civil defense, that was situated in every Yugoslav republic and was independent of the JNA, became subordinate to the JNA command (Nazor and Pušek 2018, 24). Known as "the seventh Yugoslav republic", the JNA as a federal army favored a communist and centralized Yugoslavia in which it enjoyed a highly privileged position. Accordingly, it supported Milošević's centralist aspirations and did not accept democratic changes in Croatia and Slovenia.

Just after the multi-party elections in Croatia, the JNA seized almost all weaponry stores of the Croatian Territorial Defense, which contained approximately 80,000 to 200,000 crates of weapons and ammunition by some estimates, and removed them to "stores controlled by the JNA" (Nazor 2011, 28), and subsequently distributed them to Serbian insurgents. It is important to emphasize that by 1990s almost 70% of JNA officers were Serbs (from Serbia and other Yugoslav republics), whereas only 12% of them were Croats (Nazor and Pušek 2018, 24). The dominance of Serbs in the JNA only went up after the start of the insurgency, so it can be said that by the summer of 1991 the JNA was essentially a Serbian Army.

Sporadic attacks by Serbian insurgents on Croatian police stations started in the second half of 1990 and continued in the first half of 1991 (Nazor 2011, 55). The efforts of Croatian police to establish order and peace in Croatia were hampered by the JNA that formed defensive buffer zones around Serbian areas under the pretext of wanting to secure peace in Croatia and to preserve Yugoslavia (Barić 2005, 121).

The Project of Greater Serbia

Democratically elected leaderships of Slovenia and Croatia attempted to resolve the political crisis peacefully. In order to prevent any further conflicts, they attended meetings with presidents of other Yugoslav republics and advocated for restructuring Yugoslav federation into a confederation of independent states (Milardović 1992, 761-803; Bilić 2005, 97-98). From March to June 1991 the presidents of all six republics met six times (Table 1) with the goal of finding a compromise and a peaceful solution for the political crisis, but they were unsuccessful (Nazor 2011, 56).

Table 1. Meetings of presidents of Yugoslav republics

Date of the Meeting	Place of the Meeting
March 23 1991	Split (Croatia)
April 4 1991	Belgrade (Serbia)
April 11 1991	Brdo near Kranj (Slovenia)
April 18 1991	Ohrid (Macedonia)
April 29 1991	Cetinje (Montenegro)
June 6 1991	Sarajevo (Bosnia and Herzegovina)

The repeated rejections of Milošević and his allies of all proposals for a confederation, as well as growing conflicts with the JNA, steered Croatia and Slovenia towards independence (Nazor 2011, 56). On referendum held in May 1991, 93.24% of voters, representing 83.56% of the population, opted for the independence of the Republic of Croatia and its secession from Yugoslavia (Nazor and Pušek 2018, 91). Based on the results of the referendum, the Sabor declared the country's independence on June 25, 1991 (Milardović 1992, 82). However, urged by the European Community, Croatia introduced a three-month moratorium on that decision. Slovenia also declared its independence the same day as Croatia. That provoked the JNA to attack Slovenia in a "ten-day war," only to later retreat to Croatia and prepare for further actions.

Refusing to restructure Yugoslavia as confederation of independent states, Milošević and his associates proclaimed that separation from Yugoslavia is possible but emphasized the position of Serbian leadership that only "peoples" had the right to leave Yugoslavia, and not republics. That implied changing the borders of republics established after World War II (Jović 1995, 159-161, 257-258, 262; Barić 2005, 72-73, 75-76). In that way, Milošević planned to achieve the "Greater Serbia Project" from the 19th century that proposed a western border of the Greater Serbia "deep in Croatian territory," so that all Serbs inhabiting Yugoslavia could live in one country (Nazor and Pušek 2018, 117). The evidence for this was recorded in the journal entries of one of Milošević's closest associates, former President of the SFRY's Presidency Borisav Jović (Nazor 2011, 78). Shortly after Croatia had proclaimed independence, at the beginning of July 1991, open Greater-Serbian aggression began.

Open Greater-Serbian Aggression against Croatia (July 1991 - January 1992)

From July 1991 to January 1992, Serbia, Montenegro (from October 1991), the JNA, and Serb insurgents carried out high intensity aggression against Croatia and opened multiple fronts.

Violence and Destruction by Serbian Forces

Croatia was attacked from Serbia, Montenegro, Bosnia and Herzegovina, and from inside its own territory, by the insurgent Serbs and by the JNA from its barracks situated in numerous Croatian cities and towns (Nazor and Pušek 2018, 122). The aggressor's objective was to splinter Croatian territory and occupy at least those parts of Croatia that were planned to be annexed to the Greater Serbia (Nazor and Pušek 2018, 126).

From the beginning of October 1991 these forces were carrying coordinated all-out attacks across all battlefields in Croatia. Serbian aggression entered its severest phase at that time (Nazor and Pušek 2018, 126). By the end of 1991 almost one third of Croatia was occupied and on December 19, 1991, the insurgent Serbs proclaimed "Republic of Serbian Krajina" (RSK). Its territory consisted of the occupied Croatian regions of Krajina, Eastern Slavonia, Baranja, Western Syrmia, and Western Slavonia. These areas were to be ethnically cleansed and ultimately inhabited only by Serbs. Accordingly, most of non-Serbian population was killed or expelled from the RSK, and even some Serbs who did not support Greater Serbia politics (Nazor 2011, 105-106; Barić 2005, 124).

Aggression against Croatia was characterized by disregard for war laws and customs on the aggressor's side. Serbian propaganda formed the image of Serbian nation as a nation better than others and endangered by Croats that were depicted as fascists and Ustasha whose very existence threatened Serbs. Referring to Norman Cigar's assertion, Barić (2005, 30) emphasized that such shaping of public opinion among Serbs created an atmosphere conducive to aggression against non-Serbs, especially against Croats. Accordingly, no Croatian war victim, even civilian, was perceived innocent. That kind of mentality justified mass killings and slaughter of Croats, rapes of women, as well as physical and psychological abuse of war prisoners. At the beginning of the open aggression in the summer of 1991 some villages in Eastern Slavonia, a Croatian region in the far East near border with Serbia, were burned down to the ground and the non-Serbian population was banished (Barić 2005, 124). Under the laws enacted by the Serbian insurgents, Croats who stayed in their homes were obliged to wear in public white ribbons on their arms as a sign of ethnic identification and segregation (Gregurić 1998, 377-378). Something similar had not been seen in Europe since World War II. Besides that, Serbian government conducted systematic immigration of Serbs to the occupied Croatian territory to change the ethnic image of the occupied area (Gregurić 1998, 377-378). This course of events led to retaliation by Croats and in some areas Serbs were killed and their property destroyed (Barić 2005, 137-139; Nazor and Pušek 2018, 119; Ramet 2008, 37).

The most common targets of Serbian forces were historical cultural monuments, archeological sites, religious objects, and cemeteries. Also, the very historical core of Croatia's capital, Zagreb, was damaged in the war. On the last day of the mentioned moratorium of the declaration of independence, October 7, 1991, JNA aircraft rocketed and bombed the seat of the Croatian president in Zagreb. The attack was aimed at the President of the Republic of Croatia, Franjo Tuđman; President of the SFRY Presidency Stipe Mesić; and President of the SFRY's Federal Executive Council Ante Marković, all of whom were at the meeting there at the time. The attempted assassination was unsuccessful, and it prompted Croatian leadership to call the Sabor into an extraordinary session on October 8 in the basement of the INA Petroleum Company in Zagreb. At that session, Sabor adopted the final "Decision on the separation of the Republic of Croatia from the SFRY and its independence" and severed all ties with Yugoslavia (Nazor 2011, 90, 94-95).

Croatian Army

The JNA that had been glorified in the communist period as the antifascist and liberation army was from 1991 onwards perceived by Slovenes, Croats, and later Muslims as an adversary army. There are several reasons why in Croatia the war was compared to the biblical battle between David and Goliath (Perković Paloš 2016, 95). Croatia, as a part of Yugoslavia, was legally not allowed to have its own army, thus its main forces before the open aggression were in fact units of the Ministry of Interior, i.e., police forces. In April 1991 Croatia started to form military-police units called National Guard Corps, with four of its brigades formed by the end of May of the same year and filled with volunteers (Nazor 2011, 60-61; Nazor and Pušek 2018, 89-90; Marijan 2017, 226). These were the core units of the future Croatian Army, established and developed during the war. In September 1991 the Croatian Government passed a defense law and established Headquarters of the Army and the unified line of command.

Another significant problem for Croatian defense was scarcity of weaponry and ammunition. The Croatian Territorial Defense was disarmed by the JNA in the spring of 1990. In addition, machinations of Milošević's Yugoslav government were successful in obtaining international support for the Serbian cause: on September 25, 1991, the UN declared embargo on weapons trade with all Yugoslav republics (UNSCR 1991). Since Serbia was well armed, the embargo primarily affected Croatia. Croatian inferiority of forces was reflected especially in heavy artillery (Nazor 2011, 60) and aviation. Croatian forces recaptured some of the weaponry from the JNA barracks and warehouses in September 1991, but it was not nearly enough (Nazor and Pušek 2018, 129-130).

Croatia did not have enough professional soldiers either. A substantial number of JNA officers and soldiers moved over to the Croatian side but that was not sufficient. A great number of civilians, untrained men and boys (some of them even underage), volunteered and were fighting on the front lines which very often happened to be the streets of their hometowns and villages. Croatian soldiers at the beginning of the war did not even have adequate clothes and uniforms for combat and they often joined the battlefield in their jeans and sneakers (Perković Paloš 2016, 94).

It should be noted that Croatian Army was a heterogeneous group of people, different by their social status, level of education, religion, political affiliation, but also by their nationality. Out of approximately 360,000 recruits, about 9,000 were Serbs who were Croatian citizens, did not participate in insurgency and considered Croatia their homeland. There were also a significant number of Muslims who were born and raised in Croatia and decided to fight on Croatian side, as well as more than 500 foreign volunteers, some of whom were of Croatian origin (Nazor and Pušek 2018, 158).

Symbol of Destruction: Vukovar as Croatian Guernica

Eastern Slavonia with its mixed Croatian and Serbian population was, without any doubt, one of the most critical battlefields in the war. Larger towns like Osijek and Vukovar were surrounded by villages populated by Serbian insurgents who were attacking other villages inhabited by Croats. The flat terrain of Eastern Slavonia and its physical proximity to the border with Serbia enabled easy movements of JNA tanks and troops that caused enormous destruction.

One of the prime examples of brutality and destruction by aggressor's forces was Vukovar, a baroque town on the Danube right on the river border with Serbia. Vukovar was known for its tolerance and peaceful coexistence between Croats and Serbs in the pre-war period, when it had population of 50,000. Good relations, however, significantly deteriorated during 1991, friendships and even marriages were broken, and the earlier good neighborly relations turned into deadly exchanges with guns and tanks. One of the main reasons why Vukovar today is known as a symbol of Croatian resistance was the fact that the Serbian offensive forces had 30,000 soldiers at its disposal, whereas Vukovar in some phase of its defense had only approximately 1,800 (Marijan 2002, 371). Based on those facts, military experts forecasted that the defense of Vukovar would not last more than two weeks, whereas it actually lasted three months. Because of that, at the time Vukovar was called "Croatian Stalingrad". The town showed unexpected resistance that amazed Croatia, raised its morale, and gave the nation belief that it would not fall into Serbian arms. Nevertheless, due to a gross imbalance of power the town was completely surrounded by the enemy troops in October 1991, and all attempts from Zagreb to provide weapons, ammunition, food, and medical aid were unsuccessful. Vukovar was occupied on November 18, 1991. Serbian Chetniks were captured on camera parading through the destroyed and desolated town, waving their black flag with a human skull, and singing these verses: "Milošević, send us some salad, we are going to butcher Croats" (Nazor and Pušek 2018, 152). The complete destruction of the town caused its comparison to the Spanish town of Guernica, known for its devastation in the Spanish Civil War (Letica 1991). With the fall of Vukovar, approximately 15,000 surviving Croatian civilians were banished from their town. A few days after the occupation, 266 persons (wounded civilians, defenders, and hospital staff) were taken out of Vukovar hospital that prior to the occupation was one of the most shelled town objects by the Serbian forces. 200 persons out of 266 were transported to a former farm called Ovčara where they were killed and thrown into an open mass grave. Among them were civilians, such as a prominent Croatian journalist Siniša Glavašević who was reporting from the besieged Vukovar. In 1996, all bodies were exhumed, and it was established that the youngest victim at Ovčara was 16 and the oldest 72 (Nazor and Pušek 2018, 152). Although Vukovar was not strategically significant point among Croatian battlefields in comparison to some other cities and towns, its three-month defense slowed down Serbian progress towards Zagreb, while its tragedy turned it into a symbol of the Croatian War of Independence.

International Recognition and UN Peacekeepers in Croatia

After the Sarajevo ceasefire on January 2, 1992, the aggression in Croatia was stopped "at least partly and at least in part of the territory", (Nazor 2011, 137) whereas the war carried on in Bosnia and Herzegovina. Atrocities in Vukovar and the bombing of Dubrovnik, a town in the far south of Croatia on the UNESCO's cultural heritage list since 1979, awakened international community and brought Croatia closer to international recognition. Nonetheless, during the three-month term of the Peace Conference on the Former Yugoslavia held in Hague from September 1991 and led by Lord Peter Carrington, the international community was unsuccessful in its attempt to stop aggression against Croatia and solve the Yugoslav crisis peacefully.

Croatia's path to recognition was long and difficult for several reasons. The international community was very cautious regarding formation of new national countries in Europe after World War II because it feared that it would set an example for secession of other national movements in several European countries such as Catalonia, Corsica, Scotland, Northern Ireland, and most importantly for disintegration of the Soviet Union (Bekić 2010, 341-342; Filipović 2010, 211; Glaurdić 2011, 73). Besides that, it feared the influence of the unified Germany on the Eastern Block, because Germany was the strongest advocate for Croatian and Slovene recognition (Bekić 2010, 363-364). It also should not be ignored that "the diplomatic quarantine of Croatia" (Ramet 2008, 36) was facilitated by the fact that Croatian diplomacy was in its infancy and that Yugoslav and Serbian lobby conducted very strong worldwide propaganda activity against Croatia (Perković Paloš 2018b, 168-172; 197-207).

At the beginning of October 1991, the Peace Conference convened by the UN concluded that all Yugoslav republics would be recognized according to Lord Carrington's proposal on forming "loose associations or alliances of sovereign and independent states" while preserving borders and protecting national minorities (Milardović 1992, 124-133). Carrington's proposal was similar to previous Croatian and Slovene proposals for restructuring Yugoslavia as a confederacy (Perković Paloš 2018b, 179) and Croatia accepted it. Serbia, on the other hand, rejected the proposal several times (Libal 2004, 84, 93; Glaurdić 2011, 211), because it anticipated the recognition of Croatia and preservation of Croatian borders, which clashed with the previously stated Greater-Serbian plans. Subsequently, the Badinter Arbitration Committee, formed by the Peace Conference, in December 1991 and January 1992 ruled that the Socialist Federative Republic of Yugoslavia was in the process of dissolution and that all internal borders between republics had to be respected (Nazor 2011, 131), which means they became international borders. Finally, on January 15, 1992, Croatia was internationally recognized by all the members of the European Community.

Following the Sarajevo ceasefire, the UN sent to Croatia a Special Envoy of the Secretary-General of the United Nations, Mr. Cyrus Vance. He negotiated a "Vance Plan" that provided for sending to Croatia a UN peacekeeping force, called "blue helmets". Croatian Government accepted the plan even though UN troops were to be settled within the occupied parts of Croatia instead of at Croatian borders. UN units and observers came to Croatia under the name of United Nations Protection Forces (UNPROFOR), or United Nations Confidence Restoration Operation (UNCRO) after 1995. The forces were settled in the occupied areas called United Nations Protected Areas (UNPA) where Croatian Constitution and laws were not applied and where Croatian refugees did not have the possibility of return, at least not until the war had ended. This was one of the main frustrations of Croatian authorities and the public because they feared that a permanent 'status quo' similar to Cyprus might be established (Perković Paloš 2018a, 14, 22). Although the UN mission in Croatia ensured at least some sort of peace, the occupied territory remained cut-off from Croatia and under Serbian control up until 1995.

In Search of Peace: Croatian-Serbian Negotiations

One of the main goals of the Croatian leadership from the beginning was to end the political crisis peacefully (Nazor 2011, 85-86, 149-152; Perković Paloš 2018b, 41-49). Accordingly, Croatia gave some significant concessions to Serbian insurgent leadership. For example, in May 1992, Sabor provided an opportunity for Serbs in Croatia to form two autonomous districts of Knin and Glina (Barić 2005, 165; Miškulin 2012, 177-178; Marijan 2016, 25). However, negotiations between Croatian leadership in Zagreb and the Serbian insurgent leadership in Knin did not bring any results because of diametrically opposite objectives of the two sides. While Zagreb wanted to reintegrate its occupied territory and unite it under Croatian Constitution without changing the internationally recognized borders, Serbian insurgents in Knin did not want to live in Croatia under any conditions and planned to join Serbia and Montenegro in a new Socialist Republic of Yugoslavia (Miškulin 2012, 179). Nevertheless, Croatia continued its endeavors to end the war peacefully with another peace initiative that was presented to the international community in November 1993 by Croatian president Franjo Tuđman. The initiative, however, was also ultimately rejected by the international community (Miškulin 2012, 198).

A new peace plan called Plan Z-4, initiated by the American ambassador in Croatia Peter Galbraith, the Russian ambassador in Croatia Leonid Kerestedijanc, the French ambassador in Croatia Jean-Jacques Gaillarde, and representatives of the International Conference on the Former Yugoslavia, appeared in the fall of 1994. It contained some problematic elements for Croatia. According to the Plan, Serbs in Croatia would be given a very high level of autonomy in those areas where they were in a majority before the war. They would have their own symbols, parliament, government, president, currency, and police. In return, the occupied Eastern and Western Slavonia would be reintegrated with Croatia (Barić 2005, 474). Tuđman had serious misgivings about the Plan, maintaining that Croatian leadership could only accept cultural autonomy for all Serbs in Croatia and territorial autonomy for Serbs in Knin and Glina districts, but without any elements of statehood. He stressed that he could not accept anything that would contradict the Croatian Constitution and that would give excessive concessions to insurgent Serbs. As Barić (2005, 475) emphasized, the Plan was unacceptable because it would lead to the federalization of Croatia and "Serbian autonomous unit would have possibility to separate from Croatia in the future." Nevertheless, Tuđman publicly accepted the Plan in order to continue negotiations (Radelić et al. 2006, 383) and to preserve opportunity for peaceful territorial reintegration in Slavonia. The Serbian insurgent leadership in Knin was not pleased with the Plan either and they rejected it publicly again and again until August 1995 (Barić 2005, 475-477).

The last round of negotiations reopened in Geneva on August 3, 1995, at the insistence of the representatives of the UN and International Conference on the Former Yugoslavia (Barić 2005, 517). The day before, the head of a new Serbian government in Knin Milan Babić assured Galbraith that this time he would accept the Plan. His and the Serbian leadership's change of attitude was an attempt to prevent the Croatian military actions that would liberate the occupied territory and reintegrate it with Croatia (Barić 2005, 518). However, that same day, while all of the parties were negotiating in Geneva, Serbian artillery attacked Dubrovnik's surroundings; three civilians were killed and three badly wounded (Marijan 2009, 56). This was clearly a sign that Serbs had no intention of keeping the agreement.

Having that in mind, and also all the previous Serbian obstructions of negotiations and Serbian attempts to join the Republic Serb in Bosnia and Herzegovina, the next day Tuđman gave the order to the Croatian Army, that had already liberated certain parts of the occupied Croatian territory in several actions, to launch military operation with goal to liberate the rest of the occupied territory in Croatia (Čutura and Nazor 2005, 32).

LIBERATION OPERATIONS OF THE CROATIAN ARMY

Partial Liberation Operations in 1994 and 1995

From 1993 the Croatian Army performed attack operations, but it liberated or at least attempted to liberate only small portions of the occupied territory. The first operation, called Maslenica, in January 1993 had significant strategic and moral impact on Croatia. By liberating the surroundings of the coastal city of Zadar, it "established connection between Southern and Northern Croatia" which had been broken since 1991 (Nazor 2011, 156). On the other hand, the second significant military action conducted the same year caused negative reactions from the international community. In September 1993 in the quick action called The Medak Pocket (Medački džep) Croatian forces liberated three villages that were used by Serbian artillery to attack the Croatian town of Gospić. Part of the international community accused Croatian Army for "scorched-earth tactics" as well as for the civilian victims and it urged Croatian forces to retreat to their starting positions (Nazor 2011, 156).

From the fall of 1994 to the end of July in 1995, the Croatian Army carried out military actions that liberated some strategically important parts of the occupied territory. With these actions it "gained control over the mountains and zones in the hinterland of Knin, thereby creating conditions for its liberation" (Nazor 2011, 166). At the beginning of May 1995, in a quick two-day Operation Flash (Bljesak) it liberated Western Slavonia, a significant part of the RSK; in retaliation, Serbian insurgent leadership ordered rocketing of Zagreb. The attack on Zagreb resulted in human losses. According to Marijan (2009, 48) five civilians were killed and 203 wounded. Nazor (2011, 167-168) on the other hand, stated that seven civilians were killed and 176 wounded. Despite the fact that Croatian authorities "ensured humane treatment and all civil rights to Serbian population", the majority of Serbs left Western Slavonia even before and during the Operation Flash (Nazor 2011, 168).

Previously stated military actions and operations in 1994 and 1995 were in fact a prelude to the military-police Operation Storm (Oluja). The goal of that operation was to prevent Serbian insurgent leadership from uniting the remaining occupied territory of the RSK in Croatia with Republika Srpska (RS) in Bosnia and Herzegovina, established in 1992 by the insurgent Serbs there. To achieve unification, Serbian forces had to conquer Bihać, a town in Bosnia and Herzegovina close to the Croatian border and from 1993 a UN protected zone. To the end of October 1994 Serbian forces carried out "several larger military campaigns around Bihać," so on November 12, 1994 Bosnian-Herzegovinian president Alija Izetbegović appealed to Franjo Tuđman, asking him that "Croatia would conduct measures to prevent attack on Bihać from the Croatian territory" (Marijan 2009, 43-44). Nevertheless, Serbian forces continued to attack Bihać. Its occupation would have caused a new humanitarian disaster such as the one in Srebrenica in July 1995 when Serbian forces killed about 8,000

Bosnian men and boys (Nazor 2011, 247). Therefore, in order to save Bihać, achieve Croatian territorial integrity, and end the war, a new military operation by Croatia proved to be necessary (Nazor 2011, 168). Croatian and Bosnian-Herzegovinian military cooperation was essential to ensure the success of the operation. To that end, an agreement between Croatian President Franjo Tuđman and Bosnian and Herzegovinian President Alija Izetbegović was signed in Split on July 22, 1995. The agreement made it possible for Croatia to respond to the call from Bosnia and Herzegovina to help it defend from Serbian aggression (Barić 2005, 511). A few days after, in the operation called Summer 95 (Ljeto '95), Croatian Army liberated two towns, Bosansko Grahovo and Glamoč, and cut-off the road which connected the RSK in Croatia to the RS in Bosnia and Herzegovina. The path to Knin was now open to the Croatian Army (Marijan 2009, 54). According to Croatian general Janko Bobetko (1996, 498), had Grahovo and Glamoč not been conquered by the Croatian Army, the implementation of the operation Storm certainly would have been more difficult and much slower. Apart from that, the Croatian military action stopped Serbian attempts to conquer Bihać (Barić 2005, 513). Further, in the Operation Storm, Croatian forces, together with the forces of the Fifth Corps of BH Army, finally put an end to the 1201-day siege of Bihać (Barić 2005, 521).

Operation Storm

In addition to the military operations of the Croatian Army that gradually liberated parts of the occupied Croatian territory, Operation Storm was also preceded by unsuccessful negotiations between Zagreb and Knin. Based on the fact that Serbs rejected all Croatian proposals, Zagreb estimated that it would at least have implicit approval of the USA and Germany to launch a new military operation. The goal of the Operation Storm was to liberate occupied territories and return them to the internationally recognized borders of the Republic of Croatia.

According to Marijan (2009, 136) 127,000 soldiers and policemen participated in the Operation Storm. Combined military-police operation started in early morning of August 4, 1995. The commander of Croatian forces in the Operation Storm in northern Dalmatia around Knin was Croatian general Ante Gotovina. The difference between the Storm and previous military actions and operations was that before only one part of the occupied territory was targeted, whereas in the Storm Croatian forces attacked simultaneously from thirty-one directions along the front line longer than 630 kilometers (Nazor 2011, 172, 259).

Knin was liberated on the second day of the operation on the 5th of August. When Croatian forces entered Knin, the town was already deserted. One part of Serbian population that had not left the town, took refuge in the UNCRO camp where they waited for the arrival of the Croatian Army (Barić 2005, 520). On August 8, colonel Čedomir Bulat, commander of the 21st Kordun Corps of the "Serbian Army of Krajina," surrendered to the Croatian Army near Topusko (Nazor 2011, 171, 261). In only four days, Croatian forces had liberated most of the occupied areas in Croatia. Only Eastern Slavonia, Baranja and Western Syrmia were still occupied.

Departure, not Deportation: Fate of the Serbs from "Republic of Serbian Krajina"

The liberation of Knin by Croatian forces marked the military collapse of the RSK in Croatia and announced that the end of the war was near. Mass exodus of Serbian population from Croatia to the RS and to Serbia followed. Estimates of the number of Serbs who emigrated from the RSK vary by source (Nazor 2011, 265), as shown in Table 2 below.

Fate of RSK Serbs since then has been debated among scholars, politicians, media, and the public in general. Several questions were raised on this topic: Were Serbs expelled by force or they left voluntarily? And if they were expelled, who gave the order? Did ethnic cleansing occur? Some public figures, particularly those of Serbian nationality, talk about the ethnic cleansing of the RSK Serbs (Livada 2006; Đokić Jović and Sjekavica 2012, 2-4; Pupovac 2013). The term "ethnic cleansing", which was introduced in the 1990s, indicates attempts to create ethnically homogenous territory not only by mass killings of certain group of people but also by their deportation, i.e., their forcible transfer from one place to another (Andreopoulos n.d.). Recent research by Croatian historians, however, proves that Croatian authorities did not commit nor had any intention of committing ethnic cleansing of Serbs in Croatia (Barić 2004, 441-461; 2005, 531-565; Marijan 2009, 138-139; Nazor 2011, 282). A great number of documents show that the evacuation was ordered by the Serbian insurgent leadership, and that a plan for it in case of Croatian actions existed from 1993 (Marijan 2009, 327-375).

The Supreme Defense Council of the RSK gave the order on August 4, 1995, to evacuate Serbian civilians from Dalmatia and southern Lika according to previously made plans (Barić 2005, 551-553; Marijan 2009, 139; Nazor 2011, 172-173). During the Operation Storm President Tuđman called on Serbs who had not committed war crimes to remain in their homes, declaring that all of their civil rights would be guaranteed. As for paramilitary Serbian forces, he called on them to lay down their arms, guaranteeing them amnesty (Marijan 2009, 142-143). This proclamation of President Tuđman was repeated every hour (Scheffers 2000, 108). Despite the call, the majority of Serbs left, because, according to numerous statements of Serbs leaving the RSK, they did not want to live in Croatia with Croats as their neighbors (Barić 2005, 535-542).

Unfounded claims of Silber and Little (1996, 350) that Tuđman's proclamation was not sincere and could not "obscure the true desire of the Croatian authorities to expel Serbs completely from Croatia" is an example of the authors' prejudice, because they do not present any sort of evidence. Robert R. Hayden (1996) went even further in his viewing of Serbs as the ultimate victims of the Croatian policy, ignoring the Greater-Serbian aggression on Croatia and numerous victims on the Croatian side.

Table 2. Different estimates regarding departed Serbs during and after operation Storm

Sources	**Number of Departed Serbs**
Croatian	90,000
United Nations	150,000
Serbian	200,000 – 300,000

Tragically, after the operation, crimes were committed by the Croatian side, including killings, robberies, and burning down of Serbian houses. Sources reveal, however, that it was not systematic, or planned, or encouraged by the Croatian authorities. Exactly the opposite: the orders and directives of the Croatian state and military authorities prior to the operation stated that “commanders on the field must prevent any sort of excess against civilians and their property”, that is robberies, killings, and arson had to be prevented (Barić 2005, 557). The directives of the Headquarters of the Croatian Army clearly stated: “In all units of the Croatian Army conduct consistent enforcement of international law of war regarding the relation toward prisoners and population on the occupied areas, that is why next to units of the Military Police, engage the units of the Ministry of Interior” (Bobetko 1996, 484-491). However, the Croatian authorities did not have complete control over the Army after the operation (Nazor 2011, 272; Barić 2005, 521). A videotape revealed in 2004 showed that general Ante Gotovina demanded from military police to do their job and to establish control over the situation in Knin (Barić 2005, 558). Then-President of the Croatian Government Nikica Valentić and Minister of Interior Ivan Jarnjak “helped stabilize the situation in the occupied areas and sent additional police forces, to prevent criminal acts and violence against the remaining Serbs” (Barić 2005, 559).

Goldstein (2008, 571-572) suggests, without presenting any evidence, that Croatian retaliation was “partially deliberate action in order to disable return to those Serb refugees who eventually would want to come back to their homes”; he also claims that Croatian authorities were “unacceptably tolerant” towards these crimes. However, in 1995, particularly in the second half of that year, the State Attorney’s Office of the Republic of Croatia received “significant number of charges for crimes committed during and immediately after the ‘Storm’.” These charges referred mostly to “crimes against property, but also for security threat (arson), murders and to a lesser extent for war crimes” (DORH 2011). According to the available data, Croatian authorities made efforts to bring to justice the perpetrators of crimes against Serbs committed in that period, as shown on Table 3 (DORH 2011; Nazor 2011, 301).

According to data of the State Attorney’s Office, the number of victims of the war crimes and murders during and after the Storm was 47. Out of 6,390 indicted perpetrators, 2,262 could not be located at the time but charges have been filed against them for 26 war crimes and murders (DORH 2011). For other 4,128 located perpetrators, 400 charges were dropped. Considering this data, the State Attorney’s Office concluded:

> “Data on great number of proceedings concluded with a negative decision (suspension, acquittal or refusal) demonstrate exactly the opposite of the claims that the State Attorney’ Office has not prosecuted the perpetrators of war crimes, and these data are constantly being presented. The above presented information provides a foundation to the claim that the State Attorney’s Office sometimes in the 1990s and without sufficient criticism, submitted requests for investigation against persons reported for criminal offenses.” (DORH 2011)

It should be noted that work on war crimes cases is still ongoing and will not be stopped as long as there is possibility that any one of the perpetrators or those who gave them orders is alive, since war crimes have no period of limitation (DORH 2011).

Table 3. Sanctions enforced by the Croatian authorities (as of mid-2011; DORH 2011; Nazor 2011, 301)

Number of Perpetrators	Sanctions
6390	Indicted
3728	Prosecuted
2380	Convicted

PEACEFUL REINTEGRATION AND THE END OF THE WAR

In the successful Operation Storm Croatia demonstrated enviable military power and skill. Croatian Army was evidently at that moment capable to liberate the rest of the occupied territory in Croatia and even Bosnia and Herzegovina however Tuđman opted for peaceful reintegration of the remaining occupied Croatian territory. His main reason was the position of US President Clinton's administration that a peaceful reintegration should be conducted in the region after achieving a strategic balance (Holjevac Tuković 2015, 620). In addition, according to numerous statements of Tuđman's close associates, he did not want any more war victims and casualties, nor did he want more destruction of Croatian towns (Radoš 2005, 74-75). This enabled Serbian insurgents and population to remain for the time being in Eastern Slavonia, Baranja, and Western Syrmia, which covered 4.6% of the total land territory of the Republic of Croatia (Nazor 2011, 174).

On November 12, 1995, Croatian authorities and the Serbian leadership in Eastern Slavonia, Baranja and Western Syrmia signed "the Erdut Agreement" on peaceful and gradual reintegration of that area with the Republic of Croatia. A transitional administration of the UN in Eastern Slavonia was introduced as the initial step toward the complete reintegration of that area to Croatia (Barić 2005, 530). The complete reintegration was finally realized in January 1998. As Nazor (2011, 174) emphasized, although it "provoked the dissatisfaction of most Croats expelled from the area" because of the concessions to the insurgent Serbs, Tuđman's decision "confirmed the consistency of the Croatian policy in its attempts, even in moments of victorious euphoria and military superiority, to resolve problems with the insurgent Serbs by peaceful negotiation in spite of certain painful compromises."

Tuđman's decision on the peaceful reintegration set an example for Croatian people concerning their future relations with Serbs. He understood the nation's state of mind after the aggression, pervasive destruction, killings, expulsion of Croats from their homes, and extremely inhumane treatments of Croatian war prisoners. Half a year before the finalization of the peaceful reintegration on June, 1997, Tuđman visited Vukovar via "Freedom and Return Train". On that occasion he delivered a speech on forgiveness, urging Croatian people to forgive their Serbian neighbors because "the victor who does not know how to forgive plants the seed of discord and future ills". In this speech Tuđman called for peaceful coexistence between Croats and Serbs and other ethnic communities in this region (Nazor 2011, 175).

Successful military operations and Tuđman's decision on peaceful reintegration enabled reaching a peace agreement between all parties in Dayton, Ohio, in the USA, on November 21, 1995. The Dayton Agreement ended the war in Croatia and brought it peace and territorial integrity. The Agreement also brought peace to Bosnia and Herzegovina but it was not a just peace; that republic was split into two entities, one Serbian and another Bosniak-Croatian. In that way, Serbs who accounted for about one third of the country's population received 49% percent of the territory despite the fact that Serbian leaders and Serbian policy were found to be responsible for war in the former Yugoslavia (Nazor 2011, 177).

Consequences of Serbian Aggression: Human Losses, Refugees, and War Damage

Greater-Serbian aggression against Croatia resulted in great human losses, large number of refugees and displaced persons, and significant war damage. As a result of pervasive aggression and aggressor's methods of warfare, more than half of killed persons were civilians. On the "Croatian side", on the free Croatian territory, more than 14,000 citizens were killed, while approximately 1,000 citizens were "disappeared" (Nazor and Pušek 2018, 278). According to data of the Croatian Minister of Health during the War of Independence, Andrija Hebrang (2013), 6,891 Croatian soldiers and 7,263 civilians were killed, in total 14,154. Considering that data are still incomplete and that there are noticeable differences in numbers presented by the available sources, further research needs to be conducted regarding the topic (Nazor and Pušek 2018, 278). It should be noted that at least 150 mass graves and about 1,200 individual graves of victims of Greater-Serbian aggression have been discovered. According to data from 2017, remains of 5,131 persons were exhumed (Nazor and Pušek 2018, 279).

The persecution of Croatian and other non-Serbian populations was one of the main features of the aggression. It could be claimed that Serbian policy was policy of ethnic cleansing. There were two kinds of affected persons. Croatian civilians who were banished from their homes and who were forced to move to safe areas in Croatia were called "displaced persons", whereas "refugees" were those Croats and non-Serbs who emigrated abroad from Croatia and those Bosnians-Herzegovinians who fled to Croatia (see Perković Paloš 2018b, 209-210). Displaced persons and refugees were housed mainly in hotels and tourist resorts and their expenses were covered mostly from the Croatian state budget (Perković Paloš 2018b, 213-214). Persecution of non-Serbian, mainly Croatian, population was followed by systematic immigration of Serbian population into the occupied areas in Croatia. President Tuđman addressed this topic in a letter to the Secretary-General of the UN Boutros Boutros Ghali on January 13, 1992, informing him that the native population of non-Serbian nationality (other than Croats, mainly Hungarians, Czechs, Slovenians, and Rusyns) were being forcefully deported, their homes were being burned down to the ground and destroyed, and their private property confiscated; he concluded that Serbs tried to achieve two strategic goals: to change demographic structure and permanently usurp occupied parts of Croatia. Tuđman also raised alarm that those Croats and other non-Serbs who remained in the occupied areas were forced to wear white ribbons on their arms as an identification sign, their outdoor movement was limited, and those citizens who in any way had expressed their support for duly and democratically elected local Croatian authorities were fired from their jobs. Finally, Tuđman requested of the UN Truce Supervision Organization (UNTSO), which would to stop and prevent any further immigration of Serbian population and to control the treatment of the non-Serbian population in the occupied parts of Croatia (Gregurić 1998, 377-378). Croatian authorities also objected to emigration of Serbian population from Croatia (Gregurić 1998, 299), effectively opposing ethnic cleansing on the Croatian territory regardless of the ethnicity of their citizens.

In 1992, after the escalation of the war in Bosnia and Herzegovina, Croatia received a great number of refugees from Bosnia and Herzegovina. At the beginning of July 1992, approximately 82,500,000 DEM from the Croatian budget monthly went to Bosnian-Herzegovinian refugees (Gregurić 1998, 581). With regards to that, at the beginning of June 1992, Croatian Government concluded that Croatia could not afford to sustain this level of support any longer (Gregurić 1998, 582). In July 1992, Croatia asked help from the United Nations High Commissioner for Refugees (UNHCR) in taking care of the Bosnian-Herzegovinian refugees (Perković Paloš 2018b, 240). Financial help for the care of displaced persons and refugees from 1992 was indeed provided by UNHCR, and also by European Community and "others", which were not specified. According to the Report of the Croatian Government from 1998, in the period from 1991 to 1997, the majority of funds, 88,74%, for displaced persons and refugees, was provided from the State Budget and 11,26% from the other sources (Hrvatsko zakonodavstvo 1998). Croatia dealt with the problem of the displaced persons and refugees up until 1998, the year which marked only the beginning of systematic returns to their homes. Table 4 presents data from the Report of the Croatian Government (Hrvatsko zakonodavstvo 1998).

War damage was inflicted on residential infrastructure, transport, utilities, and industry. The largest economic damage was recorded in tourism. For example, just in 1991 the number of overnight stays decreased by 80.7% (Perković Paloš 2018b, 255). The decrease and slow recovery of tourism was caused not only by fear of war but also by the fact that most hotel facilities were filled with displaced persons and refugees (Gregurić 1998, 454-455). Great environmental damage was caused by the bombing of the oil refinery in the town of Sisak, the leakage of oil from a hydroelectric power plant into the river Cetina, the mining of the river dam, and by the destruction of arable land caused by bombing and rockets (Gregurić 1998, 440).

Table 4. Displaced persons and refugees in Croatia from 1991 to 1998

Time of Registration	Registered displaced persons and refugees in Croatia		
	Displaced persons from Croatia	**Refugees from BH and SRY**	**Total in Croatia**
1991-12-01	550,000	-	550,000
1992-12-01	260,705	402,768	663,493
1993-06-01	254,791	272,869	527,660
1994-08-01	196,870	212,056	408,926
1995-05-01	210,592	188,672	399,264
1996-05-31	167,609	184,545	352,154
1997-03-01	117,721	106,750	224,471
1998-04-04	94,796	37,400	126,181

Table 5. Destroyed and damaged Roman Catholic objects

Damaged/Destroyed Objects	Number
Parish churches	266
Other churches	306
Chapels	254
Parish halls	286
Monasteries	80
Cemeteries	100
Outdoor crucifixes	134
TOTAL	1,426

In the war, 590 settlements were damaged or destroyed, as well as 195,000 to 217,009 housing units. Croatian cultural monuments were one of the aggressor's frequent targets; 2,423 of them were damaged or destroyed by the end of the war (Nazor and Pušek 2018, 279; Živković 1996, 400). Majority of them were Roman Catholic religious objects as shown in Table 5 (Nazor and Pušek 2018, 279).

In comparison, as Ramet (2008, 35) noted, only 2.5% of Serbian Orthodox churches were destroyed in those areas liberated by the Croatian Army during 1995 (35). Significant number of other religious objects in Croatia were also damaged or destroyed by the Serbian forces. This included Jewish, other Christian communities, and also Serbian Orthodox religious objects (Živković 1996, 403-415). According to recent findings, total war damage in Croatia from 1991 to 2004 was 142 billion US dollars (Nazor and Pušek 2018, 279).

The consequences of the listed material war damages shaped the reality of Croatian life during and long after the war had ended. Even more traumatic were human losses, particularly persons whose fate is still unknown and raped Croatian women whose perpetrators still have not been prosecuted and convicted. These facts are of primary importance when discussing the war and its aftermath. Issues of war reparations and justice for war victims are, unfortunately, still not resolved and they are still taking a toll on relations between Croats and Serbs in some war-affected areas in Croatia and also on relations between the Republic of Croatia and the Republic of Serbia.

CONCLUSION

Writing about the war in Yugoslavia, many authors present the image of the Balkans as a barrel of gunpowder that was about to explode due to the "ethnic hatred" of its nations and present Tuđman and Milošević as two sides of the same coin, suggesting that they fomented Croatian and Serbian nationalism, which ignited war. These simplistic interpretations of the complex events relativize culpability for the outbreak of war, and they show disregard for the chronology of events and different policies of Croatian and Serbian leaderships. The analysis of causes of war and of chronological events leading to the dissolution of Yugoslavia, briefly described in this chapter, clearly demonstrate that Serbian leader Slobodan Milošević and his associates were responsible for the outbreak of the war. Their plan was to centralize Yugoslavia and impose Serbian domination on other Yugoslav republics and, if that would fail, to form Greater Serbia and bring all Serbs into one country. Subjecting Serbs in Croatia to aggressive and chauvinist nationalistic propaganda, Milošević managed to turn them against the democratically elected Croatian leadership in 1990 and mobilized them to start the insurgency. This led to the establishment of the RSK in Croatia with the goal of separating from Croatia and uniting with Serbia so that all Serbs in Yugoslavia would live in one country.

After Croatia declared its independence, Serbia started open aggression and with the help of the Serbian-dominated JNA occupied almost one third of Croatian territory by the end of 1991. During the four-year war, Croatia opted for a peaceful solution of the crisis. Prior to its international recognition it ensured all rights for national minorities according to the standards of the European Community, and agreed to give territorial autonomy to Serbs in two districts, Knin and Glina, where they constituted the majority of population. However, the stumbling stone was the fact that Croatia wanted to reintegrate all of its territory under Croatian constitution and laws, whereas insurgent Serbs wanted to separate from Croatia and unite with Serbia. Also, all peace initiatives and plans, even those guaranteeing them high level of autonomy, were rejected by the insurgent Serbian leadership in Knin. This inevitably led to the military operations of the Croatian Army that in August 1995 liberated occupied Croatian territory.

Controversies regarding the fate of the RSK Serbs led to accusations by some that Croatian authorities conducted ethnic cleansing. However, available sources and recent findings demonstrate that it was the Serbian leadership that ordered evacuation of civilians and that evacuation started even before the Operation Storm. A majority of Serbs showed that they did not want to live in the same country as Croats. The peaceful policy of Franjo Tuđman was reflected in his decision for peaceful reintegration of the remaining occupied Croatian territory, despite the power of the Croatian Army and the public mood. His speech on forgiveness and coexistence of Croats and Serbs delivered in 1997 in the completely devastated Vukovar, the symbol of destruction during the aggression, showed consistency of his policy for sovereign, independent, and free Croatia based on democratic values in which different peoples could live in peace.

We can conclude that so called "ethnic hatred" between nations in Yugoslavia never really existed. Wars and animosities between numerous European nations also occurred in the course of the 20th century; it is not something specific to the nations that lived in Yugoslavia. What is important to emphasize is that between the nations in Yugoslavia did exist significant differences that the two Yugoslav states (Kingdom of Yugoslavia and communist Yugoslavia) just brought up to the surface. Negative experience with domination of one nation over others, killings and atrocities on all sides during World War II, and repression of their differences in the communist Yugoslavia, only deepened their distrust and animosities towards each other and opened the door to their conflicts that would mark the last decade of the 20th century.

References

Andreopolous, George J. n.d. "Ethnic cleansing." In *Encyclopadia Britannica*. Accessed January 31, 2020. http://www.britannica.com/topic/ethnic-cleansing.

Antić, Ljubomir. 2007. *Velikosrpski nacionalni programi: ishodišta i posljedice*. Zagreb: Golden marketing: Tehnička knjiga: Hrvatski institut za povijest. [*Greater-Serbian National Programs: Origins and Consequences*. Zagreb: Golden Marketing – Tehinčka knjiga: Croatian Institute of History].

Barić, Nikica. 2005. *Srpska pobuna u Hrvatskoj: 1990.-1995.* [*Serbian Rebellion in Croatia: 1990-1995*]. Zagreb: Golden marketing-Tehnička knjiga.

Bekić, Andrea. 2010. "London i Bonn – dva pola politike Europske zajednice prema priznanju Republike Hrvatske 1991. godine." *Časopis za suvremenu povijest* 42:339-366. ["London and Bonn – Two Poles of the European Community's Policy Concerning the Recognition of the Republic of Croatia in 1991." *Journal of Contemporary History* 42:339-366. Accessed February 2, 2020. https://hrcak.srce.hr/63647.

Bilić, Ivan. 2005. "Kronologija raspada SFRJ i stvaranje Republike Hrvatske do 15. siječnja 1992." ["The Chronology on the SFRY Dissolution and Creating of the Republic of Croatia until January 15, 1992"]. *National security and the future* 6:73-184. Accessed January 20, 2020. https://hrcak.srce.hr/18568.

Bobetko, Janko. 1996. *Sve moje bitke*. Zagreb: Vlastita naklada. [*All My Battles*. Zagreb: Self-publishing].

Denich, Bette. 1994. "Dismembering Yugoslavia: Nationalist ideologies and the Symbolic Revival of Genocide." *American Ethnologist* 21:367-390. Accessed January 15, 2020. doi: 10.1525/ae.1994.21.2.02a00080.

DORH – Državno odvjetništvo Republike Hrvatske [DORH – State Attorney's Office of the Republic of Croatia]. 2011. Accessed March 27, 2020. http://www.dorh.hr/PodaciOPrijavama2.

Đokić Jović, Jelena, and Marko Sjekavica. 2012. "Osvrt na presudu MSKJ-a u predmetu protiv Gotovine i dr. (s obzirom na utvrđivanje činjeničnog konteksta događaja te jedinstvenu sudsku interpretaciju u stvarnoj primjeni međunarodnog humanitarnog prava)." ["Review of the ICTY in the Case Against Gotovina et al. (Considering the Established Factual Context of Events and Unique Judical Interpretation in the Actual Application of the International Humanitarian Law"]. Accessed February 2, 2020. http://www.documenta.hr/assets/files/objave/2012%2008/2012.08.03_osvrt.pdf.

Filipović, Vladimir. 2010. "Trenutak Europe – rasprave o mogućoj intervenciji Zapadnoeuropske unije (WEU) u rat u Hrvatskoj tijekom ljeta 1991. godine". *Politička misao* 47:210-224 ["The Hour of Europe – Discussion about the Possible Intervention by the Western European Union (WEU) in the War in Croatia in 1991." *Political Thought* 27:210-224]. Accessed March 28, 2020. https://hrcak.srce.hr/66498.

Glaurdić, Josip. 2011. *Vrijeme Europe: zapadne sile i raspad Jugoslavije.* [*The Hour of Europe: Western Powers and the Breakup of Yugoslavia*]. Zagreb: Mate.

Goldstein, Ivo. 2008. *Hrvatska povijest 21.* [*Croatian History 21*] Zagreb: Europapress holding.

Goldstein, Ivo, and Slavko Goldstein. 2011. *Bleiburg i Jasenovac nisu isto.* [*Bleiburg and Jasenovac are not the same*]. Zagreb: Novi liber.

Gregurić, Franjo. 1998. *Vlada demokratskog jedinstva Hrvatske 1991.-1992.* Zagreb: Naklada Zadro. [*Democratic Unity Government of Croatia 1991-1992*].

Hayden, Robert M. 1996. "Imagined Communities and Real Victims; Self-Determination and Ethnic Cleansing in Yugoslavia." *American Ethnologist* 23:783-801. Accessed March 30,

2020. https://is.muni.cz/el/1490/podzim2014/CZS05/re/Hayden-Imagined-Communities-Real-Victims-AE-1996.pdf.

Holjevac Tuković, Ana. 2015. "Temeljni sporazum o području istočne Slavonije, Baranje i zapadnog Srijema (Erdutski sporazum) i uvjeti za njegovu provedbu." *Časopis za suvremenu povijest* 47:617-634. ["The Basic Agreement Regarding the Area of Eastern Slavonia, Baranja and Western Syrmia (The Erdut Agreement) and the Conditions for its Enforcement." *Journal of Contemporary History* 47:617-634]. Accessed January 31, 2020. https://hrcak.srce.hr/154374.

Hrvatsko zakonodavstvo [Croatian Legislation]. 1998. Izvješće Vlade Republike Hrvatske o dosadašnjem tijeku povratka i zbrinjavanju prognanika, izbjeglica i raseljenih osoba. [Report of the Government of the Republic of Croatia Regarding the Current Course of Return and Care for the Displaced Persons and Refugees]. Accessed February 3, 2020. http://zakon.poslovna.hr/public/izvjesce-vlade-republike-hrvatske-o-dosadasnjem-tijeku-povratka-i-zbrinjavanju-prognanika%2C-izbjeglica-i-raseljenih-osoba/16265/zakoni.aspx.

Jović, Borisav. 1995. *Poslednji dani SFRJ*. Beograd: Politika. [*The Last Days of the SFRY*. Belgrade: Politics].

Letica, Slaven. 1991. "Vukovar ili hrvatska Knjiga Postanka." ["Vukovar or the Croatian Book of Genesis"]. *Globus*, November 22.

Libal, Michael. 2004. *Njemačka politika i jugoslavenska kriza 1991.-1992.* [*German Policy and the Yugoslav Crisis 1991-1992*]. Translated by Zoran Bošnjak. Zagreb: Golden marketing-Tehnička knjiga.

Livada, Svetozar. 2006. *Etničko čišćenje: ozakonjeni zločin stoljeća.* [*Ethnic cleansing: A Lawful Crime of the Century*]. Zagreb: Euroknjiga.

Marijan, Davor. 2002. "Bitka za Vukovar." ["The Battle of Vukovar"]. *Scrinia slavonica* 2:367-402. Accessed January 31, 2020. https://hrcak.srce.hr/11352.

Marijan, Davor. 2009. *Oluja*. Zagreb: Hrvatski memorijalno-dokumentacijski centar Domovinskog rata. [*Storm*. Zagreb: Croatian Homeland War Memorial and Documentation Center].

Marijan, Davor. 2016. *Domovinski rat*. Zagreb: Despot infinitus: Hrvatski institut za povijest. [*Homeland War*. Zagreb: Despot infinitus: Croatian Institute of History].

Marijan, Davor. 2017. *Hrvatska 1989. – 1992. Rađanje države*. Zagreb: Hrvatski institut za povijest. [*Croatia 1989 – 1992. The Birth of the State*. Zagreb: Croatian Institute of History].

Marić, Davor. 1990. "Izmišljene opasne namjere." *Slobodna Dalmacija*. ["Fictional Dangerous Intentions." *Free Dalmatia*], April 16.

Martinić Jerčić, Natko, and Ante Nazor. 2019. "Ubojstva hrvatskih policajaca 2. svibnja 1991. – najava velikosrpske agresije na Hrvatsku." *Časopis za suvremenu povijest* 51:123-49. ["The Murders of Croatian Policemen on 2 May 1991 – Heralding the Greater Serbian Aggression on Croatia." *Journal of Contemporary History* 51:123-49]. doi: org/10.22586/csp.v51i1.8659.

"Memorandum Srpske akademije nauka i umetnosti (nacrt)." ["The Memorandum of the Serbian Academy of Science and Arts (Draft)"]. (1986). Accessed January 15, 2020. https://www.helsinki.org.rs/serbian/doc/memorandum%20sanu.pdf.

Milardović, Anđelko, ed. 1992. *Dokumenti o državnosti Republike Hrvatske: (od prvih višestranačkih izbora 1990. do međunarodnog priznanja 15. siječnja 1992.* [*Documents *on Statehood of the Republic of Croatia: (Since the First Multi-party Elections 1990 to the International Recognition January 15 1992*]. Zagreb: "Alinea."

Miškulin, Ivica. 2016. "'Napokon nešto'" ili o mirovnoj inicijativi Franje Tuđmana iz studenog 1993." In *Franjo Tuđman i stvaranje suvremene hrvatske države (1990.-1999.)*, edited by Ante Bralić, 175-198. Zadar: Sveučilište u Zadru. ["Finally Something" or About Franjo Tuđman's Peace Initiative in November 1993." In *Franjo Tuđman and Creating of the Contemporary Croatian State (1990-1999)*, edited by Ante Bralić, 175-198. Zadar: University of Zadar].

Narodne novine [*National Newspapers*]. 1990. Ustavni sud Hrvatske, Rješenje [Constitutional Court, Decision]. August 14. Accessed March 26, 2020. https://narodne-novine.nn.hr/clanci/sluzbeni/1990_08_33_677.html.

Nazor, Ante, and Dinko Čutura. 2005. *Bljesak Oluje.* Zagreb: Ministarstvo kulture Republike Hrvatske. [*A Flash of the Storm.* Zagreb: Ministry of Culture of the Republic of Croatia].

Nazor, Ante. 2011. *Velikosrpska agresija na Hrvatsku 1990-ih.* Zagreb: Hrvatski memorijalno-dokumentacijski centar Domovinskog rata. [*Greater-Serbian Aggression Against Croatia in the 90.* Zagreb: Croatian Homeland War Memorial and Documentation Center].

Nazor, Ante, and Tomislav Pušek. 2018. *Domovinski rat: Pregled političke i diplomatske povijesti.* Zagreb: Nakladni zavod Globus: Hrvatski memorijalno-dokumentacijski centar Domovinskog rata. [*Homeland War: Review of Political and Diplomatic History.* Zagreb: Publishing House Globus: Croatian Homeland War Memorial and Documentation Center].

Oberschall, Anthony. 2000. "The Manipulation of Ethnicity: From Ethnic Cooperation to Violence and War in Yugoslavia." *Ethnic and Racial Studies* 23:982-1001. Accessed January 15, 2020. doi: org/10.1080/014198700750018388.

Pavlaković, Vjeran. 2009. "Komemorativna kultura Bleiburga, 1990 – 2009." In *Kultura sjećanja 1945. Povijesni lomovi i svladavanje prošlosti*, edited by Tihomir Cipek and Sulejman Bosto, 167-194. Zagreb: Disput. ["The Commemorative Culture of Bleiburg, 1990-2009." In *Historical Fractions and Mastering the Past*, edited by Tihomir Cipek, and Sulejman Bosto, 167-194. Zagreb: Disput].

Perković Paloš, Andrijana. 2016. "Domovinski rat u Globusu i Glasu Slavonije." In *Zbornik radova znanstveno-stručnog skupa Simbol, identitet i Domovinski rat, Zagreb, 31. listopada 2014.*, edited by Željko Heimer, and Marin Sabolović, 87-103. Zagreb: Hrvatsko grboslovno i zastavoslovno društvo. ["Homeland War in Globus and Glas Slavonije." In *Proceedings of the Scientific Conference Symbol, Identity and Homeland War, Zagreb, October 31 2014*, edited by Željko Heimer, and Marin Sabolović, 87-103. Zagreb: Croatian Heraldic and Vexillological Association].

Perković Paloš, Andrijana. 2018a. "Uloga predsjednika Tuđmana na putu Hrvatske prema teritorijalnoj cjelovitosti." In *Hrvatska – put prema teritorijalnoj cjelovitosti. Zbornik radova sa znanstvenog skupa održanog na Filozofskom fakultetu u Splitu povodom obilježavanja 20. obljetnice vojno-redarstvenih operacija Bljesak i Oluja*, edited by Aleksandar Jakir, Andrijana Perković Paloš, and Marin Sabolović, 9-31. Split: Sveučilište u Splitu: Hrvatski memorijalno-dokumentacijski centar Domovinskog rata. ["The Role of President Tuđman in Croatian Path towards Territorial Integrity". In *Croatia – Path towards Territorial Integrity. Proceedings of the Scientific Conference at the Faculty of Philosophy in Split on the Occasion of Commemoration of the 20th Anniversary of the*

Military-Police Operations Flash and Storm, edited by Aleksandar Jakir, Andrijana Perković Paloš, and Marin Sabolović, 9-31. Split: University of Split: Croatian Homeland War Memorial and Documentation Center].

Perković Paloš, Andrijana. 2018b. "Vlada demokratskog jedinstva." PhD diss., Sveučilište u Splitu, Filozofski fakultet. ["Democratic Unity Government." PhD diss., University of Split, Faculty of Philisophy].

Programske zasade i ciljevi HDZ. [The Principles and Goals of HDZ]. 1990. Zagreb, Samobor: A. G. Matoš.

"Pupovac o Oluji: 'Hrvatska nije imala pravo na etničko čišćenje Srba!'." 2013. [Pupovac on Oluja: 'Croatia had no Right to Ethnic Cleansing of Serbs!'"] *Index*. Accessed August 31, 2015. http://www.index.hr/vijesti/clanak/pupovac-o-oluji-hrvatska-nije-imala-pravo-na-etnicko-ciscenje srba/693302.aspx.

Radelić, Zdenko. 2006. *Hrvatska u Jugoslaviji 1945.-1991.: Od zajedništva do razlaza. Zagreb: Školska knjiga.* [*Croatia in Yugoslavia 1945-1991: From Community to Dissolution. Zagreb: Schoolbook*].

Radelić, Zdenko, Davor Marijan, Nikica Barić, Albert Bing, and Dražen Živić. 2006. *Stvaranje hrvatske države i Domovinski rat*. Zagreb: Školska knjiga: Hrvatski institut za povijest. [*Creating the Croatian State and Homeland War*. Zagreb: Školska knjiga: Croatian Institute of History].

Radoš, Ivan. 2005. *Tuđman izbliza: svjedočenja suradnika i protivnika*. [*Tuđman Up Close: Testimonies of Associates and Opponents*]. Zagreb: Profil international.

Ramljak, O. 1990. "'I mi smo vojska'." *Slobodna Dalmacija*. ["'We are an Army too'." *Free Dalmatia*], April 9.

Ramet, Sabrina P. 2005. *Balkanski babilon* [*Balkan Babel*]. Zagreb: Alinea.

Ramet, Sabrina P. 2008. "Politics in Croatia since 1990." In *Croatia Since Independence: War, Politics, Society, Foreign Relations*, edited by Sabrina P. Ramet, Konrad Clewig, and Reneo Lukić, 31-57. Munchen: Oldenburg Verlag.

Sadkovich, James. 2010. *Tuđman: prva politička biografija*. Prevela Ivana Šimunić Mesić. Zagreb: Večernji posebni proizvodi. [*Tuđman: The First Political Biography*. Translated by Ivana Šimunić Mesić. Zagreb: Evening Special Editions].

Scheffers, Joop. 2000. *Veleposlanik u Zagrebu 1994.-1998.* [*Ambassadeur in Zagreb 1994-1998*]. Translated by Vinko Prizmić. Zagreb: Ceres.

Sekula Gibač, Janja, and Ilija Vučur. 2018. "Služba unutarnjih poslova i policajci srpske nacionalnosti na pobunom zahvaćenom području u sjevernoj Dalmaciji, Lici i na Banovini 1990. godine." *Polemos: časopis za interdisciplinarna istraživanja rata i mira* 21:13-46. ["Service of the Interior and Policemen of Serbian Nationality in the Rebelled Area of Croatia in 1990 (Northern Dalmatia, Lika and Banovina)". *Polemos: Journal of Interdisciplinary Research on War and Peace* 21:13-46]. Accessed January 21, 2020. https://hrcak.srce.hr/index.php?show=clanak&id_clanak_jezik=319586.

Silber, Laura, and Alan Little. 1996. *Smrt Jugoslavije*. [*The Death of Yugoslavia*]. Translated by Anka Katušić-Balen. Opatija: "Otokar Keršovani."

Šmidt, Josip. 1990. "Plebiscit protuustavan." *Slobodna Dalmacija* ["The Unconstitutional Plebiscite." *Free Dalmatia*]. August 18.

UNSCR - United Nations Security Council Resolutions. (1991). Resolution 713. September 25. Accessed March 27, 2020. http://unscr.com/en/resolutions/doc/713.

Živković, Ilija. 1996. *Ranjena crkva u Hrvatskoj: uništavanje sakralnih objekata u Hrvatskoj (1991.-1995.).* Zagreb: Hrvatska biskupska konferencija: Hrvatski informativni centar: Hrvatska matica iseljenika: Državna uprava za zaštitu kulture i prirodne baštine Hrvatske. [*Wounded Church in Croatia: Destruction of Sacral Objects in Croatia (1991-1995).* Zagreb: Croatian Bishops' Conference: Croatian Information Center: Croatian Heritage Foundation: State Administration for Protection of Culture and Natural Heritage of Croatia].

Žunec, Ozren. 2007. *Goli život I. – Socijetalne dimenzije pobune Srba u Hrvatskoj* [*Bare Life I – the Social Dimensions of the Serb Insurgency in Croatia*]. Zagreb: Demetra.

BIOGRAPHICAL SKETCH

Andrijana Perković Paloš, PhD

Affiliation: External Associate at the University of Split, Faculty of Humanities and Social Sciences, University of Split, Split, Croatia.

Education:

2007-2012 University of Split, Faculty of Philosophy, History and Italian Language and Literature, double studies.

2012-2018 University of Split, Faculty of Humanities and Social Sciences, Doctoral Studies in Modern Croatian History.

2018 Defense of the PhD thesis "Vlada demokratskog jedinstva" ("Democratic Unity Government") under the supervisors Professor Aleksandar Jakir and Professor Ante Nazor at the University of Split, Faculty of Humanities and Social Sciences.

Business Address: University of Split, Faculty of Humanities and Social Sciences, Department of History, Poljička cesta 35, Split, Republic of Croatia.

Research and Professional Experience:

During her graduate and postgraduate studies and teaching some courses as External Associate at the Faculty of Humanities and Social Sciences, Andrijana Perković Paloš showed interest in research of Contemporary Croatian History with emphasis on controversial questions and topics from the Croatian War of Independence. With the topic of Democratic Unity Government as her Doctoral Dissertation, Perković Paloš analyzed certain aspects of Croatian political life during the one-year mandate of the first Croatian multi-party government formed in 1991. Main fields of interests regarding further research are political, military and social history.

Professional Appointments:

2016-2018 – External Associate at the Faculty of Humanities and Social Sciences in Split, Croatia within courses "Introduction to History", "Croatian Society in the 20th century" and "Croatian History after 1945."

2013-2020 – Teacher of History and Italian Language in various Primary and High Schools in Split, Croatia

Publications from the Last 3 Years:

Articles

Perković Paloš, Andrijana. 2020. "Was the Croatian leadership in the 1990s Anti-Semitic?", ST-OPEN, in press.

Books

Perković Paloš, Andrijana. 2020. *Vlada demokratskog jedinstva* [*Democratic Unity Government*]. Hrvatski memorijalno-dokumentacijski Centar Domovinskog rata, in press.

Perković Paloš, Andrijana. 2018. *Djelovanje Matice hrvatske u Brelima od 1993. do 1997. godine.* [*Activity of the Matica Hrvatska in Brela from 1993 to 1997*]. Split: University of Split, Faculty of Philosophy.

Aleksandar Jakir, Andrijana Perković Paloš, & Marin Sabolović, editors 2018. *Hrvatska – put prema teritorijalnoj cjelovitosti, Zbornik radova međunarodnog znanstvenog skupa održanog na Filozofskom fakultetu u Splitu 26. lipnja 2015.* [*Croatia – Path Towards Territorial Integrity. Proceedings From the International Conference Held at the Faculty of Philosophy June 26th 2015*]. Split: University of Split, Faculty of Humanities and Social Sciences: Croatian Homeland War Memorial and Documentation Center.

Chapters in Books

Perković Paloš, Andrijana. 2018. "Uloga predsjednika Tuđmana na putu Hrvatske prema teritorijalnoj cjelovitosti." In *Hrvatska – put prema teritorijalnoj cjelovitosti* ["Role of the President Tuđman in Croatia's Path Towards Territorial Intergity." In *Croatia – Path Towards Territorial Integrity]*, 9-31.

Perković Paloš, Andrijana. 2017. "Suživot Hrvata i Srba tijekom srpske pobune u Hrvatskoj: primjer Sjeverne Dalmacije," In *Vojno-geografski aspekti obrambenoga Domovinskog rata. Zbornik radova znanstveno-stručnog skupa* ["Coexistence of Croats and Serbs During rhe Serb Insurgency in Croatia: Example of the Northern Dalmatia." In *Military-Geographic Aspects of the Defense Homeland War. Proceedings from the Scientific Conference*], edited by Marin Sabolović, 33-47. University of Zadar, Zadar, Croatia.

PART II: PAST IN PRESENT AND FUTURE

In: Croatia: Past, Present and Future Perspectives
Editor: Matko Marušić

ISBN: 978-1-53618-300-9

Chapter 9

CROATIAN-SERBIAN RELATIONS IN THE 19TH AND 20TH CENTURY

Mihovil Biočić*
University of Split School of Medicine
and University Hospital Split, Split, Croatia

ABSTRACT

This work outlines the main historical controversies of the Croatian 19th and 20th century, which have persisted to this day. The chapter analyzes the most important features of Croatian-Serbian relations, origins of political ideas that led to the conflicts between these two nations, and consequences of those conflicts. Presented questions concern Croatian and Serbian political ideas and impact they had on their relations from the mid 19th century through the turbulent and changing political and war situations of the 20th century. That includes Croatian-Serbian relations in the Kingdom of Yugoslavia, the complete breakdown of the Croatian-Serbian relations during World War II, with emphasis on controversies regarding the Ustashas, the Chetniks and the partisans, the suppressed and unsolved national question in Communist Yugoslavia hidden under the phrase of 'brotherhood and unity', and finally Greater-Serbian aggression on Croatia in the 1990s.

Keywords: Croatia, relations with Serbia; controversies, Croatia-Serbia; Croatia, national question; Yugoslavia, Kingdom; Independent State of Croatia; Yugoslavia, Communist rule; Greater Serbia, Croatia; Serbian Orthodox Church, Valerian's Memorandum

INTRODUCTION

The 20th century history of Croats and Croatia is inextricably linked with Serbs and Serbia. The issue is complicated and blurred by changes of political and martial settings; changing episodes of their cooperation and conflicts; wars which brought about tragedies; and hatred and controversies involved in the relations of these two nations. The aim of this

* Professor of Pediatric Surgery (retired). Corresponding Author's Email: mihovil.biocic@gmail.com.

chapter is to address briefly these questions and outline recent findings that differ significantly from the canon of the historiography from the Communist period.

The relations of Croats and Serbs and their controversies from the mid 19th to the end of the 20th century were marked by the Croatian struggle to preserve its autonomy, limited as it may have been, and in the end to achieve a free and independent Croatian state. Serbian politics, on the other hand, strived to expand Serbia's territory at the expense of other nations, among them Croatian, and establish the Greater Serbia based on ethnicity. The project of Greater Serbia (for detailed respective debates, documents, and cartographic reviews, see Čović 1993) included the 'ethnic cleansing' of the territories that Serbs wanted to incorporate into their state..

Research on the Croatian-Serbian relations and on the national question of Croatia in the two Yugoslav states, was influenced by regimes under which the history was studied. There was no free and independent research or discussions about sensitive topics from contemporary history, such as Croatian and Serbian roles in World War II. While Croatian crimes were magnified and Croats portrayed as villains, Serbs as a nation and communists as revolutionaries, and later as policy makers, were presented simultaneously as victims and heroes. Today historians have an obligation to research these topics independently and to unwind the knot that is still taking a toll on relations between Croats and Serbs, as well as Croatia and Serbia, that today are both free and independent, democratic states. Permanent peace and reconciliation in Southeast Europe can be achieved only by means of professional scientific research, analysis of acquired data, dialogue, and – above all – true desire to reach permanent peace and cooperation for a better life of all people concerned.

Croatian-Serbian Relations from the 19th Century to the End of World War I

Formation of modern European nations and building of European national states during the 19th century also impacted Croats and Serbs, whose historical path intertwined from this period to the end of the 20th century. In contrast to the Western European idea of a nation as a community of individuals, with emphasis on social and political interests of an individual person rather than on collective identity, Central and East European nations formed their identity based on language and cultural standardization (Stančić 2002, 22, 29, 38).

Croatian and Serbian National Identities

Formation of Croatian and Serbian national identities as modern European nations and establishment of their national states occurred in different political frameworks and did not happen simultaneously. Serbs achieved their independent state after liberating their territories from the Ottomans, under whom they had lived since they lost the battle of Kosovo in 1389. In contrast to other South Slav nations, Serbs were the first to establish themselves as a modern state (Antić 2007, 19). In 1878 at the Berlin Congress, the Kingdom of Serbia was internationally recognized. However, the 19th century was not only the century of independence of the Serbian nation and standardization of their language, but also the beginning of their political agenda of creating Greater Serbia. The Greater Serbia idea aimed to expand Serbian territory, i.e., "include adjacent areas that objectively belong to other nations and countries or state communities" (Antić 2007, 9). Strategically, the expansion relied on the imposition of Serbian language on other nations and the expansion of the Serbian Orthodox Church (Srpska pravoslavna crkva – SPC) to as large a territory as possible. In 1557, the Turkish Serb Mehmed-pasha Sokolović, the Grand Vizier (the first ruler after the Sultan), appointed his brother Makarija to head the Patriarchate of Peć. Since then, the Serbian Orthodox Church has spread to the territories (Croatia, Bosnia and Hercegovina, Hungary etc.) conquered by the Ottoman Empire (Štefan 1999, 11). This concept would mark a significant part of Serbian and Croatian history, as well as the history of other South Slav nations.

At the time of formation of the Kingdom of Serbia, Croatian lands were within the Austro-Hungarian Monarchy, known as the Triune Kingdom of Croatia, Slavonia and Dalmatia. For centuries, they were part of Mediterranean and Central European political, social and cultural framework but also were separated politically and administratively. The Kingdom of Croatia-Slavonia from 1867 was under the Hungarian half of Austria-Hungary, whereas Kingdom of Dalmatia was part of the Austrian half (Antić 2007, 19, 21). In such conditions, Croats strived to preserve their national identity and autonomy.

"South Slav" or "Yugoslav" Idea

Standardization of the Croatian language on the basis of Shtokavian dialect initiated the process of integration of disunited Croatian provinces and the formation of modern Croatian nation (H. Matković 1998, 16, see also Chapter 2). However, constant danger of Germanisation and Hungarisation compelled the Croatian political elite to find support for their political goals in a wider, South Slav cultural and political framework (H. Matković 1998, 16-17; Stančić 2002, 188; Kljaić 2012, 184). The Croatian idea of the formation of a common state of South Slavs emerged on the basis of their ethnic, linguistic, and cultural similarity and their common interest in the struggle for liberation against foreign rule. The difference was that Croatia was opposing Germanisation and Hungarisation, whereas Serbia already had achieved its independence from the Ottoman rule and had the upper hand and the strategy of expansion in the Greater Serbia.

While the South Slav or the Yugoslav idea in the 19th century was promulgated predominantly in cultural circles in Croatia, at the beginning of the 20th century it became the foundation of a concrete political program (H. Matković 1998, 16). However, the fact that the area where South Slavs lived in the 19th century was divided between different imperial and religious traditions was the key hidden weakness in the idea of Yugoslavism (Kljaić 2012, 184). As mentioned before, Croatian identity was developing in the Central European and Mediterranean Catholic frameworks, whereas Serbian identity was inextricably linked to its Orthodox-Byzantine heritage. Centuries-old Ottoman rule also left its mark regarding political traditions in Serbia. Conditions that compelled Croats to rely on their South Slavic neighbors in order to resist the pressure from Austrians and Hungarians turned out to be favorable for Greater-Serbian territorial aspirations.

Greater-Serbian Plans: Ideological Foundation of the Future Conflicts

Origins of the Greater-Serbian project lie in the writings of two Serbian figures from the 19th century. Considering that language was the main component of national identity at the time, it was not a coincidence that one of the best known architects of the Greater-Serbian project was philologist, linguist and one of the reformers of the Serbian language Vuk Stefanović Karadžić. In his article "Serbs All and Everywhere" ("Srbi svi i svuda") written in 1836 and published in his book "Manual for History, Language and Customs for Serbs of all Three Laws" in 1849, he claimed that all South Slavs who spoke the Shtokavian dialect were Serbs and were speaking the Serbian language (Antić 2007, 55; H. Matković 1998, 22). Since Shtokavian dialect was present in significant parts of Croatia and Bosnia and Herzegovina (BH), he "converted" the population of these lands to Serbs, claiming that Shtokavian Croats were in fact the Catholic Serbs. His goal was to assimilate great majority of the Catholic Croats and BH Muslims (Banac 1995, 85).

A minister in the Government of the Kingdom of Serbia, Ilija Garašanin, elaborated Karadžić's ideas in his secret writing "Načertanije", short for "The Program of Serbian Foreign and National policy at the end of 1844" which became public only in 1906. Garašanin used the work of a Czech linguist František Zach as a template and transformed it. According to Zach, South Slavs were a larger group of nations that were similar to each other, whereas Garašanin claimed that South Slavs were simply Serbs divided into two categories – Catholic and Orthodox. He advocated for expansion of Serbia to BH, Montenegro and Macedonia and, through Albania, to the Adriatic. A large part of the Croatian territory was also included in the Greater-Serbian program (Garašanin, n.d.; Bataković 2014, 245-260). By annexing Croatian and Slovenian lands to the future Greater Serbia, all Serbs would gather into one country (H. Matković 1998, 21-22; Antić 2007, 91, 121). It should be noted that the expansionist Serbian policy was applied not only to Croats but also to Albanians and others. The Serbian Army in the Balkan Wars in 1912 and 1913 occupied Kosovo and Albania and committed horrific crimes against Albanian civilians, among them women, children, and the elderly population (Štefan 1999, 16-19).

Expansionism became the main principle of Serbian policy (Banac 1995, 87). New Serbia was to be the successor to the medieval Serbian Empire and the basis of the Serbian domination in the Balkans. As Matković (1998, 24) pointed out, "imperialism became the foundation of the Serbian long-term policy" and they disregarded the existence of other South Slav nations or their national interests.

Because of these agendas, some political parties and politicians in Croatia, such as the founders of the Party of Rights, Ante Starčević and Eugen Kvaternik, considered this Serbian policy a serious threat. Furthermore, motivated by the lack of reactions from the Croatian political elite to Karadžić's writing, Starčević did respond to his linguistic aggression. He strongly refuted the national identity of Serbs and considered that etymologic word "Serb" derived from the Latin "servus", which means servant (Holjevac 1999, 306; Banac 1995, 92; H. Matković 1998, 24). Starčević and Kvaternik saw the future of Croats in a free and independent state (H. Matković 1998, 25-26).

Eve of World War I: "Till the Annihilation, Yours or Ours"

As Antić (2007, 115-121) noted, writings of Karadžić and Garašanin had an almost "immediate impact on political modeling of Serbs in Croatia." A Serbian newspaper from Zagreb "Srbobran" at the beginning of the 20th century claimed that all Serbs should live in one country and that should include BH, Montenegro, Kosovo, and Macedonia, as well as Dalmatia, Syrmia, Slavonia, and Lika in Croatia (Antić 2007, 123-124). Moreover, "Srbobran" proclaimed Dalmatia to be a Serbian land (Antić 2007, 130). To mobilize Serbs in Croatia, the allegations of endangerment of Serbs in Croatia were constantly repeated (Antić 2007, 124, 130).

In 1902, relations between Croats and Serbs in Croatia deteriorated. It was the year in which "Srbobran" published an article written by Serbian writer and politician Nikola Stojanović, entitled "Serbs and Croats." In this article, which is also known as "Till the annihilation, yours or ours," originally published in "Srpski književni glasnik" (Serbian Literary Magazine) from Belgrade, the author claimed that Serbs were a nation formed in medieval times, unlike Croats who, according to him, did not have their own national identity and were already on their way to become Serbs. He described Croats and Serbs as two opposite "parties" that would fight until the extermination of one of them, and predicted that in that fight Croats would be annihilated (Stojanović 1902, 1149-59; Antić 2007, 266-272). Vigorous anti-Serbian demonstrations erupted in Zagreb as a reaction to the article even though the response of Croatian politicians was muted (Artuković 2010).

Nevertheless, such aggravation of Croatian-Serbian relations did not stop cooperation of certain Croatian and Serbian political groups in Croatia. Their goal was stopping German "Drang nach Osten" by uniting Dalmatia with Croatia and Slovenia, and eventually forming independent South Slav state (Banac 1995, 100; Stančić 2002, 198-199). This led to the formation of the Croatian-Serbian Coalition on December 12, 1905. The text of the "Manifest on the Establishment of the Croatian-Serbian Coalition" can be found in H. Matković (2006, 217-218). It is important to stress that in the course of the 19th and 20th century Serbian political elite in Croatia often oscillated between support of the Croatian struggle for autonomy and cooperation with the Croatian political elite and between their blind following of Belgrade's Greater-Serbian policy; Stančić (2002, 188) noted that such shifts represented the lasting core of the conflict between Croats and Serbs in Croatia.

World War I: Framework for Croatian-Serbian Relations

International situation and territorial claims of some European countries on Croatian territory further influenced Croatian-Serbian relations. Among the members of the two military alliances formed at the eve of World War I, the Triple Alliance and the Entente, three countries strived to annex certain parts of Croatian lands. They were all neighboring countries of Italy, Serbia, and Austria-Hungary (Zöllner and Schüssel 1997, 266; Cravetto 2007, 40; Dirlmer 1999, 191). "The London Treaty" in 1915 officially sanctioned Italian aspirations towards eastern-Adriatic coast and islands. With the Treaty, members of the Entente granted Italy the right to the Croatian part of the Adriatic coast if Italy would join them. The transcript of the Treaty is published in H. Matković (2006, 219-225).

Suffice to say that Croatian politicians tried to avoid these scenarios. They feared the continuation of Croatia's subordinate position in the Austro-Hungarian Monarchy, but they also could not disregard the possible threat of fragmentation of Croatian lands between Austria-Hungary, Italy and Serbia (Stančić 2002, 204). Some Croatian politicians wanted all lands inhabited by Croats, Slovenes and Serbs to unite into one independent unit under the Habsburg dynasty (H. Matković 2006, 226). Others advocated for collaboration with Serbia and saw the future of Croatia outside of the Austria-Hungary Monarchy.

Croatian politicians Ante Trumbić and Frano Supilo, who emigrated during the war, formed the Yugoslav Committee in London with the support of the Serbian Government (Pavličević 2000, 307). It consisted of Croatian, Slovene, and Serbian politicians and strived to form a new federative South Slav state that would guarantee equality to all its nations (Stančić 2002, 205). In contrast to that, Serbia still strived to achieve Greater-Serbian plans, which meant to annex all South Slavs, except for Bulgarians, to the Kingdom of Serbia (Antić 2007, 139). The idea that Serbian people would have sovereignty, whereas Croats and Slovenes would just merge with Serbs into one nation (H. Matković 1998, 29) indicates similarities with Stojanović's proclamation on annihilation of Croats in the mentioned article "Croats and Serbs". The only difference was that Serbian Government would realize the idea through political unification, and not through war. As Antić (2007, 92) pointed out, "there is no doubt that Serbian Empire was being built on ethnic nationalism, and so it would make room for only Serbian nation. Hence the state would also be centralist." Apart from that, he noted that throughout the 20th century Serbs severely opposed the establishment of a federative state, which Croats proposed.

The Serbian Government and the Yugoslav Committee in July 1917 signed the Corfu Declaration in which they agreed to form the Kingdom of Serbs, Croats and Slovenes, emphasizing that they would decide on structuring the state after its establishment. The transcript of the Declaration is published in H. Matković (2006, 227-230). The leader of the Croatian-Serbian Coalition formed in Croatia by the end of 1905, Serbian-Croatian politician Svetozar Pribićević, tried to carry out the unification as soon as possible and without any conditions (Stančić 2002, 207). The National Council (Narodno vijeće – NV), formed in October 1918, in Zagreb, Croatia, declared itself a political representative body of South Slavs in Austro-Hungary. The document on its establishment "Program and Organization Rules of the National Council of Slovenes, Croats and Serbs" ("Pravilnik o programu i organizaciji Narodnog vijeća Slovenaca, Hrvata i Srba") is published in the book "Documents on Yugoslavia" (Čulinović 1968, 68-69). The same month the Croatian Parliament (Hrvatski sabor) broke off all legal ties to the Monarchy and proclaimed that Croatian lands would join the new state called State of Slovenes, Croats and Serbs (State of SHS) (Država Slovenaca, Hrvata i Srba – Država SHS) led by the National Council. This document can be found in Čulinović (1968, 76-77). The State that included significant parts of Austria-Hungary inhabited by Slovenes, Croats, and Serbs was only a provisory entity until the final union with Serbia (H. Matković 1998, 49-50).

The president of the National Council Anton Korošec and Serbian Government's president Nikola Pašić, in the presence of Trumbić and Serbian opposition, signed a treaty called Geneva Declaration. The Declaration proclaimed equality of the State of SHS and Kingdom of Serbia. It stated that the new state would have joint government for Foreign Affairs, Army and Navy, the State of SHS and the Kingdom of Serbia would separately govern their own Internal Affairs. This, however, was not in accordance with the Greater-

Serbian policy, so Pašić withdrew his signature and the Declaration was never ratified. The National Council was too weak to insist on the initial agreement and accepted to create a joint state with the Serbian Government (Šišić 1920, 236-237).

Pribićević, who dominated the National Council, advocated for unification of the State of SHS with the Kingdom of Serbia as quickly as possible, so he and Croatian politician Ante Pavelić (not to be confused with the Poglavnik of the Independent State of Croatia formed in World War II) led the delegation of the National Council consisting of 28 members to Belgrade (Matijević 2008, 65). Leader of the Croatian Peasant Party (CPP) (Hrvatska seljačka stranka – HSS) Stjepan Radić warned the delegates not to go to Belgrade and not to conclude any agreement on unification before the position of Croatia in the new state was determined (H. Matković 1998, 54-59).

Under pressure from Serbs, Croatian delegates gave up on their condition regarding the guarantee of equality of all nations in the common country. On December 1, 1918, Serbian king Aleksandar Karađorđević proclaimed in Belgrade the new state, the Kingdom of Serbs, Croats and Slovenes (the Kingdom of SHS). Such unification embedded into the foundation of the new country the seeds of future instability that would eventually lead to its disintegration (Stančić 2002, 208).

Croatia in the Kingdom of Serbs, Croats and Slovenes

Radić's warnings to Croatian delegates in National Council proved to be correct, as Croatia entered the new state unprepared for what was coming. One of the most notable changes was that Croatia, for centuries tied to the Habsburgs and to the Central Europe, now for the first time was bound to a state with its capital in the southeastern Europe, in Belgrade. Croatian political elites did not comprehend that they were to lead Croatia, a central European country, into the union of countries that had very different political backgrounds and traditions (Stančić 2002, 208). Consequently, they did not understand the request of Frano Supilo to postpone the unification until Serbia transformed itself (B. Boban 2019, 28). Since 1918, the year that proved to be a historic turning point for Croatia, the fate of Croatia and Croats up to the end of the 20th century would depend on Croatian-Serbian relations (Stančić 2002, 209).

First Victims of the Serbian Policy

Two events foretold Croatia's future relations and position in the new country. The first event occurred during the World War I. In 1915, the Serbian Government's president Nikola Pašić and his associates planned to form Serbian Volunteer Corps, composed of South Slav war prisoners who had fought in the Austro-Hungarian units. The majority of the Corps were to be Serbs, and only a small part were to include Croats and Slovenes. Pašić saw in the Corps an opportunity to spread the Serbian name and empower Serbian goals of expanding the Serbian ethnic lands (Knez 2017, 169). While Croatian and Slovene soldiers wanted to fight under the South Slav or Yugoslav name, Serbian officers and soldiers insisted exclusively on the Serbian name. In Odessa where the units had been organized, a number

Croatian soldiers who refused to fight under the Serbian flag and wear Serbian insignia were killed (Knez 2017, 173; Banac 1995, 122). This case was indication of the future relations in the common state of Croats and Serbs. According to the prominent Croatian writer Miroslav Krleža: "In the first ten years of the Yugoslav state: 24 political death penalties, 600 political murders, 30,000 political imprisonments, 3,000 political emigrants…" (Curać 2015).

The other event occurred only few days after the unification. As Croatian politicians were frustrated with the methods of unification, mainly because they wanted a republic and not a monarchy, on December 5, 1918 protesters, mostly members of the Croatian military units that had been part of the former Austro-Hungarian army, protested on the main square in Zagreb against the unification and applauded calls for a Croatian republic. The regime with its military units responded with arms. Thirteen people were killed and seventeen wounded. Croatian historiography calls this event "December Victims" and interprets it as a harbinger of future methods of the Belgrade regime when it came to dealing with conflicts with Croatia (Pavličević 2000, 320; Bilandžić 1999, 72; H. Matković 1998, 84; Banac 1995, 206). After that event, Croatian military units of the National Council were disbanded or joined the Serbian army (Pavličević 2000, 332-333). This event "poisoned the political mood" and "announced series of measures aiming to eliminate administrative autonomy of Croatia eventually" (Banac 1995, 207).

Serbian Domination in the Kingdom of SHS

In the new state, Croatia lost its autonomy and all ancient attributes of its statehood for the first time in history. Evidence for that is cancellation of the activity of the Croatian Parliament (Sabor), which had existed from the 13th century, the elimination of the position of Croatian 'ban' or 'viceroy' who had governed Croatia since the early medieval period, and loss of the military units (Pavličević 2000, 314, 332-333). As H. Matković (1998, 86) stressed, Serbs "from the first day imposed their domination over other nations. The loss of statehood was the source of Croatian discontent and that with the time became stimulus and focal point of the Croatian national movement." One of the indicators of the Serbian domination was their disproportionate representation in the first Government, formed December 18, 1918 and led by a Serb Stojan Protić (Table 1).

Table 1. The composition of the first government in the Kingdom of SHS (Pavličević 2000, 333; Petranović 1980, 3)

Nationality of ministers	Number (%) in the government	Percentage of population in the Kingdom of SHS
Serbs	14 (66.7)	39
Croats	4 (19.0)	23.9
Slovenes	2 (9.5)	8.5
Muslims	1 (4.8)	6.3

Already from the beginning of the mandate, the Government of the Kingdom of SHS was very severe in sanctions against all political opponents (Pavličević 2000, 345). Northwestern states Croatia and Slovenia were the most developed economically and culturally in the Kingdom of SHS, whereas the east and the south of the country (Serbia, Montenegro, Macedonia, Kosovo and BH) were underdeveloped. Thus, Belgrade manipulated economy, banking, taxing, and government funds in order to exploit these richer parts of the country. One of the examples was the exchange of the Austro-Hungarian currency 'crown' or 'krone' into the Serbian 'dinar' in 1919. As Kolar-Dimitrijević (2018, 147) pointed out, since "not all of the banknotes could be replaced at once, stamped and marked banknotes of the krone remained in circulation until early 1923 outside of Serbia proper, where a strong dinar currency was immediately created. When used for the payment of taxes and other levies to the state, these banknotes were exchanged for the dinar at a rate of 4 to 1." Accordingly, the capital of the former State of SHS and its population was reduced by 75% (Pavličević 2000, 337). This measure ruined savings of the population that lived in the areas of the former Austro-Hungary and strengthened Serbian purchasing power (Banac 1995, 214). These measures in every branch of the economy contributed to deterioration of national relations.

The Serbian Government conducted systematic policy of changing the demographics of the Croatian ethnic territory by colonizing eastern parts of Croatia – Bačka, Banat, Syrmia, Slavonia and Baranja – with Serbs and Montenegrins (Pavličević 2000, 337).

One of the few positive outcomes of the unification was the fact that almost the entire Croatian historical territory and other territories with Croatian majorities found itself in one country. However, this did not ameliorate the discontent and frustrations among Croats caused by the Treaty of Rapallo signed November 12, 1920, which granted Italy the peninsula of Istria and significant part of the Dalmatian coast. The transcript of the Treaty is published in H. Matković (2006, 275-278) and Čulinović (1968, 200-203). In addition, with the Roman Treaty signed between Benito Mussolini and Nikola Pašić in 1924, the Kingdom of SHS handed to Italy the very important Croatian port city of Rijeka, that had been previously occupied by Italian fascists, (Radelić 2006a, 23). The text of the original document can be found in H. Matković (2006, 279) and Čulinović (1968, 210).

One of the most important changes for Croatia in the new country was the fact that the Kingdom of SHS was formed of nations that prior to the unification had developed in different cultural traditions. As already mentioned, Croatia was part of the Central European and Mediterranean cultural and political tradition, BH was exposed to Islamic traditions of the Ottoman Empire whereas Serbia belonged to the Orthodox-Byzantine tradition and were also heavily influenced by Ottomans. That means that some Serbian leaders from the 19th century, who were raised in the Ottoman society, reflected their ruling style, meaning, they "introduced the despotic form of Government" (Banac 1995, 140). Banac (1995, 139) noted that these differences were most evident "in the area of Government institutions". For example, Serbian king Aleksandar Obrenović was killed in a military coup d'etat and Petar I Karađorđević was installed as the new king in stark contrast with the ways of solving political conflicts in Austria-Hungary.

The Belgrade regime did not acknowledge differences of these traditions: rather there was a strong tendency of unification and formation of the singular Yugoslav culture under the Serbian dominion. Nevertheless, despite all efforts, these different cultures could not be merged into one, so "the dissimilarity of cultural traditions still continued." Exemplary was language as an important feature of national identity and unique cultural heritage (see Chapter 2). This aggressive policy of unification, especially in language, was reinforced by the Vidovdan Constitution, proclaimed in 1921 without Croatian representatives (Pavličević 2000, 346). The Constitution legalized the centralism in the Kingdom of SHS and stated that there was only one nation in the country, but the said nation had three names – Serbian,

Croatian and Slovenian. The other assertion was that there were "three tribes of one nation" and there was only one language "Serbian-Croatian-Slovene" (H. Matković 1998, 96-97).

The Constitution was also used as a means to fight against "all attempts of establishing of national equality" (H. Matković 1998, 99). Most Serbian politicians, especially the radical ones, did not consider Yugoslavia a new state, but only expansion of the Serbian territory (Banac 1995, 207). This we can see in the position of Catholic and Serbian Orthodox Churches. By November 1920, there were several independent Orthodox churches in Croatia – Metropolis in Srijemski Karlovci, BH autonomous Orthodox Church, and Orthodox Church in Dalmatia (Lozo 2017, 102). However, in 1920, the Serbian Orthodox patriarchate was established in Srijemski Karlovci and all other Orthodox metropolis and churches in the Kingdom were incorporated in it. In that way, the Serbian Orthodox Church became dominant in the Kingdom of SHS. All Orthodox Christians in the Kingdom – Macedonians, Montenegrins, Vlachs, Croats, Bulgarians, Romanians, Albanians, etc. – were subservient to the Belgrade's Patriarch and from then on were considered Serbian Orthodox (Lozo 2017, 102). The Serbian Orthodox Church had the privileged position in the Kingdom, whereas the Catholic Church was only tolerated (Pavličević 2000, 377).

The first law after passing the Constitution was the State Protection Law in August 1921, which imposed severe penalties, even the death penalty, for every activity that one could interpret as "anti-state" (Pavličević 2000, 346). This law primarily struck the Communist Party of Yugoslavia (CPY) (Komunistička partija Jugoslavije - KPJ), and later the other parties, for instance in 1924 it struck also the Croatian Peasant Party because of its joining to the Communist International (Išek 1971, 37).

Among Serbs in Croatia, the Independent Democratic Party (IDP) (Samostalna demokratska stranka - SDS) led by Svetozar Pribićević was the strongest. As Banac (1995, 205) noted, due to Belgrade's centralism and resistance among non-Serbian nations, "the national question became the most important problem of the internal relations in Yugoslavia". The core of the national question, in fact, was "the conflict between supporters of several antagonistic national ideologies", which reflected in the struggle about the very structure of the state.

In that period the Croatian Peasant Party and its charismatic leader Stjepan Radić became the voice of Croatia. After the elections in 1920, the party gained 50 representatives in National Assembly in Belgrade and became the fourth most powerful party in the Kingdom of SHS (Pavličević 2000, 339), but also the leader of the national movement in Croatia. Radić and his party often raised the issue of the position of Croats and Croatia in the Kingdom of SHS and advocated for Croatian sovereignty as one of equal units in a federative country (H. Matković 1998, 108). The subordinate position of Croats in their relations to Serbs as well as the goal that Croats wanted to achieve in their common state was best described by Radić's statement that "a Croat wants a Serb for his brother, and not for his sovereign" (Pavličević 2000, 338). The behavior of Serbian regime towards non-Serbian nations in the Kingdom can be impressively illustrated by its treatment of Macedonians (today Republic of North Macedonia); the regime insisted that Macedonians are Serbs and forced the entire population to change their first and last names to sound as Serbian (Apostolski et al. 1969, 12-13), for example a man Grkovski Dimitar to Atanasiević Dimitrije or a woman Alačka Rada to Alačević Radojka (Mazganski 2012).

The Murder of Stjepan Radić and the Dictatorship of King Aleksandar

Belgrade's centralist policy led to collaboration of the Croatian Peasant Party and Independent Democratic Party, and the two parties formed the Peasant-Democratic Coalition (PDC) (Seljačko-Demokratska Koalicija – SDK) in 1927. Some consider this Pribićević's sudden turn as his realization that the centralist policy was the main threat to the existence of the country (Karaula, 2015, 89; Pavličević, 354). The aim of the Coalition was fighting against centralism and Serbian hegemony (Pavličević 2000, 354-356). When at the beginning of June 1928 Radić proposed reconstructing the country in a way that implied a confederation, the reaction from Belgrade was severe. The pro-regime newspaper "Jedinstvo" wrote that "Radić must be eliminated" (Pavličević 2000, 357). Soon after the threat became reality.

In the National Assembly in Belgrade, one of the People's Radical Party representatives Puniša Račić on June 20, 1928 shot with a revolver and killed two Croatian representatives and wounded three, among them Stjepan Radić. Words of the prominent Croatian sculptor Ivan Meštrović indicated the severity of the event: "I felt that that shot, fired at Radić, was really intended at the whole Croatian nation" (Meštrović 1993, 174). After the assassination there were several demonstrations in Croatia. Radić died on August 8, 1928 from complications of the gunshot wound. After his death, the new leader of the Croatian Peasant Party became Vladko Maček. The Coalition called for change of the Constitution, federalization of the country and the autonomy for Croatia (Pavličević 2000, 363).

This violent and barbaric method of solving political disputes shocked Croats and provoked widespread demonstrations which provided a pretext for King Aleksandar's decision on January 6, 1929 to abolish the Constitution, prohibit all political parties, dismiss the Assembly, and proclaim dictatorship. The transcript of the document is published in H. Matković (2006, 304-305) and Čulinović (1968, 291-292). That same year he renamed the country into the Kingdom of Yugoslavia and divided it into nine provinces ('banovinas'), so that Croatian ethnic and historical lands would be dismembered (Skupina autora 2007, 61) and Croatian historical regions would be ultimately forgotten. This was part of the plan to abolish Croatia as a political entity and suppress the Croatian identity (Jonjić 2000, 21). Displaying Croatian flags and other national symbols was prohibited, and freedom of speech was limited.

This led to retaliation by some Croatian political actors. For example, in March 1929 two young members of the Croatian Party of Rights Marko Hranilović and Matija Soldin killed one of the associates of King Aleksandar, Toni Schlegel. In the Hranilović-Soldin trial, they were sentenced to death by hanging (Jonjić 2009, 186).

Assassinations and attempts of assassinations of influential Croatian intellectuals and politicians also marked this period. Prominent Croatian historian and member of the Croatian Party of Rights Milan Šufflay was murdered in Zagreb, in 1931. His murder caused Albert Einstein and Heinrich Mann to address the League for Rights of Man to take actions against the "horrible brutality" of the Belgrade regime, asking that the League would stand up for Croats and "protect this small, peaceful and highly civilized people" (New York Times 1931a). Einstein also accused King Aleksandar of "having been implicated" in Radić's murder (New York Times 1931b).

There was also an attempted assassination of the Croatian writer Mile Budak, and in the same period Vladko Maček was imprisoned. Such conditions damaged the reputation of the country, especially in the eyes of France, which had very good relations with Yugoslavia, so King Aleksandar was urged to pass a new Constitution and to reestablish the Parliament. The King complied, however the changes did not reflect the reality of the country, which remained "dictatorship and absolutism" (Pavličević 2000, 366).

As a response, in 1932 the Peasant-Democratic Coalition passed a political program entitled "Zagrebačke punktacije" ("Zagreb Points") that condemned Serbian hegemony and suggested that things should go back to 1918 and that the country should be reconstructed in a way that would guarantee the equality of all nations in Yugoslavia (Povijest Hrvata 2007, 64-65). "Zagrebačke punktacije" was a political program not just of Croats but also of major part of Serbs in Croatia. Because of that, political persecution of the Croatian Peasant Party and Independent Demoratic Party leaders began. Maček was convicted to three years in prison on charges that he attempted to separate Croatia from Yugoslavia (Pavličević 2000, 368).

The situation in Yugoslavia concerned some Western European countries, such as the United Kingdom. Two British politicians, Ben Riley and Rhys J. Davies, visited Belgrade in September 1932. In the magazine "Manchester Guardian" of September 30, 1932, they wrote an unsigned article in which they presented a summary of conversations they had had with Maček and Trumbić. Both Croatian politicians had pleaded for secession of Croatia from Yugoslavia; however the politicians disagreed and concluded that Yugoslavia should not be dismembered. After the publication of the article, the already severe campaign of the Belgrade regime against Maček and Trumbić intensified, and even their lives were threatened. In response, Trumbić wrote an article in the "Manchester Guardian" in which he claimed that the report by the said British politicians was not accurate and he refuted their conclusions; he also elaborated on the position of Croatia in Yugoslavia, depicting different cultural and political traditions of Croatia and Serbia prior to their unification, continuing with the Serbian domination in Yugoslavia and stressing the importance of the unsolved "Croatian question", i.e., the loss of Croats' autonomy and their rights. The transcript of the Trumbić's article was published in Boban (1971, 159-176) and S. Matković and Trogrlić (2019, 338-339; 341-362).

After the first article in the "Manchester Guardian" and Trumbić's response, in October 1932 the two British politicians wrote a report for British political circles briefly describing the history of Croats as well as the status of Croatia in Yugoslavia. They wrote that the Croats settled down in these countries in the sixth century and created and organized their own State; that in the 12th century Croatia formed a personal union with Hungary and with Austria in the sixteenth century; that both unions lasted till the end of the Great War and that Croats never regained a single State; that the Croatian national character was formed under the influence of the Western nations while the Serbian character was influenced by Byzantium on one side and by the Ottoman Turks on the other (Riley and Davies 1932, see also Chapter 1).

Riley and Davies continued to describe thoroughly the status of Croatia in Yugoslavia after the unification. They wrote that the King prohibited the use of the Croatian name and Croatian national flag, dismissed all Croatian national parties as well as Croatian national institutions, banned all free manifestations of Croatian national life, swamped Croatian lands with police and his agents and supported police brutality. They also wrote about Radić's murder and the dictatorship of King Aleksandar. Riley and Davies also looked back on the status of the Croatian soldiers in the Yugoslav Army. Stating that although Croats have "always been considered one of the greatest soldiers" during the Austria-Hungary, "today they are completely excluded from the higher positions in the Yugoslav Army" and that "among numerous colonels and less numerous generals, not one Croat could be found" (Riley and Davies 1932). They concluded the report asserting that "the present state of affairs cannot last much longer," and that some changes needed to be made (Riley and Davies 1932). Such report by these British politicians shows us that political and diplomatic circles already at the beginning of the 1930s knew that the Yugoslav state was unnatural creation with an uncertain future.

Pribićević, who wanted to cooperate with the opposition to the regime inside Serbia itself, was put under house arrest. Later he emigrated to Paris and Prague. In 1933 his 'book of accusations', "The Dictatorship of King Aleksandar", which was really his personal experience and experience of Serbs from BH and Croatia in the Kingdom of Yugoslavia, was published in Paris (Pavličević 2000, 365-366). In his book he denounced the policy of Serbia at the time in very strong terms:

"I cannot condemn too severely the policy pursued by Belgrade against the Croats. I should not like at the moment, to say too much about the Serbs outside of Serbia. First of all, I will speak of the Croats. Before the World War I constantly had occasion to eulogize in the 'Srbobran' of Zagreb [former organ of Pribićević's Party in Austria-Hungary] the measure of liberty which reigned in Serbia. I constantly insisted to the Croats that they would see what liberty meant after they would be united with Serbia. Events have utterly belied my words. Instead of the home of liberty that she was before the war, Belgrade has become a center of violence, of reaction and autocracy, without its equal in ferocity and unscrupulousness in any other Balkan country; still less in the rest of Europe." (Pribićević 2000, 71).

Shortly before the New Year of 1934, Pribićević sent a letter to Serbs from Paris. Among other things, he wrote: "Serbs need to see and understand that they do not have any moral, political, national or historical rights to rule over Croats and to keep them in community with them by force (dictatorship). The historical experience has showed that [mountain] Velebit will crush in the see and Dunav (Danube), Sava and Drava will dry up before the Croatian people give up their name and their national individuality." He continued that Serbs should "recognize the right to Croats to freely decide on their own about the idea of the state union with Serbs and to decide on their future." Pribićević further stressed that he could not even imagine that "Serbs would fight Croats because they [Croats] would not live together with them, that Serbs would with fire and sword impose the common state to Croats." (Pribićević 2000, 301-307).

The attitude of Serbian political elites in the first Yugoslavia was criticized even by some Serbian communists in the second Yugoslavia. Serbian historian and Secretary of the Central Committee of the Communist Party of Serbia from 1969 to 1972, Latinka Perović once said that "Serbian nationalists did not only kill their own rulers, but also three Croatian representatives in the Parliament, including Stjepan Radić..." Then she said to Serbs: "You want the common state, and yet you kill the political representatives of the Croatian people in the Parliament!? It was the end of the first Yugoslavia." (Sejdinović 2019).

The Ustasha Movement and the Assassination of King Aleksandar

The murder of Stjepan Radić in 1928 and the King's dictatorship that followed motivated right-wing Croatian politicians who saw Croatia's future only outside of Yugoslavia. The Head of the Croatian Party of Rights Ante Pavelić claimed that Croats could not live in the same country with Serbs. During the dictatorship, Pavelić emigrated to Austria and there he connected with some other emigrants, such as Vanča Mihajlov, the leader of the Macedonian political emigration which strived to overthrow Yugoslavia as well. After Belgrade sentenced Pavelić to death in absentia, Austria expelled him but Mussolini's Italy welcomed him. There in 1930 he established Ustasha – Croatian Revolutionary Organization (Jareb 2006, 112). It was a nationalist movement with the aim of freeing Croatia from Yugoslavia by armed uprising (Jareb 2006, 114; H. Matković 2006, 319).

They conducted several actions against the Belgrade regime. One of the well-known actions of the Ustashas was the attack on the police station in Lika, Croatia in 1932. After the attack, Croats in the neighborhood were severely punished for the Ustashas' actions, and some of them even murdered under the accusation of being members of the Ustasha movement (Pavličević 2000, 370).

The best known Ustashas action was the assassination of King Aleksandar in Marseilles in 1934, in cooperation with the Internal Macedonian Revolutionary Organization (IMRO) (Vnatrešna Makedonska Revolucionerna Organizacija – VMRO). It was Ustashas first step towards the breakup of Yugoslavia and their ultimate goal of creating an independent Croatian state (Pavličević 2000, 371-372). From then on, as Pavličević (2000, 373) wrote, "Croatian and Serbian extremists encouraged the spirit of revanchism, announced new actions and predicted the near end of the unnatural alliance of Croats and Serbs in that artificial 'Versaille creation'", in other words the near end of the Kingdom of Yugoslavia.

Killings and Terror

Oppression by the Belgrade regime prompted prominent Croatian historian Ivo Pilar to compare the position of Croatia in the Kingdom of Yugoslavia to the one in Austria-Hungarian Monarchy, claiming that the Kingdom of Yugoslavia was "more a dungeon of nations than Austria-Hungary ever had been" (Pilar 1997, 17-18; Pavličević 2000, 331). His writings turned out to put him in danger. He shared the same fate with his colleague Milan Šufflay: in the fall of 1933, Pilar was found dead (Pavličević 2000, 370). In this period, Croatian-Serbian relations were aggravated even more. Serbian radicals in Croatia established Chetnik military organizations that had existed since the 19th century in Serbia itself. They were loyal to the Belgrade regime (Karaula 2014, 64, 67). Regular Serbian military units also performed some police assignments together with Gendarmes ('žandari') (a rural police) and they played a crucial role in the oppression of any kind of opposition to the Belgrade regime (Karaula 2014, 77). Chetniks and Gendarmes terrorized, tortured, and murdered Croatian peasants, especially in the period from 1935 to 1937 (Pavličević 2000, 375).

Violent conflicts and attacks occurred in numerous Croatian villages and towns. Pavličević (2000, 375) singled out three notorious "bloody episodes" from that time, known as victims of Sibinj, Vrba and Ruščica, and Senj. In Sibinj, 19 February 1935, after a mass in the village's church, local Gendarmes killed 8 Croatian peasants, and wounded, imprisoned, and beat many more of them. The day after, peasants from villages Vrbe and Ruščice protested against this attack and 5 of them were beaten by Gendarmes while one of them was shot. Two years later, Gendarmes murdered 7 young Croatian men and women who came from Sarajevo to Senj to the concert of a Croatian choir, waving Croatian flags. As Karaula (2014, 95) noted, from the beginning of 1936 "the wave of violence and terror of Chetnik troops and certain groups of Orthodox population against Croatian population continued."

As nothing was accomplished by appeals and memorandums that Croatian emigrants and the archbishop of Zagreb were writing to the League of Nations and to the Serbian Prince Pavle, the regent to the Crown Prince Petar after the death of King Aleksandar, the Croatian Peasant Party formed the Croatian Civil and Peasant Defense. The goal of this organization was the defense of Croats against the regime's brutality (Pavličević 2000, 376; Karaula 2014, 73-152).

Such conditions forced Croatian politicians to talk more and more about the "Croatian question" in Yugoslavia, which referred to the unsolved Croatian position and necessity for its solution. Belgrade could not ignore this question any more, since Croats were the second largest nation in Yugoslavia. Serbian Prince Pavle tried to solve the Croatian question "as a basic prerequisite for survival of the country," in cooperation with the mentioned Serbian Independent Democratic Party (Pavličević 2000, 377). The new President of the Government Milan Stojadinović finally recognized the existence of the "Croatian question" (H. Matković 1998, 189). That was the first step toward its resolution.

Banovina of Croatia: The First Step towards Solving the "Croatian Question"

Belgrade finally understood that solving the Croatian question – bringing back the Croatian political and territorial autonomy – was the main prerequisite for the survival of Yugoslavia. This was boosted by the international situation in 1939, primarily German forces, approaching Yugoslavia from the north and Italian from the south, that threatened Yugoslavia with a direct attack. The new President of the Yugoslav Government Dragiša Cvetković at the urging of Prince Pavle asserted that, "relations between Croats and Serbs should be solved as soon as possible." (Pavličević 2000, 380).

Negotiations between Maček and Cvetković resulted in the signing of the Agreement Cvetković-Maček, adopted and published on August 26, 1939, by which the Banovina (Banate) of Croatia was formed (Pavličević 2000, 381-382; H. Matković 1998, 205). The Banovina of Croatia exercised its own legislative, administrative, and judicial autonomy. Legislative authority was in hands of the reinstated Croatian Parliament. The office of the Croatian Ban was also restored and Ban Ivan Šubašić was appointed, but he was subjected to the King and the Sabor (Pavličević 2000, 383). In Banovina of Croatia, almost all Croatian historic lands and the territory in today's BH with a Croatian majority were united (Stančić 2002, 214; Matković 1998, 209). Notwithstanding its wide autonomy, Maček considered Banovina of Croatia to be just "the first phase of restructuring the country and anticipated its further transformation" towards full independence (H. Matković 1998, 205). From then on, Yugoslavia was a politically "asymmetric country" because the rest of it had a centralist structure (Stančić 2002, 214).

The sharpest opponents to the establishment of the Banovina of Croatia were the Serbian Orthodox Church, Serbian Cultural Club in Belgrade and most Serbs in Croatia. The Serbian newspaper "The Serbian Word", published in Zagreb, promoted the movement "Serbs, rally together!" which advocated for secession of certain parts of the Banovina of Croatia where the majority of Serbs lived (Skupina autora 2007, 101). That referred to Serbs who lived in western Slavonia, Banovina, Kordun, Lika, northern Dalmatia and part of Herzegovina. Their ultimate goal was to "separate the 'Serbian' districts" of the Banovina of Croatia and "annex them to Greater Serbia" (Regan 2010, 87). Representatives of the Serbs in northern Dalmatia wrote "The St. Vitus' Day Declaration of Dalmatian Serbs", during the celebration of the Feast of St. Vitus (Vidovdan) near the Lazarica Church in Kosovo near Knin in 1939. In the Declaration, they demanded the removal of the municipalities of Knin, Kistanje, Skradin, Obrovac, Benkovac and Zemunik from the Banovina of Croatia (Regan 2010, 99). In eastern Slavonia, for example, there was "a high number of Orthodox priests participating in anti-Banate and anti-Agreement political activity" (Regan 2010, 98).

On the other hand, one part of the Croatian Peasant Party also criticized the Agreement because it thought that Croatia did not gain enough and that Maček was too accommodating. Fierce opponents of the Agreement were Croatian far-right politicians, in fact supporters of the Ustasha movement, who did not want Croatia to stay within Yugoslavia (Povijest Hrvata 2007, 101). Nevertheless, the formation of the Banovina of Croatia indeed hugely improved the position of Croatia and Croats in the Kingdom of Yugoslavia. The Banovina of Croatia was in fact a "state within state". Legally, it was more than autonomy but less than state (Ivičević 2007, 108). Establishing the Banovina of Croatia was the first step towards federation, but the approaching war interrupted that process (H. Matković 1998, 209).

The Breakdown of the Kingdom of Yugoslavia and the Formation of the Independent State of Croatia

Complex political circumstances in Europe and Hitler's Blitzkrieg played a significant role in the evolution of Yugoslav policy and the fate of the country. In 1941, Yugoslavia was surrounded with allies of the Axis Powers. Except for Greece, Yugoslavia was the only country in the Balkans that had not joined the Axis Powers, so Hitler pressured the Yugoslav Government to take that step. Prince Pavle and the Yugoslav Government joined the Axis Powers on March 25, 1941, which provoked a coup led by Yugoslav officers with Greater-Serbian orientation. They overthrew the existing Cvetković-Maček Government, deposed Prince Pavle and elevated the young King Petar II Karađorđević to the throne (Pavličević 2000, 388).

The coup caused a German attack on Yugoslavia on April 6, 1941. Due to its internal weaknesses and conflicts, the Kingdom of Yugoslavia quickly began to succumb to the attack of the German army and of its allies. The King and the Government fled the country and Yugoslavia capitulated on April 17, 1941. As Pavličević (2000, 389) picturesquely noted, "the country which had been formed artificially in World War I, was torn down like a tower of cards." It was divided between Germany, Italy, Hungary and Bulgaria.

Such conditions provided an opportunity to solve the Croatian question outside of Yugoslavia, but the solution was inevitably linked to the Axis Powers due to the fact, that they were "creating the new European order" (Skupina autora 2007, 157). Since Maček enjoyed the support of the majority of Croats, Germany wanted him for the leader of the new Independent Croatia, but he refused the offer, not wanting to be associated with Nazi Germany (Skupina autora 2007, 157; Pavličević 2000, 401). German representatives then turned to the Ustashas and to Pavelić (Pavličević 2000, 402). The Independent State of Croatia (Nezavisna Država Hrvatska – NDH) was proclaimed on April 10, 1941, and five days after the proclamation, Ante Pavelić, the Poglavnik of the new state, entered Zagreb with approximately 250 Ustashas (Pavličević 2000, 403). Besides the NDH that comprised most of today's Croatia and BH, and was led by the Ustashas, in the dismembered Yugoslavia the Serbian state was established and led by the general of the former Royal Yugoslav Army Milan Nedić.

CROATIA IN WORLD WAR II

World War II is considered one of the greatest wars in history, not just because of the enormous human losses, but also because of the political and ideological conflicts of big European nations. Croatia was also exposed to various warring sides. It served as a battlefield on which different armies clashed – Germans, Italians, Ustashas, partisans, and Chetniks. The World War II tragedy is considered also one of the greatest tragedies of Croatian history. Comparing to other periods in Croatian history, only the Ottoman conquests and devastations of the Croatian territory in the 16th century can be placed at the same level of brutality with World War II. Besides the tragedies, this period contains by far the most controversies of the Croatian history of the 20th century that have not yet been resolved.

Croatia and Serbia under German Occupation

Both countries, the NDH and Nedić's Serbia, were under German control and conducted Nazi racial politics. NDH was a puppet state of Nazi Germany and Fascist Italy and it was divided between German and Italian zones of influences (Pavličević 2000, 400).

The first laws passed by the NDH authorities dealt with the protection of a pure Croatian state and of its territory. Already in April 17, 1941 the authorities passed the "Legal provision for the defense of the people and state", saying that violation of the "honor and life interests of the Croatian people" or endangerment of any kind of the existence of the NDH or state authorities are proclaimed as the act of "high treason".

The Holocaust in Croatia

The penalty for violation of this act was capital punishment (Crohis; H. Matković 2006, 376-377). Racial laws that NDH accepted under German pressure affected Jews and Roma (H. Matković 2006, 377-379; 380-381; 2002, 67; Skupina autora 2007, 169; Geiger 2011, 699; Pavličević 2000, 414; Goldstein 2008, 256). Consequently, almost 80% of Jews in the NDH perished. It should be stressed that the "oppression and terror against all enemies and opponents of the NDH resulted in great population losses, numerous single and mass murders, especially in camps" (Geiger 2011, 699). The symbol of suffering of Jews, Roma, Serbs, and persons that were perceived as a threat to the Croatian state was the concentration camp Jasenovac, established in August 1941 (H. Matković, 2002, 72). Other Jews were saved due to numerous petitions for protection of Jews by ordinary Croats as well as activities of the Catholic Church in Croatia led by the Archbishop of Zagreb Alojzije Stepinac (Batelja 2019; Gitman 2019a). Besides that, some of them were saved with the help of some members of the NDH authorities, while others joined the partisan troops (Gitman 2019a). In the XI chapter of her book "Eichman in Jerusalem", H. Arendt (1964) described the persecution of Jews from Serbia, Croatia, Bulgaria, Romania and Greece. Arendt stated that by Germany's orders, the NDH had to be "Judenfrei", which means cleansed of the Jews by the February 1942. However, the Germans found out that Croatian laws against Jews allowed the possibility that all Jews "who had contributed to the Croat cause" would be transformed into "Honorary Aryans" and therefore, should not be persecuted. Furthermore, the S. S. Intelligence service discovered that numerous members of the NDH leadership were married to Jewish women, including Pavelić himself, and that was the reason why the Jewish question was not prosecuted decisively in the NDH (Arendt 1964). Besides that, according to the list of generals of the NDH Army (Topalović 2001) and their biographies (Dizdar et al. 1997), among the generals there were Jews, Serbs, and Muslims. NDH had 28 (21,4%) Jewish generals: Hinko Alabanda, Ladislav Aleman, Edgar Angeli, Emanuel Balley, Oton Ćuš, Julije Fritz, Josip Gramberger, Ferdinand Halla, Dragutin Helbich, Đuro Isser, Oskar Kirchbaum, Rudolf Kraus-Tudić, Rikard Kubin, Josip Metzger, Milan Miesler, Milan Praunsperger, Julio Resch, Dragutin Rumler, Julio Sach, Julio Simonović, Nikola Steinfel, Ivan Šarnbek, Ivo Šnur, Josip Šolc, Kvintijan Tartaglia, Rudolf Wanner, Mirko Zgaga, And Božidar Zorn. Ten of the generals were Serbs who considered themselves Orthodox Croats: Milan Desović, Đuro Dragičević, Fedor Dragojlov, Đuro Grujić, Jovan Iskrić, Mihajlo Lukić, Lavoslav Milić, Dušan Palčić, Zvonimir Stimaković, Milan Uzelac. At that time, Muslims in NDH considered themselves Croats of Islamic religion and there were also three Muslim generals in the NDH army: Januz Ajanović, Salko Alikadić and Muhamed Hromić. Dizdar's biographies of these generals were written in collaboration with 48 prominent scientists, journalists, publicists, and archivists. It should be said that certain data in these two references differ which indicates the necessity of further scientific research.

The Holocaust in Serbia: Serbian Government and Serbian Orthodox Church

Serbia also accepted and conducted racial laws against Jews, as did all other Nazi puppet states. Serbian historiography and government policy, on the other hand, during the communist regime (1945-1990) distorted the historical facts and presented a thesis that the Ustashas were far more persistent and thorough than Serbs in their extermination of Jews, which resulted in stigmatization of the entire Croatian people as fascist and genocidal, while Serbs were depicted as Jewish friends (Cohen 1992).

However, some contemporary authors claim that anti-Semitism was more widespread in Serbia than in Croatia in the course of the 19th and 20th century (Lebel 2007; Pilić 2018). Serbian intellectuals in Croatia also expressed anti-Semitism. For example, a Serb from Bjelovar, in Croatia, Milan Obradović, wrote 30 booklets against Jews in which he stated that Croats were not capable to raise their voices against Jews (Vuković and Bojović 1992, 9, 31). One of the reasons was, perhaps, the fact that Jews played significant role in Croatian political and economic life at the time (Artuković 2001, 733). In the second half of the 19th century 'Srbobran' was extremely anti-Semitic oriented and it attacked Starčević's Party of Rights for its sympathy toward Jews (Vuković and Bojović 1992, 25; Artuković 2001, 733). Already in 1807, the Council for the future Serbian provinces concluded that Belgrade had to be "cleansed from Turks and Jews" (Štefan 1999, 15).

Horvatić (2019a) wrote an article on the topic in which he included some statements from the prominent Jewish-American historian Esther Gitman. Gitman claims that the main generators of anti-Semitism in the interwar Yugoslavia were not the Ustashas, but some Serbian writers (see also Chapter 5). One of the examples is the "The Protocol of the Elders of Zion", translated and published in Serbia from 1929 to 1945.

Before the war, some members of the Serbian Orthodox Church spoke positively of Nazis and Hitler. Patriarch Varnava Rosić, the head of the Serbian Orthodox Church in 1937 said that "the Führer of the great German people led struggle that served the entire mankind" but "God sent to the German people one far-sighted Führer, who represented opinion that I had accepted myself long ago. We trust Führer and his honest word (Glasnik Srpske pravoslavne patrijaršije 1937). It is important to mention that the Episcop Nikolaj Velimirović, canonized by the Serbian Orthodox Church in 2003, in 1935 in his book "The Nationalism of St Sava" glorified Hitler. He also said that "we are the children of God, people of the Aryan race to which the fate assigned the honorary role to be the main bearer of Christianity to the world…" (Horvatić 2019a; Goldstein and Goldstein 2001, 62).

The Serbian Orthodox Church welcomed the Nazis and invited the Serbian population to collaborate with them in the "Appeal to the Serbian people", published in the newspaper "Novo vreme" August 13, 1941. In this Appeal Serbian intellectuals called on people for obedience to the occupiers and collaboration with them. That Appeal was signed by 546 prominent persons, among them three episcopes and some academics who after the war would continue their work in the Serbian Academy of Science and Arts (Pilić 2018). Besides collaborating with the Nazis, the Serbian Orthodox Church made it difficult to save Jews. It proclaimed the prohibition of conversion of Jews to the Serbian Orthodoxy (Glasnik Srpske pravoslavne crkve 1942). With that proclamation, published and announced in collaboration with the German military authorities, one of the few ways of saving Jews was blocked. The Serbian Orthodox Church also refused the pleas from other endangered groups of people. For example, Serbian women who were imprisoned in the camp Banjica and sentenced to death, requested baptism for their children who had been born in the camp. The request was refused from the temporary head of the Holy Synod of the Serbian Orthodox Church Josif Cvijović (Štefan 1999, 21; Horvatić 2019 b).

According to the head of the civilian branch of the military government in Serbia Harald Turner, unlike Croatia, Serbia was by August of 1942 "the only country in which the problems of both Jews and Gypsies were solved" (Arendt 1964). Besides that, from 1941 to 1945, 51 books with anti-Semitic content were published in Serbia (Vuković and Bojović 1992, 37). American publicist of Jewish origin and adviser for the UN in BH in 1992, Philip J. Cohen, wrote an extensive letter to Rabbi Abraham Cooper of the Simon Wiesenthal Center. Among other things, he informed Cooper that the Serbian government exhibited four anti-Semitic postal stamps in the anti-Mason exhibition in Belgrade from October 22, 1941 to January 18, 1942. The stamps depicted the alleged Jewish-communist-mason conspiracy to rule the world (Cohen 1992). Furthermore, he stated that Serbs had hidden their anti-Semitic history, particularly from World War II. He asserted that the Serbian quisling government headed by the general of the Royal Army Milan Nedić collaborated with the Nazis from the beginning to the end of the World War II. Nedić collaborated closely with the local Nazi officials and personally met Hitler in his command bunker September 19, 1943 (Cohen 1992).

About 94% of the Jews in Serbia were exterminated (Cohen 1992; Shelah 1990, 288-289). This was partially due to the high level of collaboration of the Serbian government,

Serbian Orthodox Church, and the Serbian public with Nazis (Cohen 1992). A Minister in Nedić's government, Mihailo Olćan, notorious anti-Semite and anticommunist, stated that the Holocaust was justified and that "the Jews got what they deserved" (Stojić 2017). Serbs also maintained a number of concentration camps; the largest was Sajmište in Belgrade. Inexplicably, however, Sajmište is not on the list of the European concentration camps in Jerusalem; neither was it mentioned during the communist Yugoslavia, regardless of the fact that the camp was reserved strictly for Jews (Pilić 2018).

Despite its own collaboration with Nazis, the Serbian Orthodox Church accused the Catholic Church in Croatia of being collaborators and involved in the crimes of the regime (Štefan 1996; Cohen 1996). In spite of these facts, during the communist Yugoslavia, Serbs accused Croats for the Holocaust in the NDH. They wanted to impose the claim that the extermination of Jews in Serbia did not happen and to present Serbs as friends to the Jews; this was especially emphasized during the Serbian aggression on Croatia in the 1990s (Cohen 1992). The stigma they wanted to impose was that the entire Croatian nation was Ustashas and anti-Semitic.

The Policy of the Independent State of Croatia towards Serbs

The already deteriorated Croatian-Serbian relations in the Kingdom of Yugoslavia were completely destroyed during World War II due to Serbian opposition to any kind of independent Croatian state, and coming to power of the Ustashas. Although there were no organized or systematic legal provisions against Serbs as there were in the case of Jews, a severe anti-Serbian propaganda campaign began (H. Matković 2002, 69), and Serbs were exposed to "different forms of discrimination, persecution and violence" (Geiger 2011, 699). It is questionable whether the harsh Ustasha attitude to Serbs was an a priori policy or the reaction to Chetnik massacres of Croats that began already in April 1941. What is unquestionable is that soon after the proclamation of the NDH, the Ustasha authorities prohibited the use of the Cyrillic alphabet and the movement of Serbs in the country was limited. Serbs were also dismissed from work, sent to concentration camps and killed (Skupina autora 2007, 169; H. Matković 2002, 68-69). In the NDH, which, unlike the present-day Croatian state, also encompassed BH, in 1941 approximately one third of the population were Serbs. Some of them fled and others were deported to Serbia. In general, it is considered that from 200 to 250,000 of Serbs moved voluntarily or forcibly to Serbia (Pavličević 2000, 417).

In May 1941, "the legal provision on the transition from one religion to another" was passed. It provided that all those who wanted to convert to Catholicism had to have permission from the NDH authorities (Crohis, n.d.; H. Matković 2002, 69). Soon afterwards began the propaganda for conversion from Orthodoxy to Catholicism (H. Matković 2002, 69). Some of Serbs converted, mainly out of fear for their property and their lives, and some requested it because the Catholic Church attempted to save them. However, already by the end of the summer of 1941, an increasing number of Serbs were forcibly converted to Catholicism (Pavličević 2000, 417-418; H. Matković 2002, 70), regardless of the strong opposition of the Catholic bishops in Croatia to forceful conversions (H. Matković 2002, 48). In February 1942, Pavelić stated that he had nothing against Orthodoxy, but he was against the allegiance of the Orthodox Church within Croatian state to Serbia (Pavličević 2000, 418).

Right after that, the NDH leadership decided to establish Croatian Orthodox Church (Povijest Hrvata 2007, 170). The justification provided for this was the fact that Orthodox churches are closely linked to their national states, therefore Ustashas wanted to avoid the possibility of the Orthodox believers, mostly Serbs, being subjected to some other Orthodox Church outside the NDH borders and indirectly to some authorities other than Ustasha regime (Skupina autora 2007, 174).

However, by then the resistance to NDH and the Ustasha regime by the persecuted groups of population, mainly Serbs and Jews, and by the growing number of Croatian people already was in full swing and could not be stopped. Thus, the regime itself created the climate for emergence and growth of the Chetniks and the partisan movement (Skupina autora 2007, 169), even though a significant number of the Serbian population in Croatia would not accept the Croatian state under any conditions "and it did not accept it, regardless of the Ustashas" (H. Matković 2002, 73).

Resistance to the NDH and to the Ustasha Regime

Conflicts between Croats and Serbs had begun even prior to the proclamation of the NDH. They were linked to the fact that the Croatian soldiers refused to defend Yugoslavia. The exemplary case was in the Croatian town of Bjelovar. Two days before the proclamation of the NDH on April 10 1941, on April 8 the 108th Regiment of the Royal Yugoslav army rebelled, not wanting to defend Yugoslavia, and took over power in town and spontaneously proclaimed the Croatian state. Chetniks located in villages surrounding Bjelovar immediately reacted to the proclamation and murdered eleven Croatian civilians (Pavličević 2000, 401; Dizdar 2007, 602). The Ustashas in turn, promptly took their revenge, and so that pattern continued to the end of the war.

The Political Agenda and Crimes of the Chetniks

Led by Colonel Draža Mihailović, Chetniks originally operated in Serbia, then were organized in BH, Montenegro, and in certain Croatian areas where the Serbian population constituted a relative or absolute majority (H. Matković 1998, 250). In World War II Chetniks were supported by the Yugoslav Government in Exile in London (H. Matković 1998, 246). At the end of January 1942 Mihailović was appointed general and minister of Army and Navy in the Government in Exile and deputy commander-in-chief of the army (H. Matković 1998, 251). Chetniks were supported by Great Britain, but at the same time, they collaborated with Germans and Italians. Chetniks and Italian fascist forces signed an agreement in Otrić near Knin, August 11, 1941. The agreement stated that the Chetniks would not fight the Italian fascists. Mihailović also accepted this collaboration in order to eliminate the partisan movement that wanted to renew Yugoslavia, but under communist leadership (H. Matković 1998, 251).

Extremist with strong anti-Croatian sentiment from their beginning, Chetniks opposed the creation of the Banovina of Croatia in 1939 and in 1941 the NDH. In general, they opposed the idea of an independent Croatian state and rebelled against it in those areas where Serbs were a majority of the population (Stančić 2002, 219). It was clearly and openly a Greater-

Serbian organization (Matković 2002, 73). They recruited Serbian population to their units, planning to renew Yugoslavia and to establish "an ethnically clean" Greater Serbia. In June 1941, one of Mihailović's closest associates, Stevan Moljević, wrote a "Memorandum" in which he presented a plan for creating a "homogeneous Serbia" which would "comprise the entire ethnic area where Serbs lived." That meant not only the majority of the territory of the Kingdom of Yugoslavia, but also significant parts of BH as well as Croatia, Albania, Bulgaria, Romania and Hungary (H. Matković, 2006, 453-455).

One of the methods of achieving that was terror and mass killings of Croats in Croatia and Croats and Muslims in BH (Stančić 2002, 219). H. Matković (2002, 74) summarized Chetnik's activity saying: "Their main opinion was: peace and collaboration with the occupier, and extermination of the Croatian and Muslim population."

The first attempt at a Chetnik rebellion in the NDH began in May 1941, in eastern Herzegovina, but as a topic of historiography, it has been "underestimated" and has not been thoroughly researched yet (Lozo 2017, 95, 99). However, even before the organized rebellion, already in April, from the 11th to the 15th, 1941 in the wider area of Mostar, Serbs committed crimes against Croats, particularly in the settlements of Cim and Ilići (Jonjić 2011, 472) where they killed "large number of the Croatian civilians and burnt down larger number of houses" (Lozo 2017, 134). Near those settlements, Serbian forces attacked also the Croatian settlements of Radoč, Bijelo Polje, and Gnojnice; 138 houses were burnt down and eight Croatian civilians were murdered (Lozo 2017, 134). When local authorities in Čapljina, Herzegovina, accepted the new Croatian state on April 14 1941, Yugoslav military forces, Serbian volunteers from eastern Herzegovina, and Chetniks attacked Čapljina, committed violence against its Croatian population and burned down Croatian houses. On the day of the capitulation of the Yugoslav Army, April 17, Serbian forces shelled numerous Croatian houses near Čapljina; 25 Croatian civilians were murdered (Lozo 2017, 135).

In contrast to writings of the historians from the communist period and of some Croatian historians today, Lozo (2017, 134) concluded that "the first acts of violence and crimes against civilians in the area of the former Yugoslavia" were committed by "Serbs against Croats," and that they were not acts of defense. Cohen wrote that in April 1941 Serbs committed 11 unprovoked larger-scale crimes against Croats in the NDH in which 246 Croatian civilians were killed (Cohen 1996, 235). Lozo (2017, 134) mentions that in the period from the 6th to the 25th of April 1941 near Bjelovar, Serbs killed 99 Croats, among them 19 women and 17 children, which subsequently led to revenge and killings of a larger number of Serbs in that area. It is estimated that during April 1941, parts of the Yugoslav Army and Chetniks killed over 300 Croatian Catholics and Muslims (Jonjić 2011, 472-473).

The first killings of Serbs in NDH, April 28 1941, occurred in the village Gudovac next to Bjelovar, where the previously mentioned crimes against Croats took place. There, the Ustashas' retaliation resulted in massacres of 176 Serbs (Cohen 1996, 235; Lozo 2017, 134). These crimes aggravated Croatian-Serbian relations even more and led to even stronger anti-Serbian sentiment of the Ustasha government of the NDH (Jonjić 2017, 473). Probably the most notorious of all mass killing of Serbs in NDH was conducted in Glina in May 1942, when Ustashas killed 260 Serbs (Tomašević 2010, 447). These Ustasha crimes against Serbs are widely known and can be found in most historiographical works, whereas the initial Chetnik crimes are not mentioned.

June and July of 1941 were the period of organized Serbian rebellion against the NDH. In June 23/24, 1941, Serbs began their armed "St. Vitus rebellion" against the NDH authorities, centered in eastern Herzegovina (Lozo 2017, 121). In Grahovo and its surroundings, July 27, 1941, Lozo (2017, 419) stated that more than 90 Croats, mostly civilians, were murdered, whereas other authors cite that 62 Croatian civilians were killed (Jareb 2011, 764). The perpetrators were the Serbian "rebels" accompanied by Chetniks and the communist guerilla. "All Croatian houses in the settlement of Grahovo in Herzegovina and five villages in surroundings were robbed and burnt down," while the parish priest of Grahovo, Juraj Gospodnetić, after horrific torture was impaled onto the skewer and baked (Lozo 2017, 419). That same day Chetniks killed approximately 350 Croatian Catholics, and an unknown number of Muslims in Drvar, mostly civilians. 200 of the Croats who were killed were pilgrims returning from their pilgrimage, and their parish priest Waldemar Maximilian Nestor was also killed (Jareb 2011, 764; Lozo 2017, 419). These events were part of the larger rebellion against the NDH. July 27, 1941, was a significant date because during the communist Yugoslavia it was celebrated as the day of the "Uprising of the peoples of Croatia" against the Ustasha regime, as will be discussed later.

Chetniks were often bragging about their crimes and terror. The Chetniks' commandant, Ilija Trifunović Birčanin, in his report to Draža Mihailović on September 5 1942, bragged about the crimes of his troops in the area of Vrgorac in Croatia when the Chetniks "tore alive three Catholic priests. Our Chetniks murdered every man older than 15…" (Dedijer and Miletić 1990, 187). As previously stated, the main purpose of the Chetniks terror and crimes was establishment of the Greater-Serbia on the Croatian territory. This was the reason why crimes were aimed at the entire Croatian nation, which means that the plan was to exterminate Croats (Dizdar and Sobolevski 1999, 63).

The question arises: who committed the mass crimes and against whom in the area of the stated rebellion? No fascist, Nazi, Italian, German, Ustasha, or Domobran (soldier in the regular Croatian army) was killed, but only Croatian civilians, and in the most brutal and primitive way. The rebellion was organized by the members of the Chetniks of Draža Mihailović and communists from that area.

The Chetniks plan was to create Greater Serbia according to the plan of Stevan Moljević. According to that project, the first and basic duty of all Serbs was to "create and organize homogeneous Serbia, which would comprise the entire ethnic territory where Serbs lived" and enable free access to the sea. This had to be conducted with the occupation of the areas of the planned Greater Serbia and its ethnic cleansing of the Croats and Muslims (Lozo 2017, 71-94).

The Greater-Serbian Propaganda: The Valerian's Memorandum

It is well known that the Ustashas committed crimes against the Serbian population in the NDH. However, the number of casualties was magnified even in the first months of the existence of the new Croatian state. The Serbian Orthodox Church was the main force for spreading disinformation and addressed it to the Germans. The leading example was the case of the "Valerian's Memorandum of the Serbian Orthodox Church" ("Valerijanov memorandum Srpske pravoslavne crkve"). It was an official document of the Serbian Orthodox Church, signed by the Episcop Valerian Stefanović (Lozo 2017, 107).

The "Memorandum" claimed that just over a period of two months, from proclamation of the NDH on April 10 to the date of the handover of the "Memorandum" to the German authorities on June 24, 1941, about 100,000 of innocent Serbs were killed in the NDH. The "Memorandum" was provided to the German military representatives in Belgrade (SPC 1941, cf. Lozo 2017, 109). On June 28, 1941, the Serbian Orthodox Church sent a new version of the "Memorandum", where they claimed that the number of the murdered Serbs exceeded 180,000, whereas by the end of the August 1941, the third version stated that the figure of the killed Serbs was 300,000 or even higher. In addition to spreading disinformation regarding the number of killed Serbs, Lozo (2017, 121-122, 124) claims the "Memorandum's" authors also expressed their territorial aspirations towards some parts of Croatia. The reason for that claim was the fact that some areas in Croatia where Serbs made a significant part of the population (Lika, Syrmia, and BH) Memorandum named "Serbian regions". It should be noted that its authors expressed their positive view regarding Nazi Germany, glorified the "virtues" of the German army, and sought support from the German authorities (Lozo 2017, 124).

Lozo (2017, 108, 126) stated that we can be sure that by the end of June 1941, approximately 1,000 Serbs were killed in the NDH. That means less than 1% of the numbers claimed above. Another historian Igor Graovac (1992, 97) stated that in Dalmatia from April to the end of the 1941, 418 Serbian civilians were killed. This data contradict the fabricated numbers presented in the "Valerian's Memorandum."

It should be noted that even to this day no thorough and systematic research has been conducted that would answer the question of how many Serbs were killed in the NDH (Lozo 2017, 289). Lozo presented an example of how some historians accepted and published data on the topic. Influential historians from the communist period, such as B. Krizman when writing about killings of Serbs in northern Dalmatia referred to writings of another historian from that period, F. Jelić Butić. Jelić-Butić in her turn referred to the "chroniclers of Yugoslav provenance" Drago Gizdić and Sibo Kvesić. Their texts, however, do not provide any sources (Lozo 2017, 292). Neither Gizdić nor Kvesić provided any facts, such as the names of those claimed killed, the claimed perpetrators, or the context of the alleged event or the date of the execution. Besides that, there were not even any eyewitnesses, so Lozo (2017, 292) concluded that the mentioned authors formed "a chain of receiving and transmitting rumors" and that "according to the principles of the historical science their sayings we can accept as some indications for further research, but not as facts." Therefore, we can conclude that "Valerian's Memorandum" was only the first attempt to exaggerate the number of the Serbian casualties in the NDH but not the last. As it will be seen further in this chapter, it started a pattern that has persisted in the period of the communist Yugoslavia and even after its breakup in the 1990s.

Partisans

It is commonly known that partisans were fighters operating on the territory of the ruined Kingdom of Yugoslavia whose primary goal was to liberate the area from the occupiers and conduct a socialist revolution. The partisan movement was led by the communists and their goal was a) to reestablish Yugoslavia, and b) only under the communist regime modeled on the Soviet Union. Accordingly, the beginning of their war resistance was linked to the international situation, more specifically – to the relations between Germany and the Soviet Union. The Molotov-Ribbentrop Pact, officially the Treaty of Non-Aggression between

Germany and the Union of the Soviet Socialist Republics, concluded August 23, 1939, formalized the German-Soviet collaboration (The Molotov-Ribbentrop Pact 1939). The Secret Additional Protocol of the Pact also described the division of zones of the German and Soviet spheres of influence in the Baltic states and Poland. This was realized with the German invasion of Poland, which began on September 1, 1939, and followed by the Soviet invasion of Poland two weeks after that (Boćkowski 2009; Magnuski and Kolomijec 1994). On September 22, 1939 in Brest Litovsk, in the occupied Poland, Stalin's general Semyon Krivoshein called the Nazi commanders to make a toast to their common victory and to the defeat of the "capitalist England" (Magnuski and Kolomijec 1994). In the first two years of the war the Soviet Union helped the Nazis, mostly with oil, in their fight against the British and the French, while the Nazis helped the Soviets with modern technology. Four days after Wehrmacht had entered Paris, June 18, 1940, the Foreign minister of the Soviet Union Vyacheslav Molotov sent, the warmest congratulations of the Soviet Government for excellent success of the German armed forces" (Čuljak 2019). In order to help Hitler to conquer Europe, Stalin gave an order to all communist parties in Europe to sabotage the defense of their own countries and to help Hitler (Čuljak 2019). Stalin officially collaborated with the Nazis from August 23, 1939 to June 22, 1941 (Jakovina 2009).

This Pact was the reason of the passivity of the Communist Party of Yugoslavia, which did not react immediately after the occupation of Yugoslavia and proclamation of the NDH. In fact, at the beginning of war, they accused Great Britain and France as those who bore the greatest guilt for the outbreak of war (Radelić 2006a, 26). They did not act openly until 22 June 1941, when Germany attacked the Soviet Union (Pavličević 2000, 413; Stančić 2002, 220; H. Matković 1998, 254; 2002, 73).

The Comintern sent a telegram to the Central Committee of the Communist Party of Yugoslavia on June 22, 1941, "to take necessary measures to support and facilitate the just struggle of the Soviet people" (Arhiv Znaci). Several days later, on July 1, 1941, the Comintern sent another directive to the Politburo of the Central Committee of the Communist Party of Yugoslavia to fight the occupiers. "The Fatherland war led by the Soviet people against Hitler's bandit attack is a giant fight to life and death and on the result of that fight does not depend only the fate of the Soviet Union, but also the liberty of your people. The hour came when communists are obliged to raise open people's fight against the occupier. Organize, without losing not one minute, the partisan detachments and stir partisan war in the enemy's hinterland" (Petranović 1992, 180). According to Leontić (1955, 48) the communists were given the opportunity to conduct the armed uprising and "achieve their revolutionary goals." Contrary to the Ustashas, whose crucial goal was to establish and maintain the Croatian state, as it was mentioned earlier, the partisans wanted to create a communist Yugoslavia (Radelić 2006a, 27, 32).

It is important to note that Chetniks and partisans collaborated in certain matters. Exemplary was the case of the already mentioned rebellion on July 27, 1941 with the epicenter in the village Srb in Croatia. Among the rebellion leaders there were some communists, but significant number of participants were pro-Chetniks. According to some participants, the term "Chetnik" was widely accepted at the beginning of the rebellion, and only later one part of the rebels refuted it under the influence of the communists (Jareb 2011, 766). One of the reasons for the rebellion was the Ustasha regime, but their fight against the NDH as the Croatian state and mass crimes against Croats suggest that at least "one part of the uprising was motivated with hate against Croats as a nation." Some leaders and participants of the rebellion even prior to the event communicated with the Italian authorities about their collaboration (Jareb 2011, 758; Lozo 2017, 532). The violence emerged simultaneously in Srb, Drvar, Bosansko Grahovo and several places in southwestern Bosnia, and then it spread to northern Dalmatia. Because of that, we can talk about the common rebellion or uprising of the Serbian population in NDH (Jareb 2011, 759). In the place called Boričevac, the majority of Croatian civilians and NDH authorities withdrew before the rebels, but 55 Croats, among whom were 44 women and children, were murdered by the rebels (Jareb 2011, 764). The areas under the Chetnik control were "ethnically cleansed" (Jareb 2011, 764).

As previously stated, during the communist Yugoslavia the Srb rebellion was proclaimed as "the Uprising of the Peoples of Croatia." Communist historiography and public discussions from 1945 to 1990 considered the Srb rebellion as the antifascist resistance. Only after the democratic changes in 1990, crimes committed by the rebels in collaboration with the Italians and the fact that significant number of the participants later became Chetniks were presented to the public (Jareb 2011, 751-752). However, even today, various public figures glorify the "Uprising of the peoples of Croatia" in Srb regardless of the fact that not one Croat participated in the rebellion (Lozo 2017, 532). Advocates for the celebration of July 27 dissociate themselves from the crimes claiming that they were not committed by the "antifascists", which means communists. However, one of the leaders of the rebellion and prominent communist Gojko Polovina refuted these claims asserting that "in the mass of the non-combatants at that moment in the robbery and ignition participated significant number of the combatants (i.e., communists and Chetniks, a.c.), and some of them after that were great, not only as partisan fighters, but also political and military executives, commanders. I never have nor will I ever mention publicly their names" (Polovina 1988, 340, 342). From September 1941, Chetnik's and partisan's elements in the rebellion began to separate (Jareb 2011, 765).

In September and October 1941, partisan leader and head of the Communist Party of Yugoslavia Josip Broz Tito and Draža Mihailović attended two meetings regarding their collaboration. Both meetings were held in Serbia, in Struganik and Brajići. They agreed to help each other in arms, but their collaboration did not last for a long time and soon they began to fight each other (Roberts 2013, 51-52).

Tito, who according to the Comintern's orders (Petranović 1992, 180), organized resistance against the occupiers with the goal of coming to power in post-war Yugoslavia, also negotiated with Germans. At secret negotiations in Zagreb, held in order to establish a ceasefire and prisoner exchange between the Germans and the partisans, the partisan delegations consisting of three Tito's close associates – Milovan Đilas, Vladimir Velebit and Koča Popović – offered alliance to the Nazis in their fight against the British, but Germans refused the proposal (Leković 1985, 90). In as much as the communist leadership in Yugoslavia wanted to preserve the idealized image of the partisan struggle and its leaders, any mention of these negotiations was taboo in the postwar Yugoslavia until Tito himself mentioned them at the end of his life (Velebit 2002, 185-291).

What drew some of the population to partisan units led by the communists is the fact that the communists did not reveal their political aim to install communism after the war. In contrast to the extreme nationalist program of the Ustashas, the communists emphasized the idea of the federative Yugoslavia and the policy of "brotherhood and unity" (Stančić 2002, 221; H. Matković 1998, 253). Understanding that the national question was the key question to be solved in order to renew Yugoslavia and encourage Croats and Serbs to live in the same country again, the Party formed national communist parties (Communist Party of Croatia, Communist Party of Slovenia, etc.) within the Communist Party of Yugoslavia (H. Matković 1998, 251-253). The official name of the partisan forces during the war was Peoples' Liberation Army of Yugoslavia (Narodnooslobodilačka vojska Jugoslavije– NOVJ). After the war, these forces became the core of what was called from 1945 to 1951 the Yugoslav Army (Jugoslavenska armija – JA), and from 1951 the Yugoslav People's Army (Jugoslavenska narodna armija – JNA) (Marijan 2006, 25-26).

The absolute majority of Croatian voters gave their trust to the Croatian Peasant Party and Vladko Maček before World War II, and that same majority welcomed the proclamation of the Croatian state in 1941. It is important to emphasize that the Ustasha regime never really had wide support of the Croatian nation (Tomašević 2010, 395; Pavličević 2000, 413), regardless of the people's positive attitude towards the Croatian state. However, the initial enthusiasm of Croats dropped soon after the establishment of the state, for two main reasons. The first was the Roman Treaties signed between the NDH and Italy in May 1941. The Treaties obliged the NDH to cede to Italy the most developed parts of the Adriatic coast, which included the whole of Dalmatia with its cities and towns (Split, Trogir and Šibenik) and all islands except Pag, Brač and Hvar. Pavelić also agreed to demobilize the remaining coastal area under the NDH authorities (Pavličević 2000, 406). The Treaties caused indignation and desire for resistance, especially among Croats who lived along the Adriatic coastline (Pavličević 2000, 406), regardless of the fact that the Kingdom of Yugoslavia also gave some parts of the Adriatic coast to Italy in the 1920s. The second reason was the totalitarian Ustasha regime, its close ties to the Nazi Germany as well as the policy against Jews, Roma, Serbs, and all Croats who resisted Ustasha authorities (Stančić 2002, 219). Including the Chetnik terror, which was especially severe in Dalmatia, where they collaborated with the Italians, such atmosphere, as well as the passive attitude of the Croatian Peasant Party and the communist propaganda which hid the communist ultimate goals, encouraged Croatian population to join the partisans (Pavličević 2000, 431; H. Matković 1998, 245). The complicated situation in which Croats had found themselves was thus explained by Stančić (2002, 221): "Choosing between the radical options, Croatian civic forces were experiencing a crisis of conscience, so on the side of the NDH were patriots who did not agree with the Ustasha regime but they were anticommunists, and on the partisans' side there were democrats who did not accept the communist ideology, but as antifascists could not accept Croatia as a part of the fascist 'new order'."

Despite the mentioned enthusiasm of the Croatian public regarding the proclamation of the NDH, due to numerous internal and external political and military developments, the public was soon exposed to multiple conflicts, not only with Serbs, but also with other Croats in a veritable Croatian civil war – Croats found themselves on at least two warring sides. The severity of the conflict was also the consequence of the ideological clash, not only in Croatia and Yugoslavia, but also in Europe (Jonjić 2011, 473). Within the NDH, in 1943 the partisans proclaimed the Federal State of Croatia that made part of the Democratic Federal Yugoslavia. The fate of Croatia and Croats was once more, just as in 1918, determined by the set of external and internal factors (Stančić 2002, 222).

Although Yugoslav partisans have been perceived as antifascist fighters and liberators from the occupiers, the fact is that they also committed horrific crimes (Pavličević 2000, 464-467). One of the reasons is ideologically based and connected with their relationship with the

Soviet communists. Already at the beginning of war, the partisans had to be taught how to hate their enemies in order to destroy them and to be blindly submissive to the Communist Party. One of the closest of Tito's associates said: "Hate without mercy towards them, that is your program and your oath, which is your noble fervor of ideals for which you fight... Remember that the great leader of the progressive mankind comrade Stalin said: the enemy could not be defeated until he is learned – to be hated" (Đilas 1947, 32-33). The historiography under communism regarding this topic was ideologically based and this is the reason why partisan and communist crimes have been focus of researches only since the democratic changes.

One notorious example of how the partisans dealt with those perceived as enemies during and after the war were mass executions without trials. Exemplary of the many times and places that had happened was the partisans' action after entering Dubrovnik in October 18, 1944: people were arrested according to the lists previously made by OZNA (Odjeljenje za zaštitu naroda), the communist secret police modeled on the Soviet Union's NKVD (The People's Commissariat for Internal Affairs), before entering the cities and towns that the partisans proclaimed "free". Citizens of Dubrovnik did not have the right to defend themselves, nor did they know of what they were accused, but all of them had something in common: they were respectable citizens of Dubrovnik and a potential threat to the new authorities. Ante Jurjević Baja, a Croat and communist, told the Zagreb's daily newspaper "Vjesnik" in December 1992 that in 1944 there were no courts formed and that "the people's enemies had to be killed either way" (Kačić 2017, 350).

In total, Partisans killed 193 persons – almost all city's intellectual elite, only 46 of them after 13 formal trials (Kačić 2017, 45-46). Some of these victims were butchered by Herzegovinian Chetniks who had joined the Partisans just before they entered the city. Fifty-four persons were taken to the nearby small island of Daksa and killed in the night. Twenty-four priests and friars were killed. One of the executed friars, fr. Marijan Blažić, had collaborated with the Partisans (so people called him "Red Friar"). When the physician of the 24th Herzegovinian Partisan Brigade, Dr. Korlaet, saw Blažić's name on the list of the executed persons, he went to the brigade Commander Šegrt and asked: "Why did you kill padre Marijan Blažić? He was ours." Šegrt replied: "Indeed he was ours but he knew too much, and will soon cease to be ours." (Kačić 2017, 149).

The End of the War: Bleiburg, the Way of the Cross and Postwar Partisan Crimes

The fate of the defeated side was in the hands of the communists. When on May 3, 1945 Tito came to Varaždin (Croatia) in the northwestern part of Yugoslavia to visit the units of the Yugoslav Army that "performed important tasks regarding the final fight with the Croatian stench," he said that "in the new communist state they would look at the daylight only that long, that takes the road to the nearest pit" (Vjesnik jedinstvene narodnooslobodilačke fronte Hrvatske 1945a).

Crimes Against the "People's Enemies"

Two days before the capitulation of Germany, May 6, 1945, Pavelić and members of the NDH leadership fled Zagreb. Scared by the rumors of the communists' massacres in the areas they entered after German withdrawal, the NDH army and a great number of civilians, including women, children and elderly, withdrew with the NDH leadership. The fear that led to this withdrawal was also caused by the Chetniks, who for the greatest part had crossed over to the winning (partisan) side, understanding that the war was over and that the partisans were on the victorious side. Accordingly, the Chetnik units were included into the People's Liberation Army and significant number of Chetnik units was dissolved (Stančić 2002, 225). According to some historians, more than 80% of Chetniks crossed over to the partisan side (Projekt Velebit 2018).

Incorporating Chetniks into the communist military and administrative structures in Belgrade enabled "embedding of the Greater-Serbian ideology and ensuring its extension by new means – the Yugoslav communism" (Horvatić 2017). As news about the crimes of partisans and Chetniks spread, Croats and Muslims (who at the time were considered Croats of the Islam religion) fled towards Zagreb. The crucial trigger for the mass crimes at the end of, and even after the war was Tito's Command from March 1945: "To all committees of the Communist Party of Yugoslavia, to all the commissioners of the partisan detachments of the JA (Partisan Army), these day the opportunity will present for the Communist Party of Yugoslavia to take over the power on the territory of the entire state. That opportunity will last only a few days, and maybe even a few hours, and if in that time we do not execute all our enemies, that opportunity will be lost forever" (Jonjić 2007, 182).

At the beginning of May, after the German capitulation, the first to enter Zagreb after the withdrawal of the NDH authorities were members of the 45th Serbian Division (Hudelist 2013). In his article on the situation in Zagreb upon the partisan's entry into the Croatian capital Horvatić (2019c) referred to the prominent Croatian historian, publicist, diplomat, writer, antifascist, and anticommunist Bogdan Radica. Radica described the first few days in the "liberated" Zagreb: "While the enraged masses of partisans, young men intoxicated with lies and alcohol, sang about 'freedom', there was no freedom for anyone – not for the oppressed and fearful majority, not for minority, which feared anarchy, violence and terror that had been imposed on the majority. Everyone in every moment could become the victim of arbitrary violence (…) Being Serb at that time meant being in power." Some Croatian historians share that opinion. Horvatić (2016) also cites Josip Jurčević, who stated: "That was no liberation of Zagreb because it was followed by the whole series of frightening crimes conducted by the communist regime, which is proved by finding of the 850 covert execution sites in Croatia, and only in the area of Zagreb and its surroundings 120 of such mass graves have been located".

According to the testimonies, approximately 500,000 civilians escaping "the Tito's regime" wanted to "surrender and place themselves under the British protection" (Grahek Ravančić 2009, 95; Omrčanin 1986, 51), in hopes that they would be considered war prisoners. In order to save themselves, on May 8, 1945, Pavelić and his Government left the army and civilians in Rogaška Slatina and fled to the American Zone of Occupation in Austria (Grahek Ravančić 2009, 92). This puts enormous responsibility for what happened later also on Pavelić and NDH leadership (Grahek Ravančić 2009, 92-93).

Various military units (estimated 200,000) were retreating alongside civilians – German, Ukrainian, Bulgarian, Hungarian, and Croatian. Various army units fought the partisans on their way to Austria in order to keep the route open to get to the British forces in Austria (Grahek Ravančić 2009, 73-93; Dizdar 2005, 135-138).

On May 15, 1945, near the Austrian town of Bleiburg the English disarmed the majority of the army that had surrendered and extradited them over to the partisans (Grahek Ravačić 2009, 148; Pavličević 2000, 438; Stančić 2002, 225). It turned out, however, that the partisans did not respect Hague and Geneva Conventions on war prisoners, which Democratic Federal Yugoslavia, as well as the NDH and Great Britain had signed (Grahek Ravančić 2009, 112). The majority that had been disarmed, together with civilians, were driven along the Drava River through Slovenia, where mass executions without any trial were conducted (Tolstoy 1991; Prcela and Živić 2001).

Members of the British Army later justified the decision of Great Britain, saying that the civilians killed by the partisans were sympathizers of the defeated Croatian Army. However, that argument is invalid as the Article 81 of the Geneva Conventions from 1929 clearly states that even civilians who were sympathizers of a certain army, had a right to be treated as war prisoners (Tolstoy 1998). American-Croatian academician and jurist Mirjan Damaška in his book "Tito – the Secrets of the Ruler" stated that the cruel and inhumane treatment of the Croatian and Slovene prisoners was similar to those for which the German soldiers answered at the court trials in Nürnberg (Damaška 2009).

In Slovenia 600 mass graves were found, whereas in Croatia 840, where soldiers and many civilians were executed (Grahek Ravančić 2009, 199). The best known mass graves are Kočevski Rog, Tezno near Maribor, Huda Jama near Laško in Slovenia, and in Croatia Zagrebačka gora, Maceljska gora, Jazovka etc. (Grahek Ravančić 2009, 200). Other captives were forced to march in columns through Yugoslavia to prison camps, even all the way to Macedonia. Slovene researcher Roman Leljak published a book entitled "Huda Jama", based on the testimonies of eyewitnesses of the crime collected during the communist regime. Huda Jama was a coal mine pit in Slovenia that was buried under 10 concrete walls to keep the crime a secret (Leljak 2015, 15, 17), and was not known to the public during the communist regime, all until Leljak discovered and opened it to the public.

According to testimonies left by survivors of these "death marches" passing through places inhabited mostly by Serbian populations, the prisoners in columns were often insulted and abused, while at the same time the Croatian population was not given permission to help them in any way (Grahek Ravančić 2009, 202; H. Matković 2002, 94). The inhumane treatments of prisoners were also well documented (Grahek Ravančić 2009, 204-220; Prcela and Živić 2001; Smoljan and Sabljak 2000; Jurčević 2005; Vukorep 2005). These marches were later named "The Way of the Cross", referring to Christ's Way of the Cross. Months after the end of the war tens of thousands of not only members of Ustashas and Domobrans (Home Guard), the regular NDH army, and civilians were tortured and killed by the partisans.

The words of the partisan leader Josip Broz Tito regarding the partisan crimes, that "the hand of justice, the hand of revenge" reached the defeated side, is probably the best way to describe the treatment of the Bleiburg tragedy in Yugoslav politics and historiography. The entire topic of these crimes committed by the partisans at the end of the war, known as Bleiburg Tragedy, was neither known nor discussed in public during the Communist regime in Yugoslavia (Pavličević 2000, 438).

In the report to the public prosecutor of Croatia Jakov Blažević, from May 15, 1945, the public prosecutor of the district of Bania Branko Drezga, among other things, wrote that there was a necessity to spread hate toward "enemy and criminals" (Dizdar et al., 2005, 374).

Because of the rigidity of the communist regime, free academic research of the subject was not possible and the subject was never discussed publicly, only in the privacy of one's home. Regarding that, the Croatian emigrants, most of them ex-Ustashas or civilians who wanted independent Croatia and did not agree with the communist regime, began to write about this topic and publish their estimates of the number of those killed (Knezović 1960; Hećimović 1962; Omrčanin 1986, Nikolić 1988).

Free and independent research in Croatia was allowed only after the collapse of the Communist regime. Literature that has presented different estimates regarding the number of those killed, range from 50,000 to, especially in the emigrant literature, 200-250,000, 500-600,000 and to even over 1,000,000 killed and imprisoned Ustashas, Domobrans, and civilians (Geiger 2010, 699). Generally accepted data in historiography, also to a certain extent confirmed by statistical calculations, is at least 70 to 80,000, most of them Croats, whose losses are around 50 to 55,000 (Geiger 2010, 699). Although Grahek Ravančić (2009, 327) noted that the closest number of casualties is probably somewhere around 80,000, Geiger (2010, 699) suggested that according to the most recent archival and field research of mass graves in Slovenia, the final number of actual casualties related to Bleiburg could be even higher than the statistical calculations. Some of the estimates and calculations regarding the topic are presented in the Table 2.

Table 2. Number of casulties in Bleiburg and "The Way of the Cross" (Geiger 2010, 715)

Source	Year	Number	Nationality
G. J. Prpić Estimate	1975	More than 1,000,000	Mostly Croats
O. Knezović and J. I. Prcela Estimate	1960 1970	600,000	Mostly Croats
D. Crljen Estimate	1966	500,000	Mostly Croats
B. M. Karapandžić Calculation	1976	250,000	Croats, Serbs, Slovenes, Montenegrins
I. Bogdan and V. Nikolić Estimate	1963 1976	About 200,000	200,000 Croats, 12,000 Slovenes
V. Žerjavić Calculation	1992	About 70,000	45-55,000 Croats and Muslims, 8-10,000 Slovenes, 2,000 Serbs and Montenegrins
M. Portmann Estimate	2004	Around 80,000	Croats, Bosniaks, Serbs, Montenegrins, Slovenes, Germans
Z. Dizdar Estimate	2005	Around 62,000	Croats

The number of casualties is not final; there are still many open questions, similar to historiography regarding the number of casualties in other European countries (Dežman 2010). Regarding the topic of Bleiburg victims the public discourse is still very emotional and a subject of fiery public discussions. While conservative historians consider it to be one of the greatest tragedies of the Croatian people not just in recent but in all Croatian history, (N1 Hrvatska 2019; Braniteljski portal 2019), the liberal side minimizes its significance and justifies the war crimes of the victorious partisan army (Bakotin 2019).

Documents of OZNA (Odjeljenje zaštite naroda) and of KNOJ (Korpus narodne obrane Jugoslavije) prove Tito's unquestionable responsibility for war crimes (Jura 2013). Pero Simić in his book "Tito – the Phenomenon of the Century", included testimony of Jefta Šašić, Serbian partisan general and the commander of the III Department of the Yugoslav secret police OZNA, who told his best friend at the beginning of May 1945 that between May 9 and 12 Tito had called him in the middle of the night and said to him to "kill!," and then to "go to Slovenia and Austria and send my order to the commanders of out armies." Simić concluded that this is how the biggest mass crime happened – after the capitulation of Germany (Simić 2009, 221-222).

According to the testimony of the Head of the Headquarters of the JNA Koča Popović that he gave on June 6, 1945, to the News Bulletin of the Unified People's Liberation Front (Vjesnik jedinstvene i narodnooslobodilačke fronte Hrvatske) from June 6, 1945, twenty six echelons of prisoners of war passed through the route from Bjelovar in Croatia to Kovin (Voivodina, Serbia), and each of these echelons numbered from 3,000 to 5,000 prisoners. All prisoners were killed in Voivodina and thrown down into antitank trenches. At the same time, Popović received the order from Tito for the destruction of all the written records of postwar killings (*Vjesnik jedinstvene i narodnooslobodilačke fronte Hrvatske 1945c)*.

Croatian Serb and partisan Simo Dubaić publicly admitted that he was responsible for the execution of 30,000 Croats, who were sentenced to death without any trials. At the end of his life, he said: "I commanded at the Kočevski rog. I participated in execution of people by order… And then, I received a command to kill 30,000 of the domestic traitors at the Kočevski rog. The command was given by Maksimilijan Baće, Matija Maček and Jovo Kapičić, all by Tito's command" (Lopušina 1997, 122-123).

Clearly much has been learned recently about the extent and magnitude of these crimes but many remain undiscovered. It is important to emphasize that further research of postwar executions of members of the NDH armed forces, which are commonly known as Bleiburg and Victims of the Way of the Cross, needs to be conducted (Radelić 2006a, 45). However, researchers who decide to research these topics encounter many obstacles (Opačak 2019).

The Bleiburg tragedy anticipated how all civilians suspected of collaboration with the occupiers and those who were perceived to be opponents of the communist regime would be treated. After the war, the Yugoslav communist authorities established numerous prison camps where captured soldiers and civilians were imprisoned as "enemies of the people" or "war criminals." The system of prison camps where executions were conducted was one of the main means of oppression in the communist Yugoslavia. A majority of the camps were situated in the same locations and facilities where the concentration camps of the NDH had been, among them Jasenovac camp (Jurčević, 2005, 347; Horvat et al., 2015). In the camps located in Zagreb, including notorious camps Prečko and Kanal, communists tortured Croatian and German soldiers, civilians, women, and children (Šarić 2008, 341-361).

The partisans did not even make exceptions for wounded soldiers of the NDH army. Great numbers of them were taken from hospitals together with the hospital's personnel and killed without a trial, as shown in Table 3. The table does not include patients suffering from tuberculosis and casualties in the hospital Brestovac in Gračani on the periphery of Zagreb. These 210 patients, which is the official number, were taken tied with wire to the nearby execution site Obernjak where they were shot and killed mainly during the night not to be detected. In total, the communists killed 5,001 personnel and patients from Zagreb's hospitals after the so-called liberation of Zagreb (Marušić 2002; Novosel 2008) (Table 3).

Table 3. Execution of the wounded members of the Croatian armed forces from Zagreb's hospitals in May and June 1945 (B. Matković 2011, 179-214)

Hospital	Number of killed patients
The Hospital Rebro	467
The Military Hospital	500
The Military Hospital Kuniščak	1,170
Hospital Sv. Duh I [Holly Spirit Hospital I].	690
Hospital Sv. Duh II [Holly Spirit Hospital].	250
Hospital Sestre milosrdnice [Sisters of Mercy]	297
Privremena bolnica [Provisional Hospital]	285
Privremena bolnica, gimnazija časnih sestara [Provisional Hospital, Nuns' Secondary School].	550
Privremena bolnica Ratkajev prolaz [Provisional Hospital in Ratkaj's Pass].	341
Privremena bolnica Sljeme Runolist Sljeme [Provisional Hospital Edelweiss Sljeme].	91
Privremena bolnica PTS-a Sanitetski konvoj-Slovenija, Krajiška ulica [Provisional Hospital Medical Corps Convoy-Slovenia, Krajiška Street]	150
Total	4,791

On May 25, 1945, Tito ordered that refugees needed to be removed from Zagreb and its surroundings "under the armed escort of the JA units." At the time, about 220,000 civilian refugees stayed in Zagreb and they needed to be "executed without mercy because most of them were people's enemies." Furthermore, the monstrous order that Tito gave, according to Koča Popović and Gabriel Divjanović (head of the Military Court Department of the II Army of JNA) was to "kill all Croatian young men in the city and district of Zagreb, born between 1924-27, who were located in the prison camps or had not joined the partisan units." These young men who responded to the call of the Command of the city of Zagreb (Order no. 7) that invited them to join the Army, about 7,800 of them, were taken to camps Maksimir and Prečko, where they met the same fate as the prisoners in those camps (Vjesnik jedinstvene narodnooslobodilačke fronte Hrvatske 1945b).

Without disputing numerous and confirmed crimes of the Ustashas and Nazis, numerous and horrific by the methods of killing, but also magnified and increased by the communist historiography in Yugoslavia, based on the facts established so far – written evidence, excavations of the pits and forensic evidence – we can assume that communism in Yugoslavia has surpassed the magnitude of crimes of the Nazis and the Ustashas in Yugoslavia. Even worse, a majority of the communist crimes occurred in a time of peace, after the war, not just in Croatia, but also in other parts of Yugoslavia.

In April 2016, the "British Daily Mail" wrote: "Communists such as Tito, are the worst mass killers… he is responsible for murder of 570 thousand political opponents." Piero Scaruffi, professor at Stanford University in the United States in the discussion "The worst genocides of the 20th century" classified Tito as one of the 10 greatest criminals and claims that he was responsible for the death of 570,000 people (Zovko 2014). During the Government of Konrad Adenauer, Germans considered Tito "a common thug" (Borić 2015). Klaus Jacobi (journalist with "Der Spiegel") in his book "My Journal" placed Tito on the 10th place of the World's greatest killers of the 20th century. The reason for that was, as he wrote, one million and one hundred thousand victims, that he ordered to be killed after World War II (Večernji list 2004). Nigel Jones (historian and journalist with the "The Daily Mail") also place Tito at the top of the list of the greatest criminals of the 20th century (Šimić 2019; Jones 2014).

In spite of these facts, according to numerous historians in Croatia, all those who even raise these questions and discuss the nature and number of the communist crimes are labeled as "revisionists". Moreover, most every attempt to examine or reassess topics regarding Ustashas and partisans, the number of casualties in Jasenovac, and the role of Croats and Serbs in the Holocaust, are dismissed as pseudoscientific and their authors are accused of attempts to rehabilitate NDH (Goldstein 2019; Kasapović 2018). A comprehensive response to that attitude was summarized by Marijan (2019), but the dispute is far from conciliation or even a dialogue. He stated that while great emphasis is put on Jasenovac, the topic regarding Bleiburg is "completely silenced". Moreover, assertion that Jasenovac and Bleiburg victims are not the same (Goldstein and Goldstein 2019b), Marijan (2019, 411) considers an example of relativizing the Communist crimes.

Croatian historian Blanka Matković, PhD student from the University of Warwick in England stated that due to the fact that Croatian history from 1945 hither was without any systematic and thorough research, sometimes it is difficult to say what is the truth, and what needs to be researched again. Because of that, the revisionism is absolutely necessary (Marijačić 2016).

Crimes against the Catholic Church

Partisans committed numerous crimes against Catholic clergy in Croatia and BH. Partisans had an antagonistic attitude towards clergy in Croatia in accordance with the teachings of Marx that religion is the "opium for the masses", and because they considered them a threat for conducting a socialist revolution. Once again, they found their role model in the Leninist and Stalinist attitude toward religion, and the fact that several Popes in the 19th and 20th century, bishops, and theologians condemned communist ideology as well as its relations towards Church and the faithful (Jonjić 2011, 462-467). The Communist Party also strived to be "the only ideological and political authority and tried to destroy every authority outside of the Communist Party" (Radelić 2006a, 99).

As many as 664 members of the Catholic clergy were killed, which is the highest absolute number in Europe (Horvat 2009). More than 80% were killed by Yugoslav partisans (Jonjić 2011, 460).

As mentioned earlier, on July 27, 1941, the first day of the rebellion, two priests were killed – Waldemar Maximilian Nestor and Juraj Gospodnetić. The best known case was the murder by Yugoslav partisans of 12 Franciscan monks on February 7, 1945, in the monastery in Široki Brijeg; another 18 members of the monastery were killed, among them 12 teachers at a prominent high school (Jonjić 2011, 461). Evidence was found that the monks were shot in the back of the head, their bodies doused with gasoline and burnt, and thrown into an underground shelter nearby (Jonjić 2011, 462). The details of this crime became known only a few decades later.

The Catholic Church in general, and in this particular case the Catholic Church in Croatia, always defended the right of the Croatian people to its own free and independent state, and by the end of the war this viewpoint directly clashed with those who advocated for the renewal of Yugoslavia, mainly members of the Communist Party of Yugoslavia. The "Catholic Newspaper" (Katolički list), which published from 1877 to 1945, during the third anniversary of the NDH said that while the partisans claimed to be fighting against Germans,

Italians, Ustashas, and Chetniks, in reality they were fighting the Croatian people and the Croatian state. The main cause of the systematic persecution of Catholic priests and bishops during and after the war was their defense of faith and the Croatian right to an independent state and their strong influence on Croats (Jonjić 2011, 475).

The best example was the case of the Archbishop of Zagreb Alojzije Stepinac, who helped numerous Jews and Serbs persecuted and threatened by the Ustasha regime (Gitman 2019b; see also Chapter 5). Although Stepinac as a Croatian patriot welcomed the idea of an independent Croatian state he was also known as severe opponent and critic of the Ustasha regime. As a priest and bishop loyal to the teachings of the Catholic Church and to the Vatican he was also an opponent of the Communist regime. This was the reason why he strongly refuted the idea proposed by Tito to separate the Catholic Church in Croatia from Vatican. His opposition led to being sentenced to 16 years of prison for collaborating with the Ustasha. Stepinac was later sent to house arrest where he died in 1960. Autopsy of his body showed that he had been poisoned while in the prison (Pavičić 2017).

Croatia in Communist Yugoslavia

In accordance with the Marxist view on nations and national states, communists in the multinational Yugoslavia thought that by building socialism the nations and national states would become "extinct" or "die" (Stančić 2002, 229; H. Matković 1998, 297). They also expected that all unsolved national problems and current issues would also disappear. Contrary to their expectation, not only did none of this happen, but the consequences of suppressing national identities and sweeping existing conflicts under the rug only exacerbated these conflicts that would later lead to war in 1991-1995.

The Unsolved "National Question"

Communist Yugoslavia was a political, economic, and cultural battlefield of its nations, and this was particularly evident in Croatian-Serbian relations. Some of these conflicts regarding the structure of the country dated back to the Kingdom of Yugoslavia. For example, Croatia and Slovenia were persistent advocates of federalism in contrast to the reality of the established centralist policy conducted from the state center, the Serbian capital Belgrade (Stančić 2002, 229). As a result of these countervailing pressures certain periods of centralism and unitarism were followed by periods of freer manifestation of the national identity and decentralization of the country (Stančić 2002, 230) like in 1971, which, however, was brutally crushed (see Chapter 7).

One of the most evident aspects of national inequality that impacted Croats as the second largest nation in Yugoslavia, and their relations to Serbs, was the over-representation of Serbs in many state services. Although all nations in Yugoslavia were represented in the central government "in the apex of the Party and the State legislative and judicial branches in numbers corresponding to the national structure", Serbian cadres dominated in the executive branch, especially in the most "sensitive services", for example the secret service, the police, the army, and the diplomatic corps (Radelić 2006b, 22; H. Matković 1998, 335). Following the same pattern, Serbs in Croatia were overrepresented in similar positions and institutions from local to the level of the Republic of Croatia relative to the size of their population in Croatia (Stančić 2002, 229-230; Radelić 2006b, 22).

Every expression of national dissatisfaction with that situation from the Croatian side or any attempt to advocate for Croatian national interests was seen as a sign of danger of separatism. People who dared to speak up were stigmatized as nationalist and immediately linked to the Ustashas (Stančić 2002, 225). One of the examples is the case of Andrija Hebrang, a prominent Croatian communist and the Secretary General of the Communist Party of Croatia who in 1948 was imprisoned and killed due to his advocacy for Croatian national interests and opposition to the Serbian centralists in Belgrade. The authorities sought to justify his imprisonment by claiming that he collaborated with the Ustashas during the war, while the real reason was Tito's fear that Stalin would use Hebrang's help to overthrow Tito. His ultimate death was claimed to be a suicide but he was actually murdered (H. Matković 1998, 304; Radelić 2006a, 260).

Stigmatization of Croats: The Example of Jasenovac Camp

The concentration camp Jasenovac became the symbol of the Ustasha regime and the NDH and, as the Archbishop of Zagreb Alojzije Stepinac once said, "the stain in the Croatian history" (H. Matković 2006, 390). It was the place where numerous Jews, Serbs, Roma, and those Croats who opposed the Ustasha regime perished. It is also the best example of stigmatization of Croats during communist Yugoslavia. The Jasenovac tragedy for decades was used to stigmatize Croats for the crimes committed by the Ustashas. The constant increase of publicized numbers of victims in the camp, which at one point exceeded 1,000,000, suggested that all Croats were Ustashas as such an enormous crime could not have been committed by just a small group of Ustashas but had to involve the entire Croatian nation. This increase in numbers and collective genocidal stigma imposed on the Croatian people are known as "the Jasenovac myth" (Pečarić 2001; Pečarić and Razum 2018). The goal of maintaining this myth was to stigmatize all Croats and support constant feel of shame, inextricably linking it with the Croatian national consciousness and the idea of Croatian independence. At the same time, the goal was also to depict Serbs as strictly innocent victims.

As in the case of the previously mentioned Bleiburg victims, there are various estimates and calculations of the number of victims of Jasenovac. Not talking about and hiding the number of casualties in Croatia during World War II was "the greatest and the most dishonest coverup" of Croatian and Yugoslav politics and historiography. "Due to the lack of the systematic research, many even today cite arbitrary estimates, increasing or decreasing certain categories of human losses of Croatia and Yugoslavia in World War II and aftermath" (Geiger 2011, 700).

Arbitrary estimates that gradually led to the increase in the claimed number of casualties began already in 1945. After Tito claimed on May 21 in Zagreb and on May 26, 1945 in Ljubljana that 1,700,000 persons were killed in Yugoslavia during the war, the Federative People's Yugoslavia (Federativna Narodna Jugoslavija – FNRJ) officially reported to the International Reparation Commission in Paris in 1946 the number of 1,706,000. This number became official and was sanctioned by the authority of the communist government until the breakdown of Yugoslavia. Every doubt or criticism was "dangerous and punishable by law"

(Geiger 2011, 701). This was the case not only with the official number of persons killed in all of Yugoslavia, but also led to creating the mentioned "Jasenovac myth" (Geiger 2011, 709-710). To the extent there was public discussion on the topic, it lacked any scientific basis and had ideological-propagandistic foundation and agenda.

In 1945, the Yugoslav State Commission for Determination of the Crimes of Occupiers and Their Helpers delivered an assertion to the International Military Court in Nurnberg that at least 600,000 persons, mostly Serbs, but also Jews, Roma, and Croats were killed in Jasenovac, until 1943. Geiger (2011, 718) claims that such "unfounded estimate entered international circulation and became entry for all later exaggeration of the victims of the camp Jasenovac." Exemplary was the number of Serbs killed in Jasenovac that was claimed to be one million, as mentioned earlier. The topic became the main charge against the entire Croatian nation in Yugoslavia with the aim of accusing it of committing the greatest crimes and atrocities in history. Table 4 presents some estimates and calculations of the number of Serbs killed in Jasenovac.

Table 4. Estimates, calculations and list by name of Jasenovac victims (Geiger 2013, 239)

Source	Number
Report of the Yugoslav State Commission for determining crimes of occupiers and their helpers NKOJ 1945 estimate	600,000
Encyclopedia of the Lexicographic Institute, 1958 Encyclopedia of the Lexicographic Institute, 1959	500-600,000 350,000
Commission for list of war victims of the Federal Executive Council of SFRY, 1964 List by name	49,602
Military Encyclopedia, 1967 and Encyclopedia of Yugoslavia, 1971	600,000
A. Miletić, 1986/1987, Estimate	700,000
F. Tuđman, 1989, Estimate	30-40,000
R. Bulatović, 1990, Calculation	1,110,929
V. Žerjavić, 1992, Calculation	85,000
Memorial Area of Jasenovac, 2007, List by name	59,403
A. Miletić, 2010/2011, List by name and estimate	146,401 146,248

In addition to this table, the most recent number of the Jasenovac victims – 83,145 – was presented by the Memorial area of Jasenovac in 2018 (Jasenovac Memorial Site 2018).

Commission for the List of War Victims of the Federal Executive Council of SFRY (1964) primarily listed human losses caused by the occupiers and their collaborators. However, there were also people who were killed by the Western Allies and partisans but were proclaimed victims of some other perpetrator, time, and place. Exemplary was the case of Jasenovac. On the lists of names of victims of the camp Jasenovac there are persons who lost their lives in Allied bombing; died in the refuges in El Shatt and in southern Italy; were killed by the German or Italian armies; were victims of Chetniks; partisans who were killed in the battles of Neretva and Sutjeska; and even Domobrans and Ustashas (Geiger 2011, 723). Moreover, some persons were listed there twice or even more times (Geiger 2011, 723). One of the supporters of the Jasenovac Myth – Jasenovac Research Institute from New York – persistently cites number of 597,323 victims listed by name on their websites, disregarding significant difference in estimates, calculations, and controversies in the sea of existing literature (Geiger 2011, 724). It is evident that these lists are neither complete nor final.

Controversies regarding the number of Serbs killed in Jasenovac are still taking a toll on Croatian-Serbian relations. Serbian nationalists continue to increase the claimed numbers of Serbs killed in Jasenovac. According to Serbian author R. Bulatović (1990), over one million persons were killed in Jasenovac, allegedly based on the anthropologic research of the camp. In contrast to these claims, Geiger (2011, 726-7) concludes that "all field work, aerial recordings, and anthropologic research" of the camp have resulted in finding of around 1,100 to 1,500 as the highest possible number of human remains." With the increasing claimed number of Jasenovac victims, the goal has been to stigmatize the entire Croatian nation as genocidal and to impose guilt on entire new generations of Croats (Sadkovich 2010, 341). Geiger (2011, 729-30) claims that recent Serbian school textbooks uncritically have accepted the number of 600,000 or 700,000 casualties. In contrast to Serbian nationalists, Geiger (2011, 724; 2013, 220) claims that some Croatian nationalists try to minimize the number of victims in order to remove the stigma from the Croatian nation, although he does not name any of the authors.

Croatian journalist, publicist, and researcher of Serbian origin Igor Vukić, whose family had passed through Jasenovac camp, claims that in Jasenovac there were no mass murders. He stated that, other than Jews and Roma who were imprisoned there due to the racial laws, most of those interned in the camp, for example Serbs and Croats, were political opponents the NDH (Vukić 2018, 150-151). According to him, the number of 700,000 casualties of Jasenovac is "absurd" in its increase and he suggests that further research on the matter needs to be conducted (Vukić 2018, 154-155). Sources for Vukić's book included 700 archive boxes of the Yugoslav Land Commission for Determination of the Crimes of the Occupiers and their Helpers; 200 boxes of documents of the administrative and military authorities of the NDH; extensive documentation of successive Yugoslav secret police agencies OZNA (Odjeljenje za zaštitu naroda), UDBA (Uprava državne bezbednosti), and SDS (Služba državne sigurnosti); document collections from partisan sources and reliable testimonies of former camp prisoners; and also scientific papers and articles in the media.

Using computer programs, members of the Faculty of Electrical Engineering and Computing at the University of Zagreb Nikola Banić and Mladen Koić published more than 60 articles in Croatian media on inaccuracies of the official list of victims on the internet list of the Public Institution Memorial Area Jasenovac. Comparisons with similar lists of victims in other concentration camps showed that the names of many persons listed as the victims of Jasenovac are also located on the victim lists of the camps Auschwitz, Buchenwald, Dachau etc. Thousands of repetitive names of victims on the Memorial Site Jasenovac list were also found, as well serious incompatibilities of dates on years of births with statistical probabilities, systematic incongruence of length of names of victim and names of their fathers, and other (Braniteljski portal 2018).

Since the topic of Jasenovac could not be researched freely under communism and some of the mentioned recent works considerably differ from earlier research, further systematic research on the topic needs to be conducted. During the Serbian occupation of Croatia and the site of the former camp Jasenovac in 1991, the entire documentation preserved in the archives of the camp Jasenovac was plundered and sent to Belgrade and to this day still has not been returned to Croatia. Until the entire documentation on Jasenovac is made public, all kinds of manipulations and distortions of facts by the Serbian side are possible.

It should be stressed, however, that honest, objective, and unbiased further research on these topics is the only way to get closer to the truth and that even then we will probably not know the exact number of the victims. Nevertheless, it is the only way to reduce and eventually stop the distortions of contemporary history and to stop dividing the victims to "ours" and "theirs", or "less important" and "more important", to Croats and Serbs (I. and S. Goldstein and Goldstein 2011; I. Direktno 2019; Marušić 2019).

Beside the manipulations with the number of victims of the camp Jasenovac during World War II, some researchers have written about the postwar camp Jasenovac, held by the communist authorities, where members of the defeated side as well as those civilians who were considered "people's enemies" just because they did not support the communist regime, were held. S. Pilić and B. Matković have published an article in which they confirm the existence of the camp Jasenovac from 1945 to 1947 operated by the Yugoslav authorities. Their article is based on court verdicts and other accessible documents of the police and other state bodies. These documents reveal that political prisoners served their sentence in Jasenovac, which in some documents was called Institution for the Forced Labor Jasenovac (Pilić and B. Matković 2014). On May 29, 1951, CIA also revealed that Jasenovac was a communist concentration camp and that it contained about 3,000 prisoners who were opponents of the Yugoslav communist regime (Zdunić 2018). Some authors consider that the number of victims in the post-war communist camp was considerably larger than the Ustashas' (Vukić 2018, 27). Croatian historian Josip Jurčević (2005, 347) stated that "it should be emphasized that the new authorities (communist, a.c.) for establishment of their camps used almost every location and facility that during the war had been camps controlled by the defeated side. So Jasenovac, after the war was a camp used by the Yugoslav state." Former president of the Republic of Croatia Kolinda Grabar Kitarović proposed the establishment of an international scientific commission that would research the camp, but numerous historians and many of the "old guard" still in the new democratic government oppose the idea (Hina 2018).

Preserving Croatian Identity and Sovereignty

Life of a Croatian in communist Yugoslavia can be depicted as a life of struggle for equality and sovereignty, just as in the Kingdom of Yugoslavia. The communist regime systematically suppressed national cultures so they would eventually "assimilate artificially into the Yugoslav mixture permeated with the Marxist ideology" (Matković 1998, 354). The communists conducted systematic suppression of religion and national traditions "in the name of the state's stability", which "increased the frustration of those citizens who wished to express their sense of traditional values" (Radelić 2006b, 17). However, the best example to describe the communist oppression of national individuality is to use their policy regarding the language.

Struggle for Equality of the Croatian Language

The best example of the communist suppression of national identity is their policy regarding language, where we can also see similarities to the policy conducted in the Kingdom of Yugoslavia. In December 1954, "the Novi Sad Agreement" was published (Novosadski dogovor 1954; Radelić 2006a, 403). Croatian and Serbian linguists had prepared it under the Party' pressure with the goal of determining that the language of Croats and Serbs was in fact one language with two names, Serbo-Croatian or Croatian-Serbian and two "variants": western or Croatian and eastern or Serbian, which were declared equal. Despite the proclaimed equality, the Croatian language was suppressed (see Chapter 2). In the Yugoslav Peoples' Army, the Serbian "variant" was mandatory, as it was in the correspondence of the federal state institutions, federal newspaper agencies, radio and television (H. Matković 1998, 354; D. Pavličević 2000, 483; Radelić 2006a, 347-348).

The process of stronger national affirmation of the republics and autonomous provinces commenced in 1966 after Aleksandar Ranković was removed from his positions. He was the second most powerful man in the country, its vice president, and the head of the secret police UDBA. He was also the leader of the centralist current in the Party and his loss of power meant more freedom for national affirmation (H. Matković 1998, 352, 358). Having that in mind, Croatian linguists and writers had the opportunity to resist the linguistic aggression of the Novi Sad Agreement and to defend the individuality of the Croatian language (H. Matković 1998, 354). Croatian cultural institution Matica hrvatska and Croatian Society of Writers in 1967 published the "Declaration on Name and Status of the Croatian Literary Language" (Radelić 2006a, 404-05; Deklaracija o nazivu i položaju hrvatskog književnog jezika 2009). The "Declaration" was supported by sixteen more scientific and cultural institutions in Croatia and it determined that the Croatian language was not the same as the Serbian language, which in administration and public communication was in fact the "state language". The "Declaration" demanded sovereignty for the Croatian nation, requested that the Croatian language should be named Croatian Literary Language and that the federal institutions should secure the equality of all literary languages in Yugoslavia: Croatian, Serbian, Slovenian, and Macedonian (H. Matković 1998, 354-55, see also Chapters 2 and 7). With regard to that, Matica hrvatska became the pivot of the resistance to Serbian domination. In the next two or three years it increased the number of its branches and spread across all Croatia (H. Matković 1998, 355), only to be prohibited from further action at the beginning in 1972 (Radelić 2006a, 455).

Advocacy for the Decentralization of Yugoslavia

About that time, the communist leadership in Croatia started advocating for decentralization and a higher level of independence of the republics in the decision making (H. Matković 1998, 334). One of the reasons for dissatisfaction among the more developed republics of Croatia and Slovenia was "pouring of capital into the federal funds" (H. Matković 1998, 361). For that, Serbian centralists attacked Croatian leadership of nationalism.

This kind of development led to a mass national movement called the Croatian Spring, modeled on the Prague Spring of 1968. The main goal of the movement was to advocate for the national equality of Croatia. Widespread thesis among Croats was that other nations were free to express their national individuality, except for Croatia, that Serbs were the dominant nation in Yugoslavia, that they occupied most of the seats in the country's institutions, especially in the police and in the army, and that Yugoslavism was just a cover for the Greater-Serbian political agenda (Radelić 2006a, 391-392). It was the first "broad political action" outside of the Party since 1945 (Stančić 2002, 230). This was the reason why Tito perceived it as dangerous for his own monopoly on power, although at first he favored political currents in the communist leadership of Croatia that opposed the centralists from Serbia (see Chapter 7).

At the end of 1971 the Croatian national movement was stopped by the central government of Yugoslavia. Tito removed the most prominent members of the Croatian leadership from their positions and at the beginning of 1972, mass persecutions of the members of the Croatian Spring and imprisonments were conducted. Pavličević (2000, 490-491) described that: "The epilogue of the Croatian national movement was a new political emigration, crowded courts and prisons. Ensued the age of oppression, that in some nationally mixed areas had features of the anti-Croatian persecution. Thus began the "lead years" and "the Croatian silence".

Regardless of the end of the movement and severe punishments, some demands of the movement were accepted and in 1974, a new Yugoslav constitution gave more independence to the republics and more autonomy to two Serbian provinces – Voivodina and Kosovo. The Constitution expressed the right of the republics to self-determination and even to secession (Radelić 2006a, 476-477). As it will be discussed later, this was one of the main frustrations of Serbia, which felt disadvantaged by it. With this Constitution "the sovereignty of the republics became stronger than that of the federal government" (Radelić 2006b, 20). Republics became national states but at the same time, the continuing oppression by the Party suffocated every expression of the national individuality. For example, the singing of patriotic songs was punishable by law (H. Matković 1998, 373). Discussions regarding international questions were reserved only for "the narrow political top" because of their sensitivity (Radelić 2006a, 563-64). The Yugoslav prisons had been full of political prisoners since 1972. By the middle of the decade, Yugoslavia had around 4,000 political prisoners and in Europe only Albania and the Soviet Union had more (Radelić 2006a, 552).

That the "Croatian question" once again was not solved, but only suppressed, indicates the fact that up until 1981, Croats were the most numerous political prisoners in Yugoslavia. Causes for that do not have to be sought in their particular anti-communist orientation, but in their strong advocacy for greater independence of Croatia in Yugoslavia, or for complete independence (Radelić 2006a, 575). This high number of political prisoners prompted forty-five Croatian intellectuals in November 1980 to submit a petition demanding a general amnesty for all political prisoners. Among the signatories were writer and philosopher Vlado Gotovac, former rector of the University of Zagreb Ivan Supek, writer Zlatko Tomičić, and retired Army general and historian Franjo Tuđman, who will later become the first president of the free and democratic Croatia. New charges were made against Gotovac, Tuđman, and prominent economist Marko Veselica who were accused of giving interviews to foreign media about the position of Croats and Croatia in Yugoslavia. Veselica for example, was sentenced to eleven years in prison. He told a German journalist in 1981, "it is modern to constantly criticize Croatia for fascism, to stop its process of democratic expansion, to program the feeling of its constant guilt and frustration even when it is completely innocent" (Radelić 2006a, 576). During his trial, which sentenced him to three years in prison, Tuđman demanded rights for all nations to their complete freedom (Radelić 2006a, 577).

Serbian Path to Solution of the National Question: Renewal of Greater-Serbian Plans

Other developments also showed that the national question had not been solved. After Tito's death in 1980, the knot of the national question began to unravel. First Albanians in the province of Kosovo demanded that Kosovo become a republic (H. Matković 1998, 353), whereas Serbs began to oppose fiercely the Constitution that had expanded the autonomy of the provinces (Kosovo and Metohija, and Voivodina) and ultimately sought to restrict that autonomy (Radelić 2006a, 547). That period was also marked by the renewal of the program of Greater-Serbia (Stančić 2002, 234).

In 1986, the first national political program outside of the League of Communists was published. It was "Memorandum of Serbian Academy of Science and Arts" (Memorandum SANU, Draft, Autumn 1986, see also Čović 1993) whose authors introduced theses on problems of the Yugoslav economy and political system, but also very biased regarding the position of Serbs in Yugoslavia, especially those outside of Serbia, particularly in Croatia and BH. Their conclusion was that the status of Serbs in Yugoslavia had deteriorated. The authors of the "Memorandum", prominent Serbian scholars and writers, claimed that the 1974 Constitution impaired Serbia and called for the revision of the Constitution with the aim that Kosovo and Metohija and Voivodina would become once again constituent parts of Serbia. Besides that, the authors of the "Memorandum" called for any confederative principles to be left out of the Constitution. As Radelić (2006a, 550) pointed out, "the authors of the 'Memorandum' outlined one goal and two paths to achieving that goal. First was the attempt to establish one integrated Serbia, which would include Voivodina and Kosovo and to impose Serbian domination in Yugoslavia. If that was not possible, the alternative was for Serbia to annex all areas in Yugoslavia where Serbs lived in parts of Croatia and BH, and to go on their separate way, regardless of the other republics and nations in the country."

Significant was the thesis introduced by the "Memorandum" regarding the alleged endangerment of Serbs in Croatia. It stated that apart from the period of NDH, Serbs in Croatia have never been endangered as they were at that point. This proved to be a powerful trigger for Serbs in Croatia and their later attitude towards the Croatian leadership, communist or democratic, and their general attitude towards the idea of an independent Croatia. The Memorandum posited that solving the Serbian question in Yugoslavia would lead to the breakup of Yugoslavia and the creation of the Greater Serbia that would include large parts of Croatia and the entire BH.

Soon after, the new Serbian leader Slobodan Milošević accepted the program of the "Memorandum" and took leadership of the Serbian League of Communists in 1987. As Radelić (2006a, 551) explained, "in a very short time he formed coalition of the Serbian political parties, Serbian Orthodox Church, intelligentsia, and Party-state apparatus, in order to adopt constitutional changes by force." Serbs in Kosovo, who feared the Albanian majority demanding Kosovo to become republic, proved to be very useful for his plans, so with Serbian mass meetings and protests, Milošević managed to change the leadership of Montenegro and provinces of Kosovo and Voivodina. The other nations feared that he would apply the same scenario to the rest of Yugoslavia. Milošević was supported by the Yugoslav People's Army ("Jugoslavenska narodna armija" – JNA) in his attempt to centralize Yugoslavia (Barić 2005, 30-31).

The End of "Croatian Silence" and Beginning of the Serbian Insurgency in Croatia

Milošević's initiatives and attempts to take control of the League of Communists of Yugoslavia failed. At the 14th (extraordinary) Congress of the League of Communists of Yugoslavia, held in Belgrade on January 20-22, 1989, the Slovene and Croatian delegates, led by Croat Ivica Račan, left the Congress because they did not agree with Milošević's policy. This event marked the breakup of the League of Communists of Yugoslavia (Barić 2005, 32-33). In addition to its political institutions, the Yugoslav economy also broke down. The Serbian leadership began to take illegal actions. Serbs took over Yugoslav monetary system in December 1990 (Sudetic 1991). Serbian leadership also took control over the Yugoslav military, secret services, and the Yugoslav diplomacy (Nazor 2011, 44).

"Memorandum SANU", Milošević's policy and propaganda that depicted Serbs as a nation endangered by Croats, who were proclaimed Ustashas, and evoking the memory of the NDH, radicalized many Serbs in Croatia (Barić 2005, 48-49). Their mass gatherings where they chanted Milošević's name showed their acceptance of his agenda. Already in 1989, when communists still held power, Croatian Serbs organized a huge meeting in Knin on February 28, 1989, and in Dalmatian Kosovo (not to be confused with Kosovo in Serbia), near the church Lazarica, on July 9, 1989, demanded equality in the Socialist Republic of Croatia and chanted Milošević. Some of the participans wore Chetnik symbols and considered Croats to be Ustashas (Barić 2005, 42-45).

The collapse of the communist regimes in all Eastern Europe encouraged the forming of the political parties in Slovenia and Croatia as an alternative to the Communist leadership. Such developments marked the end of the "Croatian silence" in 1989. In April and May 1990, the first multiparty elections were held in Croatia, and the Croatian Democratic Union ("Hrvatska demokratska zajednica" – HDZ), led by historian and former JNA general Franjo Tuđman, won.

The policy of HDZ reflected aspirations of Croats more than those of other political parties (Nazor 2011, 28). When establishing his party, Tuđman wanted to unite three main Croatian historical political components: Croatian Party of Rights (right wing), Radić's political viewpoints (center) and Croatian left, taking only what he saw positive and fit with a new political and social framework.

The already pro-Serbian JNA opposed democratic changes and, in accordance with its centralist viewpoints, accepted Milošević's policy of centralizing Yugoslavia. In May 1990, just after the results of the election were announced, when communists led by Ivica Račan still held power, the JNA removed the arms of the Croatian Territorial Defense (TD) (Teritorijalna obrana – TO) from their armories and transferred them to its own facilities (Nazor 2011, 28). In that way, one of the Yugoslav republics, Croatia, was disarmed by the JNA. The new HDZ government was installed on May 30 1990. It brought back the traditional Croatian national symbols without the red Communist star, such as the Croatian red and white coat of arms. Serbs in Croatia perceived these as Ustasha symbols and consequently as a revival of the NDH (Nazor 2011, 35).

Regardless of attempts of the democratically elected Croatian authorities to find a peaceful solution for the Yugoslav crisis, many Serbs, from areas in Croatia where they constituted a majority of population, in August 1990 rebelled against Croatian leadership and the Croatian state in general and started an insurgency, known as the "Log revolution"

(Balvan means log in Croatian and was used because Serbs used logs to impede road traffic at the peak of tourist season). The aim of the insurgency was to separate from Croatia and unite with Serbia. The insurgents received help and arms from the JNA, albeit the latter publicly declared that it served as a buffer zone and that it strived to prevent further conflicts. Lamentations that Serbs had been excluded from the Croatian Constitution passed in December 1990 are not accurate because they were listed as national minority with all the rights of the Croatian citizens. Furthermore, democratic changes and the new democratic Croatian Constitution allowed the establishment of their own political parties as well as cultural institutions and organizations (Barić 2005, 67). Nevertheless, Serbian insurgents complained that the new Constitution downgraded their position, since the 1974 Constitution said that "the Socialist Republic of Croatia is the national state of the Croatian nation, state of the Serbian nation in Croatia and state of other nationalities that live there" (Radelić 2006a, 484). While in the 1974 Constitution Serbs were mentioned by name, unlike other nationalities in Croatia, in the new Croatian Constitution they were not constituent nation in Croatia, because the phrase "the national state" regarded only Croats (Radelić 2006a, 485).

Eventually, insurgent Serbs formed their autonomous territorial unit that was later named the Republic of Serbian Krajina (Republika Srpska Krajina – RSK), where Croatian Constitution and laws were dismissed, and Croats and other non-Serb populations were banished from their homes. Sporadic terrorist attacks of the insurgents and JNA's support of their actions, especially the brutal murders of twelve Croatian police officers, ambushed by the Serbian insurgents in Borovo Selo in eastern Slavonia, and another in the hinterland of Zadar, a coastal city in Dalmatia (Nazor 2011, 56-57), strengthened national unity and resolve among Croats.

Greater-Serbian Aggression against Croatia

Milošević's constant refusal of Slovene and Croatian proposals for restructuring the country as confederation, led Croatia to the path of independence. At the referendum in May 1990 94% voted for Croatian independence, with 85% of eligible voters, so the Croatian Parliament June 25, 1991, proclaimed Croatia's independence (Nazor 2011, 68-69). Serbs in Croatia largely boycotted the referendum and at the beginning of July 1991, joint armed forces of Serbian insurrectionists and JNA began the Greater-Serbian aggression on Croatia. Since Slovenia had no significant Serbian population in its territory, the Serbian leadership did not include Slovenia in its long-term occupation goals. The Serbian Orthodox Church incited Greater-Serbian plans for occupation of Croatia and other territories in its surroundings, so Serbian writer Mirko Kovač, who at the beginning of war had to flee to Croatia, said jokingly that the Serbian Orthodox Church was the "spiritual JNA" (Štefan 1999, 6).

From the Serbian actions in the 1991 offensive, we can see the continuity with the mentioned Greater-Serbian plans introduced in the 19th century. Serbia did not plan to stop Slovenia's and Croatia's independence, but it emphasized that only "nations" could leave Yugoslavia, and not republics. The Serbian leadership wanted Serbs in Croatia, who had illegally proclaimed their autonomy, to secede from Croatia and join Serbia so all Serbs could live in one country. This resulted in Serbian usurpation of almost one third of the Croatian territory and inclusion of those territories into the Greater-Serbia (Nazor and Pušek 2018, 117).

Croatia not only continued peace negotiations with Serbia, but the Croatian government submitted an official proposal to the federal government for a confederacy, an Alliance of Sovereign States (Rudolf 1999, 291-347). The plan was accepted by the international community and all Yugoslav republics, except for Serbia, which was superior in arms and ultimately wanted to use the opportunity for creating the Greater Serbia.

Serbia, JNA, and Montenegro conducted full-scale aggression on Croatia. Montenegro was another Yugoslav republic with puppet leadership subjected to Milošević. One of the main features of the aggressor's warfare was the complete disregard for the laws of war. The war was marked with brutal destruction of Croatian villages, such as Ćelije which was burnt to the ground, Dalj, Erdut, Aljmaš, Škabrnja, Nadin, etc., (Nazor 2011, 222, 350, 372); towns and cities, as well as cultural monuments and symbols of the Croatian history and identity. Most damaging were attacks on the Croatian towns Vukovar and Dubrovnik. In a three-month siege, most of Vukovar was flattened to the ground. In the attack and killings of civilians Chetniks particularly stood out. Dubrovnik, which had been included in UNESCO-s cultural heritage list, also was shelled. Catholic churches and other religious objects, such as Jewish, Muslim, etc., were destroyed or at least damaged by the aggression (Nazor and Pušek 2018, 279), as well as hospitals (Nazor 2008).

Maybe the best indication of Serbian warfare was their attitude towards civilians and, in general, the profile of war victims. The aggressor conducted systematic expulsion of the Croatian and other non-Serbian populations from the occupied Croatian territories (Nazor and Pušek 2018, 279). In October 1991, citizens of the Croatian far-east town of Ilok and its surroundings were forced to sign an agreement to hand over all arms to the JNA and leave the area. Estimated number of Ilok's refugees was from 8,000 to 10,250 people (Vuković 2015, 319; Gregurić 1998, 205.) Among the refugees, there were Croatian citizens of Slovakian ethnicity (Vuković 2015, 320), which proves that all non-Serbs in Croatia during the Greater-Serbian aggression were in danger. The peak of the refugee crisis happened in November 1991, after the fall of Vukovar. About 15,000 civilians were banished and at least 266 civilians, wounded soldiers, and hospital personnel were taken from the hospital, killed and thrown down into the mass grave at the former farm near Vukovar called Ovčara (Nazor and Pušek 2018, 152).

At the same time, Croatia struggled for international recognition and cooperated with the international community during the Peace Conference in Hague that lasted from September to December 1991. The Badinter Arbitration Committee, formed by the Conference, concluded in December 1991 and January 1992, that Yugoslavia was in the process of dissolution. In addition, the Arbitration Committee concluded that the borders between the republics should be respected (Nazor 2011, 131). On January 15, 1992, Croatia was internationally recognized by the members of the European Community, most countries, and in June by the United States.

From 1992 to 1995, Greater Serbian aggression continued in BH, using the same strategy as in Croatia. Insurgent Serbs established their Republic Srpska (RS), which aimed to separate that particular territory from BH and unite with Serbia and attacked Bosniaks and Croats. Numerous Bosnian-Herzegovinian refugees, both Croats and Muslims, fled to Croatia where they were taken care of. The President of Republic of Croatia Franjo Tuđman and the President of the Presidency of Bosnia and Herzegovina Alija Izetbegović on July 21, 1992, signed the "Agreement on Friendship and Cooperation between the Republic of Bosnia and Herzegovina and the Republic of Croatia." The Agreement stated that the Croatian Defense Council (HVO), formed in April 1992 in BH to protect Croats from Serbian aggression, "is an integral part of the united military of the Republic of Bosnia and Herzegovina" (Nazor 2011, 139-140). Despite the Agreement, that same year began the conflict of Muslims with BH Croats. During the conflict Croats were mostly expelled from the areas controlled by the BH Army (such as Konjic, Jablanica, Travnik, Kakanj, Fojnica, Bugojno, and Vareš as well as villages within municipalities of Zenica, Kakanj, Travnik, Novi Travnik, Visoko, Busovača, Konjic, Kiseljak, Kreševo, and Fojnica), while the Muslims were expelled from the areas controlled by the HVO (Stolac, Prozor, Kiseljak, and western Mostar) (Nazor 2011, 141-142). Both sides established concentration camps and committed crimes (Nazor 2011, 142). The conflict was eventually stopped by signing the Washington Agreement on March 18, 1994, which anticipated "the renewal of military cooperation between Croats and Muslims" (Nazor 2011, 142). After that, Croats and Muslims began their military cooperation to free Croatia and BH from the Serbian occupation.

Cooperating with the international community and giving priority to the peaceful end of the war, Croatia negotiated with Milošević and with the insurgent Serbs. On September 25, 1992, Croatian Parliament passed the "Law on Forgiveness" by which no criminal prosecution would be conducted against those who had committed crimes against the Republic of Croatia from August 17, 1990 (Pavković 2019a). This law aimed to establish peace in the occupied areas. However, it did not help, as the goals of the insurgent Serbs, who at any cost wanted to separate from Croatia and unite with Serbia, clashed with the Croatian goal of reintegrating the occupied Croatian territories.

From 1994 Croatian Army, formed and developed during the war, began to conduct actions and operations that liberated part by part the occupied territory. In August 1995 in the military-police Operation Storm ("Oluja"), Croatia liberated most of its occupied territory and announced the end of the war.

Despite President Tuđman's proclamation to the Serbs who had not committed war crimes to remain in Croatia, guaranteeing them their civil rights (Marijan 2009, 142-143), many Serbs from the RSK fled to Serbia. Different estimates regarding the number of Serbs who left Croatia vary from 90,000 to 200 or 300,000 (Nazor 2011, 265). Serbs left Croatia in the pre-planned evacuation according to the plans made by the RSK leadership from 1993 to 1995. The evacuation had begun by order of the Serbian leadership even before the operation Storm started and the majority of Serbs left because they did not want to live in Croatia with Croats as their neighbors (Marijan 2009, 327-375; Barić 2005, 551-53; 535-42). Slobodan Lazarević, lieutenant colonel of the RSK Counter-Intelligence service ("Kontraobavještajna služba" – KOS), who for the entire time of the existence of the Republic of Serb Krajina worked as a liaison officer with Belgrade, said at Milošević's trial in The Hague:

"In Krajina there were no civilian men because all of them were armed. None of us could say that we did not do something that would be violation of the laws of the Republic of Croatia. Accordingly, all of us had reason to leave Croatia. People left out of fear of revenge for the crimes against Croats. Those who were opposed to leaving were forced to do it under threat of violence by the 'Krajina's army and police'."

Lazarević is a reliable witness. According to the BBC News February 20, 2003, he was "the most blaming witness that The Hague Tribunal had ever heard," while "The Economist" said that the witness was "the real insider" who had known exactly the Serbian command chain from top (Belgrade) to bottom during the aggression on Croatia. Several times Lazarević refuted the indictment of the persecution that Tuđman and the Croatian Army in Storm "had banished 250 thousand Serbs from Krajina." He proved that emigration of Serbs had been prepared in advance and that the order had been given by the president of the RSK Milan Martić (Figure 1). Text of the order of the "Supreme Defence Council" was published in the Belgrade newspaper Politika. Lazarević stated that "if anyone is to be accused for emigration of the Croatian Serbs, than it is the former leadership of the so-called Krajina and then leadership in Belgrade… and leadership in Belgrade wanted to 'gain cheap political points'" (Dogan 2019).

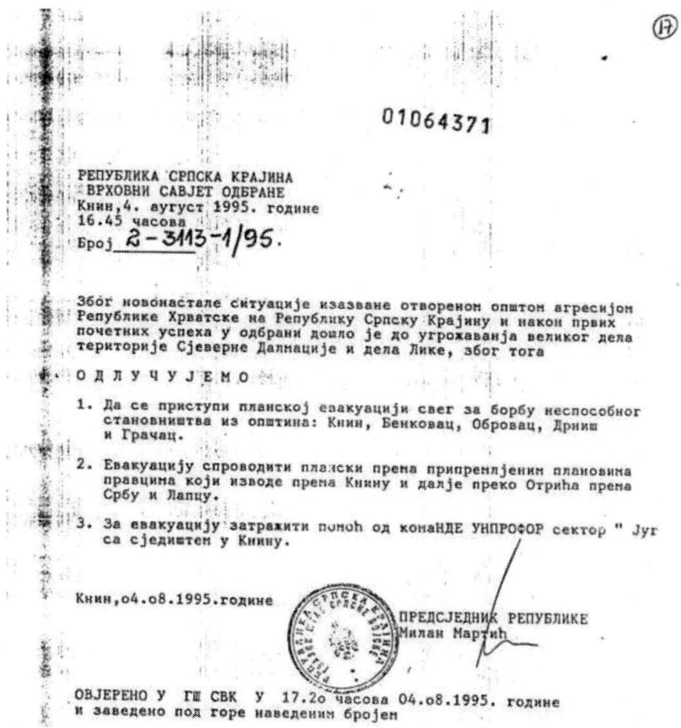

(17)

01064371

РЕПУБЛИКА СРПСКА КРАЈИНА
ВРХОВНИ САВЈЕТ ОДБРАНЕ
Книн,4. аугуст 1995. године
16.45 часова
Број 2-3113-1/95.

Због новонастале ситуације изазване отвореном општом агресијом Републике Хрватске на Републику Српску Крајину и након првих почетних успеха у одбрани дошло је до угрожавања великог дела територије Сјеверне Далмације и дела Лике, због тога

О Д Л У Ч У Ј Е М О

1. Да се приступи планској евакуацији свег за борбу неспособног становништва из општина: Книн, Бенковац, Обровац, Дрниш и Грачац.
2. Евакуацију спроводити плански према припремљеним плановима правцима који изводе према Книну и даље преко Отрића према Србу и Лапцу.
3. За евакуацију затражити помоћ од комаНДЕ УНПРОФОР сектор " Југ са сједиштем у Книну.

Книн,о4.о8.1995.године

ПРЕДСЈЕДНИК РЕПУБЛИКЕ
Милан Мартић

ОВЈЕРЕНО У ГШ СВК У 17.2о часова 04.о8.1995. године
и заведено под горе наведеним бројем

01064371

Republic of Srpska Krajina
The Supreme Defense Council
Knin, August 4, 1995.
At 4.45 pm
No. 2-313-1/95

Due to a new situation caused by open general aggression of the Republic of Croatia on the Republic of Srpska Krajina and after the first initial successes in defense, a great deal of territory of Northern Dalmatia and part of Lika is threatened, therefore we make

DECISION

1. to evacuate all for struggle incapable population according to a plan from the communities Knin, Benkovac, Obrovac, Drniš and Gračac
2. the evacuation should be performed according to the prepeared plans with the direction leading to Knin and further over Otrić towards Srb and Lapac
3. for evacuation we should seek assistance of the Unprofor Headquarters, sector "South" located in Knin

President of Republic
Milan Martić

Knin, August, 4, 1995.

Endorsed in the Headquarters of the Serbian Army Krajina and registered under above number, at 5.20 pm August 4, 1995.

Figure 1. Order for Evacuation of Croatian Serbs from the occupied parts of Croatia ("Republic Srpska Krajina") by their "president" Milan Martić. Document is in Cyrilic, and below is chapter author's translation in English.

The operation Storm liberated most of the occupied Croatian territory, but eastern Croatia – eastern Slavonia, Baranja, and westerm Syrmia – were still under Serbian control. These areas were reintegrated peacefully to Croatia in January 1998.

The victory of the Croatian Army in Croatia also made possible the end of the war in BH. However, despite the military victory of the Croatian and Bosniak forces, the Dayton Agreement legalized the existence of the Republic Srpska in BH, giving the insurgent Serbs 49% of the territory and in fact recognizing the state based on ethnic cleansing and genocide. In July 1995, Serbian forces killed about 8,000 Muslim men and boys in the Bosnian town of Srebrenica that today is part of the Republic Srpska. The rest of the territory (51%) formed the Federation of BH as a federation of Muslims and Croats (Nazor 2011, 178).

Consequences: Human Losses, Genocide Lawsuit and Memorandum 2

Because of the Serbian policy of "ethnic cleansing", Croatia was compelled to host a large number of refugees, which by the end of 1991 reached more than half a million. The number of refugees and displaced persons in Croatia constantly fluctuated according to the situation on the battlefield. Through its Office for Displaced Persons and Refugees, the Croatian Government took care of Croatian refugees and displaced persons, as well as those from BH who were fleeing to Croatia from the Serbian aggression in their country, which also declared its independence from Yugoslavia. Most of the costs for the refugees and displaced were covered by the state budget with the rest provided by humanitarian aid from abroad. This enormous effort of the Croatian state that was conducted in times when it was itself partly under occupation and in the greatest need was not rewarded financially nor recognized objectively by the later BH leadership. By mid-1992, there were 325,806 refugees and almost half of them were children. By the end of that year, there were about 350,000 refugee children. Some specific data on the suffering of children during the aggression is presented in Table 5.

Table 5. Effects of 1991-1995 war in Croatia on children (Hebrang 2013, 121-24)

The effects of the war on children		Number
Lost one parent		4,285
Lost both parents		54
Prisoners of the Serbian concentration camps		219
Missing		15
Injured		1,184
Killed	During the war	345
	In the postwar period	57

These data are not complete, and the numbers are not final yet, and the research on the topic is continuing. For these crimes against children, no one has been prosecuted.

According to the incomplete data, about 22,000 Croatian citizens were killed or "disappeared" in the war in Croatia (Nazor and Pušek 2018, 278). According to data presented by then Minister of Health Andrija Hebrang Jr, during the Greater-Serbian aggression, on the Croatian side 6,891 soldiers and 7,263 civilians were killed – in total 14,154 (Hebrang 2013; Nazor and Pušek 2018, 278). Numerous mass and individual graves directly show the severity and amount of war crimes. To date, 150 mass graves and 1,200 individual graves have been found. According to the available data, up to 2017, 5,131 remains were exhumed (Nazor and Pušek 2018, 279).

National minorities in Croatia loyal to the Croatian state also suffered great human losses and property damage at the hands of the aggressor. Among most numerous were Czechs, Slovaks, Hungarians, Rusyns, Ukranians and Italians. More than 35,000 Croatian soldiers who were members of the national minorities participated in the defense of Croatia, including about 9,000 or 10,000 Serbs loyal to the Croatian state. In addition, we can mention soldiers from the United Kingdom, France, Germany, Argentina, Austria, Italy, Hungary, Ireland, Poland, Norway, Russia, Spain, Sweden, Ukraine, etc (Radoš and Šangut 2013, 231; Nazor and Pušek 2018, 158).

Journalist Pavković estimates that about 30,000 Croatian prisoners went through approximately 70 Serbian prisoner camps (Pavković 2019b). The UN Commission of Experts in 1995 published the Final Report in which it stated that during 1991 around 480 camps for interned civilians and soldiers were established under Serbian control. According to the Commission for Imprisoned and Missing Persons of the Government of the Republic of Croatia, about 300 prisoners were killed in the camps. The prisoners, on the other hand, consider that the number was much higher. The youngest person killed was only 6 months old and the oldest 104 years (Jukic 2019). The lists of the imprisoned and killed on the territory of the state of Serbia itself have been requested from the Republic of Serbia, but Serbia denies the existence of these camps. During the Peace Conference in London on August 27, 1992, Serbian president Milošević stated that there were no more concentration camps under Serbian control. Five months later the American CIA revealed 70,000 prisoners in 135 Serbian camps (Frusca 1996, 25).

Serbian-Montenegrin aggressor killed 3,182 women, constituting 43.8% all of killed civilians, not including the missing persons. Most of the women were killed inside of their homes (Hebrang, 2013, 118, 119). Among the victims were women and men raped in the camps and outside of the camps in the occupied territories. According to the list of the Association of Women from the Croatian War of Independence, members of the JNA and Serbian-Montenegrin paramilitary units raped around 3,000 women in Croatia. The youngest raped person was 5 and the oldest 80 years of age (Hebrang 2013, 194-195). Numerous testimonies of foreign observers confirm that mass rapes were part of the politics of the Serbian "ethnic cleansing" carried out at command. More than 30,000 women in BH were raped by the Serbian forces, and humanitarian organizations asserted that those rapes had been planned in Belgrade (Frusca 1996, 41). The commander of the Third Corps of the Serbian Army Milan Dedić in a secret letter to Mihailo Kertes, close Milošević's associate, stated: "In different centers of our territory there are 1,680 of Muslim women aged from 12 to 60 (…) many of them are pregnant (…) the psychological effect is strong, which means it should be continued" (Frusca 1996, 42; Zaccaria 1994, 130). Further, Kertes stated: "The Minister of Interior of Yugoslavia will not open investigation on rapes, because it is part of the psychological-strategic pressure (…) it was agreed that certain number of young women would be transferred to the occupied territories for the purposes of the Serbian forces and officers of the UN (Frusca 1996, 42). Human Rights Commission of the European Union stated: "The Serbian rapes of Croatian and Bosniak women are not accidental, but planned by Belgrade, as strategic weapon" (Frusca 1996, 30). No one has been found responsible for these crimes yet.

Not only that Serbia did not take responsibility for the outbreak of war, but Serbian academics wrote another memorandum in 2011. The document was written by the Serbian writer and politician Dobrica Ćosić and Ljubomir Tadić and other members of the SANU. Colloquially, the document is known under the name of "Memorandum SANU II". One of the goals is to "reduce Serbia's responsibility for war" in Croatia, BH and Kosovo and bring them to give up on their announced accusations before the international courts; "bring Serbia into the same position with the war damaged neighboring states; help the secession of the Republic Serb from BH; and insist on recognition of of Serbs in Croatia, Montenegro, and Kosovo as constituent minorities" (Drugi Memorandum SANU 2011, 12-15). Once again, we can see that there is still no serious attempt from Serbia to face its recent history and crimes committed to nations surrounding it. Improving its relations with the neighbors, in particular Croats, Bosniaks, and Kosovars, Serbia will not achieve with these kinds of Memorandums that throughout the 20th century always implied territorial expansion. The first step toward catharsis and reconciliation is honest, objective, and unbiased scientific research.

CONCLUSION

Croatian history of the 20th century still is full of controversial questions. Most of these questions regard Croatian-Serbian relations from the mid-19th to the end of the 20th century that still present difficult task for historians. This task becomes even more difficult because of the manipulations and state control of history research during the communist regime in the second half of the 20th century.

The experience of political interaction between these two nations in two multinational Yugoslav states have demonstrated the main source of conflict: Croats advocated for a federative country that would guarantee equality to all nations in Yugoslavia, while Serbs advocated for expanding their territory to all lands where Serbs lived, regardless of other nations and their rights. Croats and Serbs entered the Kingdom of SHS, later renamed to the Kingdom of Yugoslavia, with such different goals, and ended up in a state where Serbs dominated. Serbian territorial pretensions were rooted in the writings of Vuk Stefanović Karadžić and Ilija Garašanin, whose political agenda of territorial expansion, of usurping others' cultural values, and not acknowledging identities of other nations was adopted by the Serbian state and people and caused all conflicts and wars in southeastern Europe in the last two centuries.

The position of Croats and Croatia in the Kingdom of Yugoslavia described in this chapter was the reason why they did not want to defend the country when the Axis Powers attacked it in 1941 and why a majority of Croats welcomed the establishment of the Independent State of Croatia. The terror and dictatorship of the Serbian king Alseksandar Karađorđević also was the trigger for the formation of the Ustasha movement that struggled for Croatian sovereignty and independence by violent means and took over power in the Independent State of Croatia with the help of the Axis Powers.

The terror of the Ustasha regime, and the intolerant and violent policy towards Serbs (and others as described in other chapter), was retaliation for the treatment of Croats in the Kingdom of Yugoslavia and for Serbian massacres of Croats at the onset of the Independent State of Croatia. Some Serbs and Serbian military units loyal to the Royal Yugoslav

Government in emigration called Chetniks, not only did not want a Croatian independent state ruled by the Ustashas but also *any* kind of independent Croatia. This can be seen by the campaigns of Serbian cultural institutions and Serbian Orthodox Church to separate from the Banovina of Croatia in 1939 and later from the NDH. Already in April 1941, before the proclamation of the NDH, Chetniks killed Croatian civilians and soon after the proclamation, in accordance with the "Memorandum" of Chetnik Stevan Moljević, they began the rebellion with the aim of creating a Greater Serbia that would usurp certain parts of Croatia by the policy of ethnic cleansing. This was the reason why they committed mass killings of Croats and Muslims in the NDH. The Ustasha regime, on the other hand, also carried out a policy of killing and deportation of Serbs and committed crimes against Serbian civilians. In the horrific episodes of bloodshed all warring parties committed crimes – Chetniks, Ustashas, and partisans and all of them at some point collaborated, or attempted to collaborate, with the German and Italian occupiers to attain or to keep power. The mass transfer of Chetniks to partisan units in 1944, when it was clear that partisans would win the war in Yugoslavia, and joint crimes of the partisans and Chetniks against Croats and Muslims during and after the war have been neglected both in Croatian and Serbian historiography.

The victory of the antifascist coalition in Europe and partisans in the area of the former Kingdom of Yugoslavia enabled communists to create a new Yugoslavia and complete a communist revolution after the war. As for the national question, under the imposed phrase of "brotherhood and unity" the communists tried to suppress national tensions. However, it turned out that national question in the multinational communist Yugoslavia could not be solved by ignoring it and not allowing any public and academic discussions about it, so the communist Yugoslavia was in a way a time bomb and its fuse were Croatian-Serbian relations. One of the most important and difficult tasks of the Yugoslav communists was to keep the national question under their control and to strike a balance between its nations. Accordingly, periods of trends toward federalization of the country alternated with centralization.

The two successive Yugoslav states could not solve the national question of their nations. Despite the fact that they declared and emphasized national equality, in reality the Serbian nation and Greater Serbian policy always dominated with the final goal of creating the Greater Serbia in which all nations would "drown" in the Serbian one. In both Yugoslav states the crucial problem was a clash of ideas of federalism, advocated by Croats and other non-Serbian nations, and unitarism, which implied Greater Serbian domination. Croatian-Serbian relations, above all other national relations, were the key for continuity or dissolution of the Yugoslav state.

One of the elements of suppression of the national question, particularly the Croatian question, was labeling all forms of manifestation of Croatian national identity as chauvinism and sympathizing with the Ustashas. Communist and later Serbian historiography imposed a genocidal stigma on the entire Croatian people by systematically magnifying the Ustasha crimes and hiding Serb and communist ones in spite of the fact that the latter were an order of magnitude bigger. Exemplary was a constant increase in the claimed numbers of victims of Jasenovac. During communist Yugoslavia, the brutal regime imposed and maintained an idealized image of the partisan fighters as liberators from the occupiers and just soldiers whose crimes against the defeated side were justified as rightful revenge, if they were spoken of at all. Only after the breakdown of the communist regime in Yugoslavia, in a free and democratic Croatia, could historians begin to research topics that had been taboo during communism. The crimes of the Ustasha regime have been acknowledged numerous times by politicians and historians in Croatia, whereas similar thing did not happen in Serbia when it comes to crimes of Serbs and communist regime.

It must be stressed that certain intellectual circles in Croatia continue to label this recent research as historical "revisionism" and as an attempt to deny the Ustasha crimes; they intentionally disregard the lack of objective or systematic research of partisan and communist crimes in Croatia, nor even any public knowledge or acknowledgement of these crimes. Moreover, every attempt to examine or reassess topics regarding Ustashas and partisans, the number of casualties in Jasenovac, the comparison of the NDH's and Nedić's Serbia towards Jews, and the role of Croats and Serbs in the Holocaust, are dismissed as pseudoscientific and their authors are accused of attempts to rehabilitate NDH (Goldstein 2019; Kasapović 2018). A comprehensive response to that attitude was summarized by Marijan (2019), but the dispute is far from reaching conciliation, or even a dialogue.

Finally, as the political moves for centralization of Yugoslavia led by Slobodan Milošević had failed and due to persistent advocacy of Slovenia and Croatia for confederacy, Milošević and his associates with the support of the JNA (Yugoslav Army) planned and conducted the aggression on Croatia with the aim of amputating parts of Croatia where Serbs formed a substantial part of the population. During the war, Croatia gained its independence, was internationally recognized, and through liberation operations and peaceful reintegration it achieved its territorial integrity.

Croatia did not want or seek the armed conflict; achieving its independence within the existing and internationally recognized borders was legal and legitimate. Croatia tried to avoid war by persistent negotiations and to achieve peace by signing all offered peace agreements. The fact is that one strong army (JNA) attacked disarmed Croatian people, and in the same time it armed the Serbian paramilitary troops, including Chetniks, that were robbing, burning down villages, destroying, raping, and expelling people and conducting in that way ethnic cleansing. Moreover, today Serbia denies its expansionist policy and continues it through the mentioned Memorandum SANU II from 2011.

The questions presented in this chapter are still taking a toll on relations between Croats and Serbs, as well as Croatia and Serbia, which today are both free and independent, democratic states. It is obvious that in democracy, peace and reconciliation between the two countries cannot be achieved without serious scientific research that will approach these events evenhandedly and dispassionately. The prerequisite for this is a sincere wish to progress towards mutual understanding and elimination of centuries-long frictions. Therefore, these open questions still wait for a thorough, systematic, and objective research and dialogue at all levels of society (see Chapter 11).

References

Antić, Ljubomir. 2007. *Velikosrpski nacionalni programi: ishodišta i posljedice.* Zagreb: Golden marketing – Tehnička knjiga: Hrvatski institut za povijest. [*Greater-Serbian National Programs: Origins and Consequences.* Zagreb: Golden Marketing – Tehinčka knjiga: Croatian Institute of History].

Апостолски, Михајло, Данчо Зографски, Иван Катарџиев, Блаже Конески, Љубен Лапе, Димитар Митрев, Христо Андонов-Полјански, уредници. 1969. *Историја на македонскиот народ (периодот меѓу двете светски војни и народната револуција 1918 – 1945), книга трета.* Скопје: Институт за национална историја. [Apostolski, Mihailo, Dančo Zografski, Ivan Katardziev, Blaže Koneski, Ljuben Lape, Dimitar Mitrev, and Hristo Andonov-Poljanski, editors. 1969. *History of the Macedonian people: The Period between the Two World Wars and the People's Revolution (1918 - 1945). Third book.* Skopje, North Macedonia: Institute of National History].

Arendt, Hannah. 1964. *Eichmann in Jerusalem. A report on the banality of evil.* New York: The Viking Press. Accessed March 1, 2020. https://platypus1917.org/wp-content/uploads/2014/01/arendt_eichmanninjerusalem.pdf.

Arhiv Znaci. Baza podataka o drugom svetskom ratu na tlu Jugoslavije [Archive Znaci. Data Base on World War 2 in Yugoslavia]. Accessed March 25, 2020. http://znaci.net/arhiv/dogadjaj/14288.

Artuković, Mato. 2001. "Židovi u srpskom tisku u Hrvatskoj potkraj 19. stoljeća." *Časopis za suvremenu povijest* 33: 725-745. ["Depictions of Jews in the Serbian Press in Croatia at the End of the 19th Century." *Journal of Contemporary History* 33: 725-745]. Accessed April 9, 2020. https://hrcak.srce.hr/208549.

Artuković, Mato. 2010. "Pitanje šteta i odštete u antisrpskim demonstracijama 1902. godine." *Časopis za suvremenu povijest* 42: 179-217. ["The Question of Damages and Compensation in the Anti-Serb Demonstrations of 1902." *Journal of Contemporary History* 42: 179-217]. Accessed February 10, 2020. https://hrcak.srce.hr/index.php?show=clanak&id_clanak_jezik=90565.

Bakotin, Jerko. 2019. "Razgovor s povodom – Ivo Goldstein: relativiziranjem ustaških zločina kriminalizira se čitav jedan narod." *Lupiga.* ["Interview with the Occasion – Ivo Goldstein: By Relativizing of the War Guilt one Entire Nation is Criminalized." *Lupiga*]. Accessed March 17, 2020. https://lupiga.com/intervjui/intervju-ivo-goldstein-relativiziranjem-ustaskih-zlocina-kriminalizira-se-citav-jedan-narod?page=2.

Banac, Ivo. 1995. *Nacionalno pitanje u Jugoslaviji: porijeklo, povijest, politika.* Translated from English Josip Šentija. Zagreb: Durieux. Originally Published: Banac, Ivo. 1988. *The National Question in Yugoslavia: Origins, History, Politics.* Ithaca, New York: Cornell University Press.

Barić, Nikica. 2005. *Srpska pobuna u Hrvatskoj: 1990.-1995.* Zagreb: Golden marketing-Tehnička knjiga. [*Serbian Rebellion in Croatia: 1990-1995*].

Bataković, Dušan T. 2014. *The Foreign Policy of Serbia (1844-1867) Ilija Garašanin's Načertanije.* Belgrade: Institut des Etudes Balkaniques. Accessed February 20, 2020. https://books.google.hr/books?id=Y5yxDwAAQBAJ&pg=PA6&lpg=PA6&dq=na%C4%8Dertanije+the+program+of+the+foreign+and+national+policy&source=bl&ots=tq7o74I_Na&sig=ACfU3U3-kEMB2OiCFLCRSX1-werpa8er3g&hl=hr&sa=X&ved=2ahUKEwizn5iR2pnoAhXh-yoKHYqnDQ0Q6AEwAHoECAcQAQ#v=onepage&q=na%C4%8Dertanije%20the%20program%20of%20the%20foreign%20and%20national%20policy&f=false.

Batelja, Juraj. 2019. *Blaženi Alojzije Stepinac – spašavanje Židova i Srba u Drugom svjetskom ratu.* [*Blessed Alojzije Stepinac – Rescue of Jews and Serbs in Second World War*]. Zagreb: Postulatura Bl. Alojzija Stepinca.

Bilandžić, Dušan. 1999. *Hrvatska moderna povijest.* [*Croatian Modern History*]. Zagreb: Golden marketing-Tehnička knjiga.

Boban, Branka. 2019. "Stavovi hrvatske političke elite prema stvaranju jugoslavenske države." *Tragovi: časopis za srpske i hrvatske teme* 2: 7-98 ["Attitudes of Croatian political elite towards formation of the Yugoslav state." *Clues: a journal for Serbian and Croatian topics* 2: 7-98]. Accessed February 21, 2020. https://hrcak.srce.hr/index.php?show=clanak&id_clanak_jezik=333440.

Boban, Ljubo. 1971. "Geneza, značenje i odjek Zagrebačkih punktacija." *Časopis za suvremenu povijest* 3: 153-209. ["Genesis, Significance and Repercussions of the Zagrebačke punktacije." *Journal of Contemporary History* 3: 153-209]. Accessed February 20, 2020. https://hrcak.srce.hr/219309.

Boban, Ljubo. 1971. "Ustaše." *Enciklopedija Jugoslavije* 8. Zagreb. ["The Ustashas." *Encyclopedia of Yugoslavia* 8. Zagreb].

Boćkowski, Daniel. 2009. "'Together Forever': The Soviet Occupation of Eastern Poland during the Second World War," 599-616. In *Okupācijas režīmi Baltijas valstīs 1940–1991. Latvijas Vēsturnieku komisijas 2008. gada pētījumi un starptautiskās konferences "Okupācijas režīmi Baltijas valstīs (1940–1990): izpētes rezultāti un problēmas" materiāli,* 2008. gada 30.–31. oktobris, Rīga. Riga: Latvijas vēstures institūta apgāds. [In *Occupation Regimes in the Baltic States 1940-1991. Research of the Commission of the Historians of Latvia, 2008 and Proceedings of the International Conference "Occupation Regimes in the Baltic States (1940–1990): Research results and problems"*, 30–31 October 2008, Riga. Riga: Lativan Institute of History. Accessed April 14, 2020. file:///C:/Users/pp/Downloads/TogetherForever-TheSovietOccupationofEastern PolandduringtheSecondWorldWar.pdf.

Borić, Gojko. 2015. "Nijemci su Tita još u Adenauerovo doba nazivali 'običnim drumskim razbojnikom'". *Cro Express.* ["Back in Adenauer's Time Germans Called Tito 'a Common Thug'". *Cro Express*]. May, 18. Accessed March 2, 2020. https://www.croexpress.eu/kolumne/4047/nijemci-su-tita-jos-u-adenaerovo-doba-nazivali-obicnim-drumskim-razbojnikom.

Borovčak, Damir. 2007. *Voliš li Hrvatsku?* Zagreb: Vlastita naklada. [*Do You Love Croatia?* Zagreb: Self-Publishing].

Bogdan, Ivo, ed. 1963. *La Tragedia de Bleiburg. Documentos sobre las matanzas en masa de los croatas en Yugoeslavia comunista en 1945.* Buenos Aires: El Instituto cultural Croatia Latinoamericano. [*The Bleiburg Tragedy. Documents on the Mass Killings of Croats in Communist Yugoslavia in 1945.* Buenos Aires: Croatian-Latinamerican Cultural Institute].

Braniteljski portal. 2018. "Video: Nikola Banić-računalni programi ne lažu: Popis žrtava Jasenovca je stvaran kao i mogućnost da nas sad pogodi meteor." [Veterans' Portal. 2018. "(Video). Nikola Banić-Computer Programs Do Not Lie: The List of Jasenovac Victims Is as Real as the Possibility of Meteor Hitting Us Right Now"]. Accessed March 17, 2020. https://www.braniteljski-portal.com/video-nikola-banic-racunalni-programi-ne-lazu-popis-zrtava-jasenovca-je-stvaran-kao-i-mogucnost-da-nas-sad-pogodi-meteor.

Braniteljski portal. 2019. "Video: Bleiburg – najveće stradanje Hrvata u povijesti svog postojanja." [Veterans' Portal. 2019. "Video: Bleiburg – the Greatest Suffering of Croats in Their History."]. 2019. Accessed March 16, 2020. https://www.braniteljski-portal.com/video-bleiburg-najvece-stradanje-hrvata-u-povijesti-svog-postojanja-2.

Bulatović, Radomir. 1990. *Koncentracioni logor Jasenovac, s posebnim osvrtom na Donju Gradinu. Istorijsko-sociološka i antropološka studija*. Sarajevo: Svjetlost. [*Concentration Camp Jasenovac, with the Special Review on Donja Gradina. Historical-Sociological and Anthropological Study*. Sarajevo: Light].

Cohen, Philip J. 1992. "Židovsko-američki publicist Philip J. Cohen: Srbija ima povijest duboko ukorijenjenog antisemitizma" ["Jewish-American Publicist Philip J. Cohen: Serbia Has History of Deeply Rooted Anti-Semitism"]. Accessed February 25, 2020. http://www.safaric-safaric.si/katas_srb/20190306_Zidovsko-americki_publicist_Philip_J_Cohen_Srbi.pdf.

Cohen, Philip J. 1996. *Serbia's Secret War: Propaganda and the Deceit of History*. Texas City: College Station, Texas A&M University Press.

Cravetto, Enrico, ed. 2007. *Povijest 15: Kolonijalna carstva i imperijalizam (1871.-1914.)*. Zagreb: Jutarnji list. [*History 15: Colonian Empires and Imperialism (1871-1914)*]. Zagreb: Morning Newspaper].

Crljen, Danijel. 1966. "Bleiburg." *Hrvatska revija* 16, edited by Vinko Nikolić. Paris: Matica hrvatska. ["Bleiburg." *Croatian Review* 16, edited by Vinko Nikolić. Paris: Matica of Croatia].

Curać, Marko. 2015. "Sto godina ubijaju nas a i dalje šutimo." *Hrvatski focus*. ["They Have Been Killing Us for Hundred Years and We Still Keep Silence." *The Croatian Focus*]. January 1. Accessed March 5, 2020. https://www.hrvatski-fokus.hr/index.php/intervjui/12578-sto-godina-ubijaju-nas-a-i-dalje-sutimo.

Crohis. n.d. Accessed March 13, 2020. https://sbplus.hr/_Data/Files/173_20110629192835724/ustzk.pdf.

Čović, Bože, editor. 1993. *Roots of Serbian Aggression. Debates / Documents / Cartographic Reviews*. Zagreb: Centre for Foreign Languages Zagreb and AGM d.o.o.

Čulinović, Ferdo. 1968. *Dokumenti o Jugoslaviji*. Zagreb: Školska knjiga. [*Documents on Yugoslavia*. Zagreb: Schoolbook].

Čuljak, Tihomir. 2019. "Cionizam, Hitler i Holokaust" ["Zionism, Hitler and the Holocaust"]. Accessed March 15, 2020. https://novenews.net/hr/znanost/cionizam-hitler-i-holokaust-155.

Damaška, Mirjan. 2009. *Tito-tajne vladara*. Zagreb: Večernji list. [*Tito – The Secrets of the Ruler*. Zagreb: Evening Newspaper].

Dedijer, Vladimir, and Antun Miletić. 1990. *Genocid nad Muslimanima 1941-1945, Zbornik dokumenata i sjećanja*. Sarajevo: Svjetlost. [*Genocide against the Muslims 1941-1945, Collection of Documents and Memories*. Sarajevo: Light].

"Deklaracija o nazivu i položaju hrvatskog književnog jezika." *2009. Kolo* 1-2. ["Declaration on the Name and Status of the *Croatian* Literary Language." *Circle* 1-2]. Accessed http://www.matica.hr/kolo/314/deklaracija-o-nazivu-i-polozaju-hrvatskog-knjizevnog-jezika-20681/.

Dežman, Jože, ed. 2010. *Prikrita grobišta. Izvješće komisije Vlade Republike Slovenije za rješavanja pitanja skrivenih grobišta 2005.-2008.* Translation in Croatian from Slovenian. Sarajevo: Hrvatsko katoličko dobrotvorno društvo. [*Concealed Grave-Yards. Report of the Committee of the Government of the Republic of Slovenia for solution of the question of the Concealed Grave-Yards 2005-2008.* Sarajevo: Croatian Catholic Philantrophical Association].

Direktno. 2019. "Goldstein o Bleiburgu i Jasenovcu: Neprihvatljivo je govoriti da su sve žrtve iste." *Direktno*. ["Goldstein on Bleiburg and Jasenovac: It is Unacceptable to Say that All Victims are the Same"]. Accessed March 17, 2020. https://direktno.hr/direkt/goldstein-o-bleiburgu-i-jasenovcu-neprihvatljivo-govoriti-da-su-sve-zrtve-iste-150765/.

Dirlmer, Ulf. 1999. *Povijest Njemačke*. [*History of Germany*]. Zagreb: Barbat.

Dizdar, Zdravko. 2005. "Prilog istraživanju problema Bleiburga i križnih putova (u povodu 60. obljetnice)." *Senjski zbornik* 32: 117-196 ["A Contribution to Research of the Problem of Bleiburg and Ways of Cross (on the Occasion of the 60th Anniversary)." *Proceedings of Senj* 32: 117-196]. Accessed March 19, 2020. https://hrcak.srce.hr/17764.

Dizdar, Zdravko. 2007. "Bjelovarski ustanak od 7. do 10.travnja 1941." *Časopis za suvremenu povijest* 39: 581-609 ["The Bjelovar Uprising of 7-10 April 1941." *Journal of Contemporary History* 39: 681-609]. Accessed February 27, 2020. https://hrcak.srce.hr/19060.

Dizdar, Zdravko, Marko Grčić, Slaven Ravlić, and Darko Stuparić. 1997. *Tko je tko u NDH*. [*Who Is Who in NDH*]. Zagreb: Minerva.

Dizdar, Zdravko, Vladimir Geiger, Milan Pojić, and Mate Rupić. 2005. *Partizanska i komunistička represija i zločini u Hrvatskoj 1944.-1946. Dokumenti.* 2. izd. Slavonski Brod. Hrvatski institut za povijest – Podružnica za povijest Slavonije, Srijema i Baranje. [*The Partisan and Communist Oppression and Crimes in Croatia 1944-1946. Documents.* 2nd ed]. Slavonski Brod: Croatian Institute of History – Section for Slavonia, Syrmia, and Baranya]. Accessed March 8, 2020. http://znaci.net/00003/665.pdf.

Dogan, Željko. 2019. "Svjedočenje agenta KOS-a o 'Oluji' koje trebaju pročitati svi Hrvati, ali i Srbi." *Maxporta*l. ["The Testimony of the KOS Agent on 'Oluja' that All Croats, and Even Serbs, Have to Read"]. Accessed March 19, 2020. https://www.maxportal.hr/vijesti/svjedocenje-agenta-kos-a-o-oluji-koje-trebaju-procitati-svi-hrvati-ali-i-srbi/.

"Drugi Memorandum SANU" ["The Second Memorandum SANU"]. 2011. *Bosnian-Herzegovinian Magazine Europa*, April, 12-15. Accessed March 18, 2020. http://www.europamagazine.info/PDF/EuropaApril2011.pdf.

Đilas, Milovan. 1947. *Članci 1941-1946*. Zagreb: Kultura. [*Articles 1941 – 1946*. Zagreb: Culture].

Frusca, Paolo. 1996. *Genocido nei Balcani nel nome della grande Serbia*. Brescia: Centro studi cattolici "Mater Eclesiae". [*The Genocide in the Balkans in the Name of the Greater Serbia*. Brescia: Center for Catholic Studies "Mater Eclesiae"].

Gabelica, Ivan. 2007. *Blaženi Alojzije Stepinac i hrvatska* država. Zagreb: Vlastita naklada. [*Blessed Alojzije Stepinac and the Croatian State*. Zagreb: Self-Publishing].

Garašanin, Ilija. n.d. *Načertanije. Program spoljašne i nacionalne politike Srbije na koncu 1844. godine* [*Načertanije. The Program of Foreign and National Policy of Serbia at the End of 1844*]. Accessed February 15, 2020. http://www.rastko.rs/istorija/garasanin_nacertanije.html.

Geiger, Vladimir. 2010. "Ljudski gubici Hrvatske u Drugome svjetskom ratu i u poraću koje su prouzročili Narodnooslobodilačka vojska i Partizanski odredi Jugoslavije/Jugoslavenska armija i komunistička vlast. Brojidbeni pokazatelji (procjene, izračuni, popisi) *Case study*: Bleiburg i folksdojčeri." *Časopis za suvremenu povijest* 43: 693-722 ["Human Losses in Croatia during the Second World War and in the Postwar Period, which were Carried out by the National Liberation Army and the Partisan Units of Yugoslavia/the Yugoslavian Army and the Communist Government. Numeric Data

(Estimates, Calculations, Lists). *Case Study*: Bleiburg and the Volksdeutsche." *Journal of Contemporary History* 43: 693-722]. Accessed February 27, 2020. https://hrcak.srce.hr/index.php?show=clanak&id_clanak_jezik=114002.

Geiger, Vladimir. 2011. "Ljudski gubici Hrvatske u Drugom svjetskom ratu koje su prouzročili 'okupatori i njihovi pomagači'. Brojidbeni pokazatelji (procjene, izračuni, popisi)." *Časopis za suvremenu povijest* 43: 699-749. ["Human Losses in Croatia during the Second World War Instigated by the 'Occupiers And Their Accomplices'. Quantitative Indicators (Estimates, Calculations, Lists)." *Journal of Contemporary History* 43: 699-749]. Accessed February 29, 2020. https://hrcak.srce.hr/76758.

Geiger, Vladimir. 2013. "Brojidbeni pokazatelji o žrtvama logora Jasenovac, 1941.–1945. (procjene, izračuni, popisi)." *Časopis za suvremenu povijest* 45 No. 2: 211-242 ["Numerical Indicators of Victims of the Jasenovac Camp, 1941-1945 (Estimates, Calculations, Lists)." *Journal of Contemporary History* 45 No. 2: 211-242]. Accessed March 14, 2020. https://hrcak.srce.hr/109878.

Gitman, Esther. 2019a. *Kad hrabrost prevlada: spašavanje i preživljavanje Židova u Nezavisnoj Državi Hrvatskoj 1941.-1945.* Drugo izdanje. Prevela Lidija Šimunić Mesić. Zagreb: Kršćanska sadašnjost. Originally published: Gitman, Esther. 2011. *When Courage Prevailed: The Rescue and Survival of Jews in the Independent State of Croatia 1941-1945.* St. Paul: Paragon House.

Gitman, Esther. 2019b. *Stepinac – Pillar of Human Rights*. Zagreb: Kršćanska sadašnjost: Hrvatsko katoličko sveučilište. [Zagreb: Christian Present: Croatian Catholic University].

Glasnik srpske pravoslavne patrijaršije 1-2 [*Herald of the Serbian Orthodox Patriarchate 1-2*]. February, 1937. Beograd.

Glasnik srpske pravoslavne crkve 2-3 [*Herald of the Serbian Orthodox Church 2-3*]. March 1, 1942. Beograd.

Goldstein, Ivo. 2008. *Hrvatska 1918-2008*. Zagreb: [*Croatia 1918-2008*]. Zagreb: Europapress holding: Novi liber.

Goldstein, Ivo. 2019a. *Kontroverze hrvatske povijest 20. stoljeća* [*Controversies of the Croatian history of the 20th century*]. Zagreb: Profile.

Goldstein, Ivo, and Slavko Goldstein. 2011. *Jasenovac i Bleiburg nisu isto*. Zagreb: Novi liber. [*Jasenovac and Bleiburg are not the Same*. Zagreb: Novi liber].

Grahek Ravančić, Martina. 2009. *Bleiburg i križni put 1945*. Zagreb: Hrvatski institut za povijest [*Bleiburg and the Way of Cross in 1945*. Zagreb: Croatian Institute of History]. Accessed March 2, 2020. http://www.znaci.net/00003/658.pdf.

Graovac, Igor. 1992. "Ljudski gubici Dalmacije 1941." *Časopis za suvremenu povijest* 24: 83-106. ["The Human Loss in Dalmatia in 1941." *Journal of Contemporary History* 24: 83-106].

Gregurić, Franjo. 1998. *Vlada demokratskog jedinstva Hrvatske 1991.-1992*. Zagreb: Naklada Zadro. [*Democratic Unity Government of Croatia 1991-1992*. Zagreb: Publishing House Zadro].

Hebrang, Andrija. 2013. *Zločini nad civilima u srpsko-crnogorskoj agresiji na Republiku Hrvatsku* Zagreb: Udruga hrvatskih liječnika dragovoljaca 1990.-1991. Zadar: Ogranak Matice hrvatske. [*Crimes against Civilians in the Serbian-Montenegrin Aggression on the Republic of Croatia*. Zagreb: Association of Croatian Volunteer Doctors 1990-1991. Zadar: Branch of the Matica of Croatia].

Hećimović, Joseph. 1962. *In Tito's Death Marches and Extermination Camps*. New York: Carlton press.

HINA. 2018. "Predsjednica o Jasenovcu. Podržavam ideju da međunarodna komisija utvrdi pravu istinu o logoru i što se u njemu događalo od '41. do '45., ali i kasnije" ["The President on Jasenovac. I support the Idea that the International Commission Establishes the Real Truth about the Camp and about What happened in it from 1941 to 1945, and Later"]. *Jutarnji list*, April, 24. Accessed March 16, 2020. https://www.jutarnji.hr/vijesti/hrvatska/predsjednica-o-jasenovcu-podrzavam-ideju-da-medunarodna-komisija-utvrdi-pravu-istinu-o-logoru-i-sto-se-u-njemu-dogadalo-od-41-do-45-ali-i-kasnije/7282015/.

Holjevac, Željko. 1999. "Jezik i nacija u hrvatskim i srpskim nacionalnim ideologijama: Starčevićeva polemika iz 1852. godine." *Migracijske i etničke teme* 15: 289-321 ["Language and Nation in Croatian and Serbian National Ideologies: Starčević's Polemics from 1852." *Migration and Ethnic Themes* 15: 282-321]. Accessed: April 17, 2020 https://hrcak.srce.hr/109432.

Horvat, Saša. 2009. "Zaboravljeni krvavi zločini. Likvidirana 664 crkvenjaka, a nijednog krivca još nema" ["The Forgotten Bloody Crimes. 664 of Executed Clergymen, and no Culprits yet"]. Accessed March 15, 2020. http://www.miljenko.info/attachments/article/1965/Zaboravljeni%20krvavi%20zlocini.pdf.

Horvat, Vladimir, Igor Vukić, Stipo Pilić, and Blanka Matković. 2015. *Jasenovački logori – istraživanja.* Zagreb: Društvo za istraživanje trostrukog logora Jasenovac. [*Jasenovac Camps – Research.* Zagreb: Association for Research of the Triple Camp Jasenovac].

Horvatić, Petar. 2016. "Titovi zločini – Hrvati ni danas ne znaju razmjere zločina u Zagrebu" *Narod.* ["Tito's Crimes – Croats do not Know of the Scale of Crimes in Zagreb Even Today." *The People*]. Accessed March 15, 2020. https://narod.hr/hrvatska/titovi-zlocini-hrvati-ni-danas-ne-znaju-razmjere-zlocina-zagrebu.

Horvatić, Petar. 2017. "27. listopada 1941. Srbija – kako je Tito surađivao s četnicima i abolirao ih zbog prelaska u partizane?" *Narod.* ["October 27, 1941 Serbia – How Tito Collaborated with the Chetniks and Abolished Them Because of Their Transfer to Partisans?" *The People*]. Accessed March 16, 2020. https://narod.hr/kultura/27-listopada-1941-srbija-tito-suradivao-s-cetnicima-abolirao-ih-zbog-prelaska-partizane.

Horvatić, Petar. 2019a. "21. kolovoza 1942. Istina o Holokaustu u Srbiji (2) – izvorni pokretači antisemitizma u Jugoslaviji nisu ustaše nego Srbija!" *Narod.* ["August 21, 1942. The Truth about the Holocaust in Serbia (2) – the Original Generators of Anti-Semitism in Yugoslavia Were Not the Ustashass but Serbia!" *The People*]. Accessed March 15, 2020. https://narod.hr/kultura/21-kolovoza-istina-o-holokaustu-u-srbiji-2-izvorni-pokretaci-antisemitizma-u-jugoslaviji-nisu-ustase-nego-srbija.

Horvatić, Petar. 2019b. "22. kolovoza 1941. Istina o Holokaustu u Srbiji (3) – skrivanje mračne antisemitske prošlosti Srbije i laži o antifašizmu." *Narod.* [*August 22, 1941.* The Truth about the Holocaust (3) – Hiding of the Dark Anti-Semitic History of Serbia and Lies on Anti-Semitism." *The People*]. Accessed March 15, 2020. https://narod.hr/kultura/22-kolovoza-1941-istina-o-holokaustu-u-srbiji-3-skrivanje-mracne-antisemitske-proslosti-srbije-i-lazi-o-hrvatskom-antisemitizmu.

Horvatić, Petar. 2019c. "24. svibnja 1945. Bogdan Radica (svibanj 1945.) – 'Biti Srbin u Zagrebu tih dana značilo je vlast'." Narod. ["May 24, 1945. Bogdan Radica (May 1945) – 'Being Serb that Day meant Being in Power'." *The People*]. Accessed March 16, 2020.

https://narod.hr/kultura/24-svibnja-1945-bogdan-radica-svibanj-1945-biti-srbin-u-zagrebu-tih-dana-znacilo-je-vlast.

Hrvatski tjednik [*The Croatian Weekly*]. 2018. "Povijesni ekskluziv - objavljujemo popis žrtava: Zemaljska komisija Hrvatske 1946. godine" ["The Historical Exclusive – We Publish a List of Victims: Land Commission of Croatia in 1946"]. Published February 8. Accessed March 16, 2020. https://hu-benedikt.hr/?p=111926.

Hudelist, Darko. 2013. "Dan oslobođenja Zagreba – 8. V. 1945" ["The Day of Zagreb's Liberation – May 5, 1945"]. *Globus*, May, 10. Accessed March 16, 2020. http://www.darkohudelist.eu/det.php?id=12.

Išek, Tomislav. 1971. "Primjena 'Obznane' na HRSS i posljedice za njene pristaše u Bosni i Hercegovini." *Časopis za suvremenu povijest* 3: 27-55. ["The Application of the 'Obznana' against the HRSS and the Consequences This Had on Its Followers in Bosnia and Herzegovina." *Journal of Contemporary History* 3: 27-55]. Accessed April 9, 2020. https://hrcak.srce.hr/219303.

Ivičević, Jozo. 2007. *Iz novije hrvatske povijesti*. Zagreb: Matica hrvatska. [*From Recent Croatian History*. Zagreb: Matica of Croatia].

Izvještaj Jugoslovenske Državne komisije za utvrđivanje zločina okupatora i njihovih pomagača Međunarodnom vojnom sudu u Nürnbergu. 1947. Beograd. [Report of the Yugoslav State Commission for Determining Crimes of Occupiers and their Helpers to the Military Court in Nürnberg. Belgrade].

Jakovina, Tvrtko. 2009. "Staljin: Od Hitlerova saveznika do krvnika Trećeg Reicha." *Jutarnji list*. ["Stalin: From Hitler's Ally and Butcher of the Third Reich." *The Morning Newspaper*]. September, 6. Accessed March 16, 2020. https://www.jutarnji.hr/vijesti/staljin-od-hitlerova-saveznika-do-krvnika-treceg-reicha/2838977/.

Jandrić, Berislav. 2006. "Prijepori saveznika oko zahtjeva Jugoslavije za izručenjem osumnjičenih za ratne zločine iz savezničkih izbjegličkih logora u Italiji 1945.-1947." *Časopis za suvremenu povijest* 38: 457-498 ["Disputes Among The Allies Concerning The Demands of Yugoslavia to Extradite Suspected War Criminals from Allied Refugee Camps In Italy, 1945 – 1947." *Journal of Contemporary History* 38: 457-498]. Accessed March 15, 2020. https://hrcak.srce.hr/7736.

Jareb, Mario. 2006. *Ustaško-domobranski pokret: od nastanka do travnja 1941*. Zagreb: Školska knjiga. [*The Ustasha-Domobran Movement: From Formation to April 194*1. Zagreb: Schoolbook].

Jareb, Mario. 2011. "Prilog raspravi o karakteru ustanka od 27. srpnja 1941. godine." *Časopis za suvremenu povijest* 43: 751-771 ["A Contribution to Discussion on the Character of the Uprising of July 27, 1941." *Journal of Contemporary History* 43: 751-771]. Accessed March 13, 2020. https://hrcak.srce.hr/76759.

"Jasenovac". 1958. *Enciklopedija Leksikografskog zavoda* 3. [*Encyclopedia of the Lexicographic Institute* 3]. Zagreb.

Jones, Nigel. 2014. "From Stalin to Hitler, the Most Murderous Regimes in the World." *Mail Online*, October 7. Accessed March 16, 2020. https://www.dailymail.co.uk/home/moslive/article-2091670/
Hitler-Stalin-The murderous-regimes.world.html.

Jonjić, Tomislav. 2000. *Hrvatska vanjska politika 1939.-1942*. Zagreb: Liber. [*Croatian Foreign Policy 1939-1942*].

Jonjić, Tomislav, editor. 2007. *Politički zatvorenik*, svibanj. Zagreb: Hrvatko društvo političkih zatvorenika. [*The Political Prisoner*, May 2007. Zagreb: Croatian Society of Political Prisoners].

Jonjić, Tomislav. 2009. "Proces Hranilović-Soldin: Prilog poznavanju postanka ustaškog pokreta." In *Hrvatska između slobode i jugoslavenstva: Zbornik radova sa znanstvenog skupa održanog 8. i 9. siječnja 2009. u Zagrebu*, edited by Tomislav Jonjić and Zlatko Matijević, 167-196. Zagreb: Zajednica udruga hrvatskih vojnih invalida Domovinskog rata Grada Zagreba. ["The Hranilović-Soldin Trial: A Contribution to the Knowledge of Formation of the Ustaša Movement." In *Croatia between Freedom and Yugoslavism: Proceedings from the Scientific Conference Held January 8 and 9, 2009 in Zagreb*, edited by Tomislav Jonjić and Zlatko Matijević, 167-196. Zagreb: The Croatian Disabled Homeland War Veterans' Association of the City of Zagreb]. Accessed February 20, 2020. https://www.tomislavjonjic.iz.hr/slike/II_hranilovicsoldin.pdf.

Jonjić, Tomislav. 2011. "Pokolj širokobrijeških franjevaca u kontekstu uspostave jugoslavenske komunističke vlasti" ["Massacre of the Franciscans of Široki Brijeg in the Context of Establishment of Yugoslav Communist Rule"]. Accessed February 27, 2020. https://www.tomislavjonjic.iz.hr/JONJIC-Pokolj%20sirokobrijeskih%20franjevaca-Zr.pdf.

Jukic, Marko. 2019. "Da se ne zaboravi: Srbijanski koncentracijski logori u Hrvatskoj i Srbiji 1991. – 1995." *Benedikt*. ["Not to be Forgotten: Serbian Concentration Camps in Croatia and Serbia 1991-1995." *Benedict*]. Accessed March 14, 2020. https://hu-benedikt.hr/?p=120458.

Jura, Ana. 2013. "Vladimir Geiger. Josip Broz Tito i ratni zločini: Bleiburg – Folksdojčeri." Review of Josip Broz Tito and War Crimes: Bleiburg and Folksdeutchers, by Vladimir Geiger. *Časopis za suvremenu povijest* 45: 549-552 [*Journal of Contemporary History* 45: 549-552]. Accessed March 17, 2020. https://hrcak.srce.hr/index.php?show=clanak&id_clanak_jezik=167311.

Jurčević, Josip. 2005. *Bleiburg: jugoslavenski poratni zločini nad Hrvatima*. Zagreb: Dokumentacijsko informacijsko središte. [*Bleiburg: Yugoslav Postwar Crimes against Croats*. Zagreb: Documentation and Information Center].

Kačić, Hrvoje. 2017. *Dubrovačke žrtve, jugokomunistički teror na hrvatskom jugu 1944. i poratnim godinama (početak Bleiburga)*. 3. dopunjeno izdanje. Zagreb: Tkanica. [*The Victims of Dubrovnik. Yugo-Communist Terror on the Croatian South in 1944 and in the Postwar Years* (the Beginning of Bleiburg. 3rd ed. Zagreb: Tkanica). https://hrcak.srce.hr/index.php?show=clanak&id_clanak_jezik=307406.

Karapandžić, Borivoje M. 1976. *Jugoslovensko krvavo proleće 1945. Titovi Katini i Gulazi*. Cleveland. [*The Yugoslav Bloody Spring 1945. Tito's Katyns and Gulags*. Cleveland].

Karaula, Željko. 2014. "Hrvatska seljačka zaštita u Kraljevini Jugoslaviji." *Doktorska disertacija*. Sveučilište u Zagrebu, Hrvatski studiji. ["Croatian Peasant Protection in the Kingdom of Yugoslavia." *PhD diss*. University of Zagreb, Faculty of Croatian Studies].

Karaula, Željko. 2015. "S Pribićevićem, Mačekom i Titom za Jugoslaviju – portret političkog djelovanje dr. Hinka Krizmana (1881. – 1958.)." *Radovi - Zavod za hrvatsku povijest* 47: 75-107. ["With Pribicevic, Macek and Tito for Yugoslavia - A Portrayal of Political Activity of Dr. Hinko Krizman (1881 – 1958)." *Journal - Institute of Croatian History* 47: 75-107]. Accessed April 10, 2020. https://bib.irb.hr/datoteka/303408.04_Karaula_RZHP_-_Hinko_Krizman.pdf.

Kasapović, Mirjana. 2018. "Genocid u NDH: Umanjivanje, banaliziranje i poricanje zločina." *Politička misao* 55: 7-32. ["Genocide in NDH: Downplaying, Banalizing and Denying Crimes." *Croatian political science review* 55: 7-32]. Accessed March 26, 2020. https://doi.org/10.20901/pm.55.1.01; https://hrcak.srce.hr/196775.

Kljaić, Stipe. 2012. "'Nikada više Jugoslavija! – jugoslavenstvo u vizijama hrvatskih nacionalističkih intelektualaca (1929.-1945.)" In Intelektualci i rat 1939.-1947. Zbornik radova s Desničinih susreta 2011. Edited by Drago Roksandić and Ivana Cvijović Javorina, 183-197. Zagreb: Filozofski fakultet u Zagrebu, Plejada. ["'Never again Yugoslavia!': Yugoslavism in the Views of the Croatian Nationalist Intellectuals. In Intellectuals and War 1939-1947." In *Proceedings from the Desnica's Meetings*. Edited by Drago Roksandić and Ivana Cvijović Javorina, 183-197. Zagreb: Faculty of Humanities and Social Sciences, University of Zagreb, Plejada].

Knez, Luka. 2017. "Odessa – san ili stvarnost izgubljenih Hrvata." *Rostra* 8: 163-181. ["Odessa – Dream or Reality of the Lost Croats." *Rostra* 8: 163-181]. Accessed February 10, 2020. https://hrcak.srce.hr/182146.

Knezović, Oton. 1960. *Pokolj hrvatske vojske 1945. Dokumenti o zvjerstvima Srba nad Hrvatima*. Chicago: Croatian Franciscan Press. [*The Massacre of the Croatian Army in 1945. Documents on Atrocities of Serbs against Croats*. Chicago. Croatian Franciscan Press].

Kolar-Dimitrijević, Mira. 2018. *The History of Money in Croatia 1527-1941*. Zagreb: Croatian National Bank. Accessed April 17, 2020. https://www.hnb.hr/documents/20182/121504/The-History-of-Money-in-Croatia.pdf/09461b90-2568-4610-9ee6-e6b47c638892.

"Koncentracioni logori." 1959. *Enciklopedija Leksikografskog zavoda* 4. ["Concentration Camps." *Encyclopedia of the Lexicographic Institute* 4]. Zagreb.

Krstić, Miloš, ed. 1969. *Zbornik dokumenata i podataka o narodnooslobodilačkom ratu naroda Jugoslavije* XIII/1. Beograd: Vojnoistorijski institut [*Collection of Documents and Dana on the National Liberation War of the Peoples of Yugoslavia* XIII/1. Belgrade: Institute of Military History]. Accessed March 15, 2020. http://www.znaci.net/00001/4_13_1_1.pdf.

Lebel, Jennie. 2007. *Until 'The Final Solution'. The Jews in Belgrade 1521-1942*. Bergenfield, NJ, U.S.: Avotaynu Inc.

Leković, Mišo. 1985. *Martovski pregovori 1943*. Beograd: Narodna knjiga. [*The March Negotiations in 1943*. Belgrade: People's book].

Leljak, Roman. 2015. *Huda jama - strogo čuvana tajna*. Zagreb: Društvo Huda jama. [*The Huda Pit – A Strictly Kept Secret*. Zagreb: Society Huda Jama].

Leontić, Boro. 1955. "Split godine 1941." *Historijski zbornik* 8: 41-67 ["Split in 1941." *Historical Collection* 8: 41-67]. Accessed March 25, 2020. http://www.historiografija.hr/hz/1955/HZ_8_3_LEONTIC.pdf.

Lopušina, Marko. 1997. *Ubij bližnjeg svog: Jugoslovenska tajna policija od 1945. do 1997*. Beograd: Narodna knjiga-Alfa [*Kill Your Neighbor: The Yugoslav Secret Police from 1945 to 1997*. Belgrade: People's book -Alfa].

Lozo, Stjepan. 2017. *Ideologija i propaganda velikosrpskoga genocida nad Hrvatima - Projekt Homogena Srbija 1941*. Split: Naklada Bošković. [*The Ideology and Propaganda of the Greater-Serbian Genocide against Croats: The Project Homogeneous Serbia 1941*. Split: Publishing House Bošković].

Magnuski, Janusz, and Maksym Kolomijec. 1994. *Czerwony Blitzkrieg. Wrzesien 1939: Sowieckie Wojska Pancerne w Polsce* [*Red Blitzkrieg: September 1939: Soviet Armed Forces in Poland*]. Warsaw: Wydawnictwo Pelta.

Marijačić, Ivica. 2016. "Mr. sc. Blanka Matković: Hrvatska je zatrovana lažima o Jasenovcu i o Drugome svjetskom ratu." *Hrvatski tjednik* ["Mr. sc. Blanka Matković: Croatia is Poisoned with Lies on Jasenovac and World War II." *Croatian Weekly*], May 16. Accessed January 30, 2020. https://www.hkv.hr/hrvatski-tjednik/23884-mr-sc-blanka-matkovic-hrvatska-je-zatrovana-lazima-o-jasenovcu-i-o-drugome-svjetskom-ratu.html.

Marijan, Davor. 2006. "Jugoslavenska narodna armija - važnija obilježja." *Polemos: časopis za interdisciplinarna istraživanja rata i mira* 9: 25-44 ["Yugoslav People's Army – Key Features." *Polemos: The Magazine for Interdisciplinary Research on War and Peace* 9: 25-44]. Accessed March 12, 2020. https://hrcak.srce.hr/17159.

Marijan, Davor. 2009. *Oluja*. Zagreb: Hrvatski memorijalno-dokumentacijski centar Domovinskog rata. [*The Storm*. Zagreb: The Croatian Memorial-Documentation Center of the Homeland War].

Marijan, Davor. 2019. "Suvremena hrvatska povijest i nevolje s revizionizmom." *Časopis za suvremenu povijest* 51: 385-421. ["Contemporary Croatian History and Troubles with Revisionism." *Journal of Contemporary History* 51: 385-421]. Accessed March 26, 2020. https://hrcak.srce.hr/225210.

Marušić, Matko. 2019. "Prof. dr. sc. Matko Marušić: Nezamislivi rasizam Ive Goldsteina traži javnu osudu." *Narod*. ["Prof. dr. sc. Matko Marušić: Inconceivable Racism of Ivo Goldstein Calls for Public Condemnation." *The People*]. Accessed March 15, 2020. https://narod.hr/hrvatska/prof-dr-sc-matko-marusic-nezamislivi-rasizam-ive-goldsteina-trazi-javnu-osudu.

Marušić, Milan, ed. 2002. *Žrtve komunističkih zlodjela u Zagrebu i na sljemenskim stratištima: Bolnica Brestovac, Gračani, Zagreb, svibanj 1945.* Zagreb: Hrvatsko žrtvoslovno društvo. [*Victims of the Communist Crimes in Zagreb and at Scaffolds on Sljeme: the Hospital Brestovac, Granačni, Zagreb, May 1945.* Zagreb: Croatian Society of Victimology].

Matijević, Zlatko. 2008. "Narodno vijeće Slovenaca, Hrvata i Srba u Zagrebu: Osnutak, djelovanje i nestanak (1918/1919)." *Fontes: izvori za hrvatsku povijest* 14: 35-66 ["National Council of Slovenes, Croats and Serbs in Zagreb: Establishment, Action and Disappearance (1918/1919)." *Fontes: Sources for Croatian History* 14: 35-66]. Accessed February 10, 2020. https://hrcak.srce.hr/29290.

Matković, Blanka. 2011. "Odvođenja i likvidacije ranjenih pripadnika Hrvatskih oružanih snaga (HOS) iz zagrebačkih bolnica 191 u svibnju i lipnju 1945. kroz arhivsko gradivo Državnog arhiva u Zagrebu." *Arhivski vjesnik* 54: 179-214 ["Arrests and Liquidations of Wounded Members of the Croatian Armed Forces (HOS) Taken from Hospitals in Zagreb by Yugoslav Armed Forces in May and June of 1945 in the Records of State Archives in Zagreb." *Archival News* 54: 179-214]. Accessed March 16, 2020. https://hrcak.
srce.hr/90525.

Matković, Blanka, and Ivan Pažanin, ed. 2011. *Zločini i teror u Dalmaciji 1943.-1948. Počinjeni od pripadnika NOV, JA, OZN-e i UDB-e. Dokumenti* [*Crimes and Terror in Dalmatia 1943-1948. Committed by the Members of NOV, JA, OZN, and UDB. Documents*]. Zagreb. Accessed March 17, 2020. http://www.znaci.net/00002/410.pdf.

Matković, Blanka, and Stipe Pilić. 2014. "Poslijeratni zarobljenički logor Jasenovac prema svjedočanstvima i novim arhivskim izvorima." *Radovi Zavoda za povijesne znanosti HAZU u Zadru* 56: 323-408 ["Postwar Prison Camp Jasenovac According to Testimonies and Recent Archival Sources." *Works of the Institute for Historical Research of the Croatian Academy of Sciences and Arts in Zadar* 56: 323-408]. Accessed March 17, 2020. https://hrcak.srce.hr/index.php?show=clanak&id_clanak_jezik=193840.

Matković, Hrvoje. 1998. *Povijest Jugoslavije: 1918.-1991.* Zagreb: Naklada Pavičić. [*The History of Yugoslavia 1918-1991.* Zagreb: Publishing House Pavičić].

Matković, Hrvoje. 2002. *Povijest Nezavisne Države Hrvatske. Drugo, dopunjeno izdanje.* Zagreb: Naklada Pavičić. [*The History of the Independent State of Croatia.* The Second Amended Edition. Zagreb: Publishing House Pavičić]. Accessed March 10, 2020. https://www.hercegbosna.org/STARO/download-hr/Matkovic_Povijest_NDH.pdf.

Matković, Hrvoje. 2006. *Na vrelima hrvatske povijesti.* Zagreb: Golden marketing-Tehnička knjiga. [*On the Sources of Croatian History.* Zagreb: Golden marketing-Tehnička knjiga].

Matković, Stjepan, and Marko Trogrlić, ed. 2019. *Političke bilješke Ante Trumbića 1930.-1938. Sv. I. 1930.-1934.* Zagreb-Split: Hrvatski institut za povijest: Filozofski fakultet u Splitu. [*Political Notes of Ante Trumbić 1930-1938, Vol. I. 1930-1934.* Zagreb-Split: Croatian Institute of History: Faculty of Humanities and Social Sciences, University of Split].

Мазгански, Јован. 2012. *Родовник на населението во селото Владимирово во периодот на Кралството на Србите, Хрватите и Словенците (1925-1941).* Канцеларија на Месната заедница во Владимирово. [Mazganski, Jovan. 2012. *List of Names and Surnames of the Population in the Village of Vladimirovo in the Period of the Kingdom of Serbs, Croats and Slovenes (1925-1941).* Vladimirovo Municipality Office].

Memorandum srpske akademije nauka i umetnosti (nacrt). Jesen 1986. [*Memorandum of the Serbian Academy of Sciences and Arts (Draft). Autumn 1986*]. Accessed March 19, 2020. https://www.helsinki.org.rs/serbian/doc/memorandum%20sanu.pdf.

Meštrović, Ivan. 1993. *Uspomene na političke ljude i događaje.* Zagreb: Nakladni zavod Matice hrvatske. [*Memories of Political People and Events.* Zagreb: Publishing House Matica hrvatska].

Miletić, Antun. 1986/1987. *Koncentracioni logor Jasenovac 1941-1945. Dokumenta, I.–III.* Beograd: Narodna knjiga. [*Concentration Camp Jasenovac 1941-1945. Documents I-III.* Belgrade: Narodna knjiga.

Miletić, Antun. 2010. *NDH – Koncentracioni logor Jasenovac 1941-1945.* Beograd. [*NDH – Concentration camp Jasenovac 1941-1945.* Belgrade].

Miletić, Antun. 2011. *Ubijeni u koncentracionom logoru Jasenovac 1941-1945.* Beograd: Gambit. [*The Assassinated in the Jasenovac Concentration Camp 1941-1945.* Belgrade: Gambit].

"The Molotov-Ribbentrop Pact 1939." Accessed March 14, 2020. https://truecostmovie.com/img/TSR/pages/section_01/1939_Molotov-Ribbentrop_Pact.pdf.

Nazor, Ante. 2008. *Grad je bio meta: bolnica, dom umirovljenika...* Zagreb: Hrvatski memorijalno-dokumentacijski centar Domovinskog rata. [*The Town Was the Target: Hospital, Retirement Home...* Zagreb: Croatian Memorial-Documentation Center of the Homeland War].

Nazor, Ante. 2011. Zagreb: *Velikosrpska agresija na Hrvatsku1990-ih.* Zagreb: Hrvatski memorijalno-dokumentacijski centar Domovinskog rata. [*Greater-Serbian Aggression on Croatia in the 90s*. Croatian Memorial-Documentation Center of the Homeland War].

Nazor, Ante, and Tomislav Pušek. 2018. *Domovinski rat: Pregled političke i diplomatske povijesti*. Zagreb: Nakladni zavod Globus: Hrvatski memorijalno-dokumentacijski centar Domovinskog rata. [*Homeland War: Review of Political and Diplomatic History*. Zagreb: Publishing House Globus: Croatian Memorial-Documentation Center of the Homeland War].

N1 Hrvatska. 2019. "Ressler: Bleiburg jedna od najvećih tragedija hrvatskog naroda." [N1 Croatia. 2019. "Ressler: Bleiburg Is On of the Greatest Tragedies of the Croatian People."]. 2019. Accessed March 17, 2020. http://hr.n1info.com/Vijesti/a403272/Ressler-Bleiburg-jedna-od-najvecih-tragedija-hrvatskog-naroda.html.

New York Times. 1931a. "Einstein Accuses Yugoslavian Rulers in Savant's Murder." Published on May 6. Accessed January 31, 2020. http://www.croatianhistory.net/etf/nyt.html

New York Times. 1931b. "Raditch Left tale of Yugoslav Plot." Published on August 23. Accessed January 31, 2020. http://www.croatianhistory.net/etf/raditch.pdf

Nikolić, Vinko.1988. *Bleiburg:uzroci i posljedice*. München – Barcelona: Knjižica Hrvatske revije. [*Bleiburg: Causes and Consequences*. München – Barcelona: Booklet of the Croatian Review].

Nikolić, Vinko, and Franjo Nevistić. 1976. *Bleiburška tragedija hrvatskog naroda*. Barcelona: Hrvatska revija. [*The Bleiburg Tragedy of the Croatian People*. Barcelona: Croatian Review].

Novosadski dogovor 1954. [*The Novi Sad Agreement 1954*]. Accessed March 18, 2020. http://govori.tripod.com/novosadski_dogovor.htm.

Novosel, Domagoj. 2008. *Gračanska kronika*. Zagreb: Župa Gračani. [*The Gračani Chronicle*. Zagreb: The Disctrict Gračani].

Omrčanin, Ivo. 1986. *Holocaust of Croatians*. Washington: Samizdat.

Opačak, Marijan. 2019. "Hebrang: Od početka istraživanja komunističkih zločina postoji jak otpor vladajućih u otkrivanju istine." *Direktno*. ["Hebrang: From the Beginning of Research of the Communist Crimes There Is a Strong Resistance from those in Power in Reveling the Truth." *Directly*]. Accessed April 27, 2020. https://direktno.hr/direkt/hebrang-od-pocetka-istrazivanja-komunistickih-zlocina-postoji-jak-otpor-vladajucih-otkrivanju-istine-165041/.

Pavičić, Darko. 2017. "Kako su ga otrovali: Kardinal osuđen na polagano umiranje." *Večernji list* ["How They Poisoned Him: The Cardinal Sentenced to Slow Dying." *Evening Newspaper*], November, 23. Accessed March 17, 2020. https://www.vecernji.hr/premium/alojzije-stepinac-juraj-batelja-komunizam-1209519.

Pavković, Mladen. 2019a. "25. rujna 1992. Donijet zakon o oprostu koji nije ispunio svoju svrhu." *Tjedno*. ["September 25, 1992. Passed the Law on Forgiveness That Did Not Fulfill Its Purpose." *Weekly*]. Accessed March 26, 2020. https://www.tjedno.hr/25-rujna-1992-donijet-zakon-o-oprostu-koji-nije-ispunio-svoju-svrhu/.

Pavković, Mladen. 2019b. "O Jasenovcu svi znaju, a o 70 tisuća Hrvata u srpskim logorima šuti i Hrvatska. *Priznajem*." ["Everyone Knows Everything about Jasenovac, and about 70 thousand of Croats in the Serbian Concentration Camps Even Croatia Is Silent." *I*

Admit]. Accessed March 16, 2020. https://priznajem.hr/novosti/hrvatska/o-jasenovcu-svi-znaju-a-o-70-tisuca-hrvata-u-srpskim-logorima-suti-i-hrvatska/97844/.

Pavličević, Dragutin. 2000. *Povijest Hrvatske. Drugo izmijenjeno i prošireno izdanje*. Zagreb: Naklada Pavičić. [*The History of Croatia. Second Revised and Amended Edition.* Zagreb: Publishing House Pavičić].

Pečarić, Josip. 2001. *Serbian Myth about Jasenovac*. Translated by Ivana Pečarić. Zagreb: Stih.

Pečarić, Josip, and Stjepan Razum. 2018. *Razotkrivena jasenovačka laž*. Zagreb: Društvo za istraživanje trostrukog logora Jasenovac. [*Exposed Jasenovac Lie*. Zagreb: Society for Research of the Tripple Jasenovac Camp].

Petranović, Branko. 1980. *Istorija Jugoslavije 1918–1978*. Beograd: Nolit. [*History of Yugoslavia 1918-1978*. Belgrade: Nolit]. Accessed April 17, 2020. http://www.znaci.net/00001/93.htm.

Petranović, Branko. 1992. *Srbija u Drugom svetskom ratu 1939-1945*. Beograd: Vojnoizdavački centar. [*Serbia in World War 2 1939-1945*. Belgrade: Military-publishing Center]. Accessed March 25, 2020. http://www.znaci.net/00001/92_4.pdf.

Pilar, Ivo. 1997. *Uvijek iznova Srbija*. [*Always and Only Serbia*]. Zagreb: Dominović d.o.o.

Pilić, Stipe. 2018. "S. Pilić: Korijeni, razmjeri i zataškavanje srpskog antisemitizma." *Portal Hrvatskog kulturnog vijeća*. ["S. Pilić: Roots, Extent and Cover-Up of the Serbian Anti-Semitism." *Portal of the Croatian Culture Council*]. Accessed March 14, 2020. https://www.hkv.hr/izdvojeno/vai-prilozi/ostalo/prilozi-graana/30165-s-pilic-korijeni-razmjeri-i-zataskavanje-srpskog-antisemitizma.html.

Poimenični popis žrtava Kcl Jasenovac 1941-1945. 2018. Spomen područje Jasenovac [*List by Name of the Victims of the Concentration Camp Jasenovac 1941-1945*. Jasenovac Memorial Site]. Accessed March 14, 2020. http://www.jusp-jasenovac.hr/Default.aspx?sid=6284.

Polovina, Gojko. 1988. *Svedočenje: sećanja na događaje iz prve godine ustanka u Lici*. Beograd: Rad. [*The Testimony: Memories on the Events from the First Year of the Uprising in Lika*. Belgrade: Rad].

Portmann, Michael. 2004. "Comunist Retaliation and Persecution on Yugoslav Territory during and after WWII (1943 - 1950)." *Tokovi istorije. Časopis Instituta za noviju istoriju Srbije* 1-2: 45-75 [*Currents of History. Journal of the Institute for Research History of Serbia* 1-2: 45-75]. Accessed March 19, https://www.inisbgd.co.rs/celo/2004_1.pdf.

Prcela, John I., and Stanko Guldescu. 1970. *Operation Slaughterhouse. Eyewitness Accounts of Postwar Massacres in Yugoslavia*. Philadelphia: Donance & Company.

Prcela, John Ivan, and Dražen Živić, ed. 2001. *Hrvatski holokaust. Dokumenti i svjedočanstva o poratnim pokoljima u Jugoslaviji*. Zagreb: Hrvatsko društvo političkih zatvorenika. [*The Croatian Holocaust. Documents and Testimonies on the Post-War Massacres in Yugoslavia*. Zagreb: Croatian Society of Political Prisoners]. Accessed March 2, 2020. http://www.pobijeni.info/userfiles/HrvatskiHolokaust.pdf.

Pribićević, Svetozar. 2000. *Izabrani politički spisi*. Izbor i uvodna studija Hrvoje Matković. Zagreb: Golden marketing-Narodne novine. [*The Selected Political Writings*. Selection and Introduction by Hrvoje Matković].

Prpić, George J. 1975. *Tragedies and Migrations in Croatian History*. Toronto.

Radelić, Zdenko. 2006a. *Hrvatska u Jugoslaviji 1945-1991: od zajedništva do razlaza.* Zagreb: Školska knjiga: Hrvatski institut za povijest. [*Croatia in Yugoslavia 1945-1991: From Communion to Dissolution*. Zagreb: School Book: Croatian Institute of History].

Radelić, Zdenko. 2006b. "Croatia 1945-1991." *Review of Croatian History* 2:13-26. Translated by Ida Jurković. Accessed March 2, 2020. https://hrcak.srce.hr/index.php?show=clanak&id_clanak_jezik=21965.

Radoš, Ivica, and Zoran Šangut. 2013. *Branili smo domovinu – pripadnici nacionalnih manjina u obrani Hrvatske.* Vukovar: Udruga pravnika Vukovar 1991. [*We defended the Homeland – Members of the National Minorities in Defense of Croatia*. Vukovar: Association of Jurists Vukovar 1991].

Regan, Krešimir. 2010. "The Serbian orthodox church and Croatian independence – activity in the Banate of Croatia." *Review of Croatian history* 4: 85-104. Accessed March 11, 2020. https://hrcak.srce.hr/index.php?show=clanak&id_clanak_jezik=100771.

Riley, Ben, and Rhys J. Davies. 1932. *The Croats under Yugo-Slavian Rule.* Accessed February 20, 2020. http://www.domovod.info/showthread.php?225-The-Croats-Under-Yugo-Slavian-Rule-The-Result-of-an-Inquiry-1932.

Roberts, Walter. 2013. *Tito, Mihailović i saveznici 1941-1945*. Beograd: Čigoja štampa. [*Tito, Mihailovic and Allies 1941-1945*. Belgrade: Čigoja Press]. Accessed April 14, 2020. http://www.znaci.net/00003/555.pdf.

Rudolf, Davorin. 1999. *Rat koji nismo htjeli: Hrvatska 1991.* Zagreb: Nakladni zavod Globus. [*The War We Did Not Want: Croatia in 1991*. Zagreb: Publishing House Globus].

Sadkovich, James J. 2010. *Tuđman. Prva politička biografija*. Zagreb: Večernji posebni proizvodi. [*Tuđman: the First Political Biography*. Zagreb: Evening Special Edition].

Sejdinović, Nedim. 2019. "Intervju – Latinka Perović: 'Srbija nastavlja politiku Slobodana Miloševića'." *Lupiga.* ["Interview – Latinka Perović: 'Serbia Is Continuing the Policy of Slobodan Milošević'." *Lupiga*]. Accessed March 12, 2020. https://lupiga.com/intervjui/intervju-latinka-perovic-srbija-nastavlja-politiku-slobodana-milosevica.

Shelah, Menachem. 1990. "Chetniks." In *Encyclopedia of the Holocaust*, Vol 1. Edited by Israel Gutman. New York: MacMillan.

Simić, Pero. 2009. *Tito: fenomen stoljeća: prva politička biografija*. Zagreb: Večernji posebni proizvodi. [*Tito: Phenomenon of the Century: The First Political Biography.* Zagreb: Evening Special Edition].

Skupina autora. 2007. *Povijest Hrvata: od 1918. do danas. 3. knjiga.* Zagreb: Školska knjiga. [Group of Authors. 2007. *The History of Croats: From 1918 to Today. The 3rd book.* Zagreb: Schoolbook].

Smoljan, Ivo, and Tomislav Sabljak, ed. 2000. *Povlačenje 1945. - krivci i žrtve*. [*The Withdrawal of 1945 - Culprits and Victims*]. Zagreb: Omega.

Smreka, Jelka, and Đorđe Mihovilović, ed. 2007. *Poimenični popis žrtava koncentracijskog logora Jasenovac 1941.-1945.* Jasenovac: Spomen područje Jasenovac. [*List by Name of the Victims of the Concentration Camp Jasenovac from 1941 to 1945*. Jasenovac: Memorial Area Jasenovac].

Sobolevski, Mihael, and Zdravko Dizdar. 1999. *Prešućivani četnički zločini u Hrvatskoj i BH 1941-1945*. Zagreb: Hrvatski institut za povijest: Dom i svijet. [*Silent Chetnik Torture in Croatia and Bosnia and Herzegovina 1941-1945*. Zagreb: Croatian Institute of History: Home and World].

Stančić, Nikša. 2002. *Hrvatska nacija i nacionalizam u 19. i 20. stoljeću*. Zagreb: Barbat [*Croatian Nation and Nationalism in the 19th and 20th Century*. Zagreb: Barbat].

Stojanović, Nikola. 1902. "Srbi i Hrvati." *Srpski književni glasnik* 2(6): 1149-59. ["Serbs and Croats." *Serbian Literate Herald* 2(6): 1149-59].

Stojić, D. 2017. "Mihailo Olćan." Acceessed March 15, 2020. https://www.zanimljivaistorija.com/2017/12/12/mihailo-olcan/.

Sudetic, Chuck. 1991. "Financial Scandal Rocks Yugoslavia." *The New York Times*, January, 10. Acessed May 14, 2019. https://en.calameo.com/books/0001117901be640dcac4f.

Šarić, Tatjana. 2008. "Osuđeni po hitnom postupku: uloga represivnih tijela komunističke vlasti u odnosu na smrtne osude u Hrvatskoj u Drugom svjetskom ratu i poraću na primjeru Fonda uprava za suzbijanje kriminaliteta Sekretarijata za unutrašnje poslove SRH." *Arhivski vjesnik* 51: 341-361. ["Sentenced under Urgent Procedure: The Role of Repressive Bodies of Communist Order During the WWII and in the Post-War Period, Ilustrated by Data from the Fonds of the Administration for the Supression of Delinquency of the Secretariat for Internal Affairs of the Socijalist Republic of Croatia." *Archival News* 51: 341-361]. Translated by Rajka Bućin. Accessed March 17, 2020. https://hrcak.srce.hr/index.php?show=clanak&id_clanak_jezik=46405.

Šimić, Damir. 2019. "Kineski i sovjetski komunistički režimi daleko najbrutalniji – Titov jugoslavenski režim u samom svjetskom vrhu." *HRSvijet*. ["Chinese and Soviet Communist Regimes By Far The Most Brutal – Tito's Yugoslav Regime at the Very Top." *CROWorld*]. Accessed March 17, 2020. http://www.hrsvijet.net/index.php/vijesti/132-hrvatska/53384-kineski-i-sovjetski-komunisticki-rezimi-daleko-najbrutalniji-titov-jugoslavenski-rezim-u-samom-svjetskom-vrhu.

Šišić, Ferdo. 1920. *Dokumenti o postanku Kraljevine Srba, Hrvata i Slovenaca 1914.-1919.* Zagreb: Matica hrvatska. [*Documents on forming of the Kingdom of Serbs, Croats and Slovenes 1914-1919*. Zagreb: Matica of Croatia].

Štefan, Ljubica. 1996. *Srpska pravoslavna crkva i fašizam*. Zagreb: Nakladni zavod Globus. [*The Serbian Orthodox Church and Fascism*. Zagreb: Publishing House Globus].

Štefan, Ljubica. 1999. *Mitovi i zatajena povijest*. Zagreb: K. Krešimir: Slovo M. [*Myths and Hidden History*. Zagreb: K. Krešimir: The Letter M].

Šumanović, Vladimir. 2019. "Ključni vojno-politički događaji u istočnoj Bosni 1942." PhD diss., Sveučilište u Zagrebu, Hrvatski studiji. ["Key Military-Political Events in the Eastern Bosnia in 1942." PhD diss., University of Zagreb, Faculty of Croatian Studies].. Accessed March 1, 2020. https://repozitorij.hrstud.unizg.hr/islandora/object/hrstud%3A1802.

Tolstoy, Nikolai. 1998. "Bleiburški pokolj." *Izlaganje na Međunarodnom znanstvenom skupu Jugoistočna Europa 1918.- 1995.* Zagreb. ["*The Bleiburg Massacre.*" *Presentation at the International Scientific Conference Southeastern Europe from 1918-1995*].

Tolstoy, Nikolai. 1991. *Ministar i pokolji. Bleiburg i Kočevski Rog 1945*. Zagreb: Nakladni zavod Matice hrvatske. [*Minister and Massacres. Bleiburg and Kočevski Rog in 1945*. Zagreb: Publishing House Matica of Croatia].

Tomašević, Jozo. 2010. *Rat i revolucija u Jugoslaviji 1941.-1945: okupacija i kolaboracija*. [*War and Revolution in Yugoslavia 1941-1945: Occupation and Collaboration*]. Zagreb: Europapress holding: Novi liber.

Topalović, Vjenceslav. 2001. *Srednja Bosna. Ne zaboravimo hrvatske žrtve 1941. – '50./1991. – 95.* Zagreb: Hrvatski informativni centar [*Central Bosnia. Let Us Not Forget Croatian Victims 1941-'50/1991-95*. Zagreb: Croatian Information Center].

"Tri razdoblja četničkih zločina u BiH 1941.-1945." *Projek Velebit*, March 9, 2018. ["Three Perioned of Chetnik's Crimes in BH 1941-1945." *Project Velebit*]. Accessed April 20, 2020. https://projektvelebit.com/tri-razdoblja-cetnickih-zlocina-bih-1941-1945/.

Tuđman, Franjo. 1989. *Bespuća povijesne zbiljnosti*. Zagreb: Nakladni zavod Matice hrvatske. [*Horrors of War*. Zagreb: Publishing House Matica hrvatska].

Večernji list [*Evening News*]. 2004. Zagreb, September 13.

Velebit, Vladimir. 2002. *Tajne i zamke Drugog svjetskog rata*. Zagreb: Prometej. [*Secrets and Traps of World War 2*. Zagreb: Prometheus].

Vjesnik jedinstvene narodnooslobodilačke fronte Hrvatske. May 20, 1945a. Zagreb.

Vjesnik jedinstvene narodnooslobodilačke fronte Hrvatske. May 26, 1945b. Zagreb.

Vjesnik jedinstvene i narodnooslobodilačke fronte Hrvatske. June 6, 1945c. Zagreb.

Vojna enciklopedija 10. 1967. "Ustaše." Beograd: Redakcija Vojne enciklopedije. [*Military Encyclopedia* 10. "The Ustashas." Belgrade: Redaction of the Military Encyclopedia].

Vukić, Igor. 2018. *Jasenovac u 2. svjetskom ratu – Labour Camp Jasenovac in World War II*. Zagreb: Društvo za istraživanje trostrukog logora Jasenovac.

Vukorep, Stanislav. 2005. *Preživjeli svjedoče*. [*The Survivors Testify*]. Zagreb: Detecta.

Vuković, Nikolina. 2015. "Ukradeni grad – o progonstvu Iloka i Iločana" ["The Stolen Town – on the Exile of the People of Ilok"]. *Scrinia Slavonica* 15: 317-339. Accessed March 19, 2020. https://hrcak.srce.hr/index.php?show=clanak&id_clanak_jezik=242523.

Vuković, Tomislav, and Edo Bojović. 1992. *Pregled srpskog antisemitizma*. [*A Review of Serbian Anti-Semitism*]. Zagreb: Alatir.

Zaccaria, Giuseppe. 1994. *Noi criminali di guera*. [*We The Criminals of War*]. Milano: Baldini&Castodi.

Zdunić, J. 2018. "Kakva pljuska za Godlsteina [sic]: Dokumenti CIA-a potvrdili da je njegova izjava o Jasenovcu bila lažna!" *Ekskluzivno*. ["What A Slap for Goldstein: the CIA Documents Confirmed that His Statement on Jasenovac Was Fake!" *Exclusive*]. Accessed March 17, 2020. http://www.ekskluzivno.me/kakva-pljuska-za-godlsteina-dokumenti-cia-a-potvrdili-da-je-njegova-izjava-o-jasenovcu-bila-lazna-3041/.

Zovko, Jure. 2014. "Predsjedniče, Drug Tito je ipak bio zločinac." *Direktno*. ["President, The Comrade Tito Was A Criminal After All!" *Directly*]. Accessed March 17, 2020. https://direktno.hr/kolumne/predsjednice-drug-tito-je-ipak-bio-zlocinac-4760/.

Zöllner, Erich, and Therese Schüssel. 1997. *Povijest Austrije*. Prevela Vlatka-Ana Dujić, and Sonja Ledinčić. [*The History of Austria*. Translated by Vlatka-Ana Dujić, and Sonja Ledinčić]. Zagreb: Barbat.

Žerjavić, Vladimir. 1992. *Opsesije i megalomanije oko Jasenovca i Bleiburga. Gubici stanovništva Jugoslavije u drugom svjetskom ratu*. [*Obsessions and Megalomania on Jasenovac and Bleiburg. The Loss of Population of Yugoslavia in World War 2*]. Zagreb: Globus.

Žrtve rata 1941 – 1945. godine. Rezultati popisa. 1966. [*The Victims of War 1941-1945. The List Results*]. Zagreb.

BIOGRAPHICAL SKETCH

Mihovil Biočić, MD, PhD

Affiliation:

Retired pediatric surgeon and university professor of pediatric surgery, University of Split School of Medicine, Split, Croatia

Education:

1965 – Secondary school in Split, Croatia;

1971 – University of Zagreb (Croatia) School of Medicine;

1979 – Pediatric surgery;

1983 – MSc from University of Zagreb School of Medicine ("Damage to kidney parenchyma after pyelonephrostomy");

1984 – General surgery;

1988 – PhD from University of Zagreb School of Medicine ("Transplantation of urinary bladder mucosa into intestine", University of Zagreb School of Medicine.

Visiting pediatric surgeon at: National Children's Hospital, Tallaght, Dublin, Ireland; Pediatric Uro-Nephrology Centre –Queen Silvia Children's Hospital and Sahlgrenska University Hospital, Goteborg, Sweden; and University Hospital Ghent, Belgium.

Research and Professional Experience:

- Pediatric urology and abdomen; research in electrolyte disbalance after urine absorption in different urine derivations; modified Grobb-Poljugan method of surgical reconstruction of penis hypospady and treatment of perforated omophalocele and gastroshizis.
- 2004 – 2011 head of Surgery course at postgraduate program at University of Split School of Medicine.
- Published 77 research reports, and had oral presentation at 16 international meetings. Coauthor in four textbooks for pregraduate and postgraduate students.

Professional Appointments:

1988- 2014: Professor of University of Split (Split, Croatia) School of Medicine. Chair of the Department of Pediatric Surgery in two mandates.

1990 – 1995: Surgeon volunteer of the Croatian Army with appointments in war hospitals in South Dalmatia and Bosnia-Herzegovina.

1990 – present: One of the founders of Croatian Democratic union in Kaštela County and in several mandates president of the Main Council of the party in Kaštela; member and President of the Kaštela County Council and President of the Assembly of Split-Dalmatia County.

1991 – 1993: President of the Directorate of University Hospital Center Split.

1993 – 2000: Director of the University Hospital Center Split and Commander of the Health Care Emergency Headquarters for Middle and North Dalmatia.

1991-1995: Organizer and commander of Mobile Surgical Teams of War Hospitals in South Croatia and Bosnia-Herzegovina.

1994 – 2001: Member of the Board for building Hospital "Dr fra Mato Nikolić" Nova Bila, Bosnia-Herzegovina.

1990: Member of Association of Veterans of Volunteers in the Croatian War of Independence.

2004: Organizer and vice-president of the First World Congress of Pediatric Surgery in Zagreb.

1995 – present: Member of the City of Kaštela Committee for Environmental Protection. The Committee succeeded in closing factory of plastics "Jugovinil" because of outdated technology and subsequent pollution (vinilchloride monomer, chlorine and other), located in the center of Kaštela. Also, the Committee has been instrumental in averting burning of the waste in cement factories in city of Kaštela and entire Split-Dalmatia County (dioxine, N-methylpyrol, heavy metals and other).

2005.-2009: President of the Kaštela City Council.

2004-2012: Member of the County Board for Equality of Sexes.

2016. – present: President of the City of Kaštela Board for Equality of Sexes.

Honors:

- For contributions to Croatian War of Independence received the following honors from the President of Republic of Croatia Dr. Franjo Tuđman:
- Commemorative Medal of the Homeland War;
- Order of Danica Hrvatska with Figure of Katarina Zrinska, 1995;
- Order of the Croatian Trefoil, 1997;
- Medal for Participation in Operation 'Summer '95', for contribution to military-police operations and for exceptional deeds.
- Letters of Thanks from:
  - Assembly of Croatian Chamber of Physicians;
  - Ministry of Defense of Republic of Croatia;
  - Ministry of Defense of Republic of Croatia, Headquarter of Split and of Knin;
  - IV Guardian Brigade;
  - Croatian Democratic Union of Lepenica-Lašva-Vrbas County in BH, and Municipality Council of Busovača in BH;
  - of President of BH Mr. Alija Izetbegović;
  - of Association of War Veterans with Disabilities from Rama, BH;
- Special Recognition of Association of War Hospitals of Croatian Defense Council (BH)
- The "Ladislav Rakovac Recognition", the highest recognition of Croatian Physicians' Association.

Publications from the Last 3 Years:

1. Biočić, Mihovil, and Marija Županović. 2015. "Uloga KB Split na južnom bojištu." U Hrvatski sanitet tijekom srpsko – crnogorske agresije na Republiku Hrvatsku 1990.-1995. Urednici Hebrang, Andrija i sur., 618-629 ["Contribution of University

Hospital Split at South Front." In *Croatian Sanitation during the Serbian – Montenegro Aggression on the Republic of Croatia 1990.-1995,* edited by Hebrang, Andrija et al., 618-629]. Vukovar – Zagreb, Medicinska naklada.

2. Biočić, Mihovil. 2018. "Otvoreno pismo predsjedniku RH Ivi Josipoviću." [Open letter to Croatian President Ivo Josipovic]. In Nazor, Ante, and Tomislav Pušek. *Domovinski rat. Pregled političke i diplomatske povijesti*, p. 209. [Homeland War. A review of political and diplomatic history, 209]. Nakladni zavod Globus, Hrvatski Memorijalno dokumentacijski centar Domovinskog rata. [Croatian War Memorial Documentation Center].
3. Biočić, Mihovil. 2018. "Obnova hrvatske države glavna je 'krivnja' hrvatske politike devedesetih", 210-211 [The reconstruction of the Croatian state was the main "guilt" of Croatian politics in the 1990s]. In Nazor, Ante, Pušek, Tomislav, editors. *Domovinski rat. Pregled političke i diplomatske povijesti.* [*Homeland War. A review of political and diplomatic history, 210-11*]. Nakladni zavod Globus, Hrvatski Memorijalno dokumentacijski centarDomovinskog rata. [Croatian War Memorial Documentation Center].
4. Biočić, Mihovil, Goran Dodig, and Marija Županović. 2019. "KB Split u obrambenom Domovinskom ratu." [KB Split in the Defensive Homeland War]. In *Kongres veterana IV. gardijske brigade. Što nam znače iskustva iz Domovinskog rata u izgradnji suvremene Republike Hrvatske?* [*Veterans Congress of the IV. Guards Brigade. What are the experiences of the Homeland War in the construction of the modern Republic of Croatia?*]. Split: Udruga veterana IV. Gardijske brigade, 24-31.
5. Biočić, Mihovil. 2017. "Zviždači antifašizmu u hrvatskoj Istri 2017." [*Whistleblowers of anti-fascism in Croatian Istria 2017*]. https://www.hrsvijet.net/index.php/vijesti/132-hrvatska/48274-zvizdaci-antifasizmu-u-hrvatskoj-istri-godine-2017. Accessed January 27, 2020.
6. Biočić, Mihovil. 2019. "*Gospodine Josipoviću, zgrožen sam Vašim riječima o predsjednici Grabar Kitarović*" ["*Mr. Josipovic, I Am Disgusted at Your Words about President Grabar Kitarović*"]. Accessed January 27, 2020. https://www.maxportal.hr/premium-sadrzaj/dr-mihovil-biocic-gospodine-josipovicu-zgrozen-sam-vasim-rijecima-o-predsjednici-grabar-kitarovic/.
7. Croactive Online. Editorial. 2019. "*Biočićev ubitačan odgovor Dejanu Joviću povodom njegovih velikosrpskih obmana izrečenih u Banskom Grabovcu.*" [*Biočić's Deletorious Reply to Dejan Jovic Regarding His Greater Serbian Deceptions Made in Banski Grabovac*]. Accessed January 27, 2020. https://croativ.net/biocice-ubitacan-odgovor-dejanu-jovicu-povodom-njegovih-velikosrbskih-obmana-izrecenih-u-banskom-grabovcu%EF%BB%BF-2520/.
8. Biočić, Mihovil. 2017. "U Splitskoj bolnici liječili smo više od 32.000 ranjenika i bolesnika iz BiH." [At University Hospital Split we treated over 32,000 wounded and sick from Bosnia-Herzegovina]. Accessed January 27, 2020. https://www.hrsvijet.net/index.php/vijesti/132-hrvatska/48656-mihovil-biocic-u-splitskoj-bolnici-smo-lijecili-vise-od-32-000-ranjenika-i-bolesnika-iz-bih.
9. Biočić, Mihovil. 2018. "Istinu treba reći do kraja. Mihovil Biočić odgovara Mirjani Nazor." *Slobodna Dalmacija* 22. siječnja, str. 17. [The Truth Must be told to the End. Mihovil Biocic Answers to Mirjana Nazor]. *Free Dalmatia* January 22, p. 17.

10. Biočić, Mihovil. 2019. "Pitam DORH je li samo Ivan Đakić kriv za govor mržnje i što je onda s Nenadom Stazićem i JUSP Jasenovac?" *Hrvatski tjednik* 769: 8-9. [I Ask DORH whether only Ivan Djakic is Guilty of Hate Speech and what about Nenad Stazic and Public Establishment Memorial Park Jasenovac. *Croatian Weekly Journal* 769: 8-9].

In: Croatia: Past, Present and Future Perspectives
Editor: Matko Marušić
ISBN: 978-1-53618-300-9

Chapter 10

UNDERSTANDING HISTORY IN CROATIA TODAY: A MISSED OPPORTUNITY IN THE FILM "DIARY OF DIANA BUDISAVLJEVIĆ"

Igor Vukić*
Society for Research of the Threefold Jasenovac Camp, Zagreb, Croatia

ABSTRACT

The makers of the film *Diary of Diana Budisavljević* (2019) chose a sensitive subject: the fate of children without parents after the breakdown of the Partisan rebellion against the Independent State of Croatia (In Croatian: Nezavisna Država Hrvatska, NDH) in the summer of 1942 on the Kozara Mountain in northwest Bosnia. The Partisans were led by communists and consisted in that area almost exclusively of Serbian people of the Orthodox Christian religion. They retreated to the mountain together with thousands of women and children. Eventually, they were captured, and some 10,000 men and 8,000 women were taken to work in factories and on farms in Germany. By agreement of German and NDH authorities, approximately 7,000 children stayed in Croatia, the majority of them ill and exhausted. They were sent to children's shelters and hospitals, waiting to be fostered in Croatian, mainly Catholic homes. Despite all efforts, about 2,000 children died by the end of that year.

Even today, this rebellion and the ensuing suffering of the Orthodox children is still being used by some historians and journalists as one of numerous subjects for false accusations against Croatia and Croats. According to historic propaganda, the Ustasha-led NDH went to war against the Orthodox population because it wanted an ethnically pure state, and the Orthodox children were mass-murdered after being transferred to concentration camps. The credit for saving several thousand children was attributed to communists who "organized a network for rescuing the children."

However, the publication of Diana Budisavljević's diary in 2003, proved this narrative to be untrue. Diana was an Austrian woman, married to a surgeon from Zagreb, Dr. Julije Budisavljević. He was an Orthodox Christian who worked in Zagreb's main hospital during the NDH regime as department head and professor at the School of Medicine. With permission from the NDH police, his wife Diana organized a group of

* Corresponding Author's Email: igor.vukic.zg@gmail.com.

friends and acquaintances to collect food and clothes for the Orthodox captives. By 1942, this group got involved in helping the children from Kozara.

The film *Diary of Diana Budisavljević* is at variance with communist historiography, but still contains a number of inaccuracies and omissions in comparison to both the diary and available historic sources. The film attributes key merits for the children's rescue to Diana Budisavljević, but does not explain how her activities were possible if the state was hostile to the entire Orthodox population.

The authors claim that they did historical research in preparation for the film, but they used the diary selectively and neglected numerous documents that testify about the activities of various institutions in the rescue action. These include several ministries, groups of physicians and nurses, the Red Cross, Caritas (a Catholic charity), and Catholic nuns. The inaccuracies and omissions are a missed opportunity to present a more accurate picture of the events and to help Croatian public to confront a sensitive topic of World War II that has been clouded in propaganda. This chapter discusses historic evidence that is at variance with this important film.

Keywords: children, rescue; Croatia; Diana Budisavljevic, Diary; Diana Budisavljevic, film; Independent State of Croatia; Jasenovac; Kozara Mountain, battle at; Ustasha, regime

INTRODUCTION

After its premiere in the summer of 2019, the film *Diary of Diana Budisavljević* attracted attention of viewers in Croatian cinemas as well as public interest. The film deals with a sensitive subject: rescuing and helping a large number of children without parents after the breakdown of the Partisan rebellion on the Kozara Mountain in the northwest Bosnia and Herzegovina in the summer of 1942. The Partisans who lead the rebellion against the newly established Independent State of Croatia (NDH) and its allies, Italy and Germany, were organized in the area of Kozara by Communist Party of Yugoslavia. With rare exceptions, mainly in the commanding staff, its troops consisted almost completely of Orthodox Serbian fighters. The Partisans took with them thousands of their wives and children (Barić 2016, 55-57).

After the united forces of the German Wermacht and NDH military destroyed Partisan defense in the summer of 1942, around 10,000 captured men and around 8,000 women were sent to work in the Third Reich. Roughly 7,000 of their children remained in Croatian shelters and camps. Those children were helped by volunteers (Petešić, 1990, 14, 123).

The central character of the *Diary of Diana Budisavljević* is one of those volunteers, who organized food collection and, together with her associates, helped provide shelter for these refugee children. Diana Budisavljević, née Obexer, was Austrian, born in Innsbruck in 1891. She married a Zagreb doctor Julije Budisavljević and came to live with him in Croatia. Julije was an Eastern Orthodox Christian. He advanced to the position of head of surgery and professor at the University of Zagreb School of Medicine and kept this job even after the forming of the Independent State of Croatia (Budisavljević 2003, 14).

The film received positive reviews and awards after its premiere. Critics and journalists wrote numerous articles and held promotional interviews, stating that this was a thoroughly researched film with ten years of research behind it. They praised the film as a huge contribution to shedding light on a time in modern Croatian history that filmmakers had known very little about until they came across Diana's diary quite accidently.

Diana Budisavljević kept a private diary during the war that became known to the public only at its publishing in Zagreb in 2003. The director of this film, of a similar name, 45-years old Dana Budisavljević, came across this diary ten years later. She previously had directed several documentaries on various topics (Art kino 2019). Someone once asked her if she was related to Diana Budisavljević and did she know about her diary: she did find some family relations to Diana's husband, but had no idea about the diary. Dana Budisavljević read the diary and was thrilled about this interesting story (Zamoda 2019). She wrote a script based on the diary and produced a documentary film *The Diary of Diana Budisavljević* at a cost of around 750,000 USD. The film was financed by a subsidy (roughly 450,000 USD) from the Croatian Audio-Visual Center, a government-backed agency in charge of financing documentaries and feature films, and by donations from other film centers in Serbia and Slovenia as well as the Euroimage fund (HAVC 2014, 67). It was 118 minutes long: documentarian sequences consisted of short videos from World War II (WWII) and conversation with four people who were 4-6 years old in 1942; with the biggest part of the film consisting of fictional scenes based on certain parts of the diary of Diana Budisavljević.

Significant Differences in Relations with the Jewish and Serbian Communities in Croatia

Children and other prisoners Diana Budisavljević helped during the war were almost all Eastern Orthodox Christian (Orthodox in further text). However, the first scenes of this film portrayed the demolition of the Zagreb synagogue. NDH authorities were undoubtedly responsible for this anti-Semitic act (Goldstein 2001, 385) but the scenes tell nothing about relation of the authorities to the Serbian minority, i.e., population of Orthodox faith. The film, which is being promoted as based on actual events, fails to show the differences of NDH policies dealing with the two minority communities.

The policy toward the Jews was mainly a consequence of the alliance with Nazi Germany and the dictates of Nazi representatives (Tomasevich 2010). The new Croatian state had no choice but to agree to German conditions; however, it tried to obtain certain concessions such as protection for Jews in mixed marriages or protection for families whose members fought for the Croatian cause (Goldstein 2001, 379-384). A certain number of Jews managed to obtain permits for entering the southern part of the country, controlled by the Italians, where they managed to preserve their lives. They were sent to detention camps in Crikvenica, Novi Vinodolski or Kupari near Dubrovnik. Then they were grouped together in the camp on the Island of Rab. The circumstances which kept them alive were due to the decision of Benito Mussolini who decided not to send the Jews to the German allies. Owing to this, many Jews from NDH survived the war (Tomasevich 2010).

At the same time, Croatian authorities proposed a plan to their German allies to place Jews in the Jasenovac concentration camp, which could be turned into a relatively big settlement with solid living conditions. Based on this idea, about which the representatives of the Jewish community spoke after the war, the Jews would work in this settlement utilizing their skills and expertise and they would be useful to the new state. According to the proposal, they would be protected from further persecution until the end of the war. Plans for the establishment of the settlement were drafted in cooperation with the representatives of the Jewish community in Zagreb (HR-HDA-a). However, Nazi representatives rejected the proposal of the Croatian Ustasha authorities.

Instead, the next year, with the help and organizational supervision of the German intelligence service, the majority of the Jewish community in the area controlled by the Germans (roughly from the northern part of Bosnia to the Croatian border with Hungary) was deported to Nazi camps in the Third Reich, mainly Auschwitz in occupied Poland. This was the summer of 1942, and mainly the Jewish communities in Osijek, Zagreb, and central Croatia were deported (Goldstein 2001, 424). The next big deportation of Jews, also to the Third Reich, followed in May 1943.

The policy toward the Serbs, that is the Orthodox population in Croatia, was quite different. Unlike the relations with the Croatian Jews, a strong political antagonism against the central Yugoslav government in Belgrade existed amongst the Ustasha between the World War I and World War II. This antagonism applied also to the Serbian population and the Serbian Orthodox Church in Croatia. The Ustasha were forced to emigrate as a consequence of their opposition to the policy of the Yugoslav King and Serbian domination in pre-war Yugoslavia (Matković 2003).

Maintaining that the Serbian Orthodox Church contributed to this and acted more as a political and not a religious organization, the new NDH government of 1941 promoted and organized forced conversions of Serbian farmers to Catholicism. Priests of the Serbian Orthodox Church were arrested and deported to Serbia (or killed in some cases) (Škiljan 2014, 161).

In agreement with the Nazi representatives (and on their initiative), NDH deported many Serbs to Serbia starting in June 1941. Among the first were the immigrants from Serbia that the former Yugoslav authority settled in Croatia between the two wars with the aim of changing the local ethnic composition. Deported Serbs were supposed to be replaced by the Sloves who were exiled from Slovenia by the Germans (Škiljan 2014, 115). The process of organized deportations of Serbs did not last long. Due to the resistance of the German occupiers in Serbia, who claimed they lacked funds to support arriving Serbs and that these people would join the rebels in Serbia, deportations were stopped in October. To that point, some 14,500 people had been moved from NDH to Serbia, compared with the initial plan of 40,000 for the first phase (Škiljan 2014, 304-306).

Regulation of the of the Status of the Serbian Orthodox Population in NDH

In some local communities, antagonisms between Catholics and Muslims (who were considered to be Croats in NDH) on one side, and the Orthodox on the other side reached its critical point. Instigated by vague recollections of earlier injustice and the crimes committed by Chetniks and the remainder of the Yugoslavian army in April 1941, as well as the opportunity of pillaging the weak (Dizdar and Sobolevski 1999), self-proclaimed guerrilla groups of Ustasha, often called "wild Ustasha," invaded Serbian villages, plundered, burned down houses, and killed villagers who did not manage to escape (Bergholz 2016). Sometimes, not even women or children were spared. By the end of July 1941, an even more violent Serbian response followed. Armed with weapons they had hidden during the short April war (actually, it was a tradition to own weapons in the hilly Bosnian region on the border of the Ottoman and the Austrian Empire, so called *Vojna krajina*), Serbian rebels committed a series of mass crimes in Croatian and Muslim villages and exiled their residents (Bergholz 2016).

The central NDH government in Zagreb tried to calm down the situation. They sent regular army (Home Guard, *Domobrans*) to disarm the Serbian rebels, sometimes even with the intention to divert the Ustasha from further actions. In some cases, Croatian authorities arrested and convicted to death some of the "wild Ustasha" to send a message to stop the violence (Obhođaš et al. 2013, 79-85).

In August 1941, attorney Savo Besarović came to Zagreb. He was an Orthodox from Sarajevo, and a school friend of NDH Chief Commander (in Croatian *Poglavnik*), Ante Pavelić (HR-HDA-b). They talked about how they could calm down the situation in the state and reach some kind of a *modus vivendi* between Croatians and the minority Serbian population. To start, several groups of captured Serbs were released immediately as a sign of good will (HR-HDA-b). In February 1942, Savo Besarović became a member of the Croatian State Parliament, which was assembled for the first time (Tko je tko u NDH 1997, 36). The Parliament did not have any real authority, but it had a certain symbolic role. Savo Besarović became afterwards minister in the NDH government and the representative of the Orthodox population. He remained in the government until the end of the war (Tko je tko u NDH 1997, 36).

As one of the measures for calming down the situation in the country, Croatian authorities encuraged the establishing of a new church organization – The Croatian Orthodox Church – to suppress the political influence of the Serbian church while preserving the same religious content already practiced by the Orthodox population in Croatia. The Croatian government also decided not to recruit Orthodox young men to the Croatian army, but to organize DO-RA regiments (Domobran working regiments). The regiments were used for building roads, cutting wood, building strongholds, etc. Young Serbs would not participate in armed conflicts so that they would not have to shoot their own relatives; at the same time, the authorities could keep an eye on them and prevent them from planning sabotages or deserting to the enemy side with weapons, etc. (Košutić 1992).

In early 1942, Serbian rebels split into two parts: the Partisans and the Chetniks. The Partisans supported communist ideology (with political commissioners based on the USSR model), and the Chetniks were royalists and nationalists (Hurem 1972). However, in Croatian areas as in Serbia, the Chetniks were inclined to wait for the end of the war without fighting, avoiding conflict with Italians and Germans, preserving their assets, and hoping for a better political situation after the war. They wanted the King and the Yugoslavian government, then in Great Britain and supported by the Western Allies, to return: they believed it would be possible to re-establish Yugoslavia in which the Serbian people would rule again (Matković 2003).

In terms of tactics, Chetniks were ready to form non-aggression pacts with the Croatian side. From the beginning of 1942, almost 30 pacts were concluded. In some places, they arranged joint fights against the communist Partisans. If one of the Chetniks died in these conflicts, his wife would receive a pension from Croatia. The wounded were treated in Croatian hospitals (Matković 2010). The film of director Dana Budisavljević does not mention this political background in the Croatian areas in which the Serb uprisings took place.

Political Attitude Instead of a Balanced Documentary

Content analysis of the diary and other documentarian sources from the period of WWII shows that the film *Diary of Diana Budisavljević* does not make a significant contribution to a relatively realistic vision of events of that period. Instead of placing events in a real historical context, and presenting them as neutrally as possible, the director and her associates tried to be as suggestive as possible and influence the audience with several well-tried film techniques.

For example, the movie is filmed in black and white. On one hand, this gives it authenticity, but creates in audience feeling of limitation, gloom, and anxiety. Many films have used the same technique, e.g., *Schindler's List* by Spielberg. Actually, at some point even this film had *Diana's List* as its working title (MFDB 2014).

Almost all scenes in the entire film were shot in winter or late fall in cold and unpleasant weather. Participants walk through thick fog, wrapped in winter coats and scarves. Witnesses are interviewed in authentic locations of former shelters, now ruined and neglected.

In reality, according to the Diary, the major and most important part of Diana's activities took place during spring and summer of 1942 (Budisavljević 2003, 69-103). The filmmakers clearly wanted to show yet another moral and political judgement about the regime of the Independent State of Croatia.

Diana's first experience with a big group of refugees was during the spring of 1942, when a larger group of children needed help after successful anti-partisan activities in Kordun. Kordun is a Croatian region located around 65 kilometers south of Zagreb. When military and administrative authorities of NDH pursued the rebels, they would sometimes evacuate civilians so the rebels would have no local support. Women and children would be transferred to temporary shelters – in this case, they were transferred from Kordun to Stara Gradiška camp. Some groups of adults would thereafter be sent to work in Germany and children would stay in the camp (Glišić 1970).

The same happened a few weeks after, during the battle on Kozara Mountain in the summer of 1942. (Kozara is located in Bosnia 120 km south-east from Zagreb). German and NDH military forces started surrounding the mountain on 15 June, and military activities ended on 15 July. During the anti-rebel activities, Kozara was surrounded by joint German-Croatian forces, supported by Italians in the south, several Chetnik units on the east side of the mountain, and river Sava on the north was patrolled by boats of the Hungarian fleet. During their withdrawal from a stronger attacker, the Partisans took with them a large number of children and women, which they described in their historical documents after the war (Samardžija 1984). After the Partisans surrendered to the German-Croatian forces, separations of prisoners took place. Around 10,000 men and 8,000 women were sent to work in Germany. About 6,000 to 7,000 children remained in the care of the Croatian state, based on a German-Croatian agreement. These children were placed in the Stara Gradiška camp in several improvised shelters and in other detention centres (Mlaka, Jablanac, Cerovljani, Bosanska Dubica). Based on the command issued by Chief Commander Ante Pavelić, the children from these centers were handed over to available shelters and children's homes (Barić 2016, 100).

Neglecting the Role of the State and Archbishop Stepinac in Helping the Children

The initial engagement of Diana Budisavljević started in October 1941. She had heard about an imprisoned group of 173 Orthodox Serbs (women and children from Bihać, Sarajevo, Mostar, and Stolac in Bosnia and Herzegovina) held in old castle Lobor around 40 kilometers from Zagreb. In an improvised camp in this castle, they were held together with a group of Jewish women and their children (Budisavljević 2003, 13). Lobor Town was governed by Karlo Heger, an earlier resident of Zagreb and a member of the German national group in Croatia (Budisavljević 2003, 18).

Serbian women and children were held there as a form of pressure on their husbands and fathers not to join the rebels against the Independent State of Croatia. Such cruel measures were more or less common in those times. But, taking hostages as a form of measure against paramilitary groups, under specific conditions, was not a violation of international human rights provisions which at that time regulated the rules of war (Barić 2012, 284-285).

When Diana Budisavljević found out about the Orthodox group in Lobor, she went for advice to the Jewish community in Zagreb – to ask if she could donate money for supporting women and children of Christian faith (Budisavljević 2003, 13). The community suggested to her to organize a campaign for collecting clothes and other necessary items for the prisoners. She hesitated at first as she had never done anything like that before and she had never been a member of any association. But then she accepted the idea. Soon afterwards the first truck with supplies travelled to Lobor, an action organized by her and managed through the Jewish municipality (Budisavljević 2003, 16).

After several shipments, Diana Budisavljević wanted to visit Lobor Town herself and check the distribution of goods. With a member of the Croatian Red Cross Anka Meleš she visited the office of Vilko Kühnel, Head of Jewish Department in Ustasha Police. This office supervised the Jewish community. "I wish to stress that the head officer was helpful then and later on," Diana Budisavljević wrote in her diary (Budisavljević 2013, 18).

In December 1941, Diana Budisavljević obtained verbal permission from NDH Minister of Internal Affairs Andrija Artuković to organize aid for prisoners, guaranteeing no one would cause her trouble (Budisavljević 2003, 21-22). Subsequently, she met with Zagreb Archbishop Alojzije Stepinac for the first time. According to her words, Stepinac was ready "to give all for the cause, but he said that nothing could be done" and explained to her he had no influence on the government (Budisavljević 2003, 20). That month, Diana Budisavljević also met with Savo Besarović, who promised her that he would speak with the authorities in favor of the Orthodox prisoners (Budisavljević 2003, 21). This is all proof that different levels of Ustasha officials and state authorities knew from the first day about the work of Diana Budisavljević, and they allowed it. The authorities could have stopped it if they had wanted to. Orthodox children up to 14 years old were soon released from Lobor Town. Ustasha police called Diana Budisavljević, asking her to take over the children and provide them with shelter (Budisavljević 2003, 27).

In March 1942, all Orthodox women from Lobor Town were boarded onto a train heading via Zagreb to Serbia. In April, an order was issued to release the remaining Orthodox women and children held in other locations, e.g., Gornja Rijeka near Križevci, Đakovo, etc. (Budisavljević 2003, 42).

Film Scenes Not All Based on Diary's Entries

The film barely describes the mentioned communications between Diana Budisavljević and the NDH authorities. Actually, it suggests she worked in secrecy and against their will. The impression of great difficulties Diana encountered during her work is reinforced with made up scenes that do not correspond to the authentic source, her diary. For example, in a scene where the Ustasha police came to Diana's apartment while she was packaging fruit and food for the prisoners, the scene is full of tension and threats shouted at Diana and her co-workers. At the end of the scene, the policeman starts throwing food packages from the table and apples roll down on the floor. According to Diana's diary entries, in reality there was not any violence or threats. The policemen came because they had received an anonymous tip that someone had been sending packages to Partisans from that apartment. They checked the activities that took place in the apartment and consulted with the police authorities that had been aware of the activities of that group. For example, during the raid, they were on the telephone with Savo Besarović and Eugen Kvaternik, who was at the time one of the most powerful persons in the system of state security. The police left the apartment and left the people in it to continue with their good work (Budisavljević 2003, 30-31). Just a day later after the described raid of Diana's apartment, she received written permission to continue her work so that her associates and protégés would avoid future misunderstandings with other authorities (Budisavljević 2003, 32).

The climax of Diana's activities followed in the summer of 1942. Despite the attempts of the Croatian authorities to control the violence and apply measures for mitigating the conflicts in the country and prevent a predominantly Serbian uprising (Bergholz 2016), the trust between the authorities and the Serbian minority was severely diminished. The measures yielded success in some areas, e.g., Knin and its surroundings (northern Dalmatia) and the areas where agreements with the local Chetnik command (northern Bosnia) were signed (Hurem 1972).

In northwest Bosnia, around the Kozara Mountain, the rebels organized in groups headed by the communists. In May 1942, the Partisans took over Prijedor, where they immediately tried and executed 200 people (Catholics and Muslims), finding them guilty of earlier killing Orthodox people (Barić 2016, 70). Besides invasions of villages and towns, where they plundered and burned down public facilities, schools, town offices, Partisan groups damaged vital roads and some commercial facilities. One of such places was an iron mine, Ljubija near Prijedor, which was for Germans a crucial resource for their war industry: for example, 150,000 tons of iron ore was excavated there just in the second half of 1941. The stoppage of production after the Partisan attacks speeded up plans for pacification of this area. (Kolar-Dimitrijević 1981). Earlier, in April 1942, NDH authorities promised the Germans to hand over the prisoners and the civilians captured in the area hit by the uprising and military actions. The Germans found them useful as a workforce of whom they had been in great shortage in factories and farms of the Third Reich. The workers were first held in camp Stara Gradiška, from where they were boarded onto trains and sent east to Zemun; from there, they were boarded onto ships on the Danube River, heading for Germany or even Norway (HR-HDA-c).

Diana Budisavljević Also Participated in Separating the Children from Their Parents

The film Diary of Diana Budisavljević suggests that the children were detained only because they were Orthodox, that is, they were of Serbian origin. It is suggested the children would have been killed or left to die in the camps as they had already suffered from typhus and dysentery. In doing so, the director of the film completely neglects the archives which show that the NDH authorities had organized shelter and aid for prisoners and refugees even while the military activities were still going on (Barić 2016, 74). Representatives of the Ministry of Health and Ministry of Social Care (Ministarstvo udružbe, in Croatian) were sent to the field from where they reported on the extent of the refugee surge. It should be pointed out that earlier on the NDH authorities had to find accommodation for many refugees who had fled from the rebellion in Herzegovina and east Bosnia and they did not have enough facilities or health resources (Crnjac 2015). After the war, a doctor from Zagreb, Nikola Vadkov, told the investigators of State Security (political police of the communist Yugoslavia known as Udba), that on 16 July 1942, he was ordered by his superior from the Ministry of Health to visit village Mlaka near Jasenovac for the purpose of helping a large number of refugees suffering from typhus and provide them with necessary medical aid (HR-HDA-d). During his stay in Mlaka, a group of nurses arrived from Zagreb to help the children. They were led by Diana Budisavljević, accompanied by a few nuns and nurses of the Croatian Red Cross.

The film does not mention either that Diana participated in separating the children from their mothers, even though Diana mentioned this in her diary (Budisavljević 2003, 73, 77, 87). According to the diary and recollections of Doctor Nikola Vadkov, Diana and her assistants told the mothers that their children would go to Zagreb where they would be placed in nice accommodation in private homes, even better than their own previous homes. Vadkov reported that Diana and the nurses brought sweets for the children, made tea, and nurtured the younger ones (HR-HDA-d).

Ustasha soldiers from the nearby Jasenovac camp, about which Yugoslavian historiographic records told terrifying stories, did not cause any trouble to Diana Budisavljević when she came for the children. Diana reports in her diary quite the opposite: "Older children came willingly; the smaller ones had to be carried. We had to search for them in piles of pillows. One young Ustasha was quite nervous about it as he was worried that "we would miss a child and they would be soaked wet from the rain." (Budisavljević 2003, 88).

The film does not mention such details either. Its director and assistants as well as the film's PR department just went on repeating the story of a woman who saved "over 10,000 children from Ustasha concentration camps."

Identities of Fostered Children Were Preserved

Every child was listed and photographed so their identities would be preserved. However, the refugee surge, especially a large group of children who fell sick on Kozara Mountain and then, weak and hungry, barely survived until the refugee centers and camps, was too much of a challenge for health authorities. Despite the attempts to help, cure, feed and clothe the young, 1,150 children died out of 7,000 children temporarily placed in Sisak and elsewhere,

(HR-HDA-e). Another 452 died in a shelter in Jastrebarsko near Zagreb, through which 3,400 children passed. The records, statistical data, and witnesses said that the death toll had plummeted after the newly arrived had been given medical help, appropriate food and clothes, and after the sick were isolated from the healthy ones (Petešić 1990, 26). These data clearly refute claims by some authors, e.g., English historian Rory Yeomans, who said that Sisak and Jastrebarsko were "concentration camps for children" or even worse "places for extermination of children" (Yeomans 2012).

After the health situation stabilized in Jastrebarsko and in other Zagreb hospitals, the children of Kozara were fostered by many Croatian families, with the assistance of the Ministry of Social Care and Caritas of the Zagreb Archdiocese. The children were accepted by many ordinary citizens of many classes and occupations, including families of Domobrans and Ustasha officers (HR-HDA-f).

The film fails to describe the role of Kamilo Bresler, social worker, advisor to the Department for Families and Children in the Ministry of Social Care in the summer of 1942. Bresler had a vital role in organizing transport and accommodation for the children, including food, medicine, and other supplies (Petešić 1990). For the purpose of helping the children of Kozara, Bresler hired numerous health workers, representatives of church orders, heads of schools for medical nurses and caretakers, as well as volunteers such as Diana Budisavljević. Bresler worked with Monsignor Pavle Jesih from the Catholic Church and Stjepan Dumić, director of Caritas of the Zagreb Archdiocese. During 1942 alone, 5,124 children of Kozara were placed in families through Caritas of the Archdiocese of Zagreb and Diocese of Đakovo (HR-HDA-f).

The End of the Film's Story

The end of the film describes a real event when new communist authorities took from Diana's apartment a file containing names and addresses of children processed by her organization. She offered her help with managing the file, which had been her main focus of work during the last two years of the war, and in re-joining the children with their families. But communists did not tolerate this kind of help from a high society woman, and of Austrian origin at that (Budisavljević 2003, 168).

The film ends here. White letters on black background of the last shot tell the audience that the file of Diana Budisavljević has never been found, suggesting that some children lost their identity and were never reunited with their parents. However, even this strong statement at the end of the film is not true. Diana's file can be found even today in the center of Zagreb. It is kept in the Croatian State Archives (HR-HDA-g), and it is available for public inspection to anyone who pays a small membership fee. The file contains names of 30,000 refugee children: Orthodox children from Kozara as well as Catholic and Muslim children refugees from other parts of the state. The file's entries were recorded by the workers of the Ministry of Social Care, Caritas, as well as Diana Budisavljević and her associates (Crnjac 2015, 11-12).

The film by Dana Budisavljević shows a recent interview with Živko Zelenbrz, one of four still-living children. Zelenbrz said he did not know his identity at the time of his arrival to the shelter. In the shelter they gave him a plate with the number 1128 engraved, which he has kept to this day. He showed the plate in the film. It is suggested that the file was lost and that Živko could not find out anything about his origin. Notwithstanding that statement, Diana's file contains the name Živko Zelenbrz, and his file carries the same number 1128. The record shows that a boy called Živko was transferred to the Institute for Deaf Children in Zagreb, one of the bigger facilities that offered temporary shelter to refugee children before foster families took them over (HR-HDA-g). Živko's foster parent was Mato Zelenbrz from Grobnička Street 20/II in Zagreb. According to the record, Živko received the surname of his foster parent, which was not unusual (HR-HDA-f). The file also contains a note 'See under Ivančević Živko' so Ivančević might have been his real last name. Who knows what could be found if one would follow these clues? Maybe a persistent researcher could discover the true identity of Živko Zelenbrz, his place of birth, name of his parents and other relatives. Maybe some of his relatives are still alive!

Chances for this are small today, but in the late 60's and early 70's, Marino Zurl, an *Arena* journalist (*Arena* was a weekly Zagreb magazine), described a series of cases of Kozara children who survived the war and who did know that their parents and relatives were still alive. He investigated part of a collection of authentic documents and files from the war still kept in their offices for some reason by some functionaries of the communist authorities, *i.e.,* Marija Šoljan Bakarić, President of the Commission for Social Activities of Women of Croatia (HR-HDA-e). Zurl tried to investigate and find other survivors who might have been convinced their relatives were dead (Zurl 1978). Even though the director of the film and her associates often claimed in the media they had investigated the archives diligently for nine years, it is really strange they did not find the file of children still kept in front of their noses in Zagreb. They claimed they had searched for witnesses and spoke to many people who were still children during the period they were fostered. In the end, they presented only four cases.

Bias and Poorly Investigated Archives

After seeing the film, it remains unclear what its authors investigated. The film does not contain a single new documentary data, while other, already known data, were used in the inaccurate context. The film relies entirely on Diana's diary, but with carefully selected passages.

Film's bias is evident in the depiction of Zagreb's Archbishop Alojzije Stepinac. Even though abundant evidence shows that he helped people in trouble during the war regardless of their faith (Gitman 2019), the film portrayed him as a coward who hesitated to help Orthodox refugees, including the ones who converted to Catholicism. Even before the war, Archbishop Stepinac founded in Zagreb a committee for helping Jews escaping from the Third Reich (Gitman 2005). The committee would take them in, give them financial aid, provided accommodation, and organized travel if they wanted so. During the war, Stepinac helped individuals and groups in danger from the NDH. Owing to his efforts, couples in mixed marriages (Jews and Catholics) were exempt from deportation. In Germany, such married couples were deported, but in Croatia, owing to Stepinac, they stayed with their families and continued working. Some were released subsequently from detention camps (Gitman 2011). Stepinac did not hesitate to preach in public condemning racism and anti-Semitism, even in the presence of German representatives. Zagreb Gestapo branch regularly commented on his speeches with a negative note. Stepinac received positive comments, even during the time of war, in the New York Times, and from the Partisans who imprisoned him for a long time after the war (Akrap 2016). Certain negativity towards Stepinac is evident in the original entries of Diana's diary; however, she also describes that, based on his decision, Caritas organized accommodation for the Orthodox children in many Catholic homes (Budisavljević 2003, 55, 64, 99).

It can be assumed that the filmmakers' portrayal of this highly placed priest sends a message of their attitude towards religion – just like the entire film it is more an expression of their political beliefs, rather than an objective view, even though they promote it as an account of real events. This was noticed by Croatian historian Nikica Barić, when he investigated documents about the refugees and children from Kozara in 1942. From the archives he concluded that the NDH definitely organized the children to be taken from concentration camps, processed, and provided with accommodation. In that sense, he finds Diana's role depicted in the film, overrated: it was possible to help the children since the regime itself, under the order of Pavelić, approved these actions and implemented them (Barić 2016, 109).

More Fact Less Fiction

What does the film Diary of Diana Budisavljević say about the society which funded and awarded the film? How is it possible in Croatia to make a film that presents events in black and white, literally and metaphorically? The film neglects many humanitarian efforts of Croatian citizens, church representatives, and state apparatus of those times. It can be concluded that this portrays freedom and maturity of contemporary Croatia which funds these projects. Promoted by journalists and film critics who praised this film, *Diary of Diana Budisavljević* was seen by around 27,000 viewers in Croatian cinemas. The most popular Croatian film of that year was seen by 78,000 people. Helped by strong PR, *Diary of Diana Budisavljević* had more viewers than usual for a documentary film.

Reactions to this film show that Croatia is in need of additional historiographic research of the WWII period and more accurate public presentation of the research results. There is already a series of books, written more recently after the fall of communism in a multi-party democratic environment, that provide a realistic depiction of these times (Barić 2012, Kevo 2009, Obhođaš et al. 2013). However, there are still many areas and themes which need to be investigated and which are obscured by the ideology and biased histories from the earlier communist period. Interesting themes are in abundance. For example, the selector of the NDH boxing representation was Afro-American Jimmy Lygett, a fact from that period that was not talked about by any warring side (Bušić 2002). Based on a similar template, film *Red tails* was made in the USA about the first black army pilots who barely got a chance to fly for the Armed Forces during WWII (IMDb 2012). Even such films can help understand historical events. Until the main controversies from the recent history are resolved, Croatia is in need of works of art like "Katyn" by Andrzej Wajda (IMDb 2007) or Spielberg's "Schindler's List," (IMDb 1993) and less like complete fiction of Tarantino's "Inglorious Bastards" (IMDb 2009).

References

Akrap, Gordan. 2016. *Kardinal Stepinac u dokumentima Gestapa i OZN-e.* [Cardinal Stepinac in Documents of Gestapo and OZNA]. Zagreb: Udruga sv. Jurja.

Art-kino. 2019. *Dana Budisavljević.* https://www.art-kino.org/en/reziseri/dana-budisavljevic.

Barić, Nikica. 2012. *Ustaše na Jadranu.* [Ustasha on Adriatic Sea]. Zagreb: Hrvatski institut za povijest.

Barić, Nikica. 2016. "Kozara 1942. – sudbina zarobljenika, civila i djece" [Kozara Mountain in 1942 – the Destiny of Captives and Children], *Pilar: časopis za društvene i humanističke studije* Vol XI, No. 2, 53-111.

Bergholz, Max. 2016. *Violence as a Generative Force: Identity, Nationalism, and Memory in a Balkan Community.* New York: Cornell University Press.

Budisavljević, Diana. 2003. *Dnevnik Diane Budisavljević 1941-1945.* [Diary of Diana Budisavljević]. Zagreb: Hrvatski državni arhiv.

Bušić, Zvonimir. 2002. *Šampioni hrvatskog i svjetskog boksa.* [Champions of Croatian and World Boxing]. Zagreb: Hrvatski športski muzej.

Crnjac, Pavao. 2015. *Oteto djetinjstvo.* [Abducted Childhood]. Zagreb: Ramska zajednica.

Dizdar, Zdravko, Sobolevski, Mihael. 1999. *Prešućivani četnički zločini u Hrvatskoj i u Bosni i Hercegovini 1941.-1945.* [Missed Chetnik Massacres in Croatia and Bosnia-Herzegovina 1941-1945]. Zagreb: Hrvatski Institut za povijest: Dom i svijet.

Gitman, Esther. 2005. *Rescue of Jews in the Independent State of Croatia, 1941–1945*, Ph.D. diss. GC of the City University New York.

Gitman, Esther. 2011. *When Courage Prevailed, The Rescue and Survival of Jews in the Independet State of Croatia 1941-1945.* St. Paul: MN, Paragon House.

Gitman, Esther. 2019. *Alojzije Stepinac – Pillar of Human Rights.* Zagreb: Croatia, Kršćanska sadašnjost and Hrvatsko katoličko sveučilište.

Glišić, Venceslav. 1970. *Teror i zločini nacističke Nemačke u Srbiji 1941-1944.* [Terror and Crimes of Naci Germany in Serbia 1941-1945]. Belgrade: Rad.

Goldstein, Ivo. 2001. *Holokaust u Zagrebu.* [Holocaust in Zagreb]. Zagreb: Novi liber.

HAVC-Hrvatski audiovizualni centar. 2014. *Godišnje izvješće.* Zagreb: HAVC 64. Uz HAVC film su financijski podržali i Slovenski filmski centar, Filmski centar Srbije, Viba Film, Grad Zagreb, MEDIA, Eurimages te Hrvatska radiotelevizija (HRT) [HAVC-Croatian Audiovisual Center. 2014. *Yearly Report.* Zagreb: HAVC 64. In addition to HAVC financial support the film received from Slovenian Film Center, Film Center of Serbia, Viba Film. City of Zagreb. MEDIA. Eurimages and Croatian Radiotelevision (HRT)]. https://www.havc.hr/hrvatski-film/katalog-hrvatskih-filmova/dnevnik-diane-budisavljevic. On film financing see also: https://www.nacional.hr/kako-je-debitantica-s-humanom-pricom-iz-ndh-nadmasila-razvikanog-generala/.

HR-HDA-a. Hrvatski državni arhiv-306 – Zemaljska komisija za utvrđivanje zločina okupatora – Glavni urudžbeni zapisnik. Mikrofilm Z-2943, dokument 935. [Croatian State Archive-306 – Country Committee on the Establishment of Crimes of the Occupiers – Main Protocol. Microfilm Z-2943, document 935].

HR-HDA-b. Hrvatski državni arhiv-306 – Zemaljska komisija za utvrđivanje zločina okupatora – Glavni urudžbeni zapisnik. Presuda Savi Besaroviću, donesena 10. rujna 1945., kutija 84, br. 305/46. [Croatian State Archive-306 – Country Committee on the

Establishment of Crimes of the Occupiers – Main Protocol. The Verdict of Savo Besarović from September 10, 1945, Box 84, No. 305/46].
HR-HDA-c. Hrvatski državni arhiv-0487 – Ministarstvo oružanih snaga. Prilog izvješću br. 242 Glavnog stožera od 30. kolovoza 1942. [Croatian State Archives-0487 Ministry of Armed Forces. Annex to Report No. 242 of the Main Headquarters of August 30, 1942].
HR-HDA-d. Hrvatski državni arhiv-1561-SDS RSUP SRH. Izjava Nikole Vadkova, 015.7.11, RZ0070725. [Croatian State Archive-1561-SDS RSUP SRH. The Statement of Nikola Vadkov, 015.7.11, RZ0070725].
HR-HDA-e. Hrvatski državni arhiv-1722 – Antifašistički front žena, kutija 8, 2, Kazalo umrle djece. [Croatian State Archive-1722 – Antifascist Front of Women, Box 8, 2, Directory of Deceased Children].
HR-HDA-f. Hrvatski državni arhiv-1012 – Osobni fond Diane Budisavljević, kutija 3, mapa 1. [Croatian State Archive-1012 – Personal Fund of Diana Budisavljević. Box 3. Portfolio 1].
HR-HDA-g. Hrvatski državni arhiv-226 – Ministarstvo zdravstva i udružbe NDH. Kartoteka djece. [Croatian State Archive-226 – Ministry of Health Care and Register NDH (Independent State of Croatia). Card-Files of Children].
Hurem, Rasim. 1972. Kriza Narodnooslobodilačkog pokreta u Bosni i Hercegovini krajem 1941 i početkom 1942. [The Crisis of People's Liberation Froant in Bosnia-Herzegovina at the End of 194 and beginning of 1942]. Sarajevo: Svjetlost.
IMDb database. Inglorius Bastards. Director Quentin Tarantino. https://www.imdb.com/title/tt0361748/?ref_=nv_sr_srsg_0.
IMDb database. Katyn. 2007. Director Andrzej Wajda. https://www.imdb.com/title/tt0879843/?ref_=nv_sr_srsg_3.
IMDb database. Red Tails. 2012. Director Anthony Hemingway. https://www.imdb.com/title/tt0485985/.
IMDb database. *Schindler's list*. Director Steven Spielberg. https://www.imdb.com/title/tt0108052/?ref_=nv_sr_srsg_0.
Jasenovac Memorial. https://www.youtube.com/user/JasenovacMemorial.
Kevo, Mario. 2009. *Veze Međunarodnog odbora Crvenog križa i Nezavisne Države Hrvatske*. Slavonski Brod, Zagreb, Jasenovac: Hrvatski institut za povijest, Hrvatski državni arhiv, JUSP Jasenovac [Connections of the International Committee of the Red Cross and Independent State of Croatia. Slavonski Brog, Zagreb, Jasenovac: Croatian Institute of History, Croatian State Archive, Public Establishment Memorial Park Jasenovac].
Kolar-Dimitrijević, Mira. 1981. "Rudnik željezne rude Ljubija za vrijeme okupacije." U: *Kozara u NOB-i i socijalističkoj revoluciji*. Prijedor: Nacionalni park Kozara, 363-377. [The Iron Mine Ljubija during Times of Occupation. In: *Kozara in People's Liberation Fighting and Socialist Revolution*. Prijedor: National Park Kozara, 363-377].
Košutić, Ivan. 1992. *Hrvatsko domobranstvo u Drugom svjetskom ratu* [Croatian Home Guard in World War II]. Zagreb: Nakladni zavod Matice hrvatske: Školska knjiga.
Matković, Hrvoje. 2003. *Povijest Jugoslavije* [History of Yugoslavia]. Zagreb: Naklada Pavičić.
Matković, Hrvoje. 2010. *Između Mačeka i Pavelića: politički portret Davida Sinčića* [Between Maček and Pavelić: Political Portrait of David Sinčić]. Zagreb: Naklada Pavičić.

MFDB – Media film database. 2014. https://mfdb.eu/en/film-dianas_list_c85277. O radnom naslovu "Dianina lista" vidi i: https://www.jutarnji.hr/kultura/film-i-tv/dianina-lista-zena-koja-je-uspjela-prevariti-sistem-i-spasiti-12.000-djece-iz-ustaskih-logora/1638099/ i https://dianaslistmovie.tumblr.com/.

Obhođaš, Amir, Mario Werhas, Bojan Dimitrijević, and Zvonimir Despot. 2013. *Ustaška vojnica 1*. [Ustasha Army I]. Zagreb: Despot Infinitus.

Petešić, Ćiril. 1990. *Dječji dom Jastrebarsko, dokumenti 1939-1947*. [Children's Domicile Jastrebarsko, Documents]. Zagreb: Kršćanska sadašnjost.

Samardžija, Dušan. 1984. *Bosanskodubičko područje u NOR-u 1941-1945*. Bosanska Dubica: Općina Bosanska Dubica. [Bosanska Dubica Area in People's Liberation War 1941-1945. Bosanska Dubica: Municipality Bosanska Dubica].

Škiljan, Filip. 2014. *Organizirana prisilna iseljenja Srba iz NDH*. [Organized Forcefull Evictions of Serbs from NDH]. Zagreb: Srpsko narodno vijeće.

Tko je tko u NDH [Who is Who in NDH]. 1997. Ur. Dizdar, Zdravko et al. Zagreb: Minerva.

Tomasevich, Jozo. 2010. *Rat i revolucija u Jugoslaviji 1941-1945.: okupacija i kolaboracija*. [War and Revolution in Yugoslavia 1941-1945: Occupation and Collabioration]. Zagreb: Europapress holding: Novi liber.

Yeomans, Rory. 2013. *Visions of Annihilation: The Ustasha Regime and the Cultural Politics of Fascism 1941-1945*. Pittsburgh: UPP.

Zamoda, Jagoda. 2019. "Zagrebačka redateljica 9 godina snimala potresnu priču..." *Gloria*, July 19. [The Director from Zagreb Has Been Making the Disturbing Film Story for 9 Years…]. https://www.gloria.hr/fokus/price/zagrebacka-redateljica-9-godina-snimala-potresnu-pricu-tko-je-kucanica-koja-je-spasila-vise-od-10-tisuca-djece/9139670/.

Zurl, Marino. 1978. *Tri jablana* [Three Poplars]. Zagreb: Mladost.

BIOGRAPHICAL SKETCH

Igor Vukić

Affiliation: Društvo za istraživanje trostrukog logora Jasenovac/Society for Research of the Threefold Jasenovac Camp, Zagreb, Hrvatska/Croatia

Education: MA in political science, Faculty of Political Science of Zagreb University, Zagreb, Croatia, 1992

Business Address: Pavlenski put 7 D, 10090 Zagreb

Research and Professional Experience: Reporter with several Croatian daily and weekly newspapers and magazines (Vjesnik, Jutarnji list, Novi list, Privredni vjesnik, Hrvatski tjednik)

Professional Appointments: independent historian

Publications from the Last 3 Years:

Books

1. *Radni logor Jasenovac/Labour camp Jasenovac*, Naklada Pavičić (publisher), Zagreb, 2018.
2. *Jasenovac iz dana u dan/Jasenovac, a chronology*, Naklada Pavičić, Zagreb, 2019.

In: Croatia: Past, Present and Future Perspectives
Editor: Matko Marušić ISBN: 978-1-53618-300-9

Chapter 11

CROATIA: FUTURE PERSPECTIVES: THE SWOT ANALYSIS

Matko Marušić*
University of Split, Split, Croatia

ABSTRACT

As part of the European Union (EU), Croatia today shares its reality and future perspectives with the other 26 member states. The majority of this country's specific problems are rooted in its troubled history and former communist regime. A Strengths – Weaknesses – Opportunities – Threats (SWOT) analysis indicates that Croatia's strength is belonging to European, Western civilization; that Croats have a strong love for their country and strong faith; that the county has remarkable natural beauty, with many national parks and parks of nature on land and at sea (https://www.croatiatraveller.com/National%20Parks/NationalParks.htm); and an important geopolitical position. The population has respect for knowledge, science and culture, as well as a strong commitment to progress, learning and improving quality of life. Weaknesses encompass the problem of declining population, which means that Croatia must address the problem of decreasing natality and curb the emigration that followed EU accession. The gap between the EU and Croatia in industrial production and productivity is closing thanks to the generations of young, educated people, a booming market economy, and considerable assistance from the EU. The most important part of the market economy is tourism that contributes almost one fifth GDP. Poor performance of industries inherited from the communist regime (e.g., shipbuilding) and the mindset and work ethic lingering from communist planned economy slow down the growth of the market economy and acceptance of competition as the driving force of progress. Similarly, serious economic and social problems arise from the misuse and mismanagement of the national health and social services. Negative influence of the political Soviet-style 'nomenklatura' continues largely because Croatia did not implement a lustration of the communist cadre after gaining independence, due to the exigencies of the 1991-1995 Croatian War of Independence. Another serious problem is corruption at all levels of society, exacerbated by a slow change of the mindset in the judicial system. EU membership represents an opportunity for Croatia because it stimulates the country to intensify the implementation

* Corresponding Author's Email: matko.marusic@gmail.com.

of the EU recommendations. Also, its geographical position provides Croatia with the opportunity to significantly contribute to the strategic cooperation with countries from Southeast Europe and the EU, and serve as a "bridge" between them. The country's natural environment is well-preserved and the modernization of industrial production does not require expensive restructuring but rather the adoption of safe and environment-friendly technologies. The membership in NATO contributes to the security of the country, reduces the expenses for defense and, at the same time, provides opportunities for the transfer of technology and development of defense industry, as well as training of defense personnel. External threats stem from old unresolved problems of the Balkan region, which concern Croatia indirectly, mostly in connection with the Croatian constitutive population in Bosnia-Herzegovina, and still existing claims of certain Serbian circles to parts of Croatia and Bosnia-Herzegovina. There are also unresolved border disputes with Bosnia-Herzegovina, Slovenia, Serbia and Montenegro.

Keywords: Croatia, faith; Croatia, future; Croatia, relations with Bosnia-Herzegovina; Croatia, relations with Slovenia; Croatia, relations with Serbia; demography, Croatia; SWAT analysis, Croatia

INTRODUCTION

Symbolically speaking, Croatian plight to win freedom and have an independent state lasted from the defeat in the battle of Gvozd Mountain in 1102 (see Chapter 1) until the victory in the battle for Knin in 1995 (see Chapter 8). These nine centuries have been marked by innumerable sacrifices, suffering and losses, but Croats never gave up. In 1990, at the first free elections in their history, they voted overwhelmingly for democracy. The first session of a democratically-elected Croatian parliament (Croatian "Sabor", which means Assembly) on May 30, 1990, marked a historic opportunity to achieve freedom and is today officially celebrated as the Statehood Day. The choice of democracy was important as it brought freedom and made it possible for Croatia to proclaim independence from Yugoslavia a year later, in 1991. International recognition and membership in the United Nations followed in 1992. Meticulous work on the reconstruction of the country after the devastating war 1991-1995 as well as consistent adherence to democratic rule ensured that Croatia would become a NATO member in 2009 and a member of the European Union in 2013. In 2020, it presided over the Council of the EU.

The nine centuries-long yearning for freedom should be remembered, respected and considered the key to understanding Croatian history, Croatia's present state and its future perspectives. That is why this book! Naturally, most of the chapters dealt with the past; here, the last chapter offers a view of the future of the Republic of Croatia based on the Strengths – Weaknesses – Opportunities – Threats (SWOT) analysis. In the context of time, Strengths and Weaknesses depict present based on the past, and Opportunities and Threats relate to the future based on past and present (Emerald Works 2020). This analysis was done by the author, on the basis of publicly available and relevant data.

STRENGTHS

Croatia has four main strengths: it is part of the European, Western civilization; Croats have a profound and abiding love for their country; the Croatian nation is of strong faith, i.e., its majority has a strong attachment to religion of the Roman Catholic Church; and Croatia has remarkable natural beauty and enjoys an important geopolitical position. As a part of the European and Western civilization, Croatia has due respect for knowledge, science and culture, as well as a strong commitment to progress, learning and improving quality of life.

Croatia Belongs to the Western World

Croats are open to the Western way of life, culture, and technology. Schools are good and young people are receptive to education. Croatian language is cherished as a source of national pride and identity, but the majority of the younger population also speaks English (Education First 2019) and often another foreign language, such as German in the North and Italian in the South. There are elite schools that offer mandatory classes in Latin and ancient Greek as well as other languages (Chinese, Japanese, Hebrew, Arabic) as electives. Culture and science are well-developed and highly valued, and sports are widespread and popular, especially soccer, basketball, handball, and water polo. Public life is safe and lively; there are no streets or areas in the country which are unsafe to enter at night. Humor is different in different parts of the country but is cherished and freely practiced everywhere. Food and water are safe. Despite the difficult history and unresolved political disputes, there is no hatred of neighbors or among different political camps or other groups within the country, and no racism or discrimination. Since the first democratic elections in 1990 until today, which includes the 1991-1995 War of Independence, there has never been a single incident of violence at elections or other political and cultural events. In 2019 Croatia ranked 13th on the global Berkeley Inclusiveness Index (Menendian et al. 2019).

Love for the Country

At the beginning of the breakup of Yugoslavia in 1990, Croatia had a poor international image, and Western democracies mourned the disappearance of Yugoslavia (Sanz 1992; Kaplan 1993; Sadkovich 2005). Reasons for this are manifold but can be summed up in terms of two factors: first, those who favored Yugoslavia for geostrategic and other reasons saw Croatian efforts to gain independence as a threat and did everything possible to suppress them; this included presenting those efforts in a negative light. Second, the communist terror after WWII silenced all Croatian intellectuals who could have been able to challenge the distorted historical and other writings with due arguments. This silence lasted until 1990, when the fall of communism allowed Croats to express their true political stance: at the referendum on independence, held on May 19, 1991, more than 3 million people (83.56%), out of approximately 3.6 million registered voters, cast their vote. Of them, 93.24% voted for independence whereas only 4.15% wanted to remain in Yugoslavia (Hrvatski Sabor 2020). Even if those citizens who abstained from voting are counted as opposing independence, the result was that 78% of Croatian citizens voted for independence. This finding is even more impressive in light of the fact that at the time Croatian citizens included 12.2% Serbs, who had been born in Croatia or had arrived from Serbia and had residence in Croatia, and that Serbian extremists had started a rebellion already in August 1990 ("Log Revolution") against the Croatian democratic government (United Nations 2007).

Love for one's country is essential for citizens' commitment to defend national, social and public security. In case of Croatia, this commitment came to the test soon after the referendum, because on Easter (March 31) 1991, the insurrection of Serbs in Croatia claimed its first casualties (Bandić 2015). It soon grew into a large-scale Serbian aggression against Croatia and Bosnia-Herzegovina which had the aim of creation of Greater Serbia; in its Judgement from 2015, International Court of Justice stated in Hague stated:

"... 442. The evidence establishes the existence, as of early 1991, of a political objective to unite Serb areas in Croatia and in BiH with Serbia in order to establish a unified territory. Moreover, the evidence establishes that the SAO Krajina, and subsequently the RSK, government and authorities fully embraced and advocated this objective, and strove to accomplish it in co-operation with the Serb leaderships in Serbia and in the RS in BiH.

445. From at least August 1991, the political objective to unite Serb areas in Croatia and in BiH with Serbia in order to establish a unified territory was implemented through widespread and systematic armed attacks on predominantly Croat and other non-Serb areas and through the commission of acts of violence and intimidation." (International Court of Justice 2015).

[Author's note: BiH – Bosna i Hercegovina, Bosnia-Herzegovina; SAO Krajina – Srpska autonomna oblast Krajina (in Croatia), Serb Autonomous Region Krajina (in Croatia); RSK – Republika Srpska Krajina, Republic of Serb Krajina (in Croatia, "Autonomous Region was transformed into "Republic" after ethnic cleansing of Croats); RS – Republika Srpska, Republic Srpska (in Bosnia and Herzegovina, still existant)].

Croats proved their love for their country at this time, when they successfully established the Croatian Army (Rohde 2015) and helped it achieve victory in the 1991-1995 war (see Chapter 8). The final operation of the war, "Operation Storm", which the Croatian army and police undertook to liberate occupied territories in August 1995, is still studied as part of U.S. military education as a well led, well trained, well equipped military operation with good political guidance, which changed the course of history because "Croatia could bat above its weight, fight above its weight" (US Department of Defense 2017).

Faith

According to the 2011 Census, Croatia had 90.42% Croats, 4.32% Serbs and no other minority exceeded 1%; of them 86.28% are Roman-Catholic, 4.44% Orthodox Christian, 1.47% Muslims, 0.34% Protestant and around 4.5% of the people are atheists or agnostics (EURYDICE 2020).

Catholic faith is inseparable from Croatian identity, which was preserved throughout the difficult history from early medieval times until the present time. This may be associated with centuries-long Christian wars with Ottoman Turks, in which religious identity was maybe a more important strategic goal than territory (see Chapter 1). By the same token, faith proved important during the War of Independence; Croatian soldiers became known worldwide as soldiers who wore a rosary and a cross around their neck (Burilović and Parlov 2013). The testimony of a high commander (later admiral) Major Ivica Tolić reads:

"There have been moments when we were in overwhelming dangers, when our body strength was waning. However, a rosary around the neck, and more so in the heart, brought about the spiritual strength so that afterward we wondered how we had endured all that." (Jurišić 1992).

In 2006 Croatian war veterans proclaimed the rosary as the symbol of the Croatian War of Independence (Jutarnji list 2006).

Faith fortifies tolerance, family life and fairness, which are important in the life of each person as well as in the nation as whole. In case of Croatia this is manifest in the high overall inclusivity of its society (Menendian et al. 2020).

Geostrategic Position and the Beauty of the Country

Croatia's strategically favorable geographic position is its location on the Mediterranean and its closeness to Western and Eastern Europe, which allows easy contacts, trade and transfer of culture and knowledge. In addition to its geographic position, Croatia has a mild climate, which is especially pleasant along the coast; the Adriatic Sea is relatively small and not prone to heavy storms; in addition, numerous islands protect the coast from waves. In general, the country's geography is varied as it includes the flat and fertile region of Slavonia, a mountainous middle part with an abundance of clean water, woods and pastures, and the very long (East) Adriatic coast with 1,244 islands, of which 67 are inhabited.

Albeit favorable, the geographic position historically has also proven to be a challenge: the country is located in Central Europe but mostly to the South and therefore farthest from the centers of European culture. Historically and culturally it belongs to Western Europe, but borders with Eastern Europe and has the traces Balkan legacy. The line of the schism of Christianity in 1054 is roughly on the Eastern border of Bosnia-Herzegovina (BH, first Croatia's eastern neighbor), and the Eastern Adriatic coast is the closest warm sea to the countries from European North and East. Historically strong powers neighbor the country; Hungary and Austria (historically the Austro-Hungarian Empire) to the northwest, Italy (Venice) to the west-southwest and Serbia to the east. Serbia was under Ottoman rule for five centuries, and the constantly shifting Ottoman-Christian frontier ran through Croatia, resulting in a centuries-long permanent war filled with many defeats and territorial losses; but country's spirit never capitulated. For that unyielding resistance, Croatia has been called both "Antemurale Christianitatis" (the Bulwark of Christendom) in the 15th century, and "Reliquiae reliquiarum olim magni et inclyti regni Croatiae" (the Remnants of the Remnants of the once great and glorious Kingdom of Croatia) since the 16th century, when Slavonia fell under Ottoman rule. Dalmatia (the southern Croatian coastal region) was under Venetian rule for four centuries. After World War I (WWI), Croatia was trapped in the Kingdom of Yugoslavia under harsh Serbian imperialistic rule (Šegedin 1993; Janjatović 2002; Matković and Trogrlić 2019) and in the communist dictatorship of Josip Broz Tito's Yugoslavia after WWII. In those times it lost half of its territory (the cause of its unusual shape today) and unknown part of population, but has continually demonstrated its will to endure and sustain its Christian and Western culture (Tanner 2010). Regardless of their political or any other position, Croats have always believed that Croatia is part of Western Europe (see Chapter 1).

WEAKNESSES

Croatia's weaknesses are numerous and include the mindset and work ethic inherited from the communist planned economy, a relatively high corruption in all levels of society, inadequate quality of higher education, an economy with a fragile basis, declining population, and internal societal frictions.

The Mindset and Work Ethic of Communist Planned Economy

The mindset and work ethic inherited from communist planned economy are strongly ingrained in Croatia, more so than in the post-communist Czech Republic, Slovakia, Hungary, or Poland. The key reason is that Croatian national and liberal intellectuals and entrepreneurs were exterminated in 1945, which was the loss from which it has been difficult to recover. From 1945 to 1990, in Tito's Yugoslavia, there was no freedom of speech, limited or no access to information other than communist propaganda, and school programs were packed with lies and partial truths so that students learned to love communism, Yugoslavia and Tito and hate or despise capitalism, despise entrepreneurship, Croatian national history, and the West. Especially devastating were the distortions of history because almost all Croatian historic attempts or ideas of national liberation were depicted as backward and wrong – chauvinist, or even fascist. Additionally, many Croatian citizens have a less negative opinion of the communist regime because in its last decade communism in Croatia was seemingly less brutal than in other countries under communist rule. The so-called worker self-management (Dubey 1975), may have also contributed to that mindset because it remained in the memory of a number of unskilled workers who contributed to the management of factories and institutions and had better pay, position and social recognition. Therefore, even today there is a portion of the population which finds life in the market economy worse than in communist "uravnilovka" (leveling), which meant administrative leveling of salaries, regardless of the type of work, job complexity, or productivity. Together with job security and lack of pressure for better productivity, this led to a relatively easy life for the unambitious, lazy, and uneducated.

From 1962 until 1965, the communist regime gradually opened the borders and those hopelessly poor (peasants from devastated villages), as well as those more ambitious or politically dissatisfied with the regime left for Western countries in search of a better and more dignified life. This was followed by the period of 1991-1995, when one third of industry and housing were destroyed during the Croatian War of Independence and the country achieved democracy and a free market economy while contending with a shortage of people able to perform sophisticated jobs, from diplomacy to the judiciary system and the business world. Patriotism and political freedom are good things but insufficient to solve everyday problems, from the personal to the state level.

The key problem may lay in the inefficiency and corruption of the judicial system. Genuine corruption caused by the communist totalitarian approach to law and justice migrated to the democratic system (1990/1991) because the communist cadre, partly also anti-Croatian, was not removed from their positions. Removal was impossible because of Serbian aggression immediately after Croatian secession from Yugoslavia. In the spirit of developed Western democracies, the judicial system was proclaimed independent ("third independent pillar of democracy"), and judges' salaries significantly increased (the idea was that they will be relieved from the pressure of corruption). Good ideas – but in practice a specific disastrous vicious circle emerged: those who are entrusted to fight corruption are free of any oversight regarding their own corruption. Once the judicial system is corrupt, no other public service can be thoroughly remedied.

Corruption as Historical Way of Life

For centuries Croats lived in states with non-Croatian governments that were hostile towards Croatia not only in the realm of politics and economy, but also in every aspect of life of common people. The state administration has never been Croatian and until 1868 was conducted in foreign languages that were also imposed in schools and public life. The systemic discrimination of native people has materialized as corruption, first as the activity of the rulers and then as the only way for the discriminated to achieve otherwise legal rights and needs. The borders were artificial and changing, exposed to permanent skirmishes, looting and wars. Croats did not see the states in which they lived and their administrations as their own. It was a kind of patriotic deed to betray the state and cheat it. The borders proved useful for smuggling, and black-market trade was the means of everyday survival. A disconnect from the assistance of political, judicial, educational, and public services forced common people to rely on families, relatives, and faithful friends instead of the rules and institutions of legal civil life. All this resulted in a mentality of 'survival by crafty management' and leaning on family and small local ('tribal') support.

The distorted "culture of survival" is difficult to eradicate even once a self-governed, free and democratic state has been achieved. Desperate because of its contemporary manifestations, this author used to bitterly say that "A Croat is ready to face an enemy tank with an iron bar, yet it is normal for him to avoid paying taxes to his own state." (This was indeed how the National Guard attacked enemy tanks at the beginning of the War of Independence in 1991: boldly stabbing an iron stick into the tracks to stop the tank, which then can be attacked with hand grenades thrown into the turret.) Furthermore, taxes are high (e.g., VAT is 25%) and pervasive, because the state provides free health care to all, pensions to a disproportionate percentage of population (even as they are low overall), and other social expenses inherited from the communist times.

It was a strange twist of fate that this tradition of mischievous behavior proved useful in the Croatian War of Independence; due to the United Nations embargo on arms, Croatia was forced to smuggle arms from abroad; this endeavor escalated to the level of successful smuggling of articles as large as tanks (Bellamy 1992).

In 2018, the Transparency International Corruption Perceptions Index placed Croatia as the 63rd least corrupt nation out of 175 countries (Transparency International 2020). However, while the country is improving in its newfound freedom and democracy, the pace is slower than many expected. Despite its current challenges, the European Union (EU) is still the key hope for improvements in Croatia. Although a number of reforms promised to the EU have only been formally implemented (e.g., the reform of university structure, OECD 2008), Croatia has advanced steadily and at an acceptable pace since its accession to the EU. However, many years of stability are needed before it comes even close to other fellow member countries.

Slow Recovery of Higher Education

As stated above, Croatian primary and secondary schools are good and young people like to study. However, some university faculties are weak – old-fashioned and insufficiently research-oriented – and yet those enroll too many students. This results in relatively insufficient quality of some components of higher education. These faculties are those which have been most strongly influenced by the totalitarian political system in the communist times: parts of faculties of political sciences, law and economics, as well as some programs in history, philosophy, and sociology. Inadequate education of their graduates deprives the young state of top intellectuals, professionals, and leaders in important areas of life, such as politics, law, social work, and some aspects of culture.

Universities have been under total communist control, from the composition of faculties and programs to the appointment of university and department heads. Limited travel and international collaboration, including international research funds, left academics with no or with distorted criteria of quality (see OECD 2008), which are still present in the general mindset and in policy (Marušić 2012, 2016).

After achieving independence and democracy in 1990, the Croatian War of Independence started in 1991 and lasted until 1995; UN peace keeping forces left the country in 1998 (see Chapter 8). There were more urgent tasks to take on during that time than to address the quality and background of university professors. The faculties have not been reevaluated nor the universities reconstructed. Nobody dared to reevaluate the academy, especially not politicians in the new democratic system. In any case there were not enough good candidates to replace those who became professors on the basis of political loyalty to the collapsed totalitarian system. In time, the old academic circles regrouped, defined criteria that suited them, and successfully kept insisting on academic independence. They continue to breed personnel identical to themselves (Obadić and Aristovnik 2011).

However, there are objective signs that the situation is improving. As shown in Figure 1, Croatian scientific productivity dropped significantly at the start of Serbian aggression in 1990/1991 only to slowly recover and reach the global average in 2015 (in 25 years!). Moreover, the young and modern University of Split, weak in the eighties, reached the global average in 2009 and subsequently surpassed the global average by roughly 40%.

The lack of high-quality personnel in certain environments triggers a vicious circle of inadequacy: poor performers do not care about increasing the quality of education and research, bad managers are not able to increase productivity, and mediocre university professors refuse international criteria of quality so university graduates suffer. Ultimately, the resistance to improvements and modernization also breeds corruption, which infects the students, too. Some of them enter the job market primed for corrupt behavior and most of them are disappointed because in reality, corruption is clearly visible as soon as one starts searching for a desirable job. The nuclei of communist thought have survived at Croatian universities, disguised but prosperous.

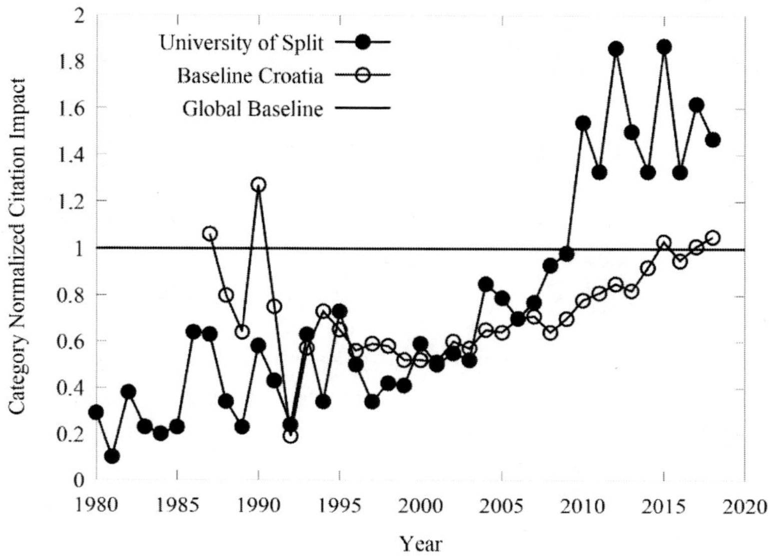

Figure 1. Growth of scientific production in Croatia and of University of Split in comparison to the global average. CINC – Category Normalized Citation Impact (based on the number of citations of scientific reports where global average for each year = 1) (Vranješ Markić 2019).

A Fragile Economic Basis

Almost all huge enterprises established under the communist regime had been artificially kept alive by state's assistance (e.g., inflation), they swiftly went bankrupt in the free-market economy which arrived in 1990. Privatization of state-owned enterprises started already in the late eighties and lasted for years, at the same time as the closures of unprofitable companies (Bendeković 2000). Since then, many Croats have blamed unfair privatization for the disappearance of their firms and jobs, but the lack of competitiveness was the key cause. During the 1991-1995 Serbian aggression 14.760 km^2 or 26% of Croatian territory was occupied, 13,583 persons were killed or went missing, and 37,180 persons were wounded. In December 1991 Croatia had 550,000 refugees and displaced persons (386,264 in 1995), and 150,000 people took refuge abroad (57,000 in 1995). One third of the country was physically destroyed (Perković and Puljiz 2001). Thousands of volunteers from 1991 returned 1995 from the battlefields to find themselves jobless. The state gave them pensions, shares and other benefits, but they retained the initial bitterness of a sudden feeling of purposelessness – after their noble sacrifice for freedom. This is the economic and social situation Croatia faced when it began rebuilding the economy in peacetime. Since then, the rate of recovery and growth of its economy showed steady, though often uneven, progress.

The Croatian currency Kuna (1 US$=6.9 HRK) was introduced in 1994 and stayed stable until today. Gross domestic product (GDP) grew by roughly 2.3% until 2019 when growth reached 3.9%. Its main component is private consumption (around 4%) and government spending (around 3%). GDP per capita grew from US$8,563 in 1995 to roughly US$13,700 from 2011-2014 (during a left-wing government), and then showed a steady growth to US$15,870 in 2018. Tourism accounts for 20% of the GDP. Industry, which currently shows only insignificant growth, is dominated by food processing, pharmaceutical industry, shipbuilding, and information technology (CEIC 2019).

Government debt was the lowest in 1995 (the first reported year, 22.6% of the GDP), and highest in 2014 (84.7%, the penult year of the left-wing government); in 2018 it decreased to 78.0% (CEIC 2019).

By the end of 2019, Croatia's economy recovered from the adverse effects of the global financial crisis. It grew by approximately 3% since 2017. Fiscal imbalances were reduced and in 2018 the annual budget was not negative for the first time. Exports of goods and services grew from below 40% of GDP in 2008 to above 50% in 2018. Exports account for 46%, whereas imports account for 44% of GDP, adding a total of 2% to GDP (World Bank in Croatia 2019).

According to the Global Competitiveness Report, Croatia ranked 68th in 2018, with 60.1% of 0-100 value, whereas the US was 1st (85.6%), Slovakia 41st (66.8%) and Albania 76th (58.1%) (World Economic Forum 2018).

From 2009 until 2019, productivity in Croatia (measured as GDP per hour over a defined period of time as the real value of production by a unit of labor) ranged from 92.4 to 111.3 points (Trading Economics 2020). It was comparable to the EURO Zone (102.10), lower than the EU (106.2) and far lower than some other post-communist countries like the Czech Republic (122.7), Slovakia (128.1) and Hungary (114.4), yet higher than that of Greece (100.1) and Germany (97.1) (Trading Economics 2020).

In general, economic development is neither steady nor even. The sources of growth are not sufficiently diversified. Tourism, sensitive to uncontrollable factors, makes up too big a share of the economy; the population is aging, emigration is high and technological modernization and adaptation is slow to new modes of work. The growth rate (approximately 2.5% on average) is too low to bring about rapid convergence with EU averages. The World Bank estimated that "… with the right set of policy actions, Croatia can increase returns on public investment by effectively using EU grant funds and attract strategic private investment to create economic opportunities. Critical reform areas include investments in human capital and natural resource management to preserve and leverage the country's natural assets. However, the success of these reforms will ultimately rely on strengthening Croatia's institutions." (World Bank in Croatia 2019).

Declining Population

During the 20th century, the Croatian population has not grown at a pace consistent with the population size and birthrate. Since the beginning of the 20th century, Croats from the poor parts of the country, primarily Southern (coastal) Croatia, emigrated in several waves to South America, USA, and Australia. Few of them ever returned home. Later came heavy losses in WWII, especially related to the communist mass murder of up to half a million Croats (see Šterc 2015, below). Starting immediately after the fall of Kingdom of Yugoslavia in April 1941, Croat civilians, especially in the Serb-Croat mixed areas, would have been massacred (see Chapter 9). Ustasha revenged and thousands innocent people perished until 1945. In addition, wherever the partisans would arrive, they would kill people according to the lists their agents and collaborator had made in advance (see city of Dubrovnik case, Kačić 2009). At the end of the WWII the armies (Ustasha and Domobran) of the Independent State of Croatia (in Croatian, Nezavisna Država Hrvatska, NDH) together with family members and anti-communists in general, retreated towards Austria to surrender to British forces, but were repelled and handed to partisans who kept killing them for months. This is called the Bleiburg Tragedy (Nikolić 1993), after the small town of Bleiburg where the retreating crowd was returned to partisans and forced to surrender (Tolstoy 1986; Marević 1993; Grubišić 2000; Mijatović 2007). The murders continued on the "Way of the Cross" ("Death Marches"), because not all captives could be killed at Bleiburg and in Slovenia, but thousands were forced to march back towards North and Middle Croatia and killed all along the way; it is estimated that only 10% survived (Grahek Ravančić 2015; Jurčević 2015). Commission of the Government of Republic of Slovenia listed 581 mass graves in Slovenia estimating 100,000 killed (Dežman 2010). Thousands of war-wounded patients from Zagreb hospitals were executed (Matković 2011). Since 1990 many horrifying mass graves were discovered in the Republic of Slovenia: Kočevski Rog (Dubajić 2006), Huda Jama (Leljak 2015), Tezno (Ferenc 2012; see also Dežman 2010; Tadić and Crnogorac 2013; Jurčević 2015; Matkovich 2017; Borovčak 2018). However, due to more or less visible resistance of circles which inherited the ideology of Communist Party of former Yugoslavia, state-level research on communist post-WWII crimes has never been conducted in Croatia and that in Slovenia was gradually extinguished. The increased mortality during WWII encompassed also killed soldiers of all sides, non-Croat civilians, and people who died of hunger, cold, and diseases.

After WWII, the tradition of working abroad continued and people would temporarily emigrate to work, mostly to Germany. Emigration was banned from 1945 and people would emigrate illegally (Šarić 2015). Starting in early 1960s the regime gradually allowed people to have passports and used that to paint a picture of a "milder regime". It also profited from getting rid of people who disliked communism and by having their money to flow back into the country, because it was mostly men who went to work abroad while their families stayed at home. Germans coined the word "Gastarbeiter", for guest workers, which in time became a colloquial Croatian expression. Hundreds of thousands of Croats worked in Germany over a period of years. An unknown portion of them ultimately took their families abroad, and most of those families never returned to Croatia (Jurić 2017).

According to the Croatian demographer Dr. Stjepan Šterc (Šterc 2015), 350,000 Croats left for the Americas at the beginning of the 20th century. In WWI, direct and indirect losses are estimated at 363,000 inhabitants, and Croatia was the only country in the region with depopulation in the first census after WWI. According to the census of 1948, the losses in WWII and in the "Bleiburg/Path of the Cross" were 639,000 people. Some 450,000 Croats emigrated when the borders were opened in the sixties. The 1991-1995 Croatian War of Independence caused direct (war casualties) and indirect (emigration) losses of 482,000 inhabitants of whom roughly 300,000 were Serbs who did not want to live in an independent Croatia and emigrated to Serbia. After Croatia joined the European Union, 150,000 inhabitants moved to work abroad (Šterc 2015).

Overall, Šterc maintains that Croatia directly or indirectly lost 2,434,000 inhabitants in the 20th century. Today, Croatia has 4.2 million inhabitants, whereas without those losses it would have had 6.7 million inhabitants (Šterc 2015). Similar calculations have been published by Mrkoci and Horvat (2008). A number of Serbian writers claim that during WWII Ustasha committed a "genocide" on Serbs, but the official Census data suggest that the Croats underwent extremely high losses (Lozo 2017): comparison of Croat and Serb populations from the census of 1931 and the census of 1948 show that during those 17 years Croatia lost 639,000 inhabitants whereas Serbia had a total growth of 802,000 inhabitants (growth rate 17%) (Šterc 2015, Lozo 2017). A review of all figures published until 2010 has been summarized by Vladimir Geiger (2010). The dim future of Croatian demography has been summarized by Akrap (2015).

Internal Social Frictions

In spite of inclusivity and tolerance of the Croatian population, there is a surprisingly high level of political strife over the history of 20th century. The reason for it is because a lustration (a bill according to which members of Communist Party and secret police are not allowed to public function of the higher level, see Horne 2014) has not been carried out. It was impossible to implement it immediately after the fall of communism as has been done in other post-communist countries like East Germany, Poland and Hungary, because the country was attacked three months after its free elections. (Elections took place in May and the Serb rebellion started in August 1990.) After the war was over (in 1995, but the last UN troops left the country in 1998), it was too late – communists recovered disguised under new name (Social Democratic Party – which officially inherited the properties of the former Communist Party) as well as by joining several other parties, and won the parliamentary majority in 2000-2003 and in 2011-2016. Today they fiercely oppose any systematic investigation of the communist slaughter of Croats after WWII, and block historic and forensic research on numerous WWII events which have been misinterpreted or simply made up (Kasapović 2018; see Lozo 2017; and Vukić 2019). This causes significant dissatisfaction among many of the population and serious division and friction between the left elite and common people.

OPPORTUNITIES

Opportunities for Croatia's future started with its independence and freedom in 1990/91. Democracy came with independence and it can open up important opportunities for any post-communist country. Despite numerous weaknesses and relative lag behind the majority of EU countries, Croatia's prospects for the future are bright. Membership in the European Union and NATO brought Croatia into developed Western world, and today Croatia has opportunities and a strategic position comparable to other EU countries.

European Union

The positive effect of the EU membership on Croatia is visible in its achievements since accession. From the start of the European Semester 2014, 51% of recommendations specific for Croatia have achieved at least "some progress" but the remaining 49% made only "limited" or "no progress" (European Commission 2019). That means that Croatia has to intensify the efforts for implementation of the recommendations, because they represent its opportunities (International Monetary Fund 2019). The European Commission (2019) and the International Monetary Fund (2019) proposed to Croatia a number of recommendations, among which repeatedly the typical are: to abort socialist (communist) inheritance and mentality; to cut back state spending; to reduce the number of employees in the public sector because of their shortage in the private sector; to increase efficacy of public administration; to reform the systems of health care, retirement and pensions; to lower VAT and continue lowering corporate taxes; and to increase mobility for inhabitants by upgrading train services. It is interesting and instructive to note that almost half of all recommendations are related to problems caused by the communist system which lasted until 1990.

International Collaborations

A favorable geographic position allows Croatia to significantly contribute to strategic cooperation with countries that are to the East of the EU and to enable their integration with the Western part of the EU (Three Seas Initiative 2019). After so many centuries without any foreign political and other official contacts, it is a satisfaction for Croats to entertain good relations with numerous countries around the world. Especially important are very good relations and cooperation with the Republic of Slovakia, which shares a similar history, mentality, and culture as well as with Hungary with which Croatia shares good deal of history, and with Israel, because Israeli intellectual, economic, technologic and science capacities are top-grade and Croats can profit greatly from any kind of cooperation with a country which showed that a nation can endure against all odds – environmental, political, economic and other. At the same time, Israel can profit from having a friendly country with abundance of clean water, a pleasant climate, cooperative intellectuals and a population with high esteem for knowledge and art (Krce 2017).

NATO

Despite the fact that active membership in NATO includes obligations and hazards, the Republic of Croatia has joined that system of regional and world security (Skok 2007). But NATO membership for Croatia means more than security, because application of NATO standards directly diminishes the expenses needed for defense of the country, opens additional business opportunities for the military industry, and enables participation of military personnel, experts, and scientists in NATO projects and acquisition of knowledge and technology. Reforms associated with NATO membership have modernized and improved flow of business, which decreases business risks and subsequently interest rates (Miščević et al. 2012). Collaboration with NATO requires the development of defense technologies against new threats to security (e.g., internet attacks), development of specific competences of the Croatian army (e.g., upgrading soldiers to the level of instructors), and formation of armed forces capable of contributing to multinational NATO formations. This collaboration adds to the capabilities of the involved personnel (e.g., learning foreign languages) and increases their earnings and standard of life (Barić 2004).

Preserved Environment

With respect to opportunities related to Croatia's natural resources and environment, the unfortunate experience with 45 years of communist/socialist rule may be seen as an opportunity, because inefficiency of communism slowed down uncontrolled industrial growth and pollution of the environment, whereas companies in dirty industries (coal, steel, plastic) all disappeared with the establishment of the open market. Although they have left a number of "open environmental wounds", the country's natural environment is generally well-preserved and the modernization of industrial production does not require painful shutting down of factories, but only the establishment of modern technologies – for which the workforce is ready. In this regard, the European Green Deal Investment Plan is a great opportunity, because it will facilitate public and private investments needed for the transition to a climate-friendly, carbon-neutral, green, competitive and inclusive economy (European Commission 2020). For Croatia, it constitutes a shortcut to modern industry and jobs, as well as the highest environmental standards. Croatia is already the 10th country in the EU with respect to the use of renewable energy for heating and cooling (Eurostat 2020). Taken all listed together, it may be said that Croatia today stands better than ever in its history, and that the prospects for the future are good.

THREATS

According to the SWOT analysis, the threats are contained in potentially harmful attributes of the political environment (Emerald Works 2020). For Croatia they may come from the neighboring countries, from Europe or from the world in general. The threats that may ensue as the threats to Europe or the world are not specific for Croatia, and will not be analyzed. The relations with the neighboring states are relevant as problems that need to be solved to improve security, trade, and cooperation and diminish the external and internal worries and frictions.

Relations with Bosnia and Herzegovina

Relations between the Republic of Croatia and the Republic of Bosnia-Herzegovina (BH) are very complicated: BH itself is a problem with its three nations (Bosniak, Serb and Croat) that are all constitutional peers (equals) and two subunits – Republic Srpska, totally dominated by Serbs because of ethnic cleansing from 1992, and Federation of BH comprising Bosniaks and Croats, with Bosniaks being significantly more numerous than Croats. Bosniaks are also the relative majority in the entire BH. Bosniaks are Slavic Muslims who became recognized as a nationality in 1968 ("People's Republic of BH" was formed in communist Yugoslavia in 1945), and they chose to be called Bosniaks in 1993 (Pickering et al. 2019). Historically, Serbs claimed them as Serbs, and Croats considered them Croats. Until the Ottoman conquests in the 15th and the 16th century, the population of what is today BH was Catholic, with a minority of the followers of the Bosnian Christian Church ("krstjani Crkve bosanske") (Šanjek 1988). There were no reports of Orthodox monasteries in BH at the time (Malcolm 1996). Recently acquired evidence from (published and unpublished) Ottoman survey registers points to the existence of a small number of Orthodox monasteries active during the late 15th and early 16th centuries in the easternmost parts of Bosnia, including the monastery of Dobrun near Višegrad (Michael Ursinus, personal communication, 2019).

The key Croatian problem with BH is the fulfillment of rights of the Croat population in BH. The constitution was meant to ensure equal representation of three constituent nations in the Presidency of BH. In reality, due to the way the electoral law was written, Bosniaks can and do outvote Croats; that leads to widespread dissatisfaction among the Croats in BH (Ivanović 2015). Republic Srpska wants to join Serbia and, if this happens, BH Croats and Croatia will find themselves in a very difficult strategic position: although Republic Srpska contains a number of areas that had Bosniak and/or Croat majorities before the 1991-1995 war, Bosniaks will not be able to claim those territories. The same applies for BH Croats. BH Croats will not want to live in the leftover half of BH under total Bosniak control; yet they are weaker than Bosniaks, whereas Croatia itself should not interfere in BH internal affairs of any kind, let alone military affairs. The only hope is that BH joins the EU and thus further develops democracy and a higher standard of living. However, it appears that only BH Croats are sincerely committed to joining the EU. Symbolically and formally, BH Croats, are already EU citizens because they also have Croatian citizenship.

Relations with the Republic of Montenegro

The relations between Croatia and the Republic of Montenegro in the 20th century had been complex because of the division of Montenegrin identity, society and politics, but in general they can be considered fair, with the exception of the 1991 aggression against Croatia. In contrast to Serbia, Montenegro accepted its responsibility for the 1991 aggression, apologized (HINA 2016) and compensated prisoners whom it kept in prisoner camps (Rašović 2018).

The Croatian peninsula of Prevlaka with its territorial waters controls the access to the bay of Boka Kotorska in Montenegro (Kapac 1992). This gives rise to a particular conflict with Montenegro. However, a temporary solution was found in the agreement that Montenegrin ships freely pass through Croatian territorial waters and that the police forces of both countries perform sea border checks in cooperation (Punda and Filipović 2015).

Relations with the Republic of Slovenia

Although the Republic of Slovenia and Croatia have historically good relations, and there is abundant economic collaboration, the disputes since the independence of both states have been surprisingly numerous and intense. They include several border disputes; the issue of Slovenian delay in building highways in the direction of Croatia and the introduction of highway tolls (both to impede travel of European tourists to Croatia); the Krško nuclear power plant (situated in Slovenia, built jointly in ex-Yugoslavia) plagued by issues regarding the division of profits, expenses, and radioactive waste disposal; Bank of Ljubljana (the bank's block of saving accounts of Croatian citizens opened before dissipation of Yugoslavia), and the ownership of Slovenian worker summer resorts built in Croatia in ex-Yugoslavia.

Most important and unpleasant are the border disputes between the two countries. The Republic of Slovenia was accepted into the EU on the basis of the Opinion 7 of the Badinter Commission from January 11, 1992 (Ragazzi 1992), in which Slovenia declared that it has no territorial disputes with any neighboring state, including the Republic of Croatia, listed specifically by its name. However, Slovenian police took control of Sveti Ilija (Sveta Gera in Slovenian) hill and fortress on the Croatian-Slovenian border as early as 1991, although they are unequivocally Croatian, and they remain in their control (Degan 2019).

The dispute with the Republic of Slovenia about Savudrijska Vala started in 1993, when a third of the Croatian territory was occupied by Serbia (and Croatia would struggle for liberation for another two years). Slovenia decided that Savudrijska Vala (Slovenians call it The Bay of Piran) is Slovenian. Croatia offered to jointly appeal to the International Court for Sea Law, but Slovenia insisted on the International Court of Justice in Hague, because that court also takes into account "the principle of justice", claiming that if Croatia closes sea access to Piran, Slovenia may starve. When Croatia refused, Slovenia blocked Croatian accession to the EU until Croatia accepted to go to Court of Justice in Hague for arbitration in 1999 (Maretić Žonja et al. 2017). The arbitration process started at the end of 2011, after Croatia signed the Contract of Accession to the EU. In June 2014, the Court announced that the verdict will be announced in 2015. However, on July 22, 2014, the media, first in Serbia and then in Croatia, published voice recordings of telephone conversations between the Slovenian arbiter at the Court, Jernej Sekolec, and the Slovenian representative Simona Drenik. These conversations revealed a conspiracy between the Slovenian arbiter at the Court and the representative of Slovenia as the litigant in the process. Arbiter Sekolec had transferred secret information to representative Drenik, which is normally available only to the (five) arbiters, and the voice records revealed that the two Slovenians arranged ways of planting documents and discussed tactics for influencing certain arbiters, aiming to affect the outcome of the verdict in favor of Slovenia. Therefore, on July 30, 2014, the Croatian government decided to dissolve the Contract on Arbitration, relying on the provision of the Vienna Convention on the Law of Treaties (United Nations 1969). But the Arbitration Court continued its work and brought the verdict that Slovenia should get 4/5 of the Bay of Piran, as Slovenia had requested (Maretić Žonja et al. 2017). Thus the problem has worsened because Slovenia insists on applying this verdict whereas Croatia does not recognize it. Slovenia had sued Croatia at the European Union Court in Luxembourg for that stance, but the suit was rejected in January 2020 (Vladisavljević 2020) and the two countries have to settle the dispute through direct negotiations.

Relations with the Republic of Serbia

The relations between the Republic of Croatia and the Republic of Serbia are tense, unpleasant and dangerous. They have deep historic roots and are weighed down by territorial aspirations of Serbian intellectuals, Government and the Church (Brandt and Čović 1991, Šegedin 1993, Cohen 1996, Tanner 2010, Lozo 2017, Pilar 2017), unhealed wounds of WWII (Lozo 2017), as well as the 1991-1995 war (Nazor 2011), unresolved issues concerning the state of Bosnia-Herzegovina (primarily the issue of Republic Srpska within BH), and the River Danube border (northeast border of Croatia).

All these issues are perceived totally differently in Croatia and Serbia, so their analysis is rather sensitive. The sensitivity is intensified by the disagreements on the interpretation of a number of historical events and relations. The leaders of the Serb minority in Croatia and certain Croatian former communists, mostly presented as various variants of the "new left", calling themselves "anti-fascists", resist to consider even historical data that are unquestionable (see Geiger 2007; and 2009), political events (Jović 2017) and Croatian language (Kordić 2010). They call any new research data "revisionism" and "revival of the Ustasha ideology", awaiting each new report with fierce opposition (Milekić 2018; Kasapović 2018). The dispute starts with Ustasha Jasenovac concentration camp because a number of Serbian authors and politicians claim that up to a million Serbs were killed there. This is in gross contrast to the review of data of respectable historians like V. Geiger (Geiger 2013) and others. The dispute is exacerbated because Serb forces took Jasenovac in 1991 and transferred the camp archives to Belgrade, with no intention of returning even a copy, and with serious restriction of access to it. Furthermore, Serbia maintains that during WWII Ustasha regime had committed genocide on the Serbian population in Croatia (and today's BH), whereas new data, revealed since Croatia gained independence, suggest that Chetnik and partisan forces had committed much heavier crimes against Croats (see Jurčević 2015 for the number, distribution and perpetrators of mass graves). Serbia also claims that in WWII the Ustasha regime of the Independent State of Croatia (which collaborated with Germany in 1941-1945), had the primary goal of extermination of Serb minority in Croatia, whereas a number of newly published studies indicate that the Serbian paramilitary Chetniks committed many massacres of Croats and Muslims (today Bosniaks) and that these crimes have been concealed during the communist regime (Dizdar and Sobolevski 1999; Dizdar 2009). There are indications that Chetniks started atrocities first, that the "cleansing" of those Croat territories which Serbia considered Serbian had been planned in advance, and that Ustasha retaliated in the remote parts of the country with Croat-Serb mixed populations who entered WWII with preexisting mutual hatred (Cohen 1996; Lozo 2017).

The Chetnik movement was founded in 1903 as an instrument of nationalist and expansionist Serbian politics. Both in royal (1918-1941) and communist (1945-1991) Yugoslavia (see Chapter 1) the Chetniks' key slogan was "to sustain Yugoslavia" which in essence represented a strategy of forming Greater-Serbia (Dizdar 2009; Jurčević 2015; Lozo 2017). In 1938 they had around 1,000 Chetnik subcommittees with more than 500,000 members. In 1940, the Chetnik Command was established within the Army of Kingdom of Yugoslavia, as 7 battalions, one within each of the in 7 Yugoslav Army groups. During the German-Italian aggression against Yugoslavia in April 1941, these forces fell apart, but they still managed to commit numerous crimes against the Croatian and Muslim populations. In Serbia, under the "Duke" Kosta Pećanac, Chetniks joined German occupation forces and in 1941 arrived in NDH to start an "uprising" against it, which resulted in numerous mass murders of Croats and Muslims. Later, communist partisans proclaimed these events as their own "uprising against fascism", although only a few of them assisted the Chetniks in spring 1941. The most known places of Chetnik mass crimes against Croats and Muslims were Kulen Vakuf, Drvar, Bosanski Petrovac, Rama, Vrgorac, Knin, Omiš, Dugopolje, Gomirje, Bosansko Grahovo, Goražde, Bileća, Gacko, Trebinje, Stolac, Nevesinje, Višegrad, Foča, Doboj, Derventa, Čapljina, to name only a few (Tomasevich 1975; Dizdar and Sobolevski 1999).

In 1990, the Serbian minority in Croatia started the "uprising" (the so-called "log-revolution") against the new Croatian government. In 1991, Chetniks, with traditional insignia and units, joined the Yugoslav Federal Army in the war against the democratic Republic of Croatia and proceeded to commit similar mass murders in the same areas – in Tordinci, Tovarnik, Saborsko, Glina, Kijevo, Škabrnja, Nadin, Petrinja, Kostajnica, Pakrac, Ćelije, Vukovar and others (Judaš and Kostović 1992). Televisions all over the world showed Chetniks marching over the devastated streets of the city of Vukovar on the day of its fall on November 18, 1991, singing victoriously a song that nobody bothered to translate up to now, perhaps because of its meaning: "Slobodan (Slobodan Milošević, president of Serbia), send us some salad, there will be plenty of meat, we will be slaughtering Croats" (in Serbian: "Slobodane šalji nam salate, bit će mesa, klat ćemo Hrvate"). Unthinkable in the 20th century Europe, but true.

However, the purpose of this chapter is not to judge numerous historical issues, but to indicate the threat from this ugly agglomerate of disputes for both countries. Finding the truth about every aspect of these Serb-Croat disputes is a prerequisite for reconciliation, and the truth can stem only from research that is rigorously performed, reviewed and published and then objectively analyzed, possibly with assistance of neutral third-party experts. In this extremely important process, no research should be forbidden or thwarted and all forensic findings should be taken in account to reach the conclusions best supported by evidence. For the time being, it suffices to read the verdict of the International Court of Justice in The Hague (above) which clearly confirms that Serbian goal of 1991-1995 aggression was creation of Greater Serbia through unification of territories in Croatia and BH with Serbia (International Court of Justice 2015).

During the Croatian War of Independence, from 1991 to 1995, Serbian minority in Croatia decreased from 11.6% to 4.5%, so Serbs accuse Croatia of ethnic cleansing. Croats, however, maintain that Serbs who left Croatia when it proclaimed independence emigrated voluntarily and according to pre-existing plans. The 1991-1995 war did not affect Serbs who remained loyal to the state of Croatia; moreover some 10,000 of them served in the Croatian Army (as did Hungarians, Albanians, Muslims, Roma and other minorities) (Butković 2010). The reason why a significant portion of Serbs who originally lived in Croatia left the country was their refusal to live in an independent Croatia in contrast to Yugoslavia, in which Croatian national identities were suppressed. In any case, all Serbs who left the country after the military successes of the Croatian army and police in liberating 25% of the country that had been occupied in the very beginning of the 1991-1995 war, were and are free to come back to their properties and jobs. If their houses and apartments had been destroyed in the war, the state of Croatia rebuilt them (Nazor 2011).

The divide within the Serbian minority in Croatia with respect to loyalty to the Republic of Croatia still exists. Most Serbs live regular, everyday lives and a bystander would not able to tell them apart from Croats and other nationalities. However, a portion of them remain in line with Greater Serbian politics and severely criticize Croatia for "revisionism", "growing pro-Fascism", or discrimination. However, the Serb minority has three reserved seats in the Croatian parliament (Sabor), out of the total of 9 seats reserved for minority representation (out of 150 Parliament seats). Their cultural and political activities are financed by the government and their major political party participates in coalitions that form the government. The general character of this friction is best described by a Croatian complaint that "they live in Croatia but pray to God that it rains in Serbia" (Bubalo 2019). Serb accusations are regularly reported by the mainstream media and disseminated abroad by Serb National Council (https://snv.hr/).

Other disputes concern borders, border traffic, archives that had been common ("Yugoslavian") and those taken by Serbia during the 1991-1995 war, the lack of cooperation in the search for persons missing in war (some 1,700 still missing on the Croatian side), compensation for war damages and prisoners of war held in camps in Serbia, and minefield plans of the Yugoslav Federal Army, inasmuch as a number of them in Croatia still remain since the war.

Another unsolved dispute is the dispute about the border along the Danube River. In ex-Yugoslavia, the judiciary systems of Croatia, Serbia and Slovenia had agreed that the "territory of a republic is composed of districts, and districts are defined as cadaster districts". In 2001 Serbia and Croatia signed the "Protocol of principles for determination of borders", which stated that "the borders will be determined on the basis of cadaster districts and relevant documentation". According to the cadaster, on the left ("Serbian") side of Danube Croatia has 115 square km of land, whereas Serbia has 9 square km on the right ("Croatian") side of the Danube. However, at present Serbia claims that the border with Croatia goes by the middle of the Danube River and subsequently all land on the left bank of the Danube is Serbian, as well as the Vukovar and Šarengrad river islands which it still keeps occupied (Veljković 2017).

Threats Common to all European Countries

There are threats to Croatia that are common for all EU countries: international political instability, climate changes, depopulation, decay of morale, and advancement of neocommunism. However, these threats are more serious for a small and vulnerable country like Croatia which, according to the 1991 census, had 4,284,889 inhabitants in a 56,542 km² area. With this respect, Croatia does and will follow the general lines of common politics of the EU in facing the listed threats. There is only one subject in which EU (and the western world in general) has not shown determination, and that is the growth of the neo-Marxist pressure in the public life. If the human rights and social tolerance will not be equal for all people regardless of their differences as openly proposed by Herbert Marcuse (Marcuse 1969), if militant feminism will suppress biological facts, "hate speech" will become a tool to constrain of freedom of speech, and the inflow of migrants from very different cultures will annul national and cultural differences, the world may become a global stage of serious political division. Croatia cannot be an exception, but it can neither offer an effective resistance nor isolated successful self-protection. The fate of the world will be decided elsewhere.

In conclusion, regardless of all Croatian weaknesses relative to other EU countries listed above, it can be said that, with respect to outside threats to the Republic of Croatia, what happens to France, Germany and Italy, will happen to Croatia. So a tormented, new and small country cannot be safer than that.

References

Akrap, Anđelko. 2015. "Demografski slom Hrvatske: Hrvatska do 2051." *Bogoslovska smotra* 85(3): 855-868. [Demographic Breakdown of Croatia: Croatia until 2051. Theologian Review 85(3): 855-868].

Bandić, Ninoslav. 2015. "Krvavi Uskrs." *Vojna povijest* ["Bloody Easter." *Military History*]. March 31. Accessed January 12, 2020. https://vojnapovijest.vecernji.hr/vojna-povijest/josip-jovic-krvavi-uskrs-1991-godine-997987.

Barić, Robert. 2004. "Transformacija NATO-a i hrvatska obrambena reforma." [Transformation of NATO and Croatian Defense Reform]. *Polemos* 7(1-2):45-89.

Bellamy, Christopher. 1992. "Croatia Built 'Web of Contacts' to Evade Weapons Embargo." *Independent*, October 10. Accessed February 20. 2020. https://www.independent.co.uk/news/world/croatia-built-web-of-contacts-to-evade-weapons-embargo-1556500.html.

Bendeković, Jadranko. 2000. "Privatization in Croatia." *Ekonomski pregled* 51(1-2):55-90.

Borovčak, Damir. 2018. *Macelj 1945. In memory of the martyrs. Commemorating 75 Years since the Crimes of Communism*. Zagreb-Đurmanec: Macelj 1945 Association.

Brandt, Miroslav, and Bože Čović. 1991. *Izvori velikosrpske agresije: rasprave, dokumenti, kartografski prikazi*. Zagreb: August Cesarec. [*Sources of the Greater-Serbia aggression: arguments, documents and cartographic images*].

Bubalo, Slavko. 2019. *Intervju Boris Milošević: Sve srpske organizacije moramo još bolje da povežemo*. Srbi.hr [*Intervju Boris Milošević: All Serbian Organizations We have to Interconnect Even Better.* Serbs.hr], August 22. Accessed February 3, 2020. https://srbi.hr/intervju-boris-milosevic-sve-srpske-organizacije-moramo-jos-bolje-da-povezemo/.

Bulatović, Radomir. 1990. *Koncentracioni logor Jasenovac, s posebnim osvrtom na Donju Gradinu. Istorijsko-sociološka i antropološka studija*. Sarajevo: Svjetlost. [*Concentration Camp Jasenovac, with the Special Review on Donja Gradina. Historical-Sociological and Anthropological Study.* Sarajevo: Light].

Burilović, Silvana, and Mladen Parlov. 2013. "Krunica u Domovinskom ratu znak vjerskog rata ili vjere u ratu?" *Služba Božja* 53(2):156-177. [Rosary in Croatian war of independence A sign of religious war or of faith in the war? *The Service of God* 53(2):156-177].

Butković, Davor. 2010. "I Srbi su branili Hrvatsku" [Serbs, too, Defended Croatia]. *Jutarnji list* November 6. Accessed November 29, 2019 https://www.jutarnji.hr/arhiva/i-srbi-su-branili-hrvatsku/1891017/.

CEIC Data Global Database. 2019. "Croatia Government Debt: % of GDP." Accessed January 7, 2020. https://www.ceicdata.com/en/indicator/croatia/government-debt--of-nominal-gdp.

Cohen, Philip, J. 1996. *Serbia's Secret War: Propaganda and the Deceit of History*. College Station, Texas A&M University Press, Texas City, TX, USA.

Degan, Vladimir-Đuro. 2019. "Spor o granicama između Hrvatske i Slovenije." *Poredbeno pomorsko pravo* 58(173):11-66. [The Boundary Dispute between Croatia and Slovenia." *Comparative Maritime Law*] 58(173):11-66.

Dežman, Jože, president of the Committee and editor. 2010. "*Prikrita grobišta. Izvješće komisije Vlade Republike Slovenije za rješavanja pitanja skrivenih grobišta 2005.-2008.*

Translation in Croatian from Slovenian. Sarajevo: Hrvatsko katoličko dobrotvorno društvo. [*Concealed Grave-Yards. Report of the Committee of the Government of the Republic of Slovenia for solution of the question of the Concealed Grave-Yards.* Sarajevo: Croatian Catholic Philantrophical Association].

Dizdar, Zdravko. 2009. "Četnički pokret na području Hrvatske i Bosne i Hercegovine (1941.-1945.)." In Ramet, Sabrina P., editor 43-66. *Nezavisna Država Hrvatska* 1941.-1945. Zagreb: Alineja. [Chetnik Movement in the area of Croatia and Bosnia-Herzegovina (1941-1945). In Ramet, Sabrina P., editor 43-66. *Independent State of Croatia* 1941-1945. Zagreb: Alineja].

Dizdar, Zdravko, and Mihael Sobolevski. 1999. *Prešućivani četnički zločini u Hrvatskoj i u Bosni i Hercegovini 1941.-1945.* Zagreb: Hrvatski institut za povijest – Dom i svijet. [*Missed Chetnik Crimes in Croatia and Bosnia-Herzegovina (1941-1945).* Zagreb: Croatian Institute for History – Home and World].

Dubajić, Simo. 2006. *Od Kistanja do Kočevskog roga. Život, greh i kajanje.* [*From Kistanje to Kočevski rog. Life, Sin and Remorse*]. Beograd: Nidda Verlag GmbH (Bad Vilbel) and Vesti d.o.o.

Dubey, Vinod. 1975. *Yugoslavia: Development with Decentralization.* Baltimore: The Johns Hopkins Press.

Education First (EPI). 2019. *EF English Proficiency Indeks. A Ranking of 100 Countries and Regions by English Skills.* Accessed January 28, 2020. https://www.ef.com/__/~/media/centralefcom/epi/downloads/full-reports/v9/ef-epi-2019-english.pdf.

Emerald Works. 2020. *MindTools. SWOT Analysis: How to Develop a Strategy for Success.* Accessed February 11, 2020. https://www.mindtools.com/pages/article/newTMC_05.htm.

European Commission. 2019. *Commission Staff Working Document. Country Report Croatia 2019 Including an In-Depth Review on the prevention and correction of macroeconomic imbalances.* Accessed January 11, 2020. https://ec.europa.eu/info/sites/info/files/file_import/2019-european-semester-country-report-croatia_en.pdf.

European Commission. 2020. *Financing the Green Transition: The European Green Deal Investment Plan and Just Transition Mechanism*, January 14. Accessed January 17, 2020. https://ec.europa.eu/commission/presscorner/detail/en/ip_20_17.

Eurostat. 2020. *Renewable Energy for Heating and Cooling.* Accessed February 18, 2020. https://ec.europa.eu/eurostat/web/products-eurostat-news/-/DDN-20200211-1.

EURYDICE. 2020. *Croatia. Population: Demographic Situation, Languages and Religions.* https://eacea.ec.europa.eu/national-policies/eurydice/content/population-demographic-situation-languages-and-religions-14_en.

Ferenc, Mitja. 2012. "Tezno – najveće prikriveno grobište u Sloveniji. O istraživanju grobišta u protutenkovskom rovu u Teznom (Maribor)." (In Croatian*). Časopis za suvremenu povijest* 44:539-69.)" [Tezno – The Biggest Hidden Mass Burial Site in Slovenia. On the Research of the Hidden Burial Site in the Antitank Ditch in Tezno (Maribor). *Journal of Contemporary History* 44:539-69].

Geiger, Vladimir. 2007. "O zborniku Bleiburg i Križni put 1945. Saveza antifašističkih boraca i antifašista Republike Hrvatske, Zagreb, 2007." *Časopis za suvremenu povijest* 39(3):809-827. [On the Collection of Papers 'Bleiburg and Way of Cross 1945 published by the Association of Antifascist Warriors and Antifascists of the Republic of Croatia, Zagreb 2007. *Journal of Contemporary History* 39(3):809-827].

Geiger, Vladimir. 2009. "U povodu knjige: Ivo GOLDSTEIN, Hrvatska 1918 - 2008., Europapress holding, Novi liber, Zagreb 2008., 931 str. – osvrt na poglavlja: 48. 'Rasap i slom NDH, Bleiburg i Križni put', 49. Obračun s narodnim neprijateljem' i 50. 'Ratni i demografski gubici'". *Časopis za suvremenu povijest* 41(1):231-252. [On the Occasion of the book: IVO GOLDSTEIN, Croatia 1918-2008, Europapress holding, Novi liber, Zagreb 2008, 931 pages – Overview of Chapters: 48. "Breakup and Breakdown of NDH (Independent State of Croatia), Bleiburg and Way of Cross", 49: "Payoff with Peoples Enemy" and "War and Demographic Losses". *Journal of Contemporary History* 41(1):231-252].

Geiger, Vladimir. 2010. "Ljudski gubici Hrvatske u Drugome svjetskom ratu i u poraću koje su prouzročili Narodnooslobodilačka vojska i Partizanski odredi Jugoslavije/ Jugoslavenska armija i komunistička vlast. Brojidbeni pokazatelji (procjene, izračuni, popisi) Case study: Bleiburg i folksdojčeri." *Časopis za suvremenu povijest* 42(3):693-722. [Human Losses of Croatia in World War II Caused by People's Liberation Army and Partisan Squads of Yugoslavia/Yugoslav Army and Communist Regime. Numerical Indicators (Estimations, Figures, Lists). Case Study: Bleiburg and Folkdeutchers. *Journal for Contemporary History* 42(3):693-722].

Geiger, Vladimir. 2013. "Numerical Indicators of the Victims of the Jasenovac Camp, 1941-1945 (Estimates, Calculations, Lists)." *Review of Croatian History* 9(1):151-187.

Grahek Ravančić, Martina. 2015. *Bleiburg i Križni put*. Zagreb: Hrvatski institut za povijest. [Bleiburg and Path of Cross. Zagreb: Croatian Institute for History].

Grubišić, Slavko. 2000. *Nad ponorom pakla: svjedočanstvo o komunističkim zločinima*. Zagreb: Hrvatsko društvo političkih zatvorenika. [Above the Abyss of the Hell: Testimony of Communist Crimes. Zagreb: Croatian Association of Political Prisoners].

Horne, Cynthia M. 2014. "Lustration, Transitional Justice, and Social Trust in Post-Communist Countries. Repairing or Wresting the Ties that Bind?" *Europe-Asia Studies*, 66(2):225-254, DOI: 10.1080/09668136.2014.882620.

HINA. 2016. *Đukanović se pokajao za 1991.: 'Napad na Dubrovnik je sramota za Crnu Goru!'* [*Đukanović Repented for 1991: 'Attack at Dubrovnik is a Shame for Montenegro'*]. net.hr, June 1. Accessed February 21, 2020. https://net.hr/danas/hrvatska/dukanovic-se-pokajao-za-agresiju-napad-na-dubrovnik-1991-je-sramota-za-crnu-goru/.

Hrvatski Sabor. 2020. 19. svibnja – *Referendum o hrvatskoj samostalnosti.* [May 19 – *Referendum on Croatian Independence*]. Accessed January 22, 2020. https://www.sabor.hr/hr/o-saboru/povijest-saborovanja/vazni-datumi/19-svibnja-referendum-o-hrvatskoj-samostalnosti.

International Court of Justice. 2015. "Application of the Convention on the Prevention and Punishment of the Crime of Genocide (Croatia v. Serbia)", *Judgment, I.C.J. Reports 2015, p. 3.* Accessed March 20, 2019. https://www.icj-cij.org/files/case-related/118/118-20150203-JUD-01-00-EN.pdf.

International Monetary Fund. 2019. "Republic of Croatia. 2018 Article IV Consultation – Press Release; Staff Report; and Statement by the Executive Director for the Republic of Croatia." Accessed January 11, 2020. https://www.imf.org/en/Publications/CR/Issues/2019/02/12/Republic-of-Croatia-2018-Article-IV-Consultation-Press-Release-Staff-Report-and-Statement-by-46594.

Ivanović, Vesna. 2015. "Postizborna Bosna i Hercegovina." *Međunarodne studije* 15(2):45-59. [Post-Elections Bosnia-Herzegovina. *International Studies* 15(2):45-59].

Janjatović, Bosiljka. 2002. *Politički teror u Hrvatskoj* 1918.-1935. Zagreb: Dom i Svijet/Institut za hrvatsku povijest. [Political Terror in Croatia 1918-1935. Zagreb: Home and World/Institute for Croatian History].

Jović, Dejan. 2017. *Rat i mit. Politika identiteta u suvremenoj Hrvatskoj*. Zagreb: Fraktura. [War and Myth. Politics of the Identity in Contemporary Croatia].

Judaš, Miloš, and Ivica Kostović, editors. 1992. *Mass killing and genocide in Croatia 1991/92: A book of evidence*. Zagreb: Hrvatska sveučilišna naklada.

Jurić, Tado. 2017. "Suvremeno iseljavanje Hrvata u Njemačku: karakteristike i motivi." *Migracijske i etničke teme* 33(3):337-371. [Contemporary Emigration of Croats to Germany: Characteristics and Motives. *Migration and Ethnic Themes* 33(3):337-371].

Jurčević, Josip. 2015. *Stogodišnji teror jugoslavenstva i komunizma u Hrvatskoj*. Zagreb: Dokumentacijsko i informacijsko središte – DIS. [*Hundred years of terror of Yugoslavianism and communism in Croatia*. Zagreb: Documentation and Information Center – DIS].

Jurišić, Mario. 1992. "Ratna krunica." [Wartime Rosary]. Split: Slobodna Dalmacija.

Jutarnji list. 2006. "Krunica proglašena simbolom Domovinskog rata." ["Rosary Proclaimed the Symbol of War of Independence"]. Accessed February 20, 2020. https://www.jutarnji.hr/arhiva/krunica-proglasena-simbolom-domovinskog-rata/3352379/.

Kačić, Hrvoje. 2009. *Dubrovačke žrtve. Jugokomunistički teror na hrvatskom jugu 1944. i poratnih godina*. Zagreb: Naklada Gea. [Dubrovnik Victims. Yugo communist Terror at Croatian South 1944 and after the War. Zagreb: Gea Edition].

Kapac, Davor. 1992. "Prevlaka". *Časopis za suvremenu povijest* 24(2):109-113. ["The Prevlaka Peninsula." *Journal for Contemporary History* 24(2):109-113].

Kaplan, Robert D. 1993. *Balkan Ghosts: A Journey through History*. New York: Picador.

Kasapović, Mirjana. 2018. "Genocid u NDH: Umanjivanje, banaliziranje i poricanje zločina." *Politička misao* 55(1):7-33. [Genocide in the Independent State of Croatia: Alleviating, Banalization, and Denial of the Crime. *Political Thought* 55(1):7-33].

Kordić, Snježana. 2010. *Jezik i nacionalizam*. Zagreb: Durieux [Language and Nationalism].

Krce, Tina. 2017. "20 years of diplomatic relations between Israel and Croatia." *The Jerusalem Post*, September 3. Accessed November 14, 2019. https://www.jpost.com/Israel-News/20-years-of-diplomatic-relations-between-Israel-and-Croatia-504130.

Leljak, Roman. 2015. *Huda jama – strogo čuvana tajna*. Zagreb: Društvo Huda jama. [*Huda Jama – Strictly Guarded Secret*. Zagreb: Association Huda Jama].

Lozo, Stjepan. 2017. *Ideologija i propaganda velikosrpskoga genocida nad Hrvatima*. Split: Naklada Bošković. [*Ideology and propaganda of Greater-Serbian genocide over Croats*. Split: Naklada Bošković].

Malcolm, Noel. 1996. *Bosnia: A Short History*. New York: New York University Press.

Marcuse, Herbert. 1969. "Repressive Tolerance". In Wolff, Robert Paul, Barrington Moore, Jr., and Herbert Marcuse. *A Critique of Pure Tolerance*, 95-137. Boston: Beacon Press. Accessed June 27, 2019. https://www.marcuse.org/herbert/publications/1960s/1965-repressive-tolerance-fulltext.html.

Maretić Žonja, Petra, Sandra Veljković, Tea Romić, and Bojan Arežina. 2017. "Arbitražni sud objavio kako treba izgledati granica na Piranskom zaljevu" [Arbitration Court Announced How Should Look The Border in Bay of Piran]. *Večernji list* June 29, 2017. Accessed January 22, 2020. https://www.vecernji.hr/vijesti/arbitraza-teritorijalni-spor-slovenija-hrvatska-1179423.

Marević. Jozo, editor. 1993. *U Bleiburgu iskra. Zbornik radova o Bleiburgu i križnom putu: znanstveni, prigodničarski i autobiografski prilozi s 1. međunarodnog znanstvenog simpozija u Bleiburgu* 15. i 16. svibnja 1993. Zagreb: Vidokrug. [*The Spark in Bleiburg. Almanac on Bleiburg and Path of Cross: Research, Occasion-Related and Autobiographic Contributions from the First Scientific Meeting in Bleiburg,* May 15 and 16, 1993. Zagreb: Vidokrug].

Marušić, Matko. 2012. *Novi zakoni o znanosti i visokom školstvu, Bologna, naša budućnost i mi.* [*New Laws on Science and Higher Education, Bologna, Our Future, and We*]. Slobodna Dalmacija. Universitas, March 7, 3(27):18-19. Accessed March 10, 2020. http://www.unizg.hr/fileadmin/rektorat/Novosti_press/universitas/universitas-27.pdf.

Marušić, Matko. 2016. "Nacrt Pravilnika o znanstvenom napredovanju? Fantastičan, samo ništa ne valja!" ["Draft of the Regulations on scientific Advancement: Phantastic, only Worth Nothing"]. *Slobodna Dalmacija. Universitas*, May 2 8(78):23. http://www.unizg.hr/fileadmin/rektorat/Novosti_press/universitas/universitas-78.pdf.

Matkovich, Blanka. 2017. *Croatia and Slovenia at the End and After the Second World War (1944-1945): Mas Crimes and Human Rights Violations Committed by the Communist Regime.* Irvine, CA: Brown Walker Press.

Matković, Blanka. 2011. "Odvođenja i likvidacije ranjenih pripadnika Hrvatskih oružanih snaga (HOS) iz zagrebačkih bolnica u svibnju i lipnju 1945. kroz arhivsko gradivo Državnog arhiva u Zagrebu." *Arhivski vjesnik* 54:179-214. [Carrying Away and Executions of Wounded Members of Croatian Defense Forces (HOS) from Zagreb Hospitals in May and June 1945. *Archives' Herald* 54:179-214].

Matković, Stjepan, and Marko Trogrlić. 2019. *Političke bilješke Ante Trumbića: 1930.-1938.* 2 sveska. Zagreb, Split: Hrvatski institut za povijest; Odsjek za povijest Filozofskog fakulteta u Splitu. [*Political Annotations of Ante Trumbić: 1930-1938,* two volumes. Zagreb and Split: Croatian Institute of History in Zagreb and Department of History of Faculty of Humanities and Social Sciences in Split].

Menendian, Stephen, Elsadig Elsheikh, and Samir Gambhir. 2019. *Inclusiveness Index: Measuring Global Inclusion and Marginality*. Berkeley, CA: Othering & Belonging Institute. Accessed January 26, 2020. https://belonging.berkeley.edu/system/tdf/2019_inclusiveness_index.pdf?file=1&force=1.

Mijatović, Anđelko. 2007. *Bleiburška tragedija i Križni put hrvatskoga naroda godine 1945.* New York, Zagreb: Hrvatski svjetski kongres. [Bleiburg tragedy and Path of Cross of Croatian people in year 1945. New York, Zagreb: Croatian World Congress].

Milekić, Sven, and BIRN. 2018. *Croatian Church Venues Host Jasenovac Camp Revisionist Events.* https://balkaninsight.com/2018/09/19/croatian-catholic-church-venues-jasenovac-revisionist-promoter-09-19-2018/. Accessed January 12, 2020.

Mišević, Petar, Tonći Lazibat, and Josip Jurčević. 2012. Utjecaj primjene NATO standarda na razvoj hrvatskog gospodarstva. *Poslovna izvrsnost Zagreb* VI(1):97-114. [Influence of Application of NATO Standards on Development of Croatian Economy." *Bussiness Excellence Zagreb* VI(1):97-114].

Mrkoci, Vladimir, and Vladimir Horvat. 2008. *Ogoljela laž logora Jasenovac* [*Bare Lie about Jasenovac Camp*]. Zagreb: Naklada E. Čić.

Nazor, Ante. 2011. *Greater-Serbian aggression against Croatia in the 1990s* (The Republic of Croatia and the Homeland War: overview of political and military developments 1990,

1991-1995/1998). *Zagreb: Hrvatski memorijalno-dokumentacijski centar Domovinskog rata.* [Zagreb: Croatian Memorial-Documentation Center of Patriotic War].

Nikolić, Vinko, editor. 1993. *Bleiburška tragedija hrvatskoga naroda.* Zagreb: Knjižnica Hrvatske revije. [*Bleiburg Tragedy of Croatian People.* Zagreb: The Library of the Croatian Review].

Obadić, Alka and Aleksander Aristovnik. 2011. "Relative efficiency of higher education in Croatia and Slovenia: an international comparison". *Amfiteatru Economic Journal* (The Bucharest University of Economic Studies, Bucharest) 13(30): 362-376.

OECD – Organisation for Economic Co-operation and Development Directorate for Education Education and Training Policy Division. 2008. "OECD Reviews of Tertiary Education. Croatia". Accessed January 15, 2020. https://www.oecd.org/education/skills-beyond-school/38814548.pdf.

Perković, Marijan, and Vlado Puljiz. 2001. "Ratne štete, izdaci za branitelje, žrtve i stradalnike rata u Republici Hrvatskoj." Ministarstvo rada i socijalne skrbi [War Damages, Costs of Care for Veterans, Victims and Suferrers in Republic of Croatia. Ministry of Labor and Social Care]. Accessed February 17, 2020. https://hrcak.srce.hr/file/47404.

Pickering, Paula, John R. Lampe, and Noel R. Malcolm. 2019. "Bosnia and Herzegovina." *Encyclopaedia Britannica.* Last modified December 9, 2019 Accessed February 21, 2020. https://www.britannica.com/place/Bosnia-and-Herzegovina.

Pilar, Ivo. 2017. *Južnoslavensko pitanje: prikaz cjelokupnog pitanja.* Švagelj, Dražen, editor. Vinkovci: Matica hrvatska, Ogranak Matice hrvatske u Vinkovcima. (Prijevod Suedlanda 1918 s njemačkog). [*South Slav Question: Presentation of the Overall Question.* (Translation of Suedland 1918 from German). Vinkovci: Branch of Matrix Croatica in Vinkovci].

Punda, Vesna, and Valerija Filipović. 2015. "Protokol o privremenom režimu uz južnu granicu (2002.) s posebnim osvrtom na odluke vlada Republike Hrvatske i Crne Gore o istraživanju i eksploataciji ugljikovodika u Jadranu." *Poredbeno pomorsko pravo* 54:(169):73-88. Accessed January 23, 2020. [Protocol on the interim regime along the southern border (2002) with special regard to the decisions of the governments of the Republic of Croatia and Montenegro on the exploration and exploitation of hydrocarbons in the Adriatic. Comparative Martime Law 54:(169):73-88]. https://hrcak.srce.hr/144389.

Ragazzi, Maurizio. 1992. "Conference on Yugoslavia Arbitration Commission: opinions on questions arising from the dissolution of Yugoslavia." *International Legal Materials* 31(6):1488-1526. https://www.jstor.org/stable/20693759.

Rašović, Renata. 2018. "Crna Gora hrvatskim logorašima isplatila 1,43 milijuna eura." [Montenegro Reimbursed Croatian Detainees with 1.43 million Euros]. *Večernji list,* October 4. Accessed February 21, 2020. https://www.vecernji.hr/vijesti/crna-gora-hrvatskim-logorasima-isplatila-1-43-milijuna-eura-1274010.

Rohde, David. 2015. "How Croatia Built Up Military Might." *The Christian Science Monitor.* Accessed January 8 2020. https://www.csmonitor.com/1995/0802/02061.html.

Sadkovich James J. 2005. (E) *Is Image Everything? American Stereotypes of Croatia.* Text for a Talk Delivered in Chicago on April 26, 2005. Accessed January 8, 2020. http://www.croatia.org/crown/articles/6254/1/E-Is-Image-Everything-American-Stereotypes-of-Croatia.html.

Sanz, Timothy. 1992. "The Yugoslav conflict: Review of the literature." *European Security* 1(3):427-441.

Skok, Dobriša. 2007. "NATO, Redefinition of Security and Croatia." *ADRIAS* 14:139-149.

Šanjek, Franjo. 1988. *Crkva i kršćanstvo u Hrvata: srednji vijek*. Zagreb: Kršćanska sadašnjost. [The Church and Christianity in Croats: Middle Ages. Zagreb: Christian Actuality].

Šarić, Tatjana. 2015. "Bijeg iz socijalističke Jugoslavije – ilegalna emigracija iz Hrvatske od 1945. do početka šezdesetih godina 20. stoljeća." *Migracijske i etničke teme* 31(2):195-220. [Escape from Socialist Yugoslavia – Illegal Emigration from Croatia from 1945 until the Beginning of Sixties of 20th Century". *Migration and Ethnical Themes* 31(2):195-220]. DOI: 10.11567/met.31.2.1.

Šegedin, Petar. 1993. *Au royaume des amés exaltes – U carstvu ponesenih duša* (French-Croatian). Zagreb: Hrvatska sveučilišna Naklada. [In the Empire of the Exalted Souls. Croatian University Press].

Šterc, Stjepan. 2015. "Na Bleiburgu umrlo 500 tisuća Hrvata, eto koliko je bilo stradanja i gdje." *Direktno*. [At Bleiburg 500,000 Croats died, this is how much and where perishing occurred. *Portal Direct*]. https://direktno.hr/direkt/na-bleiburgu-umrlo-500-tisuca-hrvata-eto-koliko-je-bilo-stradanja-i-gdje-14973/. Accessed January 12, 2020.

Tadić, Mate and Crnogorac, Želimir. 2013. *Svjedočanstva o stradanjima Hrvata*. [Testimonies on perishing of Croats]. Zagreb: DVA i DVA d.o.o.

Tanner, Marcus. 2010. *Croatia; A Nation Forged in War*. 3rd edition. Yale University Press. Accessed January 11, 2020. www.jstor.org/stable/j.ctt1npzsd.

Three Seas Initiative. 2019. "Slovenia, 5 – 6 June." Accessed January 23, 2020. https://three.si/.

Tolstoy, Nikolai. 1986. *The Minister and the Massacres*. London: Century Hutchinson.

Tomasevich, Jozo. 1975. *The Chetniks. War and Revolution in Yugoslavia 1941-1945*. Volume 1. Stanford, California: Stanford University Press.

Transparency International. 2020. "Corruption Perception Indeks 2019." Accessed January 23, 2020. https://www.transparency.org/country/HRV.

Trading Economics. 2020. "Croatia Productivity." Accessed January 22, 2020. https://tradingeconomics.com/croatia/productivity.

United Nations. 1969. "Treaty Series." Vol. 1155, p. 331. Accessed December 20, 2019. https://legal.un.org/ilc/texts/instruments/english/conventions/1_1_1969.pdf.

United Nations. 2007. International Tribunal for the Prosecution of Persons Responsible for Serious Violations of International Humanitarian Law Committed in the Territory of Former Yugoslavia since 1991. "Case No. IT-95-11-T, Prosecutor vs. Milan Martić." Accessed December 5, 2019. https://www.icty.org/x/cases/martic/tjug/en/070612.pdf.

US Department of Defense. 2017. "Remarks by Secretary Mattis in an Honor Cordon Welcoming Croatian Defense Minister Damir Krsticevic to the Pentagon." Accessed January 9 2020. https://www.defense.gov/Newsroom/Transcripts/Transcript/Article/1245735/remarks-by-secretary-mattis-in-an-honor-cordon-welcoming-croatian-defense-minis/.

Veljković, Sandra. 2017. "Granica Hrvatske i Srbije nije Dunav, već katastarska općina." *Večernji list*. [The border between Croatia and Serbia is not Danube but cadaster district. *Evening Letter* (Zagreb) July 25, 2017]. Accessed January 22, 2020.

https://www.vecernji.hr/vijesti/granica-hrvatske-i-srbije-nije-dunav-vec-katastarska-opcina-1184569.

Vladisavljević, Anja. 2020. "EU Court Denies Jurisdiction Over Slovenia-Croatia Border Dispute." *BalkanInsight*, January 31. Accessed February 2, 2020. https://balkaninsight.com/2020/01/31/eu-court-denies-jurisdiction-over-slovenia-croatia-border-dispute/

Vranješ Markić, Leandra. 2019. "Naslovnica." In: Ljutić D, Marušić M, editors. *O Sveučilištu i Gradu; u prigodi 45 godina Sveučilišta u Splitu godine 2019*. Split: Sveučilište u Splitu. [Cover Page. On the University and the City; on Occasion of 45 Years of University of Split in 2019. Split: University of Split].

Vukić, Igor. 2019. *Labour camp Jasenovac*. Zagreb: Igor Vukić.

World Bank in Croatia. 2019. "Overview". Last Updated Oct 21, 2019. Accessed January 17, 2020. https://www.worldbank.org/en/country/croatia/overview.

World Economic Forum. 2018. "The Global Competitiveness Report 2018. Competitiveness Rankings." Accessed January 6, 2020. https://reports.weforum.org/global-competitiveness-report-2018/competitiveness-rankings/.

Biographical Sketch

Matko Marušić

Affiliation: University of Split (Split, Croatia), Professor Emeritus

Education:

- Secondary school "Natko Nodilo", Split (graduated 1965).
- Zagreb University School of Medicine (1965-1970, MD).
- Postgraduate master's program – Zagreb University School of Natural Sciences and Mathematics (1971-1973, MSc).
- Postgraduate doctoral program – Zagreb University School of Medicine (1971-1975, PhD).
- 1976-1978 postgraduate training at Oak Ridge National Laboratory Oak Ridge, TN, USA.
- 1981-1984 (one year total), guest researcher at Max Planck institute for Biology, Department of Immunogenetics, Tuebingen, Germany.
- 1989 guest researcher at University of Connecticut Health Center, Farmington, CT, USA.

Business Address:

Editor-in Chief, ST OPEN overlay+ journal, University of Split, University Library, Rugjera Boškovića 31, 21000 Split, Croatia.

Research and Professional Experience:

Research

Some 200 scientific articles, which have received 3159 citations; H-index 35. Five selected publications:

1. Marušić, Matko. 1989. "Biological foundations of prediction in an unpredictable environment." *British Journal for the Philosophy of Science* 40:485-99.
2. Marušić, Matko. 1991. "Evolutionary and biological foundations of malignant tumors." *Medical Hypotheses* 34:282-7.
3. Marušić, Matko. 1994. "War and medical education in Croatia." *Academic Medicine* 69:111-113.
4. Marušić Matko, Mirjana Turkalj-Kljajić, Mladen Petrovečki, Branka Užarević, Marija Rudolf, Drago Batinić, et al. 1998. "Indirect demonstration of the lifetime function of human thymus." *Clinical and Experimental Immunology* 111:450-6.
5. Marušić Ana, Marušić Matko. 2012. "When a disaster strikes: two editors in war." *Medical Journal of Australia* 197(2):118-20.

Teaching

Professor at Medical Schools (in Zagreb and Split since 1971); courses: Physiology, Immunology, Principles of Research in Medicine, and Research Methodology at postgraduate programs.

A dozen of educational texts and textbooks.

Professional Experience:

- 1978-1982: President of the Croatian Association of Physiologists.
- 1991-2009: Founder and co-editor-in chief of Croatian Medical Journal.
- 1991-1994: Associate dean of Zagreb University School of Medicine for School Branches in Osijek and Split.
- 1993-1994: One of the organizers and leaders of the humanitarian action "White Road for Nova Bila and Silver Bosnia".
- 2009.-2011: Dean of the University of Split School of Medicine.
- 2018- present: Founder and Editor-in Chief of University of Split overlay+ scientific journal ST-OPEN.

Literary Works:

Marušić, Matko. 1987. *Snijeg u Splitu* [The Snow in the City of Split] (in Croatian). Zagreb: Školska knjiga.

Marušić, Matko. 1996. *Plaču li anđeli*? [Do Angels Cry?] (in Croatian). Zagreb: Medicinska Naklada. Translated in English: *Do Angels Cry*? Portland, WA: Ooligan Press, Portland University, 2012.

Marušić, Matko. 2003. *Škola plivanja* [Swimming lessons] (in Croatian). Zagreb: Alfa.

Marušić, Matko. 2006. *Medicina iznutra* [Medicine from Inside] (in Croatian). Zagreb: Medicinska Naklada.

Marušić, Matko. 2008. *Živjeti u Župi Radobilji* [Living in the Radobilja Parish] (in Croatian). Medicinska Naklada: Zagreb.

Marušić, Matko. 2010. *Life of an Editor*. Zagreb: Medicinska Naklada and Croatian Medical Journal.

Marušić, Matko. 2019. *Mi Hrvati* [We Croats] (in Croatian). Zagreb: Medicinska Naklada.

Other publications
Several hundreds of discussions, polemics, and analyses.

Professional Appointments:

- 1979-2008: Department of Physiology and Immunology, Zagreb University School of Medicine, Zagreb, Croatia.
- 1986-1996: Head of the Laboratory for Immunological Diagnosis, Central Clinical Laboratory, University Hospital Zagreb Rebro, Zagreb, Croatia.
- 2008-2017: Department for Research in Biomedicine and Health, University of Split School of Medicine, Split, Croatia.
- 2017-present: Retired as Professor Emeritus, University of Split, Split, Croatia.
- 2018-present: Editor-in Chief, ST-OPEN overlay+ journal, University of Split, Split, Croatia (half time).

Honors:

- 1970: University of Zagreb Student Award for Best Student.
- 1970: Jure Banović Award for Best Medical Student.
- 1994: Award of the Croatian Council of European Movement, for international cooperation.
- 1998: Croatian National Award for scientific discovery (of the lifetime function of human thymus).
- 1998: "Josip Juraj Strossmayer" Award of the Croatian Academy of Sciences and Arts, for the "Pathophysiology" textbook.
- 2000: President of Croatia Decoration of Danica Hrvatska Order with Rugjer Bošković for the overall contribution to science.
- 2005: State Award for Promotion of Science.
- 2010: "Hippocrates" Award for Struggle against Corruption in Health Care.
- 2010: "Green Cardboard Award of Croatian Movement for Patient Rights."
- 2020: City of Split Personal Award for the book "Mi Hrvati" [We Croats].

Publications from the Last 3 Years:

2017

1. Viđak, Marin, Ružica Tokalić, Matko Marušić, Livia Puljak, and Damir Sapunar. 2017. "Improving completion rates of students in biomedical PhD programs: an interventional study." *BMC Medical Education* 17:144. DOI 10.1186/s12909-017-0985-1

2018

2. Banožić, Adriana, Ivan Buljan, Mario Malički, Matko Marušić, and Ana Marušić. 2018. "Short– and long–term effects of retrieval practice on learning concepts in evidence–based medicine: Experimental study." *Journal of Evaluation in Clinical Practice*. 2018 Feb;24(1):262-263. doi: 10.1111/jep.12740.
3. Sapunar, Damir, Matko Marušić, Livia Puljak, Ivica Grković, Mario Malički M, Ana Marušić, et al. 2018. "The establishment of Medical School at Catholic University of Croatia: principles, goals, standards and organization." *Acta Medica Academica* 47(1):61-75. doi: 10.5644/ama2006-124.215.

4. Marušić, Ana, and Matko Marušić. 2018. "Explore! Dream! Discover!" *Croatian Medical Journal 59:1-2.*
5. Buljan, Ivan, Ana Jerončić, Mario Malički, Matko Marušić, and Ana Marušić. 2018. "How to choose an evidence-based medicine knowledge test for medical students? Comparison of three knowledge measures." *BMC Medical Education* 18(1). DOI: 10.1186/s12909-018-1391-z.

2019

6. Malički, Mario, Domagoj Marković, Vedran Katavić, Matko Marušić, and Ana Marušić. 2019. "Perceptions of ethical climate and research pressures in different faculties of a university: cross-sectional study at the University of Split, Croatia." *Sci Eng Ethics* 25: 231. https://doi.org/10.1007/s11948-017-9987-y.
7. Marušić M, editor. 2019. *Principles of research in medicine.* 3rd edition. Zagreb: Medicinska naklada. (ISBN 978-953-176-730-9)
8. Jurić, Diana, Ivančica Pavličević, Ana Marušić, Mario Malički, Ivan Buljan, Vedran Šarotić et al: (Matko Marušić last author). 2019. "Effectiveness of treatment of newly diagnosed hypertension in family medicine practices in South Croatia." *BMC Family Practice* 20:10. doi: https://doi.org/10.1186/s12875-019-0902-2.
9. Marušić, Matko, Vicko Tomić, Danijel, Gudelj, Elizabeth Wager, and Ana Marušić. 2019. "University repository overlay journal – increasing the quality and visibility of student research at the University of Split, Croatia." *European Science Editing* 45(2):39-41. doi:10.20316/ESE.2019.45.19007
10. Ljutić, Dragan, and Matko Marušić, editors. 2019. *"O Sveučilištu i Gradu u prigodi 45 godina Sveučilišta u Splitu."* [*On the University and the City on Occasion of 45 years of University of Split*]. (in Croatian). Split: Sveučilište u Splitu.
11. Roguljić, Marija, Tina Poklepović Peričić, Andrea Gelemanović, Anita Jukić, Dina Šimunović, Ivan Buljan, et al. (Matko Marušić 7th coauthor). 2019. "What patients, students and doctors think about permission to publish patient photographs in academic journals: a cross-sectional survey in Croatia." *Science and Engineering Ethics* 1-19| https://doi.org/10.1007/s11948-019-00134-y.
12. Buljan, Ivan, Ružica Tokalić, Matko Marušić, and Ana Marušić. 2019. "Health numeracy skills of graduate medical students: cross-sectional and controlled before-and-after study." *BMC Medical Education.* 19(1). DOI: 10.1186/s12909-019-1902-6.

About the Editor

Matko Marušić, MD, PhD

Retired Professor Emeritus of Physiology, Immunology
and Research Methodology
University of Split, Split, Croatia
Email: matko.marusic@unist.hr; matko.marusic@gmail.com

Dr. Marušić is a graduate of Zagreb University School of Medicine (1970), where he also obtained PhD (1975), and professorship at the Department of Physiology (1980). His research interest has been mostly concentrated on immunology of bone marrow transplantation, but he also published in fields of oncology, philosophy of science, and medical education. In 1998, his research team demonstrated the lifetime functioning of human thymus. In 2008 he moved to University of Split School of Medicine, Split, Croatia, where he also served as the dean (2009-2011), and in 2017 was retired as Professor Emeritus. Dr. Marušić is a devoted educator of young Croatian scientists. He was the key person in the foundation of Split University School of Medicine, and also helped the establishment of medical schools in Osijek, Mostar and at the Croatian Catholic University in Zagreb. He is the founder and Editor-in-Chief of Croatian Medical Journal (1991-2009), and ST-OPEN, an overlay+ journal of University of Split, Split, Croatia (2018-present). Dr. Marušić published seven literature books (two of his works became obligatory readings in the primary schools in Croatia), and hundreds of articles on health care, science, history and politics.

INDEX OF NAMES

A

Alexander I, King, 157
Alexander of Yugoslavia, 191
Alexander of Yugoslavia, King, 191
Angjelinović, Grga, 47
Ante Starčević, Father of the Nation, King of Croatia and Dalmatia, 39, 40, 56, 64, 66, 68, 300, 314, 354
Archbishop of Zagreb, 50, 53, 181, 198, 199, 203, 206, 212, 220, 225, 243, 313, 330, 332
Arendt, H., 313, 315, 349
Artuković, Interior Minister, 184, 195, 202, 204, 212, 257, 260, 301, 314, 349, 375
Auburger, Leopold, 82, 111, 117, 124
August Šenoa,, 40, 41, 90

B

Babukić, Vjekoslav, 93, 95, 98, 103, 125
Bagdasarov, Artur, 82, 125
Bakarić, Vladimir, 51, 64, 234, 251, 257, 379
Baram, Dan, testimony describes how Stepinac saved his life, 199
Bartol, Kašić, 24, 28, 81, 89, 95, 97, 127
Bastianini, Giuseppe, 201
Below, Otto von, 153, 154
Benedict XVI, Pope, 167
Birčanin, Ilija Trifunović, 319
Bishop of Zagreb, 24
Bjelovučić, Nikola Zvonimir, 135, 140, 141, 143
Blažević, Jakov, 210, 326
Bolle, Hermann, architect, 41
Borna, Duke, 7
Boroević, Svetozar, The Lion of Soča, v, 147, 148, 149, 150, 151, 152, 153, 154, 155, 156, 157, 158, 159, 160, 161, 163, 164, 167, 168, 170, 171
Bošković, Ruđer, xiv, 24, 28, 29, 72, 357, 408, 413
Breier, Louis, 180, 210
Brezovački, Tituš, 88
Broz, Ivan, 67, 103, 125, 264, 355
Brozović, Dalibor, 89, 90, 104, 112, 113, 118, 120, 124, 125, 251
Bučar, Franjo, 42
Budak, Mile, 307
Budiša, Dražen, 56, 254, 257
Budisavljević Diana
  The film Diary of, 370, 377
Budisavljevic, Diana, 370
Bujas, Srećko, 198, 212
Bukovac, Vlaho, 41, 70
Bulešić, Reverend Miroslav, 167
Bušić, Bruno, 55, 71, 255, 257, 260, 380, 381
Buvina, Andrew, doorways of, 16

C

Casaroli, Agostino, 226, 238
Churchill, Winston, 180, 210
Čičak, Ivan Zvonimir, 173, 254, 257
Cohen, Philip J., x, xii, 193, 210, 260, 314, 315, 316, 318, 350, 400, 401, 405
Cvijović, Josif, 315

D

Dabčević-Kučar, Savka, 55, 249, 254, 256, 257
Dalmatinac, Juraj, 18
Davies, Rhys J., 308, 361
Dedić, Milan in a secret letter to Mihailo Kertes, 345
Dedijer, Vladimir, 183, 210, 319, 351
  The first accuser, 182
Djilas, Aleksa, 175, 177, 178, 187, 188, 190, 211
Djilas, Milovan, 175, 177, 178, 187, 188, 190, 211

Dobrila, Bishop Juraj, 36, 65, 67
Đodan, Šime, 191, 211, 229, 230, 248, 252, 254, 257
Domagoj, Prince, xv, 8, 223, 260, 261, 265, 360, 414
Dominis, Marko Antony de, 18, 71
Drašković, Count Janko, 34
Drašković, Juraj, 24
Držić, Marin, 17, 66, 70
Dubaić, Simo, 328
Dubček, Alexander, 233
Duić, Stevo, 157

F

Finka, Božidar, 113, 116, 124
Franić, Frane, 226, 241
Frankopan, Fran Krsto, 13, 14, 17, 19, 20, 27, 28, 29, 71, 88
  deaths of Peter and Fran Krsto Frankopan, 27, 28, 88
Franz Ferdinand, Archduke, 3, 20, 22, 23, 36, 37, 44, 128, 136, 139, 143, 144, 314
Franz Josef I (Joseph I), 136, 137, 140, 151, 152
Freiberger, Dr. Miroslav Shalom, 198, 201
  Chief Rabbi of Croatia, 184, 198, 199, 200, 201, 203

G

Gaj, Ljudevit, 34, 35, 84, 94, 95, 100, 102, 105, 126, 131
Gandhi, Mahatma, 233
Garašanin, Ilija, 300, 301, 346, 349, 352
Glavašević, Siniša, 60, 67, 277
Gospodnetić, Juraj, 319, 330
Gotovac, Jakov, 49, 128, 257, 261, 337
Gotovac, Vladimir (Vlado), 257
Gregory of Nin, 9
Gruner, Teodor, 199, 211
Gubec, Matija, 25
Guberina, Petar, 11, 108, 119, 126
Gundulić, Ivan, 28, 74

H

Habdelić, Juraj, 88
Hamm, Josip, 81
Hanamann, Franjo, 42
Hebrang, Andrija, communist, 54, 74, 118, 127, 332, 344, 345, 353, 360, 366
Hektorović, Petar, 18, 86
Helm, Hans, 197, 200, 204, 206, 212
Herzog, Chief Rabbi, 203
Hilberg, Raul, historian, 184, 207, 211
Hötzendorf, Conrad von, 152, 153
Hrvatska, Matica, 18, 21, 30, 54, 56, 64, 65, 67, 68, 69, 70, 71, 72, 75, 108, 114, 117, 124, 125, 128, 129, 131, 132, 144, 145, 149, 160, 169, 170, 176, 191, 210, 212, 213, 234, 239, 240, 255, 258, 259, 260, 261, 262, 263, 264, 265, 270, 289, 290, 291, 292, 294, 302, 339, 349, 351, 353, 355, 356, 357, 359, 360, 361, 362, 366, 369, 381, 383, 395, 404, 406, 407, 410, 413

I

Ibrišimović, Luka, 25, 74
Ilija, Sveti, 292, 300, 319, 346, 349, 352, 400
Ivanić, Matija, 26
Iveković, Franjo, 103, 125
Iveković, Oton, 41, 103
Izetbegović, Alija, 280, 341, 366

J

Jagić, Vatroslav, 81, 103, 104, 127
Jelačić, Josip, 36, 37, 38, 40, 47, 52, 57, 71, 74, 253
Jelena "The Beautiful", xv, 10, 11, 289
Jerinić, Miho, 141, 143
John VIII, Pope, 3, 8
Jović, Josip, 58, 274, 282, 289, 290, 401, 407
Jurjević Baja, Ante, 324

K

Kačić Miošić, Andrija, 32, 73, 89, 90
Kanižlić, Antun, 89
Karađorđević, Peter I, 44, 45, 46, 48, 156, 160, 179, 186, 187, 303, 305, 312, 346
Karadžić, Vuk Stefanović, 61, 85, 89, 90, 96, 97, 98, 100, 101, 102, 103, 104, 105, 107, 115, 127, 128, 130, 300, 301, 346
Karl I Robert, 14
Karl IV, 148, 151, 155, 156, 157, 160
Kašić, Dušan, 81, 95, 97, 127, 208
Katančić, Matija Petar, 81
Katičić, Radoslav, 81, 112, 134, 251
Khuen-Héderváry, Károly, 40
King Aleksandar, 307, 308, 309, 310
  assassination of, 310
  dictatorship of, 306, 308
Klović, Juraj Julije, 18

Kluk, Lobel, Muhlo, Kosenc, and Croat, and sisters Tuga and Buga, 5
Koloman, King, 11, 12, 13, 14
Korošec, Anton, 45, 192, 198
Kostich, Lazo M
The third accuser, 183
Kostich, Lazo M., 183, 212
Kotruljević, Benedict, 17
Krešimir I, 3, 9, 10
Krešimir IV, Peter, 3, 9, 10
Krivoshein, Semyon, 321
Krleža, Miroslav, 45, 49, 68, 70, 169, 223, 239, 251, 252, 303
Krstić, Kruno, 108, 119, 126, 357
Kružić, Petar, 21
Kuharić, Franjo, 225
Kundera, Milan, 221, 239
Kustić, Živko, 223
Kvaternik, Eugen, 38, 39, 48, 300, 376
Kvaternik, Slavko, 39, 48, 50, 161, 182, 300

L

Ladan, Tomislav, 112, 251
Ladislav of Naples (Ladislav Napuljski), 15
Laginja, Matko, 36
Lazarević, Slobodan, 342
Leljak, Roman, ix, xiv, 326, 357, 395, 407
Lisinski, Vatroslav, 35
Lucić, Hanibal, xii, 18, 86
Lučić, Ivan, 29, 222, 239
Ludovik I, 15, 16, 20
Lukačić, Ivan, 29, 74

M

Maček, Vladko, viii 47, 48, 49, 50, 190, 191, 194, 213, 233, 307, 308, 311, 312, 323, 328, 382
Maksimilijan Vrhovac, Bishop of Zagreb, 33
Mann, Hinko, viii, xii, 171, 197, 307
Marcone, Giuseppe Ramiro, 197, 201
Maretić, Tomo, 103, 104, 105, 127, 128, 129, 400, 408
Marmont, Marshal, 32, 33, 71
Martić, Milan, 36, 62, 342, 343, 411
Marulić, Marko, 17, 65, 86
Mažuranić, Antun, vii, 49, 92, 93, 95, 102, 129
Mažuranić, Ivana Brlić, ix, xv, 39, 40, 41, 49, 64, 93, 102, 129
Merz, Ivan, 44
Mesić, Marko, 25, 57, 63, 275, 292, 352
Meštrović, Ivan, 9, 41, 45, 49, 50, 159, 178, 209, 213, 307, 359
Methodius, philosopher, 8, 12, 36, 83
Mihailović, Draža, 51, 317, 319, 322, 361
Mihanović, Robert Frangeš, 34, 49, 158
Miklenić, Ivan, 223, 240
Milanović, Božo, 148, 165, 167, 168, 171
Milivojević, Bishop Dionisije, 180
Milošević, Slobodan, 7, 56, 63, 238, 268, 269, 270, 271, 272, 273, 274, 276, 277, 287, 338, 339, 340, 342, 345, 348, 362, 402, 404
Mislav, Prince, 7, 8
and Prince Družak, 7
Mlinar, Miroslav, 271
the Mlinar case, 271
Moguš, Milan, 67, 82, 84, 89, 92, 113, 116, 118, 124, 125, 129
Moljević, Stevan, 317, 319, 347
Molotov, Vyacheslav, 320, 359
Muncimir, 8
Mužić, Ivan, 4, 5, 6, 7, 8, 71, 72, 225, 226, 227, 228, 229, 230, 231, 232, 233, 234, 235, 236, 237, 241, 242, 255, 262

N

Nazor, Vladimir, 13, 49, 51, 58, 60, 61, 62, 63, 71, 72, 160, 164, 166, 170, 189, 213, 269, 270, 271, 272, 273, 274, 275, 276, 277, 278, 279, 280, 281, 282, 283, 284, 285, 287, 290, 291, 293, 339, 340, 341, 342, 344, 345, 359, 366, 367, 400, 403, 409
NDH ministers Mladen Lorković and Ante Vokić, 52
Nedić, Milan, 186, 192, 208, 217, 272, 312, 313, 315, 348
Nestor, Waldemar Maximilian, 319, 330
Nicolier, Jean-Michel, 60
Nikola Banić, x, xiii, 334, 363
Nikola Jurišić, 21
Nikola Pašić, 45, 46, 303, 305
Nikola Stojanović,, 301
Njegovan, Maximilian, 155
Novak, Grgo, 17, 25, 26, 29, 33, 41, 43, 72, 73, 94, 129, 223, 233, 235, 240, 252, 256, 262

O

O'Brien, Count of Thomond, 182, 185

P

Pacel, Vinko, 102, 103

Paradžik, Ante, 254, 257, 263
Pavelić Poglavnik (Head) of NDH, xiii, 4, 48, 50, 52, 179, 181, 182, 183, 189, 191, 193, 194, 195, 196, 197, 200, 205, 206, 208, 211, 212, 213, 309, 312, 314, 316, 323, 324, 325, 380, 382
Pavelić, Ante, 4, 48, 50, 189, 191, 195, 205, 213, 217, 236, 302, 309, 312, 373, 374
Pavešić, Slavko, 112, 124, 251
Pavle, Prince, 113, 124, 191, 310, 311, 312, 378
Penkala, Slavoljub, 42, 73
Perović, Latinka, 309, 362
Peter, King, 9, 10, 47, 50, 51, 52
Pezet, Ernest, 179, 214
Phayer, Michael, 179
Pilar, Ivo, viii, xiv, 48, 135, 142, 143, 145, 310, 360, 381, 400, 409
Pius XII, Pope, 179, 180, 185, 201
Planinc, Milka, 257
Polovina, Gojko, 322, 361
Popović, Koča, 246, 261, 328, 329
Popovici, Aurel C., 135, 136, 137, 138, 139, 143, 144
Porphyrogenitus, Constantine VII, 5, 7, 9
Posavski, Ljudevit, 7
Pribićević, Svetozar, 43, 46, 47, 156, 302, 306, 308, 309, 361
Prince Trpimir, 8

R

Račan, Ivica, 56, 338, 339
Račić, Puniša, 47, 307
Rački, Franjo, 103
Radica, Bogdan, 325, 354
Ranjina. Nikša, 89
Ranković, Aleksandar, 220, 246, 248, 258, 261, 335
Rašković, Jovan, 58, 271
Reljković, Matija, 32, 70, 89
Reljković, Matija Antun, 70, 89
Rendić, Smiljana, vii, 219, 222, 223, 224, 225, 226, 227, 228, 229, 230, 231, 232, 233, 234, 235, 236, 237, 238, 240, 241, 242
Riley, Ben, 308, 361
Riley, Ben and Davies, Rhys J., 308
Rosić, Varnava, 315
Rosner, Leontine von, 151, 157

S

Šagi-Bunić, Tomislav Janko, 226
Sakcinski, Ivan Kukuljević, 27, 34, 70, 75, 92, 126, 127, 129
Salis-Seewis, Bishop, 197, 211
Šegedin, Petar, 229, 230, 389, 400, 410
Shnidman, Ronen, 185
  The fifth accuser, 184
Shomrony, Amiel, 197, 199, 200, 201, 207, 210, 212, 214
Simić, Pero, 327, 362
Souhard, Cardinal, 165
Spalatin. Christopher, 181, 214
Spinčić ,Vjekoslav, 36
Stalin, Joseph, x, 54, 164, 165, 210, 226, 238, 321, 324, 332, 355
Starčević, Šime, 39, 40, 56, 64, 66, 68, 103, 300, 314, 354
Stein, Ljudevit, 199, 214
Steiner, Sabina, 202
Stepinac, Alojzije, Archbishop of Zagreb, v, viii, xiii, 50, 53, 68, 175, 176, 177, 178, 179, 180, 181, 182, 183, 184, 185, 186, 188, 193, 194, 195, 196, 197, 198, 199, 200, 201, 202, 203, 204, 205, 206, 207, 208, 209, 210, 211, 212, 213, 214, 215, 217, 218, 220, 223, 225, 243, 313, 330, 332, 349, 352, 353, 375, 379, 381
  addressed the Ustasha authorities, 208
  campaign against Stepinac, 177
  critical of Eastern Orthodoxy, 210
  in 1936 appealed to his wealthier parishioners, 198
  no one who will say a word against me, 210
Stjepan Babić, 113, 119, 130
Stjepan Radić, viii, xviii, 3, 40, 42, 43, 46, 47, 64, 142, 144, 189, 253, 302, 306, 307, 309
  assassination of, 4
Stjepan Steiner, 199
Stockhammer, Danko, 199
Stojan Janković, 25
Stojković, Ivan, 28
Šubašić, Ivan, 49, 52, 311
Šufflay, Milan, viii, 48, 307, 310
Šulek, Bogoslav, 95, 103, 108, 116, 130
Supilo, Frano, 43, 45, 159, 302, 303
Svačić, Petar, 11

T

Tesla, Nikola, 41, 72
Tito, Josip Broz, 51, 67, 109, 164, 179, 235, 250, 256, 264, 268, 322, 326, 355, 389
Tomislav, King, 8, 9
Trifković, Srdja, 183, 214
  The second accuser, 183
Tripalo, Miko, 55, 249, 254, 255, 257, 262, 263
Trnina, Milka, 42, 74

Trpimir, 8, 9, 10, 12, 69, 70, 80
Trpimir II, 9
Trpimir, Prince (Pro duce Trepimiro), 8, 9, 10, 12, 69, 70, 80
Trumbić, Ante, 43, 45, 156, 159, 163, 164, 169, 302, 308, 358, 408
Tuđman, Franjo, ix, xiii, xviii, 46, 47, 48, 49, 50, 57, 58, 62, 63, 75, 117, 237, 240, 252, 253, 257, 261, 265, 268, 270, 271, 275, 279, 280, 282, 284, 285, 287, 288, 291, 292, 294, 333, 337, 339, 341, 342, 362, 363, 366
Tutavac, Pero, 114, 130

V

Vance, Cyrus, 61, 278
Veber, Adolfo, 95, 96, 103, 130
Velimirović, Nikolaj, 193, 215, 315
Veselica, Marko, 252, 254, 257, 260, 262, 337
Višeslav, Duke, 7, 64
Vladimir (Vlado) Gotovac, 128, 257, 261, 337
Vladimir Velebit and Koča Popović – offered alliance to the Nazis, 322
Vrančić, Faust, 18, 70, 81, 86, 131
Vukić, Igor, vi, ix, x, xiii, xv, 334, 335, 354, 364, 369, 383, 396, 411
Vuletić, Ante, 199

W

Weizsäcker, Ernst von, 184
Weltmann, Dr. Meir Tuval, 203
Wilson, Woodrow, 46, 142, 147, 148, 162, 163, 172, 189

Z

Zoranić, Petar, 86
Zrinska, Katarina, 27, 75, 88, 366
Zrinski
  deaths of Peter and Fran Krsto Frankopan, 28
Zrinski Ban Nikola
  and his brother Petar, 27
Zrinski, Ban Nikola, 27
Zrinski, Nikola Šubić, 21, 23, 28, 41, 64
Zrinski, Petar, 88
Zuroff, Efraim, x, xiii, 183, 203, 211
Zvonimir, Dmitar, 3, 10, 11, 12, 15, 72, 135, 144, 257, 314, 381, 383

Index of Terms

#

1,100 to 1,500 as the highest possible number of human remains, 333
10th meeting of the CC LCC, 250, 254
12th battle of Soča, 151, 154, 155
1510 to 1514, 26
1944, xiii, xiv, 52, 53, 164, 202, 203, 216, 223, 324, 347, 351, 356, 381, 407, 408
1960s, 219, 220, 221, 224, 226, 228, 230, 231, 234, 236, 237, 239, 245, 246, 247, 248, 249, 251, 253, 254, 258, 261, 264, 265, 395, 408
1971, 20, 55, 73, 80, 105, 106, 110, 113, 114, 127, 129, 130, 219, 220, 221, 224, 225, 229, 230, 234, 235, 239, 243, 245, 246, 247, 248, 250, 252, 253, 254, 255, 256, 257, 259, 260, 261, 262, 263, 264, 306, 308, 331, 333, 336, 350, 354, 364, 411, 412
1992, xi, 4, 22, 27, 28, 46, 47, 48, 49, 50, 61, 62, 63, 64, 68, 71, 74, 110, 113, 115, 116, 119, 121, 124, 125, 128, 130, 167, 189, 210, 220, 221, 222, 223, 233, 239, 240, 256, 263, 273, 274, 277, 278, 279, 280, 285, 286, 289, 290, 314, 315, 316, 320, 321, 322, 324, 327, 333, 341, 342, 344, 345, 350, 353, 360, 364, 373, 382, 383, 386, 387, 389, 391, 398, 399, 400, 402, 404, 407, 410
1998, vii, xiv, 12, 42, 48, 49, 52, 55, 56, 58, 63, 69, 70, 71, 74, 81, 95, 96, 116, 117, 124, 131, 132, 133, 134, 196, 217, 222, 239, 248, 249, 259, 263, 275, 284, 286, 289, 290, 292, 299, 300, 302, 303, 304, 305, 306, 311, 312, 317, 321, 322, 323, 326, 331, 332, 335, 336, 337, 341, 343, 353, 358, 363, 392, 396, 409, 412, 413, 417
52 mass graves and hundreds of individual ones, 60
520 petitions on behalf of Jews, 195
80% of Chetniks crossed over to the partisan side, 325

A

academy, xiv, 10, 11, 18, 30, 65, 66, 69, 74, 75, 88, 92, 93, 115, 116, 132, 134, 151, 173, 233, 238, 250, 265, 269, 290, 315, 358, 392, 413
acceptance and defense of, 200
adoption of market economy, 246
Adriatic, 3, 5, 6, 7, 9, 10, 12, 13, 15, 21, 22, 23, 27, 31, 33, 39, 41, 46, 54, 59, 67, 84, 90, 143, 147, 155, 159, 160, 163, 189, 201, 229, 239, 300, 301, 323, 381, 389, 409
Adriatic Sea, 6, 7, 9, 12, 13, 23, 27, 39, 41, 155, 381, 389
aggression against Bosnia and Herzegovina, 61
Agrarian Reform, 54
agreement Cvetković-Maček, 311
agreement in Otrić, 317
all-girls school, 35
allies, 5, 27, 28, 44, 51, 52, 53, 159, 160, 164, 165, 188, 274, 312, 333, 355, 361, 370, 371, 373
amendments, 56, 57, 250, 252, 261, 272
amendments to the constitution of Yugoslavia, 250
American Senators, 179
ancient culture, 5
animosity between Serbs and Croats, 188
Anjou Dynasty, 15
annual budget, 394
anti-semitism, 191, 350, 354, 360, 364
anti-Serbian demonstrations, 41, 301
apostolic Constitution *Sollicitudo Ecclesiarum*, 183
Arpadović dynasty, 10, 11, 13, 14
Arpadović reign, 13
assassinations, 4, 44, 47, 48, 55, 188, 189, 275, 307, 309, 310
atheism, 180, 193, 222, 227, 232
attack on the police station in Lika, 309

Auschwitz, 186, 202, 211, 334, 372
Austria-Hungary, v, 25, 44, 64, 135, 136, 139, 140, 141, 142, 143, 144, 148, 155, 156, 158, 159, 160, 162, 167, 169, 188, 299, 301, 302, 305, 308, 309, 310
Austrian town of Bleiburg, 325
Austro-Hungarian Compromise, 91, 135, 143
Austro-Hungarian Empire, 45, 46, 148, 151, 156, 159, 160, 162, 167, 169, 187, 389
Austro-Hungarian fleet, 155
authoritarian dictator, 235
Avar-Slavic invasion, 5
AVNOJ, 51, 52

B

Badinter Commission, 400
Balkan legacy, 389
Balkan Wars, 43, 144, 168, 300
Banovina of Croatia, 30, 31, 33, 35, 39, 43, 49, 79, 108, 311, 312, 317, 347
baptismal font of Duke Višeslav, 7
Baška (Baščanska) Tablet, 10, 13, 67, 85
Battle of Kobarid, 154
Battle of Sisak, 22, 74
Belgrade, xiii, 3, 20, 24, 25, 46, 47, 49, 50, 52, 54, 56, 57, 63, 66, 69, 81, 94, 107, 109, 111, 140, 143, 157, 164, 165, 171, 187, 189, 190, 192, 193, 211, 213, 214, 215, 216, 238, 245, 250, 254, 256, 269, 274, 290, 301, 302, 303, 304, 305, 306, 307, 308, 309, 310, 311, 314, 315, 319, 325, 331, 332, 334, 338, 342, 345, 349, 355, 357, 359, 360, 361, 363, 372, 381, 401
Berlin Congress, 43, 298
BH Croats, 399
Bjelovar, 158, 314, 317, 318, 328, 351
Bjelovučić, 135, 140, 142
Black Hand, 44, 48
black-market, 391
Bleiburg tragedy, 326, 328, 350, 359, 395, 409
Boka Kotorska, 26, 28, 73, 399
border disputes, 386, 399, 400
borders, 22, 30, 53, 56, 62, 89, 92, 102, 113, 152, 161, 166, 167, 170, 171, 188, 221, 255, 269, 274, 278, 279, 281, 317, 341, 348, 389, 390, 391, 395, 403
Boričevac, 322
Borovo Selo, 58, 340
Bosanska Dubica, 374, 383
Bosnia-Herzegovina, 151, 159, 166, 185, 213, 268, 365, 367, 381, 382, 386, 388, 389, 398, 401, 405, 407
Bosniaks, 327, 341, 346, 398, 399, 401
Bosnian Christian Church, 398
Branimir, 3, 8, 12, 64, 80, 170, 218, 222
BRANIMIRO COM (ES) DVX CRVATORV(M)., 8
Bribirska glavica, 14
Bunjevci and Šokci from Hungary, 36
Byzantine-influenced, 12

C

Cadorna, 152, 155, 170
Caritas, 176, 185, 370, 378, 380
cartographic reviews, 298, 351
casualties, 152, 155, 185, 284, 319, 320, 327, 329, 332, 334, 348, 388
Cathedral of Šibenik, 18
Catholic Church, 10, 18, 45, 53, 80, 141, 176, 177, 180, 183, 184, 187, 194, 195, 198, 200, 204, 205, 207, 208, 209, 210, 213, 214, 219, 220, 222, 223, 225, 226, 227, 228, 229, 230, 231, 232, 235, 237, 238, 239, 242, 270, 306, 313, 316, 330, 331, 378, 387
Catholic intellectuals, 224, 227, 231
Catholic laypeople, 219, 220, 221, 222, 223, 225, 228, 230, 234, 237, 240
Catholic press, 223, 224, 226, 229, 231, 235
census of 1910, 163
Central Committee, 46, 114, 234, 246, 249, 309, 321
centralist policy, 28, 234, 245, 306, 331
Cerovljani, 374
Chakavian, 82, 85, 86, 87, 88, 89, 90, 95, 96, 123, 131
Chakavian Literary-Language Stylization, 86
Chetnik and Partisan terror, 51
Chetnik military organizations, 310
Chetnik(s), 21, 51, 52, 66, 109, 114, 186, 270, 277, 297, 310, 313, 316, 317, 318, 319, 321, 322, 323, 324, 325, 330, 333, 339, 341, 346, 348, 354, 362, 363, 372, 373, 374, 376, 381, 401, 402, 405, 410
Chetniks and partisans collaborated, 321
children, ix, 18, 19, 30, 49, 172, 173, 199, 201, 217, 300, 315, 318, 322, 324, 328, 344, 365, 369, 370, 371, 372, 374, 375, 377, 378, 379, 380, 381, 382, 383
Christmas Constitution, 57, 123
Christomarxists, 227
church, 5, 7, 8, 9, 10, 12, 13, 15, 16, 17, 18, 21, 24, 26, 28, 29, 30, 73, 75, 81, 83, 85, 87, 88, 90, 97, 98, 101, 129, 137, 146, 150, 157, 171, 174, 176, 177, 178, 180, 181, 182, 183, 184, 195, 196, 199, 200, 201, 202, 204, 207, 208, 209, 213, 220, 222, 224, 225, 226, 227, 228, 230, 231, 234, 237, 238, 239, 241, 293, 299, 305, 310, 311, 315, 316, 317,

319, 330, 331, 339, 340, 361, 372, 373, 378, 380, 400, 409, 410
church of St. Spas, 12
Church Slavonic, 73, 75, 83, 87, 88, 90, 98, 129
CIA also revealed that Jasenovac was a communist concentration camp, 335
CIA reports, 256
civil rights, 36, 42, 43, 53, 257, 270, 280, 282, 342
Collapse of the NDH and the Bleiburg Tragedy, 52
Collapse of the SFRY, 55
colonizing eastern parts of Croatia, 305
Comintern, 321, 322
Commission for Imprisoned and Missing Persons, 345
communism, v, viii, xv, 4, 56, 167, 176, 177, 180, 181, 189, 191, 193, 195, 201, 209, 217, 219, 220, 221, 228, 232, 233, 237, 238, 239, 240, 259, 261, 322, 324, 325, 329, 334, 347, 390, 395, 398, 404, 407
communist authorities, 221, 224, 228, 236, 239, 243, 248, 255, 270, 328, 334, 378, 379
communist block, 220
communist dictatorship, 180, 228, 255, 259, 389
communist government, 54, 219, 234, 248, 258, 332, 352
communist guerilla, 164, 318
communist monopoly, 225, 235
Communist Party of Yugoslavia, 53, 109, 306, 321, 322, 325, 330, 370
communist rule, 4, 53, 57, 164, 220, 221, 223, 228, 232, 237, 247, 258, 356, 390
communist Yugoslavia, xi, xiii, 102, 109, 148, 165, 166, 167, 175, 179, 221, 222, 225, 227, 233, 242, 267, 268, 271, 288, 297, 316, 319, 320, 321, 322, 328, 331, 332, 335, 347, 350, 377, 398
concentration camp Jasenovac, xii, xiv, 253, 313, 332, 350, 359, 360, 362
concordat, 227
conflict of Muslims with BH Croats, 341
conformism, 231
Congress of Vienna in 1814, 33
conservative, 227, 232, 251, 327
Constitution, xiv, 47, 54, 55, 56, 57, 106, 123, 139, 189, 195, 246, 251, 252, 261, 269, 272, 278, 279, 305, 306, 307, 337, 338, 339, 340
Constitution of Yugoslavia, 246
controversies, viii, x, xii, 74, 288, 297, 298, 313, 333, 353, 380
conversion, 173, 193, 200, 204, 315, 316
Corfu Declaration, 45, 302
corruption, 67, 385, 390, 391, 392, 410, 413
Corruption Perceptions Index, 391
Council of Trent, 24, 80
countries in the Austro-Hungarian Monarchy, 4
coup led by Yugoslav officers, 312
craftsman Radovan, 16
crimes against Croats, 270, 318, 342, 401
criminal charges, 257
crisis created by Nazi Germany, 177
Croat, 5, 7, 35, 51, 64, 80, 100, 126, 143, 147, 149, 151, 157, 160, 161, 164, 175, 179, 189, 190, 206, 233, 236, 306, 308, 313, 322, 324, 338, 388, 391, 394, 396, 398, 399, 401, 402
Croatia during World War II, 49
Croatia in the First World War, 43
Croatia in the First Yugoslavia, 45
Croatia in the Second Yugoslavia, 52
Croatia regained its national symbols, 57
Croatia tried to avoid war by persistent negotiations, 348
Croatia was internationally recognized, 61
Croatia within the Austro-Hungarian Monarchy, 38
Croatian Army, 177, 276, 280, 281, 283, 284, 287, 288, 326, 342, 344, 357, 365, 388, 402
Croatian as a Slavic language, 80
Croatian Catholic movement, 141
Croatian character of Istria, 165
Croatian Civil and Peasant Defense, 310
Croatian Committee, 45
Croatian communist elite, 234
Croatian Cyrillic, 17, 80, 83, 85
Croatian Defense Council, 341, 366
Croatian Democratic Union, 63, 117, 270, 339, 366
Croatian dialects, 80, 85, 86, 95, 123
Croatian emigration, 31, 55, 114, 140, 222, 240, 247, 255, 258
Croatian forces liberated, 61, 280
Croatian generals, 63, 111
Croatian grammar, 24, 79, 81, 96, 97, 115, 116, 123, 126, 127, 129
Croatian humanist intellectuals, 18
Croatian identity, 148, 150, 165, 232, 235, 299, 307, 335, 388
Croatian intellectuals, viii, 17, 54, 55, 96, 103, 114, 135, 245, 246, 249, 252, 254, 257, 258, 307, 337, 387
Croatian intellectuals were charged and sentenced, 257
Croatian Kingdom, 4, 9
Croatian Lands under French Rule, 32
Croatian language, v, viii, ix, xvii, 8, 10, 11, 30, 32, 33, 34, 35, 36, 38, 41, 55, 66, 67, 70, 72, 73, 79, 80, 81, 82, 85, 88, 89, 90, 91, 92, 93, 94, 95, 96, 97, 101, 103, 104, 105, 106, 107, 108, 109, 110, 111, 112, 113, 114, 115, 116, 117, 118, 119, 122, 123, 124, 125, 126, 127, 128, 129, 130, 131, 132,

133, 134, 141, 157, 206, 207, 209, 229, 233, 235, 236, 251, 261, 299, 335, 336, 387, 401
Croatian Language Days, 112
Croatian leadership, 189, 255, 256, 267, 268, 271, 272, 273, 275, 279, 288, 294, 336, 338, 339
Croatian literary language, 79, 83, 86, 89, 90, 100, 102, 103, 104, 105, 112, 113, 115, 123, 124, 125, 126, 127, 128, 129, 130, 131, 132, 133, 247, 250, 260, 261, 262, 336, 351
Croatian literature, 16, 17, 19, 41, 94, 103, 104, 115, 125, 128, 129, 132
Croatian National Guard (Croatian Zbor narodne garde, ZNG), 58, 59
Croatian national identity, 79, 97, 107, 157, 250, 253, 347
Croatian national movement, 233, 246, 247, 250, 252, 256, 257, 258, 304, 336
Croatian national question, 232, 239
Croatian National Revival, 33, 35, 74, 144
Croatian noble families, 13, 14
Croatian Orthodox Church, 141, 170, 316, 373
Croatian Orthography, 103, 113, 114, 116, 118, 124, 125, 127
Croatian Parliament, vii, xi, xiii, 3, 20, 21, 29, 30, 31, 34, 46, 47, 50, 56, 57, 59, 91, 104, 112, 139, 140, 142, 189, 270, 302, 304, 311, 340, 342
Croatian Parliament (Consilium regium), 30
Croatian partisans, 233
Croatian Party of Rights, 43, 56, 59, 68, 139, 142, 160, 307, 309, 339
Croatian peasant lived in the hope, 191
Croatian Peasant Party, viii, 3, 47, 48, 49, 50, 160, 189, 191, 194, 233, 253, 302, 306, 307, 310, 312, 323
Croatian Peasants' Revolt in 1573, 25
Croatian People's Peasant Party, 42, 43, 47
Croatian policemen were ambushed and killed, 58
Croatian Principalities in the 9th Century, 7
Croatian question, v, 48, 49, 135, 139, 141, 143, 144, 308, 310, 311, 312, 337, 347
Croatian Red Cross, 375, 377
Croatian Republican Peasant Party (HRSS), 47, 354
Croatian scripts and orthography, 80
Croatian Shtokavian Literary-Language Stylization, 88
Croatian Shtokavian stylization, 85, 90
Croatian silence, 55, 80, 114, 118, 257, 270, 337, 338, 339
Croatian silence, the, 55, 80, 114, 118, 257, 270, 337, 338, 339
Croatian Social Liberal Party, 56
Croatian Spring, vii, 54, 55, 56, 80, 113, 114, 221, 224, 230, 234, 245, 246, 247, 248, 249, 250, 252, 253, 255, 256, 257, 258, 259, 260, 261, 262, 263, 264, 336
Croatian Spring, 1971, 54, 113
Croatian standard language, 71, 80, 82, 85, 117, 118, 120, 121, 126, 128, 129
Croatian state, vii, 3, 4, 6, 7, 8, 10, 15, 50, 55, 58, 73, 108, 111, 117, 135, 139, 140, 142, 143, 144, 148, 167, 189, 195, 197, 211, 212, 253, 260, 264, 271, 283, 285, 291, 292, 313, 316, 317, 318, 319, 321, 323, 330, 339, 344, 345, 352, 366, 371, 373, 374, 378, 381, 382
Croatian State Archives, 195, 211, 212, 264, 378, 382
Croatian Territorial Defense, 57, 273, 276, 339
Croatian Vukovians, 96, 97, 98, 99, 100, 103, 104, 107
Croatians from Gradišće, 36
Croatian-Serbian Coalition, 142, 301, 302
Croatia-Serbia, 297
Croats and Serbs, 46, 79, 96, 97, 101, 102, 104, 118, 141, 142, 187, 188, 210, 268, 277, 284, 287, 288, 294, 298, 301, 302, 303, 310, 311, 317, 322, 329, 334, 335, 346, 348
Croats and Slovenes, 106, 147, 152, 163, 187, 188, 302, 303
Croats Felt Betrayed and Cheated, 189
Croats in BH, 399
Croats living in the Diaspora, 189
Culture and Literacy in the Early Middle Ages, 12
currency, 47, 248, 279, 304, 393
Cvetković–Maček Agreement, 49

D

Dajla, 167, 170, 171, 174
Đakovo, 375, 378
Dalmatia, 3, 5, 7, 8, 10, 12, 13, 14, 15, 17, 21, 25, 26, 29, 31, 32, 33, 34, 35, 37, 39, 41, 43, 49, 50, 59, 62, 67, 71, 72, 75, 84, 86, 91, 92, 129, 136, 139, 140, 141, 142, 143, 147, 155, 157, 158, 159, 161, 162, 163, 164, 167, 168, 187, 188, 201, 233, 235, 272, 281, 282, 290, 292, 294, 299, 301, 305, 311, 320, 321, 323, 340, 343, 353, 358, 365, 376, 389
Dalmatian songs, 233
Danube River, 376, 403
Dayton Agreement, 61, 62, 284, 344
Dayton Peace Conference, 166
declaration, 45, 54, 55, 58, 72, 80, 109, 112, 126, 142, 147, 160, 200, 247, 250, 251, 252, 260, 261, 262, 275, 302, 311, 336, 351
Declaration of Corfu, 160

Declaration on the Status and Name of the Croatian Literary Language, 54, 80, 109, 112
declining population, 385, 390, 394
de-Croatization, 79, 80
demands for greater independence, 247
Democratic Federal Yugoslavia, 51, 323, 326
democratic government, 43, 57, 271, 335, 388
demography, 169, 386, 396
demonstrations, 40, 74, 307, 349
departure, 55, 84, 203, 224, 231, 235, 240, 282
diary, viii, 44, 72, 205, 215, 369, 370, 371, 374, 375, 376, 377, 379, 380, 381
dictatorship, 3, 4, 47, 48, 176, 179, 189, 221, 259, 262, 306, 307, 308, 309, 346
differences between Croatian and Serbian, 80
diplomatic relations, 220, 225, 226, 231, 239, 240, 243, 407
discrimination, 60, 179, 181, 316, 387, 391, 403
displaced persons, 285, 286, 290, 344, 393
disproportionate representation, 304
distortions of history, 390
documentary film, 371, 380
Domagoj, xv, 8, 223, 260, 261, 265, 360, 414
Domobran, 319, 355, 373, 395
Domobran working regiments, 373
Drinković, 156, 169
Dubrovnik, v, 5, 13, 15, 16, 17, 18, 26, 27, 28, 29, 32, 59, 61, 65, 66, 69, 70, 71, 73, 74, 89, 91, 93, 126, 140, 141, 144, 159, 253, 277, 279, 324, 341, 356, 371, 395, 406, 407
Dubrovnik in 16th and 17th century, 26
Dubrovnik in October 18, 1944, 324

E

Eastern Front, 147, 152
economic reform, 234, 246, 248, 253
elections, 4, 35, 37, 52, 56, 57, 63, 116, 117, 137, 168, 254, 256, 259, 263, 269, 270, 273, 291, 306, 339, 387, 396, 407
elections for the first Constitutional Assembly, 52
Eltz castle in Vukovar, 29
emigration, 22, 41, 42, 55, 64, 114, 140, 147, 222, 224, 231, 255, 258, 261, 286, 309, 336, 342, 346, 385, 394, 395, 407, 410
emphasis on issues of Croatian history and national symbols, 253
Entente, 152, 156, 160, 161, 216, 301
entire library was saved, 201
entrepreneurs were exterminated, 390
environment, 88, 149, 157, 218, 270, 380, 386, 398, 412
Erdut Agreement, 62, 284, 290
establish the Greater Serbia, 298
ethnic, 59
ethnic cleansing, 51, 167, 282, 285, 288, 289, 292, 298, 319, 344, 345, 347, 348, 388, 398, 402
ethnic imbalances, 163
EU membership, 385, 396
European Commission, 122, 396, 398, 405
European Green Deal, 398, 405
exchange of the Austro-Hungarian currency, 304
Execution of the wounded members of the Croatian armed forces, 328
existential fears, 219, 228
extermination, viii, 301, 314, 316, 318, 353, 378, 401

F

faith, vii, 5, 7, 8, 22, 65, 84, 100, 101, 147, 150, 157, 167, 175, 181, 208, 216, 225, 230, 237, 330, 371, 375, 379, 385, 386, 387, 388, 389, 404
fall of communism, 4, 380, 387, 396
Federal People's Republic of Yugoslavia (FNRJ), 53, 332
federalism, vii, 47, 135, 141, 144, 234, 248, 331, 347
Federation of BH, 344, 398
Field Marshal, v, 92, 147, 148, 153, 155, 157, 158, 161, 163, 164, 167, 170, 171
film, vi, ix, 61, 369, 370, 371, 373, 374, 376, 377, 378, 379, 380, 381, 383
filmmakers, 371, 374, 380
first Croatian book, 13
First World War, 4, 43, 44, 45, 66, 168, 169, 171, 180
fleet of Dubrovnik, 27
Foibe Massacres, 167
formal and informal pressures, 237
former farm near Vukovar called Ovčara, 341
Fourteen Points, 162, 172
Frankish missionaries, 7
free elections, 386, 396
Free Territory of Trieste, the, 53, 165, 166
freedom and respect, 177
freedom of speech, viii, 36, 219, 247, 307, 390, 403
future, v, vi, viii, ix, xi, 18, 22, 38, 45, 76, 92, 97, 107, 122, 139, 160, 165, 167, 175, 176, 182, 188, 191, 202, 218, 227, 239, 257, 269, 271, 273, 276, 279, 284, 289, 295, 300, 302, 303, 304, 308, 309, 314, 376, 385, 386, 396, 398, 408

G

Gastarbeiter, 55, 395
GDP, 385, 393, 394, 405

Genealogy of the Boroević, 149
generals of the NDH Army, 314
Geneva Conventions from 1929, 326
Geneva Declaration, 302
Glagolitic, 7, 8, 9, 10, 12, 13, 16, 20, 24, 73, 76, 80, 83, 84, 85, 86, 87, 141, 233
Glagolitic masses, 9
Glagolitic script, 7, 8, 9, 10, 12, 17, 20, 83, 84, 141, 233
Global Competitiveness Report, 394, 411
Golden Bull, 14
Gornja Rijeka near Križevci, 375
government debt, 405
Grahovo and its surroundings, 318
Grand Anti-Masonic Exhibition, 192
Great Turkish War, 24
Greater Austria, 135, 137
Greater Serbia, 4, 55, 56, 58, 100, 142, 160, 268, 273, 274, 275, 287, 290, 297, 298, 299, 300, 311, 317, 319, 338, 340, 341, 347, 352, 367, 388, 402, 403
Greater-Serbian aggression, 59, 72, 267, 268, 274, 282, 285, 291, 297, 340, 341, 344, 359, 409
Greater-Serbian Aggression against Croatia, 274, 291, 340
guerrilla groups, 372
Gvozdansko, 21, 65

H

Habsburg Dynasty on the Croatian Throne, 20
Habsburg Monarchy, 4, 25, 37, 39, 136, 144, 145, 149, 153
HDZ, 56, 63, 117, 118, 270, 271, 292, 339
HDZ, Croatian Democratic Union, led by Franjo Tuđman, 56
higher education, 134, 140, 255, 390, 392, 408, 409
historians, viii, ix, xi, 4, 5, 18, 34, 48, 50, 140, 143, 157, 158, 175, 178, 179, 182, 183, 184, 185, 186, 187, 188, 192, 199, 203, 210, 222, 225, 230, 253, 256, 261, 264, 265, 267, 270, 282, 298, 307, 309, 310, 314, 318, 320, 325, 327, 329, 330, 335, 337, 339, 346, 347, 350, 369, 378, 380, 401
Holocaust, x, xiii, xv, 184, 192, 198, 211, 212, 214, 216, 218, 313, 314, 315, 316, 329, 348, 351, 353, 354, 360, 361, 362, 381
Holy League, 24
Home Guard (Domobrani), 47, 50, 140, 177, 326, 373, 382
Homeland War, 4, 29, 63, 64, 65, 71, 72, 73, 76, 115, 116, 267, 290, 291, 292, 294, 356, 357, 359, 366, 367, 409
honorary Aryans, 194, 314
honorary citizen, 42, 157, 158
Horoathos or Horuathus, 4
hostilities between the Croats and the Serbs, 237
Hranilović-Soldin trial, 307, 356
Hrvatski gospodarski glasnik, 252
Hrvatski tjednik, xiv, 171, 174, 252, 253, 257, 261, 354, 357, 367, 383
huge meeting in Knin, 339
Hum inscription, 13
humane image of Yugoslavian socialism, 228
humane socialism, 220, 221
humane version of socialism, 221
humor, 243, 387
Hundred-Year Croatian-Turkish War, 149
Hungarian-Croatian Kingdom, 4
Hungarization, 40
Hungarization of Croatia, 40
Hungary, 3, 11, 12, 13, 14, 15, 19, 20, 21, 22, 25, 27, 28, 29, 31, 32, 37, 38, 39, 40, 41, 43, 44, 49, 50, 61, 81, 133, 135, 136, 137, 139, 140, 141, 142, 143, 146, 148, 152, 154, 159, 164, 187, 188, 203, 226, 265, 299, 302, 305, 308, 312, 318, 345, 372, 389, 390, 394, 396, 397

I

ideological opponent, 220
ideology of Greater Serbia, 51
Illyrian movement, 34, 35, 74, 91, 93, 95, 106
Illyrian Provinces, 33
immigrants from Serbia, 372
imposed constitution (Oktroirani Ustav), 37, 48
Inclusiveness Index, 387, 408
independent Croatia, 36, 39, 48, 177, 191, 194, 250, 298, 310, 312, 316, 317, 326, 330, 338, 346, 395, 402
independent Croatian Church, 177
independent Orthodox churches in Croatia, 305
independent State of Croatia (Nezavisna Država Hrvatska or NDH), xi, xii, xiii, 50, 52, 74, 79, 108, 109, 129, 167, 176, 184, 185, 186, 191, 194, 196, 197, 198, 200, 201, 205, 206, 211, 212, 213, 217, 236, 237, 270, 271, 272, 297, 302, 312, 313, 316, 317, 318, 319, 320, 321, 323, 324, 325, 326, 328, 329, 330, 332, 334, 338, 339, 346, 348, 351, 353, 356, 358, 369, 370, 371, 372, 373, 374, 375, 376, 377, 379, 380, 381, 382, 383, 395, 401, 405, 406, 407
industry, 137, 193, 286, 376, 386, 390, 394, 397, 398
inequalities, 190, 265
inner emigration, 220, 230
intellectuals who were expelled from public life, 230
International Court, 388, 400, 402, 407

International Court of Justice, 388, 400, 402, 407
International Criminal Tribunal, 62, 63, 402
international image, 387
International Monetary Fund, 397, 407
international recognition, 4, 8, 61, 128, 167, 267, 277, 288, 291, 341
intervention, 37, 58, 165, 196, 198, 201, 202, 221, 256, 268, 269, 272, 289
Irredenta, 157
islands, 5, 6, 9, 10, 13, 14, 26, 32, 49, 50, 158, 161, 162, 164, 165, 301, 323, 389, 403
Isonzo, 148, 152, 153, 154, 158, 168, 171, 172
Israel, 183, 184, 199, 201, 203, 217, 362, 397, 407
Istria, 3, 5, 7, 8, 9, 10, 12, 15, 16, 24, 26, 31, 32, 35, 36, 39, 41, 75, 91, 136, 139, 140, 141, 142, 143, 148, 155, 156, 158, 161, 162, 164, 165, 167, 168, 171, 260, 305, 367
Istrian Catholic clergy, 148, 165, 167
Istrian territory, 13
Italian aspirations, 155, 163, 301
Italian forces, 148, 152, 154
Italian front, 147, 152, 154, 157
Italian irredentistic aspirations, 163
Italian occupation, 51, 147, 161, 163, 168
Italy, 4, 7, 9, 18, 27, 44, 45, 46, 47, 48, 49, 50, 51, 52, 53, 61, 80, 86, 140, 147, 148, 152, 155, 156, 158, 159, 160, 161, 162, 163, 164, 165, 166, 167, 168, 171, 188, 192, 193, 194, 201, 202, 203, 301, 302, 305, 309, 312, 313, 323, 333, 345, 355, 370, 389, 404
Izvestia, 159

J

Jablanac, 374
January 15, 1992, Croatia was internationally recognized, 278, 341
Jasenovac, ix, x, xii, xiii, xiv, xv, 51, 289, 328, 330, 332, 333, 334, 335, 347, 348, 350, 353, 354, 355, 358, 359, 360, 361, 362, 364, 368, 369, 370, 371, 377, 382, 383, 384, 401, 404, 406, 408, 411
Jasenovac concentration camp, 359, 371, 401
Jasenovac Research Institute, x, 333
Jasenovac victims, ix, 333, 363
Jasenovac, victims in, ix, 50
Jastrebarsko, 378, 383
Jewish community, 184, 186, 198, 199, 201, 202, 353, 371, 372, 375
Jewish Department in Ustasha Police, 375
Jewish-Catholic relations, 176
Jews, 50, 141, 179, 180, 181, 184, 185, 186, 189, 191, 192, 193, 194, 195, 196, 197, 198, 199, 200, 201, 202, 203, 204, 205, 206, 207, 208, 209, 210, 211, 212, 214, 215, 216, 217, 313, 314, 315, 316, 317, 323, 330, 332, 334, 348, 349, 353, 357, 371, 372, 379, 381
Jews (Croatian Jews), 184, 372
Jews who had converted to Catholicism, 197
Jezik, 67, 68, 71, 114, 115, 118, 124, 125, 126, 127, 128, 131, 132, 133, 134, 353, 407
JNA, 56, 57, 58, 59, 60, 61, 116, 248, 251, 267, 269, 272, 273, 274, 275, 276, 277, 288, 323, 328, 329, 338, 339, 340, 341, 345, 348
JNA as Serbian Army, 273
Judenfrei, 193, 313
judicial system, 138, 385, 391

K

Kaykavian, 82, 85, 86, 87, 88, 91, 93, 94, 95, 96, 123, 127, 130
Kaykavian Literary-Language Stylization, 88
key motives of communist politics toward the churches, 222
kill all Croatian young men in the city and district of Zagreb, born between 1924-27, 329
Kingdom of Serbs, 3, 46, 47, 106, 123, 143, 145, 156, 157, 160, 161, 162, 163, 169, 187, 188, 191, 214, 302, 303, 359
Kingdom of Serbs, Croats and Slovenes, 46, 106, 123, 143, 145, 156, 187, 188, 302, 303, 359
Kingdom of Yugoslavia, 4, 47, 48, 49, 50, 51, 106, 107, 108, 109, 123, 143, 148, 156, 164, 168, 189, 190, 191, 227, 232, 233, 236, 240, 268, 288, 297, 307, 308, 310, 312, 316, 318, 320, 323, 331, 335, 346, 347, 356, 389, 394, 401
Klis, 8, 15, 21, 22
Korčula Statute, 17
Košice, 151, 152
Kotor Cathedral, 29
Kozara Mountain, 369, 370, 374, 376, 377, 381
Kraglski Dalmatin, 32, 94
Krbavsko Field, 20
Kulin Ban Charter, 13

L

language, vii, viii, 10, 30, 32, 34, 35, 38, 40, 54, 55, 67, 68, 71, 76, 79, 80, 81, 82, 83, 85, 86, 87, 88, 89, 90, 91, 92, 93, 95, 96, 97, 100, 101, 102, 103, 104, 105, 106, 107, 108, 109, 110, 111, 112, 113, 114, 115, 116, 117, 118, 119, 120, 121, 122, 123, 124, 125, 126, 127, 128, 129, 130, 131, 132, 133, 134, 138, 140, 141, 142, 163, 165, 187, 191, 235,

236, 251, 293, 298, 300, 305, 335, 336, 354, 387, 407
later to become Orthodox Serbs, 187
Latin, xvii, 8, 12, 16, 17, 24, 34, 80, 81, 83, 84, 85, 87, 91, 92, 93, 94, 97, 100, 105, 110, 112, 113, 115, 119, 120, 121, 126, 129, 131, 140, 215, 300, 387
Lavoslav Schwarz, 202
Law on Forgiveness, 342, 360
League of Communist of Croatia, 246
League of Communists of Yugoslavia, 56, 109, 114, 115, 117, 235, 245, 246, 269, 338
liberalization, 220, 228, 230, 235, 245, 246, 248, 249, 252, 258, 259, 261, 262, 264
Liberation Operations of the Croatian Army, 280
lies and partial truths, 390
Lobor Town, 375
log-revolution, 402
London Treaty, the, 301
Londoner, 113, 116

M

Macedonians, 186, 306
main strengths, 387
many Croatian intellectuals were sentenced, 257
many of the clergy of Zagreb wore the yellow star, 197
Marxism, 219, 222, 226
mass crimes, xvi, 319, 321, 325, 373, 401
mass graves in Slovenia, 327, 395
mass movement, 55, 262
mass national movement called the Croatian Spring, 336
mass slaughter, 232
member of the European Union, vii, 4, 386
membership in the United Nations, 386
Memorandum of Serbian Academy of Science and Arts, 338
memorandum SANU, 267, 270, 338, 339, 346, 348, 352
mental ghetto on the margins of society, 230
Mid-Sixties in Yugoslavia, v, 219
mild climate, 389
Military Academy, 151, 190
Military Frontier, 22, 23, 27, 30, 31, 34, 36, 40, 149, 150
Military Order of Maria Theresa, 153, 157
mindset and work ethic(s), 385, 390
minority communities, 371
mixed marriages, 199, 200, 207, 212, 371, 379
Mlaka, 374, 377
Molotov-Ribbentrop Pact, 320, 359
monarchy, 3, 25, 37, 38, 39, 40, 41, 42, 43, 44, 45, 47, 52, 91, 92, 93, 101, 106, 107, 135, 136, 139, 140, 141, 142, 143, 144, 147, 149, 151, 152, 156, 157, 158, 160, 161, 163, 169, 170, 176, 190, 203, 220, 232, 299, 302, 303, 310
Muslim, 25, 51, 141, 189, 314, 318, 341, 344, 345, 373, 378, 401

N

Naputak (Advisory), 46
Narodne novine, 93, 94, 102, 106, 127, 200, 213, 240, 272, 291, 361
national anthem of Croatia, 34
National Council of Slovenes, Croats and Serbs, 142, 156, 169, 302, 358
national identities, 232, 236, 248, 298, 331, 402
national identity, vii, 54, 87, 103, 147, 149, 221, 232, 233, 299, 300, 301, 305, 331, 335
national issues, 246, 248
National Party in Croatia, 139, 141
national question, 64, 103, 136, 139, 142, 144, 210, 234, 246, 268, 297, 298, 306, 322, 331, 337, 347, 349
nationalist, 105, 190, 194, 232, 236, 254, 268, 289, 309, 322, 356, 401
NATO, vii, 4, 386, 396, 397, 404, 409, 410
NATO member, 386, 397
negation of an independent Croatian nation, 232
neo-Marxist pressure, 403
new course, 42, 71
no two South Slavic regions developed in a similar fashion, 187
Nobel Prize, 42, 49
Novi Sad Agreement, 79, 102, 109, 110, 111, 112, 113, 114, 251, 335, 336, 359
Novine Horvatszke, 34

O

objective research and dialogue, 348
Odessa, 303, 356
opera, 21
Operation, 62
Operation Flash, 61, 280
Operation Flash (Bljesak in Croatian), 280
Operation Maestral, 62
Operation Storm, 62, 267, 268, 280, 281, 282, 284, 288, 342, 388
opportunities, 9, 217, 385, 386, 394, 396, 397, 398
ornaments called, 12

Orthodox, 10, 22, 147, 149, 150, 157, 171, 174, 175, 177, 180, 190, 193, 194, 207, 208, 237, 287, 299, 300, 305, 310, 311, 314, 315, 316, 319, 340, 353, 369, 370, 371, 372, 373, 375, 376, 377, 378, 379, 388, 398
Orthodox children, 369, 375, 378, 380
Orthodox Christian, 306, 369, 370, 371, 388
Ottoman conquests, 4, 17, 21, 22, 27, 313, 398
Ottoman Empire, 16, 19, 20, 24, 25, 44, 136, 149, 168, 188, 232, 299, 305
Ottoman rule, 16, 17, 19, 21, 24, 25, 27, 149, 186, 187, 299, 389
Ottoman-Christian frontier, 389
Ovčara, 60, 277
Ozalj Literary Circle, 27, 88
Ozalj Literary Circle of Writers, 27

P

Pacta Conventa, 11
Paris Agreement, 61
Paris Peace Conference, 148, 161, 165
parliament (Sabor, 4, 12, 403
partisans, ix, xiii, 21, 51, 52, 186, 203, 232, 233, 235, 297, 313, 320, 321, 322, 323, 324, 325, 326, 329, 330, 333, 347, 348, 354, 369, 370, 373, 374, 376, 379, 394, 401
party purge, 235, 256, 258
Patriarchate of Constantinople, 157
Patriarchate of Srijemski Karlovci, 149, 157
Peace Conference, 147, 277, 278, 341, 345
Peace of Vasvar, 27
peaceful reintegration, 61, 62, 284, 288, 348
peaceful reintegration ended on January 15, 1998, 62
Peasant-Democratic Coalition, 306, 307
persona non grata, 186
Piave river, 155
pillar of human rights, 204
plan was to exterminate Croats, 319
Plan Z-4, 279
Plenum of the Student Union of Split, 255
policy and plans to create Greater Serbia, 272
political judgement, 374
political pluralism, 247, 252, 262
political prisoners since 1972., 337
population censuses, 165
port of the Imperial Navy, 41
postwar camp Jasenovac, 334
Pragmatic Sanction of 1712, 29
Prague Spring, 221, 234, 336
Praxis group, 231
Prevlaka, 399, 407
priests and nuns continue wearing this sign, 196
Principality of Croatia, 6
privatization, 393, 404
productivity, 230, 385, 390, 392, 394, 410
propaganda of Greater Serbia, 51, 57
prosecutions, vii, 38, 39, 176
provisional government, 51, 52
public life, ix, 38, 50, 53, 112, 116, 183, 216, 224, 235, 257, 270, 391, 403

R

race laws, 50
racial laws, 109, 314, 334
racism, 179, 358, 379, 387
radical nationalist movement, 189
rate of taxation, 190
reconciliation,, 402
referendum on independence, 387
reform movement, v, 245, 246, 253, 254, 255, 256
refugees, 5, 22, 52, 176, 193, 201, 216, 278, 283, 285, 286, 290, 329, 341, 344, 374, 377, 378, 379, 380, 393
regime, vii, ix, x, xiv, 47, 48, 50, 164, 175, 176, 177, 178, 180, 182, 183, 186, 187, 191, 193, 194, 196, 197, 198, 199, 201, 203, 205, 206, 219, 220, 222, 225, 226, 227, 228, 229, 230, 231, 233, 235, 236, 237, 240, 245, 253, 254, 257, 258, 269, 271, 272, 273, 304, 305, 306, 307, 308, 309, 310, 314, 316, 317, 319, 320, 321, 323, 325, 326, 327, 328, 330, 332, 334, 335, 346, 347, 362, 369, 370, 374, 380, 383, 385, 390, 393, 395, 401, 406, 408, 409
relations with Bosnia-Herzegovina, 386
relations with Serbia, 297, 386
relations with Slovenia, 386
Relief Committee for Refugees, 185
religion, 22, 36, 38, 39, 53, 60, 83, 84, 101, 127, 141, 177, 180, 181, 182, 186, 187, 193, 200, 207, 208, 213, 219, 220, 222, 229, 232, 276, 314, 316, 325, 330, 335, 369, 380, 387
Reliquiae reliquiarum, 22, 389
renewable energy, 398, 405
repression of Croats, 233
Republic of Croatia became a full member of the European Union, 63
Republic of Croatia entered NATO in 2009, 63
Republic of Serbian Krajina, 58, 61, 62, 63, 275, 282, 340
Republic Srpska, 341, 343, 344, 388, 398, 399, 401, 402
rescue, 185, 198, 199, 203, 208, 211, 214, 215, 217, 218, 349, 353, 370, 381
Resolution of Rijeka, 43
Resolution of Zadar, 43

revisionism, xii, 168, 330, 358, 401, 403
Rijeka, 24, 27, 31, 34, 37, 39, 41, 43, 67, 68, 73, 94, 95, 124, 125, 130, 133, 139, 140, 141, 142, 159, 161, 162, 163, 164, 165, 167, 224, 253, 260, 305
Rijeka philology school, 95
Roman missionaries, 7
Roman Treaties, 323
Rosary, 404, 407
Royal Academy, 30, 93
Royal Council of Dalmatia, 30
Royal Council of Dalmatia, Croatia, and Slavonia 1767, 30

S

Sabor, vii, xi, xiii, 3, 4, 91, 92, 93, 104, 189, 270, 271, 272, 274, 275, 279, 304, 311, 386, 387, 406
Sajmište, 315
satellite regimes, 164
Sava, 22, 23, 25, 33, 90, 152, 159, 163, 309, 315, 374
Savudrijska Vala, 400
schism of Christianity, 389
schools, 24, 36, 38, 40, 93, 95, 103, 104, 107, 110, 111, 116, 119, 130, 140, 293, 376, 378, 387, 391, 412, 417
scientific productivity, 392
Second Vatican Council, 220, 223, 224, 228, 238
Second World War, xiii, xiv, 217, 220, 232, 233, 234, 235, 236, 237, 253, 349, 350, 352, 408
Second Yugoslavia, 4, 55
secondary schools, 28, 392
secret police, 38, 157, 180, 192, 220, 229, 246, 324, 327, 334, 336, 357, 396
Serb Democratic Party in Croatia,, 58
Serbian academics wrote another memorandum in 2011, 345
Serbian Academy of Sciences and Arts, 55, 58, 59, 359
Serbian aggression, 61, 62, 148, 267, 268, 275, 281, 285, 316, 341, 344, 351, 388, 391, 392, 393
Serbian cadres dominated, 331
Serbian elite, 192
Serbian forces, 59, 274, 275, 277, 280, 282, 287, 318, 344, 345
Serbian hegemony, 47, 306, 307
Serbian insurgency, 267, 270, 272, 273, 338
Serbian minority, 4, 22, 59, 136, 270, 371, 376, 402, 403
Serbian Orthodox Church, 141, 157, 227, 236, 269, 297, 299, 305, 311, 314, 315, 316, 319, 338, 340, 346, 353, 363, 372
Serbian propaganda, 192, 267, 271, 273, 275, 316, 319
Serbian rebels, 373
Serbian troops rocketed Zagreb, 61
Serbs and Croats were not the same people, 187
Serbs had been prepared in advance and that the order had been given, 342
Serbs took over Yugoslav monetary system, 339
Serbs, rally together!, 311
series of frightening crimes, 325
severe and unlawful measures, 194, 207
SFRJ, 53, 55, 289, 290
Shtokavian, 34, 79, 80, 82, 85, 86, 87, 88, 89, 90, 93, 94, 95, 96, 97, 100, 102, 103, 104, 118, 119, 123, 299, 300
Sibinj, victims of, 310
simony, 157
Široki Brijeg, xiii, 330, 356
Sisak, 19, 22, 31, 34, 70, 261, 286, 377
six republics, 53, 232, 245, 268, 273
Sklavinija, 6
Slav, 43, 45, 143, 147, 151, 160, 299, 303
Slavonia, 9, 10, 13, 14, 15, 21, 24, 25, 31, 32, 34, 39, 42, 49, 59, 60, 61, 66, 67, 90, 91, 92, 129, 136, 139, 140, 141, 142, 143, 146, 159, 237, 275, 276, 279, 280, 281, 284, 290, 299, 301, 305, 311, 340, 343, 352, 389
Slovakia, 22, 27, 49, 61, 137, 138, 145, 390, 394, 397
smuggling, 391
Soča battlefront, 148
Soča river, 44, 148, 161, 163, 168
Social Democratic Party, 117, 396
Socialist Republic of Croatia, 54, 57, 245, 339, 340
Socialist Yugoslavia, vii, 239, 243, 245, 265, 410
Society of Writers of Croatia, 250, 253
South Slav, 82, 96, 111, 126, 139, 141, 142, 143, 146, 147, 156, 158, 159, 161, 162, 163, 186, 187, 188, 189, 190, 191, 215, 298, 299, 300, 301, 302, 303, 409
South Slav problem, 162
South Tyrol, 159, 162, 163, 171
split with Stalin, 220
sports, 42, 387
Srebrenica, 19, 61, 280, 344
Srpanjske žrtve (The July Victims), 35
St. Cross in Nin, 12
Stara Gradiška camp, 374
State of Slovenes, 46, 64, 106, 143, 188, 302
State of Slovenes, Croats and Serbs, 46, 64, 106, 143, 188, 302
State Security Administration, 53, 114
state-controlled media, 231

Statehood Day, 57, 386
Stepinac – Tito, 179, 214
stigmatization of Croats, 332
stigmatized as nationalist, 331
struggle for equality of the Croatian Language, 335
student protest, 246
students, viii, 8, 12, 40, 54, 76, 124, 129, 236, 245, 247, 249, 253, 254, 255, 257, 258, 262, 263, 365, 390, 392, 414, 415
stylization, 82, 85, 86, 87, 88, 90, 93, 94, 95, 97, 100, 106, 110, 118, 123
Šubašić, 52
suffer and die for the faith, 175, 176
SWAT analysis, 386
system of prison camps where, 328
systematic, 119, 174, 235, 253, 275, 283, 285, 286, 305, 316, 320, 330, 332, 334, 335, 341, 348, 388, 396
systematic expulsion of the Croatian and other non-Serbian populations, 341

T

Tanjug, 235, 236
tanks, 60, 277, 391
targets of repression was Matica, 257
Tatar invasion, 14
termination of legal ties with SFRY, 59
The battle for Vukovar, 59
The declaration of a Serbian dictatorship, 189
The evacuation had begun by order of the Serbian leadership, 342
The Hvar rebellion, 26
The Independent State of Croatia, 4, 164, 236, 312
The Montreal Gazette, 181
The New York Times Editorial, 180
The Proclamation of Croatian Independence and State Sovereignty, 58
The second accuser, 183
The third accuser, 183
The two successive Yugoslav states could not solve the national question, 347
The Way of the Cross, 326, 327
The worst genocides of the 20th century, 329
Theresianum, 151
tie or cravat, 23
tombstones (Croatian stećci), 18, 68
total war damage in Croatia, 63, 287
Treaty of Karlowitz, 149
Treaty of London, 46, 47, 147, 148, 152, 156, 157, 158, 159, 162, 163, 166
Treaty of Osimo, 166, 167
Treaty of Rapallo, 47, 161, 163, 164, 305
Treaty of Rome, 47, 50, 161, 163
trialism, v, 135, 140, 141, 142, 143, 144
trials, xiii, 26, 53, 176, 257, 261, 265, 324, 326, 328
tridialect Croatian stylization, 86
Trieste, 36, 137, 138, 140, 141, 143, 148, 155, 156, 158, 161, 164, 165
Tripartite Pact, 49, 50, 52
Triple Alliance, 158, 301
Triple Entente, 45, 46, 148, 158, 160, 161
Triune Kingdom, 136, 139, 140, 142, 299
Triune Kingdom of Croatia, 136, 139, 140, 142, 299
Trpimirović Dynasty, 8
Turkish Conquests in Croatia, 19
Turks, 17, 20, 21, 22, 25, 34, 149, 186, 308, 314, 389
two autonomous provinces, 53, 268, 269

U

U.S. diplomats after the trial, 178
Ugri (Hungarians), 7, 9, 11, 35, 37, 38, 39, 40, 41, 42, 60, 91, 140, 152, 186, 285, 299, 345, 402
unification, v, 32, 33, 34, 35, 36, 43, 46, 51, 95, 102, 109, 110, 129, 136, 139, 141, 142, 143, 147, 156, 160, 163, 186, 187, 188, 189, 190, 191, 280, 302, 303, 305, 308, 402
uniform Croatian alphabet and language, 32
unitarism, 79, 107, 113, 115, 118, 245, 250, 252, 254, 255, 259, 331, 347
unitaristic language policy, 80
United States Congress, 181
United States of Greater Austria, 135, 136, 137, 143, 144
universal values, 207
university(ies), xi, xv, 18, 24, 28, 30, 40, 44, 49, 64, 65, 66, 67, 68, 72, 75, 76, 79, 81, 110, 126, 131, 132, 134, 136, 137, 140, 145, 146, 147, 157, 168, 172, 173, 181, 197, 210, 211, 213, 214, 217, 218, 238, 239, 242, 243, 245, 247, 249, 251, 253, 254, 258, 260, 262, 263, 264, 291, 292, 293, 294, 297, 329, 330, 334, 337, 349, 350, 353, 356, 359, 363, 364, 365, 366, 367, 370, 381, 383, 385, 392, 393, 405, 408, 409, 410, 411, 412, 413, 414, 417
University of Zagreb, 24, 30, 40, 64, 72, 131, 132, 136, 140, 145, 157, 242, 243, 245, 249, 253, 254, 263, 264, 334, 337, 356, 363, 364, 365, 370, 413
UNPROFOR, 61, 278, 343
until extermination, yours or ours, 188
uprising against fascism, 401
Uprising of the Peoples of Croatia, the, 322
Urbarium, 30
Uskoks, 22
Ustasha, viii, ix, 4, 48, 50, 53, 109, 175, 176, 177, 178, 182, 183, 184, 185, 186, 190, 191, 192, 194,

195, 196, 197, 198, 199, 202, 203, 205, 206, 207, 208, 209, 210, 213, 236, 237, 253, 255, 270, 271, 272, 275, 309, 310, 312, 316, 317, 318, 319, 321, 323, 330, 332, 339, 346, 347, 348, 355, 369, 370, 372, 373, 375, 376, 377, 378, 381, 383, 394, 395, 401
basic characteristic of the Ustasha regime, 191
comprehensive Ustasha ideology, 193
crimes against Serbs, 318
Croatian Revolutionary Movement, 48
Croatian Revolutionary Organization, 4, 309
harsh attitude to Serbs, 316
radical nationalist movement, 189
voluntary militia, 50
war crimes, 236

V

VAT, 391, 397
Vatican, 61, 166, 167, 177, 179, 180, 185, 187, 197, 199, 201, 202, 206, 207, 209, 222, 223, 225, 226, 227, 231, 238, 239, 240, 331
Venetian rule, 15, 26, 389
Versailles Peace Conference, 161
Veselica, 252, 257, 262, 337
vicious circle of inadequacy, 392
Victory in the War of Independence, 61
Vienna Literary Agreement, 92, 101, 102, 123
Vinodol Code, 17
Višeslav, 7, 64
Vjesnik, 64, 109, 173, 209, 252, 324, 328, 329, 363, 383
Vjesnik u srijedu, 252
Vlach, 22, 68, 149
Vlach Statutes, 22
Voice of the Council, the, 210, 219, 223, 224, 226, 234, 236, 238, 239, 240, 242, 243
Vojnomir, 7
volunteers, 25, 51, 60, 276, 318, 365, 370, 378, 393
Vukovar, 13, 17, 31, 42, 58, 59, 60, 62, 67, 71, 76, 132, 134, 276, 277, 284, 288, 290, 341, 361, 366, 402, 403
Vukovar hospital, 60, 277
Vukovianism, 79, 96, 101, 104

W

war casualties, 395
war with Hungary, 37
Washington Agreement, 342
Way of the Cross, 67, 324, 326, 328, 395
Western civilization, 177, 233, 385, 387
Western Croatian Kingdom in the Carpathian Mountains, 5
white, 4, 5, 7, 8, 9, 10, 11, 14, 72, 272, 275, 285, 339, 374, 378, 380, 412
White Croatia, 5, 7, 8, 10, 11, 14
White Croatia around the city of Krakow, 5
White, Western Croatian Kingdom in the Carpathian Mountains, 5
who is once baptized, need not be re-baptized, 195
women and men raped, 345
worker self-management, 390
workers self-management, 220, 221
working abroad, 395
World War, viii, xii, xiv, 3, 19, 21, 43, 47, 49, 56, 64, 106, 135, 142, 143, 145, 147, 148, 151, 152, 158, 164, 167, 168, 169, 171, 175, 176, 177, 179, 183, 184, 185, 187, 189, 191, 193, 196, 200, 202, 209, 210, 216, 222, 270, 271, 272, 274, 275, 278, 288, 297, 298, 301, 302, 303, 309, 312, 313, 315, 316, 317, 323, 329, 332, 334, 349, 351, 357, 360, 364, 372, 382, 389, 406
World War I, 3, 47, 106, 135, 142, 143, 147, 148, 151, 152, 158, 167, 168, 175, 176, 298, 301, 303, 312, 389
World War II, x, 148, 164, 168, 175, 177, 179, 183, 184, 185, 189, 191, 193, 196, 200, 202, 209, 298, 313, 315, 316, 317, 323, 329, 332, 334, 349, 351, 357, 360, 364, 382

Y

Yad Vashem, 176, 199, 212, 214
Young Bosnia, 44
Young Yugoslavia, 48
Yugoslav Club, 45, 142
Yugoslav Comittee in London, 45
Yugoslav Committee, 45, 46, 142, 147, 156, 159, 160, 161, 163, 302
Yugoslav Federal Army, 4, 402, 403
Yugoslav idea, 101, 104, 112, 135, 299
Yugoslav State Commission for Determination of the Crimes of Occupiers and Their Helpers, 332
Yugoslav succession, 167
Yugoslavian communists, 220, 221, 222, 228, 232, 233, 237
Yugoslavian Marxist intellectuals, 231

Z

Zadar philology school, 95
Zagreb philology school, 92, 95, 96, 97, 98, 99, 101, 103, 104, 105, 106

Zagreb school, 95, 96, 126, 365
ZAVNOH, 51
Zemun, 140, 143, 158, 216, 376
ZNG, 58, 59
zone A, 164, 165
zone B, 164, 165
Zones A and B, 165
Zrin, 15, 70, 150
Zrinski-Frankopan Resistance in 1671, 27